BIG DATA AND GLOBAL TRADE LAW

This collection explores the relevance of global trade law for data, big data and cross-border data flows. Contributing authors from different disciplines including law, economics and political science analyze developments at the World Trade Organization and in preferential trade venues by asking what future-oriented models for data governance are available and viable in the area of trade law and policy. The collection paints the broad picture of the interaction between digital technologies and trade regulation as well as provides in-depth analyses of critical to the data-driven economy issues, such as privacy and AI, and different countries' perspectives. This title is also available as Open Access on Cambridge Core.

MIRA BURRI is a senior lecturer at the University of Lucerne and the principal investigator of the research project 'The Governance of Big Data in Trade Agreements.' For more than a decade now, she has worked in the area of digital trade law, publishing a number of key studies and advising governments, the European Parliament and NGOs on the topic.

T0384582

Big Data and Global Trade Law

Edited by

MIRA BURRI

University of Lucerne

Shaftesbury Road, Cambridge CB2 8EA, United Kingdom

One Liberty Plaza, 20th Floor, New York, NY 10006, USA

477 Williamstown Road, Port Melbourne, VIC 3207, Australia

314–321, 3rd Floor, Plot 3, Splendor Forum, Jasola District Centre, New Delhi – 110025, India

103 Penang Road, #05–06/07, Visioncrest Commercial, Singapore 238467

Cambridge University Press is part of Cambridge University Press & Assessment, a department of the University of Cambridge.

We share the University's mission to contribute to society through the pursuit of education, learning and research at the highest international levels of excellence.

www.cambridge.org
Information on this title: www.cambridge.org/9781108825924

DOI: 10.1017/9781108919234

First published 2021

A catalogue record for this publication is available from the British Library

Library of Congress Cataloging-in-Publication data
NAMES: Burri, Mira, editor.
TITLE: Big data and global trade law / edited by Mira Burri, University of Lucerne.
DESCRIPTION: Cambridge, United Kingdom ; New York, NY : Cambridge University Press, 2021.
IDENTIFIERS: LCCN 2020046984 (print) | LCCN 2020046985 (ebook) | ISBN 9781108843591 (hardback) | ISBN 9781108825924 (paperback) | ISBN 9781108919234 (epub)
SUBJECTS: LCSH: Transborder data flow—Law and legislation. | Big data. | Data protection—Law and legislation. | Foreign trade regulation. | World Trade Organization. | Blockchains (Databases)—Law and legislation. | Artificial intelligence—Law and legislation.
CLASSIFICATION: LCC K4305 .B54 2021 (print) | LCC K4305 (ebook) | DDC 343.08/15—dc23
LC record available at https://lccn.loc.gov/2020046984
LC ebook record available at https://lccn.loc.gov/2020046985s

ISBN   978-1-108-84359-1   Hardback
ISBN   978-1-108-82592-4   Paperback

Contents

Figures

Tables

Contributors

Susan Ariel Aaronson is Research Professor of International Affairs at the Elliott School of International Affairs of the George Washington University and Director of the Digital Trade and Data Governance Hub. Aaronson is also a cross-disciplinary fellow and a senior fellow at the think tank Center for International Governance Innovation (CIGI) in Canada. Aaronson was previously the Carvalho Fellow at the Government Accountability Project and the Minerva Chair at the National War College.

Aaronson's research examines the relationship between economic change and human rights. She is currently directing projects on mapping data governance, and writing on comparative advantage in data, data and national security, and the US approach to stimulating AI. Her research has been funded by the Hewlett, MacArthur, Ford, and Rockefeller Foundations, governments, such as those of the Netherlands, United States, and Canada; the United Nations, the International Labour Organization, and the World Bank; and US corporations including Ford Motor and Levi Strauss. Aaronson is a frequent speaker on public understanding of globalization issues and international economic developments. She regularly comments on international economics on 'Marketplace' and was a monthly commentator on 'All Things Considered' and 'Morning Edition'. She has also appeared on CNN, the BBC, and PBS to discuss trade and globalization issues. Aaronson was a guest scholar in economics at the Brookings Institution (1995–1999) and a research fellow at the World Trade Institute (2008–2012).

In recent years, she has been a pro bono advisor to the UN Special Representative on Transnational Corporations and Human Rights and the Congressional Human Rights Caucus. She has also consulted for the International Labour Organization; the World Bank; Free the Slaves; the Ford Foundation; the Extractive Industries Transparency Initiative; the Progressive Policy Institute; the Stanley Foundation; several corporations; and the governments of Canada, Belgium, and the Netherlands, among others.

Mira Burri is Professor of International Economic and Internet Law and managing director for internationalization at the Faculty of Law of the University of Lucerne. She teaches international intellectual property, media, Internet, and trade law. Prior to joining the University of Lucerne, Mira Burri was a senior fellow at the World Trade Institute at the University of Bern, where she led a project on digital technologies and trade governance as part of the Swiss National Centre of Competence in Research (NCCR): Trade Regulation. Mira received her law degree from the University of Sofia and a Master of Advanced European Studies (MAES) from the Europe Institute of the University of Basel. Her doctoral thesis dealt with EU competition law and was awarded the Professor Walther Hug prize (2006/2007). Mira completed her habilitation in 2015 with *venia docendi* for international economic law, European and international communications and media law, as well as Internet law.

Mira's current research interests are in the areas of digital trade, culture, copyright, data protection, and Internet governance. Mira is the principle investigator of the project 'The Governance of Big Data in Trade Agreements', sponsored by the Swiss National Science Foundation. She consults the European Parliament, UNESCO, the WEF, EFTA and others on issues of digital innovation and cultural diversity. Mira has co-edited publications *Free Trade versus Cultural Diversity* (Schulthess, 2004); *Digital Rights Management: The End of Collecting Societies?* (Stämpfli et al., 2005); *Intellectual Property and Traditional Cultural Expressions in a Digital Environment* (Edward Elgar, 2008); *Governance of Digital Game Environments and Cultural Diversity* (Edward Elgar, 2010), and *Trade Governance in the Digital Age* (Cambridge University Press, 2012). She is the author of *Public Service Broadcasting 3.0* (Routledge, 2015). Mira's publications are available at http://ssrn.com/author=483457.

Anupam Chander is Professor of Law at Georgetown University. The author of the widely reviewed book, *The Electronic Silk Road* (Yale University Press, 2013), Chander is an expert on the global regulation of new technologies. A graduate of Harvard College and Yale Law School, he clerked for Chief Judge Jon O. Newman of the Second Circuit Court of Appeals and Judge William A. Norris of the Ninth Circuit Court of Appeals. He practised law in New York and Hong Kong with Cleary, Gottlieb, Steen & Hamilton. He has been a visiting law professor at Yale, the University of Chicago, Stanford, Cornell, and Tsinghua.

Anupam Chander previously served as the director of the California International Law Center and Martin Luther King Jr. Professor of Law at UC Davis. A member of the American Law Institute, he has also served on the Executive Council of the American Society of International Law, where he co-founded the International Law and Technology Interest Group. He serves as a judge of the Stanford Junior International Faculty Forum. A recipient of Google Research Awards and an Andrew Mellon grant on the topic of surveillance, he has worked with ICTSD/ World Economic Forum expert groups on the digital economy. He serves as an

Adjunct Senior Research Scholar at Columbia University's School of International and Public Policy, a faculty advisor to Georgetown's Institute for Technology Law and Policy, and as a faculty affiliate of Yale's Information Society Project.

Manfred Elsig is Professor of International Relations, Deputy Managing Director and Director of Research of the World Trade Institute of the University of Bern. Between 2013 and 2017 he was the director of the NCCR Trade Regulation. He studied at the universities of Bern and Bordeaux and earned a degree in political science. He worked from 1997 to 1999 at the Swiss Federal Office for Foreign Economic Affairs. He later joined the Political Science Institute at the University of Zurich and received his PhD (Dr. Phil) in 2002 with a dissertation on European Union trade policy. From 2002 to 2004 he worked for the UBS financial services group and as a personal advisor to the Minister of Economy of Canton Zurich. In 2004–2005 he was a teaching fellow at the International Relations Department at the London School of Economics and Political Science. From 2005 to 2009, he worked as a postdoc fellow at the World Trade Institute and at the Graduate Institute of International and Development Studies in Geneva. From 2009 to 2013 he was an assistant professor at the World Trade Institute.

Manfred's research focuses primarily on the politics of international trade, regional trade agreements, European trade policy, international organizations, US–EU relations, and private actors in global politics. He has published in international peer-reviewed journals including *International Studies Quarterly, European Journal of International Relations, European Union Politics, Journal of European Public Policy, Journal of Common Market Studies, Review of International Organizations, Review of International Political Economy*, and *World Trade Review*. He has been visiting lecturer/visiting professor at the University of Zurich, the University of Geneva, the Graduate Institute of International and Development Studies, the London School of Economics and Political Science, and the Thunderbird School of Global Management. His courses include international political economy, international relations theories, international institutions, globalization and European integration, and research methods.

Martina F. Ferracane is Max Weber Fellow at the European University Institute and Research Associate at the European Center for International Political Economy (ECIPE). Martina is passionate about policymaking and technological innovation. She has been awarded a PhD on the topic of cross-border data flows at University of Hamburg, where she has also received a postdoctoral scholarship to investigate the topic of creative pedagogy in the digital era. In her academic career, she has been affiliated with the European University Institute (Policy Leaders Fellow in 2018 and currently Max Weber Fellow), Columbia University and the California International Law Center. On top of regulatory issues connected to data flows, including trade governance, cybersecurity, and privacy, her work covers topics related to digital transformation, digital education, and entrepreneurship.

Martina founded and manages the FabLab Western Sicily, a non-profit organization which brings creative digital education to Sicilian kids and she was listed in 'Forbes 30 under 30' for her work with Oral3D, a start-up she co-founded in the area of 3D printing and dentistry. For her work in these areas, she was listed in 2018 among the fifteen most influential Italian women on digital issues. She acts regularly as a consultant on digital trade and data flows for several institutions, including the United Nations, the European Commission, WEF, and the World Bank. More about Martina's work can be found at www.martinaferracane.com.

Emmanuelle Ganne is Senior Analyst in the Economic Research and Statistics Division of the World Trade Organization, where she leads WTO's work on blockchain. She is the author of a recently published WTO book entitled *Can Blockchain Revolutionize International Trade?*. Ganne is also WTO's lead on micro- , small- and medium-sized enterprises. Prior to this, she held the position of Vice President and Managing Director for Europe at the Allam Advisory Group (AAG), a team of former C-level executives and senior diplomats that specializes in helping businesses expand their operations globally. Before joining AAG, she held various positions at the WTO, including as counsellor to Director-General Pascal Lamy, and in the Accessions Division where she assessed trade policies of governments wishing to join the WTO and advised them on how to improve their business environment.

Before joining the WTO in 2002, Emmanuelle Ganne worked for the Organisation of Economic Cooperation and Development, putting in place the Stability Pact Anti-Corruption Initiative, which assisted South Eastern European states curb corruption. Ganne was a 2009 Yale World Fellow.

Henry S. Gao is Associate Professor of Law at Singapore Management University. With law degrees from three continents, he started his career as the first Chinese lawyer at the WTO Secretariat. Before moving to Singapore in late 2007, he taught law at the University of Hong Kong, where he was also the Deputy Director of the East Asian International Economic Law and Policy Program. He has taught at the IELPO programme in Barcelona and the Academy of International Trade Law in Macau, and was the academic coordinator to the first Asia-Pacific Regional Trade Policy Course officially sponsored by the WTO. Widely published on issues relating to China and the WTO, Gao's research has been featured by CNN, BBC, *The Economist*, *Wall Street Journal*, and *Financial Times*. He has advised many national governments as well as the WTO, the World Bank, the Asian Development Bank, APEC, and ASEAN on trade issues. He sits on the Advisory Board of the WTO Chairs Programme, which was established by the WTO Secretariat in 2009 to promote research and teaching on WTO issues in leading universities around the world. He is also a member of editorial board of *Journal of Financial Regulation*, which was launched by Oxford University Press in 2014. Gao is currently working on issues relating to digital trade, WTO reform, and the Belt and Road Initiative.

Urs Gasser is Professor of Practice and Executive Director of the Berkman Klein Center for Internet and Society at Harvard University. In addition to his appointments at Harvard, Gasser has had visiting professorships at the Singapore Management University School of Law, the University of Zurich Faculty of Law, KEIO University, and the University of St. Gallen, and taught at Fudan University School of Management. He serves as a trustee on the boards of the Digital Asia Hub, and the Research Center for Information Law at the University of St. Gallen. He was formerly a member of the International Advisory Board of the Alexander von Humboldt Institute for Internet and Society in Berlin, a trustee of the NEXA Center for Internet and Society at the Polytechnic of Turin, a Fellow at the Gruter Institute for Law and Behavioral Research, and served as a senior advisor to the World Economic Forum's Future of the Internet Initiative, where he currently is a member of the Global Future Council on New Metrics. He currently also serves as a member of the German Digital Council, appointed by Angela Merkel. Urs Gasser is the co-author of *Born Digital: Understanding the First Generation of Digital Natives* (Basic Books, 2008 and 2016, with John Palfrey) that has been translated into ten languages (including Chinese), and co-author of *Interop: The Promise and Perils of Highly Interconnected Systems* (Basic Books, 2012, with John Palfrey). Recent book publications include *Remembering and Forgetting in the Digital Age* (Springer, 2018, co-editor) and *Big Data, Health Law, and Bioethics* (Cambridge University Press, 2018, co-editor).

Gasser's research and teaching activities focus on information law, policy, and society issues and the changing role of academia in the digitally networked age. Current projects – several involving the Global Network of Internet and Society Centers, which he helped to incubate – focus on the governance of evolving and emerging technologies, such as cloud computing, the Internet of Things, augmented reality, and artificial intelligence, with a particular interest in privacy and security issues and the broader implications of these technologies, including questions of agency and autonomy. As a longer term research interest, he studies the patterns of interaction between law and innovation, and innovation with the legal system in the digital age. Gasser frequently acts as a commentator on digital technology, policy, and society issues for the US and European media.

Daniel J. Gervais is Milton R. Underwood Chair in Law and Director of the Intellectual Property Program, Vanderbilt Law School. He also holds a Chair in Information Law at the University of Amsterdam and a Professor II position at the University of Oslo. His work focuses on international intellectual property law, having spent ten years researching and addressing policy issues as a as legal officer at the World Trade Organization, as head of the Copyright Projects section of the World Intellectual Property Organization, and Deputy Secretary General of International Confederation of Societies of Authors and Composers, and Vice Chair of the International Federation of Reproduction Rights Organizations. He is

the author of *The TRIPS Agreement: Drafting History and Analysis*, a leading guide
to the text that governs international intellectual property rights (5th edition, 2021).

Before joining Vanderbilt Law School in 2008, Daniel Gervais served as acting
dean and vice dean of the Common Law Section at the University of Ottawa. Before
entering the academy, he practised law as a partner with the technology law firm BCF
in Montreal. He was also a consultant with the Paris-based Organisation for Economic
Cooperation and Development. He has been a visiting professor at numerous international universities and a visiting scholar at Stanford Law School. In 2012, he was the
Gide Loyrette Nouel Visiting Chair at Sciences Po Law School in Paris. He served for
ten years as editor-in-chief of the peer-reviewed *Journal of World Intellectual Property*.
In 2012, he was the first North American law professor admitted to the Academy of
Europe. In 2017–2019 he served as Chairman of the International Association for the
Advancement of Teaching and Research in Intellectual Property (ATRIP). He is a
member of the American Law Institute, where he serves as an Associate Reporter on
the Restatement of the Law, Copyright project.

Kristina Irion is Associate Professor at the Institute for Information Law (IViR),
University of Amsterdam. She is also the coordinator of the Research Master's
programme in Information Law and faculty organizer of the Annual IViR
Summer Course on Privacy Law and Policy. Until 2017, she was Associate
Professor at the School of Public Policy at Central European University in
Budapest. Irion obtained her Dr. iuris degree in EU competition law in the
communications sector from the Martin Luther University, Halle-Wittenberg, and
holds a Master's degree in Information Technology and Telecommunications Law
from the University of Strathclyde, Glasgow. Before academia, she worked as a part-
time legal officer at the Data Protection Authority in Berlin and as Senior
Regulatory Counsel for a German mobile network operator. Irion also gained
working experience as a trainee at the European Commission in Brussels and was
a visiting fellow at the Electronic Privacy Information Center (EPIC) in
Washington, DC.

Kristina Irion is an expert in information law and governance, data markets, and
cross-border data flows. In 2016, she lead-authored a highly influential study which
identifies possible tensions between EU data protection law and free trade agreements. As a Marie Curie Fellow, she accomplished her individual research project
on *Governing Digital Information*, which explores how cloud computing transforms
the (legal) relationship between individuals and their personal records. Irion was key
personnel of four collaborative European research projects on privacy, independent
media supervisory authorities, and building functioning media institutions. She
frequently provides expertise to the European Parliament and the European
Commission, the Council of Europe, the OECD, and civil society organizations.

Sebastian Klotz is Doctoral Fellow at the World Trade Institute of the University of
Bern and a visiting researcher at the University of Oxford's Department of Politics

and International Relations. His research focuses on the governance of regulatory-standard setting and international trade. In this context, he explores the relationship between international standard–setting bodies and multilateral as well as plurilateral trade agreements. He presented his ongoing research at leading conferences including ECPR, EPSA, PEIO, and IPES.

Before joining the World Trade Institute, Sebastian worked as a Carlo Schmid Fellow and Trade and Competitiveness Consultant for the Office of the Chief Economist of the International Trade Centre, the joint agency of the United Nations Conference on Trade and Development, and the World Trade Organization. Prior to joining the International Trade Centre, he gathered work experience at the ifo Institute for Economic Research, the German–Mexican Chamber of Commerce and Industry and the University of Strathclyde.

Sebastian holds a Master in International Trade, Finance and Development jointly awarded by the Barcelona Graduate School of Economics, the Universitat Pompeu Fabra, and the Autonomous University of Barcelona in Spain. He completed his undergraduate studies at the University of Strathclyde and Tec de Monterrey, and graduated with a Bachelor's in Economics with First Class Honours.

Patrick Leblond is Associate Professor and CN-Paul M. Tellier Chair on Business and Public Policy in the Graduate School of Public and International Affairs, University of Ottawa. He is also Senior Fellow at the Centre for International Governance Innovation (CIGI), Research Associate at CIRANO, and Affiliated Professor of International Business at HEC Montréal. Owing to his training and experience in business, economics and international relations, Leblond's expertise relates to questions relating to global economic governance and international and comparative political economy, more specifically those that deal with international finance, international economic integration as well as business-government relations. His regional expertise focuses on Europe and North America. Before joining the University of Ottawa in 2008, Patrick was assistant professor of international business at HEC Montréal and director of the Réseau Économie Internationale (REI) at the Centre d'Études et de Recherches Internationales de l'Université de Montréal (CERIUM). He was also visiting scholar at the Institute for Research on Public Policy (IRPP). Before embarking on his academic career, Patrick worked in accounting and auditing for Ernst & Young (he holds the title of Chartered Accountant), as well as in corporate finance and strategy consulting for Arthur Andersen & Co. and SECOR Consulting.

Neha Mishra is a lecturer at the Australian National University's College of Law. Previously she was a Postdoctoral Fellow at the Centre for International Law, National University of Singapore. Mishra completed her doctoral thesis at the University of Melbourne. Her doctoral thesis investigated how international trade agreements apply to government measures restricting cross-border digital data flows, and whether trade law can effectively align trade with Internet policy objectives. In course of her doctoral candidature, Mishra held visiting research positions at the Max Planck Institute Luxembourg and the World Trade Organization. She previously practised law with Herbert Smith Freehills LLP in London and Economic Laws Practice in Delhi. She also served as a lecturer at National Law School of India University, where she was teaching competition law and public international law. Mishra has completed her undergraduate degree in law from the National Law School Bangalore, LLM in Public International Law from the London School of Economics, and Master's in Public Policy from the National University of Singapore. During her studies in Singapore, Neha Mishra interned with the Government Relations Teams at eBay Singapore and Microsoft Singapore, working on a wide variety of legal and policy issues related to Internet and digital trade regulation. She has published extensively in the field of international trade law, especially in relation to digital trade and cross-border data flows, as well as presented her research at various international fora.

Andrew D. Mitchell is Professor at the Faculty of Law, Monash University, and a member of the Indicative List of Panelists to hear WTO disputes. He has previously practised law with Allens Arthur Robinson (now Allens Linklaters) and consults for states, international organizations and the private sector. Andrew has taught law in Australia, Canada, Indonesia, Singapore, and the United States and is the recipient of five major grants from the Australian Research Council (including a Future Fellowship) and the Australian National Preventive Health Agency. He has published over 140 academic books and journal articles and is a series editor of the Oxford University Press International Economic Law Series and an editorial board member of the *Journal of International Economic Law* and the *Journal of International Dispute Settlement*. He has law degrees from Melbourne, Harvard, and Cambridge and is a barrister and solicitor of the Supreme Court of Victoria.

Rodrigo Polanco is Senior Researcher and Lecturer and Academic Coordinator of Advanced Master's Programmes at the World Trade Institute, University of Bern. He is also a legal advisor at the Swiss Institute of Comparative Law, and a visiting professor at the University of Chile. He is a former assistant professor of International Economic Law at the University of Chile Faculty of Law, where he also served as the director of international affairs, and a former postdoctoral researcher at the University of Lucerne. He was a researcher and a coordinator of the SECO Project (which supported development of Regional Competence Centres for Trade Law and Policy in Peru, South Africa, Vietnam, Indonesia, and Chile) and of the SNIS Project (*Diffusion of International Law: A Textual Analysis of International Investment Agreements*). Rodrigo Polanco is also a published scholar and legal practitioner with experience in both the public and private sectors. He specializes in economic and international law, investment law, trade law, and air and space law. He holds a bachelor and a master of laws from Universidad de Chile School of Law, an LLM in International Legal Studies from New York University

School of Law, and a PhD from the University of Bern. He is also a co-founder of Fiscalía del Medio Ambiente (FIMA), a Chilean non-profit organization working in public interest environmental cases, and teaching local communities and members of the judiciary on environmental law. He serves as member of the editorial board of their environmental law journal (*Justicia Ambiental*).

Xavier Seuba is Associate Professor of Law and Academic Coordinator and Scientific Responsible at the Center for International Intellectual Property Studies (CEIPI), University of Strasbourg. Xavier is also Coordinator of the CEIPI-BETA Project on the Law and Economics of Intellectual Property. He studied Law at the Universidad de Navarra and, after completing a master's degree and an Advanced Studies Diploma in International Studies at Universitat Pompeu Fabra (2003), he received his doctorate in 2008 from this university with a thesis on health protection and the international regulation of pharmaceutical products. He teaches courses at various European and American universities for graduate and postgraduate students on Public International Law, International Economic Law, Intellectual Property Law, International Human Rights law, and International Health Law. His areas of technical expertise include pharmaceutical policies and law, intellectual property law, and technical standards regulation. In the area of intellectual property law, he predominantly works on issues related to patents and intellectual property enforcement. Xavier Seuba has advised several national governments on intellectual property and pharmaceuticals legislation, on issues of policy design, and in the context of free trade agreements negotiations. He has also been consultant for several international organizations, including the World Health Organization, the Pan-American Health Organization, the European Union, the Inter-American Development Bank, the Central America Integration System, the United Nations Office of the High Commissioner for Human Rights and the United Nations Conference for Trade and Development. He has authored numerous papers, articles, book chapters, and books in his areas of expertise.

Aurelia Tamò-Larrieux is a Postdoctoral Fellow at the University of St. Gallen. Her research interests include privacy, especially privacy by design, data protection, social robots, automated decision-making, and trust in automation. Aurelia has published her PhD research on the topic of data protection by design and default for the Internet of Things in the book *Designing for Privacy and its Legal Framework* (Springer, 2018). Currently, she is working on her postdoctoral thesis with the working title *Trust the Machine: Towards Trust-Enhancing Regulation of Algorithmic Systems*.

Florent Thouvenin is Professor of Law and Chair for Information and Communication Law at the Center for Information Technology, Society, and Law (ITSL), University of Zurich. Florent Thouvenin completed his undergraduate, PhD and postdoctoral studies at the University of Zurich. He was a research assistant at the ETH Zurich and the University of Zurich, practised law at a Zurich corporate law firm, and was a senior fellow in a research project at the University of Zurich, as well as an assistant professor at the University of St. Gallen. His research focuses on copyright and matters of privacy and data protection in the digital society. The question at the forefront of his research is whether and how our privacy and data protection must be approached differently through the prism of the law and technology in the information society. His other research projects include the relationship between information and power, exclusive rights and access to data, and the growing personalization of advertising, agreements and pricing. Among other things, Florent Thouvenin is the chairman of the Center for Information Technology, Society and Law's Steering Committee and director of the University of Zurich's Digital Society Initiative. He is also the managing director and a member of the Board of the Swiss Forum for Communications Law.

Joris van Hoboken is Associate Professor at the Institute for Information Law (IViR), University of Amsterdam and Professor of Law at the Interdisciplinary Research Group on Law Science Technology and Society (LSTS), Vrije Universiteit Brussel. Van Hoboken works on the intersection of fundamental rights protection and the governance of platforms and Internet-based services. More generally, his research addresses law and policy in the field of digital media, electronic communications and the Internet, with a focus on the fundamental rights to data privacy and freedom of expression and transatlantic relations. He is a specialist in data privacy and the regulation of Internet intermediaries and algorithmic governance. Among other appointments, van Hoboken is a member of the European Commission's Observatory on the Online Platform Economy, and a member of the Steering Group of the Transatlantic High-Level Working Group on Content Moderation Online and Freedom of Expression.

Previously, Joris van Hoboken was a postdoctoral research fellow at the Information Law Institute (ILI) at New York University, School of Law (2013–2016), a visiting scholar at the NYU Stern Center for Business and Human Rights (2015–2016), and a lecturer at CornellTech (2016). In 2008, he was a visiting scholar at the Berkman Klein Center for Internet and Society at Harvard University. Between 2007 and 2017, van Hoboken served on the board of directors of the Dutch digital rights organization Bits of Freedom.

Joris van Hoboken obtained his PhD from the University of Amsterdam on the topic of search engines and freedom of expression (2012) and has graduate degrees in Law (2006, University of Amsterdam, cum laude) and Theoretical Mathematics (2002, University of Amsterdam, cum laude). For his PhD thesis, he received the award of the Praemium Erasmianum Foundation. Van Hoboken is a regular speaker at international events and conferences and has conducted research for the European Commission, ENISA, UNESCO, Upturn, and The Open Society Foundation. His work has been covered in NRC *Handelsblad, De Correspondent,* the Dutch evening news, *Bloomberg News*, the *Wall Street Journal*, and the *Financial Times*.

Svetlana Yakovleva is Postdoctoral Researcher at the Institute for Information Law (IViR), University of Amsterdam, and Senior Legal Adviser at De Brauw Blackstone Westbroek, Amsterdam. Svetlana Yakovleva's primary research interests lie at the intersection of data privacy and cybersecurity law, human rights and international trade law. Her recent research proposes a way to balance the fundamental right to data privacy and the liberalization of international trade. Her research has been published in several well-known journals, such as *Common Market Law Review*, *University of Miami Law Review*, and *World Trade Review*. She received a degree in law (cum laude) from the National Research University Higher School of Economics (Moscow) in 2005. She also holds an LLM degree in Law and Economics (EMLE) from the Erasmus University, Rotterdam, and the University of Hamburg (2007), and a research master degree in information law from the IViR (2016). Between 2007 and 2014, Yakovleva worked at the Moscow office of Debevoise & Plimpton LLP, as independent legal counsel and as corporate legal counsel for Allianz Partners Russia. She also provided legal and methodological advice for the e-Government project of the Russian Government.

Abbreviations

AANZFAT	ASEAN–Australia–New Zealand Free Trade Area
AEO	authorized economic operators
AI	artificial intelligence
ANTAI	National Authority of Transparency and Access to Information (Panama)
APEC	Asia-Pacific Economic Cooperation
ASEAN	Association of Southeast Asian Nations
B2B	business to business
B2C	business to consumer
BCR	Binding Corporate Rules
BOPCOM	Balance of Payment Committee (IMF)
BverGE	Bundesverfassungsgericht (German Constitutional Court)
CAC	Cyberspace Administration of China
CARIFORUM	Caribbean Forum
CBPR	Cross-Border Privacy Rules
CCPA	California Consumer Privacy Act
CDPA	Copyright, Design and Patents Act (UK)
CEFTA	Central European Free Trade Agreement
CEPA	Closer Economic Partnership Agreement (between New Zealand and Singapore)
CERNET	China Education and Research Network
CETA	Comprehensive Economic and Trade Agreement (between Canada and the EU)
CFREU	Charter of Fundamental Rights of the European Union
ChAFTA	China–Australia Free Trade Agreement
CHINAGBNET	China Golden Bridge Network
CHINANET	China Public Computer Network

CJEU	Court of Justice of the European Union
CLOUD Act	Clarifying Lawful Overseas Use of Data Act (US)
CNIL	Commission Nationale de l'Informatique et des Libertés (French Data Protection Authority)
CPC	UN Central Product Classification
CPTPP	Comprehensive and Progressive Agreement for Trans-Pacific Partnership
CSIS	Centre for Strategic and International Studies
CSTNET	China Science and Technology Network
CTS	Council for Trade in Services
CUSMA	Canada–United States–Mexico Agreement
DEPA	Digital Economy Partnership Agreement (between Chile, New Zealand and Singapore)
DGCE	General Directorate of Electronic Commerce (Panama)
DL	deep learning
DNA	deoxyribonucleic acid
DPA	data protection authority
DPIA	data privacy impact assessment
DPO	data protection officer
DSCI	Data Security Council of India
DSU	Dispute Settlement Understanding
DTE	Digital Trade Estimates
DTL	distributed ledger technology
DTRI	Digital Trade Restrictiveness Index
DUNS	Data Universal Numbering System
EAEU	Eurasian Economic Union
EC	European Communities/European Community
ECFI	European Court of First Instance
ECLI	European Case Law Identifier
EDI	electronic data interchange
EDPB	European Data Protection Board
EDPS	European Data Protection Supervisor
EDRi	European Digital Rights
EEA	European Economic Area
EFF	Electronic Frontier Foundation
EFTA	European Free Trade Association
EPA	Economic Partnership Agreement
EPC	Electronic Product Code
EPO	European Patent Office
EU	European Union
E-WTP	Electronic World Trade Platform

FCA	Financial Conduct Authority
FINMA	Finanzmarktaufsicht (Swiss Financial Market Supervisory Authority)
FTA	free trade agreement
FTC	Federal Trade Commission
GATS	General Agreement on Trade in Services
GATT	General Agreement on Tariffs and Trade
GB	gigabyte
GCC	Gulf Cooperation Council
GDP	gross domestic product
GDPR	General Data Protection Regulation (EU)
GFIN	Global Financial Innovation Network
GSBN	Global Shipping Business Network
GTAP	Global Trade Analysis Project
GVC	global value chain
IAPP	International Association of Privacy Professionals
ICANN	Internet Corporation for Assigned Names and Numbers
ICC	International Chamber of Commerce
ICO	Initial Coin Offerings
ICRIER	Indian Council for Research on International Economic Relations
ICT	information and communication technology
ICTSD	International Centre for Trade and Sustainable Development
IDB	Inter-American Development Bank
IDEA	International Digital Economy Agreement
IEEE	Institute of Electrical and Electronics Engineers
IEFT	Internet Engineering Task Force
IEL	international economic law
IGF	Internet Governance Forum
ILO	International Labour Organization
IMF	International Monetary Fund
INATBA	International Association for Trusted Blockchain Applications
IoT	Internet of Things
IP	intellectual property
IPRs	intellectual property rights
ISIC	International Standard Industry Classification
ISO	International Organization for Standardization
ISP	Internet service provider
IT	information technology
ITA	Information Technology Agreement
ITIF	Information Technology and Innovation Foundation

ITU	International Telecommunication Union
JORF	Journal Officiel de la République Française (government gazette of the French Republic)
JSI	Joint Statement on Electronic Commerce Initiative
LAC	Latin American countries
LDC	least-developed country
MASP	Multi-annual Strategic Plan
MEI	Ministry of Electronic Industry (China)
MFN	most favoured nation
MII	Ministry of Information Industry (China)
MIIT	Ministry of Industry and Information Technology (China)
ML	machine learning
MPS	Ministry of Public Security (China)
MPT	Ministry of Posts and Telecommunications (China)
NAFTA	North American Free Trade Agreement
NASSCOM	National Association of Software and Services Companies (India)
NBER	National Bureau of Economic Research (USA)
NCTS	New Computerised Transit System
NDPA	General Directorate of Transparency, Access to Public Information and Protection of Personal Data (Peru)
NFA	National Food Authority (Philippines)
NIST	National Institute of Standards and Technology (USA)
NPC	National People's Congress (China)
NRDB	National Register of Data Bases (Colombia)
NT	national treatment
OAS	Organization of American States
OECD	Organisation for Economic Co-operation and Development
OJ	Official Journal of the European Union
OSS	open-source software
P2P	peer-to-peer
PAAP	Pacific Alliance Additional Protocol
PAFTA	Peru–Australia Free Trade Agreement
PatA	Swiss Federal Act on Patents for Inventions
PDLP	Personal Data Protection Law (Peru)
PETs	Privacy-Enhancing Technologies
PII	Personally Identifiable Information
PIPEDA	Personal Information Protection and Electronic Documents Act
PoET	proof of elapsed time
PoS	proof of stake
PoW	proof of work

PPM	process and production method
PRODHAB	Agency for the Protection of Data of Inhabitants (Costa Rica)
PTA	preferential trade agreement
QR Code	Quick Response Code
RCEP	Regional Comprehensive Economic Partnership
R&D	research and development
ReCAPTCHA	Reverse Completely Automated Public Turing test to Tell Computers and Humans Apart
RFID	Radio Frequency Identification
RGPD	Le Règlement Général sur la Protection des Données (GDPR)
SAD	Single Administrative Document
SAFTA	South Asian Free Trade Area
SIC	Superintendence of Industry and Commerce (Colombia)
SMEs	small- and medium-sized enterprises
SPS	WTO Agreement on Sanitary and Phytosanitary Measures
SQL	Structured Query Language
StGB	Schweizerisches Strafgesetzbuch (Swiss Criminal Code)
TAPED	Trade Agreement Provisions on Electronic Commerce and Data
TBT	WTO Agreement on Technical Barriers to Trade
TDM	text and data mining
TFA	Trade Facilitation Agreement
TFP	total factor productivity
TiSA	Trade in Services Agreement
TPA	Trade Promotion Agreement
TPP	Trans-Pacific Partnership Agreement
TRIPS	WTO Agreement on Trade-Related Aspects of Intellectual Property Rights
TTIP	Transatlantic Trade and Investment Partnership
UDHR	Universal Declaration of Human Rights
UK	United Kingdom
UN	United Nations
UN/CEFACT	United Nations Centre for Trade Facilitation and Electronic Business
UNCITRAL	United Nations Commission on International Trade Law
UNCTAD	United Nations Conference on Trade and Development
UNIDROIT	International Institute for the Unification of Private Law
UNIS	United Nations Information Service
UNT	Universal Trade Network
US	United States
USITC	United States International Trade Commission

USMCA	United States–Mexico–Canada Agreement
VPN	Virtual Private Network
WCO	World Customs Organization
WEF	World Economic Forum
WIPO	World Intellectual Property Organization
WTO	World Trade Organization
ZKP	Zero-Knowledge Proof

Introduction

Mira Burri[*]

Data has been conceptualized as the 'new oil'[1] and although this is a flawed statement, it catches well the high value attached to data as a driver of economic growth and innovation, and as a force of change in all facets of societal life.[2] The implications of data and data analytics are multiple and some of them can be far-reaching.[3] At a micro level, for instance, the value of data changes the traditional relationship between consumers and producers. While in the past, companies sold products to their customers in return for money and some negligible data, '[t]oday, transactions – and indeed every interaction with a consumer – produce valuable information. Sometimes the data itself is so valuable that companies such as *Facebook, LinkedIn, Pinterest, Twitter*, and many others are willing to offer free

[*] The book is the result of an international conference held at the University of Lucerne in November 2018, as part of the project 'Big Data and Trade Governance: Design, Diffusion and Implications', which forms part of the National Research Programme (NRP) 75: Big Data, sponsored by the Swiss National Science Foundation (SNF). The support of the SNF is kindly and gratefully acknowledged, as well as the intellectual support of all conference participants who challenged our views, pushed us further in our thoughts and provided invaluable feedback. Rahel Schär is to be thanked for her great work on the manuscript.
For the guidance of the reader, all websites, unless otherwise noted, have been last accessed on 1 July 2020. The book does not address the Covid-19 pandemic.
[1] *The Economist*, 'The World's Most Valuable Resource Is No Longer Oil, But Data', *print edition*, 6 May 2017.
[2] J. Manyika et al., *Big Data: The Next Frontier for Innovation, Competition, and Productivity* (Washington, DC: McKinsey Global Institute, 2011); J. Manyika et al., *Digital Globalization: The New Era of Global Flows* (Washington, DC: McKinsey Global Institute, 2016); V. Mayer-Schönberger and K. Cukier, *Big Data: A Revolution That Will Transform How We Live, Work, and Think* (New York: Eamon Dolan/Houghton Mifflin Harcourt, 2013).
[3] For a brief introduction on big data applications and review of the literature, see M. Burri, 'Understanding the Implications of Big Data and Big Data Analytics for Competition Law: An Attempt for a Primer', in K. Mathis and A. Tor (eds), *New Developments in Competition Behavioural Law and Economics* (Berlin: Springer, 2019), 241–263.

services in order to obtain it'.[4] Data has also become essential in terms of competition and market power. Some firms – like Apple, Google, Amazon, Facebook, Microsoft or Baidu – have had a sizeable first-mover advantage in the field and become 'analytics leaders', while at the same time establishing themselves as some of the most valuable companies in the world, as they benefit from double-sided markets.[5] The capacity to handle data has increasingly turned into a competitive advantage not only for companies but also for countries and plays out as a power move in the global political economy. For instance, China unveiled in 2016 that it is in possession of the world's fastest supercomputer, which was forty times more powerful than the fastest computer of 2010, only to be overcome by the United States in the following years by two IBM-built supercomputers.[6] The ongoing battle between China and the US with regard to 5G dominance is equally revealing.[7] Overall, companies as well as governments are increasingly encouraged to use the potential of data and to mobilize their resources aptly, so as to make the data-driven economy real.[8]

Accordingly, data has emerged as an important topic in contemporary law and policy – on the one hand, because it is critical to understand whether and how different societal areas have been affected by digital transformations, including by recent and disruptive phenomena like big data and artificial intelligence (AI), and on the other hand, because governance toolkits, including legal rules, need to adapt to reflect these implications. Despite the urgency attached to both these tasks and the intensified mobilization of research and policy efforts to address them, the topic of data-driven transformation has been explored in a fragmented manner and with a different depth of enquiry by different social sciences. This is somewhat understandable, as the regulation of data cannot be neatly contained in one policy domain but is affected by multiple, often non-hierarchically organized, regimes of both soft and hard legal nature, in both national and international contexts. The difficulty of pinpointing the regulatory subject matter of 'big data'[9] and of 'AI'[10] adds another

---

[4] N. Henke et al., *The Age of Analytics: Competing in a Data-Driven World* (Washington, DC: McKinsey Global Institute, 2016), at 26.

[5] Ibid. See Burri, note 3, for reference on double-sided markets.

[6] www.top500.org/list/2016/06/ and www.top500.org/lists/2019/11/.

[7] See, e.g., H. Sender, 'US–China Contest Centres on Race for 5G Domination', *Financial Times*, 25 January 2019.

[8] See, e.g., Manyika et al. (2016), note 2; Henke et al., note 4; J. Bughin et al., *Digital Europe: Pushing the Frontier, Capturing the Benefits* (Washington, DC: McKinsey Global Institute, 2016).

[9] See, e.g., Mayer-Schönberger and Cukier, note 2; B. van der Sloot, D. Broeders, and E. Schrijvers (eds), *Exploring the Boundaries of Big Data* (Amsterdam: University of Amsterdam Press, 2016).

[10] See, e.g., High-Level Expert Group on Artificial Intelligence, *A Definition of AI: Main Capabilities and Scientific Disciplines* (Brussels: European Commission, 2019). J. Fjeld et al., *Principled Artificial Intelligence: Mapping Consensus in Ethical and Rights-Based Approaches to Principles for AI* (Cambridge, MA: Berkman Klein Center for Internet and Society, 2020);

level of complexity and requires a deep understanding of the existing rules, which often, on their face, do not explicitly refer to data, and even less so to big data or AI, and may often stem from much older regulatory contexts and rationales.

One area of law and policy, which has so far been only marginally explored and has been particularly slow in reacting to digital transformation is trade law. At this juncture, neither do we have a full understanding of the implications of digitization for the entire body of global trade rules, nor do we know how the current set of rules impacts on the conditions for data-driven innovation and on data governance in general. At the same time and crucially, we have not seen any radical legal adaptation, and whatever changes have occurred can be categorized as incremental and limited in their impact, as stemming exclusively from bilateral or regional trade deals. The rules under the multilateral forum of the World Trade Organization (WTO) are still in their state of 1994 and accordingly tailored to regulate trade in tangible goods and brick-and-mortar businesses. To put it plainly, despite living in times of the 'Fourth Industrial Revolution', which epitomizes the deep impact of data across all sectors of the economy and the disruptive character of digitization,[11] we have trade rules grounded at 1.0.

The increased dependence on data has also brought about a new set of concerns. The impact of data collection and data use upon privacy has been particularly widely acknowledged by scholars and policymakers alike.[12] The risks have only been augmented in the era of big data and AI, which presents certain distinct challenges to the protection of personal data. While the tensions around data and privacy protection have in the beginning been exclusively thematized at the national level, the discourse has gradually received an international[13] as well as an international

---

The White House, Draft Memorandum to the Heads of Executive Departments and Agencies: Guidance for Regulation of Artificial Intelligence Applications, Executive Office of the President, 2020; T. Wischmeyer and T. Rademacher (eds), *Regulating Artificial Intelligence* (Berlin: Springer, 2020).

[11] L. Floridi, *The Fourth Revolution: How the Infosphere Is Reshaping Human Reality* (Oxford: Oxford University Press, 2014); K. Schwab, *The Fourth Industrial Revolution* (New York: Portfolio, 2017).

[12] See, e.g., P. M. Schwartz and D. J. Solove, 'The PII Problem: Privacy and a New Concept of Personally Identifiable Information', *New York University Law Review* 86 (2011), 1814–1894; O. Tene and J. Polonetsky, 'Big Data for All: Privacy and User Control in the Age of Analytics', *Northwestern Journal of Technology and Intellectual Property* 11 (2013), 239–273; The White House, *Big Data: Seizing Opportunities, Preserving Values* (Washington, DC: Executive Office of the President, 2014); U. Gasser, 'Recoding Privacy Law: Reflections on the Future Relationship among Law, Technology, and Privacy', *Harvard Law Review* 130 (2016), 61–70; S. B. Pan, 'Get to Know Me: Protecting Privacy and Autonomy under Big Data's Penetrating Gaze', *Harvard Journal of Law and Technology* 30 (2016), 239–261.

[13] See, e.g., C. Kuner, 'Data Nationalism and Its Discontents', *Emory Law Journal* 64 (2015), 2089–2098; S. J. Deckelboim, 'Consumer Privacy on an International Scale: Conflicting Viewpoints Underlying the EU–US Privacy Shield Framework and How the Framework Will Impact Privacy Advocates, National Security, and Businesses', *Georgetown Journal of International Law* 48 (2017), 263–296.

trade aspect.[14] The reason for this is twofold: first, it has become increasingly evident that cross-border data flows are absolutely essential, particularly in the age of big data, and this is true not only for digital enterprises but also for more conventional businesses like logistics or manufacturing companies.[15] The development of AI is also critically dependent on data inputs[16] and the realization of the data-driven economy, which is high on the agenda of governments around the world, can otherwise be hindered.[17] At the same time, it is a fact that the national regulation of data, with regard to privacy, national security or intellectual property protection, may constitute a significant barrier to trade.[18] 'Data protectionism' seems to be on the rise, especially as, post Snowden, states find it necessary to localize different elements of data flows so as to ensure jurisdictional control and enforceability of national rules.[19]

Despite the well-founded centrality of the data protection–trade topic, it should be noted that it constitutes merely one piece of the puzzle of data governance[20] and

---

[14] See, e.g., S. A. Aaronson, 'Why Trade Agreements Are Not Setting Information Free: The Lost History and Reinvigorated Debate over Cross-border Data Flows, Human Rights and National Security', *World Trade Review* 14 (2015), 671–700; S. Yakovleva, 'Should Fundamental Rights to Privacy and Data Protection Be a Part of EU's International Trade "Deals"?' *World Trade Review* 17 (2018), 477–508; M. Burri, 'Privacy and Data Protection', in D. Bethlehem et al. (eds), *The Oxford Handbook on International Trade Law*, 2nd edn (Oxford: Oxford University Press, forthcoming 2021); S. Yakovleva, 'Privacy Protection(ism): The Latest Wave of Trade Constraints on Regulatory Autonomy', *University of Miami Law Review* 74 (2020), 416–519.

[15] See, e.g., Manyika et al. (2011), note 2.

[16] See, e.g., K. Irion and J. Williams, *Prospective Policy Study on Artificial Intelligence and EU Trade Policy* (Amsterdam: Institute for Information Law, 2019); A. Goldfarb and D. Trefler, 'Artificial Intelligence and International Trade', in A. Agrawal, J. Gans, and A. Goldfarb (eds), *The Economics of Artificial Intelligence: An Agenda* (Chicago: The University of Chicago Press, 2019), 463–492.

[17] Centre for International Governance Innovation (CIGI), *Special Report: Data Governance in the Digital Age* (Waterloo: CIGI, 2018); European Commission, Artificial Intelligence for Europe, COM(2018) 237 final, 25 April 2018.

[18] United States International Trade Commission, *Digital Trade in the US and Global Economies*, Part 1, Investigation No 332–531 (Washington, DC: USITC, 2013); United States International Trade Commission, *Digital Trade in the US and Global Economies*, Part 2, Investigation No 332–540 (Washington, DC: USITC, 2014); World Economic Forum, 'Exploring International Data Flow Governance: Platform for Shaping the Future of Trade and Global Economic Interdependence', WEF *White Paper*, 2019.

[19] M. Bauer et al., *The Economic Importance of Getting Data Protection Right: Protecting Privacy, Transmitting Data, Moving Commerce* (Brussels: ECIPE, 2013); E. van der Marel, H. Lee-Makiyama, and M. Bauer, 'The Costs of Data Localisation: Friendly Fire on Economic Recovery', *ECIPE Occasional Paper* 3 (2014); Kuner, note 13; A. Chander and U. P. Lê, 'Data Nationalism', *Emory Law Journal* 64 (2015), 677–739; World Economic Forum, note 18.

[20] I. Brown and C. T. Marsden, *Regulating Code* (Cambridge, MA: MIT Press, 2013); R. H. Weber, *Realizing a New Global Cyberspace Framework* (Zurich: Schulthess, 2014); A. Agrawal, J. Gans, and A. Goldfarb (eds), *The Economics of Artificial Intelligence: An Agenda* (Chicago: The University of Chicago Press, 2019); Irion and Williams, note 16; L. DeNardis, *The Internet in Everything: Freedom and Security in a World with No Off Switch* (New Haven, CT: Yale University Press, 2020).

there are various other tensions, such as those in the area of other fundamental rights and key public interests, that have become exposed and need regulatory attention.[21] Overall, there is a distinct need to identify apposite and workable mechanisms in global trade law that can manage the trade-offs and reconcile the economic and non-economic interests that states pursue and can ensure the proper safeguarding of vital societal values.

It should be underscored in this context that whereas it is evident that digital technologies have had an impact on the economy as well as on social and cultural practices, they have at least equally strongly affected the law and patterns of governance in general. Governance models have in general become less state centred, and there is a proliferation of regulatory forms that involve multiple stakeholders, with varied types of supervisory and controlling functions entrusted to the state.[22] Trade law venues need to take into account this evolution and become permeable to multi-stakeholder involvement framed within a transparent framework,[23] which may reduce the general skepticism as to the appropriateness of trade forums and effectively tackle their deficiencies as to democratic participation and accountability.[24] Analogies to Internet governance processes may be useful in this regard;[25] the recent discourse on AI technologies clearly demands such public engagement and seeks to endorse respect for human autonomy, prevention of harm, fairness and explainability.[26] As data governance is intrinsically linked to the

---

[21] See, e.g., P. Margulies, 'Dynamic Surveillance: Evolving Procedures in Metadata and Content Collection after Snowden', *Hastings Law Journal* 66 (2014), 1–76; S. I. Vladeck, 'Big Data before and after Snowden', *Journal of National Security Law and Policy* 7 (2014), 333–339; Aaronson, note 14; S.-Y. Peng, 'Cybersecurity Threats and the WTO National Security Exceptions', *Journal of International Economic Law* 18 (2015), 449–478 N. Zhang, 'Trade Commitments and Data Flows: The National Security Wildcard Reconciling Name Record Transfer Agreements and European GATS Obligations', *World Trade Review* 18 (2019), 49–62.

[22] See, e.g., V. Mayer-Schönberger, 'The Shape of Governance: Analyzing the World of Internet Regulation', *Virginia Journal of International Law* 43 (2003), 605–673; O. Lobel, 'The Renew Deal: The Fall of Regulation and the Rise of Governance in Contemporary Legal Thought', *Minnesota Law Review* 89 (2004), 262–390; C. T. Marsden, *Internet Co-regulation: European Law, Regulatory Governance and Legitimacy in Cyberspace* (Cambridge: Cambridge University Press, 2011); M. Latzer, N. Just, and F. Saurwein, 'Self- and Co-regulation: Evidence, Legitimacy and Governance', in M. Price and S. Verhulst (eds), *Handbook of Media Law* (Abingdon: Routledge, 2012), 373–397; U. Pagallo, P. Casanovas, and R. Madelin, 'The Middle-Out Approach: Assessing Models of Legal Governance in Data Protection, Artificial Intelligence, and the Web of Data', *The Theory and Practice of Legislation* 7 (2019), 1–25.

[23] See, e.g., World Economic Forum, note 18.

[24] M. Burri, 'The Governance of Data and Data Flows in Trade Agreements: The Pitfalls of Legal Adaptation', *UC Davis Law Review* 51 (2017), 65–132; also S. Cho and C. R. Kelly, 'Are World Trading Rules Passé?', *Vanderbilt Journal of International Law* 53 (2013), 623–666.

[25] See, e.g., N. Mishra, 'Building Bridges: International Trade Law, Internet Governance, and the Regulation of Data Flows', *Vanderbilt Journal of Transnational Law* 52 (2019), 463–509.

[26] See, e.g., Irion and Williams, note 16; High-Level Expert Group on Artificial Intelligence, note 10; Fjeld et al., note 10.

functioning of the Internet as a generative end-to-end platform,[27] it may also be important to consider, and where possible integrate, its underlying and comple-mentary principles of Internet openness, security and privacy,[28] as well as to contem-plate the use of middle-out approaches of governance that combine top-down and bottom-up regulation.[29] While the WTO has been so far unresponsive to such governance shifts, preferential trade agreements (PTAs) may offer suitable venues, with more open and flexible procedural frameworks and participatory and co-regulatory elements, as the recent Digital Economy Partnership Agreement (DEPA) between Chile, New Zealand and Singapore at least partially suggests.

The book is set against this backdrop and under the title 'Big Data and Global Trade Law' seeks to explore the relevance of global trade law for data, big data and cross-border data flows. It analyzes how the regulatory landscape is evolving by tracing developments at the WTO and in preferential trade venues and asks what future-oriented models for data governance are available and viable in the area of trade law and policy. To befit this ambitious objective, the book collects contribu-tions by renowned scholars that have worked in the area of trade, law and techno-logical change for quite some time now and who were asked to reflect on the 'big switch' from analogue to digital and on the future of global trade law under the conditions of the data-driven economy. Equally critical for the value of the book is its cautious selection of topics, which aims to provide both a broader picture of the interaction between digital technologies and trade regulation and the therewith triggered governance challenges, as well as to look at discrete problems and issues in different domains of global data governance.

The book is structured along four thematic parts. Part I seeks to properly set the scene for the book's discussion and the individual enquiries. In an attempt to provide a good understanding of the phenomenon of big data and its interface with trade law, Chapter 1 (Burri) explores the regulation of data flows in global trade law, in particular by tracing the critical developments in PTAs over the course of the last two decades. The chapter is based on extensive empirical research reflected in author's own dataset, which analyzes more than 340 PTAs across 90 different criteria that may impact data governance. Chapter 2 (Elsig and Klotz) complements this legal analysis by offering an insight from the perspective of international relations and political science and explains the diffusion of different models of data flow regulation and the role of different factors, such as notably power, that may be driving this diffusion. Chapter 3, written by an economist and trade policy expert (Ferracane), looks at the costs of data protectionism – a phenomenon which is on

---

[27] See, e.g., R. S. Whitt, 'A Deference to Protocol: Fashioning a Three-Dimensional Public Policy Framework for the Internet Age', *Cardozo Arts and Entertainment Law Journal* 31 (2013), 689–768, at 717–729. J. L. Zittrain, *The Future of the Internet – and How to Stop It* (New Haven, CT: Yale University Press, 2008).

[28] Mishra, note 25.

[29] Latzer et al., note 22; Pagallo et al., note 22.

the rise in recent years as many states seek to keep data within their borders. Chapter 4, the final chapter within this introductory part, by Andrew Mitchell and Neha Mishra, explores the potential of the multilateral forum of the WTO to tackle key elements of data governance, such as ensuring technological neutrality or the protection of fundamental interests and values, such as privacy.

Part II moves on to explore the newer phenomena of the data-driven economy, as the practical reality of trade is certainly no longer about plain e-commerce (as in buying things online) but about digital trade. Anupam Chander kicks off the discussions with a visionary piece on AI and trade. The discourse is continued by Emmanuelle Ganne, who explores blockchain's practical implications for global trade and its regulation, and highlights the many opportunities that blockchain could offer, if properly embedded and governed. The following chapters charter the unknown territories in intellectual property (IP) law with regard to AI – first, in terms of mapping the IP interfaces with the different underlying AI technologies, such as data mining or algorithms (Gervais) under the regime of the WTO Agreement on Trade-Related Aspects of Intellectual Property Rights (TRIPS), and second, by again highlighting the challenges as well as the opportunities before legal adaptation in terms of border enforcement of intellectual property rights (Seuba).

Part III looks at the contestations within the broad topic of data governance by exposing, on the one hand, some of the constraints of global trade law, as naturally centred on economic rationales, and by exploring, on the other hand, the complex rights' and interests' clashes in the age of big data. Chapter 9 (Gasser) reflects on the protection of privacy in a data-driven world and the future relationship between law and technology, asking us to 'reimagine' the law–tech interface in full consideration of the affordances of the digital medium. Yakovleva and van Hoboken look at the triangle of data protection, AI and trade and explore the concept of algorithmic learning deficit, whereby a sole focus on privacy protection may not suffice. Kristina Irion pushes the debate further and offers the European perspective on how to ensure individual rights and freedoms in a world in which everything flows.

Part IV seeks to bundle different global perspectives on big data and trade and provides thoughtful enquiries on how different countries have positioned themselves in the area of digital trade governance. Chapter 12 (Gao) offers a unique and in-depth study of China's distinct approach towards data regulation, which can also help understand (and accommodate) China's stance on these issues on the international scene. Polanco continues the comparative analyses by adding the perspective of Latin America on digital trade governance and asking where, to what extent and why certain levels of regulatory convergence can be observed, and to what extent international commitments may be constraining domestic policy space, in particular with regard to data protection. Leblond takes the latter discussion a step further and seeks to expose the tensions between global trade deals and the national level by looking at the challenges two important trade treaties, the Comprehensive and Progressive Agreement on Transpacific Partnership (CPTPP) and the United

States–Mexico–Canada Agreement (USMCA), pose to Canadian data regulation. Chapter 15 (Thouvenin and Tamò-Larrieux) challenges key approaches to data governance by looking at the concepts of data ownership and data access rights and by asking whether and how they can be useful tools for promoting the European Union's Digital Single Market. The book ends with a provocative short piece by Susan Aaronson, who tells us that 'data is different' and urges policymakers to think differently about its governance and citizens to take an active part in the decision-making about their data.

Overall, the book offers a collection of expertise and viewpoints that address both the micro and macro level of global trade governance in the era of big data. While the answers given and recommendations made may differ, all contributors agree that both swift responses and apt regulatory design are needed to meet the challenge of rapid technological changes and make global trade law fit for the new data-driven economy. The changes demanded seem to go beyond mere adjustments in services classification or market access commitments (although these are needed too), and go in a bolder direction of rethinking, or as Gasser calls it,[30] 'reimaging', the relationship between law and technology, as to attain a legal design that balances between national and international domains, economic and non-economic interests and the different stakeholders' positions. There is some 'down-to-earth' WTO legal interpretation involved, as well as some 'blue sky' thinking, which also begs us to pay attention to the quality of rules and their potential impact, and may also trigger a rethinking of structures and processes of international rule-making in the interest of preserving legitimacy and of protecting global public goods in an interdependent world, while taking into account the pervasive as well as the enabling role of technology.

The timing of the book is critical as well as opportune, as issues of data governance are central to regulatory agendas and there are initiatives to advance different forms of international cooperation, as evidenced by the reinvigorated efforts under the WTO and other forums, and innovative agreements, such as the DEPA. It is our hope that this publication can not only contribute but help shape these discussions beyond biased stakeholders' opinions and persisting scholarly and policy disconnect.

---

[30] See Chapter 9 in this volume.

PART I

Global Trade Law and Policy in the Age of Big Data

1

Data Flows and Global Trade Law

*Mira Burri**

A INTRODUCTION

Information has always been a valuable as well as often sensitive asset for companies, states and citizens. In this sense, the link between data flowing across borders and the need to protect certain national interests is not entirely new and has been made before.[1] In particular during the late 1970s and the 1980s, as satellites, computers and software were profoundly changing the dynamics of communications, the trade-offs between allowing data to flow freely and asserting national jurisdiction became apparent. Echoing concerns of large multinational companies, some states worried that barriers to information flows might hinder economic activities and looked for mechanisms that could prevent the erection of such barriers. Non-binding solutions were found under the auspices of the Organisation for Economic Co-operation and Development (OECD) in the form of principles that sought to balance the free flow of data with the national interests in the fields of privacy and security.[2] Yet, as the OECD itself points out, while this privacy framework endured, the situation then was profoundly different from the challenges in the realm of data governance we face today.[3] Ubiquitous digitization and the societal embeddedness of digital media have changed the volume, the intensity and, indeed, the nature of data flows.[4]

* Mira Burri is Professor of International Economic and Internet Law and Managing Director Internationalization, Faculty of Law, University of Lucerne. Contact: mira.burri@unilu.ch.

[1] See, e.g., C. Kuner, 'Regulation of Transborder Data Flows under Data Protection and Privacy Law: Past, Present and Future', OECD Digital Economy Paper No 187 (2011); S. A. Aaronson, 'Why Trade Agreements Are Not Setting Information Free: The Lost History and Reinvigorated Debate over Cross-Border Data Flows, Human Rights and National Security', *World Trade Review* 14 (2015), 671–700, at 672, 680–685.

[2] OECD, *Guidelines for the Protection of Personal Information and Transborder Data Flows* (Paris: OECD, 1980).

[3] OECD, *The OECD Privacy Framework: Supplementary Explanatory Memorandum to the Revised OECD Privacy Guidelines* (Paris: OECD, 2013).

[4] See J. Manyika et al., *Big Data: The Next Frontier for Innovation, Competition, and Productivity* (Washington, DC: McKinsey Global Institute, 2011); V. Mayer-Schönberger and

The value of data, as well as the risks associated with data collection, data processing, data use and reuse, by both companies and governments, has dramatically changed. Beyond the flawed mantra of data being the 'new oil',[5] many studies point at the vast potential of data as a trigger for more efficient business operations, highly innovative solutions and better policy choices in all areas of societal life.[6] This transformative potential refers notably not only to 'digital native' areas, such as search or social networking, but also to brick-and-mortar or physical businesses, such as in manufacturing or logistics.[7] Overall, the implications of big data availability and analytics are multiple and some of them far reaching.[8]

Recent enquiries have shown that not only the sheer amount of data and our dependence on it have exponentially increased but also the ways governments assert control over global data flows have changed.[9] Exerting jurisdiction over online matters beyond borders, as exemplified by the seminal French judgment in the *Yahoo!* case,[10] or Internet censorship, as practised by China and many other states,[11] are well-known examples of control. Yet, the new generation of Internet controls seeks to keep information from going *out* of a country, rather than stopping it from

K. Cukier, *Big Data: A Revolution That Will Transform How We Live, Work, and Think* (New York: Eamon Dolan/Houghton Mifflin Harcourt, 2013); J. E. Cohen, 'What Privacy Is For', *Harvard Law Review* 126 (2013), 1904–1933, at 1920–1921.

[5] *The Economist*, 'The World's Most Valuable Resource Is No Longer Oil, but Data', 6 May 2017.

[6] See, e.g., Manyika et al., note 4; Mayer-Schönberger and Cukier, note 4; N. Henke et al., *The Age of Analytics: Competing in a Data-Driven World* (Washington, DC: McKinsey Global Institute, 2016).

[7] See, e.g., Manyika et al., note 4.

[8] There are no clear definitions of small versus Big Data. Definitions vary and scholars seem to agree that the term of Big Data is generalized and slightly imprecise. One common identification of Big Data is through characteristics of volume, velocity, and variety, also referred to as the '3-Vs'. Increasingly, experts add a fourth 'V' that relates to the veracity or reliability of the underlying data, as well as a fifth 'V' that relates to its value. See Mayer-Schönberger and Cukier, note 4, at 13. For a brief introduction on Big Data applications and review of the literature, see M. Burri, 'Understanding the Implications of Big Data and Big Data Analytics for Competition Law: An Attempt for a Primer', in K. Mathis and A. Tor (eds), *New Developments in Competition Behavioural Law and Economics* (Berlin: Springer, 2019), 241–263.

[9] See A. Chander, 'National Data Governance in a Global Economy', UC Davis Legal Studies Research Paper No 495 (2016), at 2; also A. Chander and U. P. Lê, 'Data Nationalism', *Emory Law Journal* 64 (2015), 677–739.

[10] Tribunal de Grande Instance de Paris, *Ligue contre le racisme et l'antisémitisme et Union des étudiants juifs de France c. Yahoo! Inc. et Société Yahoo! France (LICRA v. Yahoo!)*, R6 00/05308 (2000). For more on the case, see also J. Goldsmith and T. Wu, *Who Controls the Internet? Illusions of a Borderless World* (Oxford: Oxford University Press, 2001), at 49–64; M. H. Greenberg, 'A Return to Lilliput: The *LICRA v. Yahoo* – Case and the Regulation of Online Content in the World Market', *Berkeley Technology Law Review* 18 (2003), 1191–1258.

[11] See, e.g., R. Deibert et al. (eds), *Access Denied: The Practice and Policy of Global Internet Filtering* (Cambridge, MA: MIT Press, 2008); R. Deibert et al. (eds), *Access Controlled: The Shaping of Power, Rights, and Rule in Cyberspace* (Cambridge, MA: MIT Press, 2010); R. Deibert et al., *Access Contested: Security, Identity, and Resistance in Asian Cyberspace* (Cambridge, MA: MIT Press, 2011).

entering the sovereign state space. Governments increasingly 'localize' the data within their jurisdictions for a variety of reasons.[12] To be sure, this kind of erecting barriers to data flows impinges directly on trade and may endanger the realization of an innovative data economy. The provision of any digital products and services, cloud computing applications or, if we think in more future-oriented terms, the Internet of Things (IoT) and artificial intelligence (AI), would not function under restrictions on the cross-border flow of data.[13] Data protectionism also comes at a certain cost for the countries adopting such measures.[14]

At the same time, while it may often be true that higher levels of data protection will amount to a trade barrier, one cannot disregard the legitimate desire of countries to safeguard the fundamental rights of their citizens, public interests and values that matter for their constituencies. The impact of data collection and data use upon privacy protection in particular has been, in recent years, widely acknowledged by scholars and policymakers alike, as well as felt on the ground by regular users of digital products and services.[15] The risks have only been augmented in the era of big data, which presents certain distinct challenges to the protection of personal data and, by extension, to the protection of personal and family life.[16]

---

[12] United States International Trade Commission, *Digital Trade in the US and Global Economies*, Part 1, Investigation No 332-531 (Washington, DC: USITC, 2013); United States International Trade Commission, *Digital Trade in the US and Global Economies*, Part 2, Investigation No 332-540 (Washington, DC: USITC, 2014). For a country survey, see Chander and Lê, note 9.

[13] See Chander, note 9, at 2. See also Chapter 5 in this volume.

[14] See Chapter 3 in this volume.

[15] See P. Ohm, 'Broken Promises of Privacy: Responding to the Surprising Failure of Anonymization', *UCLA Law Review* 57 (2010), 1701–1777; P. M. Schwartz and D. J. Solove, 'The PII Problem: Privacy and a New Concept of Personally Identifiable Information', *New York University Law Review* 86 (2011), 1814–1894; O. Tene and J. Polonetsky, 'Big Data for All: Privacy and User Control in the Age of Analytics', *Northwestern Journal of Technology and Intellectual Property* 11 (2013), 239–273; The White House, *Big Data: Seizing Opportunities, Preserving Values* (Washington, DC: Executive Office of the President, 2014); U. Gasser, 'Perspectives on the Future of Digital Privacy', *Zeitschrift für Schweizerisches Recht* 135 (2015), 335–448; U. Gasser, 'Recoding Privacy Law: Reflections on the Future Relationship among Law, Technology, and Privacy', *Harvard Law Review* 130 (2016), 61–70; C. J. Bennett and R. M. Bayley, 'Privacy Protection in the Era of "Big Data": Regulatory Challenges and Social Assessments', in B. van der Sloot, D. Broeders and E. Schrijvers (eds), *Exploring the Boundaries of Big Data* (Amsterdam: University of Amsterdam Press, 2016), 205–227; S. B. Pan, 'Get to Know Me: Protecting Privacy and Autonomy under Big Data's Penetrating Gaze', *Harvard Journal of Law and Technology* 30 (2016), 239–261; Council of Europe, Guidelines on the Protection of Individuals with Regard to the Processing of Personal Data in a World of Big Data, Strasbourg, T-PD(2017)01, 23 January 2017. See also Chapter 9 in this volume.

[16] The protection of privacy and family life are fundamental human rights enshrined in a number of international and regional acts, such as the Council of Europe's European Convention on Human Rights. The Charter of Fundamental Rights of the European Union (CFREU) distinguishes between the right of respect for private and family life in Article 7 and the right to protection of personal data, which is explicitly enshrined in Article 8. This distinction is no coincidence but reflects the heightened concern of the EU and translates into a positive duty to implement an effective protection of personal data and to regulate the transmission of such

Indeed, big data puts into question the very distinction between personal and non-personal data. On the one hand, it appears that one of the basic tools of data protection – that of anonymization, i.e. the process of removing identifiers to create anonymized datasets – is only of limited utility in a data-driven world, as in reality it is now rare for data generated by user activity to be completely and irreversibly anonymized.[17] On the other hand, big data enables the reidentification of data subjects by using and combining datasets of non-personal data, especially as data is persistent and can be retained indefinitely with the presently available technologies.[18]

Big data also puts into question the fundamental elements of existing privacy protection laws, which often operate upon requirements of transparency and user's consent.[19] Equally is data minimization as another core idea of privacy protection challenged, as firms are 'hungry' to get hold of more and more data.[20] These challenges have not been left unnoticed and have triggered the reform of data protection laws around the world, best exemplified by the European Union's General Data Protection Regulation (GDPR).[21] The reform initiatives are, however, not coherent and are culturally and socially embedded, reflecting societies' deep understandings of constitutional values, relationships between citizens and the state, and the role of the market, to name but a few.[22] The striking divergences both in the perceptions and the regulation of privacy protection across nations and in particular between the fundamental rights approach of the EU and the more market-based, non-interventionist approach of the United States[23] have also meant that conventional forms of international cooperation and an agreement on shared standards of data protection have become highly unlikely.

data. See Charter of Fundamental Rights of the European Union, OJ C [2010] 83/2; also M. Burri and R. Schär, 'The Reform of the EU Data Protection Framework: Outlining Key Changes and Assessing Their Fitness for a Data-Driven Economy', *Journal of Information Policy* 6 (2016), 479–511.

[17] The White House, note 15, at 14.
[18] Ibid., at 14–15; also Ohm, note 15 and Chapter 9 in this volume.
[19] I. S. Rubinstein, 'Big Data: The End of Privacy or a New Beginning?', *International Data Privacy Law* 3 (2013), 74–87, at 78.
[20] Tene and Polonetsky, note 15.
[21] Regulation 2016/679 of the European Parliament and of the Council of 27 April 2016 on the Protection of Natural Persons with Regard to the Processing of Personal Data and on the Free Movement of Such Data, and Repealing Directive 95/46/EC (General Data Protection Regulation), OJ L [2016] 119/1 [hereinafter: GDPR].
[22] See, e.g., A. Chander, M. E. Kaminski and W. McGeveran, 'Catalyzing Privacy Law', University of Colorado Law Legal Studies Research Paper No 25 (2019).
[23] See, e.g., J. Q. Whitman, 'The Two Western Cultures of Privacy: Dignity versus Liberty', *The Yale Law Journal* 113 (2004), 1151–1221; P. M. Schwartz, 'The EU–US Privacy Collision: A Turn to Institutions and Procedures', *Harvard Law Review* 126 (2013), 1966–2009; P. M. Schwartz and D. J. Solove, 'Reconciling Personal Information in the United States and European Union', *California Law Review* 102 (2014), 877–916.

Against this backdrop of a complex and contentious regulatory environment, data and cross-border data flows in particular have become one of the relatively new topics in global trade law discussions. Many questions have been raised in this context, for instance, whether and how do the existing trade rules apply to data flows? How should they be classified – as a good or a service, and if categorized as a service, under which services sector do they fall? How do we address new trade barriers, such as localization measures? How can we reconcile the free flow of data and countries' privacy, national security and other public interest concerns? How do we ensure that trade law accommodates the data-driven economy and enables global trade for the benefit of all? Which are the appropriate forum and the decision-making processes for moving the global data economy agenda ahead? Many of these questions are still open and this chapter will not give satisfactory answers to them all. It will nonetheless provide valuable information and insights about the current state of global trade law that may help policymakers down the road. In this sense, the chapter has a two-prong objective: first, it seeks to clarify the interfaces between the data-driven economy and existing trade law; second, and more importantly, it traces the regulatory responses and the emerging legal design in preferential trade agreements (PTAs) with regard to digital trade and data flows in particular.

B WTO LAW AS PRE-INTERNET LAW

While PTAs are in the spotlight of this chapter, the multilateral forum of the World Trade Organization (WTO) cannot be simply ignored – on the one hand, because it matters in its own right as a set of hard and enforceable rules on trade in goods, services and intellectual property (IP) protection, and on the other hand, because PTAs are in many senses only an addition to these rules. Politically speaking, the failings of the multilateral system on certain issues have prompted action on those issues in the preferential venues and this is particularly evident in the area of digital trade, as revealed later.

The WTO agreements, the fundamental basis of international trade law, were adopted during the Uruguay Round (1986–1994) and came into force in 1995.[24] Despite some adjustments – such as Information Technology Agreement (ITA),[25] its update in 2015 and the Trade Facilitation Agreement,[26] WTO law has not

---

[24] General Agreement on Tariffs and Trade 1994, 1867 U.N.T.S. 187; 33 I.L.M. 1153 (1994), entered into force 1 January 1995 [hereinafter: GATT]; General Agreement on Trade in Services, 1869 U.N.T.S. 183; 33 I.L.M. 1167 (1994), entered into force 1 January 1995 [hereinafter: GATS]; Agreement on Trade-Related Aspects of Intellectual Property Rights, 1869 U.N.T.S. 299; 33 I.L.M. 1197 (1994), entered into force 1 January 1995 [hereinafter: TRIPS].

[25] WTO, Ministerial Declaration on Trade in Information Technology Products, WT/MIN(96)/16 (1996).

[26] WTO, Protocol Amending the Marrakesh Agreement Establishing the World Trade Organization, Decision of 27 November 2014, WT/L/940 (2014), entered into force on 22 February 2017 following the ratification by two-thirds of the WTO membership.

fundamentally changed and is still very much in its pre-Internet state.[27] One could, of course, argue that laws need not change with each and every new technological invention.[28] And indeed, the law of the WTO lends credence to such an argument because it is in many aspects, both in the substance and in the procedure, flexible and resilient. WTO law can be qualified as relatively 'hard', as it involves deep intervention in domestic regulatory regimes and can impose certain sanctions for breach of obligations.[29] It is furthermore based on powerful principles of non-discrimination, such as the most-favoured nation (MFN) and the national treatment (NT) obligations, that address all areas of economic life and could potentially tackle technological developments better than new made-to-measure regulatory acts. Many of the rules with regard to the application of the basic principles, with regard to standards, trade facilitation, subsidies and government procurement do also operate in a technologically neutral way.[30]

Another advantage of WTO law that may be highlighted is that despite its high degree of legalization and focus on economic rules, it also permits some flexibilities. One of those relates to the so-called general exceptions clauses formulated under Article XX of the General Agreement on Tariffs and Trade (GATT) 1994 and Article XIV of the General Agreement on Trade in Services (GATS), which allow WTO members to adopt measures that would otherwise violate their obligations and undertaken commitments, under the condition that these measures are not be applied in a manner that would constitute a means of arbitrary or unjustifiable discrimination between countries where like conditions prevail, or a disguised restriction on trade. Particularly interesting for this chapter's discussion on data flows are the possibilities that Article XIV of the GATS may open for maintaining existing and adopting new data restrictions. Article XIV enumerates different grounds as possible justifications and includes two specific categories that are of pertinence for our topic: (a) those relating to public order or public morals[31] and

---

[27] M. Burri, 'The Governance of Data and Data Flows in Trade Agreements: The Pitfalls of Legal Adaptation', *UC Davies Law Review* 51 (2017), 65–132.

[28] See famously, F. H. Easterbrook, 'Cyberspace and the Law of the Horse', *The University of Chicago Legal Forum* 1996 (1996), 207–216.

[29] G. C. Shaffer and M. A. Pollack, 'Hard vs. Soft Law: Alternatives, Complements, and Antagonists in International Governance', *Minnesota Law Review* 94 (2010), 706–799, at 715.

[30] See M. Burri and T. Cottier (eds), *Trade Governance in the Digital Age* (Cambridge: Cambridge University Press, 2012); for an overview, see M. Burri, 'The International Economic Law Framework for Digital Trade', *Zeitschrift für Schweizerisches Recht* 135 (2015), 10–72.

[31] Article XIV(a) GATS. For an analysis, see J. C. Marwell, 'Trade and Morality: The WTO Public Morals Exception after *Gambling*', *New York University Law Review* 81 (2006), 802–842; M. Wu, 'Free Trade and the Protection of Public Morals: An Analysis of the Newly Emerging Public Morals Clause Doctrine', *Yale Journal of International Law* 33 (2008), 215–250; P. Delimatsis, 'The Puzzling Interaction of Trade and Public Morals in the Digital Era', in M. Burri and T. Cottier (eds), *Trade Governance in the Digital Age* (Cambridge: Cambridge University Press, 2010), 276–296.

(b) those that are necessary to secure compliance with laws or regulations,[32] including such on 'the protection of the privacy of individuals in relation to the processing and dissemination of personal data and the protection of confidentiality of individual records and accounts'.[33] Under this provision, it has been argued, for instance, that the rules of the GDPR may be found to violate the obligations of the EU under the GATS.[34]

Finally, in terms of evolution of norms, it can be maintained that the WTO possesses the advantage of a dispute settlement system that can foster legal evolution.[35] There is strong evidence in the WTO jurisprudence for both the capacity of the dispute settlement mechanism and for the relevance of the Internet in trade conflicts.[36] The *US–Gambling*[37] case is a great example in this context, as it confirmed that the GATS commitments apply to electronically supplied services and clarified key notions of services regulation, such as likeness and the scope of the 'public morals/public order' defence under Article XIV of the GATS.[38]

---

[32] Article XIV(c) GATS. For a commentary of Article XIV GATS, see T. Cottier, P. Delimatsis and N. Diebold, 'Article XIV GATS: General Exceptions', in R. Wolfrum, P.-T. Stoll and C. Feinäugle (eds), *Max Planck Commentaries on World Trade Law. Vol. 6: Trade in Services* (Leiden: Martinus Nijhoff Publishers, 2008), 287–328; H. Andersen, 'Protection of Non-trade Values in WTO Appellate Body Jurisprudence: Exceptions, Economic Arguments, and Eluding Questions', *Journal of International Economic Law* 18 (2015), 383–405.

[33] Article XIV(c)(ii) GATS.

[34] For a fully-fledged analysis, see R. H. Weber, 'Regulatory Autonomy and Privacy Standards under the GATS', *Asian Journal of WTO and International Health Law and Policy* 7 (2012), 25–47; K. Irion, S. Yakovleva and M. Bartl, *Trade and Privacy: Complicated Bedfellows?* (Amsterdam: Institute for Information Law, 2016), at 27–33. See also Chapter 4 in this volume.

[35] See, e.g., G. Sacerdoti et al. (eds), *The WTO at Ten: The Contribution of the Dispute Settlement System* (Cambridge: Cambridge University Press, 2006). For the current crisis of the WTO dispute settlement, see J. Pauwelyn, 'WTO Dispute Settlement Post 2019: What to Expect?', *Journal of International Economic Law* 22 (2019), 297–321.

[36] In fact, several major GATS cases have had a substantial Internet-related element. See WTO Panel Report, *Mexico – Measures Affecting Telecommunications Services (Mexico – Telecommunications)*, WT/DS204/R, adopted 2 April 2004; Panel Report, *United States – Measures Affecting the Cross-Border Supply of Gambling and Betting Services (US – Gambling)*, WT/DS285/R, adopted 10 November 2004; Appellate Body Report, *United States – Measures Affecting the Cross-Border Supply of Gambling and Betting Services (US – Gambling)*, WT/DS285/AB/R, adopted 7 April 2005; Panel Report, *China – Measures Affecting Trading Rights and Distribution Services for Certain Publications and Audiovisual Entertainment Products (China – Publications and Audiovisual Products)*, WT/DS363/R, adopted 12 August 2009; Appellate Body Report, *China – Measures Affecting Trading Rights and Distribution Services for Certain Publications and Audiovisual Entertainment Products (China – Publications and Audiovisual Products)*, WT/DS363/AB/R, adopted 21 December 2009; WTO Panel Report, *China – Certain Measures Affecting Electronic Payment Services (China – Electronic Payment Services)*, WT/DS413/R, adopted 31 August 2012.

[37] Ibid. In *US – Gambling*, Antigua brought a claim against the United States alleging that its restrictions on cross-border gambling services violated its obligations under the GATS. The Panel and the Appellate Body's findings focused on the violation of the US obligations for market access under Article XVI GATS.

[38] M. Krajewski, 'Playing by the Rules of the Game? Specific Commitments after *US – Gambling and Betting* and the Current GATS Negotiations', *Legal Issues of Economic Integration* 32

Yet, plainly assuming that the WTO's 'adaptive governance'[39] works will be flawed. Indeed, there are many reasons to question it and be rather sceptic about the match between the existing WTO rules, their implementation and evolution, and contemporary digital trade. Apart from the current political context, which may prevent new and forward-looking rule-making,[40] there are important hindrances in applying the GATS in the digital environment. In particular, the GATS commitments are based upon old pre-Internet classifications of services and sectors, and these have become increasingly disconnected from trade practices.[41] For instance, as the WTO law presently stands, it is unclear whether previously unknown things, such as online games, should be categorized as goods or services (and thus whether the more binding GATT or the GATS apply). Provided that no physical medium is involved and one decides consequently to apply the GATS, the classification puzzle is by no means solved: Online games, for instance, as a new type of content platform, could be potentially fitted into the discrete categories of computer and related services, value-added telecommunications services, entertainment or audiovisual services. One may also be unsure when there is an electronic data flow intrinsic to the service whether to classify this flow separately or as part of the traditional services.[42] Classification is by no means trivial,[43] as each category implies a completely different set of duties and/or flexibilities for the WTO members. If online platforms and the services they offer were to be classified as computer services, for example, states would lack any wiggle-room whatsoever and would have to grant full access to foreign services and services suppliers and treat them as they treat domestic ones — because of the high level of existing commitments under the GATS of

(2005), 417–447; S. Wunsch-Vincent, 'The Internet, Cross-Border Trade in Services, and the GATS: Lessons from *US–Gambling*', *World Trade Review* 3 (2006), 1–37; P. Delimatsis, 'Don't Gamble with GATS–The Interaction between Articles VI, XVI, XVII and XVIII GATS in the Light of the *US–Gambling* Case', *Journal of World Trade* 40 (2006), 1059–1080.

[39] R. Cooney and A. T. F. Lang, 'Taking Uncertainty Seriously: Adaptive Governance and International Trade', *European Journal of International Law* 18 (2007), 523–551; also A. T. F. Lang and J. Scott, 'The Hidden World of WTO Governance', *European Journal of International Law* 20 (2009), 575–614.

[40] For an analysis of crisis of the WTO, see, e.g., M. Elsig, M. Hahn and G. Spilker (eds), *The Shifting Landscape of Global Trade Governance* (Cambridge: Cambridge University Press, 2019).

[41] See Burri and Cottier, note 30.

[42] For a discussion of the application of technology neutrality to services classification, see S.-Y. Peng, 'GATS and the Over-the-Top Services: A Legal Outlook', *Journal of World Trade* 50 (2016), 21–46. One recent article argues a bit oddly that data should be classified separately as a good in analogy to electricity. See R. S. Neeraj, 'Trade Rules for the Digital Economy: Charting New Waters at the WTO', *World Trade Review* 18 (2019), 121–141.

[43] See R. H. Weber and M. Burri, *Classification of Services in the Digital Economy* (Berlin: Springer, 2012); S.-Y. Peng, 'Renegotiate the WTO Schedule of Commitments? Technological Development and Treaty Interpretation', *Cornell International Law Journal* 45 (2012), 403–430; I. Willemyns, 'GATS Classification of Digital Services – Does "The Cloud" Have a Silver Lining?', *Journal of World Trade* 53 (2019), 59–82.

virtually all WTO members.[44] On the other hand, were online games classified as audiovisual services, most WTO members would have the policy space to maintain and adopt restrictive and discriminatory measures.[45] The evolutionary interpretation of schedules of specific commitments, as affirmed in *China–Audiovisual Products*, while a positive development, does not necessarily help much to achieve legal certainty in such situations.[46] Neither does the finding that the GATT and the GATS are not mutually exclusive.[47]

The classification dilemma, as particularly critical for digital trade, is an illuminating example of this state of paralysis but by far not the only one. Many other issues, although discussed in the framework of the 1998 WTO Work Programme on Electronic Commerce, have been left without a solution or even a clarification.[48] For instance and as a minimum for advancing on the digital trade agenda, there is still no agreement on a permanent moratorium on customs duties on electronic transmissions and their content.[49] Against the backdrop of pre-Internet WTO law and despite the recent reinvigoration of the e-commerce negotiations under the 2019 Joint Statement Initiative,[50] many of the disruptive changes underpinning the data-driven economy have demanded regulatory solutions outside the ailing multilateral trade forum. States around the world have used in particular the venue of preferential trade agreements to fill in some of the gaps of the WTO framework, clarify its applications and beyond that, address the newer trade barriers and accommodate their striving for seamless digital trade. Quite naturally for developments in

---

[44] For all members' commitments in the sector, see www.wto.org/english/tratop_e/serv_e/computer_e/computer_e.htm

[45] The EU has strongly argued for such a classification, so as to be able to maintain its supporting schemes. The promotion of local content in digitally delivered services is however not limited to Europe. The Chinese Ministry of Culture reportedly has classified online games as 'cultural products' supports the domestic industry. See USITC (2013), note 12, at 5–7.

[46] In *China – Publications and Audiovisual Products*, note 36, at para. 396. The Appellate Body found that the terms in China's Schedule 'are sufficiently generic that what they apply to may change over time'.

[47] As confirmed by WTO Appellate Body Report, *European Communities – Regime for the Importation, Sale and Distribution of Bananas (EC – Bananas)*, WT/DS27/AB/R, adopted 9 September 1997; WTO Appellate Body Report, *Canada – Certain Measures Affecting the Automotive Industry (Canada – Autos)*, WT/DS139/AB/R, WT/DS142/AB/R, adopted 31 May 2000.

[48] S. Wunsch-Vincent and A. Hold, 'Towards Coherent Rules for Digital Trade: Building on Efforts in Multilateral versus Preferential Trade Negotiations', in M. Burri and T. Cottier (eds), *Trade Governance in the Digital Age* (Cambridge: Cambridge University Press, 2012), 179–221, at 181.

[49] The moratorium has only been temporarily extended several times, the last time for a period of two years following a decision taken in 2019. In recent years, there has even been a push by India and South Africa to rethink the scope, definition and impact of the moratorium. See WTO, Work Programme on Electronic Commerce – Review of Progress, Report by the Chairperson, WT/GC/W/780, 25 July 2019.

[50] WTO, Joint Statement on Electronic Commerce, WT/L/1056, 25 January 2019. As of 29 March 2019, 77 WTO Members support the initiative. For details, see M. Burri, 'Towards a New Treaty on Digital Trade', *Journal of World Trade* 55 (2021), 77–100.

preferential trade, the framework that has emerged as a result and now regulates contemporary digital trade is not coherent. It is neither evenly spread across different countries, nor otherwise coordinated. Indeed, it is messy and fragmented both with regard to the substantive rules and the agreements' membership.

In the following section, the chapter provides an overview of the developments in PTAs in the last two decades in the area of digital trade governance. The information stems from our own dataset *TAPED: Trade Agreement Provisions on Electronic Commerce and Data*,[51] which ran a detailed mapping and coding of all PTAs that include chapters, provisions, annexes or side documents that directly or indirectly regulate digital trade. In the subsequent section, we look at the new rules on free data flows and their design across different PTAs. We then analyze in more detail the most sophisticated template for digital trade rules that we have so far – that of the Comprehensive and Progressive Agreement for Trans-Pacific Partnership (CPTPP) and some subsequent developments in the United States–Mexico–Canada Agreement (USMCA). In the final section, the chapter offers some thoughts about the current state of global digital trade law and the prospects of governing data flows.

C EVOLUTION OF DIGITAL TRADE PROVISIONS IN PTAS

I *Overview and Some Emerging Trends*

From the 347 PTAs agreed upon between 2000 and 2019 and reviewed in TAPED, 184 PTAs have provisions related to digital trade.[52] The largest number of provisions is found in e-commerce and intellectual property chapters; overall, the provisions remain however highly heterogeneous, addressing various issues ranging from customs duties and paperless trading to personal data protection and cybersecurity. The depth of the commitments and the extent of their binding nature can also vary significantly. For instance, if one looks at the top countries that have entered into

---

[51] See M. Burri and R. Polanco, 'Digital Trade Provisions in Preferential Trade Agreements: Introducing a New Dataset', *Journal of International Economic Law* 23 (2020), 187–220. The TAPED dataset is available to all to use and further develop under the creative commons (attribution, non-commercial, share-alike) licence at the University of Lucerne website (www .unilu.ch/taped). For some previous attempts with a limited number of agreements, see, e.g., S. Wunsch-Vincent, 'Trade Rules for the Digital Age', in M. Panizzon, N. Pohl and P. Sauvé (eds), *GATS and the Regulation of International Trade in Services* (Cambridge: Cambridge University Press, 2008), 497–529; Wunsch-Vincent and Hold, note 48; J.-A. Monteiro and R. Teh, 'Provisions on Electronic Commerce in Regional Trade Agreements', WTO Working Paper No 11 (2017).
[52] The tables and figures in this section include treaties until end of 2019 at time of writing. The US–Japan Digital Trade Agreement has been covered but not the Digital Economy Partnership Agreement (DEPA) between Chile, Singapore and New Zealand and the EU–Vietnam FTA.

PTAs with e-commerce provisions,[53] the European Union occupies the first place with Singapore, yet it is only in the very recent EU PTAs[54] that there is a dedicated chapter on e-commerce and some substantive provisions – beforehand e-commerce provisions were only few, part of the services chapters and limited to mere GATS-level commitments and cooperation pledges.[55]

Putting the digital trade provisions along a chronological line, it is evident that the inclusion of provisions in PTAs referring explicitly to electronic commerce is not a recent phenomenon, although it has evolved significantly in the past eighteen years. The first e-commerce provision dates back to the 2000 Free Trade Agreement (FTA) between Jordan and the United States.[56] Almost at the same time, New Zealand and Singapore agreed upon the Closer Economic Partnership Agreement (CEPA), including an article on paperless trading. Two years later, the Australia–Singapore FTA (SAFTA), concluded on 17 February 2003, was the first PTA to have a dedicated chapter on e-commerce. At the moment of this writing, specific provisions applicable to e-commerce can be found in 109 PTAs, mostly in dedicated chapters (79) (for details, see Table 1.1). The last eight years have witnessed a significant increase in the number of agreements with digital trade provisions. As shown in Figure 1.1, digital trade provisions are, on average, included in more than 68 per cent of all PTAs that were concluded between 2010 and 2019 and despite the fall in agreed upon deals, more of them include digital trade provisions. The rise in the total number of PTAs with such norms is driven mainly by bilateral PTAs: 84 per cent of total PTAs since 2000 and involves both developed and developing countries.[57]

Among the PTAs with digital trade provisions, it is evident that the number and level of detail have also increased significantly over the years, as depicted in Figure 1.2. In 2019, 13 is the average number of provisions found in e-commerce chapters of PTAs, with an average number of 2,527 words (see Table 1.2).

At the moment of writing, the Singapore–Australia Free Trade Agreement (SAFTA), updated in 2016, is the PTA in force with the highest number of provisions in an e-commerce chapter (19 in total), with 2,997 words. As of 2020, the USMCA

---

[53] The overall list will look like this: (1) Singapore – 22 PTAs; (2) EU – 22 PTAs; (3) Australia – 15 PTAs; (4) United States – 14 PTAs; (5) Chile – 13 PTAs; (6) Canada – 12 PTAs; (7) Colombia – 11 PTAs; (8) South Korea, Japan and Peru – 10 PTAs; (9) Panama, Costa Rica and New Zealand – 8 PTAs. See also Chapter 2 in this volume.

[54] EU–Canada Comprehensive Economic Trade and Investment Agreement (CETA), EU–Singapore FTA, EU–Vietnam FTA, EU–Japan FTA, EU–Indonesia FTA, EU–Philippines FTA and EU–Mexico FTA.

[55] See, e.g., M. Burri, 'The Regulation of Data Flows in Trade Agreements', *Georgetown Journal of International Law* 48 (2017), 408–448.

[56] Article 7 US–Jordan FTA.

[57] Following the UN country classification, 48 per cent of the PTAs with digital trade provisions were negotiated between developed and developing countries, and 49 per cent were negotiated between developing countries. Only 3 per cent of PTAs negotiated between developed countries include digital trade provisions. See also Chapter 2 in this volume.

TABLE 1.1. *PTAs concluded with digital trade provisions per year (2000–2019)*

Year	Total PTAs	WTO notified	Digital trade provisions	E-commerce chapters	% PTAs with digital trade provisions
2000	20	8	2	0	10.00
2001	23	12	2	0	8.70
2002	26	8	4	0	16.00
2003	30	10	6	3	20.69
2004	29	14	6	6	21.43
2005	17	10	5	4	33.33
2006	26	13	7	6	31.82
2007	20	13	4	4	29.41
2008	24	27	9	6	40.91
2009	23	21	6	3	19.05
2010	14	18	5	3	50.00
2011	19	15	2	2	18.75
2012	8	20	3	3	33.33
2013	14	22	9	6	64.29
2014	14	12	10	7	88.89
2015	10	10	6	5	50.00
2016	11	14	7	5	71.43
2017	6	18	3	2	33.33
2018	9	7	9	10	100.00
2019	4	0	4	4	100.00
Total	347	272	109	79	

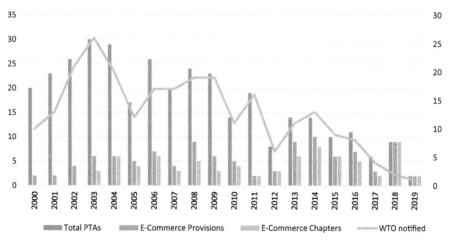

FIGURE 1.1. Evolution of PTAs with digital trade provisions (2000–2019)

TABLE 1.2. *PTAs with e-commerce chapters: average number of provisions and words (2000–2019)*

Year	Total PTAs	E-commerce chapters	Average number of articles	Average number of words
2000	20	2	1	91
2001	23	2	1	838
2002	25	4	4	168
2003	29	6	8	395
2004	28	6	6	606
2005	15	5	5	541
2006	22	7	6	801
2007	17	5	7	753
2008	22	9	7	606
2009	21	4	5	606
2010	10	5	3	313
2011	16	3	3	318
2012	9	3	3	233
2013	14	9	7	640
2014	9	8	8	1,073
2015	10	5	8	842
2016	7	5	10	1,390
2017	6	2	2	357
2018	10	10	12	1,697
2019	4	4	13	2,527

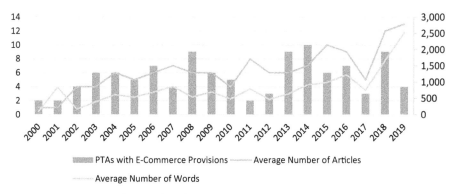

FIGURE 1.2. PTAs with digital trade provisions: average number of articles and words

would overtake SAFTA, as the current text of its Digital Trade chapter has also 19 articles but comprising 3,206 words. The new dedicated digital trade agreements go well beyond: the US–Japan Digital Trade Agreement has 5,346 words, and the Digital Economy Partnership Agreement (DEPA) between Chile, Singapore and New Zealand contains 10,887 words.

II *Overview of Data-Related Rules in PTAs*

One can in general speak of the relevance of trade rules for data and data flows, as they matter for data in at least three ways: (i) because they regulate the cross-border flow of data by regulating trade in goods and services as well as the protection of intellectual property; (ii) because they may install certain beyond the border rules that demand changes in domestic regulation – for example, with regard to procedures with electronic signatures or data protection; and (iii) finally, because trade law can limit the policy space that regulators have at home.[58] Thinking of the layered structure of the Internet, one also ought to take into account the entire set of global economic law rules that regulate *infrastructure* (e.g. rules with regard to communication networks and services, technical standards and IT hardware) and *applications* and *content* (such as software, computer and audiovisual services), so as to understand the existing regulatory environment with regard to data flows.[59] In addition to this generic trade law framework, whose rules are found both in WTO law and in the WTO-plus preferential agreements, the last decade has also witnessed the emergence of entirely new rules that explicitly regulate data flows. This section provides a brief overview of these rules.

It needs to be mentioned at the outset that there is no common agreement on a definition of data flows in PTAs, despite the wide-spread rhetoric around the term and its frequent use in reports and studies.[60] One of the first agreements that targets data – the South Korea–United States FTA – stressed in its Article 15.8 'the importance of the *free flow of information* in facilitating trade, and acknowledging the importance of protecting personal information' and encouraged the Parties 'to refrain from imposing or maintaining unnecessary barriers to *electronic information flows* across borders'.[61] Later agreements, such as the CPTPP and the USMCA, that are analyzed in more detail later, speak of '*cross-border transfer of information by electronic means*, including personal information'[62] and this has become the most common wording thus far. The new generation of EU FTAs have been cautious with regard to data and has only recently started to promote the inclusion of

---

[58] See in this sense Burri, note 27; F. Casalini and J. López González, 'Trade and Cross-Border Data Flows', OECD Trade Policy Papers No 220 (2019).

[59] Such a delineation corresponds to the well-known layered model of the Internet (see, e.g., T. Wu, 'Application-Centered Internet Analysis', *Virginia Law Review* 85 (1999), 1163–1204; Y. Benkler, 'From Consumers to Users: Shifting the Deeper Structures of Regulation toward Sustainable Commons and User Access', *Federal Communications Law Journal* 52 (2000), 561–579; K. Werbach, 'A Layered Model for Internet Policy', *Journal of Telecommunications and High Technology Law* 1 (2002), 37–67. For a full-fledged analysis of the trade rules applicable to all layers, see Burri, note 30.

[60] See, e.g., W. J. Drake, 'Background Paper for the Workshop on Data Localization and Barriers to Transborder Data Flows', *World Economic Forum* (2016); Casalini and González, note 58.

[61] Emphases added.

[62] Article 14.11 CPTPP and Article 19.11 USMCA (emphasis added).

provisions on the '*free flow of data*'.[63] In essence, what can be maintained is that so far in the trade policy discourse and in the treaty language, there has not been any clear definition but despite the different terms used, there seems to be a tendency for a broad and encompassing definition of data flows (i) where there are bits of information (data) as part of the provision of a service or a product and (ii) where this data crosses borders, although the data flows do not neatly coincide with one commercial transaction and the provision of certain service may relate to multiple flows of data. In this sense, '[t]he geography of data flows is very different from the geography of trade flows'.[64] In addition, it may be noted that there has not been a distinction between different types of data – for instance, between personal and non-personal data, personal or company data or machine-to-machine data.[65] Yet, personal information is commonly included explicitly in the data-related provisions in PTAs,[66] whereby the potential clashes with domestic data protection regimes become evident.

Overall, specific data-related provisions are a relatively new phenomenon and can be found primarily in dedicated e-commerce chapters of PTAs and only in a handful of agreements. The rules refer to both the free cross-border flow of data and to banning or limiting data localization requirements. Provisions on the cross-border flow of data can be also found in chapters dealing with discrete services sectors, where data flows are inherent to the very definition of those services[67] – this is particularly valid for the telecommunications and the financial services sectors, as shown in Table 1.3.

---

[63] See, e.g., Article 8.81 EU–Japan FTA and the following section. See also S. Yakovleva, 'Should Fundamental Rights to Privacy and Data Protection Be a Part of EU's International Trade "Deals"?' *World Trade Review* 17 (2018), 477–508.

[64] OECD, 'Trade and Cross-Border Data Dlows', OECD Trade Policy Brief (2019). As the OECD (ibid., at 1) further clarifies: 'the actual flow of data reflects individual firm choices: accessing the OECD library from Paris, for instance, actually means contacting a server in the United States (the OECD uses a US-based company for its web services). Moreover, with the cloud, data can live in many places at once, with files and copies residing in servers around the world'.

[65] For instance, Sen classifies data into personal data referring to data related to individuals; company data referring to data flowing between corporations; business data referring to digitised content such as software and audiovisual content; and social data referring to behavioural patterns determined using personal data (see N. Sen, 'Understanding the Role of the WTO in International Data Flows: Taking the Liberalization or the Regulatory Autonomy Path?', *Journal of International Economic Law* 21 (2018), 323–348, at 343–346). Aaronson and Leblond categorize data into personal data, public data, confidential business data, machine-to-machine data and metadata, although they do not specifically define each of these terms (see S. A. Aaronson and P. Leblond, 'Another Digital Divide: The Rise of Data Realms and Its Implications for the WTO', *Journal of International Economic Law* 21 (2018), 245–272). The OECD has also tried to break the data into different categories. See OECD, 'Data in the Digital Age', OECD Policy Brief, March 2019.

[66] It is typically defined as 'any information, including data, about an identified or identifiable natural person'. See, e.g., Article 19.1 USMCA.

[67] For example, banking and other financial services are commonly understood to include the provision and transfer of financial information, and financial data processing and related software by suppliers of other financial services (see Annex 10-A, Article 10.20 Singapore–US FTA; Article 117.9 Chile–EC AA; Annex IV-A Japan–Singapore FTA; Annex 2.1 New Zealand–

TABLE 1.3. *Overview of data-related provisions in PTAs*

		Data flows		
	General	Financial services	Telecommunication services	Data localization
Soft commitments	16	0	1	1
Hard commitments	12	70	64	11
Total number of provisions	28	70	65	12

1 Rules on Data Flows

If we look at the evolution of data flow provisions in PTAs, there has been a sea change over the years. Non-binding provisions on data flows appeared early. Already in the 2000 Jordan–US FTA, the Joint Statement on Electronic Commerce highlighted the 'need to continue the free flow of information', although it fell short of including an explicit provision in this regard. The first agreement having such a provision is the 2006 Taiwan–Nicaragua FTA, where as part of the cooperation activities, the parties affirmed the importance of working 'to maintain cross-border flows of information as an essential element to promote a dynamic environment for electronic commerce'.[68] A similar wording is used in the 2008 Canada–Peru FTA,[69] the 2011 Korea–Peru FTA,[70] the 2011 Central America–Mexico FTA,[71] the 2013 Colombia–Costa Rica FTA,[72] the 2013 Canada–Honduras FTA,[73] the 2014 Canada–Korea FTA,[74] and the 2015 Japan–Mongolia FTA.[75] In the same line, in the 2010 Hong Kong–New Zealand FTA, the parties agreed to ensure that 'their regulatory regimes support the free flow of services, including the development of innovative ways of developing services, using electronic means'.[76]

A slightly stronger commitment can be found in the 2007 South Korea–US FTA, where the parties, after 'recognizing the importance of the free flow of information

Singapore CEPA). The same is true for telecommunication services, which are defined as including, inter alia, data transmission typically involving the real-time transmission of customer supplied information between two or more points without any end-to-end change in the form or content of the customer's information, or simply including the transfer of data by electronic means (see Article 9.16(18) Singapore–US FTA; Annex IV-B Japan–Singapore FTA).

[68] Article 14.05(c) Nicaragua–Taiwan FTA.
[69] Article 1508(c) Canada–Peru FTA.
[70] Article 14.9(c) Korea–Peru FTA.
[71] Article 15.5(d) Central America–Mexico FTA.
[72] Article 16.7(c) Colombia–Costa Rica FTA.
[73] Article 16.5(c) Canada–Honduras FTA.
[74] Article 13.7(c) Canada–Korea FTA.
[75] Article 9.12(5) Japan–Mongolia FTA.
[76] Chapter 10, Article 2.1(h) Hong Kong–New Zealand FTA.

in facilitating trade, and acknowledging the importance of protecting personal information', stated that they *'shall endeavor* to refrain from imposing or maintaining unnecessary barriers to electronic information flows across borders'.[77] More recently and as typically for EU-led agreements, the parties have agreed to consider in future negotiations commitments related to cross-border flow of information. Such a clause is found in the 2018 EU–Japan EPA,[78] and in the modernization of the trade part of the EU–Mexico Global Agreement, currently under negotiation. In the latter two agreements, the parties commit to 'reassess' within three years of the entry into force of the agreement, the need for inclusion of provisions on the free flow of data into the treaty. This signals a repositioning of the EU on the issue of data flows, as well as EU's wish to couple this in due time with the high data protection standards of the GDPR.[79] The EU follows this model of endorsing and protecting privacy as a fundamental right also in its proposals for digital trade chapters in the currently negotiated trade agreements with Australia, New Zealand and Tunisia,[80] as well as in the EU proposal for WTO rules on electronic commerce.[81]

The first agreement having a binding provision on cross-border information flows is the 2014 Mexico–Panama FTA. According to this treaty, each party 'shall allow its persons and the persons of the other Party to transmit electronic information, from and to its territory, when required by said person, in accordance with the applicable legislation on the protection of personal data and taking into consideration international practices'.[82] A much more detailed provision in this regard is found in the 2015 amended version of the Pacific Alliance Additional Protocol (PAAP),[83] which was modelled along the negotiated text of the 2016 Transpacific Partnership Agreement (TPP) and which has since then largely influenced all subsequent agreements having data flows provisions, such as notably the CPTPP and the USMCA[84] – both endorsing a strong protection of the free flow of data, as discussed in more detail later.

---

[77] Article 15.8 Korea–US FTA (emphasis added).

[78] Article 8.81 EU–Japan EPA.

[79] See European Commission, Horizontal Provisions for Cross-Border Data Flows and for Personal Data Protection in EU Trade and Investment Agreements, February 2018, available at: https://trade.ec.europa.eu/doclib/docs/2018/may/tradoc_156884.pdf.

[80] Interestingly the 2020 EU–Vietnam FTA includes no provisions on data flows and only three most cooperation provisions on e-commerce. See Articles 8.50–8.52 EU–Vietnam FTA.

[81] WTO, Joint Statement on Electronic Commerce: EU Proposal for WTO Disciplines and Commitments Relating to Electronic Commerce, Communication from the European Union, INF/ECOM/22, 26 April 2019. See also Chapter 10 in this volume.

[82] Article 14.10 Mexico–Panama FTA.

[83] Article 13.11 PAAP (2015).

[84] Such as the 2016 Chile–Uruguay FTA (Article 8.10), the 2016 Updated Singapore–Australia FTA (chapter 14, Article 13), the 2017 Argentina–Chile FTA (Article 11.6), the 2018 Singapore–Sri Lanka FTA (Article 9.9), the 2018 Australia–Peru FTA (Article 13.11), the 2018 Brazil–Chile FTA (Article 10.12) and the 2019 Australia–Indonesia FTA (Article 13.11).

2 Data Localization

In recent years, some PTAs have started to include specific provisions on data localization, by either banning or limiting requirements of data localization or data use. An important difference with the data flows provisions analyzed earlier is that almost all the provisions on data localization found in PTAs are binding.[85] The first agreement with such rules is the 2015 Japan–Mongolia FTA. The provision stipulates that neither party shall require a service supplier of the other party, an investor of the other party, or an investment of an investor of the other party in the area of the former party, to use or locate computing facilities in that area as a condition for conducting its business.[86] Later the same year, the 2015 amended version of the PAAP, and as strongly influenced by the parallel TPP negotiations, included a similar provision on the use and location of computer facilities.[87] In 2016, the TPP included a clear ban on localization, which was then replicated in the CPTPP and the USMCA. The diffusion of these norms is clearly discernible in subsequent PTAs, such as the 2016 Chile–Uruguay FTA[88] and the 2016 Updated SAFTA,[89] which closely follow the CPTPP template.[90]

3 Privacy and Data Protection

Eighty-one PTAs in our dataset include provisions on privacy, usually under the concept of 'data protection'. Yet, the way personal data is protected varies considerably and can include a truly mixed bag of binding and non-binding provisions (see Table 1.4), which is symptomatic of the very different positions of the major actors

[85] One of the few provisions on data localization that are not directly binding is found in the 2017 Argentina–Chile FTA, where the parties merely recognize the importance of not requiring a person of the other party to use or locate the computer facilities in the territory of that party, as a condition for conducting business in that territory and pledge to exchange good practices and current regulatory frameworks regarding servers' location. See Article 11.7 Argentina–Chile FTA.

[86] Article 9.10 Japan–Mongolia FTA.

[87] Article 13.11*bis* PAAP (2015).

[88] Article 8.11 Chile–Uruguay FTA.

[89] Chapter 14, Article 15 SAFTA.

[90] Some variations can be found in the 2019 Australia–Indonesia FTA, where a party may promptly renew a measure in existence at the date of entry into force of the agreement or amend such a measure to make it less trade restrictive, at any time (Article 13.12(2)). Additionally, the Australia–Indonesia FTA stipulates that nothing in the agreement shall prevent a party from adopting or maintaining any measure that it considers necessary for the protection of its essential security interests (Article 13.12(3)(b)). A second variation is found in the 2018 Singapore–Sri Lanka FTA, the 2018 Australia–Peru FTA and the 2018 Brazil–Chile FTA, which slightly deviate from the CPTPP, as there is no least restrictive measure requirement mentioned. See correspondingly Article 9.10 Singapore–Sri Lanka FTA; Article 13.12 Australia–Peru FTA; Article 10.13 Brazil–Chile FTA.

TABLE 1.4. *Overview of privacy-related provisions in PTAs*

Total number of provisions	89
Soft commitments	81
Hard commitments	8

and the inherent tensions between the regulatory goals of data innovation and data protection.[91]

Earlier agreements dealing with privacy issues consist of non-binding declarations. The 2000 Jordan–US FTA Joint Statement on Electronic Commerce, for instance, merely declares it necessary to ensure the effective protection of privacy regarding the processing of personal data on global information networks, yet states also that the means for privacy protection should be flexible and parties should encourage the private sector to develop and implement enforcement mechanisms, such as guidelines and verification and recourse methodologies, recommending the OECD Privacy Guidelines as an appropriate basis for policy development.[92] Similarly, the 2001 Canada–Costa Rica FTA includes a provision on privacy as part of the Joint Statement on Global Electronic Commerce, with both parties agreeing to share information on the functioning of their respective data protection regimes.[93] Later agreements include cooperation activities on enhancing the security of personal data in order to improve the level of protection of privacy in electronic communications and avoid obstacles to trade that requires transfer of personal data.[94] These activities include sharing information and experiences on regulations, laws and programmes on data protection[95] or the overall domestic regime for the protection of personal information;[96] technical assistance in the form of exchange of

[91] See, e.g., Schwartz, note 23; Schwartz and Solove, note 23. See also Chapter 10 in this volume.
[92] Jordan–US, Joint Statement on Electronic Commerce, 7 June 2000, Article II.
[93] Canada–Costa Rica FTA, Joint Statement on Global Electronic Commerce.
[94] Article 13.1 and Article 99(d) EC–Moldova AA.
[95] Article 10.8.5 and Article 10.15(b) Brazil–Chile FTA; Article 14.5.2 Central America–Korea FTA; Article 11.5.5 and Article 11.9(b) Argentina–Chile FTA; Article 8.7.4 and Article 8.13(b) Chile–Uruguay FTA; Article 13.6(1) EAEU–Vietnam FTA; Article 9.12(2) Japan–Mongolia FTA; Article 13.7(b) Canada–Korea FTA; Article 13.10(2) Australia–Japan FTA; Article 14.11(b) Mexico–Panama FTA; Article 13.8(2) and Article 13.12(b) PAAP; Article 11.7(b) Singapore–Taiwan FTA; Article 16.5(b) Canada–Honduras FTA; Article 34 EU–Central America FTA; Article 15.5(b) Central America–Mexico FTA; Article 14.7(2)(b) Korea–Peru FTA; chapter 10, Article 9.1(c) ASEAN–Australia–New Zealand FTA; Article 82.2(a) Japan–Switzerland FTA; Article 1507.1(b) Canada–Colombia FTA; Article 1508(b) Canada–Peru FTA; Article 14.8(b) Colombia–Northern Triangle FTA; Article 14.5(b) Panama–US FTA; Article 12.5(b) Chile–Colombia FTA; Article 14.05(b) Nicaragua–Taiwan FTA; Article 13.4(b) Panama–Singapore FTA; Article 14.5(b) CAFTA–DR–US; Article 15.5(b) Chile–US FTA.
[96] Article 13.3(1)(b)(i) Australia–Indonesia FTA; Article 19.14(1)(a)(i) USMCA; Article 13.14(b)(i) Australia–Peru FTA; Article 9.12(c)(i) Singapore–Sri Lanka FTA; Article 9.9(c) Singapore–

information and experts;[97] research and training activities;[98] the establishment of joint programmes and projects;[99] maintaining a dialogue;[100] holding consultations on matters of data protection;[101] or in general, other cooperation mechanisms to ensure the protection of personal data.[102]

PTAs have also dealt with personal data protection with reference to the adoption of domestic standards. While some merely recognize the importance or the benefits of protecting personal information online,[103] in several treaties parties specifically commit to adopt or maintain legislation or regulations that protect the personal data or privacy of users,[104] in relation to the processing and dissemination of data,[105] which may also include administrative measures,[106] or the adoption of non-discriminatory practices.[107] Few agreements include qualifications of this commitment, in the sense that each party shall take measures it deems appropriate and necessary considering the differences in existing systems for personal data protection,[108] that such measures shall be developed insofar as possible,[109] or that the

Turkey FTA; Article 13.5 China–Korea FTA; Article 16.6(2) Colombia–Costa Rica FTA; Article 1506.2 Canada–Colombia FTA.

[97] Article 30 Chile–EC AA.
[98] Article 10.8(1)(b) Korea–Vietnam FTA.
[99] Article 30 Chile–EC AA.
[100] Article 163.1(e) Colombia–EU–Peru FTA.
[101] Article 16.10(1) Australia–Chile FTA.
[102] Article 14.7(1)(a) Central America–Korea FTA; Annex-B, Article 2(e) Colombia–Israel FTA; Article 19.7(1)(b) Colombia–Panama FTA; Article 12.6(1)(c) Colombia–Korea FTA; Article 13 Armenia–EU CEPA; Article 15 EC–Ukraine AA; Article 14 EC–Georgia AA.
[103] Article 13.7(1) Australia–Indonesia FTA; Article 10.2(5)(f) and Article 10.8.1 Brazil–Chile FTA; Article 8.78(3) EU–Japan EPA; Article 14.5(1) Central America–Korea FTA; Article 16.2(2)(e) Canada–Honduras FTA.
[104] Article 13.7(2) Australia–Indonesia FTA; Article 10.8.2 Brazil–Chile FTA; Article 19.8(1–2) USMCA; Article 13.8(1–2) Australia–Peru FTA; Article 9.7(1–2) Singapore–Sri Lanka FTA; Article 11.5(1–2) Argentina–Chile FTA; Article 16.4 CETA; chapter 14, Article 9.1-2 Australia–Singapore FTA (2016); Article 8.7(1–2) Chile–Uruguay FTA; Article 14.8(1–2) TPP/CPTPP; Article 9.7(1-2) Singapore–Turkey FTA; Article 13.5 China–Korea FTA; Article 13.5 EAEU–Vietnam FTA; Article 10.6(1) Korea–Vietnam FTA; Article 9.6(3) Japan–Mongolia FTA; Article 13.8(1) Australia–Japan FTA; Article 15.8 Australia–Korea FTA; Article 14.8 Mexico–Panama FTA; Article 13.8(1) PAAP; Article 19.6 Colombia–Panama FTA; chapter 9, Article 2 (d)(i) New Zealand–Taiwan; Article 12.3 Colombia–Korea FTA; Article 55 Chile–China FTA (2018); Article 15.8(1) Australia–Malaysia FTA; Article 1506.1 Canada–Colombia FTA.
[105] Annex II, Article 1(c)(i) Central America–EFTA; Annex XVI, Article 1(c)(i) EFTA–GCC FTA; Annex I, Article 1(c)(i) EFTA–Colombia FTA; Annex I, Article 1(c)(i) EFTA–Peru FTA.
[106] Article 16.6(1) Colombia–Costa Rica FTA; Article 14.7 Korea–Peru FTA; chapter 10, Article 2.1 (f) Hong Kong–New Zealand FTA; chapter 10, Article 7.1-2 ASEAN–Australia–New Zealand FTA; Article 16.8 Australia–Chile FTA; Article 1507 Canada–Peru FTA.
[107] Article 13.6(3) Australia–Indonesia FTA; Article 10.8(3) Brazil–Chile FTA; Article 19.8(4) USMCA; Article 13.8(3) Australia–Peru FTA; Article 11.5(3) Australia–Chile FTA; chapter 14, Article 9.3 Australia–Singapore FTA (2016); Article 14.8(3) TPP/CPTPP.
[108] Article 12.8(1) Australia–China FTA; Article 11.7(1)(j) Chile–Thailand FTA; chapter 14, Article 7.1 Australia–Singapore FTA (2003).
[109] Annex-B, Article 3 Colombia–Israel FTA.

parties have the right to define or regulate their own levels of protection of personal data in pursuit or furtherance of public policy objectives, and shall not be required to disclose confidential or sensitive information.[110] Some PTAs add that in the development of online personal data protection standards, each party shall take into account the existing international standards,[111] as well as criteria or guidelines of relevant international organizations or bodies[112] – such as the APEC Privacy Framework and the OECD Guidelines on Transborder Flows of Personal Data (2013);[113] or to accord a high level of protection compatible with the highest international standards in order to ensure the confidence of e-commerce users.[114] In a handful of treaties, the parties commit to publish information on the personal data protection it provides to users of e-commerce,[115] including how individuals can pursue remedies and how businesses can comply with any legal requirements.[116] Certain agreements put special emphasis on the transfer of personal data, stipulating that it shall only take place if necessary for the implementation, by the competent authorities, of agreements concluded between the parties,[117] or that the countries need to have an adequate level of safeguards for the protection of personal data.[118] Some treaties add that the parties will encourage the use of encryption or security mechanisms for the personal information of the users, and their dissociation or anonymization, in cases where said data is provided to third parties.[119]

PTA parties have also employed more binding options to protect personal information online. A first option is to consider the protection of the privacy of individuals in relation to the processing and dissemination of personal data and the

---

[110] Article 18.1(2)(h) and Article 18.16(7) EU–Japan EPA.

[111] Article 8.57(4) EC–Singapore FTA; Article 11.5(1-2) Argentina–Chile FTA; Article 8.7(2) Chile–Uruguay FTA.

[112] Article 13.7(3) Australia–Indonesia FTA; Article 13.8(2) Australia–Peru FTA; Article 16.4 CETA; chapter 14, Article 9.2 Australia–Singapore FTA (2016); Article 14.8(2) TPP/CPTPP; Article 12.8(2) Australia–China FTA; Article 10.6(2) Korea–Vietnam FTA; Article 13.8(2) Australia–Japan FTA; Article 139.2 EC–Ukraine AA; Article 127.2 EC–Georgia AA; Article 15.8 Australia–Korea FTA; Article 14.8 Mexico–Panama FTA; Article 11.7(j) Chile–Thailand FTA; Article 19.6 Colombia–Panama FTA; Article 16.6(1) Colombia–Costa Rica FTA; Article 12.1(2) and Article 12.3 Colombia–Korea FTA; Article 201.2 EU–Central America FTA; Article 15.8(2) Australia–Malaysia FTA; chapter 10, Article 7.3 ASEAN–Australia–New Zealand FTA; Article 16.8 Australia–Chile FTA; Article 10.5 New Zealand–Thailand FTA; Article 1106 Australia–Thailand FTA; chapter 14, Article 7.2 Australia–Singapore FTA (2003).

[113] Article 19.8(2) USMCA.

[114] Article 197.2 Armenia–EU CEPA; Article 162.2 Colombia–EU–Peru FTA; Article 119.2; Chile–EC AA and Article 202 CARIFORUM–EC EPA.

[115] Article 10.8(4) Brazil–Chile FTA.

[116] Article 19.8(5) USMCA; Article 13.8(4) Australia–Peru FTA; Article 9.7(3) Singapore–Sri Lanka FTA; chapter 14, Article 9.4 Australia–Singapore FTA (2016); Article 8.7(3) Chile–Uruguay FTA; Article 14.8(4) TPP/CPTPP; Article 9.7(3) Singapore–Turkey FTA.

[117] Article 13.2 EC–Moldova AA.

[118] Article 10.6(2) Korea–Vietnam FTA.

[119] Article 10.8(6) Brazil–Chile FTA; Article 11.5(6) Argentina–Chile FTA; Article 8.7(5) Chile–Uruguay FTA.

protection of confidentiality of individual records as an exception in specific chapters of the agreement – such as for trade in services,[120] investment or establishment,[121] movement of persons,[122] telecommunications[123] and financial services.[124] Certain agreements, mostly EU led, even have special chapters on protection of personal data, including the principles of purpose limitation, data quality and proportionality, transparency, security, right to access, rectification and opposition, restrictions on onward transfers, and protection of sensitive data, as well as provisions on enforcement mechanisms, coherence with international commitments and cooperation between the parties in order to ensure an adequate level of protection of personal data.[125] The USMCA was the first US-led PTA to include such a provision that recognizes key principles of data protection.[126]

A second option lets countries adopt appropriate measures to ensure the privacy protection while allowing the free movement of data, establishing a criterion of 'equivalence' – meaning that countries agree that personal data may be exchanged only where the receiving party undertakes to protect such data in at least an equivalent, similar or adequate way to the one applicable to that particular case in the party that supplies it. This has been largely the EU approach and to that end, parties commit to inform each other of their applicable rules and negotiate reciprocal general or specific agreements.[127]

---

[120] Article 69.1(c) Japan–Singapore FTA.

[121] Article 135.1(e)(ii) Chile–EC AA; Article 83.1(c)(ii) Japan–Singapore FTA.

[122] Article 95.1(c)(ii) Japan–Singapore FTA.

[123] Article 18.3(4) USMCA; Article 8.44(4) EU–Japan EPA; Article 12.4(4) Australia–Peru FTA; Article 8.3(4) Singapore–Sri Lanka FTA; Article 10.3(4) Argentina–Chile FTA; Article 10.3(4) Australia–Singapore FTA (2016); Article 8.3(5) Singapore–Turkey FTA; Annex 5, Article 3 Japan–Mongolia FTA; Article 13.3(4) Korea–Peru FTA; Article 13.2(4) Panama–US FTA; Annex VI, Article IX(a) Japan–Switzerland FTA; Article 13.02(4) Nicaragua–Taiwan FTA; Article 11.3(4) Korea–Singapore FTA; Article 13.2(4)(b) Morocco–US FTA; Article 13.2(4) Chile–US FTA.

[124] Annex 17-A USMCA; Article 8.63 EU–Japan EPA; Article 8.45 EU–Vietnam FTA; Article 8.54 (2) EC–Singapore FTA; Article 10.21 Australia–Peru FTA; Article 185 Armenia–EU CEPA; Article 13.15(4) CETA; Annex 9-B Australia–Singapore FTA (2016); Annex 11-B TPP/CPTPP; Article 10.12 Singapore–Turkey FTA; Annex 4, Article 11 Japan–Mongolia FTA; Article 129.2 EC–Ukraine AA; Article 118.2 EC–Georgia AA; chapter 10, Annex on Financial Services, Article 7.2 ASEAN–Australia–New Zealand FTA; Annex VI, Article VIII Japan–Switzerland FTA; Annex XVI – financial services, Article 8 EFTA–Colombia FTA; Article 245 EC–Moldova AA; Article 135.1(e)(ii) Chile–EC AA.

[125] Chapter 6, Articles 61–65 Cameroon-EC Interim EPA; chapter 6, Articles 197–201 CARIFORUM-EC EPA. Other agreements merely recognize principles for the collection, processing and storage of personal data such as prior consent, legitimacy, purpose, proportionality, quality, safety, responsibility and information, but without developing this in detail: Article 11.2(5)(f), footnote 1, Argentina–Chile FTA; Article 8.2(5)(f), footnote 3, Chile–Uruguay FTA.

[126] Article 19.8(3) USMCA; see also below.

[127] Article 8.54(2) EC–Singapore FTA; Articles 9.2 and 11.1 Understanding 3 on Additional Customs-Related Provisions; Protocol on Mutual Administrative Assistance on Custom Matters, Article 10 EC–Ghana EPA; Protocol 5 on Mutual Administrative Assistance on Custom Matters, Article 10.2

A third, less used, option leaves the development of rules on data protection to a treaty body. For example, in the 2012 Colombia–EU–Peru FTA (which also now includes Ecuador), the Trade Committee may establish a working group with the task of proposing guidelines to enable the signatory Andean Countries to become a 'safe harbour' for the protection of personal data. To this end, the working group shall adopt a cooperation agenda that defines priority aspects for accomplishing that purpose, especially regarding the respective homologation processes of data protection systems.[128]

D SUBSTANTIVE DEVELOPMENTS IN DIGITAL TRADE GOVERNANCE

As evident from the earlier overview, the regulatory environment for data flows has been substantially shaped by PTAs. The United States has played a key role in this process and has sought to endorse liberal rules in implementation of its 'Digital Agenda'.[129] The agreements reached since 2002 with Australia, Bahrain, Chile, Morocco, Oman, Peru, Singapore, the Central American countries,[130] Panama, Colombia and South Korea, all contain critical WTO-plus (going above the WTO commitments) and WTO-extra (addressing issues not covered by the WTO) provisions in the broader field of digital trade. The emergent regulatory template on digital issues is not however limited to US agreements but has diffused and can be found in other FTAs, as evident from the earlier overview. Singapore, Australia, Japan and Colombia have been among the major drivers of this diffusion but as earlier mentioned, the issues covered and the levels of legalization may still vary substantially.[131]

Key aspects of digital trade are typically addressed in (i) specifically dedicated e-commerce chapters; (ii) the chapters on cross-border supply of services; and (iii) the IP chapters. The electronic commerce chapters show by far the most substantial evolution over time – moving from less to more binding and from a mere compensation for the lack of progress in the WTO towards new (and partially innovative) digital trade rule-making. In the former sense, they have included a clear definition of 'digital products', which treats digital products delivered offline equally as those delivered online, so that technological neutrality is ensured. The chapters also recognize the applicability of WTO rules to electronic commerce, and establish a permanent moratorium on duties on the import or export of digital products by

---

Bosnia and Herzegovina–EC SAA; Article 45 and Protocol No 7 Algeria EC Euro-Med Association Agreement.

[128] Article 109(b) Colombia–EU–Peru FTA.

[129] See S. Wunsch-Vincent, 'The Digital Trade Agenda of the US: Parallel Tracks of Bilateral, Regional and Multilateral Liberalization', *Aussenwirtschaft* 58 (2003), 7–46.

[130] The DR–CAFTA includes Costa Rica, El Salvador, Guatemala, Honduras, Nicaragua and the Dominican Republic.

[131] See Chapter 2 in this volume.

electronic transmission. Critically, the e-commerce chapters, especially those of US-led agreements, ensure both MFN and NT for digital products trade; discrimination is banned on the basis that digital products are 'created, produced, published, stored, transmitted, contracted for, commissioned, or first made available on commercial terms outside the country's territory' or 'whose author, performer, producer, developer, or distributor is a person of another party or a non-party'.[132]

The e-commerce chapters do also include rules that go beyond the WTO and next to provisions on IT standards and interoperability, cybersecurity, electronic signatures and payments, paperless trading and e-government, the rules on data flows are the most illustrative example in this context. In the following two sections, we look more closely at the most advanced template for digital trade chapters endorsed by the CPTPP and slightly further developed by the USMCA, including also some remarks on the dedicated US–Japan Digital Trade Agreement.

I *The CPTPP*

The Comprehensive and Progressive Agreement for Transpacific Partnership (CPTPP; also known as the TPP11 or TPP 2.0)[133] was agreed upon in 2017 among eleven countries in the Pacific Rim[134] and entered into force on 30 December 2018. The CPTPP represents 13.4 per cent of the the global gross domestic product, or $13.5 trillion, making it the third largest trade agreement after the North American Free Trade Agreement and the single market of the European Union.[135] Beyond the broader economic impact and, more importantly, for the discussion of this chapter, the CPTPP chapter on e-commerce created the most comprehensive template so far in the landscape of PTAs. It comprises eighteen articles and includes a number of new features.[136] It is fair to note that the e-commerce chapter of the CPTPP 'survived' the TPP negotiations in its entirety and without any change, so in a sense it still very much reflects the efforts of the United States in the domain of digital trade rule-making.

The CPTPP sought for the first time to explicitly restrict the use of data localization measures. Article 14.13(2) prohibits the parties from requiring a 'covered person

---

[132] See, e.g., Article 14.3 US–Singapore FTA; Article 16.4 US–Australia FTA. For a more comprehensive analysis, see Burri and Polanco, note 51.

[133] The Comprehensive and Progressive Agreement for Transpacific Partnership, available at: http://international.gc.ca/trade-commerce/trade-agreements-accords-commerciaux/agr-acc/cptpp-ptpgp/text-texte/index.aspx?lang=eng.

[134] Australia, Brunei, Canada, Chile, Japan, Malaysia, Mexico, New Zealand, Peru, Singapore and Vietnam.

[135] Z. Torrey, 'TPP 2.0: The Deal without the US: What's New about the CPTPP and What Do the Changes Mean?', *The Diplomat*, 3 February 2018.

[136] Such as provisions on domestic electronic transactions framework, personal information protection, Internet interconnection charge sharing, location of computing facilities, unsolicited commercial electronic messages, source code, and dispute settlement. See Articles 14.5, 14.8, 14.12, 14.13, 14.14, 14.17, and 14.18 CPTPP respectively.

to use or locate computing facilities in that Party's territory as a condition for conducting business in that territory'. The soft language from the US–South Korea FTA on free data flows is now framed as a hard rule: '[e]ach Party shall allow the cross-border transfer of information by electronic means, including personal information, when this activity is for the conduct of the business of a covered person'.[137] The rule has a broad scope and most data that is transferred over the Internet is likely to be covered, although the word 'for' may suggest the need for some causality between the flow of data and the business of the covered person.

Measures restricting digital flows or localization requirements under Article 14.13 CPTPP are permitted only if they do not amount to 'arbitrary or unjustifiable discrimination or a disguised restriction on trade' and do not 'impose restrictions on transfers of information greater than are required to achieve the objective'.[138] These non-discriminatory conditions are similar to the test formulated by Article XIV GATS and Article XX GATT, which, as earlier noted, is meant to balance trade and non-trade interests. The CPTPP test differs from the WTO norms in one significant element: while there is a list of public policy objectives in the GATT and the GATS (such as public morals or public order), the CPTPP provides no such enumeration and simply speaks of a 'legitimate public policy objective'.[139] This permits more regulatory autonomy for the CPTPP signatories. However, it also may lead to overall legal uncertainty. Further, it should be noted that the ban on localization measures is somewhat softened with regard to financial services and institutions.[140] An annex to the financial services chapter has a separate data transfer requirement, whereby certain restrictions on data flows may apply for the protection of privacy or confidentiality of individual records, or for prudential reasons.[141] Government procurement is also excluded.[142]

Pursuant to Article 14.17, a CPTPP member may not require the transfer of, or access to, source code of software owned by a person of another party as a condition for the import, distribution, sale or use of such software, or of products containing such software, in its territory. The prohibition applies only to mass-market software or products containing such software.[143] This means that tailor-made products are excluded, as well as software used for critical infrastructure and those in commercially negotiated contracts.[144] The aim of this provision is to protect software

---

[137] Article 14.11(2) CPTPP.

[138] Article 14.11(3) CPTPP.

[139] Article 14.11(3) CPTPP.

[140] See the definition of 'a covered person' in Article 14.1, which is said to exclude a 'financial institution' and a 'cross-border financial service supplier'.

[141] The provision reads: 'Each Party shall allow a financial institution of another Party to transfer information in electronic or other form, into and out of its territory, for data processing if such processing is required in the institution's ordinary course of business'.

[142] Article 14.8(3) CPTPP.

[143] Article 14.17(2) CPTPP.

[144] Article 14.17(2) CPTPP.

companies and address their concerns about loss of IP or cracks in the security of their proprietary code.[145]

These provisions illustrate an important development this chapter alluded to earlier, namely, the evolution of digital trade rules that go beyond the WTO and do not simply entail a clarification of existing bans on discrimination or more liberal commitments. It is also evident that the new rules do not merely set higher standards, as is generally anticipated from trade agreements; rather, they shape the regulatory space domestically and may even lower certain standards. A commitment to lower standards of protection is particularly palpable in the field of privacy and data protection.

Article 14.8(2) requires every CPTPP party to 'adopt or maintain a legal framework that provides for the protection of the personal information of the users of electronic commerce'. No standards or benchmarks for the legal framework have been specified, except for a general requirement that CPTPP parties 'take into account principles or guidelines of relevant international bodies'.[146] A footnote provides some clarification in saying that '[f]or greater certainty, a Party may comply with the obligation in this paragraph by adopting or maintaining measures such as a comprehensive privacy, personal information or personal data protection laws, sector-specific laws covering privacy, or laws that provide for the enforcement of voluntary undertakings by enterprises relating to privacy'.[147] Parties are also invited to promote compatibility between their data protection regimes.[148] Overall, there is a priority given to trade over privacy protection. This commitment had been pushed by the United States, which subscribes to a relatively weak and patchy protection of privacy. Timewise, this insertion can be linked to the *Schrems I* judgment of the Court of Justice of European Union (CJEU) that struck down the EU–US Safe Harbor Agreement.[149]

The CPTPP contains also rules on consumer protection,[150] network neutrality[151] and spam control,[152] although these are fairly weak. The same is true for the newly

---

[145] It is interesting to note that China does demand access to source code from software producers selling in its market, so this provision may be interpreted as a reaction to this.

[146] Article 14.8(2) CPTPP.

[147] Article 14.8(2) CPTPP.

[148] Article 14.8(5) CPTPP.

[149] C-362/14, *Maximilian Schrems v Data Protection Commissioner and Digital Rights Ireland Ltd*, [2015], ECLI:EU:C:2015:650. Maximillian Schrems is an Austrian citizen, who filed a suit against the Irish supervisory authority (the Data Protection Commissioner), after it rejected his complaint over Facebook's practice of storing user data in the United States. The plaintiff claimed that his data was not adequately protected in light of the recent NSA revelations and this, despite the existing agreement between the EU and the United States – the 'Safe Harbor' scheme – that expressly sought to ensure that the United States provides for an adequate level of protection of the transferred personal data.

[150] Article 14.17 CPTPP.

[151] Article 14.10(a) CPTPP.

[152] Article 14.14 CPTPP.

introduced rules on cybersecurity under Article 14.16, which identifies a relatively limited scope of activities for cooperation, in situations of 'malicious intrusions' or 'dissemination of malicious code', and capacity-building of governmental bodies dealing with cybersecurity incidents.

II *The USMCA*

After the withdrawal of the United States from the TPP, there was some uncertainty as to the direction it will follow in its trade deals in general and on matters of digital trade in particular. The renegotiated NAFTA, now referred to as 'United States–Mexico–Canada Agreement' (USMCA), casts the doubts aside. The USMCA has a comprehensive electronic commerce chapter, which is now also properly titled 'Digital Trade' and follows all critical lines of the CPTPP in ensuring the free flow of data through a clear ban on data localization (Article 19.12), providing a non-discrimination treatment for digital products (Article 19.4) and a hard rule on free information flows (Article 19.11).

The USMCA appears particularly interesting in two aspects. The first one is that it keeps the clause on exceptions that permits the pursuit of certain non-economic objectives. Article 19.11 specifies, very much in the sense of the CPTPP, that parties can adopt or maintain a measure inconsistent with the free flow of data provision, if this is necessary to achieve a legitimate public policy objective, provided that the measure (a) is not applied in a manner which would constitute a means of arbitrary or unjustifiable discrimination or a disguised restriction on trade; and (b) does not impose restrictions on transfers of information greater than are necessary to achieve the objective.[153] Furthermore and departing from the standard US approach, the USMCA signals abiding to some data protection principles. While Article 19.8 remains soft on prescribing domestic regimes on personal data protection, it recognizes principles and guidelines of relevant international bodies. Article 19.8 recognizes 'the economic and social benefits of protecting the personal information of users of digital trade and the contribution that this makes to enhancing consumer confidence in digital trade'[154] and requires from the parties to 'adopt or maintain a legal framework that provides for the protection of the personal information of the users of digital trade. In the development of its legal framework for the protection of personal information, each party should take into account principles and guidelines

---

[153] Article 19.11(2). There is a footnote attached, which clarifies, 'A measure does not meet the conditions of this paragraph if it accords different treatment to data transfers solely on the basis that they are cross-border in a manner that modifies the conditions of competition to the detriment of service suppliers of another Party'. The footnote does not appear in the CPTPP treaty text.

[154] Article 19.8(1) USMCA.

of relevant international bodies, such as the APEC Privacy Framework and the OECD Recommendation of the Council concerning Guidelines Governing the Protection of Privacy and Transborder Flows of Personal Data (2013)'.[155]

The parties also recognize key principles of data protection, which include limitation on collection; choice; data quality; purpose specification; use limitation; security safeguards; transparency; individual participation; and accountability,[156] and aim to provide remedies for any violations.[157] This is interesting because it may go beyond what the United States has in its national laws on data protection and also because it reflects some of the principles the European Union has advocated in the domain of the protection of privacy. One can of course wonder whether this is a development caused by the 'Brussels effect', whereby the EU 'exports' its own domestic standards and they become global,[158] or whether we are seeing a shift in US privacy protection regimes as well.[159]

Finally, three innovations of the USMCA may be mentioned. The first refers to the inclusion of 'algorithms', the meaning of which is 'a defined sequence of steps, taken to solve a problem or obtain a result'[160] and has become part of the ban on requirements for the transfer or access to source code in Article 19.16. The second novum refers to the recognition of 'interactive computer services' as particularly vital to the growth of digital trade. Parties pledge in this sense not to 'adopt or maintain measures that treat a supplier or user of an interactive computer service as an information content provider in determining liability for harms related to information stored, processed, transmitted, distributed, or made available by the service, except to the extent the supplier or user has, in whole or in part, created, or developed the information'.[161] This provision is important, as it seeks to clarify the liability of intermediaries and delineate it from the liability of host providers with regard to IP rights' infringement.[162] It also secures the application of Section 230 of

---

[155] Article 19.8(2) USMCA.

[156] Article 19.8(3) USMCA.

[157] Article19.8(4) and (5) USMCA.

[158] See A. Bradford, 'The Brussels Effect', *Northwestern University Law Review* 107 (2012), 1–68; A. Bradford, *The Brussels Effect: How the European Union Rules the World* (Oxford: Oxford University Press, 2020).

[159] For a great analysis, which argues that a convergence of standards of protection is unlikely, see Chander et al., note 22; for a different opinion, see E. Büyüksagis, 'Towards a Transatlantic Concept of Data Privacy', *Fordham Intellectual Property, Media and Entertainment Law Journal* 30 (2019), 139–221.

[160] Article 19.1 USMCA.

[161] Article 19.17(2) USMCA. Annex 19-A creates specific rules with the regard to the application of Article 19.17 for Mexico, in essence postponing its implementation for three years.

[162] On intermediaries' liability, see, e.g., S. K. Katyal, 'Filtering, Piracy, Surveillance and Disobedience', *The Columbia Journal of Law and the Arts* 32 (2009), 401–426; U. Gasser and W. Schulz (eds), *Governance of Online Intermediaries* (Cambridge, MA: Berkman Center for Internet and Society, 2015).

the US Communications Decency Act,[163] which insulates platforms from liability but has been recently under attack in many jurisdictions, including in the United States, in the face of fake news and other negative developments related to platforms' power.[164] The third and rather liberal commitment of the USMCA parties regards open government data. This is truly innovative and very relevant in the domain of domestic regimes for data governance. In Article 19.18, the parties recognize that facilitating public access to and use of government information fosters economic and social development, competitiveness and innovation. 'To the extent that a Party chooses to make government information, including data, available to the public, it shall endeavor to ensure that the information is in a machine-readable and open format and can be searched, retrieved, used, reused, and redistributed.'[165] There is in addition an endeavour to cooperate, so as to 'expand access to and use of government information, including data, that the Party has made public, with a view to enhancing and generating business opportunities, especially for small and medium-sized enterprises'.[166]

The US approach towards digital trade issues has been confirmed also by the recent US–Japan Digital Trade Agreement (DTA), signed on 7 October 2019, alongside the US–Japan Trade Agreement.[167] The DTA can be said to replicate almost all provisions of the USMCA and the CPTPP,[168] including the new USMCA rules on open government data,[169] source code[170] and interactive computer services[171] but notably covering also financial and insurance services as part of the scope of agreement. A new provision has been added with regard to ICT goods that use cryptography,[172] which complements the source code provisions and is similar to

---

[163] Section 230 reads: 'No provider or user of an interactive computer service shall be treated as the publisher or speaker of any information provided by another information content provider' and in essence protects online intermediaries that host or republish speech.

[164] See, e.g., L. Feine, 'Big Tech's Favorite Law Is Under Fire', *CNBC*, 19 February 2020. For an analysis of the free speech implications of digital platforms, see J. M. Balkin, 'Free Speech Is a Triangle', *Columbia Law Review* 118 (2018), 2011–2055.

[165] Article 19.18(2) USMCA.

[166] Article 19.8(3) USMCA.

[167] For the text of the agreements, see https://ustr.gov/countries-regions/japan-korea-apec/japan/us-japan-trade-agreement-negotiations/us-japan-digital-trade-agreement-text.

[168] Article 7: Customs Duties; Article 8: Non-discriminatory Treatment of Digital Products; Article 9: Domestic Electronic Transactions Framework; Article 10: Electronic Authentication and Electronic Signatures; Article 14: Online Consumer Protection; Article 11: Cross-Border Transfer of Information; Article 12: Location of Computing Facilities; Article 16: Unsolicited Commercial Electronic Messages; Article 19: Cybersecurity US–Japan DTA. Some things are missing in the US–Japan DTA, when compared to the USMCA – such as rules on paperless trading, net neutrality and the mention of data protection principles.

[169] Article 20 US–Japan DTA.

[170] Article 17 US–Japan DTA.

[171] Article 18 US–Japan DTA. A side letter recognizes the differences between the US and Japan's systems governing the liability of interactive computer services suppliers and parties agree that Japan need not change its existing legal system to comply with Article 18.

[172] Article 21.3 US–Japan DTA.

Annex 8-B, section A.3 of the CPTPP chapter on technical barriers to trade, which addresses practices by several countries, in particular China, that impose bans on encrypted products or set specific technical regulations that restrict the sale of such products.[173]

E CONCLUSION

The era of big data has ushered in new challenges for global trade law. Policymakers are faced with the extremely difficult task to match the existing, largely analogue-based, institutions and rules of international economic law with the dynamic, scruffy innovation of digital platforms[174] and data that flows regardless of state borders. At the same time, and this only makes the task more taxing, it is evident that the regulatory framework that will be chosen will have immense effects on innovation and the fate of the data-driven economy,[175] as well as on fundamental rights beyond the province of the economy, such as the protection of citizens' privacy. Despite the importance and the urgency of finding appropriate governance solutions, global trade law has not undergone a radical overhaul so far and legal adaptation has been slow and patchy, as this chapter showed. PTAs have become the preferred venue, where digital trade rules have been adopted – on the one hand, so as to compensate for the lack of progress under the umbrella of the WTO and on the other hand, and more importantly, so as to create new rules that address new trade barriers, such as data localization measures; new and pressing concerns, such as the acute need to interface trade and personal data protection mechanisms, and overall, to provide a regulatory environment that is conducive to the practical reality of digital trade and that provides a level of legal certainty for all actors involved. It has been the chapter's objective to provide a better understanding of this newly emerged governance landscape by tracing broader developments and trends, by looking in particular at the data-related rules across PTAs and analyzing more closely the most sophisticated templates of e-commerce chapters so far, as found in the CPTPP and the USMCA.

The understanding of the existing rules on digital trade and their evolution over time is absolutely essential for future attempts of individual states and of the

---

[173] See H.-W. Liu, 'Inside the Black Box: Political Economy of the Trans-Pacific Partnership's Encryption Clause', *Journal of World Trade* 51 (2017), 309–334.

[174] Y. Benkler, 'Growth-Oriented Law for the Networked Information Economy: Emphasizing Freedom to Operate Over Power to Appropriate', in Kauffman Taskforce on Law, Innovation and Growth (ed), *Rules for Growth: Promoting Innovation and Growth through Legal Reform* (Kansas City: Kauffman Foundation, 2011), 313–342; P. K. Yu, 'Trade Agreement Cats and Digital Technology Mouse', in B. Mercurio and N. Kuei-Jung (eds), *Science and Technology in International Economic Law: Balancing Competing Interests* (Abington: Routledge, 2014), 185–211.

[175] A. Chander, 'How Law Made Silicon Valley', *Emory Law Journal* 63 (2014), 639–694; see generally J. L. Zittrain, *The Future of the Internet – and How to Stop It* (New Haven, CT: Yale University Press, 2008).

international community to grapple with the digital challenge. It may be important also for other governance actors, such as companies, think tanks, non-governmental organizations and even individual citizens who wish to more actively engage in the rule-making processes in trade agreements, which by definition tend to be behind closed doors and with little to none stakeholder involvement.[176] The experience gathered in PTAs may also be invaluable for the ongoing reinvigorated efforts in the WTO to reach an agreement on electronic commerce, as well as in new bolder deals that go beyond existing commitments and look at a range of emerging issues, such as digital identity, AI, electronic invoicing and open data, such as those covered under the DEPA.

As a final thought, one may stress that the data economy has placed higher demands on regulatory cooperation.[177] As the complexity of the data-driven society rises, enhanced regulatory cooperation seems indispensable for moving forward, since data issues cannot be covered by the mere 'lower tariffs, more commitments' stance in trade negotiations but entail the need for reconciling different interests and the need for oversight. In this context, while the paths for engaging in and advancing regulatory cooperation would ideally be followed in the multilateral forum,[178] preferential trade venues can serve as governance laboratories. The way forward may be truly bright but remains highly (and perhaps unfortunately so) dependent on the role that the key players, the United States, the EU and China, are willing to assume.

---

[176] For a general critique, see S. Cho and C. R. Kelly, 'Are World Trading Rules Passé?'. *Vanderbilt Journal of International Law* 53 (2013), 623–666, at 623–627; for a more contextualized critique, see Burri, note 27.

[177] T. J. Bollyky and P. C. Mavroidis, 'Trade, Social Preferences, and Regulatory Cooperation: The New WTO-Think', *Journal of International Economic Law* 20 (2017), 1–30, at 11–13 (Bollyky and Mavroidis discuss the need for regulatory competition in the context of global value chains; their argument is only strengthened in the domain of overall digital trade and data flows).

[178] Ibid., at 21. See also Chapter 4 in this volume.

2

Data Flow-Related Provisions in Preferential Trade Agreements

Trends and Patterns of Diffusion

*Manfred Elsig and Sebastian Klotz**

A INTRODUCTION

Innovation in information and communication technology (ICT) has been one of the key drivers of economic globalization. As a result, the volume of goods and services and, therefore, cross-border data flows have been increasing at an exceptional speed. The World Trade Organization (WTO) and its members have early on realized the importance of establishing global rules for guiding these processes. Already at its Second Ministerial Conference in 1998, the WTO adopted the Declaration on Global Electronic Commerce and called for the establishment of a work programme on e-commerce. The work programme has been implemented by four of the WTO's bodies which have regularly reported on the developments,[1] and the General Council has periodically reviewed the progress of the programme. Based on the minutes of the meetings of the General Council, Figure 2.1 maps the number of interventions by WTO members related to the topic of e-commerce. The data shows important variation in terms of attention given to the topic over time. After a substantial interest on e-commerce–related issues in the late 1990s and the early 2000s, the preoccupation with the topic dropped dramatically from 2003 until around 2011. Overall attention has only picked up again in the past few years. In preparation for the Eleventh Ministerial Conference (MC11) in Buenos Aires in December 2017, e-commerce was back on the table and the subject of many of the interventions made in the General Council.

* Manfred Elsig is Professor of International Relations and Deputy Managing Director and Director of Research of the World Trade Institute, University of Bern. Contact: manfred .elsig@wti.org. Sebastian Klotz is a doctoral fellow at the World Trade Institute, University of Bern and a visiting researcher at the University of Oxford. Contact: sebastian.klotz@wti.org.
[1] These bodies include the Council for Trade in Services, the Council for Trade in Goods, the Council for Trade-Related Aspects of Intellectual Property Rights (TRIPS), the Committee on Trade and Development; for details on the work by these bodies and updates, see www.wto.org/ english/tratop_e/ecom_e/ecom_e.htm.

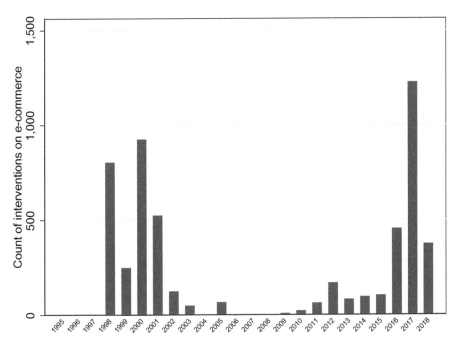

FIGURE 2.1. Interventions on e-commerce in the WTO General Council, 1995–2018
Source: Authors' illustration based on the WTO General Council meeting minutes (WT/GC/M/1-WT/
GC/M/174) available on the WTO website.

Following intensified discussions, seventy-six WTO members issued a joint statement on e-commerce during the World Economic Forum meeting in Davos in January 2019 in which they 'confirm [their] intention to commence WTO negotiations on trade-related aspects of electronic commerce', 'seek to achieve a high standard outcome that builds on existing WTO agreements and frameworks with the participation of as many WTO Members as possible' and 'continue to encourage all WTO Members to participate in order to further enhance the benefits of electronic commerce for businesses, consumers and the global economy'.[2]

Notwithstanding the newly found interest in e-commerce topics at the multilateral level, we observe that the WTO has been rather passive in its approach to address the data-related changes in the world economy. If regulatory solutions have been promoted, it was mostly driven by unilateral or extraterritorial approaches by the main trading powers. Given the absence of progress in rule-making in the WTO for some time now and a growing set of unilateral policies, the negotiators of preferential trade agreements (PTAs) have themselves attempted to shape the rule book for the twenty-first-century world economy – rules that would address needs resulting from an ever more integrated and data-driven economy. The first PTA that

[2] WTO, Joint Statement on Electronic Commerce, WT/L/1056, 25 January 2019.

had an electronic-commerce provision was the Jordan–US PTA in 2000 and the first data flow provisions go back to the Korea–US PTA concluded in 2007. So, these types of provisions are a rather recent phenomenon in trade agreements, but it clearly shows that WTO members have shifted the venue for rule-making from the WTO to the world of PTAs starting in the early 2000s.[3]

This chapter focuses on data-related provisions in PTAs and explores trends and patterns over time. We attempt to map clusters and models that have emerged. Related to this, we also focus on who the 'rule-makers' are in this regulatory area. If PTAs are best understood as 'laboratories' for global rule-making, we investigate in this chapter which governments are pivotal in pushing regulatory ideas and templates.

The chapter is organized as follows: first, we provide a short discussion of the literature that provides the backbone and rationale for the data collection. We then present particular indicators aggregated from the data that attempt to capture various salient dimensions of data flow–related provisions in PTAs. This is followed by an enquiry into the trends over time using these indicators, exploring the rule-makers' roles through both text-as-data analyses and manual coding of data-related design features. Finally, we graphically explore bivariate relationships that speak to potential explanations why we would expect to see variation in PTA design in this domain. The chapter concludes by outlining possible next research avenues in the area of digital trade governance.

B A LOOK AT STATE OF THE ART

Various strands of literature in international relations and political economy provide the backbone for collecting and analyzing PTA design features – some of them address general debates regarding the move towards more law, the relationship between multilateralism and regionalism or on rule-making versus rule-taking, the role of diffusion and debates specific to data flows and regulatory responses. We have mapped some of these debates in this chapter.

The call for more fine-grained information on the content of international agreements has been around for quite a while. Both the legalization as well as the rational design literatures provide useful guidance for choosing the types of design features to focus on.[4] Both literatures develop indicators and propose measures to account for treaties' scope, degree of obligation as well as flexibility features. In particular in the trade literature on PTAs, various indicators have been further developed – such as with regard to the depth of an agreement which captures the

---

[3] See Chapter 1 in this volume for more details.

[4] J. Goldstein et al., 'Introduction: Legalization and World Politics', *International Organization* 54 (2000), 385–399; B. Koremenos, C. Lipson and D. Snidal, 'The Rational Design of International Institutions', *International Organization* 55 (2001), 761–799.

degree to which measures may lead to increased market integration[5] or with regard to various types of flexibility tools which allow for legally imposing barriers, normally for a limited period of time.[6] These conceptualizations are also insightful when mapping data flow provisions as part of PTAs.

Another strand of literature to which this chapter speaks is the work on regime complexity, which is usually defined as a set of non-hierarchical overlapping institutions.[7] The universe of PTAs with over one thousand agreements, where all WTO members are participating actors, serves as an interesting laboratory of how regime complexity affects the behaviour of states both in collaborative and conflictive fashions. Linked to the concept of regime complexity is the emerging attention given to diffusion drivers and effects,[8] which asks the essential questions of why states sign PTAs; what the role of competition with other trading nations is; how learning and mimicking from neighbouring countries impact the decision to engage in PTAs, or whether PTA signature and the treaty commitments are a result of coercion by powerful states that aim to have their templates and models reflected in as many treaties as possible. Both, the regime complexity theories and diffusion theories, provide strong testimony to how international treaties are interdependent and serve as a cautionary note of analyzing single agreements in isolation of other treaties. Within the study of international institutions and international trade, additional debates have emerged, focusing on the groups of countries that promote their own rules ('rule-makers') and the ones that are on the receiving end of global regulation ('rule-takers'). This chapter focuses on the conditions under which rules diffuse using a mix of methods, including textual analyses.[9]

Finally, research on trade and data flows can build on the work that has zoomed in on the relationship between the promotion of liberalization and a government's objective to protect public interests. While the early trade literature focused on various linkages, such as trade and human rights and trade and environment,[10] more recently

5 A. Dür, L. Baccini and M. Elsig, 'The Design of International Trade Agreements: Introducing a New Dataset', *The Review of International Organizations* 9 (2014), 353–375.
6 L. Baccini, A. Dür and M. Elsig, 'The Politics of Trade Agreement Design: Revisiting the Depth-Flexibility Nexus', *International Studies Quarterly* 59 (2015), 765–775.
7 D. W. Drezner (ed), *All Politics Is Global: Explaining International Regulatory Regimes* (Princeton, NJ: Princeton University Press, 2007); K. J. Alter and K. Raustiala, 'The Rise of International Regime Complexity', *Annual Review of Law and Social Science* 14 (2018), 329–349.
8 B. A. Simmons, F. Dobbin and G. Garrett, 'Introduction: The International Diffusion of Liberalism', *International Organization* 60 (2006), 781–810; F. Gilardi, 'Transnational Diffusion: Norms, Ideas and Policies', in T. Risse, W. Carlsnaes and B. A. Simmons (eds), *Handbook of International Relations* (Thousand Oaks, CA: SAGE Publications, 2012), 453–477.
9 W. Alschner and D. Skougarevskiy, 'Mapping the Universe of International Investment Agreements', *Journal of International Economic Law* 19 (2016), 561–688.
10 E. M. Hafner-Burton, 'Trading Human Rights: How Preferential Trade Agreements Influence Government Repression', *International Organization* 59 (2005), 593–629; T. Bernauer and Q.

the concept of optimal protection of individual rights related to data protection has become more central. Following the old idea of 'embedded liberalism',[11] we are interested in how liberalization in data flows related to trade and services goes hand in hand with governments' demands for flexibility or escape instruments to protect citizens' interests in terms of privacy, and therefore pursuing social goals.

C DESIGN DIMENSIONS AND RELATED CONCEPTS

In recent years, research on trade agreements has made substantial progress by unpacking the various design features in PTAs to explore variation across treaties.[12] We follow this work by zooming in on data-relevant provisions. The data presented below is based on seventy-four single variables focusing, on the one hand, on the electronic commerce chapters and, on the other hand, on data-relevant provisions in other PTA chapters, including services, intellectual property rights and specific rules on ICT, data localization and similar content. The data is then aggregated to produce a number of indicators measuring various key dimensions derived from the earlier literature discussion. In the following, we briefly describe the different concepts and the types of variables that we draw upon to construct these.

I *Scope*

This concept measures the attention paid to data-related provisions. Scope is different from depth, as it does not capture the degree of obligation and commitment, but rather provides information about the extent to which the topic is covered within the agreement.[13] Therefore, we construct two different measures for scope or coverage: Scope 1 is the word count for the electronic commerce chapter; scope 2 is the number of total provisions found in the electronic commerce chapter. Scope 1 has a maximum of 3,206 words and the average value is 793. Scope 2 is an additive index which ranges from 0 to 74.

II *Depth of Data Flow Facilitation*

This measure comes closest to what is in the literature described as the depth of the agreement.[14] In this case, depth is thought of in relation to commitments, which

Nguyen, 'Free Trade and/or Environment Protection?', *Global Environmental Politics* 15 (2015), 105–129.
[11] J. G. Ruggie, 'International Regimes, Transactions, and Change: Embedded Liberalism in the Postwar Economic Order', *International Organization* 36 (1982), 379–415.
[12] Dür et al., note 5.
[13] Koremenos et al., note 4.
[14] G. W. Downs, D. M. Rocke and P. N. Barsoom, 'Is the Good News about Compliance Good News for Cooperation?', *International Organization* 52 (1996), 379–406; Dür et al., note 5.

tend to make trading easier when data transfer is involved. Here we create an additive index of seventeen variables that include rules for facilitating trade and providing for a regulatory environment to foster trade in data – these range from free movement of data commitments, promoting paperless trading and electronic signatures, and advocating self-regulation of the private sector to abstain from data localization measures. This additive indicator ranges from o to 17.

III *Flexibility*

As the literature on international institutions suggests that deeper commitments are also more flexible,[15] we constructed one indicator that focuses on eight escape and flexibility measures that we detected in the agreements' texts. These include both general and specific exceptions to commitments as well as reservations. The flexibility indicator ranges from o to 8.

IV *Consumer Protection*

An important and more specific flexibility instrument consists of explicitly foreseeing ways to protect consumer interests. This indicator ranges from o to 4 and includes elements of individual rights in relation to data protection, Internet Governance principles, data localization measures or addressing spam.

V *Non-discrimination*

This indicator measures how much attention treaty drafters have directed to general principles related to non-discrimination, such as treating domestic and foreign actors equally as well as following the most favoured nation (MFN) clause. On top, we add references to the WTO commitments and the need for technology neutrality. The higher the indicator, the more negotiators embed trade agreements within the multilateral trading system aiming for more consistency across treaties.[16] The indicator ranges from o to 7.

VI *Regulatory Cooperation*

The final indicator measures the degree to which treaty drafters advocate various forms of regulatory cooperation. We compile commitments that call for cooperation on transparency, international alignment in regulatory fora or working together on

---

[15] Baccini et al., note 6.
[16] T. Allee and M. Elsig, 'Are the Contents of International Treaties Copied-and-Pasted? Evidence from Preferential Trade Agreements', *International Studies Quarterly* 63 (2019), 603–613.

cybersecurity issues. In addition, we explore whether the treaty mentions working groups or committees to implement the electronic commerce commitments. This indicator is a proxy for how much regulatory cooperation is foreseen in the treaty text. The indicator ranges from 0 to 13.

D DESCRIBING TRENDS AND PATTERNS IN DIGITAL TRADE GOVERNANCE

In this section we discuss briefly the evolution of PTAs over time. We provide some descriptive statistics based on the indicators developed earlier, derive a better idea about who the rule-makers are and explore a number of bivariate relations which are suggestive about potential interdependence between design features, but also between treaty content and domestic practice.

The first agreement referring to electronic commerce was signed in 2000. Therefore, we deal with a rather novel issue area for trade regulation. There are no observations prior to 2000 while discussions within the WTO had been going on for a while. This is suggestive to the possibility that governments have prioritized the multilateral arena while then slowly turning to PTAs either because of lack of progress in the WTO (see Figure 2.1), or because of learning effects and development of various government strategies and potentially implicit models. Figure 2.2 shows the steady increase of e-commerce provisions, e-commerce chapters and provisions on free data flow both in absolute numbers and relative to the number of PTAs signed per year.

In total, we have identified ninety-nine PTAs that have at least one data-related provision. Table 2.1 provides the summary statistics for the different indicators outlined earlier and confirms the notion of considerable heterogeneity among PTAs.

In the following figures, we zoom into a selection of indicators and illustrate their evolution over time. Figure 2.3 shows the Scope1 indicator, which captures the number of words related to the regulation of e-commerce and data flows. The median and range of the count of words varies considerably over time. We also observe a number of outliers, including Jordan–Singapore 2004, the Central European Free Trade Agreement (CEFTA) in 2006 and Australia–Japan 2015. The latter one is an outlier for that year but is following an upward trend. We also observe large variation in the years 2016–2018.

In Figure 2.4 we show the second scope indicator, based on the number of provisions related to the regulation of e-commerce and data flows. Again, we observe that scope increases; however, this does not occur gradually. In most years, we notice a considerable range of provisions as well as a number of outliers. Compared to other PTAs signed in 2006, CEFTA has only few provisions related to the regulations of e-commerce and data flows. In 2007, the same is true for the PTA between Japan and Thailand. In contrast, the Panama–US PTA in 2007 includes a rather

TABLE 2.1. *Summary statistics on the indicators*

Variable	Obs	Mean	Std. Dev.	Min	Max
Scope 1	99	793.2	669.2	17	3,209
Scope 2	99	22.9	10.5	2	46
Depth	99	6.5	3.5	0	15
Flexibility	99	3.3	2.1	0	8
Consumer protection	99	1.6	0.8	0	3
Non-discrimination	99	3.0	1.7	0	6
Regulatory cooperation	99	4.3	2.7	0	12

Source: Authors' calculation based on the TAPED database.

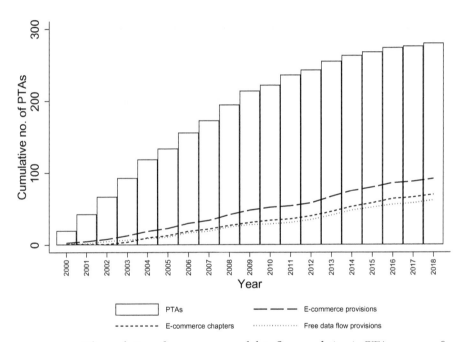

FIGURE 2.2. The evolution of e-commerce and data flow regulation in PTAs, 2000–2018.
Source: Authors' illustration based on the TAPED database. The TAPED database traces all data-relevant norms in trade agreements and is available at https://unilu.ch/taped. See also M. Burri and R. Polanco, 'Digital Trade Provisions in Preferential Trade Agreements: Introducing a New Dataset', *Journal of International Economic Law* 23 (2020), 187–220.

large number of provisions on this topic. The PTA between Colombia and Costa Rica presents the top outlier in 2013, the PTA between Central America and the European Free Trade Association (EFTA) the bottom outlier. Malaysia–Turkey and Canada–Ukraine present the two outliers in 2014 and 2016, respectively.

Over time, we also detect an increase in the depth (Data Flow Facilitation) indicator (Figure 2.5). Following the above trend, the 2006 CEFTA agreement

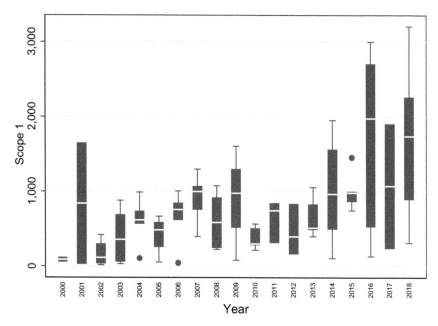

FIGURE 2.3. The Scope 1 indicator, 2000–2018.
Source: Authors' illustration based on the TAPED database.

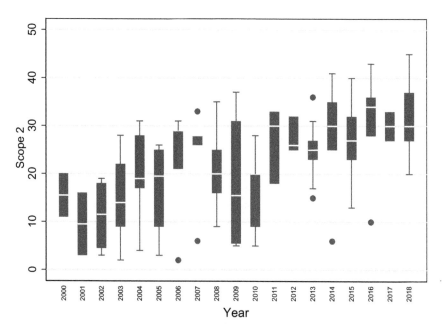

FIGURE 2.4. The Scope 2 indicator, 2000–2018.
Source: Authors' illustration based on the TAPED database.

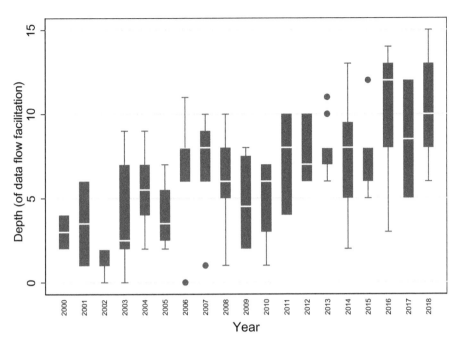

FIGURE 2.5. The depth indicator, 2000–2018.
Source: Authors' illustration based on the TAPED database.

and the 2007 Japan–Thailand PTA indicate substantially shallower commitments than other agreements in these respective years. The outlier PTAs having substantially deeper commitments in 2013 than other agreements signed in that year are Colombia–Costa Rica as well as Colombia–Panama, most likely inspired by their commitments in one of their recent trade agreements with a rule-maker. In 2015, we observe in Mongolia's first ever PTA with Japan also deeper commitments in terms of data flow facilitation.

Turning to our flexibility indicator (Figure 2.6), we observe that already between 2004 and 2008 PTAs included higher levels of flexibility. Again, CEFTA presents the outlier in 2006, which is not surprising as it also scored low on scope and depth. The bottom outlier in 2015 is the PTA between Canada and Ukraine, which might be explained by the low trade flows in goods and services with substantial data content between the two countries. The top outlier in the same year is the PTA between Australia and Singapore, which could be a result of two countries with usually deep agreements.

E OF RULE-MAKERS AND CENTRAL ACTORS

The previous sections discussed the various indicators and illustrated their variation over time. In this section, we take a closer look at the signatory countries. In total,

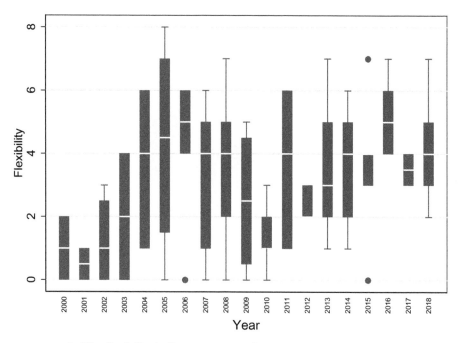

FIGURE 2.6. The flexibility indicator, 2000–2018.
Source: Authors' illustration based on the TAPED database.

eighty-two countries (counting the EU as one actor) are involved in the ninety-nine PTAs which have data flow–related provisions since 2000. As illustrated in Figure 2.7, there is considerable heterogeneity in terms of the number of PTA partners by signatory and the degree of scope measured by the number of provisions. Since 2000, the EU has signed eighteen PTAs with thirty-eight partner countries and, on average, included twenty-three provisions on e-commerce and data flows. Mongolia (MGN) has only signed one PTA (with Japan). In this PTA, however, there are forty provisions on e-commerce and data flows. The United States has signed fewer agreements than the EU, but on average their scope is substantially higher. We also observe that the average scope of agreements with European countries is significantly lower than treaties with countries of the Americas. Oceania is also above average in terms of scope. Finally, African signatories of PTAs are not yet addressing data flow–related provisions. This is surprising given the potential of e-commerce for developing countries.

To illustrate this network of PTAs, we combine the average Scope 2 indicator and the count of PTA partner countries for each signatory country and represent this in Figure 2.8 using instruments of network analysis. In this network, the size of each country is proportional to its weighted centrality. That is, the size of each country is proportional to the product of the number of PTA partners and the average number

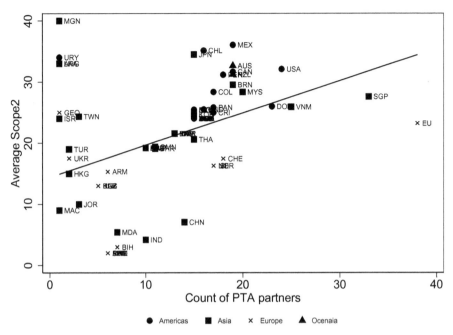

FIGURE 2.7. The Scope 2 indicator and the count of PTA partners.
Source: Authors' illustration based on the TAPED database.

of provisions on e-commerce and data flows included in all its PTAs. The width of the links is proportional to the number of e-commerce and data flow provisions in a given PTA. Figure 2.8 highlights that there are some countries that are central to this PTA network and therefore potentially influential in diffusing certain regulatory models on e-commerce and data flows. The European Union, the United States and Singapore stand out, but also other countries, such as Australia, Canada or Mexico, are pictured as central actors.

To investigate the patterns that can be graphically observed in the earlier network, we zoom into the subset of PTAs that have not only at least one provision on e-commerce and data flows but a full chapter. Out of the ninety-nine PTAs signed since 2000, seventy-two have a chapter related to e-commerce and data flows. Seven of these PTAs are signed between Latin American countries and only available in Spanish, leaving us with sixty-three PTAs that are available in the English language. Since Singapore and Australia renewed their 2003 PTA in 2016, we only include the latter PTA in this analysis – leaving us with a subset of sixty-two PTAs.

Relying on text-as-data analysis, we compare these sixty-two PTA chapters in the English language to detect potential patterns, more precisely, by employing the plagiarism software WCopyfind to measure the textual overlap between the PTA chapters. The programme allows for a number of refinements. We follow the

54 Manfred Elsig & Sebastian Klotz

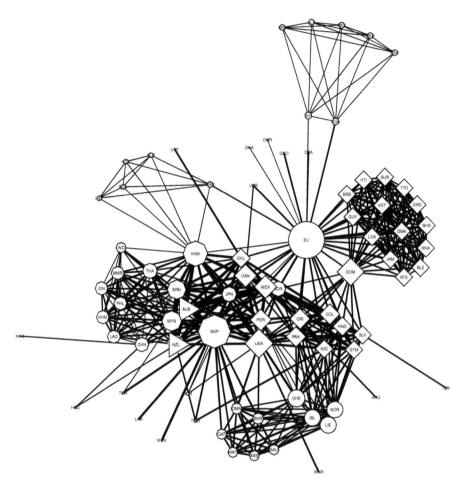

FIGURE 2.8. The network of PTAs regulating e-commerce and data flows.
Source: Authors' illustration based on the TAPED database. Note: Blue-Asia, White-Americas, Red-Europe, Green-Oceania.

convention to use a minimum of six consecutive identical words for a match.[17] All punctuation, outer punctuation, numbers, letter case and non-words are ignored. It should be pointed out that WCopyfind only reports the PTAs that have a minimum of matches between PTAs. In our case, the PTAs between Jordan and Singapore (2004), Canada and Jordan (2009), the Eurasian Economic Union (EAEU) and

[17] T. Allee and A. Lugg, 'Who Wrote the Rules for the Trans-Pacific Partnership?', Research and Politics 3 (2016), 1–9; T. Allee, M. Elsig and A. Lugg, 'Is the European Union Deal with Canada New or Recycled? A Text-as-Data Approach', Global Policy 8 (2017), 246–252; T. Allee, M. Elsig and A. Lugg, 'The Ties between the World Trade Organization and Preferential Trade Agreements: A Textual Analysis', Journal of International Economic Law 20 (2017), 333–363.

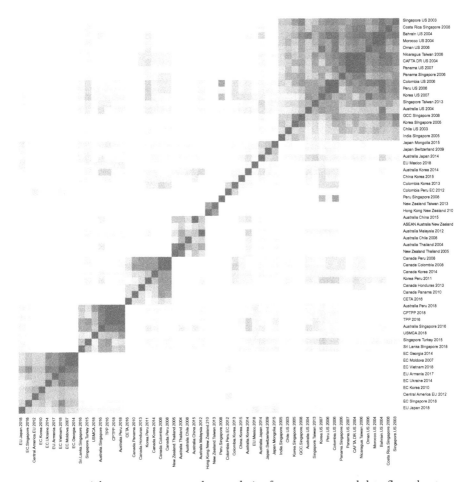

FIGURE 2.9. A heat map on text-as-data analysis of e-commerce and data flow chapters in PTAs.
Source: Authors' illustration based on PTA texts collected for the TAPED database.

Vietnam (2015) and between Canada, and the Ukraine (2016) appear to have too little overlap with the other PTAs and were consequently dropped by the programme.

The heat map (Figure 2.9) provides a number of interesting insights. In terms of interpretation, the map colours the squares darker, the higher the textual overlap between the e-commerce and data flow chapters of two respective PTAs is. In Figure 2.9, the PTA chapters are hierarchically clustered, meaning PTAs are grouped together into clusters. The clusters and their PTAs are fairly distinct from each other and the PTAs within a cluster are broadly similar to each other. Figure 2.9 suggests that there are five main clusters. The top right cluster indicates that the United States and Singapore take similar approaches when designing their e-commerce chapters. This is likely to be the case because they have signed a PTA with one another in 2003. Out of the eighteen PTAs that are identified to be in this cluster, the United States and Singapore have signed eleven and seven, respectively. Interestingly, their PTA partners overlap only partly. While the United States and Singapore both have PTAs with South Korea and Panama, the other PTA partners are distinct. It is also interesting to note that Singapore already signed its PTAs with South Korea and Panama in 2005 and 2006 respectively, while the United States only signed its agreements with the two countries in 2007. The second PTA cluster can be found in the centre of Figure 2.9. These six PTAs appear to be following the Australian approach. Indeed, Australia is a signatory of five of these PTAs; the sixth PTA is between New Zealand and Thailand in 2004. Down and to the left is the third distinct cluster of PTAs. Out of the seven PTAs identified to be in this cluster, Canada has signed six. Somewhat surprisingly, the 2011 PTA between South Korea and Peru seems to follow a similar approach to the Canadian PTAs in this cluster. Figure 2.9 also shows that the Comprehensive Economic and Trade Agreement (CETA) between the Canada and the EU is closer to previous Canadian agreements than to EU agreements (the cluster at the bottom left). The second last cluster includes the Trans-Pacific Partnership Agreement (TPP, 2016) and the Comprehensive and Progressive Agreement for Trans-Pacific Partnership (CPTPP, 2018), as well as a number of other agreements that the (CP)TPP members have signed. Interestingly, the e-commerce chapter of the recently negotiated agreement between the United States, Mexico and Canada (USMCA, 2018) is also found to be very close to the (CP)TPP. The last cluster in the bottom left corner of Figure 2.9 includes recent agreements by the EU. Overall, the text-as-data analysis presented helps detect the small group of countries which seem to be the rule-makers in the area of digital trade.

F ZOOMING IN ON THE RULE-MAKERS

In this section we compare these rule-makers by focusing on the number of provisions (Scope 2) and differentiate these provisions in terms of their legal language and overall 'bindingness'. The legal language provides clues as to whether we expect more or less obligation based on words such as 'should', 'shall', or 'may'. We differentiate between high and low obligation. Figure 2.10 provides an overview for five identified rule-makers (United States, EU, Australia, Canada and Singapore). The figure shows the average and maximum count of total provisions, as well as the average and maximum count of that have a high level of bindingness. The maximum scores might be more intuitive to interpret as countries potentially do not negotiate in their future agreements commitments below the ones already agreed upon.

For scope and depth, we observe that for the so-called rule-maker group, roughly half of all commitments are phrased in legal terms that suggest high obligation. In

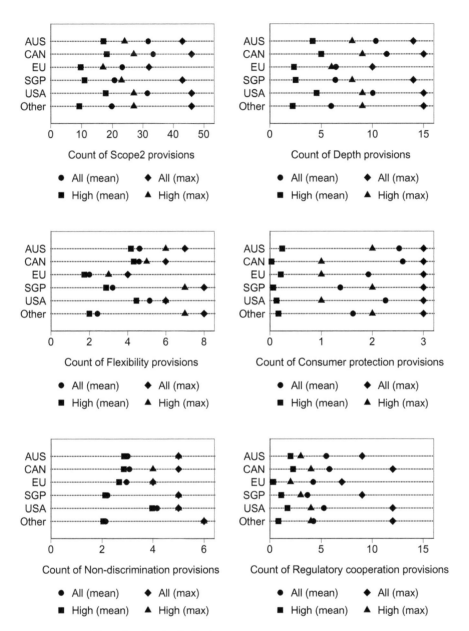

FIGURE 2.10. Dot plots for the indicators.

Note: In the figure on non-discrimination provisions, High(max) is equal to All(max) for Australia, the EU, Singapore, the United States and others, which is why only the All (max) indicator is shown.

Source: Authors' illustration based on the TAPED database.

terms of the average and maximum values for scope and depth, the EU scores lower than the other rule-makers as well as other countries. We observe a similar pattern for the flexibility indicator. Of the rule-makers, it is in particular Singapore which includes a considerable number of flexibility-related provisions. For the indicator related to consumer protection, we in particular detect that Singapore and Australia agree on legal language that signals higher obligation and therefore allows for stronger rights to protect individuals. The non-discrimination provisions are overwhelmingly commitments which come with high obligation based on the reading of the legal language. By contrast, when we turn to regulatory cooperation, we observe that the legal wording signals rather low levels of obligation, therefore these features of the treaties are practically not enforceable in case of disagreement among PTA members.

G EXPLORING EXPLANATIONS FOR TREATY DESIGN

In this section we provide graphical descriptions of a number of bivariate relations to address potential explanations for variation in PTA design. The first group of graphs (Figure 2.11) addresses the question as to whether PTA design is largely endogenous; in other words, many of the design features are related to each other, as suggested by some authors. We focus on the depth variable and explore how this is correlated with other indicators. First, we see that scope and depth are highly correlated, which is not surprising. PTAs that are paying more attention to data-related issues are also deeper. Second, deeper agreements are also going hand in hand with PTAs that advocate regulatory cooperation. This could also be interpreted as negotiators are forward-looking, promising to engage in regulatory discussion to accompany the rapidly changing regulatory environment. Deeper agreements are also more flexible, and provide for more consumer protection rights and non-discrimination clauses.

Another set of explanations can be situated at the domestic level and relates to a different set of questions: To what degree are domestic policies mirrored in international law commitments? Are countries using international law as a commitment device to bring about domestic regulatory change or are we rather witnessing a screening effect in which commitments largely reflect domestic practice suggesting some cheap talk in relation to signing agreements?[18]

To address such questions, we discuss how PTA design relates to domestic digital policies. We rely on the recently published Digital Trade Restrictiveness Index (DTRI) by the European Centre for International Political Economy (ECIPE). The DTRI covers a range of fiscal, establishment, data and trading restrictions related to digital trade for sixty-four economies worldwide. The index ranges between zero and one, where zero indicates a fully open digital economy and one indicates a virtually closed digital economy. Between the TAPED database and the

---

[18] J. von Stein, 'Do Treaties Constrain or Screen? Selection Bias and Treaty Compliance', *American Political Science Review* 99 (2005), 611–622.

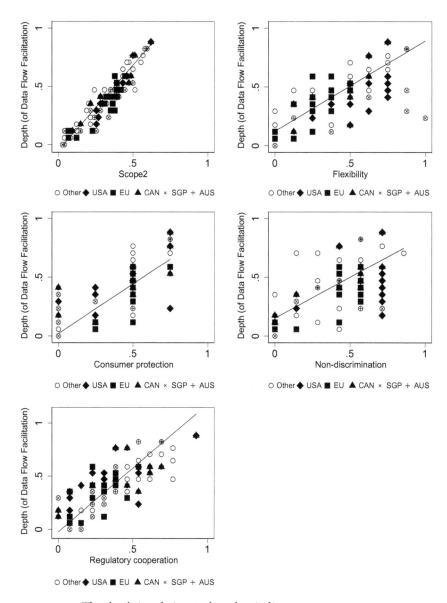

FIGURE 2.11. The depth in relation to the other indicators.
Source: Authors' illustration based on the TAPED database.

DTRI, we have an overlap of thirty-one countries.[19] Figure 2.12 illustrates how our main indicators relate to the DTRI. All indicators are negatively correlated with the

---

[19] The relatively little overlap is due to the fact that the DTRI includes individual member states which in TAPED are grouped as EU.

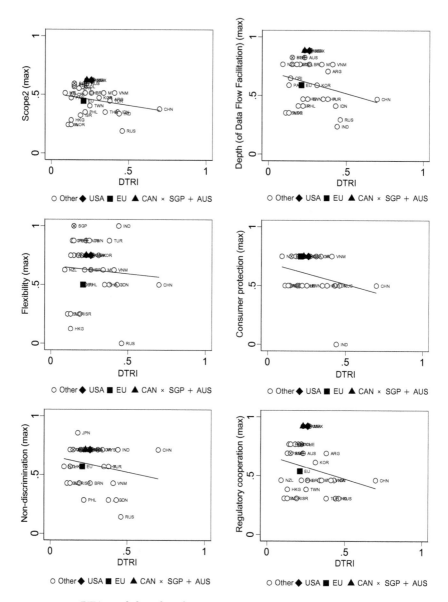

FIGURE 2.12. PTAs and digital trade restrictiveness.
Source: Authors' illustration based on the TAPED and the DTRI databases.

DTRI.[20] As for those indicators that are about scope, depth and various obligations, a negative correlation casts doubts about prima facie evidence that a commitment

---

[20] Scope 2: −0.2208, Depth: −0.2483, Flexibility: −0.0746, Consumer protection: −0.2892, Non-discrimination: −0.2132, Regulatory cooperation: −0.2639.

story is at play here. More interesting are downward trends for flexibility and consumer protection; countries with lower restrictions aim for more flexibility. This would rather suggest that these countries aim to keep policy space in this area, whereas countries with higher restrictions paradoxically demand less flexibility providing some support for the idea of a commitment device. Overall, we also observe that the rule-makers, with the exception of the EU, are substantially above the trend lines.

H CONCLUSION

Data flow provisions have entered the universe of PTAs in the past fifteen years, although, only a third of all PTAs have commitments related to this area. This chapter presented a number of indicators related to PTA design and has mapped the design evolution over time. Letting the data speak, we discovered a number of leading actors (rule-makers) and sets of overlapping models of treaties based on textual analysis. However, we seem to be at the beginning of a period where data-relevant provisions will only increase in importance as many classic trade and trade-related provisions, such as tariffs, become relatively less important.

What are the next steps in understanding design and design variation in the domain of digital trade? First, research may explore explanations to account for variation in design based on political economy models and arguments rooted in the international relations literature; for instance, what roles do commitment concerns or power asymmetry play in agreeing upon new rules? Which interest groups are pivotal for pushing new rules? How does the competition between exporter interests and consumer protection interests define government positions entering into PTA negotiations? Second, research should pay more attention to the evolving competition among models that are being developed, in particular starting with the CPTPP and how this will affect the creation and promotion of other models, such as that of the EU. Are these models complementary or are they creating regulatory barriers? Related to this, it can be asked how leading promoters of models use PTAs to diffuse their preferred models and what the impacts on non-PTA members are when they negotiate PTAs. It would be also pertinent to explore to what degree new domestic initiatives, such as the EU General Data Protection Regulation, impact on PTA design and push for updating existing PTAs.[21]

Finally, the following questions need to be raised: What is the impact of these commitments on state behaviour? How do they assist in creating new domestic

---

[21] See, e.g., M. Burri, 'Privacy and Data Protection', in D. Bethlehem et al. (eds), *The Oxford Handbook on International Trade Law*, 2nd edn (Oxford: Oxford University Press, 2021).

policies and laws on the role of data in trade and how do they inhibit government action to restrict trade in light of consumer protection concerns? Also, more generally, how do these commitments directly or indirectly impact trade flows in goods and services and investment-location decisions for firms with large data components in their business models?

3

The Costs of Data Protectionism

Martina F. Ferracane[*]

A INTRODUCTION

Movement of data across borders is central to today's economy: it enables people to instantly connect with each other, companies to do business smoothly and governments to offer new, more efficient services to their citizens. The Internet has fundamentally changed what, with whom and how trade is conducted, and today virtually all cross-border transactions make use of the Internet or some digital component.[1] The exponential growth in data being exchanged cross-border is not set to slow down.[2] Yet, cross-border data flows are also raising both economic and political concerns related to the concentration of data, data sovereignty, privacy, law enforcement, and national security. This has posed the question of whether countries should insist that companies process data within their jurisdictions, and already many countries have enacted restrictions on the transfer of data across borders.[3]

The enactment of these measures has been a topic of hot discussions across the world. On the one hand, there are actors arguing that data should flow freely and

---

[*] Max Weber Fellow at the European University Institute, Research Associate at European Center for International Political Economy (ECIPE). Contact: martina.ferracane@eui.eu.

[1] There are several reports on how data flows are impacting production and trade. See, e.g., M. Rentzhog and H. Jonströmer, *No Transfer, No Trade: The Importance of Cross-Border Data Transfer for Companies Based in Sweden* (Stockholm: Kommerskollegium, 2014); M. Rentzhog, *No Transfer, No Production – A Report on Cross-Border Data Transfers, Global Value Chains, and the Production of Goods*, 3rd edn (Stockholm: Kommerskollegium, 2015).

[2] McKinsey estimates that cross-border data flows were 45 times larger in 2015 than in 2005. J. Manyika et al., *Digital Globalization: The New Era of Global Flows* (Washington, DC: McKinsey Global Institute, 2016). TeleGeography also estimates an annual compound growth rate of global bandwidth use of approximately 40 per cent between 2009 and 2013. See TeleGeography, Global Bandwidth Research Service (2015), at Executive Summary.

[3] M. F. Ferracane, 'Restrictions on Cross-Border Data Flows: A Taxonomy', ECIPE Working Paper No 1 (2017).

that any restriction creates unnecessary costs for businesses and the economy while also limiting the freedom of expression of people online.[4] On the other hand, certain stakeholders argue that these measures are legitimate to protect important policy objectives, such as privacy and security.[5]

These discussions are not new. In fact, already in the 1980s, some companies started to worry about the potential trade-restrictive impact of new policy measures affecting the use and transfers of data justified under the rationale of national security and privacy. Yet, the debate is still open today with claims by the business community that restrictions on the transfer and use of data (both personal and non-personal) are put in place without a proper analysis of the trade-inhibiting effects and with little guarantee that security and privacy concerns are actually addressed.[6]

The discussions on the trade-restrictive impact of data policies have intensified in the past years with the increasing importance of data flows for trade. As stated by the Swedish National Board of Trade, today 'trade cannot happen without data being transferred from one location to another'.[7] Restrictions on the movement of data in practice affect not only firms in the digital sector, but in virtually any sector of the economy.[8] In fact, firms of all sizes and across all sectors use data.[9] This is even more the case considering that data per se does not have much intrinsic value, but rather acquires it when processed (often along with other data) and used to offer services, improve business efficiency or take management decisions. Therefore, it does not surprise that restrictions on data flows are perceived by companies as trade restrictions.[10] Former European Trade Commissioner Malmström also notably stated that 'restrictions on cross-border data flows inhibit trade of all kinds: digital and

[4] See, e.g., R. D. Atkinson, 'International Data Flows: Promoting Digital Trade in the Twenty-first Century', *Testimony of Robert D. Atkinson, Founder and President, The Information Technology and Innovation Foundation before the House Judiciary Committee, Subcommittee on Courts, Intellectual Property and the Internet*, 3 November 2015.

[5] Privacy and security are listed among the main motivations for governments to impose restrictions on the cross-border transfer of data in several studies. Among recent studies, see, e.g., F. Casalini and J. López González, 'Trade and Cross-Border Data Flows', OECD Trade Policy Papers No 220 (2019); WTO, *World Trade Report 2018: The Future of World Trade: How Digital Technologies Are Transforming Global Commerce* (Geneva: WTO, 2018); A. Mattoo and J. P. Meltzer, 'International Data Flows and Privacy: The Conflict and Its Resolution', *Journal of International Economic Law* 21 (2018), 769–789.

[6] S. Stone, J. Messent, and D. Flaig, 'Emerging Policy Issues: Localisation Barriers to Trade', OECD Trade Policy Papers No 180 (2015).

[7] Rentzhog and Jonströmer, note 1.

[8] See, e.g., M. Mandel, 'Data, Trade and Growth', *Progressive Policy Institute Policy Brief*, 24 April 2013; and D. Castro and A. McQuinn, 'Cross-Border Data Flows Enable Growth in All Industries', *Information Technology and Innovation Foundation*, February 2009.

[9] Rentzhog, note 1.

[10] See, e.g., Rentzhog and Jonströmer, note 1; United States International Trade Commission, Digital Trade in the US and Global Economies, Part 2, Investigation No 332-540, Publication 4485 (Washington, DC: USITC, 2014).

nondigital, products and services. We cannot just pretend that this doesn't exist, or that data has nothing to do with global trade'.[11]

While companies have advocated the removal of data policies and the free flow of data across borders, it is yet not clear how different types of data policies impact trade, and some governments have also argued that certain policies would rather support trade by enhancing consumers' confidence.[12] This chapter addresses the question by looking at whether data policies create a distortion on trade in services. It does so by providing a summary of the main empirical evidence on the costs of restrictions on cross-border transfers of data and domestic restrictions on the use of data. The latter category is also included in the analysis because domestic restrictions on the use of data could have an indirect impact on trade as a result of lower productivity for local firms and limited access to innovation.

The first category of restrictions on cross-border transfer of data deals with all measures that raise the cost of conducting business across borders. These measures either mandate companies to keep data within a certain border or impose additional requirements for data to be transferred abroad. More specifically, these measures include bans to transfer data abroad, local processing requirements, local storage requirements, and conditional flow regimes.[13] The common feature of these measures is that they create 'thick' digital borders between countries. The second group of data policies relates to the use of data domestically and includes all measures that impose certain requirements for firms to access, store, process, or more generally make any commercial use of data within a certain jurisdiction. These measures apply to both local and foreign firms alike and include data retention requirements, administrative requirements, such as the need to prepare a Data Privacy Impact Assessment (DPIA) and to hire a Data Protection Officer (DPO), data breach notifications to government authorities, and the requirement to provide government with direct access to personal data.

B COUNTRIES THAT IMPOSE STRICTER DATA POLICIES

Before exploring the empirical evidence on the costs of data protectionism, this section gives a brief introduction on the level of data restrictions imposed all over the world. The indicator used in the analysis is the Data Restrictiveness Index developed in Ferracane et al.,[14] which is based on the information available in the Digital Trade Estimates (DTE) database of the European Center for International Political Economy (ECIPE).[15]

---

[11] C. Malmström, 'Trade in a Digital World', *Speech at the Conference on Digital Trade, European Parliament*, 17 November 2016, available at http://trade.ec.europa.eu/doclib/docs/2016/november/tradoc_155094.pdf.

[12] See, e.g., UNCTAD, Data Protection Regulations and International Data Flows: Implications for Trade and Development, UNCTAD/DTL/STICT/2016/1, April 2016.

[13] For a detailed taxonomy, see M. F. Ferracane, note 3.

[14] M. F. Ferracane, J. Kren, and E. van der Marel, 'Do Data Policy Restrictions Impact the Productivity Performance of Firms and Industries?', ECIPE DTE Working Paper No 1 (2018).

[15] DTE Database, available at https://ecipe.org/dte/database.

The Data Restrictiveness Index summarizes the level of restrictiveness on data policies in over sixty economies and varies between zero (completely open) and one (virtually restricted) with higher levels indicating increasing levels of data restrictiveness.[16] In the analysis, data policies are defined as those regulatory measures that restrict the commercial use of electronic data. The study is limited to those measures implemented at the national or supranational level (such as in the European Union), while other restrictions imposed by local public entities are not taken into account. Data policies are divided into two main categories: (i) cross-border data policies and (ii) domestic data policies, as defined earlier. The data policies implemented in the countries are analysed and aggregated in the Data Restrictiveness Index through a detailed methodology, presented in Section E. The types of measures included in the analysis are listed in Table 3.1, with the respective weights assigned in the analysis, which are estimated based on experts' input.

The index shows a clear trend of increasing data restrictiveness globally, driven both by raising restrictions on domestic use of data and on transfers of data (Figure 3.1).

The index shows that Russia, China, and Turkey are the most restrictive countries when it comes to the regulatory environment for using and transferring electronic data (Figure 3.2). These countries are followed by two major European economies, France and Germany, which also show high levels of restrictions on data policies.[17] Interestingly, on the one hand, all five countries are relatively large, often with a strong manufacturing base compared to their services activities. On the other hand, small services-oriented economies are found to have a more open regime on data policies.

The analysis only focuses on costs of using and transferring data, while it does not take into account regulatory policies that can support data-intensive activities, such as the existence of a basic framework of data protection and consumer protection for online transactions. Future analyses should take into account these policies to have a full perspective on the ease of using and transferring data in different countries. Nevertheless, the Data Restrictiveness Index is an important step forward in the analysis of the national regimes on data policies and the development of much-needed empirical evidence on the costs of protectionism.

C EMPIRICAL EVIDENCE ON THE COST OF DATA PROTECTIONISM

The economic literature that discusses the cost of data policies from a trade perspective is scarce.[18] This is probably due to the fact that the topic is relatively

---

[16] A detailed methodology for constructing the index can be found in Ferracane et al., note 14.
[17] The analysis refers to the year 2017. Since the GDPR came into force in May 2019, France and Germany were required to lift some of these restrictions and therefore are likely to have a lower score in the Data Restrictiveness Index today.
[18] Other empirical research on electronic data has focused more specifically on the economics of privacy and on consumers' understanding and decisions regarding the trade-offs associated with the privacy and the sharing of personal data. See among others A. Acquisti, C. Taylor, and L. Wagman, 'The Economics of Privacy', *Journal of Economic Literature* 52 (2016).

TABLE 3.1. *Categories covered in the Data Restrictiveness Index and their weights*

Categories		Types of measures	Weights
1	**Cross-border flow measures**		0.5
	1.1	Ban on transfer or local processing requirement	0.5
	1.2	Local storage requirement	0.25
	1.3	Conditional flow regime	0.25
2	**Domestic regulatory measures**		0.5
2.1	**Data retention**		0.15
	2.1.1	Minimum period	0.7
	2.1.2	Maximum period	0.3
2.2	**Subject rights on data privacy**		0.1
	2.2.1	Burdensome consent requirement	0.5
	2.2.2	Right to be forgotten	0.5
2.3	**Administrative requirements on data privacy**		0.15
	2.3.1	Data protection impact assessment (DPIA)	0.3
	2.3.2	Data protection officer (DPO)	0.3
	2.3.3	Data breach notification	0.1
	2.3.4	Government access to personal data	0.3
2.4	**Sanctions for non-compliance**		0.05
	2.4.1	Monetary fine above 250,000 EUR or set as a percentage of revenue	0.5
	2.4.2	Jail time	0.5
2.5	**Other restrictive practices related to data policies**		0.05
	2.5.1	Other restrictive practices related to data policies	1

Source: M. F. Ferracane, J. Kren, and E. van der Marel, 'Do Data Policy Restrictions Impact the Productivity Performance of Firms and Industries?', ECIPE DTE Working Paper No 1 (2018).

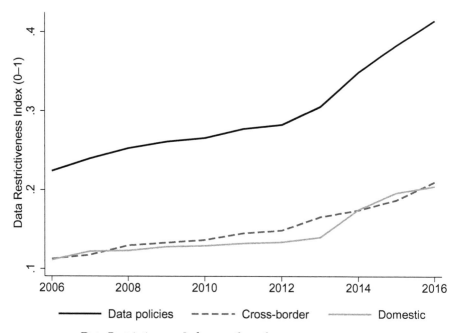

FIGURE 3.1. Data Restrictiveness Index, 2006–2016.
Note: The index covers sixty-four countries representing more than 95 per cent of value-added content of gross exports.
Source: M. F. Ferracane, J. Kren, and E. van der Marel, 'The Cost of Data Protectionism', *VoxEU*, 25 October 2018.

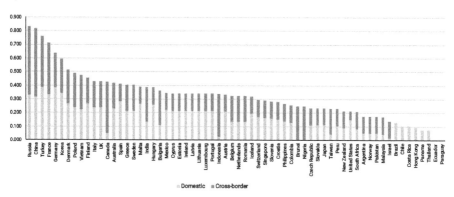

FIGURE 3.2. Data Restrictiveness Index, by country (2017).
Source: M. F. Ferracane, J. Kren, and E. van der Marel, 'The Cost of Data Protectionism', *VoxEU*, 25 October 2018.

new. Yet, the lack of in-depth empirical analysis is surprising given the extent to which trade in services today relies on data flows and considering the sizable portion of all trade in services being traded over the Internet. There are two main streams of research on data flows: one looks at the costs of data policies on local companies (mainly in terms of productivity); the other looks at the costs of these policies on foreign companies, and therefore more directly on trade.

The following section presents the empirical evidence on the costs of data protectionism on local companies in terms of jobs, productivity, and Gross Domestic Product (GDP). If data restrictions on the use and transfer of data lead to higher costs for conducting data-intense activities, then they would be detrimental for the development of local companies, impacting their productivity and, in turn, creating trade distortions. The subsequent section presents the empirical evidence on data protectionism and services trade, and therefore on whether data restrictions could create a trade barrier for foreign companies.

I *Foregone Gains for Local Companies*

A first set of empirical research looks at the costs of data restrictions on local firms. While it has been argued that data policies could support the development of a local information technology (IT) industry by shielding local incumbents from competition, there is no empirical evidence supporting this claim.[19] Instead data policies are found to have a negative impact on productivity and GDP.

Some studies look at the impact of data policies on jobs. While strict data policies might lead to the creation of data centres in the country imposing them, the construction of data centres is not expected to create a significant number of jobs. In most cases, data centres contain expensive high-tech equipment that is often imported and creates construction work only in the short term while employing relatively few full-time staff. In fact, the number of jobs associated with data centres has been decreasing sharply, as data centres become more automated.[20] A 2008 report found that Yahoo, Ask.com, Intuit, and Microsoft hired a total of 180 workers for their facilities – an average of 45 workers per facility.[21] Other media reports from 2011 showed that a massive USD 1 billion data centre Apple built to help power its cloud computing products created only 50 new full-time jobs.[22] In 2015, the media

---

[19] This logic would follow the 'infant industry argument' that some governments have put forward as a justification for restricting transfers of data cross-border. If that were the case, certain restrictions on data flows could be interpreted as a form of 'digital industrial policy'. See Casalini and López González, note 5; see also a similar argument made in J. Selby, 'Data Localization Laws: Trade Barriers or Legitimate Responses to Cybersecurity Risks, or Both?', *International Journal of Law and Information Technology* 25 (2017), 213–232; L. Tuthill, 'Cross-Border Data Flows: What Role for Trade Rules?', in P. Sauvé and M. Roy (eds), *Research Handbook on Trade in Services* (Cheltenham: Edward Elgar Publishing, 2016), 357–382; M. Langenegger, 'Cloud Mini-Series Part 1: The Transformative Potential of Cloud Computing', *Project Disco*, 26 March 2014.

[20] N. Cory, 'Cross-Border Data Flows: Where Are the Barriers, and What Do They Cost?', *Information Technology and Innovation Foundation*, 1 May 2017.

[21] R. Miller, 'The Economics of Data Center Staffing', *Informa: Data Center Knowledge*, 18 January 2008; D. Ohara, '# of Data Center Employees (Yahoo, Ask.com, Intuit, and Microsoft) in Washington Columbia Basin', *Green Data Center Blog* 2.0, 10 January 2008.

[22] H. Blodget, 'The Country's Problem in a Nutshell: Apple's Huge New Data Center in North Carolina Created Only Fifty Jobs', *Business Insider*, 28 November 2011; M. S. Rosenwald, 'Cloud Centers Bring High-Tech Flash But Not Many Jobs to Beaten-Down Towns', *The Washington Post*, 24 November 2011.

reported that Apple's USD 2 billion global command centre in Mesa, Arizona, would employ 150 full-time personnel, and create between 300 and 500 construction and trade jobs.

Another study looks specifically at one policy framework regarding data, the General Data Protection Regulation (GDPR) of the European Union, and its impact on jobs. Christensen et al. use calibration techniques to evaluate the impact of the GDPR proposal on small- and medium-sized enterprises (SMEs) and con-clude that SMEs that use data rather intensively are likely to incur substantial costs in complying with these new rules.[23] The authors compute these results using a simulated dynamic stochastic general equilibrium model and show that up to 100,000 jobs could disappear in the short run and more than 300,000 in the long term.

Therefore, the establishment of local data centres does not appear to lead to new jobs created in the country. Certain local companies providing data processing services would nevertheless benefit from such measures as they could leverage on a larger pool of data to process.[24] Yet, the empirical evidence suggests that the higher costs for processing data locally and the consequent loss of productivity in the overall economy would outweigh the benefits accrued to a small set of actors.[25] When data restrictions apply, local companies are not free to use the most convenient data processing provider globally and have to pay for more expensive or even duplicate services when they transfer data needed for day-to-day activities, for example, for human resources management. The higher costs of data processing are widespread and affect all businesses and consumers that are denied access to certain innovative services. The additional costs have a trickle-down impact on the macroeconomic performance of those countries implementing such rules.[26]

A study by the Leviathan Security Group finds that in many countries, which are considering or have considered restrictions on cross-border transfer of data, local companies would be required to pay 30–60 per cent more for their computing needs

---

[23] L. Christensen et al., 'The Impact of the Data Protection Regulation in the EU', *The European Financial Review*, 19 June 2013.

[24] For example, Selby (note 19) mentions that the local processing requirement imposed in the Russian data protection law has also resulted in a surge of business for Russian-based data hosting centres, including those operated by Orange and IXcellerate.

[25] See, e.g., M. Bauer et al., 'The Costs of Data Localisation: Friendly Fire on Economic Recovery', ECIPE Occasional Paper No 3 (2014); M. Bauer et al., 'Unleashing Internal Data Flows in the EU: An Economic Assessment of Data Localisation Measures in the EU Member States', ECIPE Policy Brief No 3 (2016).

[26] Another weakness in the infant industry argument is that not all countries are adequate to host data centres (for example, in cases of unreliable power networks, bad weather, earthquakes, and hot summer months) and therefore reliance on local solutions in such cases could significantly hurt the local digital economy in case of infrastructure failures. See Selby, note 19.

than if they used services located outside the country's borders.[27] The methodology used by the Leviathan Security Group compares the prices offered by local providers with the cheapest secure alternative option offered worldwide. In Brazil, for example, at the low end for 1-GB-equivalent servers, Microsoft's price in 2015 was USD 0.024 per hour. The lowest worldwide price for 1-GB-equivalent servers – USD 0.015 per hour – would save Brazilian customers 37.5 per cent on their server costs when compared to a Brazil-exclusive solution. For a 2-GB-equivalent server, a Brazil-located solution would cost USD 0.08 per hour, and the cheapest price globally would be USD 0.03 per hour – a saving of 62.5 per cent. Averaged across the types of servers, a customer located in Brazil would pay 54.6 per cent less by using cloud servers outside Brazil instead of Brazil-located cloud computing resources.[28] Therefore, it emerges that, while certain local companies would benefit from offering their services to other local companies, overall a vast majority of local companies would incur higher costs for data processing, leading to lower productivity for the economy.

Another set of studies looks at the impact of data policies on productivity of local firms. A study by Bauer et al.[29] is the first to explore how regulatory policies related to electronic data affect total factor productivity (TFP), albeit at an industry level.[30] The authors make a first attempt at analysing this linkage econometrically by setting up a data regulatory index using existing indices of services regulation. They look at different types of policies relating to both the use and the transfer of data. The authors calculate the costs of data policies for domestic firms by establishing a link between regulation in data services and TFP at the industry-level in downstream sectors across a small set of countries. They find that stricter data policies tend to have a stronger negative impact on the downstream performance of industries that are more data intense.

A more rigorous assessment of the empirical relationship between data policies and productivity is provided by Ferracane et al.[31] The authors use firm-level TFP data across a set of developed countries and the Data Restrictiveness Index presented in the previous section. TFP is considered the most important factor for long-run GDP growth and it represents the part of economic output accounted for by efficiency and technology. The results confirm that restrictive data policies

---

[27] Leviathan Security Group, *Quantifying the Cost of Forced Localization* (Seattle, WA: Leviathan Security Group, 2015).

[28] The Leviathan Security Group study also finds that if a European cloud were put in place, cloud computing at 4 GB and above would be consistently 10.5 per cent more expensive than accessing cheaper alternatives worldwide. However, for 1 GB and 2 GB services companies would not have to pay more, as the world's lowest-cost data centres were located in the EU in 2015, when the study was done.

[29] Bauer et al., note 25.

[30] See M. Bauer et al., 'A Methodology to Estimate the Costs of Data Regulation', *International Economics* 146 (2016), 12–39.

[31] Ferracane et al., note 14.

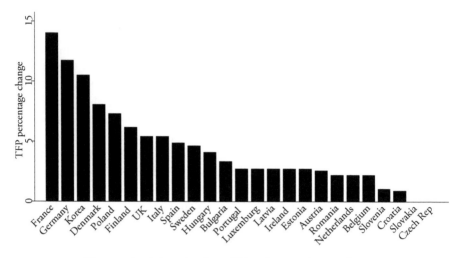

FIGURE 3.3. Firm productivity gains from lifting data restrictions, by country.
Source: M. F. Ferracane, J. Kren, and E. van der Marel, 'The Cost of Data Protectionism', *VoxEU*, 25 October 2018.

significantly harm the productivity of firms active in data-intense sectors, especially for local companies in industries and services sectors more reliant on data.

Ferracane et al.[32] is also the first empirical study to analyse cross-border and domestic data policies separately. Both types of restrictions are found to have a significant negative impact on productivity. Yet, restrictions on the domestic use of data have a marginally stronger impact on productivity compared to policies on the cross-border movement of data. Therefore, measures implemented at the domestic level with the objective to raise trust of consumers on digital services are not found to have any positive impact on productivity of firms and are rather expected to lead to a loss of productivity of local firms. On average, the study predicts that lifting data restrictions would generate a positive impact on the productivity performance of local firms with a TFP increase of about 4.5 per cent across countries (Figure 3.3), with stronger benefits in data-intensive sectors such as retail and information services.[33]

To contextualise the magnitude of this gain in productivity, we can compare the results with a study by Iootty and others,[34] who explored the potential impact of

[32] Ibid.
[33] The results are obtained using firm-level TFP developed by D. Ackerberg, K. Caves, and G. Frazer, 'Identification Properties of Recent Production Function Estimators', *Econometrica* 83 (2015), 2411–2451. Various other firm-level TFP measures common in the literature are also employed in Ferracane et al. (note 14) and provide similar results.
[34] M. Iootty, J. Kren, and E. van der Marel, 'Services in the European Union: What Kinds of Regulatory Policies Enhance Productivity?', World Bank, Policy Research Working Paper No 7919 (2016).

policy reform in services using a similar approach. The predicted TFP gains that these authors obtained from lowering services restrictions are around 3 per cent. The higher gains from reforming data restrictions can be explained by the important role of intangible assets in today's economy.

Finally, some studies look at the impact of data policies on GDP. Bauer et al.[35] employ the econometric results on TFP presented earlier in a general equilibrium analysis using the Global Trade Analysis Project (GTAP) to estimate the wider macroeconomic impact. The study measures the impact of data policies on exports, GDP, and lost consumption owing to higher prices and displaced domestic demand. The impact of proposed or enacted data restrictions on GDP is found to be substantial in all seven countries analysed in the study: Brazil (−0.2 per cent), China (−1.1 per cent), EU (−0.4 per cent), India (−0.1 per cent), Indonesia (−0.5 per cent), the Republic of Korea (−0.4 per cent), and Vietnam (−1.7 per cent). If these countries also introduced economy-wide data localisation requirements, GDP losses would be even higher: Brazil (−0.8 per cent), the EU (−1.1 per cent), India (−0.8 per cent), Indonesia (−0.7 per cent), and the Republic of Korea (−1.1 per cent). Yet, from this study it remains unclear whether the effect can be assigned to the cross-border or the domestic component of data policies.[36]

Another study from Manyika et al. of 2016 looks at the contribution of cross-border data flows to GDP and finds that it has overtaken that of flows in goods in the current wave of globalisation.[37] The study states that data flows today account for USD 2.8 trillion of the total increased world GDP over the last decade, thereby exerting a larger impact on growth than traditional goods trade. Interestingly, this work does not dedicate special attention to the interlinkages that exist between data flows and trade in services but takes the former as being a separate channel that impacts the economy independent from services.

From this analysis, it emerges that data policies are not expected to create new jobs in the local economy nor to develop the local industry in data-intense sectors. On the contrary, it appears that these policies tend to lower the level of productivity of local companies and, in particular, domestic restrictions on the use of data are expected to have a stronger impact on productivity. This is not to say that local governments should remove any domestic restrictions on the use of data. These measures might be necessary for important policy objectives, such as privacy and security. Yet, the governments need to take into account the costs of these measures on local companies when designing and implementing them.

---

[35] Bauer et al., note 25.
[36] Ibid. Another study by Bauer et al. uses a computable general equilibrium GTAP model to estimate the economic impact of the GDPR and finds that this law could lead to losses up to 1.3 per cent of the EU's GDP as a result of a reduction of trade between the EU and the rest of the world. M. Bauer et al., *The Economic Importance of Getting Data Protection Right: Protecting Privacy, Transmitting Data, Moving Commerce* (Brussels: ECIPE, 2013).
[37] Manyika et al., note 2.

II *The Foregone Gains for Foreign Companies*

Turning to the impact of data policies on foreign companies and trade in services, the evidence is even more scarce. A study conducted in 2014 by the US International Trade Commission (USITC) looks at a set of restrictions on trade including restrictions on data flows. The study estimates that removing foreign barriers on digital trade would lead to an increase in US GDP of up to USD 41.4 billion.[38] The econometric model used in the analysis relies on surveys of US firms to identify restrictions to digital trade and to rank countries that enact these restrictions in order to estimate the impact that removing these measures would have on certain sectors and the overall US economy.[39] Yet, this study looks at a broader set of restrictions than data policies, including policies on platforms and content access.

Earlier work from Freund and Weinhold points to the facilitating role of the Internet on trade in services.[40] The authors state that an increase in Internet penetration by 10 per cent has the effect of increasing the growth of services trade by 1.1 percentage point for imports and 1.7 percentage point for exports. These conclusions are closely related to the question of whether data flows influence trade in services to the extent that restrictions on data can constitute a restriction on the use of the Internet.

In addition to these studies, some scholars have focused more generally on the link between data flows and trade in services. Recent work by Goldfarb and Trefler discusses the potential theoretical implications of data policies on international trade and how these policies relate to the existing models of international trade. Although this discussion is put in a wider context of artificial intelligence (AI), the authors make clear that an expanded AI industry, in which data flows are an important factor, would have clear implications for services trade.[41] Similarly, Goldfarb and Tucker point out that privacy regulations may harm innovative activities, particularly in services.[42] They present the results of previous case studies they undertook with respect to two services sectors, namely health services and online advertising. In

---

[38] USITC, note 10.

[39] The USITC sent questionnaires to a stratified random sample of nearly 10,000 firms in seven digitally intensive industries. The questionnaires asked firms how they used the Internet and how the Internet had changed their business practices, sales, and productivity. The questionnaires also asked firms about their experiences with foreign restrictions and impediments to digital trade. The survey had a response rate of nearly 41 per cent. Of the more than 3,600 companies that responded, 80 per cent were SMEs.

[40] C. Freund and D. Weinhold, 'The Internet and International Trade in Services', *American Economic Review* 92 (2002), 236–240.

[41] A. Goldfarb and D. Trefler, 'AI and International Trade', NBER Working Paper No 24254 (2018).

[42] A. Goldfarb and C. Tucker, 'Privacy and Innovation', in J. Lerner and S. Stern (eds), *Innovation Policy and the Economy* (Chicago: University of Chicago Press, 2012), 65–89.

short, both studies show that there are strong linkages between the effective sourcing and deployment of data, the services economy, and trade in services.

Mattoo and Meltzer[43] provide anecdotal evidence on the cost of GDPR on Indian firms presenting a survey by NASSCOM-DSCI in 2013.[44] The survey finds that the requirements for cross-border transfer of personal data lead to a significant loss of business opportunities for Indian firms, with nearly two-fifths of the surveyed services exporters claiming lost commercial opportunities of more than USD 10 million and another third estimating a loss between USD 1 million and 10 million.

Ferracane and van der Marel is the first empirical study that investigates more directly the impact of data policies on trade in services and confirms the findings from the NASSCOM-DSCI survey.[45] The authors investigate whether stricter data policies on use and transfers of data inhibit trade in services. The study analyses econometrically whether data policies reduce the imports of services, and in particular whether data-intense services, such as computer services, technical services, intellectual property (IP) rights, and research and development (R&D) services, are affected. For the analysis, the authors rely on the Data Restrictiveness Index presented earlier and a methodology adapted from Ferracane et al.[46] Restrictions on the cross-border movement of data are found to significantly reduce imports of services, while no statistically significant evidence is found regarding domestic data policies. This is unsurprising, as generally restrictions at the border have a direct impact on trade, while domestic restrictions only indirectly impact trade. The analysis predicts that if countries lifted their restrictions on the cross-border flow of data, the imports of services would rise on average by 5 per cent across all countries, with obvious benefits for local companies and consumers, who could access cheaper and better online services from abroad (Figure 3.4).[47] Moreover, if the two most restricted countries – Russia and China – were to remove restrictions on the cross-border movement of data, they would experience a staggering increase of services imports by more than 50 per cent.[48]

These numbers amount to a substantial size of foregone gains from trade by putting in place restrictive data policies. To compare, total commercial services exports increased by around 7 per cent in 2017.[49] Most of these trade gains would

---

[43] Mattoo and Meltzer, note 5.

[44] *Survey of the Impact of EU Privacy Regulation on India's Services Exporters* (New Delhi: NASSCOM and DSCI, 2013).

[45] M. F. Ferracane and E. van der Marel, 'Do Data Flows Restrictions Inhibit Trade in Services?', ECIPE DTE Working Paper No 2 (2018).

[46] Ferracane et al., note 14.

[47] We obtain this conclusion by computing the marginal effects using the coefficient results from Ferracane and van der Marel, note 45. This method is common in the empirical trade literature using econometric techniques.

[48] To be more precise, we estimate the average and country-specific increase in imports in case the countries in our study reduced their data restrictions to the average of the three countries with the lowest level of data restrictions. This gives a more realistic approach to policy reform.

[49] WTO, 'Strong Trade Growth in 2018 Rests on Policy Choices', *Press Release*, 12 April 2018.

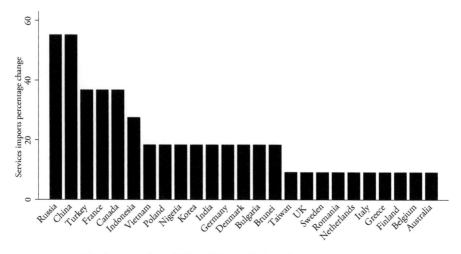

FIGURE 3.4. Trade gains from lifting data restrictions, by country.
Source: M. F. Ferracane, J. Kren, and E. van der Marel, 'The Cost of Data Protectionism', *VoxEU*, 25 October 2018.

be seen in data-intense sectors, such as computer services, financial and insurance services, as well as telecom and R&D services.

D DATA PROTECTIONISM AND THE WORLD TRADE ORGANIZATION

The empirical evidence presented in this chapter shows that data policies do restrict trade in services. Restrictions that apply to the cross-border movement of data have a more direct inhibiting effect on trade in services, while they also create trade distortions by impacting the productivity of local companies and industries, although to a marginally lower extent than policies related to the domestic use of data. On the other hand, domestic data policies are associated with lower productivity for local firms, and therefore impact trade only indirectly.

Yet, the evidence available is still scarce, especially in relation to the impact of data policies on trade. Ferracane and van der Marel[50] is the first study to delve in-depth into the impact of data policies on trade in services and the findings are in line with the expectation of businesses that indeed these measures reduce imports of services. The analysis predicts that, if countries lifted their restrictions on data (in particular restrictions on cross-border data flows), the imports of services would rise on average by 5 per cent.

Given the relevance of data policies for trade, it is not unlikely that a country could bring a claim before the World Trade Organization (WTO) to challenge certain data restrictions. The debate on whether data restrictions represent a trade

---

[50] Ferracane and van der Marel, note 45.

barrier that could potentially be challenged at the WTO is, however, still in its infancy.[51] It is urgent to undertake further empirical analyses to assess the costs of these measures. This analysis should also focus on identifying which types of data policies are mostly responsible for restricting trade and also investigate whether and how restrictive data policies affect developing countries and their growth potential in the long run.

A WTO dispute could have a profound impact on the way in which the Internet develops and eventually on our society. If a dispute were to arise, the analysis could not prescind from an informed discussion on the necessity of the measures to achieve important policy objectives. While certain data policies might be necessary to protect the privacy of citizens and national security, more research is needed to assess which measures enable countries to best protect these important non-economic policy priorities and which instead create unnecessary costs on the domestic economy and on foreign companies.

The policy implications to take into account when regulating data flows are complex and include, on top of trade aspects, also technical issues related to the Internet architecture and Internet governance, human rights including data privacy and freedom of expression, development issues connected to data sovereignty as well as potentially public order issues connected to the suppression of political dissidents.[52] However, it is not yet clear how data policies contribute to achieving any of these policy objectives and these restrictions risk creating unnecessary fragmentation of the Internet.

The plurilateral discussions currently on-going at the WTO under the Joint Statement on Electronic Commerce Initiative (JSI) might offer a fertile ground for informed discussions that could engage Internet governance institutions and other stakeholders for a better understanding not only of the costs of data policies on trade in services but also on the technical effectiveness of these policies to achieve their desired objective. If anything, countries should be in a position to carefully weigh the negative impact of certain measures in order to strike the right balance between different policy priorities, without creating excessive costs for firms and, eventually, consumers.

The WTO could provide a much-needed arena for a transparent and informed dialogue on data policies, their costs and their effectiveness in achieving certain policy objectives. As stated by Selby, there is a need to 'distinguish rhetorical claims from underlying realpolitik as to identify potential reasons why it is such a contested policy issue'.[53] Engaging the relevant stakeholders is indispensable for such an

---

[51] S. Hodson, 'Applying WTO and FTA Disciplines to Data Localization Measures', *World Trade Review* (2018), 1–29; also S. A. Aaronson, 'What Are We Talking about When We Talk about Digital Protectionism?', *World Trade Review* (2018), 1–37, at 16 (referring to the lack of accurate statistics to measure how such policies make it harder for firms to compete in foreign markets).
[52] See Chapter 4 in this volume.
[53] Selby, note 19.

informed discussion to take place, and more empirical research is needed both in relation to the costs of data policies for the economy and on the actual effectiveness of these measures in achieving the desired policy objective. Failure to do so could lead to a fragmentation of rules on data, with consequences that go well beyond trade.[54]

E ANNEX

The data policy index covers those data policies considered to impose a restriction on the cross-border movement and the domestic use of data. The methodology to build on the measures is listed in the Digital Trade Estimates (DTE) database, which is available on the ECIPE website (https://ecipe.org/dte/database/). Starting from the DTE database, these policies are aggregated into an index using a detailed weighting scheme, which looks at the trend of data policies for the years 2006–2016. The database and index are updated with new regulatory measures found in certain countries.

While certain policies on data flows can be legitimate and necessary to protect the privacy of the individual or to ensure national security, these policies nevertheless create a cost for trade and are therefore included in the analysis. The criteria for listing a certain policy measure in the DTE database are the following: (i) it creates a more restrictive regime for online versus offline users of data; (ii) it implies a different treatment between domestic and foreign users of data; and (iii) it is applied in a manner considered disproportionately burdensome to achieve a certain policy objective. Each policy measure identified in any of the categories receives a score that varies between zero (completely open) and one (virtually closed), reflecting their scope and level of restrictiveness. A higher score represents a higher level of restrictiveness in data policies. The data policy index also varies between zero (completely open) and one (virtually closed). The higher the index, the stricter the data policies implemented in the country.

The index is composed of two sub-indexes that cover two main types of policy measures: one sub-index covers policies on the cross-border movement of data and one sub-index covers policies on the domestic use of data. Analysing these two sub-indexes separately provides additional information on whether the impact of data policies on services trade varies depending on the nature of the policies. The full data policy index is measured as the sum of these two sub-indexes. This annex presents in detail the composition of the two sub-indexes. It shows which policy measures are found in each of the sub-indexes and the scheme applied to weigh and score each measure.

The list of measures included in the two sub-indexes is summarised in Table 3.1 presented earlier. As shown in the table, the sub-indexes are measured as a weighted

---

[54] See also along the same line, Chapter 4 in this volume.

average of different types of measures. The weights are intended to reflect the level of restrictiveness of the types of measures in terms of costs for digital trade. The first sub-index on cross-border data flows covers three types of measures, namely (i) a ban on data transfer or a local processing requirement for data; (ii) a local storage requirement, and (iii) a conditional flow regime. The second sub-index covers policies affecting the domestic use of data, divided in the following subcategories: (i) data retention requirements, (ii) subject rights on data privacy, (iii) administrative requirements on data privacy, (iv) sanctions for non-compliance, and finally, (v) other restrictive practices related to data policies.

The main sources used to create the database are national data protection legislations. Otherwise, information is obtained from legal analyses on data policies and regulations from high-profile law firms and from Stone et al.[55] Occasionally corporate blogs and business reports were also taken into consideration, as they can have useful information on the de facto regime faced by the company when it comes to the movement of data. All sources for each of the measures are listed in the ECIPE DTE database.

I Sub-index on Cross-Border Data Flows

The first sub-index covers those policy measures restricting cross-border data flows. Restrictions on cross-border data flows are divided in three groups: (i) ban on data transfer or a local processing requirement for data; (ii) local storage requirement; and (iii) conditional flow regime. As shown in Table 3.1, the category of bans on data transfer and local processing requirements has a score of 0.5, while the other two categories have a score of 0.25 each. The sum of the scores of these categories can go from 0 up to 1, which reflects a situation of virtually closed regime on cross-border data flows. This score is multiplied by 0.5 to create the final sub-index on cross-border data flows. The sub-index therefore goes from 0 (completely open) to 0.5 (virtually closed).

The scoring of these measures follows the scope in terms of sectoral and geographical coverage as well as the type of data affected. If a ban on transfer or a local processing requirement applies to a specific subset of data (for instance, when it applies to health records or accounting data only), this measure receives a score of 0.5. A similar score is also assigned when the restriction only applies to specific countries (for instance, when data cannot be sent for processing only to a specific country). On the other hand, when the measure applies to all personal data or data of an entire sector (such as financial services or telecommunication sector), then a score of 1 is given. Measures targeting personal data also receive the highest score because it is often hard to disentangle personal information versus non-personal

---

information, and therefore measures targeting personal data often end up covering the vast majority of data in the economy.

If there are two measures scoring 0.5, the score is 1. If there are more additional measures, the score for this category still remains 1. This score is then weighted by 0.5 which is the weight assigned to the category of bans on data transfer and local processing requirements. For the category of local storage requirements, a similar methodology applies. When data storage is only for specific data as defined earlier, this measure receives a score of 0.5, whereas when the data storage applies to personal data or to an entire sector, it receives a score of 1. As mentioned before, the score goes up to 1 maximum and is then weighted by 0.25, which is the weight assigned to the category of local storage requirements.

For the conditional flow regimes, the measures receive a score of 0.5 in cases in which they apply to specific data, but they receive a score of 1 in case conditions that apply to personal data or an entire sector. The final score is then weighted by 0.25, which is the weight assigned to the category of conditional flow regimes.

II *Sub-index on Domestic Use of Data*

The sub-index on domestic use of data index covers a series of subcategories of policies affecting the domestic use of data. These are (i) data retention requirements, (ii) subject rights on data privacy, (iii) administrative requirements on data privacy, (iv) sanctions for non-compliance, and finally, (v) other restrictive practices related to data policies. Given that each of these sub-categories contains, in turn, additional subcategories, they will be presented separately. For the calculation of the sub-index, the weights assigned to the categories are shown in Table 3.1.

The categories with the highest weights (and therefore those which are considered to create higher costs for digital trade) are data retention and administrative requirements on data privacy, which are assigned a weight of 0.15 each. The category of subject rights on data privacy is assigned a score of 0.1, while the other two categories of sanctions for non-compliance and other restrictive practices are assigned a score of 0.05.

The sum of the scores of these categories can go up to 0.5, which reflect a situation of virtually closed regime on domestic use of data. The sub-index therefore goes from 0 (completely open) to 0.5 (virtually closed). As mentioned earlier, the data policy index is measured as the sum of the two sub-indexes and therefore score for the final data policy index goes from 0 to 1.

1 Data Retention

The first category belonging to the sub-index on domestic use of data deals with measures related to data retention, which are measures regulating how and for how long a company should keep certain data within its premises. Data retention measures can define a minimum period of retention or a maximum period of retention. In the first case, the companies (often telecommunication companies) are required to retain a set of data of their users for a certain period, which can go up to two years or more in some cases. These measures can be quite costly for the companies and they are assigned a weight of 0.7. On the other hand, the measures imposing a maximum period of retention are somewhat less restrictive and prescribe the company not to retain certain data when it is not needed anymore for providing their services. They are therefore given a weight of 0.3. The country receives a score of 1 in each of the two subcategories when there is one or more measures implemented, while 0 is assigned in case of absence of these measures. Therefore, if a country implements one or more data retention requirements for a minimum period of time and no data retention requirements for a maximum period of time, the score will be 0.7. Alternatively, if the country only implements one requirement of maximum period of data retention, the score will be 0.3.

2 Subject Rights on Data Privacy

The second category belonging to the sub-index on domestic use of data covers measures related to subject rights on data privacy. The rights of the data subject are often a legitimate goal in itself, but they can nonetheless represent a cost for the firm when they are implemented disproportionately or in a discriminatory manner. This is the reason why they are covered in the index. However, they only form a smaller part of the sub-index with a weight of 0.1 as their cost on businesses is significantly low compared with other measures. Two categories of measures are identified regarding data subject rights, which are (i) a burdensome consent for the collection and use of data (with a weight of 0.5) and (ii) the right to be forgotten (with also a weight of 0.5).

If one of the measures applies, a score of 1 is given whereas a score of 0 is assigned otherwise. Regarding the first measure on the consent for the collection and use of data, a score of 1 is given only when the process for requesting consent is considered as disproportionately burdensome. This is the case when the consent has to be always written and explicit or when consent is required not only for the collection of data, but also for any transfer of data outside the collecting company. If this is not the case, then a score of 0 is assigned. Additionally, if the consent is required only in case of transfer across borders, this measure is instead reported in the first sub-index under conditional flow regime and scored accordingly.

3 Administrative Requirements on Data Privacy

The third category belonging to the sub-index on domestic use of data covers administrative requirements on data privacy. Measures included in this category are (i) the requirement to perform a data privacy impact assessment (DPIA) (with a weight of 0.3); (ii) the requirement to appoint a data protection officer (DPO) (with as well a weight of 0.3); (iii), the requirement to notify the data protection authority in case of a data breach (with a weight of 0.1); and finally (iv) the requirement to allow the government to access the personal data that is collected (with also a weight of 0.3).

For the scoring, the first three measures receive a score of 1 when a measure applies and 0 otherwise. In the case of the fourth measure, which is the requirement to allow government to access collected personal data, a full score of 1 is assigned only when the government has an open access to data stored by companies in at least one sector of the economy. However, if a government has only access to escrow or encryption keys, but still notifies access to the data, an intermediate score of 0.7 is assigned. Government direct access to data handled by the company or the use of escrow keys may, in fact, create remarkable consumer dissatisfaction that may lead to the user's termination of service demand. Finally, if the government has to follow the same procedure that it would follow for offline access to data – that is, the presence of a court decision or a warrant, or when the request follows a judicial investigation process – then the score is 0.

4 Sanctions for Non-compliance

The fourth category of the sub-index on domestic use of data covers measures which impose a sanction for non-compliance. These measures cover both pecuniary and penal sanctions with a weight of 0.5 for each of them. The pecuniary sanctions are not considered a restriction per se, but they are accounted for in the sub-index when (i) they are above 250,000 EUR; (ii) companies have explicitly complained about disproportionately high fines or discriminatory enforcement of sanctions; and (iii) they are expressed as a percentage of a company's domestic or global turnover. In fact, in all these cases, the sanctions have the capacity of putting a company out of business and might play an important role in the economic calculation of a company. We also list under this section those instances in which the infringement of data privacy rules can be sanctioned by closing down the business. The application of penal sanctions, such as jailtime as a result of infringement of data privacy rules, is included as a restriction. Instances in which penal sanctions are assigned as a result of identity theft and similar illegal actions are obviously not included. If any of these measures applies, then the score is 1.

5 Other Measures

Finally, the last category takes up all those measures which are related to domestic use of data, but do not fit under any of the aforementioned categories. All these measures are assigned a score of 1.

4

WTO Law and Cross-Border Data Flows

An Unfinished Agenda

Andrew D. Mitchell and Neha Mishra*

A INTRODUCTION

The tension between protecting free data flows and protecting goals such as privacy and cybersecurity is vexing Internet and trade policymakers. Laws and regulations hindering data flows across borders ('data restrictive measures' or 'data restrictions') are often trade restrictive,[1] and some of these measures can violate World Trade Organization (WTO) and Preferential Trade Agreements (PTAs) obligations.[2] However, countries can justify these measures under exceptions in international trade agreements that allow governments to implement measures necessary to achieve their domestic policy objectives,[3] arguably including policies for the stability and security of the domestic Internet.[4] Nonetheless, the inherent contradiction

---

* Andrew Mitchell is Professor of Law at Monash University. Contact: andrew.mitchell@monash.edu. Neha Mishra is Lecturer at the Australian National University College of Law. Contact: Neha.Mishra@anu.edu.au.
[1] W. Reinsch, 'A Data Localization Free-for-All?', *Centre for Strategic and International Studies Blog*, 9 March 2018, available at www.csis.org/blogs/future-digital-trade-policy-and-role-us-and-uk/data-localization-free-all; N. Cory, 'Cross-Border Data Flows: Where Are the Barriers, and What Do They Cost?', *Information Technology and Innovation Foundation*, May 2017, available at www2.itif.org/2017-cross-border-data-flows.pdf.
[2] This article refers to both direct data restrictive measures, such as data localisation laws and explicit data storage requirements, and indirect restrictions, such as conditional restrictions on data transfer based on ensuring security or privacy.
[3] See, e.g., General Agreement on Trade in Services, 1869 U.N.T.S. 183; 33 I.L.M. 1167 (1994), entered into force 1 January 1995 [hereinafter: GATS], at Preamble, para. 4; Article XIV; Article XIVbis.
[4] See generally S. Wunsch-Vincent, 'The Internet, Cross-Border Trade in Services, and the GATS: Lessons from US – Gambling', *World Trade Review* 5 (2006), 319–335; H. V. Singh, A. Abdel-Latif, and L. Tuthill, 'Governance of the International Trade and the Internet: Existing and Evolving Regulatory Systems', Global Commission on Internet Governance Paper No 32 (2016); T. Wu, 'The World Trade Law of Censorship and Internet Filtering', *Chicago Journal of International Law* 7 (2006), 263–287.

between the globality of the Internet and the (often) inward-looking data restrictive measures creates uncertainties for data-driven sectors.[5]

Modern-day digital services, such as cloud computing services, play an important role in facilitating businesses across the global supply chain, particularly by enabling them to expeditiously and efficiently move data across countries.[6] Some experts have even argued that data should be included as a 'fifth item to the traditional list of issues addressed by trade policy: movement of goods, persons, services, capital, and data'.[7] Yet, a contradictory narrative exists, emphasising the importance of legal checks on cross-border data flows, especially the regulatory advantages of data territoriality, to inter alia ensure privacy, security and ethical use of data.[8]

This article adopts a holistic perspective on the relevance of international trade law to data flows by (i) exploring the different regulatory issues pertaining to data flows that directly relate to international trade law; and (ii) recommending a framework in WTO law incorporating legal obligations on cross-border data flows alongside other relevant disciplines that enhance trust in the Internet ecosystem. Many contemporary electronic commerce issues are covered in recent PTAs; however, these PTAs often take different approaches, for example, on issues of cross-border data flows and data protection.[9] In the long run, such varied approaches may lead to fragmented rules on trade in digital services.[10] In contrast, the WTO being the only multilateral trade institution in the world, with a membership of 164 countries, is better suited to develop coherent, balanced and representative rules for a data-driven economy, as discussed further in this article. Moreover, electronic commerce–related issues are now more prominent at the WTO, including under the joint statement initiative, providing a timely opportunity to WTO members to develop new and relevant rules on data flows.[11]

---

[5] C. Kuner, *Transborder Data Flows and Data Privacy Law* (Oxford: Oxford University Press, 2013), at 159.

[6] J. Manyika et al., *Digital Globalization: The New Era of Digital Flows* (Washington, DC: McKinsey Global Institute, 2016); United Nations, 'Big Data for Sustainable Development', 9 December 2019, available at www.un.org/en/sections/issues-depth/big-data-sustainable-devel opment/index.html.

[7] D. Ciuariak and M. Ptaskhina, *The Digital Transformation and the Transformation of International Trade* (Geneva/NewYork: ICTSD/IDB, 2018), at vi.

[8] A. Clement, 'Canadian Network Sovereignty: A Strategy for Twenty-First-Century National Infrastructure Building', in CIGI (ed), *Special Report: Data Governance in the Digital Age* (Waterloo: CIGI, 2018), at 26–33, at 31. See also R. H. Weber and E. Studer, 'Cybersecurity in the Internet of Things: Legal Aspects', *Computer Law and Security Report* 32 (2016), 715–728.

[9] See A. D. Mitchell and N. Mishra, 'Data at the Docks: Modernizing International Trade Law for the Digital Economy', *Vanderbilt Journal of Entertainment and Technology Law* 20 (2018), 1073–1134, at 1086–1087. See also Chapter 1 in this volume.

[10] See, e.g., M. Burri, 'The Governance of Data and Data Flows in Trade Agreements: The Pitfalls of Legal Adaptation', *University of California Davis Law Review* 51 (2017), 65–132, at 99–110.

[11] See WTO, Joint Statement on Electronic Commerce, WT/L/1056, 25 January 2019; WTO, Joint Statement on Electronic Commerce, WT/MIN(17)/60, 13 December 2017. See also WTO, Declaration on Global Electronic Commerce, WT/MIN(98)/DEC/2, 20 May 1998.

This article explores various elements required within the WTO framework to address the policy ramifications of data restrictive measures, focusing on General Agreement on Trade in Services (GATS). However, we acknowledge that our research query is cross-cutting and other issues might be relevant including the alignment of GATS with General Agreement on Tariffs and Trade 1994 (GATT 1994),[12] Agreement on Technical Barriers to Trade (TBT)[13] and Agreement on Trade-Related Aspects of Intellectual Property Rights (TRIPS).[14] Further, where relevant, we also refer to applicable electronic commerce rules in different PTAs.

The first section explores the multilayered policy framework governing data flows and cross-border data flows identifying various policy goals typically associated with data restrictions. The following section then explains the trade-related aspects of data flow regulation by focusing on two interconnected topics: (i) the special nature of digital trade and trade in data that makes it harder to apply existing GATS provisions to digital services and (ii) those aspects of data flows that are trade related and, thus, should be addressed in a trade law framework. Finally, the last section proposes a novel WTO framework on data flows by identifying the foundational principles for data regulation and the legal provisions necessary to enable security, predictability and certainty in data flows. This section also discusses the feasibility of implementing this proposal at the WTO.

The article concludes that the WTO framework can and should evolve to accommodate the policy challenges of a data-driven economy, including adoption of binding provisions on free cross-border data flows; prohibition on data localisation; and introducing relevant provisions facilitating business and consumer trust in the digital ecosystem such as online consumer protection, privacy and cybersecurity. This framework should also include provisions centred on the specific needs of developing countries, such as providing them with technical assistance and capacity-building support, as well as facilitating digital inclusion and development. We, however, acknowledge various political constraints in adopting our proposal wholesale at the WTO, given the political sensitivity of the issues involved, and the policy preference of various countries to use PTAs to negotiate rules on data flows. Nonetheless, we believe that the existing WTO framework remains better suited and more relevant in achieving greater balance, coherence and consistency in trade rules on data flows, and that sufficient incentives exist for WTO members to meaningfully engage in reforming WTO rules to make them more relevant to the data-driven economy.

---

[12] General Agreement on Tariffs and Trade 1994, 1867 U.N.T.S. 187; 33 I.L.M. 1153 (1994), entered into force 1 January 1995 [hereinafter: GATT].

[13] Agreement on Technical Barriers to Trade, 1869 U.N.T.S. 299, 33 I.L.M. 1125 (1994), entred into force 1 January 1995 [hereinafter: TBT].

[14] Agreement on Trade-Related Aspects of Intellectual Property Rights, 1869 U.N.T.S. 299; 33 I.L.M. 1197 (1994), entered into force 1 January 1995 [hereinafter: TRIPS].

B REGULATING DATA FLOWS: A MULTILAYERED
POLICY FRAMEWORK

Notwithstanding the economic benefits of free data flows, countries restrict data flows to address various policy concerns. This section first discusses the most common rationales for imposing data restrictive measures, such as privacy and cybersecurity protection.[15] It then covers other aspects of data transfer that concern governments, such as illegal and unauthorised data access by foreign countries, trade secrets theft, and consumer risks in electronic transactions. Finally, the section discusses how data restrictive measures can relate to achieving domestic economic development.

I *Privacy and Cross-Border Data Flows*

With increasing digitalisation of services, privacy concerns have become significant.[16] Fifty-eight percent of all countries have now adopted or are in the process of adopting data protection laws.[17] Many of these laws contain provisions affecting cross-border data flows. Perhaps, the most prominent example is the European Union (EU) General Data Protection Regulation (GDPR).[18] The GDPR sets various conditions for cross-border transfer of data; for example, routine data transfers are only allowed to those countries having an equivalent level of data protection as the EU. Further, the GDPR provides for mechanisms, such as Standard Contractual Clauses and Binding Corporate Rules, prescribing additional mechanisms for individual companies to transfer personal data outside the EU,[19] and a right to be forgotten, allowing individuals to demand Internet platforms to delink their data to make it untraceable online.[20] The intended aim of these restrictions is preventing circumvention of EU's data protection laws and increasing individuals'

---

[15] S. A. Aaronson, 'What Are We Talking about When We Talk about Digital Protectionism?', *World Trade Review* 1 (2018), 1–37, at 11.

[16] See, e.g., Centre for International Governance Innovation, *2018 CIGI-Ipsos Global Survey on Internet Security and Trust* (Waterloo: CIGI, 2018); General Assembly of the United Nations, The Right to Privacy in the Digital Age, 71st Session, A/C.3/71/L.39/Rev.1, adopted 21 November 2016.

[17] UNCTAD, UNCTAD Global Cyberlaw Tracker: Summary of Adoption of E-Commerce Legislation Worldwide, available at https://unctad.org/en/Pages/DTL/STI_and_ICTs/ICT4D-Legislation/eCom-Global-Legislation.aspx.

[18] Regulation 2016/679 of the European Parliament and of the Council of 27 April 2016 on the Protection of Natural Persons with Regard to the Processing of Personal Data and on the Free Movement of Such Data, and Repealing Directive 95/46/EC (General Data Protection Regulation, GDPR), OJ L [2016] 119/1.

[19] See generally A. Mattoo and J. P. Meltzer, 'International Data Flows and Privacy: The Conflict and Its Resolution', *Journal of International Economic Law* 21 (2018), 769–789, at 775–776.

[20] Article 17 GDPR.

control over personal data processing. Other countries, such as Russia[21] and China,[22] have introduced explicit data localisation laws to protect privacy.

No international consensus exists on the best means to achieve online privacy, owing to the distinct socio-cultural perspectives on privacy across countries.[23] For example, the EU strongly advocates privacy as a fundamental human right,[24] including arguing for a blanket exemption for privacy laws in trade agreements.[25] EU's domestic framework has been emulated by other non-EU countries, including India.[26] However, not all countries share a similar perspective on privacy. For instance, in China (which has adopted GDPR-like provisions), privacy is viewed as a matter of information security.[27] To the contrary, in the United States (US) and broadly, under the Asia-Pacific Economic Cooperation (APEC) Privacy Framework,[28] privacy is protected as a consumer right.[29] Finally, several developing countries are yet to implement a privacy or data protection law; thus, data management is solely the prerogative of digital service suppliers in these countries.

II *Cybersecurity and Cross-Border Data Flows*

The relationship between cybersecurity and data restrictions is a relatively under-explored area,[30] although one-third of new trade-related concerns relate to

---

[21] Article 18(5) Портал персональных данных Уполномоченного органа по защите персональных данных [Federal Law No. 242-FZ of 21 July 2014 on Amendments to Certain Legislative Acts of the Russian Federation with Regard to Specifying the Procedure for the Processing of Personal Data in Data Telecommunications Networks].

[22] Article 37 Cybersecurity Law of the People's Republic of China [Zhonghua Renmin Gongheguo Wangluo Anquan Fa], adopted 7 November 2016, available at: www.chinalawinfo.com.

[23] Kuner, note 5, at 33–34.

[24] G. Buttarelli, 'Less Is Sometimes More', *European Data Protection Supervisor Blog*, 18 December 2017, available at https://edps.europa.eu/press-publications/press-news/blog/less-sometimes-more_en.

[25] European Commission, Horizontal Provisions for Cross-Border Data Flows and for Personal Data Protection in EU Trade and Investment Agreements, February 2018, available at https://trade.ec.europa.eu/doclib/docs/2018/may/tradoc_156884.pdf [hereinafter: Horizontal Provisions].

[26] Government of India, Ministry of Electronics and Information Technology, The Personal Data Protection Bill 2018, available at https://meity.gov.in/content/personal-data-protection-bill-2018.

[27] See, e.g., J.-A. Lee, 'Hacking into China's Cybersecurity Law', *Wake Forest Law Review* 53 (2018), 57–104, at 99–103.

[28] APEC, *APEC Privacy Framework* (Singapore: APEC Secretariat, 2005).

[29] C. Bulford, 'Between East and West: The APEC Privacy Framework and the Balance of International Data Flows', *I/S: Journal of Law and Policy* 3 (2007–2008), 705–722, at 707–709; See APEC, note 28, at Foreword; S. Yakovleva, 'Should Fundamental Rights to Privacy and Data Protection Be a Part of the EU's International Trade "Deals"?', *World Trade Review* 1 (2017), 477–508.

[30] See S. Y. Peng, 'Cybersecurity Threats and the WTO National Security Exceptions', *Journal of International Economic Law* 18 (2015), 449–478; M. F. Ferracane, 'Data Flows and National Security: A Conceptual Framework to Assess Restrictions on Data Flows under GATS Security Exception', *Digital Policy, Regulation and Governance* 21 (2019), 44–70.

cybersecurity.[31] The predominant motive behind cybersecurity measures is shielding a country's citizens and infrastructure against potential risks arising from poor cybersecurity practices. These risks may relate to consumer risks, such as compromising personal data through unauthorised hacking or cyberattacks; risks threatening public order (but not creating a war-like situation) resulting from security failures in ubiquitous technologies such as Internet of Things (IoT) and cloud computing; network attacks on the domain name system; and finally, national security risks arising from attacks on a country's critical infrastructure including a cyberwar-like situation.[32] For example, both the Chinese and Vietnamese cybersecurity law, which inter alia mandate data localisation, equate cybersecurity to different national interests in cyberspace, covering issue-areas varying from data security to ensuring control over domestic data flows.[33]

Several experts argue that ensuring security through data restrictive measures is largely ineffective. First, divergent cybersecurity laws (including technical standard requirements) across countries make it harder for suppliers of digital products to adopt best-in-class standards and practices in security.[34] For example, indigenous cybersecurity standards (particularly those that are not interoperable with globally recognised standards) hamper the ability of companies to 'reduce network latency and maintain redundancy for critical data',[35] and detect potential cyber risks.[36] Similarly, data localisation on grounds of security increases costs for companies in replicating their systems across different countries.[37] Second, data flow restrictions eventually increase concentration of data in specific servers, making targeting in cyberattacks much easier.[38] Finally, as long as countries remain connected to the global network, data (whether stored locally or otherwise) remains vulnerable to cyberattacks (such as distributed denial of service attacks). In restricting data storage/processing to specific jurisdictions, these risks cannot be eliminated.[39]

---

[31] WTO, 'Members Debate Cyber Security and Chemicals at Technical Barriers to Trade Committee', *WTO News*, 15 June 2017, available at www.wto.org/english/news_e/news17_e/tbt_20jun17_e.htm.
[32] C. Kuner, 'Reality and Illusion in EU Data Transfer Regulation Post Schrems', *German Law Journal* 18 (2017), 881–918, at 897.
[33] United States Trade Representative, *2016 National Trade Estimate Report on Foreign Trade Barriers* (Washington, DC: Office of the US Trade Representative, 2016), at 91; WTO, Measures Adopted and under Development by China Relating to Its Cybersecurity Law, Communication from the United States, S/C/W/274, 26 September 2017; *Luật an ninh mạng* [Law 24 on Cybersecurity], Law No 24/2018/QH14 (Vietnam). See also Chapter 12 in this volume.
[34] *Digitalization for All: Future-Oriented Policies for a Globally Connected World*, Joint B20 Statement, 2017, at 11.
[35] Business Software Alliance, 'Cross-Border Data Flows', 2017, available at www.bsa.org/~/media/Files/Policy/BSA_2017CrossBorderDataFlows.pdf.
[36] H. J. Brehmer, 'Data Localization: The Unintended Consequences of Privacy Litigation', *American University Business Review* 67 (2018), 924–969, at 967.
[37] Ibid., at 965.
[38] A. Chander and U. P. Lê, 'Data Nationalism', *Emory Law Journal* 64 (2015), 677–739, at 717.
[39] Ibid., at 715.

III Protecting Consumer Rights through Data Restrictions

The discussion of the relationship between cross-border data transfers and protecting consumer rights is often subsumed under privacy-related discussions such as obtaining informed user consent for data use/processing and data interoperability across different digital media. However, protecting consumers also relates to other issues such as reliability of data analytics and prohibiting discriminatory treatment of certain consumer groups.[40] For example, the increased use of artificial intelligence (AI) raises concerns regarding exclusion of minority groups through biased algorithms.[41] Another online consumer-protection related issue is ensuring integrity and authenticity of electronic commerce transactions.[42]

Regulatory frameworks addressing online consumer protection at an international/transnational level are absent because rights and remedies available to consumers are largely addressed through contracts and domestic laws.[43] The growth of digital trade, however, necessitates a coherent international framework rather than isolated domestic laws to address disputes related to cross-border e-commerce transactions.[44] Cross-border aspects of online consumer protection include issues such as failed delivery of services or inadequate quality, misuse of consumer data, and misinformation regarding specific digital products and services.[45] Since these issues can relate to cross-border activities of both service suppliers and consumers, incompatible or weak domestic frameworks often pose a hindrance to protecting consumer rights transnationally.

Governments have so far not explicitly adopted data restrictions based on consumer protection laws (e.g. to ensure a higher standard of data ethics or protection of consumers in one-sided digital service contracts). However, certain domestic laws like the GDPR incorporate elements of consumer protection such as restricting data-based consumer profiling.[46] Further, the e-Privacy Directive in the EU imposes requirements for cookies that can obstruct the free cross-border flow of data.[47] Poor

---

[40] M. Scrage, 'Big Data's Dangerous New Era of Discrimination', *Harvard Business Review*, 29 January 2014.

[41] L. Enochs, 'Policy Is Crucial in Curbing Discriminatory Artificial Intelligence', *CIGI*, 6 June 2018, available at www.cigionline.org/articles/policy-crucial-curbing-discriminatory-artificial-intelligence.

[42] See OECD, *Consumer Protection in E-Commerce: OECD Recommendations* (Paris: OECD Publishing, 2016).

[43] See generally K. McGillivray, 'A Right Too Far? Requiring Cloud Service Providers to Deliver Adequate Data Security to Consumers', *International Journal of Law and Information Technology* 25 (2017), 1–25, at 5–12.

[44] See generally B. Wylie and S. Macdonald, 'What Is a Data Trust?', *CIGI*, 9 October 2018, available at www.cigionline.org/articles/what-data-trust.

[45] See OECD, note 42.

[46] See Articles 21 and 22 GDPR.

[47] Article 5(3) of Directive 2002/58/EC of the European Parliament and of the Council of 12 July 2002 Concerning the Processing of Personal Data and the Protection of Privacy in the

cybersecurity practices of digital service providers can also pose a challenge to online consumer protection. For example, certain countries prescribe technical standards for cloud service providers in order to ensure adequate quality of cloud services for Internet users within the country.[48] Such measures, however, inhibit global business models/practices of cloud service providers, thereby restricting the free flow of data and significantly increasing compliance costs for foreign companies, in turn raising prices and reducing choice for consumers.[49]

IV *Access to Data for Law Enforcement*

Governments consider ready access to data a priority as the Internet is critical for carrying out different human activities, including criminal ones. However, the legal position on access to extraterritorial digital data is unsettled.[50] Consequently, different governments have adopted measures to increase regulatory control over data including data localisation laws. For example, the Indian government announced that payment service providers offering services in India must localise their data operations so as to ensure regulatory oversight over all financial transactions.[51] Additionally, certain governments have tried to exercise greater control over encryption in order to obtain access to data.[52] Selby has argued that data restrictive measures are primarily driven by the competition between governments to achieve more intelligence by controlling data flows, especially given the monopoly of American technology companies.[53]

The dispute involving Microsoft and the US government is an example of the difficulties associated with accessing data located outside one's borders.[54] In this dispute, the US government issued a warrant for data located on Irish servers for domestic law enforcement activities, which Microsoft refused to comply with

---

Electronic Communications Sector, OJ L [2002] 201/37; see also L. Coll and R. Simpson, *The Internet of Things and Challenges for Consumer Protection* (London: Consumers International, 2016), at 41.

[48] See, e.g., China is developing domestic standards for cloud computing under the Information Security Technology – Security Capability Requirements of Cloud Computing Services.

[49] Z. Fan and A. Gupta, 'The Dangers of Digital Protectionism', *Harvard Business Review*, 30 August 2018.

[50] K. Eichensehr, 'Data Extraterritoriality', *Texas Law Review* 95 (2017), 145–160, at 152.

[51] Reserve Bank of India, Storage of Payment System Data Notification, RBI/2017-18/153, 6 April 2018, available at www.rbi.org.in/scripts/NotificationUser.aspx?Id=11244&Mode=0.

[52] See, e.g., A. Reikis, 'Australian Bill to Create Back Door into Encrypted Apps in "Advanced Stages"', *The Guardian*, 12 April 2018; see also US Library of Congress, 'Government Access to Encrypted Communications: France', 10 January 2016, available at www.loc.gov/law/help/encrypted-communications/france.php.

[53] J. Selby, 'Data Localization Laws: Trade Barriers or Legitimate Responses to Cybersecurity Risks, or Both?', *International Journal of Law and Information Technology* 25 (2017), 213–232, at 231–232.

[54] *Microsoft Corporation v. United States*, 584 U. S.__(2018).

because the warrant related to data located outside the United States.[55] One of the key issues highlighted through this dispute was the ineffectiveness of Mutual Legal Assistance Treaties (MLATs) or letters rogatory to obtain legal access to extraterritorial data. While MLATs are time consuming and only exist between specific countries, letters rogatory are discretionary and thus unreliable.[56] This case was finally resolved by the adoption of the Clarifying Lawful Overseas Use of Data (CLOUD) Act containing a procedure for obtaining extraterritorial data based on principles of comity through executive action.[57]

V Digital Industrial Policy in Developing Countries

The use of data restrictive measures as digital industrial policy is becoming popular in certain countries in Africa and India.[58] The main argument is that most developing countries are unable to benefit from global digital value chains as the intellectual property (IP) and critical data resources are largely owned by companies in developed countries.[59] In other words, public ownership of data is considered vital to achieve domestic economic interests.[60] Thus, developing countries have argued that they should be able to adopt digital industrial policies, including data localisation and content filtering measures.[61] UNCTAD has further supported this approach, including advocating that developing countries should not be compelled to support the moratorium on customs duties on electronic transmissions (which is a fundamental requirement for free flow of data), as it would cause significant tariff losses.[62]

---

[55] J. Daskal, 'Microsoft Ireland Argument Analysis: Data, Territoriality, and the Best Way Forward', *Harvard Law Review Blog*, 28 February 2018.

[56] S. P. Mulligan, *Cross-Border Data Sharing under the CLOUD Act* (Washington, DC: Congressional Research Service, 2018), at 12–14.

[57] Ibid., at 9–10.

[58] See, e.g., WTO, Work Programme on Electronic Commerce: Moratorium on Customs Duties on Electronic Transmissions, Communication from India and South Africa, WT/GC/W/747, 12 July 2018 [hereinafter: Communication from India and South Africa]; WTO, Work Programme on Electronic Commerce: Report of Panel Discussion on 'Digital Industrial Policy and Development', Communication from the African Group, JOB/GC/133, 21 July 2017 [hereinafter: Communication from the African Group].

[59] UNCTAD, Adapting Industrial Policies to a Digital World for Economic Diversification and Structural Transformation, 2nd Session, 19 and 20 March 2018, Geneva, TD/B/C.I/MEM.8/5, 12 February 2018, at paras. 29–30; UNCTAD, *Trade and Development Report 2018: Power, Platforms and the Free Trade Delusion* (Geneva/New York: United Nations Publications, 2018) [hereinafter: UNCTAD Development Report], at 70–72, 77–78.

[60] B. Fang, *Cyberspace Sovereignty: Reflections on Building a Community of Common Future in Cyberspace* (Singapore: Springer, 2018), at 358–359.

[61] Communication from the African Group, note 58; UNCTAD Development Report, note 59, at 69, 84, 89, 109.

[62] UNCTAD, *Rising Product Digitalisation and Losing Trade Competitiveness* (Geneva/New York: United Nations Publications, 2017), at 16–17; UNCTAD, *Digital Economy Report: Value Creation and Capture: Implications for Developing Countries* (Geneva/New York: United Nations Publications, 2019), at xix.

India and Africa have expressed public support for UNCTAD's position on digital industrial policy at the WTO on numerous occasions,[63] although certain studies indicate that these policies are unlikely to be effective.[64] Unsurprisingly, certain developing countries, including Nigeria and Indonesia, have adopted data restrictive measures to create opportunities for domestic players.[65]

C TRADE-RELATED ASPECTS OF DATA GOVERNANCE

The discussion in the previous section indicates the complex, multilayered nature of data governance, and the need for a holistic and multidimensional trade framework on cross-border data flows. While not all governance issues related to data transfers are trade related, certain issues including online consumer protection, cybersecurity and privacy, as discussed later, are necessary to ensure a stable regulatory framework for digital trade. Being atypical of trade agreements, these issues are not explicitly covered in WTO agreements, such as the GATS.

I *Applying WTO Disciplines to Data Restrictive Measures*

Several scholars have examined how GATS applies to data restrictive measures and this section does not replicate such efforts.[66] For example, if a dispute were to arise on a data restrictive measure, legal obligations on national treatment and domestic regulation would be relevant if the measure favoured domestic services and service suppliers or imposed unreasonable compliance requirements on foreign services and service suppliers.[67] Similarly, restricting or banning cross-border data flows in sectors where members have made explicit GATS commitments could violate market access obligation.[68] GATS also encourages transparency of regulations.[69] Lastly, the general exceptions in Article XIV GATS can be relevant in distinguishing

---

[63] Communication from India and South Africa, note 58; WTO, Work Programme on Electronic Commerce: The E-Commerce Moratorium and Implications for Developing Countries, Communication from India and South Africa, WT/GC/W/774, 4 June 2019.

[64] M. Farid Badran, 'Economic Impact of Data Localization in Five Selected African Countries', *Digital Policy, Regulation and Governance* 20 (2018), 337–357; E. van der Marel, H. Lee-Makiyama, and M. Bauer, 'The Costs of Data Localisation: A Friendly Fire on Economic Recovery', ECIPE Occasional Paper No 3 (2014). See Chapter 3 in this volume.

[65] Chander and Lê, note 38, at 701–703.

[66] See, e.g., A. Mitchell and J. Hepburn, 'Don't Fence Me In: Reforming Trade and Investment Law to Better Facilitate Cross-Border Data Transfer', *Yale Journal of Law and Technology* 19 (2017), 182–237; M. Burri, 'The Regulation of Data Flows through Trade Agreements', *Georgetown Journal of International Law* 48 (2017), 407–448; S.-Y. Peng and H.-W. Liu, 'The Legality of Data Residency Requirements: How Can the Trans-Pacific Partnership Help?', *Journal of World Trade* 51 (2017), 183–204, at 199.

[67] Mitchell and Hepburn, note 66, at 195–206.

[68] Ibid.

[69] Article III GATS.

blatantly protectionist data restrictive measures (which are impermissible) from legitimate policy measures (falling within the scope of these exceptions). Thus, theoretically, the principles underlying GATS support an open environment for data flows without restraining WTO members from regulating the Internet for legitimate reasons.[70]

However, applying the pre-Internet era GATS disciplines to data-related disputes is challenging. Wu terms this as the 'problem of interpretative technological transla-tion',[71] i.e. applying GATS to technologies not envisioned at the time these rules were framed.[72] First, cross-border data flows relate to not only trade in services but also trade in goods.[73] Segregating the goods-related and services-related aspect of measures can be challenging when services form an integral part of a good (e.g. IoT). Second, interpreting whether a member's commitments in its GATS Schedule on national treatment and market access cover data flows in a certain sector is tough due to the cross-cutting nature of digital services.[74] Third, the proximity of service suppliers and consumers in the digital supply chain leads to highly intrusive (and sometimes, inefficient) data restrictive measures that are also trade inhibiting.[75]

II *Trade-Related Aspects of Data Flows*

Given that GATS is not sufficiently adaptable to a data-driven economy, we delve deeper into aspects of data regulation that are trade related but remain inadequately addressed in GATS.

1 Privacy Protection and GATS

As discussed earlier, privacy protection is the most common rationale for imposing data restrictions. Arguably, GATS acknowledges the importance of privacy protec-tion under the exceptions contained in Article XIV(c)(ii) GATS:

> (N)othing in this Agreement shall be construed to prevent the adoption or enforce-ment by any Member of measures:
> (c) necessary to secure compliance with laws or regulations which are not incon-sistent with the provisions of this Agreement including those relating to:

---

[70] J. López González and J. Ferencz, *Digital Trade and Market Openness* (Paris: OECD Publishing, 2018), at 6.
[71] Wu, note 4, at 264.
[72] Ibid.
[73] Aaronson, note 15, at 6–7.
[74] L. Tuthill and M. Roy, 'GATS Classification Issues for Information and Communication Technology Services', in M. Burri and T. Cottier (eds), *Trade Governance in the Digital Age* (Cambridge: Cambridge University Press, 2012) at 157–178, at 167; R. H. Weber and M. Burri, *Classification of Services in the Digital Economy* (Berlin: Springer, 2012), at 49.
[75] Aaronson, note 15, at 6–7.

(ii) the protection of the *privacy of individuals in relation to the processing and dissemination of personal data* and *the protection of confidentiality of individual records and accounts.*[76]

Further, paragraph 5(d) of GATS Telecommunications Annex states:

[A] Member may take such measures as are necessary to ensure the *security and confidentiality of messages*, subject to the requirement that such measures are not applied in a manner which would constitute a means of arbitrary or unjustifiable discrimination or a disguised restriction on trade in services.[77]

The exceptions for 'protection of privacy of individuals' in Article XIV(c)(ii) GATS and 'ensuring security and confidentiality of messages' in the Telecommunications Annex indicate that WTO members were aware of and recognised the fundamental importance of privacy as a policy objective and, therefore, considered them permissible even if they violated trade obligations of a WTO member. Further, Article XIV (c)(ii) GATS does not prevent members from choosing a specific standard of privacy/data protection, but rather requires examination of whether the adopted measure/standard on data protection is indeed necessary to achieve compliance with domestic privacy/data protection laws.

However, Article XIV(c)(ii) GATS cannot ensure that all WTO members adopt a sound and robust framework on data protection/privacy, but only protects their right to impose restrictions/measures to safeguard privacy of individuals and/or protect confidentiality and security of electronic transmissions. Online privacy is a fundamental precondition for open, transparent and secure flows of data across borders.[78] For example, consumers are likely to engage in digital trade only when they trust that the digital service suppliers adequately prevent unauthorised access or misuse of their data. Similarly, GATS does not address trade barriers resulting from variations in privacy frameworks across countries, as it does not specifically mandate WTO members to develop mutually compatible frameworks on privacy. For example, the mechanism available under Article VII GATS for mutual recognition of 'standards or criteria for the authorization, licensing or certification of services suppliers' has never been utilised for ensuring compatibility of privacy/data protection frameworks of WTO members.[79]

---

[76] Emphasis added. Additionally, 'public morals' under Article XIV(a) GATS can be interpreted to cover privacy.

[77] Emphasis added.

[78] See generally N. Mishra, 'Building Bridges: International Trade Law, Internet Governance, and the Regulation of Data Flows', *Vanderbilt Journal of Transnational Law* 52 (2019), 463–509, at 492–494.

[79] Article VII:1 GATS.

2 Cybersecurity and GATS

Another common rationale for imposing data restrictions is protecting security of data or the cyber networks within a country. This rationale is also related to broader national security requirements.[80] Like privacy protection, cybersecurity may be covered under Article XIV GATS, although cybersecurity is obviously not explicitly mentioned.[81] However, the exception could apply if a cybersecurity measure is necessary to maintain public order (Article XIV(a) GATS).[82] For example, certain studies suggest that the entire public utility network of a country (e.g. electricity supply) can be brought down by malware attacks by targeting smart devices used at home.[83] Another issue (particularly in trade in goods) is restrictions on encryption or forced adoption of specific encryption standards and its adverse impact on foreign suppliers.[84] Such measures are detrimental to enhancing trust of Internet users and are likely to render digital products more vulnerable to cyber intrusions.[85]

Further, Article XIV(c)(ii) GATS could be interpreted to cover certain data/Internet security measures:

> (N)othing in this Agreement shall be construed to prevent the adoption or enforcement by any Member of measures:
>
>> (c) necessary to secure compliance with laws or regulations which are not inconsistent with the provisions of this Agreement including those relating to:
>>
>>> (i) the prevention of *deceptive and fraudulent practices* or to deal with the effects of a *default on services contracts*;
>>> (iii) *safety*.[86]

Domestic laws related to 'deceptive and fraudulent practices', 'default on services contracts' and 'safety' in Article XIV(c) GATS can be creatively and flexibly interpreted to cover both cybersecurity and consumer protection–related measures. For example, a government can ban insecure and unencrypted services or impose data

---

[80] See, e.g., Law 24 on Cybersecurity of Vietnam, note 33.
[81] For the purposes of this article, we leave aside the issue of cyber wars and their relevance under Article XIV*bis* GATS because little evidence exists whether cyberattacks constitute armed attack or an emergency in international relations.
[82] Article XIV(a), footnote 5 GATS.
[83] General Electric, 'The Impact of Cyber Attacks on Critical Infrastructure', *GE Digital*, 2017, available at www.ge.com/digital/sites/default/files/download_assets/the-impact-of-cyber-attacks-on-critical-infrastructure-infographic.pdf; CISCO and the Chertoff Group, 'Addressing Critical Infrastructure Cyber Threats for State and Local Governments: Application of a Treat-Centric Approach through the NIST Cybersecurity Framework', 2015, available at www.cisco.com/c/dam/global/en_sg/assets/pdfs/govt_n_critical_infra_2169_cistcg_cisco_white_paper_v4-1.pdf.
[84] See generally R. Buddish, H. Burkert, and U. Gasser, 'Encryption Policy and Its International Impacts: A Framework for Understanding Extraterritorial Ripple Effects', Aegis Paper No 1804 (2018).
[85] D. Castro and A. Mcquinn, 'Unlocking Encryption: Information Security and the Rule of Law', *Information Technology and Innovation Foundation*, March 2016, at 2, 6.
[86] Emphasis added.

flow restrictions on foreign companies (particularly in sensitive sectors) to ensure that consumer data is not wrongfully used abroad. Further, since Article XIV(c) GATS is not exhaustive, a member may argue that its data restrictive measure is necessary to ensure compliance with domestic cybersecurity laws.

Like online privacy, cybersecurity is an essential component of ensuring free and open environment for global digital trade. However, the earlier mentioned exceptions do not require WTO members to adopt regulatory frameworks or enhance international cooperation on cybersecurity. While certain discussions at the WTO have centred on ensuring that technical compliance requirements for digital products are in conformity with international technical standards (such as under the TBT agreement),[87] similar requirements have not been explicitly included in GATS.

3 Online Consumer Protection and Digital Trade

In addition to privacy protection and cybersecurity, online consumer protection is also important to ensure an open, transparent and secure environment for digital trade and data flows.[88] For example, when buying online, consumers directly interact with service suppliers, and thus may be more vulnerable to one-sided contracts. Further, protecting Internet users from fraudulent transactions, breaches, spam and malware attacks, and data misuse by service providers and third-party advertising services is important for digital trade.[89] In case of divergent consumer protection laws across countries (e.g. rules related to enforcement and authentication of electronic contracts), businesses and consumers both face legal uncertainty when transacting online.[90] While multinational companies such as Amazon can tailor consumer contracts on a country-by-country basis and even build local servers (where such laws exist), smaller companies cannot do so.

GATS does not set any requirements for countries to adopt consumer protection laws in order to ensure adequate quality or security of services and arguably only provides for an exception under Article XIV(c)(ii) GATS to restrict data flows in consumer interests. For achieving liberalisation of digital trade, adopting internationally recognised models of consumer protection and active international cooperation on online consumer protection among WTO members is more beneficial and effective than unilateral domestic restrictions. However, to date, these questions have not been addressed at the WTO.

---

[87] See WTO, 'WTO Members Start Review of Technical Barriers to Trade Agreement', *WTO News*, 8 and 9 November 2017, available at www.wto.org/english/news_e/news17_e/tbt_15nov17_e.htm; WTO, Committee on Technical Barriers to Trade, Minutes of the Meeting of 8–9 November 2017, G/TBT/M/73, 6 March 2018.
[88] See, e.g., WTO, Joint Statement on Electronic Commerce: Establishing an Enabling Environment for Electronic Commerce, Communication from the European Union, JOB/GC/188, 16 May 2018, at para. 1.3.
[89] Ibid., at para. 2.3.
[90] Consumers International, note 47, at 40–41.

4 GATS Compatibility of Digital Industrial Policy

Certain countries, as discussed earlier, impose data restrictions as a tool of industrial policy. GATS prohibits members from imposing data restrictive measures in those sectors where they have made explicit commitments on national treatment and market access,[91] and also prohibits arbitrary and discriminatory measures that are unconnected to domestic regulatory objectives.[92] However, given the importance of protecting developing countries' interests at the WTO, especially their meaningful integration into the global economy,[93] WTO members can consider if certain data restrictive measures are beneficial to developing countries and least-developed countries (LDCs). For example, some developing countries/LDCs may argue that they need more time to open specific sectors to global competition. However, a necessary part of bridging the digital divide between developed and developing countries involves improving domestic access to high-quality and competitively priced digital services and platforms.[94] Data restrictive measures reduce consumer access to competitive digital services and could backfire in the long run and inhibit the growth of developing countries. Thus, investigating the necessity of data restrictive measures to enable digital development of developing countries is important.[95]

5 Data-Related Issues Outside the Scope of WTO Law

Certain aspects of data regulation cannot be addressed by WTO law even if they have a trade-restrictive impact. For example, in examining whether a measure is necessary to protect public morals under Article XIV(a) GATS, WTO panels and the Appellate Body have taken a deferential stance towards online censorship, as in *China – Publications and Audiovisual Products*.[96] Thus, WTO members are largely free to adopt measures censoring content online provided they comply with Article XIV(a) GATS. Given that the evaluation of the data content is based on the specific socio-cultural circumstances of each country, leaving out such issues from the ambit of trade agreements is judicious. However, further dialogues in the Internet policy and international human rights community on the necessity and the most appropriate tools for online censorship might better inform the application of Article XIV(a) GATS. WTO law also cannot address the international cooperation framework for

---

[91] See Article XVI and Article XVII GATS.
[92] Article XIV GATS. See also Article VI:1 and 5 GATS.
[93] Article IV and Preamble GATS.
[94] See generally The World Bank, *World Development Report 2016: Digital Dividends* (Washington, DC: The World Bank, 2016).
[95] See, e.g., WTO, 'Data Localization: Balancing Trade Disciplines and National Policy Objectives', Discussions at the WTO Public Forum 2018, session on audio file, 4 October 2018, available at www.wto.org/audio/pf18session76.mp3.
[96] Appellate Body Report, *China – Measures Affecting Trading Rights and Distribution Services for Certain Publications and Audiovisual Entertainment Products (China – Publications and Audiovisual Products)*, WT/DS363/AB/R, adopted 21 December 2009, at paras. 240–243.

accessing extraterritorial data as it is better addressed by international treaties such as MLATs or other initiatives, such as the CLOUD Act, as mentioned earlier.

D DEVISING A WTO FRAMEWORK ON DATA FLOWS

An ideal digital trade framework should facilitate free data flows, digital innovation, and healthy competition in the global digital market without interfering with a country's right to legitimately regulate the Internet.[97] In this section, we propose a WTO framework on data regulation addressing various trade-related aspects of data flows that fits better into such an ideal digital trade framework. The suggested framework is similar to certain recent PTAs but with specific modifications that adapt to the diversity of the WTO membership. The following first section discusses the foundational principles of data regulation in international trade law, while the subsequent section advances our proposals for reform in WTO law.

I *Foundational Principles of Data Regulation in International Trade Law*

1 Fostering Digital Trust at a Domestic and Transnational Level

WTO disciplines should enable 'digital trust', which in turn requires preserving user privacy, protecting consumers against spam, fraudulent transactions and cybersecurity attacks, and facilitating business trust, for example, providing adequate IP protection and a competitive environment for digital innovation.[98] To contribute to digital trust, the WTO framework should (i) facilitate increased transnational dialogues and international regulatory coordination and cooperation on relevant issues, such as data flows, cybersecurity and privacy; and (ii) safeguard policy space necessary for countries to enable and maintain Internet trust in domestic cyberspace, provided they meet the requirements of reasonableness (e.g. under Article VI GATS) and are not disguised protectionist measures (e.g. evaluation under Article XIV GATS). In our view, this two-fold approach to enable digital trust will promote 'trustworthy information relationships' in the global ecosystem for cross-border data transfers.[99] However, we do not argue that WTO rules are alone sufficient to ensure digital trust but rather that they could contribute to the global framework for data regulation.[100]

---

[97] See generally López González and Ferencz, note 70, at 37.
[98] B. Chakrovorthi, 'Trust in Digital Technology Will Be the Internet's Next Frontier, for 2018 and Beyond', *The Conversation*, 4 January 2018; J. Hoffmann, 'Constellations of Trust and Distrust in Internet Governance', in European Commission, *Trust at Risk: Implications for EU Policies and Institutions* (Brussels: European Commission, 2017), 85–98, at 9–13.
[99] Idea borrowed from N. Richards and W. Hartzog, 'Privacy's Trust Gap: A Review', *Yale Law Journal* 126 (2017), 1180–1224, at 1186–1187.
[100] S. A. Aaronson, 'Why Trade Agreements Are Not Setting Information Free: The Lost History and Reinvigorated Debate over Cross-Border Data Flows, Human Rights, and National Security', *World Trade Review* 14 (2015), 671–700, at 679.

2 Ensuring Interoperability and Transparency to Facilitate Free Flow of Data

WTO disciplines should ensure interoperability and transparency of Internet regulations/regulatory frameworks to facilitate data flows and greater accountability in digital networks. These twin objectives are particularly important for highly beneficial but risky technologies such as AI and IoT.[101]

Article VII GATS provides for mutual recognition of 'standards or criteria for the authorization, licensing or certification of services suppliers'. Although non-binding, Article VII:5 GATS recognises the need for more international coordination between WTO members on domestic regulations pertaining to licensing, certification or authorisation of service suppliers:

Wherever appropriate, recognition should be based on multilaterally agreed criteria. In appropriate cases, members shall work in cooperation with relevant intergovernmental and non-governmental organisations towards the establishment and adoption of common international standards and criteria for recognition and common international standards for the practice of relevant services trades and professions.

Varying standards of privacy and security across countries create impediments to cross-border data flows. While harmonising privacy and cybersecurity laws can be difficult and perhaps impossible due to the divergence of views/practices across different systems, cooperation and interoperability between different regulatory systems is achievable.[102] The WTO can learn from the experience of other international institutions such as United Nations Commission on International Trade Law (UNCITRAL) and the International Institute for the Unification of Private Law (UNIDROIT) that have used similar techniques in various areas of public and private international law respectively to obtain interface between different regulatory frameworks.[103] Further, developing new rules under Article VI:5 GATS relating to 'qualification requirements and procedures, technical standards and licensing requirements' on data flows can incentivise greater recognition of regulatory frameworks among WTO members.[104]

Another fundamental requirement that must be addressed in WTO law is transparency of data regulations. Despite a binding legal mechanism under Article III GATS, several WTO members adopt ambiguously worded data restrictive measures, causing considerable uncertainty for businesses and consumers alike. More mechanisms should be devised to increase governmental accountability at the WTO for their data

---

[101] S. A. Aaronson, 'Data Minefield? How AI Is Prodding Governments to Rethink in Data', *CIGI*, 3 April 2018, available at www.cigionline.org/articles/data-minefield-how-ai-prodding-governments-rethink-trade-data.

[102] See generally A. O. Sykes, 'Regulatory Competition or Regulatory Harmonization? A Silly Question?', *Journal of International Economic Law* 3 (2000), 257–264.

[103] Ibid.

[104] J. P. Trachtman, 'Lessons for GATS Article VI from the SPS, TBT and GATT Treatment of Domestic Regulation', SSRN Publication (2002), at 34, available at https://papers.ssrn.com/sol3/papers.cfm?abstract_id=298760.

regulations, including effective use of the Trade Policy Review mechanisms and discussions in various WTO committee meetings. Through such informal and open dialogues, members may be able to build international cooperation on relevant issues, thereby automatically reducing the tendency to adopt opaque data regulations.

3 Exploring New Regulatory Approaches in WTO Law

The third fundamental component necessary to adapt WTO law to the data-driven economy is to explore innovative and inclusive approaches in digital trade and data regulation that consider the multi-stakeholder nature of the Internet governance regime, particularly the central role of private sector in ensuring openness and security of data flows.[105] Different experts have argued that the regulatory framework for data flows requires a more sophisticated approach than traditional multilateral processes. For instance, Shackelford and others argue that majority of privacy and security issues related to digital technologies require poly-centric governance, including a self-regulatory approach in highly technical areas.[106] Kuner emphasises the significance of private sector instruments (including codes of practice and contractual clauses) in regulating cross-border data flows,[107] and argues that regulation of data flows is 'a form of legal pluralism', with no single authoritative framework.[108] Segura-Serrano argues that data regulation requires a hybrid approach involving a mixture of prescriptive and self-regulatory approaches.[109]

Adopting a co-regulatory or hybrid regulatory approach (involving the private sector and multi-stakeholder organisations) at the WTO can be challenging. For example, the WTO has not traditionally liaised with multi-stakeholder institutions, such as those prevalent in Internet policy community. Similarly, WTO rules do not refer to private standards or industry best practices although they may be commonplace in the digital world.[110] However, the WTO can liaise with multilateral institutions in relevant areas. For instance, under GATT, various mechanisms are established for consultation with the International Monetary Fund (IMF) for areas related to currency valuation and exchange.[111] Similarly, regarding applying WTO

---

[105] L. DeNardis, 'Five Destabilizing Trends in Internet Governance', *I/S: A Journal of Law and Policy* 12 (2015), 113–133, at 115.

[106] S. J. Shackelford et al., 'When Toasters Attack: A Polycentric Approach to Enhancing the Security of Things', *University of Illinois Law Review* 2 (2017), 415–475, at 439.

[107] Kuner, note 5, at 159.

[108] Ibid., at 160.

[109] A. Segura-Serrano, 'Internet Regulation and the Role of International Law', in A. Von Bogdandy, R. Wolfrum, and Ch. E. Philipp (eds), *Max Planck Yearbook of United Nations Law*, Vol. 10 (Leiden: Brill, 2006), 191–272, at 199–200.

[110] See generally J. Pauwelyn, 'Rule-Based Trade 2.0? The Rise of Informal Rules and International Standards and How They May Outcompete WTO Treaties', *Journal of International Economic Law* 17 (2014), 739–751, at 739.

[111] See, e.g., Article XV GATT.

disciplines to environmental issues, WTO members have undertaken various commitments to engage with multilateral environmental institutions.[112] There is no reason why a similar approach cannot be followed in the area of Internet and data regulation where multi-stakeholder institutions and private sector play a key role, for example, in technical standard-setting.

More specifically, some form of regulatory innovation is essential at the WTO to respond to the needs of data-driven sectors. For example, in certain cases, multi-stakeholder discussions involving Internet experts can enable a more balanced evaluation of cyber risks in digital services and the necessity of certain trade restrictive measures to address these cyber risks. This approach might be more effective than imposing unilateral data restrictions, which are not only highly trade restrictive but also have limited impact on ensuring digital trust and innovation.[113]

II *Reforms in the WTO Framework for Data Regulation*

The next section discusses various rules that we think should be included in a new WTO framework governing data flows. Many of the proposed rules in our framework somewhat resemble the rules in certain recent PTAs, such as the United States–Mexico–Canada Agreement (USMCA) and Comprehensive and Progressive Agreement for Trans-Pacific Partnership (CPTPP). However, we incorporate additional suggestions and modifications to make these rules more balanced and representative of interests of developing countries, as well as address fundamental public policy challenges in data regulation, including protecting regulatory autonomy of WTO members, as and when necessary.

1 Horizontal Obligation on Cross-Border Data Flows and Data Localisation

WTO law should incorporate horizontal obligations on ensuring free flow of data for the purposes of conducting regular business transactions and to prohibit forced data localisation. Data flows are fundamental for the growth of the digital economy and are required for both services and manufacturing sectors. In the age of cloud computing, when companies manage data resources in real time based on server capacities and real-time demands on server space, prohibitions on cross-border data flows and geographical restrictions on data storage can be a significant trade barrier.

---

[112] See, e.g., 'Relevant WTO Provisions: Text of 1994 Decision', available at: www.wto.org/english/tratop_e/envir_e/issu5_e.htm; see also 'Relevant WTO Provisions: Text of Services Decision', available at www.wto.org/english/tratop_e/envir_e/issu6_e.htm.

[113] Experts have also proposed technological or principles-based solutions to privacy and security issues. See J.-S. Bergé, S. Grumbach, and V. Zeno-Zencovich '"The Datasphere", Data Flows beyond Control, and the Challenges for Law and Governance', *European Journal of Comparative Law and Governance* 5 (2018), 144–178, at 156; Kuner, note 5, at 168.

Thus, we recommend a horizontal obligation for enabling cross-border data flows for purposes of conducting businesses and prohibition on data localisation measures.

Provisions on data flows can be found in recent PTAs, such as Peru–Australia Free Trade Agreement (PAFTA),[114] USMCA, CPTPP, etc.[115] We discuss the CPTPP later as successive PTAs contain similar provisions. Article 14.11(2) CPTPP states: 'Each Party shall allow the cross-border transfer of information by electronic means, including personal information, when this activity is for the conduct of the business of a covered person.' Further, CPPTPP Article 14.13(2) provides,: 'No Party shall require a covered person to use or locate computing facilities in that Party's territory as a condition for conducting business in that territory.'

Both these provisions are, however, rightly subject to an exception in Article 14.11(3) and Article 14.13(3) CPTPP, respectively to 'adop[t] or maintai[n] measures' inconsistent with Article 14.11(2) and Article 14.13(2) in order to achieve a 'legitimate public policy objective', provided that such measure is 'not applied in a manner which would constitute a means of arbitrary or unjustifiable discrimination or disguised restriction on trade' and 'does not impose restrictions on transfers of information/the use or location of computing facilities, greater than required to achieve the objective'. We recommend a similar provision within the WTO framework.

Although Article 14.11(3) and 14.13(3) CPTPP are similar to Article XIV GATS and Article XX GATT, clarifying the scope of 'legitimate public policy objective' with an illustrative list will be helpful. For example, the list should specify that cybersecurity, privacy, online consumer protection and protecting public order qualify as 'legitimate public policy objectives'. Further, the exceptions available under Article XIV and Article XIV*bis* GATS should clearly remain applicable for examination of data restrictive measures. For example, a WTO member should remain free to restrict data flows or require data localisation if it is necessary for achieving compliance with domestic laws, for protecting public morals or maintaining public order, or to protect essential security interests.

Given the delicate issues involved in data regulation, clarity in obligations and exceptions on data flows ensures that policy space of WTO members remains untouched. For example, in the Financial Services Chapter of the USMCA, a provision clearly acknowledges the data access to regulators should not be prohibited by data localisation measures. Article 17.20(1) states in this regard:

> No Party shall require a covered person to use or locate computing facilities in the Party's territory as a condition for conducting business in that territory, so long as the Party's financial regulatory authorities, for regulatory and supervisory purposes, have immediate, direct, complete, and ongoing access to information processed or stored on computing facilities that the covered person uses or locates outside the Party's territory.

---

[114] Peru–Australia Free Trade Agreement (PAFTA), signed 12 February 2018.
[115] Horizontal Provisions, note 25.

This provision is extremely helpful in clarifying both that (i) regulatory and supervisory authorities should have access to data for authorised and legal purposes; and that (ii) data localisation is not essential to ensure access to data.

2 Enabling International Cooperation on Cybersecurity Issues

Provisions related to relevant trade-related aspects of cybersecurity should be included in WTO law to facilitate an open and secure environment for cross-border data flows. However, we do not recommend that such rules prescribe any specific standards for cybersecurity.

First, WTO members should consider a mandatory requirement for international cooperation on cybersecurity issues.[116] This is not entirely new to the WTO; for instance, WTO members have taken concrete action to ensure greater international cooperation on trade-related environmental issues.[117] Further, given the unique role of private sector in devising and implementing cybersecurity standards, WTO rules should also provide for international cooperation between its members and non-state organisations that play a key role in international governance (including multi-stakeholder bodies).[118] For example, relevant institutions should be consulted at the stage of developing these rules and, later, if trade dispute related to a cybersecurity measure were to arise.[119] Although a little unconventional, recent years have seen WTO being more open to liaise with non-state entities, especially on digital issues. For example, in 2017, a new initiative was launched by WTO and two private sector–led multi-stakeholder institutions, World Economic Forum and Electronic World Trade Platform (e-WTP) entitled 'Enabling Electronic Commerce' to facilitate public–private dialogues on electronic commerce issues.[120]

Second, rather than enforcing domestic cybersecurity standards, WTO members should be encouraged to give preference to internationally recognised standards and best practices in cybersecurity over indigenous cybersecurity standards. Such

---

[116] In this context, see Articles 24, 25, 27, and 31 Convention on Cybercrime. See also Article 14.16 CPTPP.

[117] WTO, Relevant WTO Provisions: Text of 1994 Decision, available at www.wto.org/english/tratop_e/envir_e/issu5_e.htm; Y. Wang, 'UNEP and WTO Announce Initiative to Align Trade with Sustainable Development', *SDG Knowledge Hub*, 30 January 2018.

[118] See generally K. Karachalios and K. McCabe, *Standards, Innovation, and Their Role in the Context of the World Trade Organization* (Geneva: ICTSD/WEF, 2014).

[119] The latter is possible under the WTO Framework. See Marrakesh Agreement Establishing the World Trade Organization, 1867 U.N.T.S. 3, entered into force 1 January 1995, Annex 2 (Understanding on Rules and Procedures Governing the Settlement of Disputes, DSU), at Article 13.

[120] WTO, 'World Economic Forum and eWTP Launch Joint Public-Private Dialogue to Open Up E-Commerce for Small Business', *WTO News*, 11 December 2017, available at www.wto.org/english/news_e/news17_e/ecom_11dec17_e.htm.

provisions are atypical of trade agreements, especially for trade in services.[121] Recent PTAs, such as the USMCA, recognise the importance of adopting internationally recognised cybersecurity standard. Article 19.15(2) states that:

> Given the evolving nature of cybersecurity threats, the Parties recognize that *risk-based approaches may be more effective than prescriptive regulation* in addressing those threats. Accordingly, each Party shall endeavor to employ, and encourage enterprises within its jurisdiction to use, *risk-based approaches that rely on consensus-based standards and risk management best practices* to identify and protect against cybersecurity risks and to detect, respond to, and recover from cybersecurity events.[122]

However, adopting a similar provision in the WTO framework will be much tougher and is not recommended because of lack of consensus on whether a risk-based approach is most appropriate to address cyber risks.

Finally, all WTO members should be required to adopt a basic level of cybersecurity regulation to prevent countries from becoming havens for criminal or illegal use of digital services and data. This requirement should not prevent members from adopting stricter regulations on cybersecurity as long it is not arbitrary, discriminatory or unreasonable.

3 Requiring Privacy Frameworks and Promoting Mutual Recognition Mechanisms

Requiring all WTO members to adopt a basic regulatory framework for protection of personal information or privacy protection is fundamental for ensuring free flow of data. Meltzer and Mattoo argue that the privacy exception available under Article XIV(c)(ii) GATS is insufficient as it pressurises WTO panels to adjudicate on sensitive privacy issues, which is particularly difficult given that 'data-source countries' are unlikely to 'accept one-sided limits on their right to protect privacy'.[123] To deal with this uncertainty and distrust in other members' privacy frameworks, many countries introduce stringent privacy measures that decrease competitiveness and efficiency of both foreign and domestic digital businesses. Mattoo and Meltzer argue that increasingly more countries are likely to seek bilateral arrangements, such as the data transfer agreement between the EU and the United States (EU–US Privacy Shield) to enable cross-border data flows while ensuring privacy remains protected abroad.[124] They also argue that international recognised standards and guidelines,

---

[121] G. Gari, 'What Can International Standards on Services Do for GATS?', *E15 Initiative*, September 2015, available at http://e15initiative.org/blogs/what-can-international-standards-on-services-do-for-gats/.

[122] Emphasis added.

[123] Mattoo and Meltzer, note 19, at 789.

[124] Ibid., at 786–788. The EU–US Privacy Shield was invalidated in 2020 by the European Court of Justice, raising significant concerns regarding a future data transfer arrangement between the EU and the United States.

such as the OECD Privacy Framework, provide a basis for aligning privacy laws across countries.[125] However, we see more widespread benefits if, under the ongoing plurilateral negotiations, WTO members considered a provision requiring adoption of a basic domestic privacy framework in line with internationally recognised standards and guidelines.

Recent PTAs contain rules on privacy/data protection, although two different approaches can be seen in EU-led PTAs and US-led PTAs.[126] For example, the USMCA contains the following provision (building on a similar provision in CPTPP):

> To this end, each Party shall adopt or maintain a legal framework that provides for the protection of the personal information of the users of digital trade. In the development of its legal framework for the protection of personal information, each Party should take into account *principles and guidelines of relevant international bodies, such as the APEC Privacy Framework and the OECD Recommendation of the Council concerning Guidelines governing the Protection of Privacy and Transborder Flows of Personal Data (2013)*.[127]

The specification of OECD and APEC privacy principles as benchmarks could be controversial in a multilateral context, given that they are considered lenient in comparison to the GDPR and similar frameworks. To the contrary, EU FTAs are generally cautious in specifying appropriate rules on data protection, although they require full compatibility with international standards, in the sense that 'the Parties agree that the development of electronic commerce must be fully compatible with the international standards of data protection, in order to ensure the confidence of users of electronic commerce'.[128]

The EU has advocated an even stronger provision on privacy protection in a recent proposal on data flows: 'Each Party may adopt and maintain the safeguards it deems appropriate to ensure the protection of personal data and privacy, including through the adoption and application of rules for the cross-border transfer of personal data. Nothing in this agreement shall affect the protection of personal data and privacy afforded by the Parties' respective safeguards.'[129]

This provision provides a carte blanche for countries to adopt a privacy framework, irrespective of their trade commitments. We recommend a more balanced provision in WTO law, somewhere in between the lenient provision in USMCA and the provision proposed by EU, which could also increase disguised protectionist

---

[125] Ibid.
[126] As per Wu, about one-third of PTAs contain a provision requiring data protection for electronic commerce. See M. Wu, *Digital Trade-Related Provisions in Regional Trade Agreements: Existing Models and Lessons for the Multilateral Trade System* (Geneva/Washington, DC: IDB/ICTSD, 2017), at 20. See also Chapter 1 in this volume.
[127] Article 19.8(2) USMCA (footnote omitted; emphasis added).
[128] Article 7.48(2) EU-Korea FTA.
[129] But see Horizontal Provisions, note 25.

measures. The PAFTA offers an example of a more balanced framework on privacy that accommodates varying perspectives. It provides in Article 13.8(2): 'To this end, each Party shall adopt or maintain a legal framework that provides for the protection of the personal information of the users of electronic commerce. In the development of its legal framework for the protection of personal information, each Party should take into account principles and guidelines of relevant international bodies.'

Such a provision will provide ample opportunity for WTO members to discuss appropriate principles and guidelines in relevant institutions as well as accommodate evolving norms in this field.[130] Further, such a provision does not inhibit members from undertaking institutional innovations to protect privacy beyond the basic requirements, provided they are not arbitrary or discriminatory in nature.[131]

Additionally, WTO members should be encouraged to use the mechanism available under Article VII GATS to develop mutual recognition schemes for privacy certifications of different members to ensure greater interoperability within the multilateral system. However, in the short run, they are likely to be bilateral or regional initiatives between like-minded members till greater consensus evolves on privacy issues. Finally, WTO could liaise with institutions dealing with international cooperation for development of privacy rules/standards and cross-jurisdictional privacy enforcement, such as International Conference of Data Protection and Privacy Commissioners.

4 Incorporating Consumer Trust Enhancing Measures

Consumer trust is a fundamental requirement for digital trade. This requires not only strong domestic laws but also persistent international cooperation and engagement across relevant stakeholders, such as private companies, consumer advocacy organisations and consumer protection agencies. Further, the types of risks faced by consumers is also changing in a digital world and includes dangerous cybercrimes, such as distributed denial of service attacks, phishing attacks, hacking, identity theft and cyberstalking.[132] Dealing with these issues requires WTO's engagement with other relevant institutions, such as the International Consumer Protection Enforcement Network, UNCITRAL and other regional bodies with expertise on consumer protection issues, such as the OECD.

---

[130] Some have argued for an international treaty on data protection under the auspices of the WTO – this would exceed the competence of the WTO. See generally J. R. Reidenberg, 'Resolving Conflicting International Data Privacy Rules in Cyberspace', *Stanford Law Review* 52 (2000), 1359–1362, at 1315.

[131] See generally D. A. Hyman and W. E. Kovacic, 'Implementing Privacy Policy: Who Should Do What?', *Fordham Intellectual Property, Media and Entertainment Law Journal* 29 (2019), 1117–1149.

[132] OECD, *Consumer Protection in E-Commerce: OECD Recommendations* (Paris: OECD Publishing, 2016), at paras. 48–49. See also Interpol, Cybercrime, available at www.interpol .int/Crimes/Cybercrime.

WTO rules do not address online consumer protection issues directly and, hence, we recommend new rules to integrate this dimension in WTO framework. First, all WTO members should be required to adopt a basic regulatory framework on online consumer protection, including providing sufficient remedies to e-commerce users and ensuring that businesses provide adequate quality of digital products. The UNCITRAL Model Law on Electronic Commerce could be incorporated by reference in WTO law. Second, WTO members should adopt a mandatory cooperation mechanism for addressing the transnational aspects of online consumer protection, including information sharing and providing assistance for cross-border enforcement of consumer protection laws.[133] Implementing such provisions might require systematic changes to domestic laws of several developing countries and, therefore, they might need technical assistance, as earlier noted.

Several PTAs already contain provisions on online consumer protection, although many of them are non-binding.[134] Further, these provisions are loosely worded and do not incentivise countries to develop meaningful cooperation on online consumer protection issues. Being a multilateral institution, the WTO is better placed to facilitate increased dialogue between consumer protection (and other relevant) regulators to ensure effective international cooperation in the field.

5 Enabling Digital Innovation and Promoting Business Trust

WTO rules should also incorporate mechanisms to improve business trust to support a data-driven economy. For example, interoperable and transparent standards in data regulation can facilitate business trust. To achieve this, WTO members could consider adoption of TBT-like disciplines in context of trade in services. For instance, all members should be required to adopt only such technical standards in their digital services that are consistent with internationally recognised standards.[135] Further, unreasonable standards constituting unnecessary barriers to trade and more burdensome than necessary to achieve a policy objective such as ensuring privacy or security should be prohibited.[136] Such provisions could reduce the use of indigenous domestic standards that disrupt data flows.

WTO members could also be required to consider/use only internationally recognised standards in framing domestic regulations, including imposing standards for data security and privacy.[137] This obligation could be difficult to implement in

---

[133] See OECD, *Consumer Protection Enforcement in a Global Digital Marketplace* (Paris: OECD Publishing, 2018), at 10.

[134] Article 19.7(3) USMCA.

[135] In the context of definition of 'international standardizing body' in the TBT, see Appellate Body Report, *United States – Measures Concerning the Importation, Marketing and Sale of Tuna and Tuna Products*, WT/DS381/AB/R, adopted 16 May 2012, at paras. 353, 357, 359.

[136] See, e.g., Article 2.2 TBT.

[137] See Annex 8-B, Section A CPTPP.

practice because multi-stakeholder and private sector–driven standards are prominently used in data operations but have little recognition in WTO law. For example, the data routing architecture of the Internet is largely based on protocols established by the Internet Engineering Task Force (IETF), a multi-stakeholder organisation developing voluntary Internet standards. Similarly, cybersecurity standards are largely developed by private sector. In fact, experts argue that Internet-related standards function better when they are open and driven by market competition rather than unilateral measures.[138] To address this gap, an arrangement similar to the TBT Code of Good Practice could be adopted in context of GATS.[139] This would provide an opportunity for private or multi-stakeholder standards to gain greater recognition at the WTO while ensuring that these standards are being formulated with transparency, participation and accountability.[140] For example, the International Organization for Standardization (ISO), a private standard-setting organisation, has a strong partnership with WTO and plays an instrumental role in harmonising standards in goods through contributions to the WTO committee meetings and providing reports to WTO members.[141]

Additionally, certain PTAs, such as the CPTPP and USMCA, include provisions to enhance business trust in the context of digital services by protecting the source code and vital digital assets of foreign companies from unauthorised disclosure.[142] In the USMCA, this provision is extremely broad and prohibits governments from requiring access to both source code and algorithms as a condition of market access.[143] However, similarly worded provisions can pose problems in the multilateral context because (i) many developing countries consider technology transfer as an important prerequisite for bridging the existing digital divide between developing and developed countries (an issue requiring further debate and negotiations);[144] and (ii) certain countries fear that algorithms and technical codes underlying digital services may be discriminatory, insecure or allow unauthorised data access to certain countries or groups, and therefore, should be scrutinised further.[145]

To address the above concerns, we recommend a provision in WTO law that would prohibit forced disclosure of source code and algorithm, but subject to an

---

[138] OECD, OECD Guidelines for Cryptography Policy, adopted on 27 March 1997, available at www.oecd.org/sti/ieconomy/guidelinesforcryptographypolicy.htm#preface.
[139] Annexes 3 and 4 TBT.
[140] See Annex 3 TBT. See also WTO ISO Standards Information Gateway: List of Standardizing Bodies, available at https://tbtcode.iso.org/sites/wto-tbt/list-of-standardizing-bodies.html.
[141] See generally S. Charnovitz, 'International Standards and the WTO', GW Law Faculty Publications and Other Works Paper No 394 (2005).
[142] Article 19.16 USMCA; Article 14.17 CPTPP.
[143] Article 19.16(1) USMCA.
[144] See generally R. S. Neeraj, 'Trade Rules on Source Code – Deepening the Digital Inequities by Locking Up the Software Fortress', Centre for WTO Studies Working Paper CWS/WP/200/37 (2017), 1–37, at 25–36.
[145] See generally B. Goodman and S. Flaxman, 'European Union Regulations on Algorithmic Decision-Making and a "Right to Explanation"', AI Magazine 38 (2017), 50–57.

exception allowing governments to access this information for regulatory purposes, such as checking for discriminatory algorithms, auditing security of digital services and for judicial proceedings or governmental investigations.[146] Article 19.16(2) USMCA is a good example as it has been carefully constructed to ensure that governments can access source code and algorithms for regulatory purposes, such as checking for discriminatory algorithms, for patent applications/disputes,[147] for criminal investigations, and auditing security standards of digital services as part of domestic investigations or inspections. However, it does not specify that parties could be required to modify the source code, for example, when an investigation reveals that a company has violated domestic laws or if the security standards are below par, or where the algorithms are discriminatory.

6 Relevance of Special and Differential Treatment for Developing Countries and LDCs

Certain developing countries have claimed that data restrictive measures are necessary to develop their domestic digital sector and protect their economic and social interests, for instance preventing tariff losses resulting from the moratorium on customs duties on electronic transmissions. The WTO is an excellent forum for developing countries to present evidence on the benefits of data restrictive measures in the short run vis-à-vis the losses to their domestic consumers and businesses as well as other measures necessary to promote greater digital inclusion. However, where exceptions are made for developing countries and LDCs to impose data restrictive measures, such as through special and differential treatment, they should be evidence-based and time-bound.

Certain developing countries and LDCs may have inadequate capacity to enforce a framework for data regulation due to insufficient expertise on privacy and cybersecurity. Such members should be provided additional time to make a binding commitment on data flows. For instance, the Trade Facilitation Agreement allows for staggered implementation of obligations, so as to provide more time to developing countries and LDCs to initiate reforms in their domestic system before being fully bound.[148] Further, WTO members should also agree on mandatory technical assistance programmes and capacity-building support for developing countries and LDCs with inadequate regulatory capacity on relevant issues. None of the PTAs deal with development-related concerns in digital trade, particularly enforcing stronger obligations on developed partners to assist developing countries and LDCs. This deficiency can, however, be addressed better through the ongoing WTO plurilateral

---

[146] See, e.g., Article 19.16(2) USMCA.
[147] Article 14.17(4) CPTPP.
[148] See WTO, UNCTAD E-Commerce Week: Summary of the Session 'Digital Trade as If Development Mattered', Communication from Cambodia and Japan, JOB/GC/185, 27 April 2018.

initiative, which also brings together several developing countries and LDCs (e.g. under the Friends of E-commerce for Development.)

III *The Path Ahead for Rules on Data Flows at the WTO*

WTO members are currently considering two separate mechanisms to reform WTO rules on electronic commerce. First, GATS itself could be reformed using existing mechanisms. For example, under Article XVIII GATS, members could adopt additional commitments on data flows, akin to the Telecommunications Reference Paper.[149] WTO members could also consider adopting dedicated domestic regulations on electronic commerce under Article VI GATS. Certain members have argued for expanding existing GATS commitments on digital services, particularly for computer and related services, where commitments should be made at a two-digit level to increase the scope of commitments.[150] Second, under the joint statement initiative initiated in the last WTO Ministerial Conference and the follow-up negotiations launched at the Davos conference, members are considering a plurilateral agreement on electronic commerce covering different digital trade issues, including data flows and data localisation. The more likely outcome is the adoption of a plurilateral agreement containing electronic commerce–specific rules, like the electronic commerce/digital trade chapters in certain recent PTAs, such as the USMCA and CPTPP.

Despite WTO members making various proposals for reform under the joint statement initiative (including some reforms that we propose in this article), constraints exist in achieving these reforms in practice. First, as regards regulating data, WTO members have varied views; as discussed earlier, while some members support the incorporation of provisions on the free flow of data, others have refrained from this approach to safeguard policy objectives, such as privacy protection, Internet sovereignty and cybersecurity. Aaronson and Leblond argue that the varying approaches to data regulation has resulted in three different 'data realms', reflecting the policy orientation of the United States, China and EU.[151] Implementing a horizontal provision on cross-border data flows and prohibition on data localisation may therefore be difficult to achieve in practice, at least in the short run. The divided approach in data regulation could be one of the key reasons why countries prefer to address data-related rules in PTAs rather than at the WTO, as PTAs provide them greater flexibility in devising rules consistent with their domestic regulatory objectives.

---

[149] Mitchell and Mishra, note 9, at 1127.

[150] See, e.g., WTO, GATS 2000: Computer and Related Services (CPC 84), Communication from the European Union, S/CSS/W/34/Add.1, 15 July 2002, at para. 10.

[151] S. A. Aaronson and P. Leblond, 'Another Digital Divide: The Rise of Data Realms and Its Implications for the WTO', *Journal of International Economic Law* 21 (2018), 245–272, at 245.

Second, the deficiency of binding international frameworks on cybersecurity, online consumer and data/privacy protection poses a major challenge in facilitating cross-border data flows, and may further breed mistrust among countries. Therefore, even if reformed WTO rules required all members to adopt basic frameworks on privacy protection, online consumer protection, and cybersecurity consistent with international standards, legal uncertainty will arise with regard to the appropriate international standard(s) in these areas of regulation. As it is outside the scope of the WTO to set standards or norms in these areas, the success of the proposed rules on privacy, cybersecurity and other related areas is contingent on the development of robust approaches in non-trade fora, including relevant regional, transnational and multistakeholder bodies.

Third, the emerging voice of developing countries and LDCs, especially with regard to special and differential treatment in implementing trade commitments on electronic commerce, might face some opposition at the WTO. Given the political backlash against certain countries misusing their 'developing country' status, some members might object to introducing a development dimension in provisions on data flows. However, as indicated in our proposal, further studies are necessary to understand the development implications of data-driven growth, including the regulatory capacity of developing countries/LDCs to respond to these challenges and introduce relevant provisions accordingly.

Finally, the extent to which the existing architecture of GATS can accommodate new rules on data flows is unclear. For example, if a new plurilateral agreement were to be designed, WTO members would have to determine the legal relationship between this agreement and GATS, including whether the existing GATS commitments would apply.[152] Similarly, given the uncertainty in applying the general exceptions in the context of data restrictive measures,[153] further dialogue is necessary among the WTO members to clarify on the scope/applicability of the exceptions applicable to data restrictive measures.

Despite these constraints, we propose that the WTO can and should play a central role in devising trade rules for the digital age. Although the electronic commerce chapters in PTAs can fill gaps in WTO rules on digital trade in the short run, they are likely to divide the global framework for data regulation, as is already evident in the divergent approaches taken by countries on data flows and data protection in their PTAs. Further, certain areas of reform proposed in this article require a high level of international regulatory cooperation. The WTO, with its widespread worldwide membership, is much better suited to act as a site for facilitating such international regulatory cooperation as compared to regional bodies.[154] Further, as

---

[152] Mitchell and Mishra, note 9, at 1128–1129.

[153] N. Mishra, 'Privacy, Cybersecurity, and GATS Article XIV: A New Frontier for Trade and Internet Regulation?', *World Trade Review* 19 (2019), 1–24, at 1.

[154] J. P. Meltzer, 'A WTO Reform Agenda: Data Flows and International Regulatory Cooperation', Global Economy and Development Working Paper 130 (2019), at 17–18.

suggested by the increased vigour of negotiations under the joint statement initiative, WTO members have shared interests in promoting digital trade. Given the central role of data flows in the digital economy, sufficient incentives therefore exist for WTO members to engage in negotiating rules on cross-border data flows and related issues. Therefore, we believe that despite certain pragmatic and political constraints, our proposed WTO framework on data flows remains both relevant and timely.

E CONCLUSION

The future of trade in digital services and data entails complex and uncertain policy challenges.[155] Thus, balancing different regulatory concerns is fundamental to ensure a coherent and sustainable regulatory framework for data flows. Being the leading multilateral trade institution, the WTO is well placed to undertake several of the required reforms to bring about better balance between promoting free flow of data while protecting a secure and stable regulatory environment for data and addressing commercial interests of consumers and businesses. However, the WTO cannot deal with all pertinent issues related to data transfer, or act on its own. Instead, the WTO needs to reframe its policy approach to engage with more relevant international and multi-stakeholder institutions and develop disciplines that address relevant dimensions of data regulation.

In this article, we recommend a comprehensive framework on data flows that covers a large range of areas that is atypical of most existing international trade agreements. Our recommendations are more comprehensive than the disciplines incorporated in the USMCA and CPTPP. However, as digital trade continues to grow, WTO law will need to respond to new policy challenges arising with increased data flows. In order to do so, WTO members must consider a comprehensive and balanced regulatory framework, where provisions for free cross-border data flows and prohibition on data localisation are complemented with relevant disciplines on online consumer protection, privacy and cybersecurity. Such an approach would facilitate openness as well as business and consumer trust in digital trade. This framework should also include rules addressing the specific needs of developing countries and LDCs to enable their inclusion into the digital economy. Although such a comprehensive framework will require increased participation, goodwill and commitment of countries, particularly under the ongoing joint statement initiative at the WTO, we believe it can eventually be more meaningful and sustainable.

---

[155] Shackelford et al., note 106, at 429.

PART II

From E-Commerce to Big Data and AI

Emerging Issues in Global Trade Law

5

Artificial Intelligence and Trade

*Anupam Chander**

A. INTRODUCTION

When Lily Leong stepped outside that morning on July 1, 2025, the voice in her ear guided her to the nearest Lime ebike, only two blocks away. Her work was fifteen kilometers away in Jakarta's business district and her Samsung Universe One had woken her that morning, timing its gentle intrusion based on her sleep cycle. Her phone had reported that it was a good day to bike to work and had run through the day's appointments. As she walked, her Bose headset would gently interrupt her latest K-Pop favorite, Girls Next Generation, to tell her which way to turn ('Right after the Starbucks'). She was hoping to be able to save enough money by the end of the year to buy the Bose AR Glasses that would show her route without interrupting GNG's 'In a Funk'. On her ebike, the voice guided her around the construction site building a new skyscraper. She saw the Komatsu robot erecting the steel girders that framed the building. The construction site was marked as a Human Exclusion Zone, an 'HEZ,' with prominent signs depicting a diagonal line crossing out a human being. Humans supervised from a protected shelter across the street, staring at screens that connected them to cameras and robots. She stopped the ebike to frame a photo with an idle human in the foreground and the robot construction worker lifting a heavy steel beam in the background and uploaded it to Instagram.

As she arrived at the skyscraper where she worked, the glass turnstile whisked open, a screen displaying the photo from her first day at work two years earlier when she had long hair. In the elevator she put her hand to her mouth to muffle her laugh at the latest fad on TikTok – the #PetTwin challenge, where people showed their pets wearing hairstyles and clothes matching themselves using images generated by an app. Coming to her standing desk somewhere among the hundreds of desks on the

* Anupam Chander is Professor of Law at Georgetown Law. Contact: ac1931@georgetown.edu. The author thanks Sandeep Chandy for excellent research assistance.

fortieth floor, she sent a text to Xiaoice in Chinese about some issue she was having with her loud neighbor at work, and the Microsoft AI responded with suggestions on how to politely indicate her concern. Her Lenovo computer identified her through an iris scan, and a program automatically queued up her first task for the day – an appeal of the bank's automated denial of a housing loan in Germany.

Invisible strings pulled by invisible computers across the world shaped Leong's morning. Her Samsung phone relied on computers in Seoul to awaken her with useful information about the day. The voice telling her which turn to make for a safer biking route was Google's Singapore computer. A Bose computer in Massachusetts played songs that it thought she would like. The Komatsu heavy machinery installing the steel girders and pouring the concrete was guided by Nvidia AI based out of Santa Clara, California, coordinating with Komatsu computers in Tokyo. Instagram's California computers promoted her photo to followers, after scanning it for illegality. The facial recognition system was the work of Hikvision operating through computers in Shenzhen, China. The TikTok videos on her phone were selected for her by the Shanghai-based enterprise using leased Amazon servers in the United States. Microsoft ran its Xiaoice chatbot out of Beijing. The AI making the initial credit decision lived on Ping An Technologies' servers in Shenzhen. Even less visible were the various smart city sensors and actuators operated by various unnamed companies in China, the United States, and Singapore – these systems operated the traffic signals, routed the garbage trucks, and deployed city resources.

Even if this scenario imagines the near future, the technologies mentioned largely exist today. Artificial intelligence (AI) is already crossing borders, learning, making decisions, and operating cyber-physical systems.[1] It underlies many of the services that are offered today – from customer service chatbots to customer relations software to business processes. AI is already powering trade today.

This chapter considers AI regulation from the perspective of international trade law. Because of the near-universal reach of trade rules, the focus here will be on the World Trade Organization (WTO) agreements. My argument unfolds as follows. Section B argues that foreign AI should be regulated by governments – indeed that

---

[1] The WTO describes AI as follows: 'One way to look at AI is as the latest form of automation. However, instead of substituting machine power for manual labour, as in the past, the use of AI involves substituting the computing ability of machines for human intelligence and expertise. Human abilities that were once thought to be out of the reach of machines, such as making a medical diagnosis, playing chess or navigating an automobile, are now either routine or well within reach. Two uses of AI – analogous to the weak AI and strong AI distinction – may be distinguished here, i.e. AI which aids the production of goods and services, and AI which helps to generate new ideas. Examples of the former use of AI include guiding robots in warehouses, optimizing packing and delivery, and detecting whether loan applicants are being truthful. Examples of the latter use of AI are analysing data, solving mathematical problems, sequencing the human genome, and exploring chemical reactions and materials.'
See WTO, *World Trade Report 2018: The Future of World Trade: How Digital Technologies are Transforming Global Commerce* (Geneva: WTO, 2018), at 30 (references omitted).

AI must be what I will call 'locally responsible'. Section C then refutes arguments that trade law should not apply to AI at all and shows how the WTO agreements might apply to AI, using two hypothetical cases – a medical diagnostic AI-based system and an insurance coverage decision-making AI. The analysis will reveal how the WTO agreements leave room for governments to insist on locally responsible AI, while at the same time promoting international trade powered by AI.

B AI'S KANGAROO PROBLEM, OR WHY REGULATE AI?

In 2018, President Emmanuel Macron announced that France will send regulators to sit inside Facebook to evaluate how the company combats hate speech on its services.[2] The regulators will meet with Facebook decision-makers not only in its offices in France, but in Facebook's offices in Dublin, Ireland, and Menlo Park, California.[3] President Macron called this 'smart regulation' and hoped to extend the model to the rest of 'GAFA' members – Google, Apple, and Amazon.[4]

But what about decisions made by AI? Indeed, while it has hired legions of human content moderators, Facebook is also depending on AI to make content moderation decisions. When Mark Zuckerberg testified before Congress in 2017, he cited 'artificial intelligence' more than thirty times in his deposition.[5] 'Over the long term,' Zuckerberg offered, 'building AI tools is going to be the scalable way to identify and root out most of this harmful content.'[6] So, just as it may be appropriate for France to demand that Facebook's human decision-makers in Ireland or California comply with its laws – at least with respect to information destined for France – it is appropriate for France to demand that Facebook's AI decision-makers follow its laws on hate speech.

Governments have good reasons to regulate trade powered by AI. Imagine a dystopian turn to the sci-fi scenario in the introduction: your phone is listening in without permission and pushing advertising based on what it hears, your music app is selling your movements, the robot builder builds an insecure structure, the social network's algorithms promote hate speech because they engender more engagement, the chatbot starts giving dangerous medical advice, the credit decisions are racially discriminatory, or the smart city is a massive surveillance system in the service of a repressive government.

---

[2]   M. Rosemain, M. Rose, and G. Barzic, 'France to 'Embed' Regulators at Facebook to Combat Hate Speech,' *Reuters*, 12 November 2018, available at www.reuters.com/article/us-france-facebook-macron/france-to-embed-regulators-at-facebook-to-combat-hate-speech-idUSKCN1NH1UK.
[3]   Ibid.
[4]   Ibid.
[5]   D. Harwell, 'AI Will Solve Facebook's Most Vexing Problems, Mark Zuckerberg Says. Just Don't Ask When or How,' *The Washington Post*, 11 April 2018 (noting Zuckerberg's promotion of artificial intelligence in connection with decisions related to removing speech for fake news, hate speech, discriminatory ads, and terrorist propaganda).
[6]   Ibid.

With respect to the broad array of services now increasingly powered by AI, there are many legitimate (by which I mean non-protectionist) reasons why a government might seek to regulate the underlying AI. AI operates quite differently from human beings, raising both new issues and also old issues in a new way. AI operates at a different scale, using a different evaluation process, without emotion and judgment. Some may see being subject to decisions taken by AI as an attack on their dignity, while others may worry about who will be held accountable for AI decisions.[7] Regulations built for a world of human reasoning, emotion, and judgment may not equal a world where decisions are made by AI.

How is automated decision-making different? First, and obviously, it is done by computers rather than humans, and thus lacks traditional qualities of human judgment, empathy, and emotion, though it might offer facsimiles of any of these qualities. Second, the ability to transmit real-time data has enabled far more personalized cross-border decision-making than ever before – whether by humans or AI. Third, because it is computerized, it may be done at enormous scale. Fourth, while AI might not be programmed with invidious bias, it might learn that bias from the real-world data it receives – without even knowing perhaps to be mindful of the possibility of such bias.[8]

Decision-making from abroad, of course, predates the rise of AI. Banks, credit card companies, insurance companies, and the like have long relied on decisions made abroad. While there is nothing per se novel about decision-making or information processing across borders, the fact that the Internet now touches almost all of our daily activities increases the opportunities for AI-based decision-making, including decision-making across borders. AI changes the nature, scope, and scale of foreign decision-making. We are entering into a world in which your credit, your job prospects, your insurance claim, the news you read, and even the dates you go on are determined by faceless computers in a distant land.

There is a reason to believe that AI systems will make more mistakes as they cross borders. First, AI might be designed for different environments, nurtured on data from polities that might behave differently. This is a form of the well-known problem that AI trained on, say, a largely white (and male) population, might perform poorly with respect to other populations. Imagine, for example, an AI trained to recognize threats in the United States, but which fails to understand the context of threats in Myanmar – to possibly tragic consequences. Second, because of immense commercial pressures to claim the first mover advantage – attracting both media and venture capital, AI is being rolled out before it is ready. Because machine learning systems benefit from larger datasets, the opportunity to engage more people across the globe will tempt companies to apply their systems ever more broadly. Third, the quality of

7   M. E. Kaminski, 'Binary Governance: Lessons from the GDPR's Approach to Algorithmic Accountability,' *Southern California Law Review* 92 (2019), 1529–1616 (identifying concerns animating calls for regulating algorithmic decision-making).
8   Liu v. Uber Technologies Inc., 20-cv-07499, District Court, N.D. California; A. Chander, 'The Racist Algorithm?', *Michigan Law Review* 115 (2017), 1023–1045.

AI's judgments will be hard to assess because firms have incentives to proclaim the effectiveness of their AI while individual users cannot amass the overall data necessary to evaluate it. Like the problem of legal transplants – which can prove unsuited in new social, cultural and legal contexts – AI transplants might prove problematic.[9]

Thus, there may be special reasons to distrust foreign AI, which may not have been trained on local conditions. I call this 'AI's Kangaroo Problem' in reference to the Volvo case, where Volvo realized that its 'Large Animal Detection' system initially failed to recognize kangaroos because of their jumping, and then began training its system with films of 'kangaroos' roadside behaviour.'[10] When a Tesla, apparently on autopilot, slammed into a stopped tow truck on a Russian road, one news account offered a conjecture: 'Tesla cars [may not be] trained on Russian roads and vehicles.'[11] More generally, AI will often need to be culturally or environmentally sensitive and an AI 'trained' on the behavior of the US population may well produce erroneous results when applied in China, or vice versa.

AI's Kangaroo Problem makes it especially urgent for governments to monitor foreign AI. Of course, higher transparency and accountability obligations on foreign firms than those imposed on domestic firms will invite scrutiny as a discriminatory measure – and so governments should be careful that any special scrutiny is properly justified. One question in this regard will be about a specific set of rules that are only triggered by size. If local companies are all likely to remain smaller than the threshold, there is the possibility of exploiting size triggers to disfavor foreign competitors. Furthermore, focusing only on the world's biggest Internet companies may or may not be justified because of their impact – but it is also important to remember that some of the most pernicious applications of AI might escape scrutiny if we limit our regulatory attention to a handful of enterprises.

Overall, today, decisions about people and machines are being made by machines. AI helps people file tax returns, it helps offer or deny loans, it matches individuals for dating, it makes investment decisions, sorts through job applications, and delivers search results. Given that AI is making decisions that affect people's lives, governments should insist on what we might call 'locally responsible AI.'

C AI AND TRADE LAW

Does trade law apply at all to AI? A skeptic might offer two arguments – the first textual and the second conceptual. First, the WTO agreements and the scheduled

---

[9] On the inadequacy of legal transplants, see, e.g., P. Legrand, 'The Impossibility of 'Legal Transplants',' *Maastricht Journal of European and Comparative Law* 4 (1997), 111–124; M. Siems, 'Malicious Legal Transplants,' *Legal Studies* 38 (2018), 103–119.
[10] BBC, 'Volvo's Driverless Cars 'Confused' by Kangaroos,' *BBC News*, 27 June 2017, available at www.bbc.com/news/technology-40416606.
[11] B. Templeton, 'Another Alleged Tesla Autopilot Failure Raises Questions on Tesla Training System,' *Forbes*, 12 August 2019.

commitments of the WTO members that form an integral part of the treaties nowhere mention AI, and thus should not be interpreted to cover this new technology.[12] Applying trade law to this new sphere would violate the sound expectations of the parties. Second, AI is simply a method of doing something, the skeptic might assert, and the trade agreements focus on what is actually provided rather than the process used to provide it – a version of the process/product distinction elaborated for goods.[13] After all, if trade law does not scrutinize whether a particular decision made by a company is made by an individual or a committee, then why should it pay attention to the decision-making process at all?

Can the WTO agreements apply to AI decision-making? Even if AI techniques were not widely used when the WTO agreements were negotiated, the General Agreement on Trade in Services (GATS)[14] does not limit itself to the technologies in use in 1994. GATS proves relevant through three characteristics: First and most importantly, GATS focuses on measures regulating services without regard to the technologies by which those services are provided.[15] Its first substantive sentence declares, '[t]his Agreement applies to measures by Members affecting trade in services.'[16] Second, the GATS applies to technologies that may have not been on the minds of the negotiators.[17] When China sought to deny that it had included *electronic* distribution of audiovisual material in its WTO commitments in the *China – Audiovisual Products* case, the WTO Appellate Body ruled decisively that it was indeed covered.[18] As I have noted elsewhere, 'By subsuming an electronic version of the service within a services commitment and by interpreting treaty

[12] R. Zhang, 'Covered or Not Covered: That Is the Question,' WTO Working Paper No 11 (2015), at 14–17. 'A more far-reaching interpretation was that any service 'unforeseen' at the time of commitments could not be considered as covered by it, even if the definition in the CPC covered the 'unforeseen' service.' Ibid.

[13] See G. Cook, 'Humpty Dumpty and the Illusion of 'Evolutionary Interpretation' in WTO Dispute Settlement,' in G. Abi-Saab et al. (eds), *Evolutionary Interpretation and International Law* (Oxford: Hart Publishing, 2019). See also Appellate Body Report, *China – Measures Affecting Trading Rights and Distribution Services for Certain Publications and Audiovisual Entertainment Products (China – Audiovisual Products)*, WT/DS363/AB/R, adopted 21 December 2009. In *China – Audiovisual Products* (at para. 396), the Appellate Body found that the terms in China's Schedule 'are sufficiently generic that what they apply to may change over time.'

[14] General Agreement on Trade in Services, 1869 U.N.T.S. 183; 33 I.L.M. 1167 (1994), entered into force 1 January 1995 [hereinafter: GATS].

[15] WTO, Work Programme on Electronic Commerce – Progress Report to the General Council, S/L/74, 27 July 1999, at 4; see also WTO Panel Report, *United States – Measures Affecting the Cross-Border Supply of Gambling and Betting Services (US – Gambling)*, WT/DS285/R, adopted 10 November 2004 and WTO Appellate Body Report, *United States – Measures Affecting the Cross-Border Supply of Gambling and Betting Services (US – Gambling)*, WT/DS285/AB/R, adopted 7 April 2005.

[16] Article I:1 GATS.

[17] See generally S.-Y. Peng, 'Renegotiate the WTO 'Schedules of Commitments'?: Technological Development and Treaty Interpretation,' *Cornell International Law Journal* 45 (2012), 403–430.

[18] *China – Audiovisual Products*, note 12, at para. 412.

commitments in a dynamic form, the treaty can take account of changing technologies."[19] If a term is listed in a sufficiently generic fashion, it should be interpreted to cover activities that were not commercialized at the time of the listing.[20] Indeed, when it determined that electronic distribution of audiovisual recordings was covered by China's commitments, the Appellate Body observed that it was not necessary that such electronic distribution was feasible at the time when China acceded to the WTO.[21] Thus, a generic commitment for market access for insurance decision-making under mode 1 (cross-border supply) should be read to cover AI-based decision-making as well. Third, as *China – Audiovisual Products* decision makes clear, the GATS applies to electronically mediated services – a fact essential to enable it to cover AI-powered services. Fourth, the GATS schedules explicitly include a variety of computer and related services in their ambit, with at least seventy-seven countries committing to liberalize trade in 'data processing services.'[22] The end result is that when a government measure affects the ability of a foreign company to supply AI-based services into that country, GATS is applicable.

The second objection challenges the idea that AI can be reached by trade law on the ground that *how* a decision is made with respect to any service is not a proper subject of trade law. This is a version of the controversial process and production methods (PPMs) distinction from the realm of goods,[23] where an importing government may not be able to inquire into the process by which a product is produced, only evaluating its quality as it arrives at the border.[24] Steve Charnovitz divides PPMs into three types: (i) the how-produced standard; (ii) the government policy standard; and (iii) the producer characteristics standard.[25] Translating this into the domain of services, it

---

[19] A. Chander, *The Electronic Silk Road: How the Web Binds the World Together in Commerce* (New Haven, CT: Yale University Press, 2013), at 156.

[20] *China – Audiovisual Products*, note 12, at para. 396; Cook, note 12.

[21] *China – Audiovisual Products*, note 12, at para. 396.

[22] R. Berry and M. Reisman, 'Policy Challenges of Cross-Border Cloud Computing,' *Journal of International Commerce and Economics* 4 (2012), 1–38, at 22 (noting that sixty countries have commitments on 'on-line information and/or data processing,' while seventy-six have commitments for data processing). My review with Usman Ahmed finds at least seventy-seven countries with 'CPC 843' commitments for data processing services, though some of these commitments may be narrower than all data processing services. See U. Ahmed and A. Chander, 'Information Goes Global: Protecting Privacy, Security, and the New Economy in a World of Cross-Border Data Flows,' *E15 Expert Group on the Digital Economy Think Piece* (2015). For all commitments and exceptions of the WTO members for computer and related services, see www.wto.org/english/tratop_e/serv_e/computer_e/computer_e.htm.

[23] The term 'processes and production methods' originated in the GATT agreement of 1979 on Technical Barriers to Trade and referred to product standards focused on the production method rather than product characteristics. For example, a law prohibiting the landing of fish caught using a driftnet entails a PPM. By contrast, a law prohibiting the sale of fish smaller than a prescribed size does not constitute a PPM.

[24] S. Charnovitz, 'The Law of Environmental 'PPMs' in the WTO: Debunking the Myth of Illegality,' *Yale Journal of International Law* 27 (2002), 59–110, at 64–65.

[25] Ibid., at 67.

would mean that the importing government treats the foreign service provider differently because of (i) how it produced the service; (ii) the law governing that service in the exporting country; or (iii) the characteristics of the foreign service provider, respectively.

With respect to services, however, regulation often focuses on both, the provider and the process used, as it may be difficult to regulate the service directly. Licensing requirements, for example, often seek to assure that the individual performing the task has the relevant education, ethics, and experience to perform the service. In general, how a service is produced may be important to evaluate its quality – such as knowing whether an accountant or an engineer or a cybersecurity expert has followed the standard protocols.[26] Of course, much of the process used to provide the service could be inscribed in the service itself but it is often difficult to see the mark of that process directly. Thus, we often use other measures to evaluate the service – such as the prominence of the firm or the education of its employees or their use of a widely accepted method.[27] This is no less true with AI. Demands for explainability, for example, which have become common nowadays,[28] are often ultimately about a form of due process, including the ability to challenge a decision that one feels is unjust.

The following two sections explore two specific scenarios of the interaction between AI and international trade rules.

I *Scenario One: Dr. AI*

Imagine if a country bars unlicensed medical diagnosis, and interprets this requirement to bar all AI-based medical diagnosis, as there is no process for licensing an AI. What if a foreign company wishes to offer AI-based medical diagnosis into that country? Could it rely on the GATS commitments to liberalize trade in data-processing services to argue that the ban on AI medical diagnosis violated that country's WTO obligations?[29]

---

[26] Chander, note 18, at 146 ('The measure of the quality of a service often involves not just the appraisal of the outcome but also the appraisal of the process by which the service was produced'); see also K. Nicolaidis and S. K. Schmidt, 'Mutual Recognition 'on Trial': The Long Road to Services Liberalization,' *Journal of European Public Policy* 14 (2007), 717–734, at 719 ('for services almost all regulations have to do with processes').

[27] The WTO secretariat's Trade in Services division similarly observes: 'Services are intangible and their supply often requires an interaction between the service supplier and consumer. This implies that consumers frequently cannot appreciate the quality of the service until they have consumed it.' See WTO Trade in Services Division, Disciplines on Domestic Regulation Pursuant to GATS Article VI:4 – Background and Current State of Play, June 2011, available at www.wto.org/english/tratop_e/serv_e/dom_reg_negs_bckgddoc_e.doc.

[28] See, e.g., U. Gasser and V. A. F. Almeida, 'A Layered Model for AI Governance,' *IEEE Internet Computing* 21 (2017), 58–62; A. Deeks, 'The Judicial Demand for Explainable Artificial Intelligence,' *Columbia Law Review* 119 (2019), 1829–1850.

[29] Of course, the aggrieved corporation could not seek to enforce GATS itself but could pressure its home state to do so.

The first step in making such a claim is to establish that the country had in fact committed to liberalize trade in such AI-based medical diagnosis services in the first instance. The market access and national treatment obligations, as we have said, rest on a nation's GATS schedule. This, in turn, raises difficult questions of classification. Suppose an AI performs the task of assessing whether a skin lesion is cancerous and does so via a smartphone app. Many but not all WTO members used the United Nations' Central Product Classification (CPC) in its provisional 1991 version[30] to schedule their liberalization commitments. The CPC has been revised numerous times since but these updates have not been reflected in the law of the WTO.[31] Under the CPC scheme, human health services are classified as 'CPC 931,' with subdivisions for 'general' (93121) and 'specialized' (93122) health services, as well as other subdivisions. But perhaps the AI could be seen as a 'data processing service' (CPC 843) or a 'database service' (CPC 844) at the same time – after all the AI is an immense data processor and may rely on significant database functions? The GATS classification is designed to be exclusionary – that is, any given service should fall only under one category[32] but it can be difficult to place many technologically powered services within the classification framework existing at the time of the WTO's founding.

The CPC itself provides interpretative rules, including two rules relevant here:

1. The category that provides the most specific description shall be preferred to categories providing a more general description; and
2. Composite services consisting of a combination of different services which cannot be classified by reference to (a) shall be classified as if they consisted of the service which gives them their essential character, in so far as this criterion is applicable.[33]

---

[30] United Nations, Provisional Central Product Classification (CPC), UN Statistical Papers, Series M, No 77, Ver.1.1, E.91.XVII.7, 1991 [hereinafter: CPC]. The CPC is a classification based on the physical characteristics of goods or on the nature of the services rendered. Each type of good or service distinguished in the CPC is defined in such a way that it is normally produced by only one activity as defined in International Standard Industry Classification of all Economic Activities (ISIC). The CPC covers products that are an output of economic activities, including transportable goods, non-transportable goods and services.

[31] See R. H. Weber and M. Burri, *Classification of Services in the Digital Economy* (Berlin: Springer, 2012), at 19.

[32] A. D. Mitchell and N. Mishra, 'Data at the Docks: Modernizing International Trade Law for the Digital Economy,' *Vanderbilt Journal of Entertainment and Technology* 20 (2018), 1073–1134, at 1090 ('in a country's schedule, commitments on a service sector or subsector are exclusive; thus, a specific digital service (like the search engine services of Google) cannot be simultaneously classified under computer and related services (more specifically, data processing services), telecommunications services (online information and data processing services), and advertising services'). See also *US–Gambling*, note 14.

[33] CPC 1991, at 28.

If we assume that 'medical diagnostic service' is more specific than 'data processing service,' then an AI-based medical diagnostic service should properly be classified as a 'medical diagnostic service.' Thus, a commitment under CPC 843 for a data processing service is likely insufficient to grant a foreign AI medical diagnostic service provider market access and national treatment in that country without a relevant CPC 931 human health service commitment.

In *China–Electronic Payments*, the panel, however, questioned this approach, arguing that 'the matter is not so obvious that we could confidently determine, without undertaking a detailed examination, [which service] is 'more specific' in relation to the services at issue.'[34] Yet, the panel's preferred approach largely reached the same conclusion. The panel recognized 'electronic payment services for payment card transactions' as an 'integrated service' that included other services that could be provided independently.[35] The relevant classification in such cases would be the one describing the integrated service.[36]

What if a country has left medical services unbound, but has bound data processing services for both market access and national treatment? Would a foreign AI medical diagnostic provider be able to benefit from that data processing commitment? It seems likely that it would only be able to claim them for providing data processing but not for the medical diagnostic service itself, which would have required a CPC 931 commitment.

The scheduling guidelines adopted by the WTO's Council for Trade in Services in 2001 distinguish between a committed service and input services to that committed service.[37] The scheduling of a committed service does not imply that the input services are also equally committed when used for purposes other than the committed, composite service. It seems sensible, however, to assume that the input services are automatically committed when provided as an input into the committed service – that is, it should not be possible for a WTO member to specify that a foreign medical diagnostic provider (presuming that medical diagnostic services are committed) must use domestic AI. Otherwise, the commitment of the integrated service would be less meaningful because one could establish a variety of requirements for the inputs into that service that would greatly erode the commitment. Then if members specify medical diagnosis, they need not specify all the input services needed to supply a medical diagnosis. In our hypothetical case of 'Dr. AI,' if the data processing or database service is an input service to the AI-based medical diagnostic

---

[34] WTO Panel Report, *China – Certain Measures Affecting Electronic Payment Services (China–Electronic Payment Services)*, WT/DS413/R, adopted August 31, 2012, at para. 7.71.

[35] Ibid., at paras. 7.55–7.62, and 7.188.

[36] Ibid.

[37] WTO, Guidelines for the Scheduling of Specific Commitments under the General Agreement on Trade in Services (GATS), S/L/92, 23 March 2001, at 25 ('It is understood that market access and national treatment commitments apply only to the sectors or subsectors inscribed in the schedule. They do not imply a right for the supplier of a committed service to supply uncommitted services which are inputs to the committed service').

service, then a commitment under CPC 931 for such a service would include the data processing or database service.

II *Scenario Two: Claims Adjuster AI*

Imagine a country that bans automated decision-making for insurance coverage decisions. This would go beyond the right to object to a decision made by an automated algorithm under the European Union's General Data Protection Regulation (GDPR).[38] Such a scenario would be reminiscent of the genetic engineering debate in trade law – where Europe rejected genetically modified food outright, while the United States insists on their safety.[39]

Imagine also that domestic insurance providers are not technologically minded, while foreign competitors are more likely to use AI. So the burden of the rule largely falls on foreign providers. Assume that the country banning AI has made market access and national treatment commitments for the relevant insurance products under the Annex on Financial Services, but has limited those to mode 3 (commercial presence), as countries often are reluctant to allow for cross-border trade in financial services because of prudential regulation of financial institutions to ensure, among other things, their safety and soundness.

Might the foreign country of that foreign insurance provider with a domestic establishment have a claim? The foreign home might challenge the absolute bar as a violation of that importing state's market access commitments. A ban might be seen as a zero quota, and thus a numerical limitation on the number of providers – which will be a violation of the GATS market access obligation contained in Article XVI:2.[40]

The foreign country might also argue that the ban violates the national treatment requirement by effectively preferring domestic insurance providers, which do not use AI for decisions. A central question in answering this question is whether the AI-based insurance service was 'like' the non-AI based insurance service. While guidance on the interpretation of 'likeness' when it comes to services is limited,[41]

---

[38] Regulation 2016/679 of the European Parliament and of the Council of 27 April 2016 on the Protection of Natural Persons with Regard to the Processing of Personal Data and on the Free Movement of Such Data, and Repealing Directive 95/46/EC (General Data Protection Regulation, GDPR), OJ L [2016] 119/1 [hereinafter: General Data Protection Regulation or GDPR], at Article 22(1): data subjects 'have the right not to be subject to a decision based solely on automated processing, including profiling, which produces legal effects concerning him or her or similarly significantly affects him or her.'
[39] See WTO Panel Report, *European Communities – Measures Affecting the Approval and Marketing of Biotech Products (EC–Biotech)*, WT/DS921/R, adopted 21 November 2006; see also M. A. Pollack and G. C. Shaffer, *When Cooperation Fails: The International Law and Politics of Genetically Modified Foods* (Oxford: Oxford University Press, 2009).
[40] WTO Panel Report, *US – Gambling*, note 14, at para. 239.
[41] The US argued that online gambling was unlike real world gambling because 'in virtual casinos, the result is generated by a software algorithm' rather than physical movement. The 'online casino is an illusion – a 'virtual reality' environment in which outcomes are controlled

the Appellate Body has indicated that the 'fundamental purpose' of the likeness comparison is 'to assess whether and to what extent the services and service suppliers at issue are in a competitive relationship.'[42]

If a tribunal concludes that the AI ban violates either market access or national treatment commitments, the importing nation will argue that the ban is justified by considerations of privacy, public order, or even public morals (with respect to the latter, the argument would be that having such important decisions made as insurance denial about someone by an AI would be an affront to human dignity). Article XIV of the GATS permits a derogation that is 'necessary to protect public morals or to maintain public order'[43] but the 'public order exception may be invoked only where a genuine and sufficiently serious threat is posed to one of the fundamental interests of society.'[44] One focal point of the analysis will be whether the ban is *necessary* to protect public order. The exporting nation might argue that an alternative WTO-consistent that achieves the same ends is reasonably available, and thus an outright ban is not necessary.[45] It might for instance point to the German approach as such an alternative: Germany explicitly recognizes automated decision-making for insurance decisions but requires the insurance company to offer human review for any negative decisions.[46]

In summing up, even if existing trade law does have mechanisms to reduce protectionist barriers to trade in AI, there remains substantial room for disagreement over whether any particular rule that burdens trade in AI can be justified. The examples above point to some of the debates and critical questions, such as: Is AI medical diagnosis 'like' human medical diagnosis? Can an AI-based insurer be banned on the grounds that it is likely to be biased or opaque? The rules as they

---

by a computer rather than by the laws of the physical world,' the US insisted (see WTO Panel Report, *US–Gambling*, note 14). Because of the exercise of judicial economy, however, the dispute settlement body did not reach the issue of national treatment and thus, 'there is up until today no jurisprudence on how such characteristics on the method of supply should be evaluated' with respect to services. See N. Diebold, *Non-discrimination in International Trade in Services: 'Likeness' in WTO/GATS* (Cambridge: Cambridge University Press, 2010), at 252.

[42] WTO Appellate Body Report, *Argentina – Measures Relating to Trade in Goods and Services*, WT/DS453/R, adopted 9 May 2016, at paras. 6.33–6.34.

[43] Article XIV(a) and Article XIV(b) GATS.

[44] Article XIV GATS.

[45] WTO Panel Report, *US–Gambling*, note 14, at paras. 306–307: 'A comparison between the challenged measure and possible alternatives should then be undertaken, and the results of such comparison should be considered in the light of the importance of the interests at issue. It is on the basis of this 'weighing and balancing' and comparison of measures, taking into account the interests or values at stake, that a panel determines whether a measure is 'necessary' or, alternatively, whether another, WTO-consistent measure is 'reasonably available.'' The exporting country can also argue that the challenged measure is arbitrary or is an unjustifiable discrimination between countries where like conditions prevail, or a disguised restriction on trade in services, as specified in the chapeau of Article XIV GATS.

[46] G. Malgieri, 'Automated Decision-Making in the EU Member States: The Right to Explanation and Other 'Suitable Safeguards' in the National Legislation,' *Computer Law and Security Review* 35 (2019), 1–26, at 7–8.

stand do not give clear answers to such questions. Internationally agreed frameworks for responsible AI might offer a process to protect national regulatory goals while enabling trade in AI.

D CONCLUSION

Governments across the world are struggling to keep up with technology. The rise of AI decision-making, in everything from cars to media to business processes, challenges regulatory capacity. Governments must regulate AI in order to further traditional regulatory goals, such as consumer protection, privacy, and law enforcement. Governments can, however, craft or enforce AI rules that disfavor foreign enterprises. The regulation of AI should not be used to create yet another behind-the-border trade barrier.

6

Blockchain's Practical and Legal Implications for Global Trade and Global Trade Law

*Emmanuelle Ganne**

A INTRODUCTION

Technology is not only transforming international trade, it is also pushing the boundaries of regulation. The cross-border nature of the Internet challenged existing regulatory approaches, raised new regulatory issues and gave rise to new forms of governance. Digital technologies that leverage the Internet are challenging existing approaches even further. Among those, one technology, blockchain, keeps making the headlines. A game changer for some, the most overhyped technology for others. Few technologies have sparked so much debate.

Often associated with Bitcoin because it was first implemented as the technology underpinning the famous cryptocurrency, blockchain is much more than Bitcoin.[1] In fact, by making it possible for actors along the supply chain to interact on a peer-to-peer basis in quasi real time and in a highly secure and trusted environment, this technology could have a major impact on many facets of international trade and deeply transform it. Blockchain could facilitate international trade transactions and help implement World Trade Organization (WTO) agreements, and it could foster the digitalization of trade.

Yet, technology is only a tool. A number of regulatory issues deserve the attention of policymakers for this potential to be realized. It is therefore critical that government officials educate themselves to understand the technology, its potential, but also its limitations, and keep an eye on developments. This chapter discusses the measures that should be taken to promote the development of a regulatory

---

* Emmanuelle Ganne is a Senior Analyst at the World Trade Organization. Contact: emma-nuelle.ganne@wto.org. The opinions expressed in this chapter are those of the author. They are not intended to represent the positions or opinions of the WTO or its members and are without prejudice to members' rights and obligations under the WTO. Any errors are attributable to the author.

[1] This chapter focuses on the technology itself, not on cryptocurrency applications.

framework conducive to the development of the technology and the role that the WTO could play in this respect.

The chapter's first section describes blockchain's key features and discusses how this technology can be used to facilitate transactions in various areas of global trade and help implement WTO agreements. It examines the potential impact of this technology on international trade. The second section looks at discrete regulatory issues that deserve the attention of regulators for blockchain to truly transform international trade. The last section discusses measures that should be taken to promote the development of a regulatory framework conducive to the development of the technology and the role that the WTO could play in this respect. The chapter argues that the WTO is uniquely positioned to play a pivotal role in ensuring that a conducive governance framework is put in place to allow blockchain to be used to its full potential in the area of international trade.

B UNDERSTANDING BLOCKCHAIN'S PRACTICAL IMPLICATIONS FOR INTERNATIONAL TRADE

In spite of the many headlines on blockchain, the technology, its functioning and potential to transform business beyond the world of cryptocurrencies and of finance more generally remains difficult for many to apprehend. This section seeks to provide a basic understanding of how the technology works and discusses its practical implications for international trade and the implementation of WTO agreements.

I *Blockchain: A Complex World*

The catchy word of blockchain conceals a complex reality. The term blockchain is now often used in a generic way to refer to distributed ledger technology (DLT) and this chapter follows this practice. Strictly speaking, however, blockchain is only one type of DLT – one that combines transactions in blocks and links them in a linear way. While there are many different types of DLTs, all possess a number of key characteristics that render them particularly useful as a facilitator of a wide range of international trade processes.

A blockchain, or distributed ledger, is a shared and synchronized digital database that is maintained by an algorithm and stored on multiple 'nodes', i.e. computers connected to the network that store a local version of the ledger. Unlike traditional databases, distributed ledgers have no central data store or entity controlling the network. They function on a peer-to-peer basis without the need for the intermediaries who traditionally authenticate transactions. Data added to the ledger are shared with all participants in quasi real time, verified and validated ('mined' in the context of blockchain technology) by anyone with the appropriate permissions on the basis of the consensus protocol of the ledger, and timestamped. Therefore, participants in

TABLE 6.1. *Types of blockchain platforms*

Blockchain types	Level of centralization	Read	Write	Example
Public permissionless	Highly decentralized	Anyone	Anyone	Bitcoin
Public permissioned	Highly decentralized	Anyone	Authorized participants	Sovrin
Consortium permissioned	Partially-decentralized	Authorized participants	Authorized participants	Tradelens
Private permissioned	Centralized	Authorized participants	Authorized participants	Company blockchain

Source: Author.

a distributed ledger have all access to the same information at any time. In other words, a distributed ledger is a shared, trusted record of transactions that all participants can access and check at any time, but that no single party can control (unless it is fully private – see Table 6.1), which allows people with no particular trust in each other to collaborate without relying on trusted intermediaries. Distributed ledgers ensure immediate, across the board transparency.

A distributed ledger is secured using a blend of proven cryptographic techniques. Data entered onto the blockchain are 'hashed', i.e., converted into a new digital string of a fixed length using a mathematical function, and encrypted to ensure data integrity, prevent forgery, and guarantee that the message was created and sent by the claimed sender and was not altered in transit. Records are also linked to one another; attempting to alter the ledger is a difficult endeavour as previous blocks or records of transactions would also have to be altered for the changes to remain undetected. Because of the distributed nature of blockchain, falsifying data or compromising the whole network would require compromising a large number of nodes, which would be practically very hard.

These different characteristics make distributed ledger technology highly secure and difficult to hack – which led *The Economist* to call blockchain a 'trust machine'.[2] They also render DLT a particularly helpful technology to remove frictions from global trade by making it possible for the many stakeholders involved in international trade transactions to interact in a more efficient way.

Distributed ledgers are, to date, the most secure type of databases,[3] but this is not to say that they are completely immune from tampering or cyberattacks. A distributed ledger can be compromised if a validator or a pool of validators control

---

[2] 'The Trust Machine: The Promise of the Blockchain', *The Economist*, 31 October 2015.
[3] However, not all distributed ledgers provide the same level of security. More centralized ledgers are less resilient to outside attacks, and there is a greater risk of human tampering with data.

more than 50 per cent of the network's computing power, which is called the '51 per cent attack'. With computing power capacity of some blockchains being increasingly aggregated, the risks are certainly growing. In fact, in July 2019, two mining pools of the Bitcoin network, one reputed the most difficult to hack, carried out a 51 per cent attack on the network in an apparent effort to stop an unknown miner from taking coins that they were not supposed to have access to in the wake of a code change.[4] While the attack was arguably conducted with a view of doing something good for the community, not to reward the attacker or steal funds, it has led to heated debates in the information technology (IT) community as to the severity of the potential consequences of such attacks. Advances in quantum computing could in the long term also represent a threat to blockchain as blockchain's resilience relies on encryption and algorithms, whose strength is based on computing power. 'Post-quantum' algorithms that would be resistant to quantum computing are being actively researched.

1 A Multitude of Distributed Ledger Technologies

In spite of these common characteristics and as noted earlier, DLTs are very diverse and there is a multitude of consensus protocols. Consensus protocols govern the way transactions are validated and records are added to the network and differ in terms of energy consumption and rapidity at which blocks or transactions can be validated. Some of the most well-known consensus protocols include proof-of-work (PoW), which is used by Bitcoin; proof-of-stake (PoS), which is being considered by Ethereum, another well-known public blockchain, and Proof of Elapsed Time (PoET) used by Hyperledger Sawtooth. Proof-of-work requires that the participants who validate blocks, the 'miners', show that they have invested significant computing power to solve a hard cryptographic puzzle. Miners compete with each other to validate a block and add it to the blockchain. The miner who validates the new block is rewarded with Bitcoins. The level of difficulty of the mathematical problem increases as blocks are mined to ensure that only one block can be mined every ten minutes. The big disadvantage of proof-of-work is its high level of energy consumption – which researchers estimated to be as high as that of a country like Ireland.[5] Proof-of-stake algorithms were developed to overcome the disadvantage of PoW in terms of energy consumption. PoS replaces the mining operation with rewards in proportion to the amount of the validators' 'stake' in the network (i.e. ownership or assets of cryptocurrency in the network). As for Proof of Elapsed Time, it uses a

---

[4] One of these two pools is said to have controlled at some point more than 50 per cent of the hashing power on its own. See A. Hertig, 'Bitcoin Cash Miners Undo Attacker's Transactions with "51% Attack"', available at www.coindesk.com/bitcoin-cash-miners-undo-attackers-transactions-with-51-attack.

[5] K. O'Dwyer and D. Malone, 'Bitcoin Mining and Its Energy Footprint', National University of Ireland Maynooth Working Paper (2014).

random leader election model, or a lottery-based election, with the protocol randomly selecting the next leader to finalize the block. These are merely a few examples of the many different consensus protocols that exist in practice.

In addition, while the most well-known DLT, blockchain, combines transactions in blocks and chains them in a linear way – hence the term 'blockchain' – an increasing number of models of transaction flows are being developed, which move away from the concept of 'blocks' – or even from both concepts of 'blocks' and 'chain'. The so-called 'New kids not on the blocks' include IOTA,[6] Ripple[7] and Hedera Hashgraph.[8] In IOTA, for example, transactions are not grouped into blocks and each transaction is linked to two previous transactions as part of the validation process to form a 'tangle'.

Despite these important technical issues, the technology itself is only one part of the story and the term 'blockchain' is often used to refer to the platforms that are being developed for specific applications, the nature of which varies greatly. While blockchain was originally envisioned as a decentralized network open to everyone, a number of platforms have emerged that are controlled by a company or a group of companies forming a consortium and whose access is limited to authorized participants.

2 Various Types of Blockchain Platforms

Distributed ledgers are often classified as public versus private or 'permissioned' versus 'permissionless'. Under the category of private blockchain or ledger, there is a subtype called 'consortium' that is sometimes considered as a type of blockchain in its own right.[9] These two classifications are at times conflated and it is not uncommon for people to associate public with permissionless and private/consortium platforms with permissioned platforms. The reality is, however, slightly more complicated, as some public platforms can be permissioned (see Table 6.1).[10]

In essence, a permissionless blockchain is a platform that is open to anyone, with no restrictions imposed on who can access the platform and validate transactions, while a permissioned blockchain is a platform in which access is restricted. The distinction between public, consortium and private blockchains is linked to the degree of decentralization. A public platform is a platform that is highly decentralized, with no specific entity/entities managing the platform. Transactions are public and individual users can maintain anonymity and no user is given special privileges

---

[6] www.iota.org.
[7] https://ripple.com.
[8] www.hedera.com. For details, see E. Ganne, *Can Blockchain Revolutionize International Trade?* (Geneva: WTO, 2018).
[9] V. Buterin, 'On Public and Private Blockchains', *Ethereum Blog*, 7 August 2015, available at https://blog.ethereum.org/2015/08/07/on-public-and-private-blockchains/.
[10] Ganne, note 8.

over any decision. In contrast, in a private blockchain, the permissions to validate and add data to the ledger are controlled by one entity that is highly trusted by the other users, and participants are identified. The term 'blockchain' in the context of private ledgers is controversial and disputed, as such highly centralized ledgers have little in common with the original idea behind blockchain. A consortium blockchain is a 'partially decentralized' platform[11] that operates under the leadership of a group rather than a single entity and in which participants are identified. One of the distributed ledger technologies often used for private or consortium platforms is Hyperledger Fabric,[12] which was developed by IBM, and donated to the Hyperledger Project of the Linux Foundation, and has been designed to cater to the needs of participating companies.

Private and consortium platforms provide for greater scalability but at the expense of decentralization. Public platforms, on their side, are highly decentralized and provide for a high level of security, but this comes at the cost of efficiency and scalability. This is what Vitalik Buterin, founder of Ethereum, called the 'blockchain trilemma' – i.e., the impossibility to achieve scalability, decentralization and security simultaneously in a blockchain. At most, two of these properties can be achieved. Other researchers articulate the trilemma around a slightly different set of concepts: decentralization, correctness and cost efficiency,[13] but the conclusion remains the same: you cannot have it all.

3 Automation via Smart Contracts

A particularly interesting feature of the blockchain universe is the possibility to use smart contracts, i.e. computer programmes that automatically enforce themselves (self-execute) without the intervention of a third party when specific conditions are met (based on the 'if ... then...' logic; e.g., if the goods are unloaded at port of X, then funds are transferred). Smart contracts state the obligations of each party to the 'contract', as well as the benefits and penalties that may be due to either party under different circumstances. However, unlike the name suggests, smart contracts are neither smart, as there is no cognitive or artificial intelligence component to them, nor are they contracts in a legal sense.

Smart contracts go back many years. Cryptographer Nick Szabo introduced them first in various publications during 1994–1997,[14] but their use outside of blockchain

---

[11] Buterin, note 9.
[12] www.hyperledger.org/projects/fabric.
[13] J. Abadi and M. Brunnermeier, 'Blockchain Economics', Princeton University Working Paper (2018).
[14] Nick Szabo defined smart contracts as 'a set of promises, specified in digital form, including protocols within which the parties perform on the other promises.' The general objectives of smart contract design are to satisfy common contractual conditions (such as payment terms, liens, confidentiality and even enforcement), minimize exceptions both malicious and accidental, and minimize the need for trusted intermediaries'. See N. Szabo, 'Smart Contracts:

makes them subject to the same problems as centralized databases – that is, a single point of failure and the possibility to change the data easily. When used in the context of blockchain they inherit blockchain's key properties, such as immutability.

II *Blockchain: A Potentially Transformative Impact on International Trade*

The transparent, highly secure and quasi-immutable nature of blockchain makes it an interesting tool to facilitate a number of processes related to international trade. A myriad of proofs of concepts and pilot projects leveraging the technology have been developed in virtually all areas of international trade, from trade finance to border procedures and the management and enforcement of intellectual property rights, to cut costs, streamline procedures, and help move away from heavy paper-based processes, with an increasing number of projects now entering the production phase. The potential of this technology to transform international trade is indeed significant.[15]

1 Blockchain's Potential Impact on International Trade Transactions

International trade has seen little innovation since the invention of the container by Malcolm McLean in 1955. Goods are still transported across oceans in the same old way, requiring paper and labour-intensive processes. In a now well-known experiment, shipping company Maersk followed a container of roses and avocadoes from Mombasa in Kenya to Rotterdam in the Netherlands in 2014 to document the maze of physical processes and paperwork that impact every shipment. Around 30 actors and more than 100 people were involved throughout the journey, leading to more than 200 interactions.[16] The shipment generated a pile of paper 25 cm high and the cost of handling it was higher than the cost of moving the container.[17] One of the critical documents went missing, only to be found later amid a pile of paper.[18] The system is overall slow, costly and inefficient. The use of blockchain opens incredible opportunities to cut costs and improve processes, and to truly digitize procedures that are still analogue.

A BLOCKCHAIN CAN MAKE TRADE PROCESSES MORE EFFICIENT AND LESS COSTLY Because it allows all actors to interact in real time in a highly secure

Building Blocks for Digital Markets', *Extropy: The Journal of Transhumanist Thought* 16 (1996), 50–53, at 51. Available at: https://archive.org/details/extropy-16/page/50/mode/2up?q=a+computerized+protocol+that+executes+terms
[15] Ganne, note 8.
[16] F. Landon, 'Maersk, Avocados and the Global Trade Paperchase', *SeaTrade Maritime News*, 29 November 2017.
[17] I. Allison, 'Shipping Giant Maersk Tests Blockchain-Powered Bill of Lading', *International Business Times*, 14 October 2016.
[18] K. Park, 'Blockchain Is about to Revolutionize the Shipping Industry', *Bloomberg*, 18 April 2018.

environment, blockchain can make processes more efficient and less costly. Once added to the ledger, information is available to all participants simultaneously, and the nature of the technology gives participants the guarantee that the information cannot be tampered with, thereby generating trust.

In one of the first economic studies on blockchain, Catalini and Gans consider that the use of blockchain affects two key costs in particular: (i) verification costs, i.e. the ability to verify the attributes of a transaction cheaply and (ii) networking costs, i.e., the ability to bootstrap and operate a marketplace without the need for a traditional intermediary.[19] Other costs, such as coordination and processing costs, financial intermediation and costs related to foreign exchange could be affected as well.[20] While the potential impact on trade costs has not been thoroughly researched yet, various studies by actors in the field estimate that the potential savings from full digitalization using blockchain could represent between 15 and 30 per cent of the costs of the processes concerned.[21] The reduction in trade costs can be particularly interesting for small- and medium-sized enterprises (SMEs) who face higher fixed costs than large companies.

The potential efficiency gains of blockchain have led many actors involved in international trade to build consortia to leverage the opportunities that the technology opens. IBM and Maersk were the first ones to open the race with their platform Tradelens[22] that aims to connect the various parties involved in international trade – from freight forwarders to government authorities and banks – and to digitize the supply chain from end to end, with a view to streamlining and facilitating procedures. The platform is now fully operational and claims to process ten million events a week. Others are following suit.

Numerous initiatives have also been launched in the area of trade finance: Contour, Komgo, We.trade, eTradeConnect are some of the bank-led projects that aim to address deficiencies of trade finance processes using distributed ledger technology. Traditional trade finance, in particular letter of credit transactions, is labour and paper intensive and involves multiple players, generating much inefficiency. Research by the Boston Consulting Group found that more than twenty players are usually party to a single trade finance transaction throughout the process, with data captured in ten to twenty documents, creating approximately five thousand data field interactions, but that only 1 per cent of these interactions creates value. The remaining 85–90 per cent of the transactions simply consist of 'ignore/

[19] C. Catalini and J. S. Gans, 'Some Simple Economics of the Blockchain', MIT Sloan Research Paper No 5191-16 (2019).

[20] Ganne, note 8.

[21] Accenture, *Banking on Blockchain – A Value Analysis for Investment Banks* (New York/London: Accenture, 2017); I. Allison, 'Maersk and IBM Want ten Million Shipping Containers on the Global Supply Blockchain by Year-End', *International Business Times*, 8 March 2017.

[22] www.tradelens.com/.

transmit to the next party' actions.[23] Not surprisingly, banks see blockchain as a potential tool to reduce coordination costs between the multiple actors involved in a letter of credit transaction. The first results of initiatives using DLT to process letters of credit seem encouraging, arguably reducing the time needed to process letter of credit transactions from on average of five to ten days to a matter of hours.[24]

Yet, all these projects are still in their early stages, being at best a two or three of years. It remains to be seen whether these various platforms will effectively generate the expected outcomes and manage to scale up to become viable business projects.

B TOWARDS PAPERLESS TRADE? Efforts to digitize trade have so far been impeded by what is usually referred to in the blockchain world as the 'double-spend problem', i.e. the possibility to spend a digital asset twice, which translates in the non-currency world as the possibility to make multiple copies of digital files. This is particularly important in the case of international trade, as a document like the bill of lading represents ownership of the goods. It is critical to ensure that an electronic bill of lading can be transferred from one holder to another in a manner that guarantees that there is only one holder at any moment in time and that multiple copies cannot be put in circulation. Simple digitization through PDFs, for example, does not provide these assurances. However, blockchain does. Not only does it provide the guarantee that there exists only one copy of the document, but it also allows tracing the transfer of the file along the journey. In 2018, Accenture completed a proof of concept to digitize bills of lading in cooperation with APL Ltd. (owned by the world's third largest container line), the logistics company Kuehne + Nagel, and Danish customs.[25] The proof of concept arguably led to an 80 per cent reduction in efforts associated with managing data related to the bill of lading.[26] While these numbers are difficult to check, the key characteristics of blockchain make it a potentially interesting tool to solve some of the problems associated with electronic bills of lading.

---

[23] Boston Consulting Group and Swift, 'Digital Innovation in Trade Finance – Have We Reached a Tipping Point?', 19 October 2017, available at www.swift.com/news-events/news/digital-innovation-in-trade-finance-have-we-reached-a-tipping-point.

[24] In a proof of concept carried out in 2016, Barclays and fintech startup Wave completed a letter of credit transaction for a shipment of cheese and butter from Ireland to the Seychelles in less than four hours while it usually takes about ten days. See Barclays, 'The Blockchain Revolution in Trade Finance', 30 September 2016, available at www.barclayscorporate.com/insights/innovation/blockchain-revolution-in-trade-finance/. In May 2018, HSBC completed a live letter of credit operation, reducing the time needed to process the transaction to around twenty-four hours. See D. Weinland, 'HSBC Claims First Trade-Finance Deal with Blockchain', *The Financial Times*, 13 May 2018.

[25] 'APL Tests Blockchain Solution', *The Maritime Executive*, 17 March 2018, available at www.maritime-executive.com/article/apl-tests-blockchain-solution.

[26] Author's interview with Accenture in 2018.

Before the advent of blockchain, digitization efforts of companies like essDocs and Bolero mainly focused on digitizing payments and information, essentially via scanned PDF documents. They did little, however, to digitize the transactions themselves.[27] By allowing participants in the network to interact in real time in a highly secure environment, blockchain opens the door to the true digitization of transactions. While the rise of the Internet had a profound impact on the way we communicate, blockchain has the potential to impact transactions. Sometimes called the 'Internet of value', blockchain and distributed ledger technologies are best described in my view as the 'Internet of transactions'. By breaking the various silos that currently exist between the many parties involved in cross-border trade transactions, blockchain could give rise to a 'global asset web' and bring trade globalization to another level.

Beyond these generic considerations on the potential impact of blockchain on international trade, this technology can prove particularly useful for the implementation of the various WTO agreements, as will be explained in the following section.

2 Blockchain Can Help Implement WTO Agreements[28]

Blockchain could help implement various provisions of the recently adopted Trade Facilitation Agreement (TFA). In particular, it could prove useful to enhance inter-agency cooperation, as it allows all participants to interact directly and in quasi real time (Article 8 TFA).[29] It could improve the efficiency of customs clearance processes and reduce the need for manual verification. Requests for advance rulings (Article 3 TFA), if submitted through a blockchain platform, would be securely stored on the blockchain, in a permissioned ledger, and remain accessible at all times by authorized stakeholders, including all customs offices located in the territory, throughout the validity period of the ruling, thereby facilitating the release and clearance process. The sharing of required data on the ledger in real time could facilitate pre-arrival processing and expedited release of goods (Article 7.1 and 7.8 TFA). The use of smart contract could help optimize risk management (Article 7.4 TFA) – customs documents submitted via the system would be immediately and automatically analyzed and assessed on the basis of pre-determined selectivity criteria encoded in a smart contract – and post clearance audit (Article 7.5 TFA), the tamper-proof nature of the technology making it possible to easily track and audit transactions. Blockchain could also help handle temporary admission of goods processes (Article 10.9 TFA). It has also been argued that blockchain could help

---

[27] H. Castell, 'Blockchain in Trade: Are We Missing the Point?', *TXF News*, 8 January 2018.
[28] This section focuses on multilateral WTO agreements. It is worth noting, however, that DLT can also prove interesting in the context of government procurement. See Ganne, note 8.
[29] World Customs Organization, 'Blockchains', Information Management Sub-Committee, 72nd Meeting, 19 April 2017.

administer single windows in a more efficient way (Article 10.4 TFA).[30] Finally, blockchain could facilitate revenue collection through the use of smart contracts and the management of authorized operators status (Article 7 TFA).

In fact, the potential of the technology to facilitate these processes is already being tested. The European Commission carried out a successful proof-of-concept in cooperation with the International Chamber of Commerce (ICC) related to ATA-carnets used for the temporary admission of goods.[31] The Republic of Korea's customs authority is working with e-commerce companies to leverage the technology to accelerate customs clearance of e-commerce goods from these companies, share information in real time, generate automated import customs clearance report to authorities, and prevent fraud and smuggling.[32] A project called Cadena is also underway between Mexico, Peru and Costa Rica with the support of the Inter-American Development Bank to create a common platform for the management of authorized operators (or authorized economic operators, AEOs). Cadena aims to automate the process of sharing AEO data among the parties and remedy some of the problems faced in the implementation of AEO mutual recognition agreements. The problematic areas include manual processes of sharing sensitive and/or confidential data with low standards of security and integrity; the difficulty to establish the provenance and traceability of the data and to guarantee secure access; the inability to grant AEO benefits in real time; and the inability to react in real time when a suspension occurs, with all the consequences that this may have on the security of the supply chain.[33]

Blockchain could also help implement the Import Licensing Agreement in a more efficient way, in particular the provisions on application for import licenses (Article 1.6) and automatic import licensing (Article 2). This information, once added to the ledger, would be directly accessible to all relevant stakeholders – thereby limiting the number of agencies to approach – and the use of smart contracts could automate the granting of licenses. It could also help administer import and export licenses. Such licenses are normally delivered for a set period of time. Storing an import or export licence on a blockchain platform would save the importer or exporter the trouble of having to keep the licence in a safe place to avoid losing it and would allow customs authorities to easily check the authenticity and validity of the permit.[34] Using fake permits would no longer be

[30] Ganne, note 8; Inter-American Development Bank and World Economic Forum, 'Windows of Opportunity: Facilitating Trade with Blockchain Technology', *White Paper*, July 2019.
[31] Z. Saadaoui, 'Digitization of ATA Carnets: How the Blockchain Could Enhance Trust', WCO *Magazine*, 2018.
[32] S. Das, 'Korea Customs Service to Pilot Blockchain-Based Import Customs Platform', CCN, 6 June 2018, available at www.ccn.com/korea-customs-service-blockchain-customs-clearance-platform/.
[33] S. Corcuera-Santamaria, 'Blockchain Platform to Implement MRAs for AEO Programs', *IV AEO Global Conference Kampala*, Uganda, 14–16 March 2018.
[34] Ganne, note 8.

possible.[35] The use of a smart contract could even allow the parties to go one step further by automatically rendering an import/export licence invalid upon expiration of its validity period. This could help fight fraud and avoid situations, as the one with the Philippines in 2016, when the Department of Agriculture cancelled and recalled all import permits on meat products to tackle meat import fraud, having found that old permits were being recycled to smuggle imports.[36]

In the context of the Technical Barriers to Trade (TBT) and Sanitary and Phytosanitary Measures (SPS) agreements, the traceability and transparency features of blockchain can prove interesting to help assess sanitary risks (Article 5 SPS Agreement), prove conformity assessment and manage conformity assessment procedures (Article 5 TBT Agreement), and demonstrate compliance with standards. While traditional labelling systems can be easily manipulated, blockchain provides a highly secure system to prove key characteristics of the products concerned. Numerous start-ups and well-established companies, such as Provenance,[37] Verified Organic[38] or Bext360[39] are turning to blockchain to assert ethical, organic or quality claims. The use of blockchain is also being explored for the granting of e-phyto-certificates to help streamline the approval workflow of such certificates.[40]

Blockchain could facilitate assessment of origin, be it for the purposes of the WTO Agreement on Rules of Origin that applies to non-preferential rules of origin or for the purposes of a preferential trade agreement between two or more parties. Various companies, such as EssDocs[41] and VCargoCloud in Singapore,[42] as well as chambers of commerce in Singapore and Dubai, are testing the technology in relation to certificates of origin.[43] If blockchain traceability from farm or factory to

[35] In December 2017, the National Food Authority (NFA) of the Philippines issued a warning against individuals or entities using fake or fabricated rice import permits following a report that some unscrupulous individuals or parties were selling spurious permits allegedly issued by the NFA under the 2017 minimum access volume private sector rice import scheme. See www.nfa.gov.ph/35-news/1053-nfa-warns-against-fake-rice-import-permits.
[36] A. Fortune, 'Philippines Takes on Meat Import Fraud through Permit Recall', *GlobalMeat News*, 23 November 2016.
[37] www.provenance.org/.
[38] www.verifiedorganic.io/.
[39] www.bext360.com/.
[40] 'Antwerp Blockchain Pilot Pioneers with Secure and Efficient Document Workflow', *Port of Antwerp*, 18 June 2018, available at www.portofantwerp.com/en/news/antwerp-blockchain-pilot-pioneers-secure-and-efficient-document-workflow.
[41] essDOCS, 'Introducing essCert – A Next Generation eCO Solution', *essDOCS News*, 31 May 2018, available at: www.essdocs.com/blog/introducing-esscert-next-generation-eco-solution.
[42] www.vcargocloud.com/.
[43] An important point to note when it comes to certificates of origin is that authentication from chambers of commerce does not attest to the true origin of the product, only to the statement provided to the chambers of commerce by the exporter, leading some to argue that such authentication would, in reality, not be truly necessary. Blockchain would not change this state of affairs. Arguably, the benefits of a blockchain-based system when issuing certificates of origin would be limited to proving that the certificate is authentic – i.e. that it has been delivered by the pertinent authority – and has not been tampered with (Ganne, note 8).

shelf becomes more widely used, the determination of origin could become much easier. One could even imagine a day when certification of origin would rely on blockchain data to be determined directly at the border, without the need for a certificate or origin – provided the systems put into place are accessible by customs authorities and not confined to the internal supply chain of companies.

Another area where blockchain could have a significant impact is intellectual property (IP). Beyond blockchain's potential to provide proof of existence and ownership and to ease registration of IP rights,[44] which are issues of great importance to right holders but not directly relevant in the context of the WTO, as it is the World Intellectual Property Organization (WIPO) that administers the relevant treaties, blockchain can facilitate the implementation of various provisions of the Agreement on Trade-Related Aspects of Intellectual Property Rights (TRIPS). In particular with regard to Articles 51 and 52 TRIPS, blockchain can be of help. Article 51 requests members to put in place procedures to enable right holders to request the suspension by the customs authorities of the release into free circulation of goods that they suspect infringe IP rights. Right holders initiating such procedures must, under Article 52, provide adequate evidence that there is prima facie infringement of the right holder's right. In the same spirit, Article 58 gives WTO members the possibility to authorize customs officials to act upon their own initiative, ex officio, to suspend the release of goods for which there is evidence that IP rights are being infringed.

The difficulty is proving prima facie evidence of infringement. Most customs officials lack expertise in detecting counterfeit goods. Blockchain, when used in combination with QR codes or chips embedded in products to trace provenance, can offer an interesting tool to demonstrate prima facie evidence of infringement. If a brand uses blockchain to record the history of its products, the absence of a tag or an incorrect tag on the product would make it easier for the right holder to provide adequate evidence of infringement and for enforcement officers to detect counterfeits.[45] Various start-ups, such as Provenance, Blockpharma, Blockverify, VeChain and Seal, to name just a few, already offer blockchain-based solutions to help companies producing luxury or fashion products, as well as pharmaceuticals and electronics, fight counterfeit.

Management of IP rights has also been a subject of discussions at the WTO General Council. In December 2016, Brazil submitted a communication calling for 'a decision on the management of copyright towards fair payment for authors and performers' in which WTO members would 'stress the importance of transparency in the remuneration of copyright and related rights in the digital environment'.[46] In

---

[44] Ganne, note 8.
[45] R. Burstall and B. Clark, 'Blockchain, IP, and the Fashion Industry', *Managing Intellectual Property*, 23 March 2017.
[46] WTO, Electronic Commerce and Copyright, Submission by Brazil, JOB/GC/113, 15 December 2016.

a follow-up submission circulated in September 2018, Brazil and Argentina noted that 'information technology could and should facilitate access to real-time data on the use and remuneration of right holders'.[47] Fair remuneration is a particularly acute problem for authors and performers, who often struggle to be paid for their creation, or when they do, often see a large part of their revenue captured by intermediaries, such as record companies, performance rights organizations and streaming digital service providers like Spotify, in the case of music. Blockchain-enabled contracts attached to a creation could allow 'smart management' of IP rights, enabling authors and performers to be paid upon use of their work. UK pop singer Imogen Heap showed the way in 2017 by attaching a smart contract to two of her songs to automatize payments of royalties. She is now working on the creation of a Creative Passport to 'help musicians make money again'.[48]

As this quick overview of blockchain's potential to digitize trade transactions and make trade processes more efficient shows, blockchain's impact on international trade is likely to be wide-ranging and significant. However and as mentioned at the outset of this chapter, technology is only a tool. Without a regulatory environment conducive to its large-scale deployment, the opportunities that blockchain opens to make international trade more efficient could remain unrealized. The next section looks at various regulatory issues that deserve policymakers' particular attention if blockchain is to realize its full potential.

C REGULATORY CONSIDERATIONS AROUND BLOCKCHAIN

Code needs law for recognition, and ultimately, for large-scale adoption. Legal recognition and compliance with existing legal systems is required if blockchain and blockchain-based applications are to be accepted by users as a way to transact with one another and are to have a real value and real-world impact.

Since blockchain belongs to a large category of digital technologies, some of the regulatory issues that it raises are common to other digital technologies – such as for instance the importance of ensuring free data flows.[49] The key characteristics of blockchain, especially its quasi immutability, the ability to use smart contracts, and the possibility for users to have control over their data, opens new opportunities. But they also give rise to specific regulatory issues that deserve particular attention. This section focuses on such issues in the context of legal recognition of e-signatures, e-documents and blockchain transactions; applicable law, liability and enforcement; as well as data localization and data privacy.

---

[47] WTO, Electronic Commerce and Copyright, Submission by Brazil and Argentina, JOB/GC/200/Rev.1, 24 September 2018.
[48] I. Heap, 'Blockchain Could Help Musicians Make Money Again', *Harvard Business Review*, 5 June 2017.
[49] See Chapter 1 in this volume.

I *Legal Recognition of E-Signatures, E-Documents and*
Blockchain Transactions

The large-scale deployment of blockchain requires more than the technology. It requires frameworks that, among other things, recognize e-signatures and e-documents, and clarify the legal status of blockchain transactions.[50] As earlier noted, blockchain has the potential to accelerate the digitalization of trade and to help move towards truly paperless trade. However, full digitization can only become reality if legislation provides for e-authentication methods and for the recognition of e-signatures, e-documents and e-transactions. The adoption of the Model Law on Electronic Signatures in 2001 and the Convention on the Use of Electronic Communications in International Contracts in 2005 – both developed by the United Nations Commission on International Trade Law (UNCITRAL) – was a first step. However, only a limited number of countries have legal provisions for such recognitions: the former treaty has been enacted by thirty-two states, while the latter by eleven states only. Even in countries that provide for such recognitions, commercial buyers, importers or authorities often continue to request paper copies. In many other countries, national legislation has to be adjusted to authorize the access and sharing of information with another administration, even at the national level.[51] The issue of recognition of e-signatures and e-documents is being discussed at the WTO in the context of the WTO Joint Statement on Electronic Commerce that was launched at the Buenos Aires Ministerial Conference in December 2017 and the importance of the issue has been reaffirmed by a series of initiatives in 2019 and 2020.

An important development was the adoption of the UNCITRAL Model Law on Electronic Transferable Records on 13 July 2017,[52] which enables the use of electronic transferable records and sets out the conditions that must be met if an electronic record is to be treated as a transferable document, i.e., a document that entitles the holder to claim fulfilment of the obligation indicated in the document, such as in the case of bills of lading. The principle of neutrality embodied in the Model Law allows the use of all methods and technologies, including distributed ledger technology, to be accommodated.[53] If transposed into national legislation, this text could open the way to the legal use of blockchain for international trade transactions. To date, however, only three jurisdictions have enacted it,[54] and there

---

[50] Ganne, note 8.
[51] Ibid.
[52] United Nations Information Service (UNIS), 'UN Commission on International Trade Law Adopts the UNCITRAL Model Law on Electronic Transferable Records', *Press Release*, 17 July 2017.
[53] K. Takahashi, 'Blockchain Technology for Letters of Credit and Escrow Arrangements', *Banking Law Journal* 135 (2018), 89–103.
[54] Bahrain, Singapore and Abu Dhabi Global Market, a recently-created commercial free zone in the heart of the UAE's capital city.

is still a long way to go towards making this blockchain-enabled environment for transactions real.

Besides general issues related to the legal recognition of e-signatures, e-documents and e-transactions, the legal status of blockchain transactions and smart contracts remains still uncertain, not the least because of a lack of a unanimous definition of the terms 'blockchain' and 'smart contract'.[55] As noted earlier, the term blockchain is often used in its generic sense to refer to DLT but also employed interchangeably to refer to blockchain protocols, services, business applications and platforms, thus creating an unfortunate confusion, especially outside the world of blockchain experts. Initiatives have been launched in various international fora to develop common definitions; work is underway, for instance, at the International Telecommunication Union (ITU) and the International Organization for Standardization (ISO).[56]

Blockchain transactions also raise classification questions[57] – for instance: Does information stored on a blockchain platform representing ownership or the existence of an asset prove real ownership or the real existence of that asset? What is the legal status of blockchain registries?[58] Are existing legal and regulatory frameworks capable of comprehending the growing variety of blockchain applications, concept and use cases?[59] While smart contracts are not legal contracts per se, to what extent can they be legally binding?[60] Various governments are now working on or considering legislation to address blockchain and recognize the legal validity of blockchain and blockchain transactions, smart contracts and financial instruments issued on a blockchain platform. In the United States, since 2018, several states have been working on bills to give legal recognition to blockchain transactions, most of them in the form of legislative amendments. The State of Arizona, for example, passed a bill that qualifies blockchain-enabled signatures as valid electronic signatures.[61] In

---

[55] This chapter focuses on the technology itself, not on cryptocurrencies. One should note, however, that the legal status of cryptocurrencies also varies considerably from country to country. While some countries have explicitly allowed the use of Bitcoin, others have restricted or banned it.

[56] The ITU Telecommunication Standardization Sector established a Focus Group on Application of Distributed Ledger Technology in May 2017 that looks at definition issues and aims to develop a standardization roadmap for interoperable DLT-based services. (See www.itu .int/en/ITU-T/focusgroups/dlt/Pages/default.aspx. As for the ISO, it created a committee in 2016 that also looks at definition and standardization issues; see www.iso.org/committee/ 6266604.html.)

[57] K. Werbach 'Trust, but Verify: Why the Blockchain Needs the Law', *Berkeley Technology Law Journal* 33 (2018), 487–550.

[58] R. Herian, *Legal Recognition of Blockchain Registries and Smart Contracts* (Brussels: EU Blockchain Observatory and Forum, 2018).

[59] Ibid.

[60] R3 and Norton Rose Fulbright, 'Can Smart Contracts Be Legally Binding Contracts', R3 and Norton Rose Fulbright White Paper, November 2016.

[61] N. De, 'Arizona's Governor Signs Latest Blockchain Bill into Law', *CoinDesk*, 5 April 2018, available at www.coindesk.com/arizonas-governor-signs-latest-blockchain-bill-into-law.

Europe, Malta adopted a law in July 2018 to regulate distributed ledger technologies and virtual financial assets, with the goal of promoting Malta as a 'blockchain island';[62] France introduced two bills recognizing blockchain technology in 2016 and 2017.[63] Private sector initiatives are also exploring ways to make smart contracts more flexible.[64] Indeed, one of the fundamental reasons often mentioned to argue that smart contracts cannot, as they currently exist, be considered a wholly viable alternative to existing forms of contracts, is their immutability that goes counter to traditional contract law.[65] Greater flexibility can remedy this.

Overall, despite these various initiatives, there is no coordinated position world-wide on the legal status of blockchain and blockchain-based applications, which gives rise to a risk of regulatory fragmentation that could undermine the deployment of a technology that is built on the premise of breaking silos.

II *Applicable Law, Liability and Enforcement Issues*

Both permissionless and permissioned blockchain applications raise specific issues in terms of applicable jurisdiction, liability and enforcement, although in slightly different terms. As nodes can be located anywhere in the world, establishing which laws and regulations apply to a given application can be challenging, particularly in the case of public permissionless blockchains. Although one could argue that every transaction falls under the jurisdiction of the location of each participant in the network, the anonymous nature of public permissionless block-chains makes it extremely difficult, if not almost impossible, to identify the process-ing entity and to pinpoint the place where the contentious transaction was made. The problem is less acute in the case of permissioned blockchains, as participants are known, and the governing law can be determined as part of the governance structure of the blockchain platform.[66]

Blockchain applications also raise issues related to liability and the resolution mechanism in case of conflict, technical problems or unintentional action. While in a private/consortium blockchain, there is clear ownership and responsibility, this

---

[62] A. Alexandre, 'Malta Passes Blockchain Bills into Law, "Confirming Malta as the Blockchain Island"', *Cointelegraph*, 5 July 2018, available at https://cointelegraph.com/news/malta-passes-blockchain-bills-into-law-confirming-malta-as-the-blockchain-island.

[63] In 2016, France introduced legislative changes to recognize certain mini-bonds issued on blockchains, and in December 2017, it passed a new order to allow for the registration and the transfer of financial securities through distributed ledger technology. See Utilisation d'un dispositif d'enregistrement électronique partagé pour la représentation et la transmission de titres financiers, ordonnance No 2017-1674 (2017).

[64] The *ERC1538: Transparent Contract Standard* developed by Ethereum designers, for example, seeks to make contract terms ('functions') possible. See N. Mudge, 'ERC1538: Transparent Contract Standard #1538', *GitHub*, 31 October 2018, available at https://github.com/ethereum/EIPs/issues/1538.

[65] Herian, note 59; R3 and Norton Rose Fulbright, note 61.

[66] Ganne, note 8.

is not the case in a public blockchain. Furthermore, the ability to enforce smart contracts via traditional means is limited, not least because it requires the parties to the transaction to be known, which in the case of public permissionless blockchains is challenging. Assuming the parties to a given smart contract are known, the only way to reverse the undesirable outcomes of the coded and executed smart contract would be to create a new smart contract. In the case of permissioned blockchains, rules governing the functioning of the platform, the use of smart contracts and dispute resolution can be established as part of the governance structure of the platform, but the issue remains wide open in the case of public permissionless blockchains.

Specific liability frameworks may also have to be developed to address the needs of certain types of transactions. In the context of international trade, letters of credit, for example, are governed by a specific set of rules developed by the ICC – the Uniform Customs and Practice for Documentary Credits (UCP600). In a blockchain system using smart contracts, who would have liability at each stage of the process? Likewise, information required for customs clearance usually has to be submitted by a single declarant, who is liable. In a blockchain system, information can be added by various stakeholders making it impossible to pin down a single declarant, unless the regulatory framework is adjusted to clarify liability issues.[67]

Beyond liability issues, another important point is the extent to which blockchain-based transactions can be considered admissible evidence by a court.[68] An interesting development in this respect is the ruling by China's Supreme Court, in September 2018, that evidence authenticated with blockchain is binding in legal disputes.[69] While this ruling is an undeniable step forward, it will not solve all issues. Indeed, unless the true identity of the participant in the transaction is identified, which in the case of public blockchains is complicated, courts may have concerns about blockchain-based transactions being admissible evidence.

III *Cross-Border Data Flows, Data Localization and Data Privacy Issues*

The increased digitization of our economies, fuelled by the rise of the Internet and of digital technologies, such as artificial intelligence (AI), has brought the issue of cross-border data flows to the forefront of trade policy.[70] Despite the growing importance of data and data flows for economic activity, many countries have

---

[67] Ibid.
[68] J. S. Cermeno, 'Blockchain in Financial Services: Regulatory Landscape and Future Challenges for Its Commercial Application', BBVA Research Paper No 16 (2016).
[69] M. Huillet, 'China's Supreme Court Rules That Blockchain Can Legally Authenticate Evidence', *Cointelegraph*, 7 September 2018.
[70] See Chapter 1 in this volume.

adopted measures that impose requirements or restrictions on data flows.[71] These requirements can either be explicitly required by law or can be the result of a series of restrictions that make it de facto impossible to transfer data, such as local storage requirements, local processing of the data or government approval to transfer data. Some countries prohibit all data transfers, while others target specific sectors or services. As for barriers to cross-border data flows, they typically involve restrictions on the transfer of personal data to jurisdictions deemed to provide a lower level of data protection, as well as limitations on information that governments consider 'sensitive'. Governments' motivations for putting in place such policies are diverse and include the wish to protect citizens' privacy, ensure access to data for the purposes of law enforcement, and promote the local economy, as well as potential cybersecurity concerns. It is pertinent to ask to what extent blockchain transactions are likely to be affected by such policies.

1 Data Localization Restrictions Can Impact Blockchain, Although to a Limited Extent

Because of their distributed nature, blockchains de facto fulfil local storage and local data processing requirements: in a blockchain, all participants in the network have a local copy of the transactions and every fully participating node must process every transaction. Requirements that take the form of government approval to transfer data would however impede the participation of entities or individuals from the countries concerned in cross-border blockchain applications and thereby undermine the potential of this technology to create a global asset web. Hence, although certain types of requirements on data flows may not directly affect them, blockchain applications are not completely immune from restrictions in this area. The cross-border nature of blockchain does require free cross-border data flows. Lack of a common approach on these issues, and the regulatory fragmentation that would result from it, would ultimately impede the development of a technology that holds high promises to facilitate cross-border transactions at a global level. Discussions on this issue are taking place in the context of the WTO joint initiative on e-commerce.[72] However, at the time of writing, it remained uncertain how potential obligations would shape up, as the position of participants in the initiative differ substantially on the issue of data flows and data localization.

---

[71] See Chapter 3 in this volume.
[72] See the proposals submitted by Brazil (INF/ECOM/27); Canada (INF/ECOM/34); the European Union (INF/ECOM/22); Republic of Korea (INF/ECOM/31); Japan (INF/ECOM/20); Singapore (INF/ECOM/25); Chinese Taipei (INF/ECOM/24); and the United States (INF/ECOM/23).

2 Data Privacy

With the rise of the digital economy, issues related to data privacy have become a key concern. Blockchain opens new opportunities in this respect and is an interesting innovation for personal data management, but it also gives rise to an intense debate regarding the potential non-compliance of blockchain with data protection regulations, in particular the EU's General Data Protection Regulation (GDPR).[73] The relationship between blockchain and data privacy is, therefore, both promising and challenging.

A BLOCKCHAIN AS A NEW TOOL FOR DATA SOVEREIGNTY AND PROTECTION Blockchain is often presented as an opportunity or catalyst for better personal data protection and new forms of identity management. While in today's world, service providers like Instagram, Snapchat and Facebook control our online identity and use our data without us necessarily knowing it, sometimes even misusing it,[74] blockchain gives users control over their data, allowing them to manage and share it only with trusted parties. This is often referred to as 'self-sovereign identity', whereby the usage of one's personal data is controlled by the owner of the identity.[75] Various companies, such as Sovrin, are now offering services leveraging blockchain to allow individuals to collect, hold and choose which identity credentials to use – such as a driver's license or employment credential – without relying on individual siloed databases that manage the access to those credentials.[76]

One must, however, distinguish here between public and consortium/private blockchains. While public blockchains enable the users themselves to implement the principle of 'privacy by design' at an individual level,[77] consortium/private blockchains provide for this principle at the platform level, as the privacy protection levels are determined by the management of the platform. On such platforms, participants are known and identified, but permissions to read and write some of the data added to the platform can be restricted to certain participants in order to protect confidentiality. Blockchain is thus an interesting innovation for personal data management but it also raises some challenges.

---

[73] Regulation 2016/679 of the European Parliament and of the Council of 27 April 2016 on the Protection of Natural Persons with Regard to the Processing of Personal Data and on the Free Movement of Such Data, and Repealing Directive 95/46/EC [hereinafter: General Data Protection Regulation or GDPR], OJ L [2016] 119/1.

[74] J. Sadowski, 'Companies Are Making Money from Our Personal Data, But at What Cost?', *The Guardian*, 31 August 2016.

[75] O. Jacobovitz, 'Blockchain for Identity Management', Ben-Gurion University Technical Report 02 (2016); C. Sullivan and E. Burger, 'E-Residency and Blockchain', *Computer Law and Security Review* 33 (2017), 470–481.

[76] https://sovrin.org.

[77] A. Biryukov et al., 'Deanonymisation of Clients in Bitcoin P2P Network', Cornell University Working Paper (2014).

B COULD DATA PROTECTION REGULATIONS BLOCK BLOCKCHAIN? Data protection legislations have flourished around the world with the objective of giving individuals greater control over the way their data is processed and ensuring that their data is safe and secure. Almost 60 per cent of countries have put in place legislation to secure the protection of data and privacy, and another 10 per cent have draft legislation.[78] Probably the most well-known of these laws is EU's GDPR, whose entry into force on 25 May 2018 has unleashed heated discussions regarding the possible incompatibility of blockchain with GDPR provisions, leading some to claim that GDPR could 'block' or 'kill' blockchain.[79]

The GDPR applies to the processing of all personal data of data subjects in the European Union, unless data has been anonymized, with personal data defined as 'any information relating to an identified or identifiable natural person'.[80] The process of anonymization requires not only to make it impossible to identify the person, but it must also be irreversible.[81] Non-anonymous data, including 'pseudonymous' data, remains subject to the GDPR. The question therefore arises whether blockchain characteristics make it possible to anonymize data, which would exempt blockchain data from the scope of the GDPR. There is an intense debate within the community regarding the various techniques that could be used to anonymize data. The use of asymmetric encryption (private and public key encryption) does not ensure irreversibility. Research has shown that public keys can be traced back to the IP address to de-anonymize users – although the problem is not inherent to the technology and could be addressed by fixing the technical design of the blockchain.[82] Hashing, which is heavily used in blockchain, offers better prospects, but does not guarantee full anonymization. Although hashing is a non-reversible encryption technique, reversibility and linkability risks can exist under specific circumstances, making it still possible to identify users.[83] Such risks need to be assessed on a case-by-case basis.[84] More advanced cryptographic techniques are being developed that can be viable in the mid-term, such as Zero-Knowledge Proof (ZKP), which allows one party to produce a proof of statement without disclosing the data underlying that statement. This method makes it possible,

---

[78] UNCTAD, 'Data Protection and Privacy Legislation Worldwide', available at: https://unctad .org/en/Pages/DTL/STI_and_ICTs/ICT4D-Legislation/eCom-Data-Protection-Laws.aspx.

[79] S. Johnson 'Will GDPR Compliance Kill Blockchain?', *Medium*, 4 July 2018; A. Toth, 'Will GDPR Block Blockchain?', *World Economic Forum*, 24 May 2018.

[80] Article 4(1) GDPR.

[81] T. Lyons, L. Courcelas and K. Timsit, *Blockchain and the GDPR* (Brussels: European Union Blockchain Observatory and Forum, 2018).

[82] Biryukov et al., note 79.

[83] A reversibility risk could exist, for example, if the original data is of a known and relatively small size (although some techniques exist to mitigate this risk). A linkability risk can exist if the recorded hash is the same every time because a given user orders a transaction, making it possible to analyze times and frequency and to uncover personal data. See Lyons et al., note 83.

[84] Ibid.

for example, to prove that person X lives in Geneva without disclosing their exact address.

Two key provisions of the GDPR seem a priori incompatible with blockchain, namely the 'right to rectification' and the 'right to be forgotten' – i.e., the right to rectify or obtain the erasure of personal data.[85] Indeed, the quasi-immutable nature of blockchains makes it very difficult to update, erase, change or correct data. The GDPR, however, does not specify what constitutes erasure. Some in the community argue that a possible solution is to keep personal data off the chain, with only its evidence (cryptographic hash) exposed to the chain, thereby maintaining the integrity of the transaction while making it possible to erase the transaction itself. The deletion of the data stored externally would mean that the hash stored on the blockchain would point to a location that has been deleted. In addition, in a report published in September 2018, the French National Commission on Informatics and Liberty (CNIL) noted that some encryption techniques, coupled with key destruction, can potentially be considered erasure, 'without resulting in strictly identical effects'.[86]

Beyond these two most well-known and emblematic provisions of the GDPR, other GDPR provisions stand in tension with the way blockchains operate. Indeed, whereas the GDPR was designed for a world where data is centrally collected, stored and processed, blockchains decentralize these processes.[87] Under the GDPR 'data controllers' (the party that determines the purposes and means of processing particular personal data) and 'processors' (party responsible for processing personal data on behalf of the controller, such as an outsourced provider) have distinct obligations. Determining "who is what" is necessary to assess obligations but can be challenging in a blockchain context.

Data controllers have obligations to process personal data lawfully or face stiff consequences that can be fines as high as EUR 20 million or 4 per cent of a company's worldwide annual turnover,[88] and they should do everything to ensure that the data is secure. They also have obligations in terms of where the data processing takes place. Under the GDPR, personal data can only be transferred to third countries if they are deemed to provide data protection that is 'adequate' or equivalent to that in the EU, for example, if the organization receiving the data is covered by an agreement The ECJ declared this agreement invalid in July 2020 or where bespoke contractual protections are put in place, such as the EU's 'model clauses'. Whereas identifying the controller and processor is relatively easy in traditional cloud computing systems –

---

[85] Articles 16 and 17 GDPR.
[86] CNIL, 'Blockchain et RGPD: quelles solutions pour un usage responsable en présence de données personnelles ?', *Commission Nationale de l'Informatique et des Libertés (CNIL)*, 24 September 2018.
[87] M. Finck, *Blockchain Regulation and Governance in Europe* (Cambridge: Cambridge University Press, 2019).
[88] Article 83(5) GDPR.

typically those uploading personal data to the cloud environment are the controllers
and the operators of the cloud system are the processor – the collective processing of
data in the context of blockchains makes it difficult to define whether the users are
controllers or processors. This is particularly true for public permissionless blockchains.[89] While it is generally admitted that protocol developers should not be considered data controllers because they simply created the tool, there is a debate regarding
validating or participating nodes[90] and smart contract users. As for network users, it is
generally admitted that if they submit personal data as part of a business activity, they
could be considered data controllers, but if they submit their own personal data for their
own personal use, they are likely to fall under the household exemption of the GDPR.[91]
The debate has not been settled yet, which has implications for other rights of data
subjects under the GDPR, in particular the right of access – i.e., the right for users to
enquire of a data controller if their personal data is being processed and if it is, to receive
certain details about how this is being done.[92] If the controller is not identified, users
cannot properly exercise their rights.

Blockchain GDPR compliance issues are critically important both because of the
extraterritorial nature of the GDPR,[93] but also because of the cross-border nature of
most blockchain platforms. Interestingly, while blockchains and the GDPR seem
incompatible at a conceptual level, both pursue the same goal of giving individuals
more control over their personal data, but through different mechanisms. Some
have argued that consideration could be given to whether the GDPR's underlying
objectives could be achieved through means other than those originally envisaged to
avoid asphyxiating the development of a technology that holds great promises.[94]
CNIL, who was one of the first authorities to officially address the matter,
announced that it would work cooperatively with other European data protection

[89] In the case of private/consortium blockchains, controllers can be identified as part of the
governance design structure of the blockchain platform. CNIL actually recommends that
blockchain consortiums identify the controller or joint controllers early on in the project.
[90] Some argue that these nodes are simply running the protocol in the hope of winning a reward,
and that they do not determine the purpose of means of processing. Others, however, note that
they should be considered controllers because they are actively running the software and may
influence how the platform evolves, for example by choosing – or not – to run a new version of
a protocol that is being released.
[91] Lyons et al., note 83.
[92] Article 15 GDPR.
[93] A non-EU organization can fall in the scope of the GDPR if it is offering goods or services to
individuals in the EU. A Canadian web shop with a website in French and English that
processes multiple orders a day from individuals in the EU and ships to the EU would fall in
the scope of the GDPR, even though that web shop has no establishment in the EU and is not
performing any data processing activities within the EU. Whether the services offered are paid
or for free does not matter. In other words, a Canadian free cloud storage service must comply
with all the obligations of the GDPR, if the service is also offered to users within the EU.
[94] M. Finck, 'Blockchains and Data Protection in the European Union', *European Data Protection
Law Review* 4 (2018), 17–35.

authorities 'to suggest a strong and harmonized approach'.[95] It may also be worth noting that blockchain's built-in tracking and auditability functions could help organizations comply more easily with other GDPR provisions on internal record-keeping requirements.[96]

While the GDPR only has limited direct relevance to international trade in goods, as most information contained in trade documents relates to companies, not individuals, it could nevertheless impact trade in specific situations, when the contact details of a person at a firm need to be given (e.g., for exports of dangerous goods). Ultimately, the need to find a compromise between ensuring legal protection of personal data and encouraging innovation is one issue that regulators need to grapple with, as the current discussions in the European Union but also on trade negotiation tables show.[97]

D DEVISING A WAY FORWARD

Blockchain is a promising technology whose impact on international trade could be multifaceted and significant. While the years immediately following the release of the first distributed ledger technology have been years of exploration through proofs of concepts, many of which did not go beyond the concept stage, projects have now started to move into production. Gartner predicts that the phase of 'irrational exuberance, few high profile successes' that we have experienced, will be followed between 2022 and 2026 by a phase of 'larger focused investments, many successful models', and that after 2026 the technology will be a 'global large-scale economic value-add', which could deliver US$30 trillion of value worldwide by 2030.[98] Given the potentially significant impact that the technology could have on economic activity and international trade, it is important that regulators start thinking about the practical and legal implications of blockchain on international trade and ways to support the deployment of the technology while preserving their legitimate right to regulate.

This section discusses the need for the creation of a regulatory environment conducive to the development of the technology through polycentric co-regulation. It then proposes various actions that could be taken at the level of the WTO.

I *The Need for a Conducive Regulatory Environment*

While regulating too early is not desirable as it could stifle the development of a technology that is still maturing – or worse, fail to adequately regulate its use –

---

[95] CNIL, note 88.
[96] Ibid.
[97] Ganne, note 8. See also Chapter 9 in this volume.
[98] R. Kandaswamy and D. Furlonger, 'Blockchain-Based Transformation', A Gartner Trend Insights Report, 27 March 2018.

legislators cannot afford to do nothing in the face of the rapid changes that are under way. Regulation can be important, if not indispensable, for the large-scale deployment of the technology.

1 Regulation as an Enabler

Technology and regulation are often 'posed as adversaries'.[99] Yet, technology and innovation need regulation to thrive. The history of the Internet shows that companies might eventually welcome regulation, as it allows them to operate in a more predictable environment and to build consumer confidence.[100] Code needs to be legally recognized to build value and trust.[101] This holds true for blockchain as well. Blockchain has the potential to truly digitize trade transactions, but it is only a tool. As seen in the previous sections, without a regulatory framework that provides, for example, for the legal recognition of e-signatures, e-documents and blockchain transactions, and that clarifies liability issues, digitization of trade will remain wishful thinking and technology adoption will not occur.

Legal certainty not only allows stakeholders to evolve within a more predictable environment and gives them tools to achieve what they are thriving for, it also stimulates innovation. The Porter hypothesis, formulated by the economist Michael Porter in 1995, suggests that strict environmental regulations induce efficiency and encourage innovations that help improve commercial competitiveness. Yet, over-regulating would be counterproductive and would asphyxiate innovation. Striking the right balance is critical.

2 The Challenge of Blockchain Regulation

The rise of the Internet challenged regulators to think out of the box and to devise new regulatory approaches. Regulating blockchain is likely to be equally, if not more, challenging, given the intrinsic characteristics of the technology.[102] First, blockchain is inherently transnational by nature, which means that unilateral action anchored in territorial jurisdiction makes little sense and could, in the absence of global coordination, lead to damaging regulatory fragmentation. Second, blockchains are decentralized networks that function on a peer-to-peer basis, rendering their evolution hard to predict. This is different from the Internet, which although with a distributed architecture has physical elements – in particular the regulatory

---

[99] Finck, note 96.
[100] J. Wiener, 'The Regulation of Technology, and the Technology of Regulation', *Technology in Society* 26 (2004), 483–500.
[101] Finck, note 96.
[102] Ibid.

access points are centralized, making its regulation possible.[103] Third, in a traditional environment the decentralized and distributed nature of blockchain, combined with its high level of security and immutability, allow actors who would not transact directly because of lack of trust, to interact on a peer-to-peer basis. This is particularly important in the case of international trade where transactions involve dozens of actors along the supply chain who usually hold their own registries and follow their own processes. Blockchain has the potential to break these sectoral silos but will only be able to do so if regulation is developed at a cross-sectoral level. As noted earlier, various consortia have emerged to facilitate trade finance, transportation and logistics. However, these platforms follow their own logic and, for the time being, do not talk to each other – be it at the technological level, or at the level of semantics, data models and processes.[104] Fourth, public blockchains are built on the premise of greater anonymity and last but not least, the world of blockchain is a multifaceted and fast evolving world. It is therefore critical that regulators proactively educate themselves, closely follow developments and work with the private sector to devise collective solutions to build a regulatory environment that promotes the technology rather than impedes it. Critically, regulating blockchain does not mean regulating the technology itself but rather its specific use cases.

Regulatory approaches followed so far vary widely across jurisdictions, not only between national jurisdictions, but sometimes even between federal and state jurisdictions, as in the case of the United States. Many jurisdictions have opted for a wait-and-see approach to allow time to observe developments, with some taking a proactive observatory approach. This is the case of the European Union, which launched the EU Blockchain Observatory Forum in February 2018 to actively monitor developments, collect use cases and consult with experts and practitioners in the field before developing specific policies.[105] Some have chosen to issue guidance, such as the guidelines on Initial Coin Offerings (ICO) published by Switzerland,[106] while others have developed new legislation, either in the form of amendments to existing laws or standalone legislation, such as the Liechtenstein 'Tokens and TT Service Providers Law', also referred to as Blockchain Act, which entered into force in January 2020.

Various jurisdictions have also launched regulatory 'sandboxes', i.e. government-backed initiatives that allow live time-bound testing of innovations under a regulator's oversight. Regulatory sandboxes aim at testing and encouraging innovation by minimizing legal uncertainty while allowing regulators to stay abreast of new business ideas and products, and to learn where they might need to update or fill

[103] A. Guadamuz, *Networks, Complexity and Internet Regulation: Scale-Free Law* (Cheltenham: Edward Elgar, 2011), at 89.
[104] For more information on this issue, see Ganne, note 8.
[105] www.eublockchainforum.eu/.
[106] 'FINMA Publishes ICO Guidelines', *Swiss Financial Market Supervisory Authority (FINMA)*, 16 February 2018.

in gaps in existing regulatory frameworks. Typical features of regulatory sandboxes include customized rules for each firm/business proposal, rather than a one-size-fits-all approach; a limited number of customers/clients, testing for a limited time period, and safeguards for consumer protection (such as requirements to obtain informed consent); restricted authorization/licensing, individual guidance, waivers/modifications to rules for that project, and no enforcement action letters.[107] The UK Financial Conduct Authority (FCA) introduced the first regulatory sandbox specific to blockchain in 2016.[108] Other have followed the UK approach: among them are Australia, Canada, Denmark, Honk Kong, China, Malaysia, South Africa, Switzerland, Chinese Taipei, and more recently Brazil.[109] While regulatory sandboxes break new ground, one of their key drawbacks is their limited jurisdictional scope. Of greater interest would be the creation of a multi-jurisdictional regulatory sandbox. This is what the Global Financial Innovation Network (GFIN), which was formally launched in January 2019, aims to do.[110]

Finally, some jurisdictions have chosen the path of regulatory cooperation.[111] Singapore regulators are working with the Hong Kong Monetary Authority to develop a transnational blockchain-based trade finance system.[112] Twenty-one EU member states and Norway have signed a declaration on the establishment of a European Blockchain Partnership in April 2018, in the context of which they agreed to cooperate closely to prevent fragmented approaches, and ensure interoperability and wider deployment of blockchain-based services.[113]

While testing and flexibility are important, in particular in the early days of technological innovation, so is some degree of regulatory convergence as the technology matures and projects move into the production phase. The transnational nature of blockchain means that regulatory action cannot be confined to the national level. When it comes to international trade, its potential cross-sectoral impact means that it cannot be confined to certain sectors either. A transnational, trans-sectoral approach is necessary.

---

[107] K. Agarwal, 'Playing in the Regulatory Sandbox', *New York University Journal of Law and Business Online*, 8 January 2018.

[108] 'Regulatory Sandbox', *Financial Conduct Authority (FCA)*, 11 May 2015, available at www.fca.org.uk/firms/regulatory-sandbox.

[109] D. Aguilar, 'Brazilian Financial Authorities Announce Regulatory Sandbox for Blockchain', *CoinDesk*, 17 June 2019, available at www.coindesk.com/brazil-financial-authorities-announce-regulatory-sandbox-for-blockchain.

[110] The GFIN is a network of thirty-eight financial regulators and related organizations. See 'Global Financial Innovation Network (GFIN)', *Financial Conduct Authority (FCA)*, 31 January 2019, available at www.fca.org.uk/firms/global-financial-innovation-network.

[111] Finck, note 96.

[112] E. Barreto, 'Hong Kong, Singapore to Link Up Trade Finance Blockchain Platforms', *Reuters*, 25 October 2017.

[113] European Commission, 'European Countries Join Blockchain Partnership', *Press Release*, 10 April 2018.

II *The Need for Blockchain Polycentric Governance*

Because of its decentralized and distributed nature, blockchain requires a matching decentralized and distributed governance system, which some experts call poly-centric co-regulation[114] or polycentric governance.[115] This is a system whereby regulation is entrusted to parties which are recognized in the field and relies on the fragmentation of authority and power sharing.[116]

The multi-stakeholder approach that governs the Internet provides an interesting model of polycentric governance that could serve as an inspiration for blockchain governance. Internet governance relies on a series of 'global governance networks' that bring together companies, civil society organizations, software developers, academics and governments and that operates on consensus.[117] These networks include Standards networks, which are non-state, non-profit organizations in charge of developing technical specifications and standards; knowledge networks that conduct research and propose new ideas to help solve global problems; delivery networks, such as the Internet Corporation for Assigned Names and Numbers (ICANN), which is a public–private partnership that delivers Internet domain names and is dedicated to preserving the operational stability of the Internet; policy networks that inform the policy debate and support policy development; advocacy networks that seek to influence the agenda or policies of governments, corporations and other institutions; watchdog networks; and networked institutions, such as the Internet Society, which defines itself as a 'global cause-driven' organization dedi-cated to ensuring that the Internet remains 'open, globally connected and secure'.[118]

Some networks have started to emerge in the blockchain space, such as the Blockchain Research Institute,[119] the Blockchain Interoperability Alliance,[120] and the International Association for Trusted Blockchain Applications (INATBA).[121] But much remains to be done to put in place a proper governance system that would bring together companies, civil society organizations, software developers, academics, think-tanks, governments and international organizations in various

---

[114] Finck, note 96.
[115] S. Shackelford et al., 'When Toasters Attack: A Polycentric Approach to Enhancing the Security of Things', *University of Illinois Law Review* 2 (2017), 415–475, at 439.
[116] See Chapter 4 in this volume.
[117] D. Tapscott and A. Tapscott, 'Realizing the Potential of Blockchain: A Multistakeholder Approach to the Stewardship of Blockchain and Cryptocurrencies', World Economic Forum White Paper, June 2017.
[118] See www.internetsociety.org/.
[119] www.blockchainresearchinstitute.org/.
[120] S. Higgins, 'New Alliance Sets Out to Boost Blockchain Interoperability', *CoinDesk*, 28 November 2017, available at www.coindesk.com/new-alliance-sets-out-to-boost-blockchain-interoperability.
[121] https://inatba.org/.

configurations in an effort to develop collective solutions to existing challenges and thereby support the large-scale deployment of the technology.

III *What Role for the WTO?*

Because it is the only global body that deals with all aspects of international trade, the WTO is uniquely positioned to promote and contribute to the development of a 'trade-enabling' regulatory framework for blockchain. Some issues of direct relevance to blockchain are already being discussed at the WTO in the context of the Joint Statement initiative on electronic commerce, in particular the recognition of e-signatures, e-documents, as well as the question of cross-border data flows. However, more could be done to specifically address the needs of the blockchain space in relation to international trade. In particular, the WTO could choose to actively monitor developments in that sphere, foster multi-stakeholder cooperation and governance, and promote regulatory advances.

1 Monitoring Blockchain Developments Related to International Trade

The world of blockchain is evolving extremely fast. One of the challenges for regulators is to keep abreast of developments, be they at the legislative level or at the level of applications for international trade. Fostering transparency of WTO members' trade regime lies at the heart of the WTO work and over the years has become an increasingly important feature of the global trading system.[122] Monitoring of legislative developments related to blockchain could be performed as part of the WTO Trade Policy Review process to keep track of the evolution of the blockchain regulatory environment at the national level. In addition, standalone reports that would provide regular updates on latest developments at the level of applications (creation of blockchain consortia, developments in trade finance, etc.) would allow regulators to get a better understanding of the scope of the changes. Such reports could be prepared in the context of the WTO committees work or as part of the research function of the WTO. Closely monitoring developments at these two levels would help trade officials build expertise in an area that remains very complex for many to apprehend.

---

[122] All WTO agreements contains provisions on transparency and members have called for enhanced transparency provisions in virtually every negotiation held since the establishment of the WTO. Transparency issues are also a central feature of current discussions on WTO reform. Transparency goes hand in hand with monitoring of trade policies. The monitoring function of the WTO has evolved significantly since the 1980s. The original 'regular and systematic review of developments in the trading system' via Secretariat notes was replaced by the Trade Policy Review Mechanism, and a new trade monitoring mechanism was put in place following the 2008 global financial crisis to counter off protectionist pressure and ensure adherence to WTO rules. See P. Pedersen et al., 'WTO Trade Monitoring Ten Years on Lessons Learned and Challenges Ahead', WTO Staff Working Paper No 07 (2018).

2 Fostering Multi-stakeholder Cooperation and Governance

Given the transformative impact that blockchain technology could have on international trade and its transnational and trans-sectoral nature, fostering a multi-stakeholders' dialogue that brings together companies, governments and international organizations, as well as civil society organizations, academics and think-tanks to try and develop collective solutions to existing challenges is of paramount importance.[123] Being a global player on international trade, the WTO could be a catalyst for such a dialogue on trade issues. It could play the role of convener or facilitator on issues related to international trade with a view to promoting a coordinated approach for blockchain and global trade. The creation of a WTO Global Trade and Blockchain Forum[124] that brings together representatives from the private sector, governments, civil society organizations and international organizations working on trade and blockchain issues is a step in that direction.

Greater coordination among international organizations working on trade-related blockchain projects would also be welcome. Virtually all international organizations are conducting work on blockchain, often in a siloed manner. Discussions are taking place at the WCO and UN/CEFACT to look into the potential of the technology for border procedures and trade facilitation. Both the ISO and the ITU have put in place working groups to discuss issues related to definitions and standards, as noted earlier. The Organisation for Economic Co-operation and Development (OECD) created a Blockchain Knowledge Center, and the World Bank is involved in various blockchain projects with the support of their Blockchain Center. In April 2020, the International Chamber of Commerce launched Digital Standards Initiative (DSI) with the support of Enterprise Singapore and the Asian Development Bank to develop digital standards to establish a globally harmonized, digitized trade environment.[125] Different UN organizations are also working on various blockchain projects. To promote synergies and ensure a minimum level of coordination between the various initiatives taken at an international level, an informal expert group composed of high-level officials of the various international organizations working on blockchain projects could be established – along the lines of the WTO Expert Group on Trade Finance that meets once a year.

3 Promoting a Conducive Regulatory Environment

Finally, various actions could be taken at a regulatory level to foster the move to paperless trade. References to the UNCITRAL Model Laws on Electronic

[123] Ganne, note 8.
[124] The first edition took place in Geneva on 2 and 3 December 2019.
[125] 'Digital Trade Standards Initiative launches under the umbrella of ICC', *ICC News*, 3 April 2020.

Transferable Records (2017), on Electronic Commerce (1996, revised in 1998), and on Electronic Signatures (2001), and to the Convention on the Use of Electronic Communications in International Contracts (2005) could be incorporated in WTO law to foster their transposition into national law. As noted earlier, various international organizations, such as ISO and the ITU, are working on developing blockchain standards, including standard definitions. Other organizations, like UN/CEFACT and the ICC DSI, are developing digital standards specifically related to trade. As is the case for TBT and SPS, WTO members could be invited to use such standards when designing national legislation relevant to blockchain and trade. Beyond monitoring through the Trade Policy review mechanism, a more proactive approach could also be followed, whereby WTO members would be encouraged to notify to the WTO any regulatory changes pertinent to blockchain.

The most natural fit for such provisions would, in the current context, be the ongoing Joint Statement Initiative on e-commerce/digital trade, with the obvious drawback that these discussions do not involve all WTO members.[126] If the political context permits, one could at some point envisage the incorporation of such provisions in a multilateral document, which could take the form of a Code of Good Practice, along the lines of the TBT Code of Good Practice annexed to the TBT Agreement.

E CONCLUSION

The future of trade depends as much on technological progress as on the way regulation will shape technological innovation. The transnational nature of blockchain is pushing existing boundaries and challenging traditional regulatory approaches. Its global nature requires global regulatory approaches. In a world where people can transact on a peer-to-peer basis across jurisdictions, regulatory action cannot be confined to the national level. Blockchain could have a major impact on international trade. By making it possible to break existing sectoral silos, it could bring trade globalization to another level – provided regulatory action takes place at a cross-sectoral level. A transnational, trans-sectoral approach that involves the various stakeholders involved in international trade, from traders, shippers, banks, government authorities, but also international organizations, academics and civil society organizations, is necessary for blockchain's full potential to be realized.

The WTO is uniquely positioned to foster and contribute to this multi-stakeholders' dialogue. It can help raise awareness and understanding of the technology by monitoring blockchain developments and can play a pivotal role in promoting the

---

[126] As of March 2019, seventy-seven WTO members have joined the e-commerce initiative.

development of a conducive regulatory and governance framework to support the large-scale deployment of a technology that holds high promises to truly transform international trade. Where the blockchain adventure will ultimately take us is difficult to predict, but one thing is certain: regulation will play a key role in shaping the outcome.

7

TRIPS Meets Big Data

*Daniel J. Gervais**

'Artificial intelligence is another emerging area focusing in IPR protection, used mostly in the tech industry, producing new products and services every year. Artificial intelligence (AI) will redefine how individuals think about daily life, and start-ups will need to start leveraging AI to get ahead.'[1]

Even as the United States is playing 'hard ball' at the World Trade Organization (WTO) in the area of dispute settlement, the quote demonstrates its willingness to engage in discussions on the topic of artificial intelligence at the WTO. The United States is not alone. In this chapter, I review some of the work done at on AI and big data in the WTO and in particular under the Agreement on Trade-Related Intellectual Property Rights (TRIPS),[2] and reflect on how this work is likely to progress. I begin, however, by defining the topic.

A DEFINING BIG DATA AND AI[3]

The term 'big data' can be defined in a number of ways. A common way to define it is to enumerate its three essential features, a fourth that, though not essential, is increasingly typical, and a fifth that is derived from the other three (or four). Those

---

* Daniel J. Gervais, PhD, MAE, is the Milton R. Underwood Chair in Law and Director of the Intellectual Property Program,Vanderbilt Law School, as well as Professor of Information Law, University of Amsterdam. Contact: daniel.gervais@vanderbilt.edu.
[1] Summary of Statement by the United States, Council for Trade-Related Aspects of Intellectual Property Rights, Minutes of Meeting held in the Centre William Rappard, 8–9 November 2018, IP/C/M/90/Add.1, 15 January 2019, at para. 363.
[2] Agreement on Trade-Related Aspects of Intellectual Property Rights, 1869 U.N.T.S. 299; 33 I.L.M. 1197 (1994), entered into force 1 January 1995 [hereinafter: TRIPS].
[3] An earlier version of this part of the chapter appeared in the *Journal of Intellectual Property, Information Technology and Electronic Commerce Law* in 2019.

features are volume, veracity, velocity, variety, and value.[4] 'Volume' or size is, as the
term big data suggests, the first characteristic that distinguishes big data from other
('small data') datasets. Because big data corpora are often generated automatically,
the question of the quality or trustworthiness of the data ('veracity') is crucial.
'Velocity' refers to 'the speed at which corpora of data are being generated, collected
and analyzed'.[5] The term 'variety' denotes the many types of data and data sources
from which data can be collected, including Internet browsers, social media sites
and apps, cameras, cars, and a host of other data-collection tools.[6] Finally, if all
previous features are present, a big data corpus likely has significant 'value'.

The way in which 'big data' is generated and used can be separated into two
phases.[7] First, the creation of a big data corpus requires processes to collect data
from sources such as those mentioned in the previous paragraph. Second, the
corpus is analysed, a process that may involve Text and Data Mining (TDM).[8]
TDM is a process that uses an AI algorithm. It allows the machine to learn from the
corpus; hence the term 'machine learning' (ML) is sometimes used as a synonym of
AI in the press.[9] As it analyses a big data corpus, the machine *learns and gets better at
what it does*. This process often requires human input to assist the machine in
correcting errors or faulty correlations derived from, or decisions based on, the
data.[10] The processing of corpora of big data is done to find correlations and
generate predictions or other valuable analytical outcomes. The found correlations
and insight can be used for multiple purposes, including targeted advertising and
surveillance, though an almost endless array of other applications is possible. To take
just one different example of a lesser known application, a law firm might process
hundreds or thousands of documents in a given field, couple ML with human
expertise, and produce insights about how they and other firms operate, for instance,
in negotiating a certain type of transaction or settling (or not) cases.

A subset of machine learning, known as *deep learning* (DL), uses neural networks,
a computer system modelled on the human brain.[11] This implies that any human

---

[4] J. Cano, 'The V's of Big Data: Velocity, Volume, Value, Variety, and Veracity', *XSNet*, 11
March 2014.
[5] Ibid.
[6] The list includes 'cars' as personal vehicles are one of the main sources of (personal) data with
up to 25 gigabytes per hour of driving.
[7] The two components are not necessarily sequential. They can and often do proceed in parallel.
[8] See M. Montagnani, 'Il text and data mining e il diritto d'autore', *Annali Italiani del diritto
d'autore, della cultura e dello spettacolo* 26 (2017), 376–395.
[9] C. Kozyrkov, 'Are You Using the Term 'AI' Incorrectly?', *Hackernoon*, 26 May 2018.
[10] How IP will apply to the work involved in the human training function of machine learning is
one of the interesting questions at the interface of big data and IP. The term 'training data' is
used in this context to suggest that the machine training is supervised (by humans). See B. D.
Ripley, *Pattern Recognition and Neural Networks* (Cambridge: Cambridge University Press,
1996), at 354.
[11] With the 'deep learning model, the algorithms can determine on their own if a prediction is
accurate or not … through its own method of computing – its own "brain", if you will'.

contribution to the output of deep learning systems is often 'second degree' and the proximate cause of the output is not the programmer. When considering the possible intellectual property (IP) protection of outputs of such systems, this separation between humans and the output challenges core notions of IP law, especially authorship in copyright law and inventorship in patent law.

ML and DL can produce high value outputs. Such outputs can take the form of analyses, insights, correlations, and may lead to automated (machine) decision-making. It can be expected that those who generate this value will try to capture and protect it, using IP law, technological measures and contracts. One can also expect competitors and the public to try to access those outputs for the same reason, namely their value. In many cases, big data corpora are protected by secrecy, a form of protection that relies on trade secret law combined with technological protection from hacking, and contracts. A publicly available corpus, in contrast, must rely on erga omnes IP protection – if it deserves protection to begin with. Copyright protects collections of data; the sui generis database right (in the European Union, EU) might apply; and data exclusivity rights in clinical trial data may be relevant.

The *outputs* of the processing of big data corpora may contain or consist of subject matter that facially could be protected by copyright or patent law. Big data technology can be – and in fact is – used to create and invent. For example, a big data corpus of all recent pop music can find correlations and identify what may be causing a song to be popular. It can use the correlations to write its own music.[12] The creation of (potentially massive amounts of) new literary and artistic material without direct human input will challenge human-created works in the marketplace. This is already happening with machine-written news reports.[13] Deciding whether machine-created material should be protected by copyright could thus have a profound impact on the market for creative works. If machine created material is copyright-free, machines will produce free goods that compete with paid ones – that is, those created by humans expecting a financial return. If the material produced by machines is protected by copyright and its use potentially subject to payment, this might level the commercial playing field between human and machine, but then who (which natural or legal person) *should* be paid for the computer's work? Then there will be border definition issues. Some works will be created by human and machine working together. Can we apply the notion of joint authorship? Or should we consider the machine-produced portion (if separable) copyright-free, thus limiting the protection to identifiably human-authored portions?

B. Grossfeld, 'A Simple Way to Understand Machine Learning vs Deep Learning', *ZenDesk*, 18 July 2017.

[12] See G. Hadjeres and F. Pachet, 'DeepBach: A Steerable Model for Bach Chorales Generation', *arXiv:1612*, 3 December 2016, 1–20, at 1.

[13] See C. Underwood, 'Automated Journalism – AI Applications at *New York Times*, *Reuters*, and Other Media Giants', *eMerj*, 17 November 2019, available at https://bit.ly/2Q84BTV.

If such major doctrinal challenges – each with embedded layers of normative inquiries – emerge in the field of copyright, big data poses existential threats in the case of patents. AI tools can be used to process thousands of published patents and patent applications and used to *expand the scope of claims in patent applications*. This poses normative challenges that parallel those enunciated earlier: Who is the inventor? Is there a justification to grant an exclusive right to a machine-made invention? To whom? There are doctrinal ones as well. For example, is the machine-generated 'invention' disclosed in such a way that would warrant the issuance of a patent?

It gets more complicated. If AI machines using patent-related big data can broaden claim scope or add claims in patent applications, then within a short horizon they could be able to *predict the next incremental steps in a given field of activity* by analysing innovation trajectories. For example, they might look at the path of development of a specific item (car brakes, toothbrushes) and 'predict' or define a broad array of what *could* come next. Doctrinally, this raises questions about inventive step: If a future development is obvious to a machine, is it obvious for purposes of patent law? Answering this question poses an epistemological as well as a doctrinal challenge for patent offices. The related normative inquiry is the one mentioned earlier, namely whether machine-made inventions (even for inventions the scope [claims] of which were merely 'stretched' using big data and AI) 'deserve' a patent despite their obviousness (to the machine).

This use of patent and technological big data could lead to a future where machines pre-disclose incremental innovations (and their use) in such a way that they constitute publicly available prior art and thus make obtaining patents impossible on a significant part of the current patentability universe. Perhaps even the best AI system using a big data corpus of all published patents and technical literature will not be able to predict the next pioneer invention, but very few patents are granted on ground-breaking advances. AI systems that soon will be able to predict *most* improvements to currently patented inventions, which tend to be only incrementally different from the prior art would wreak havoc with the patent-based incentive system.[14] Let us take an example: It is possible that deep-learning algorithms could parse thousands of new molecules based on those recently patented or disclosed in applications and even predict their medical efficacy. If such data (new molecules and predicted efficacy) were available and published, it would significantly hamper the patentability of those new molecules due to lack of novelty.

The unavailability of patents would dramatically increase the role of data exclusivity rights – the right to prevent reliance in clinical data submitted to obtain marketing approval – in the pharmaceutical field.[15] If this prediction of future

[14] See S. Y. Ravid and X. Liu, 'When Artificial Intelligence Systems Produce Inventions: An Alternative Model for Patent Law at the 3A Era', *Cardozo Law Review* 39 (2018), 2215–2263, at 2254; T. Baker, 'Pioneers in Technology: A Proposed System for Classifying and Rewarding Extraordinary Inventions' *Arizona Law Review* 45 (2003), 445–466.
[15] See D. Gervais, 'The Patent Option', *North Carolina Journal of Law and Technology* 20 (2019), 357–403.

inventions by AI became an established practice in fields where this separate protection by data exclusivity is unavailable, the very existence of the incentive system based on patents could be in jeopardy.

B BIG DATA IN THE WTO'S WORK

Big data has slowly made its way past the imposing iron gates of rue de Lausanne and into the WTO. Big data has made appearances in various WTO committees and at the General Council. At the committee level, it showed up in the work that the WTO is doing on 'electronic commerce', based on a Work Programme on that topic adopted by the General Council on 25 September 1998.[16] The Work Programme required the Committees on Trade in Goods and Trade in Services, the Council for TRIPS and the Committee for Trade and Development to 'examine and report' on how electronic commerce might impact each of those trade sectors.[17]

In the area of intellectual property, work began quickly after the adoption of the Work Programme. In 1998, the Secretariat published a note reflecting the thinking on IP, just a few years after the adoption of the TRIPS Agreement. The note stated that intellectual property plays an important role also in promoting the development of the infrastructure of [electronic communications networks], i.e. software, hardware and other technology that make up information highways. It provides protection to the results of investment in the development of new information and communications technology, thus giving the incentive and the means to finance research and development aimed at improving such technology. In addition, a functioning intellectual property regime facilitates transfer of information and communications technology in the form of foreign direct investment, joint ventures and licensing.[18]

Along the same lines, but in a much more recent discussion of AI and big data in the Committee on Regional Trade Agreements, in response to a question from Canada as to whether there were 'effective measures to curtail repetitive infringement of copyright and related rights on the Internet' in the China–Korea Free Trade Agreement (FTA), China and Korea stated in their joint response that China would '[p]romote the cooperation of electric [sic]-commerce Big Data between the government and the industries to ensure the efficiency of information searching and evidence obtaining'.[19] Here big data and AI were seen as adjuncts for copyright

---

[16] WTO, Work Programme on Electronic Commerce, WT/L/274, 30 September 1998.
[17] Ibid.
[18] WTO, General Council, WTO Agreements and Electronic Commerce: Note by the Secretariat, WT/GC/W/90, 14 July 1998.
[19] WTO, Committee on Regional Trade Agreements, Free Trade Agreement between China and the Republic of Korea (Goods and Services): Questions and Replies, WT/REG370/2, 6 November 2017, at 3.

enforcement. One might question whether what seems a high protectionist view is always warranted in the face of empirical data about open innovation models, for example.

Some WTO members have suggested a broader role. Japan, for example, mentioned the need to address issues of 'digital protectionism', noting that the digital economy has contributed to global economic growth. Furthermore, the Fourth Industrial Revolution, realised with the utilisation of the latest technology such as the Internet of Things and Big Data will permeate countless aspects of the world economy and people's lives .... However, a number of challenges still remain to be addressed in order to maximize the benefits from this trend. ... Among others, it is indispensable to address emerging "digital protectionism"'.[20]

Though it is not clear exactly what Japan had in mind in this statement, digital protectionism is often shorthand for an attempt to restrain regulatory autonomy on the protection of personal data and data localization.[21]

In a so-called 'non paper', Brazil also raised the question whether 'usage of big data' would require a debate on concepts like universal jurisdiction or choice of jurisdiction applicable to electronic commerce.[22] Developing countries have also had their say. India underscored the need for developing countries 'to maintain policy space to formulate a policy on ownership, use and flow of data in sunrise sectors like cloud computing, data storage, hosting of servers as well as in big data analytics'.[23] They are, therefore, committed to reinvigorate work on the multilateral track, with its non-negotiating mandate, to understand these issues.[24] Rwanda's more sombre observation was that 'empirical evidence showed that the digital market was highly concentrated and that only a few companies worldwide were dominating the digital market, specializing in management and development of data centers and exploiting [B]ig [D]ata'.[25] It noted that only a few developing countries were able to catch up.[26] Finally, UNCTAD sought support to assist WTO members in adapting 'domestic IP frameworks to recent technological developments in big data solutions

[20] WTO, Work Programme on Electronic Commerce, Non-paper for the Discussions on Electronic Commerce/Digital Trade from Japan, JOB/GC/100, 25 July 2016, at paras. 2.1 and 2.2.
[21] See Chapter 1 in this volume and see S. Yakovleva, Privacy Protection(ism): The Latest Wave of Trade Constraints on Regulatory Autonomy, University of Miami Law Review 74 (2020), 416–519.
[22] WTO, Exploratory Work on Electronic Commerce, Non-paper from Brazil, NF/ECOM/3, 25 March 2019, at 5.
[23] WTO, General Council, Minutes of the Meeting held in the Centre William Rappard on 18 October 2018, Statement by India, WT/GC/M/174, 20 November 2018, at 41.
[24] Ibid.
[25] See WTO, *Aid for Trade Global Review 2017: Promoting Trade, Inclusiveness and Connectivity for Sustainable Development: Summary Report* (Geneva: WTO, 2017), at 203; also WTO, General Council, Minutes of the Meeting held in the Centre William Rappard on 26 July 2017, WT/GC/M/168, 22 September 2017, at 7.248.
[26] Ibid.

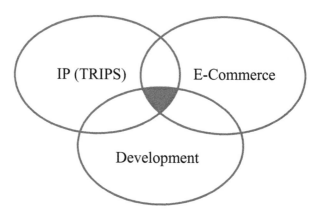

FIGURE 7.1. WTO work on AI and big data in thematic areas

and artificial intelligence'.[27] At this juncture, administratively the work on AI and big data at the WTO looks something as depicted below (Figure 7.1).

The future work of the WTO may progress in a number of different directions. It could usefully review how IP rights are actually used in the area of AI and big data, thus at least providing empirical data for future discussions. If the adoption of 'TRIPS 2.0' remains on the distant horizon, it seems clear that AI and big data issues will be on the table if and when it happens. In the intersection between IP and development, providing this type of analysis could be helpful to policymakers and development-focused international organizations outside the WTO as they develop domestic policies to facilitate the growth of AI and big data–based industries. The e-commerce and IP intersection includes how trade secret and other forms of IP apply to big data corpora. Again, more detailed work on this issue, whether comparative in nature or more theoretical, could open a useful window on various policy decisions.

In the next (and last) part of the chapter, I review a few areas in which the WTO could make analytical progress to make future discussions more productive, paying specific regard to the TRIPS Agreement.

C ADAPTING INTELLECTUAL PROPERTY TO BIG DATA AND AI

I *Intellectual Property Rights Protection of Big Data Software and Corpora*

Human-written AI software code used to collect (including search and social media apps), store and analyse big data corpora is considered a literary work eligible for copyright protection, subject to possible exclusions and limitations. That much is

---

[27] WTO, Council for Trade-Related Aspects of Intellectual Property Rights, Minutes of Meeting held in the Centre William Rappard on 5–6 June 2018, Statement by UNCTAD, IP/C/M/89/Add.1, 13 September 2018, at 38.

already in TRIPS.[28] The TRIPS Agreement also protects '[c]ompilations of data or other material, whether in machine readable or other form', which might seem like mandatory protection for big data corpora.[29] This is however not necessarily so. Indeed, Article 10.2 TRIPS imposes a condition for such protection, namely that the compilations 'by reason of the selection or arrangement of their contents constitute intellectual creations shall be protected as such'.[30] This condition is a way of stating that the compilation must be 'original' as the term is defined in international copyright law.

TRIPS incorporates most of the substantive provisions of the Berne Convention, to which 179 countries were party as of April 2021.[31] The convention contains important hints as to what constitutes an 'original' work. In its Article 2, when discussing the protection of 'collections', it states that '[c]ollections of literary or artistic works such as encyclopaedias and anthologies which, by reason of the *selection and arrangement of their contents, constitute intellectual creations* shall be protected *as such*, without prejudice to the copyright in each of the works forming part of such collections'.[32] This is the language that was reused in Article 10.2 TRIPS.

Selection and arrangement are exemplars of what copyright scholars refer to as 'creative choices'.[33] Creative choices need not be artistic or aesthetic in nature, but it seems they do have to be human.[34] Relevant choices are reflected in the particular way an author describes, explains, illustrates, or embodies their creative contribution. In contrast, choices that are merely routine (e.g., the choice to organize a directory in alphabetical order) or significantly constrained by external factors, such as the function a work is intended to serve (e.g., providing accurate driving directions), the tools used to produce it (e.g., a sculptor's marble and chisel), and the practices or conventions standard to a particular type of work (e.g. the structure of a

---

[28] This is recognized, for example, in Article 10(1) TRIPS, which provides that '[c]omputer programs, whether in source or object code, shall be protected as literary works under the Berne Convention (1971)'.

[29] Article 10.2 TRIPS.

[30] Ibid.

[31] Berne Convention for the Protection of Literary and Artistic Works of 9 September 1886, last revised at Paris on 24 July 1971, and amended on 28 September 1979 [hereinafter: Berne Convention]. On membership of the Berne Union, see www.wipo.int/treaties/en/ShowResults .jsp?lang=en&treaty_id=15.

[32] Article 2.5 Berne Convention (emphasis added).

[33] See D. Gervais and E. F. Judge, 'Of Silos and Constellations: Comparing Notions of Originality in Copyright Law', *Cardozo Arts and Entertainment Law Journal* 27 (2009), 375–408.

[34] Deciding whether big data corpora are protectable in the absence of an identifiable human author is a debate well beyond the scope of this paper. See P. B. Hugenholtz, J. P. Quintais, and D. Gervais, Trends and Developments in Artificial Intelligence: Challenges to the Intellectual Property Rights Framework (Amsterdam: Institute for Information Law, 2021); D. Gervais, 'The Machine As Author', Iowa Law Review 105 (2019), 2053–2106. This statement from the United States Copyright Office is also interesting: 'Examples of situations where the Office will refuse to register a claim include: ... The work lacks human authorship'. See United States Copyright Office, *Compendium of US Copyright Office Practices*, 3rd edn (Washington, DC: United States Copyright Office, 2017), at 22.

sonnet) are not creative for the purpose of determining the existence of a sufficient degree of originality.

When the Berne Convention text was last revised on substance in 1967,[35] neither publicly available 'electronic' databases nor any mass-market database software was available. The 'collections' referred to in the convention are thus of the type mentioned by the convention drafters: (paper-based) anthologies and encyclopaedias. When 'electronic' databases started to emerge in the 1990s, data generally had to be indexed and re-indexed regularly to be useable. The TRIPS Agreement, signed in 1994 but essentially drafted in the late 1980s up to December 1990, is a reflection of this development.[36] The data in typical (relational or 'SQL') databases in existence at the time generally was 'structured' in some way, for example via an index, and that structure might qualify the database for (thin) copyright protection in the database's organizational layer. Older databases also contained more limited datasets ('small data').

Facebook, Google, and Amazon, to name just those three, found out early on that relational databases were not a good solution for the volumes and types of data that they were dealing with. This inadequacy explains the development of open source software (OSS) for big data: the Hadoop file system, the MapReduce programming language, and associated non-relational ('noSQL') databases, such as Apache's Cassandra.[37] These tools and the data corpora they helped create and use may not qualify for protection as 'databases' under the SQL-derived criteria mentioned earlier. This does not mean that no work or knowhow is required to create the corpus, but that the type of structure of the dataset may not qualify. As the CJEU explained in *Football Dataco*, 'significant labour and skill of its author ... cannot as such justify the protection of it by copyright under Directive 96/9, if that labour and that skill do not express any originality in the selection or arrangement of that data'.[38] Indeed, big data is sometimes defined in *direct contrast* to the notion of SQL databases implicitly reflected in the TRIPS Agreement and the EU Database Directive discussed in the next section. Big data software is unlikely to 'select or arrange' the data in a way that would meet the originality criterion and trigger copyright protection.

---

[35] An Appendix for developing countries was added in Paris in 1971 but it did not modify the definition of 'work'.

[36] For a longer description of the negotiating history, see D. Gervais, *The TRIPS Agreement: Drafting History and Analysis*, 5th edn (London: Sweet and Maxwell, 2021), at Part I.

[37] See A. Reeve, 'Big Data and NoSQL: The Problem with Relational Databases', *Dell Technologies InFocus*, 7 September 2012, available at https://infocus.dellemc.com/april_reeve/big-data-and-nosql-the-problem-with-relational-databases/. It is worth noting that it is because code is protected by copyright (see TRIPS Agreement, Article 10.1) that owners of code can licence it and impose open source terms.

[38] C-604/10, *Football Dataco Ltd and others v. Yahoo!* [2012], ECLI:EU:C:2012:115, at 42.

Finally, it is worth noting that, in some jurisdictions, even absent copyright protection for big data, other IP-like remedies might be relevant, such as the tort of misappropriation applicable to 'hot news' in US law, or the protection against parasitic behaviour available in a number of European systems.[39] This might apply to information generated by AI-based TDM systems that have initially high but fast declining value, such as financial information relevant to stock market transactions, as data 'has a limited lifespan – old data is not nearly as valuable as new data – and the value of data lessens considerably over time'.[40]

In EU law, there is also a sui generis right in databases.[41] This right is not subject to the originality requirement,[42] but, according to Professor Bernt Hugenholtz, the way in which big data coprora are structured (or not) 'squarely rules out protection – whether by copyright or by the *sui generis* right – of (collections of) raw machine-generated data'.[43] The directive also mentions, however, that if there is an *investment* in obtaining the data, that investment may be sufficient for the corpus to qualify as a database.[44] The Court of Justice of the European Union (CJEU) defined 'investment' in obtaining the data as 'resources used to seek out existing materials and collect them in the database but does not cover the resources used for the creation of materials which make up the contents of a database'.[45] Professor Hugenholtz explains that 'the main argument for this distinction, as is transparent from the decision, is that the Database Directive's economic rationale is to promote and reward investment in database production, not in generating new data'.[46] This casts doubt on whether the notion of investment is sufficient to warrant sui generis protection of big data corpora, though Matthias Leistner suggested caution in

---

[39] See V. Smith Ekstrand and C. Roush, 'From "Hot News" to "Hot Data": The Rise of "FinTech", the Ownership of Big Data, and the Future of the Hot News Doctrine', *Cardozo Arts and Entertainment Law Journal* 35 (2017), 303–339.

[40] D. Sokol and R. E. Comerford, 'Antitrust and Regulating Big Data', *George Mason Law Review* 23 (2016), 1129–1161, at 1138.

[41] Directive 96/9/EC of the European Parliament and of the Council of 11 March 1996 on the Legal Protection of Databases, OJ L [1996] 77/20 [hereinafter: Database Directive]. See also D. J. Gervais, 'The Protection of Databases', *Chicago-Kent Law Review* 82 (2007), 1101–1168.

[42] See P. B. Hugenholtz, 'Intellectual Property and Information Law', in J. J. C. Kabel and G. J. H. M. Mom (eds), *Essays in Honour of Herman Cohen Jehoram* (The Hague/London/ Boston: Kluwer Law International, 1998), 183–200.

[43] P. B. Hugenholtz, 'Data Property: Unwelcome Guest in the House of IP', in P. Drahos, G. Ghidini, and H. Ullrich (eds), *Kritika: Essays on Intellectual Property*, Vol. 3 (Cheltenham: Edward Elgar, 2018), 65–77. See also E. Derclaye, 'The Database Directive', in I. Stamatoudi and P. Torremans (eds), *EU Copyright Law* (Cheltenham: Edward Elgar, 2014), 298–354, at 302–303.

[44] Article 7(1) Database Directive.

[45] C-46/02, *Fixtures Marketing Ltd v. Oy Veikkaus Ab* [2004], ECLI:EU:C:2004:694; C-203/02, *British Horseracing Board v. William Hill Organization* [2004], ECLI:EU:C:2004:695; C-338/ 02, *Fixtures Marketing Ltd v. Svenska Spel AB* [2004], ECLI:EU:C:2004:696; C-444/02, *Fixtures Marketing Ltd v. Organismos prognostikon agonon podosfairou AE (OPAP)* [2004], ECLI:EU:C:2004:697.

[46] Hugenholtz, above note 43.

opining that 'the sweeping conclusion that all sensor- or other machine-generated data will typically not be covered by the sui generis right is not warranted'.[47]

II *Text and Data Mining*

The WTO could usefully consider the need for TDM exceptions, and how they mesh with the three-step test contained in Article 13 TRIPS, as many WTO members have adopted or are considering adopting exceptions for this purpose. TDM software used to process corpora of big data might infringe rights in databases that are protected either by copyright or the EU sui generis right, thus creating a barrier to TDM.[48] The rule that copyright works reproduced in a big data corpus retain independent copyright protection has not been altered. This means that images, texts, musical works, and other copyright subject-matter contained in a big data corpus are still subject to copyright protection until the expiry of the term of protection. This is clearly reflected in Article 10.2 TRIPS, second sentence: 'Such protection, which shall not extend to the data or material itself, shall be without prejudice to any copyright subsisting in the data or material itself'.

Geiger et al. opined that '[o]nly TDM tools involving minimal copying of a few words or crawling through data and processing each item separately could be operated without running into a potential liability for copyright infringement'.[49] This might explain why several jurisdictions have introduced TDM limitations and exceptions. Four examples should suffice to illustrate the point. First, the German Copyright Act contains an exception for the 'automatic analysis of large numbers of works (source material) for scientific research' for non-commercial purposes.[50] A corpus may be made available to 'a specifically limited circle of persons for their joint scientific research, as well as to individual third persons for the purpose of monitoring the quality of scientific research'.[51] The corpus must also be deleted once the research has been completed.[52] Second, France introduced an exception

---

[47] M. Leistner, 'Big Data and the EU Database Directive 96/9/EC: Current Law and Potential for Reform', *SSRN Publication* (2018), available at https://ssrn.com/abstract=3245937.

[48] See D. L. Rubinfeld and M. S. Gal, 'Access Barriers to Big Data', *Arizona Law Review* 59 (2017), 339–381, at 368.

[49] C. Geiger, G. Frosio, and O. Bulayenko, *The Exception for Text and Data Mining (TDM) in the Proposed Directive on Copyright in the Digital Single Market – Legal Aspects, Report to the European Parliament's Committee on Legal Affairs* (Brussels: European Parliament, 2018), at 6. See also C. Geiger, G. Frosio, and O. Bulayenko, 'The EU Commission's Proposal to Reform Copyright Limitations: A Good but Far Too Timid Step in the Right Direction', *European Intellectual Property Review* 40 (2018), 4–15, at 6.

[50] Copyright Act of 9 September 1965 (*Federal Law Gazette* I, 1273), as last amended by Article 1 of the Act of 28 November 2018 (*Federal Law Gazette* I, 2014), Article 60(d).

[51] Ibid.

[52] Ibid.

in 2016 allowing reproduction, storage, and communication of 'files created in the course of TDM research activities'.[53] The reproduction must be from lawful sources.[54] Third, the UK statute provides for a right to make a copy of a work 'for computational analysis of anything recorded in the work', but prohibits dealing with the copy in other ways and makes contracts that would prevent or restrict the making of a copy for the purpose stated above unenforceable.[55] Fourth and finally, the Japanese statute contains an exception for the reproduction or adaptation of a work to the extent deemed necessary for 'the purpose of information analysis ("information analysis" means to extract information, concerned with languages, sounds, images or other elements constituting such information, from many works or other much information, and to make a comparison, a classification or other statistical analysis of such information)'.[56]

The examples in the previous paragraph demonstrate a similar normative underpinning, namely a policy designed to allow TDM of the data contained in copyright works. They disagree on the implementation of the policy, however. Based on those examples, the questions that policymakers considering enacting an explicit TDM exception or limitation should include

1. whether the exception applies to only one (reproduction) or all rights (including adaptation/derivation);
2. whether contractual overrides are possible;
3. whether the material used should be from a lawful source;
4. what dissemination of the data, if any, is possible; and
5. whether the purpose of TDM is non-commercial.

The answers to all five questions can be grounded in a normative approach, but they should be set against the backdrop of the three-step test, which, as explained later, is likely to apply to any copyright exception or limitation.

As to the first question, if allowing TDM is seen as a normatively desirable goal, then the right holder should not be able to use one right fragment in the bundle of copyright rights to prevent it. In an analysis of the rights involved, Irini Stamatoudi came to the conclusion that right fragments beyond reproduction and adaptation were much less relevant.[57] Still, it would seem safer to formulate the exception or

---

[53] Geiger et al., note 49, at 830.

[54] Law No. 2016-1231 § for a Digital Republic and Article L122-5 of the Intellectual Property Code.

[55] Added by the Copyright and Rights in Performances (Research, Education, Libraries and Archives), Regulations 2014, 2014 No 1372, available at www.legislation.gov.uk/uksi/2014/1372/regulation/3/made.

[56] Copyright Law of Japan (translated by Y. Oyama et al.), at Article 47 *septies*, available at www.cric.or.jp/english/clj/doc/20161018_October,2016_Copyright_Law_of_Japan.pdf.

[57] I. A. Stamatoudi, 'Text and Data Mining', in I. A. Stamatoudi (ed), *New Developments in EU and International Copyright Law* (Deventer: Wolters Kluwer, 2016), 262–282.

limitation as a non-infringing *use*, as for example in section 107 (fair use) of the US Copyright Act.[58]

Second, for the same reason, contractual overrides should not be allowed. One can hardly see how they can be effective unless perhaps there was only one provider of TDM for a certain type of work. Even if a provision against contractual overrides was absent from the text of the statute, the restriction could be found inapplicable based on principles of contract law.[59]

Third, the lawful source element contained in French law is facially compelling. It seems difficult to oppose a requirement that the source of the data be legitimate. There are difficulties in its application, however. First, it is not always clear to a *human* user whether a source is legal or not; the situation may be even less clear for a machine. Second, and relatedly, if the source is foreign, a determination of its legality may require an analysis of the law of the country of origin, as copyright infringement is determined based on the lex loci delicti – and this presupposes a determination of its origin (and foreignness) to begin with. Perhaps a requirement targeting sources that the user *knows or would have been grossly negligent in not knowing* were illegal might be more appropriate.

The last two questions on the list are somewhat harder. Dissemination of the data, if such data includes copyright works, could be necessary among the people interested in the work. German law makes an exception for a 'limited circle of persons for their joint scientific research', and 'third persons for the purpose of monitoring the quality of scientific research'.[60] This is a reflection of a scientific basis of the exception, which includes project-based work by a limited number of scientists and monitoring by peer reviewers. This would not allow the use of TDM to scan libraries of books and make snippets available to the general public, as Google Books does, for example. An interpretation of the scope of the exception might depend on whether the use is commercial, which in turn might vary according to the definitional approach taken: is it the commercial nature of the *entity* performing the TDM that matters, or the specific use of the TDM data concerned (i.e., is that specific use monetized)?

The EU was considering a new, mandatory TDM exception as part of its digital copyright reform efforts.[61] Article 3, which contains the proposed TDM exception, has been the focus of intense debates. The September 2018 (Parliament) version of the proposed TDM exception maintained the TDM exception for scientific

[58] The US Copyright Act reads in part as follows: 'the fair use of a copyrighted work ... is not an infringement of copyright'. US Copyright Act of 1976, 17 U.S.C. §§ 101–810 [hereinafter: US Copyright Act].

[59] See for example Lucie Guibault's detailed analysis of the possible application of the German *Sozialbindung* principle in this context. L. Guibault, *Copyright Limitations and Contracts: An Analysis of the Contractual Overridability of Limitations on Copyright* (The Hague/London/Boston: Kluwer Law International, 2002), at 224–225.

[60] See Copyright Act of 9 September 1965, note 50.

[61] Geiger et al., note 49, at 832–833. The research for this part of the chapter was completed.

research proposed by the commission but adds an optional exception applicable to the private sector, not just for the benefit of public institutions and research organizations.[62] Members of the academic community have criticized the narrow scope of the commission's proposed exception, which the Parliament's amendments ameliorated.[63] The European Copyright Society opined that 'data mining should be permitted for non-commercial research purposes, for research conducted in a commercial context, for purposes of journalism and for any other purpose'.[64] The final text of Article 3 in the now adopted directive states that EU member states must provide for an exception in their domestic laws for 'reproductions and extractions made by research organizations and cultural heritage institutions in order to carry out, for the purposes of scientific research, text and data mining of works or other subject matter to which they have lawful access',[65] as well as for 'reproductions and extractions of lawfully accessible works and other subject matter for the purposes of text and data mining'.[66]

One should note, finally, that when a technological protection measure (TPM) or 'lock' such as those protected by Article 11 of the 1996 WIPO Copyright Treaty, is in place preventing the use of data contained in copyright works for TDM purposes, the question is whether a TDM exception provides a 'right' to perform TDM and thus potentially a right to circumvent the TPM or obtain redress against measures designed to restrict it.[67] This might apply to traffic management (e.g. throttling) measures used to slow the process down. Those questions are worth pondering, but they are difficult to answer, especially at the international level.[68]

III The Three-Step Test

The three-step test sets boundaries for exceptions and limitations to copyright rights. The original three-step test is contained in Article 9(2) of the Berne Convention. Instead of enumerating acceptable exceptions and limitations, Berne negotiators

---

[62] The Parliamentary version and the commission's proposal are compared in amendments 64 and 65 of European Parliament, Amendments Adopted by the European Parliament on 12 September 2018 on the Proposal for a Directive of the European Parliament and of the Council on Copyright in the Digital Single Market (COM(2016)0593 – C8–0383/2016 – 2016/0280 (COD)), OJ C [2019] 433/248.

[63] See, e.g., M. Senftleben, 'EU Copyright Reform and Startups – Shedding Light on Potential Threats in the Political Black Box', March 2017, at 9, available at https://bit.ly/2kiJgFq.

[64] European Copyright Society, 'General Opinion on the EU Copyright Reform Package', 24 January 2017, available at https://bit.ly/2k2k3jD.

[65] Article 3 of Directive 2019/790 of the European Parliament and of the Council of 17 April 2019 on Copyright and Related Rights in the Digital Single Market and Amending Directives 96/9/EC and 2001/29/EC, OJ L [2019] 130/92.

[66] Ibid., at Article 4.

[67] WIPO Copyright Treaty, adopted in Geneva on 20 December 1996, entered into force 6 March 2002.

[68] For a brief discussion, see Geiger et al., note 49.

decided to introduce this test which allows countries party to the convention to make exceptions to the right of reproduction (i) 'in certain special cases'; (ii) 'provided that such reproduction does not conflict with a normal exploitation of the work'; and (iii) 'does not unreasonably prejudice the legitimate interests of the author'. The test was extended to all copyright rights by the TRIPS Agreement, with the difference that the term 'author' at the end was replaced with the term 'right holder'.[69]

The test was interpreted in two panel reports adopted by the WTO Dispute Settlement Body. The first step ('certain special cases') was interpreted to mean that 'an exception or limitation must be limited in its field of application or exceptional in its scope'. In other words, 'an exception or limitation should be narrow in quantitative as well as a qualitative sense'.[70] The normative grounding to justify a TDM exception is fairly clear. Indeed, exceptions and limitations have already been introduced in major jurisdictions. A well-justified exception or limitation with reasonable limits and a clear purpose is likely to pass the first step.

The second step (interference with normal exploitation) was defined as follows: First, exploitation was defined as any use of the work by which the copyright holder tries to extract/maximize the value of their right. 'Normal' is more troublesome. Does it refer to what is simply 'common', or does it refer to a normative standard? The question is particularly relevant for new forms and emerging business models that have not, thus far, been common or 'normal' in an empirical sense. If the exception is used to limit a commercially significant market or, a fortiori, to enter into competition with the copyright holder, the exception is prohibited.[71]

Could a TDM exception be used to justify scanning and making available entire libraries of books still under active commercial exploitation? The answer as regards the full text of books is negative, as this would interfere with commercial exploitation. For books still protected by copyright *but no longer easily available on a commercial basis*, the absence of active commercial exploitation would likely limit the impact of the second step, however, subject to a caveat. Some forms of exploitation are typically done by a third party under licence and do not need any active exploitation *by the right holder*. For example, a film studio might want the right to make a film out of a novel no longer commercially exploited. That may in turn

---

[69] Article 13 TRIPS. The test is now used as the model for exceptions to *all copyright rights* in TRIPS; Article 10(1) and (2) WIPO Copyright Treaty; Article 16(2) WIPO Performances and Phonograms Treaty, adopted on 20 December 1996; Article 13(2) Beijing Treaty on Audiovisual Performances, adopted 24 June 2012; and Article 11 of the Marrakesh Treaty to Facilitate Access to Published Works for Persons Who Are Blind, Visually Impaired or Otherwise Print Disabled, adopted 27 June 2013. Interestingly, in TRIPS, it is also the test for exceptions to industrial design protection (Article 26(2)) and patent rights (Article 30).

[70] Panel Report, United States – Section 110(5) of the US Copyright Act (US – Section 110(5) Copyright Act), WT/DS160/R, adopted 15 June 2000, at 6.109 (emphasis added and citations omitted). The second case was decided in Panel Report, Canada – Patent Protection of Pharmaceutical Products, WT/DS114/R, adopted 17 March 2000.

[71] P. Goldstein, *International Copyright: Principles, Law, and Practice* (Oxford: Oxford University Press, 1998), at 295.

generate new demand for the book. This is still normal exploitation. One must be careful in extending this reasoning too far, for example, by assuming that every novel will be turned into a movie.

One way to pass the second step is for a TDM exception to allow limited uses that do not demonstrably interfere with commercial exploitation, such as those allowed under the German statute. Another example is the use of 'snippets' from books scanned by Google for its Google Books project, which was found to be a fair use by the US Court of Appeals for the Second Circuit. This is important not just as a matter of US (state) practice but because at least the fourth US fair use factor ('the effect of the use upon the potential market for or value of the copyrighted work') is a market-based assessment of the impact of the use resembling the three-step test's second step.[72] The Second Circuit noted that this did not mean that the Google Books project would have *no* impact, but rather that the impact would not be meaningful or significant.[73] It also noted that the type of loss of sale created by TDM 'will generally occur in relation to interests that are not protected by the copyright. A snippet's capacity to satisfy a searcher's need for access to a copyrighted book will at times be because the snippet conveys a historical fact that the searcher needs to ascertain'.[74] In the same vein, one could argue that the level of interference required to violate the second step of the test must be significant and should be a use that is relevant from the point of view of commercial exploitation.

The third step (no unreasonable prejudice to legitimate interests) is perhaps the most difficult to interpret. What is an 'unreasonable prejudice', and what are 'legitimate interests'? Let us start with the latter. 'Legitimate' can mean sanctioned or authorized by law or principle. Alternatively, it can just as well be used to denote something that is 'normal' or 'regular'. The WTO Panel Report concluded that the combination of the notion of 'prejudice' with that of 'interests' pointed clearly towards a legal-normative approach. In other words, 'legitimate interests' are those that are protected by law.[75] Then, what is an 'unreasonable' prejudice? The presence of the word 'unreasonable' indicates that *some level or degree* of prejudice is justifiable. Hence, while a country might exempt the making of a small number of private copies entirely, it may be required to impose a compensation scheme, such as a levy, when the prejudice level becomes unjustified.[76] The WTO panel concluded that 'prejudice

---

[72] The fourth fair use factor contained in the US Copyright Act reads as follows: 'the effect of the use upon the potential market for or value of the copyrighted work ...'.
[73] *The Authors Guild v. Google, Inc.*, 804 F.3d 202 (2d Cir, 2015), cert. denied 136 S.Ct. 1658.
[74] Ibid.
[75] Panel Report, note 70, at paras. 6.223–6.229. In para. 6.224, the Panel tried to reconcile the two approaches: '[T]he term relates to lawfulness from a legal positivist perspective, but it has also the connotation of legitimacy from a more normative perspective, in the context of calling for the protection of interests that are justifiable in the light of the objectives that underlie the protection of exclusive rights'.
[76] WIPO, *Records of the Intellectual Property Conference of Stockholm: June 11 to July 14, 1967*, Vol. 1 (Geneva: WIPO, 1971), at 1145–1146.

to the legitimate interests of right holders reaches an unreasonable level if an exception or limitation causes or has the potential to cause an unreasonable loss of income to the copyright holder'.[77] Whether a TDM exception is liable to cause an unreasonable loss of income to copyright holders is analytically similar to the second step of the test as interpreted by the WTO panels. It is not, however, identical: The owner of rights in a work no longer commercially exploited may have a harder case on the second step. It is not unreasonable, however, for a copyright holder, to expect some compensation for some uses of a protected work even if it is not commercially exploited. For example, the owner of rights in a novel may expect compensation for the republication by a third party or translation of the book. The major difference between the second and third step as interpreted by the two WTO dispute-settlement panels in this regard is that the third step condition may be met by compensating right holders. This could allow the imposition of a compulsory licence for specific TDM uses that overstep the boundary of free use – for example, to make available significant portions of, or even entire, protected works that are no longer commercially exploited subject to a series of conditions such as the existence of any plan or preparation by the right holder to exploit the work.

D CONCLUSION

Multilateral trade rules, such as the General Agreement on Tariffs and Trade (GATT) 1947 began as an effort to facilitate trade in goods by removing tariff and non-tariff barriers. In 1995, with the establishment of the WTO, this was extended to services and IP protection. IP is perhaps the odd man out, as GATT Article XX considers IP as not much more than an acceptable barrier to trade. Moreover, IP is often not traded per se but rather embedded in a good or service. Data is arguably a new area of trade, as data, especially big data corpora and the inferences that can be derived from their analysis by AI machines, have become a commodity in themselves, but with special features, including the fact that many corpora are based on personal data.[78] Given its trajectory as a multilateral organization that addresses all main areas of trade, it would be normal for the WTO to extend its normative reach in trade in data. As it does so, it will need to see whether the rules contained in the TRIPS Agreement are up to the task of supporting the data economy, which must begin by a massive data gathering and analysis phase, as the GATT did when preparing the TRIPS Agreement. In this chapter, I offered a few suggestions on areas in which it could shine its analytical spotlight to illuminate a path for future negotiations.

---

[77] Panel Report, US – Section 110(5) Copyright Act, note 70, at para. 6.229.
[78] See S. Yakovleva, 'Should Fundamental Rights to Privacy and Data Protection Be a Part of the EU's International Trade "Deals"?', *World Trade Review* 17 (2018), 477–508, at 478; also Chapter 1 in this volume.

8

Big Data, AI and Border Enforcement of Intellectual Property Rights

Impact on Trade Flows

*Xavier Seuba**

A DIGITALIZATION OF INTELLECTUAL PROPERTY ENFORCEMENT

Customs surveillance of intellectual property (IP) is 'an efficient way to quickly and effectively provide legal protection to the right-holder',[1] since it makes it possible to 'nip the infringements in the bud'.[2] The World Trade Organization's (WTO) Agreement on Trade-Related Aspects of Intellectual Property Rights (TRIPS) introduced, back in 1995, the first comprehensive multilateral regulation on border measures applicable to goods protected by intellectual property rights (IPRs).[3] Since then, global trade flows have increased,[4] new trade agreements regulating IP have substantially modified international intellectual property law[5] and, most importantly for this chapter's discussion, technology has drastically changed the means and mechanisms of customs enforcement.

---

* Associate Professor of Law, Academic Coordinator and Scientific Responsible, Center for International Intellectual Property Studies (CEIPI), University of Strasbourg. Contact: xavier .seuba@ceipi.edu.
1 See Regulation No 608/2013 of the European Parliament and of the Council of 12 June 2013 Concerning Customs Enforcement of Intellectual Property Rights and Repealing Council Regulation No 1383/2003, OJ L [2013] 181/15 [hereinafter: EU Regulation No 608/ 2013], at Recital 4, Preamble.
2 See M. C. E. J. Bronckers, D. W. F. Verkade, and N. M. McNelis, *TRIPS Agreement: Enforcement of Intellectual Property Rights* (Luxemburg: Publications Office of the EU, 2000), at 20.
3 See Articles 51–60 Agreement on Trade-Related Aspects of Intellectual Property Rights, 1869 U.N.T.S. 299; 33 I.L.M. 1197 (1994), entered into force 1 January 1995 [hereinafter: TRIPS].
4 See E. Ortiz-Ospina and D. Beltekian, 'Trade and Globalization', *Our World in Data*, 2018, available at https://ourworldindata.org/trade-and-globalization.
5 See R. Valdés and R. Tavengwa, 'Intellectual Property Provisions in Regional Trade Agreements', WTO Staff Working Paper No 21 (2012); X. Seuba, 'Intellectual Property in Preferential Trade Agreements: What Treaties, What Content?', *The Journal of World Intellectual Property* 16 (2013), 1–22; P. Roffe and X. Seuba (eds), *Global Perspectives and Challenges for the Intellectual Property System: Current Alliances in International Intellectual Property Lawmaking* (Geneva/Strasbourg: CEIPI/ICTSD, 2017).

Technological developments increase the possibilities of identifying and detaining goods infringing IPRs, and make it more feasible to 'assess in advance and control where required', which is the ideal pattern of action from a customs' risk management perspective.[6] However, assessing in advance and acting when appropriate does not always match well with fundamental intellectual property principles (territoriality), global trade norms (freedom of transit), global intellectual property rules (Articles 51 and 52 TRIPS), and due process requirements. This chapter, in light of these basic norms and principles, explores some of the challenges and opportunities brought by artificial intelligence (AI), big data and distributed ledger technologies to customs enforcement of IPRs.[7]

B HOW ARTIFICIAL INTELLIGENCE TRANSFORMS INTELLECTUAL PROPERTY ENFORCEMENT

Fuelled by a profusion of digitized data and rapidly advancing computational processing power,[8] AI techniques and functional applications[9] give rise to unprecedented opportunities of innovation and creativity, and also bring about important challenges to intellectual property protection.[10] Three major areas stand out.

First, the use of AI techniques to generate innovative and creative products has prompted discussion concerning the need, extent and legal grounds for the IP protection of products developed thanks to AI.[11] Second, regarding the means that enable

[6] European Commission, Communication on the EU Strategy and Action Plan for Customs Risk Management: Tackling Risks, Strengthening Supply Chain Security and Facilitating Trade, COM(2014) 0527 final, 21 August 2014.

[7] See also Chapter 6 in this volume.

[8] WIPO, *WIPO Technology Trends 2019: Artificial Intelligence* (Geneva: WIPO, 2019), at 13.

[9] AI techniques include machine learning, deep learning, fuzzy logic, logic programming, neutral networks, latent representation and unsupervised learning. AI functional applications include computer vision (including image recognition and biometrics), natural language processing (including semantics and sentiment analysis), speech processing (speech-to-speech and speaker recognition), robotics, control methods. See WIPO, note 8, at 31.

[10] On policy issues, see the interview with the Director General of WIPO Francis Gurry. WIPO, 'Artificial Intelligence and Intellectual Property: An Interview with Francis Gurry', *WIPO Magazine*, September 2018. WIPO has also made available a website on 'Artificial Intelligence and Intellectual Property' with information and practical resources, available at www.wipo.int/about-ip/en/artificial_intelligence/.

[11] As H. Pihlajamaa underlines, AI poses challenges to inventorship and ownership, patent eligibility, assessment of inventiveness, and sufficiency of disclosure. See H. Pihlajamaa, 'Summary of Feedback by EPC Contracting States: Legal Aspects of Patenting Inventions Involving Artificial Intelligence (AI)', Committee on Patent Law of the European Patent Office, 20 February 2019. A vast body of literature already addresses these challenges. See, e.g., T. L. Butler, 'Can a Computer Be an Author – Copyright Aspects of Artificial Intelligence', *A Journal of Communications and Entertainment Law* 4 (1982), 707–748; A. Lauber-Rönsberg and S. Hetmank, 'The Concept of Authorship and Inventorship under Pressure: Does Artificial Intelligence Shift Paradigms?', *Journal of Intellectual Property Law and Practice* 14 (2019), 570–579; R. Abbott, 'I Think, Therefore I Invent: Creative Computers and the Future of Patent Law', *Boston College Law Review* 57 (2016), 1079–1126; N. Shemtov,

creation and innovation, the intellectual property protection of AI techniques and functional applications per se has skyrocketed in recent years.[12] Third, the use of AI, big data and distributed ledger technologies also impacts IP enforcement. The increase of available information and the changes in the techniques used to make such information useful impact fundamental aspects of intellectual property enforcement. These changes revolve around three concepts: authority, automation and centralization.

A substantial change concerns the authority in charge of law enforcement and the process of privatization of law enforcement by means of delegation of public authority.[13] A telling example is that of online intermediaries,[14] which have acquired a central role in managing behaviour in the digital environment.[15] From free speech to access to information, many issues are mediated by search engines, websites and social networks. Their power also expands to intellectual property enforcement, since online intermediaries not only identify infringement, but also produce the information regarding the infringing activity, the infringers, the channels of commerce and its financial aspects.[16] Intermediaries furthermore use algorithms to remove allegedly infringing content upon notice of infringement, as well as to ex ante monitor, filter, block and disable access to content automatically flagged as infringing.[17]

A Study on Inventorship in Inventions Involving AI Activity (Munich: EPO, 2019). See also Chapter 7 in this volume.

[12] P. Cupitt, 'Patenting Artificial Intelligence at the European Patent Office', *CIPA Journal*, April 2019.

[13] For examples, see WIPO, Study on Approaches to Online Trademark Infringements, WIPO/ACE/12/9 REV. 2, 31 July 2017, at 9–12.

[14] G. Frosio, 'Why Keep a Dog and Bark Yourself? From Intermediary Liability to Responsibility', *Oxford International Journal of Law and Information Technology* 25 (2017), 1–33; European Commission, Communication on Online Platforms and the Digital Single Market Opportunities and Challenges for Europe, COM(2017) 555 final, 28 September 2017. On the responsibility of intermediaries themselves, see, e.g., K. Weatherall, 'Internet Intermediaries and Copyright – A 2018 Update: A Policy Paper for the Australian Digital Alliance', Parliament of Australia: Copyright Amendment (Service Providers) Bill 2017, Submission 37, 11 February 2018; E. Rosati, 'The CJEU Pirate Bay Judgment and Its Impact on the Liability of Online Platforms', *European Intellectual Property Review* 39 (2017), 737–748; J. Ginsburg and J. A. Budiardjo, 'Liability for Providing Hyperlinks to Copyright-Infringing Content: International and Comparative Law Perspectives', *Columbia Journal of Law and the Arts* 41 (2018), 153–224.

[15] M. Perel and N. Elkin-Koren, 'Black Box Tinkering: Beyond Transparency in Algorithmic Enforcement', *Florida Law Review* 69 (2017), 181–221, at 190. This is a power that platforms do not necessarily wish to have. Google 'didn't ask to be the decision maker' on deletions, as Google's Executive President Eric Schmidt stated. See A. White, 'Google EU Ruling Response Vetted as Complaints Pile Up', *Bloomberg*, 18 September 2014.

[16] For instance, Chinese giant Alibaba leads the use of big data analytics and machine learning and sets a cutting-edge standard in the area. Alibaba automated systems flag a product as counterfeit. Next, the system pools financial and commercial information and identities counterfeiters, and probably the manufacturing site and movement of funds. See Alibaba, *Alibaba IPR Protection Handbook* (Hangzhou: Alibaba, 2019).

[17] For a list of authors and works that have discussed the function of Internet intermediaries as gatekeepers, see M. Perel and N. Elkin-Koren, 'Accountability in Algorithmic Copyright Enforcement', *Stanford Technology Law Review* 19 (2016), 473–533, at 480 and 485.

Privatization leads to the convergence of law enforcement and adjudication powers.[18] Private stakeholders that identify infringing products also apply the corresponding sanctions of destroying infringing goods and cutting access to the Internet. The conventional way of functioning has been drastically altered. Customs officials, police and judges have always been part of the enforcement process, which encompasses a variety of interrelated activities. However, the substitution of these actors by private operators gives rise to the concentration of functions in the hands of a single actor. While this may certainly enhance efficacy and may be the adequate response to the volume of current trade, it also raises concerns from the point of view of independence, accountability[19] and fair trial standards.

A second and related phenomenon concerns automation – that is, the fact that machines themselves implement the law. Computers use machine learning techniques to derive legal consequences, implement orders and reach conclusions from a database of primary sources.[20] In addition to automated processes that apply to all branches of the law, there are sui generis types of automation applicable to IP. For instance, machines may respond to copyright-based Internet takedown requests, and may also determine the existence of trademark infringement thanks to image recognition.[21] The changes brought about by AI do not merely impact the online environment but also the manner in which judges adjudicate IP cases, lawyers practice IP law and authorities, including customs authorities, identify infringement. While due process concerns arise,[22] many start-ups have developed applications that are transfiguring law practice,[23] in particular those that enable the automation of time-consuming processes, such as conducting research, writing memos, undertaking due diligence and collecting evidence.[24] Automation of the

[18] Ibid., at 481.
[19] Ibid., at 477.
[20] S. Morse, 'Government-to-Robot Enforcement', *University of Illinois Law Review* 5 (2019), 1497–1525.
[21] For instance, in 2014 WIPO added image-search to its Global Brand Database, allowing users to search for visually similar trademark from among the millions of images in the collection. See WIPO, 'WIPO Launches Unique Image-Based Search for Trademarks, Other Brand Information', *Press Release*, 12 May 2014. Private developers have brought to the market applications that allow to conduct similar analyses, among them, *TrademarkNow*, *TrademarkVision*, *MikeTM Suite* and *LawPanel's Aila*. Other applications allow to spot fakes just by scanning with a phone device. This is, for instance, the case of *Entrupy* and *Goat*.
[22] D. K. Citron and F. Pasquale, 'The Scored Society: Due Process for Automated Predictions', *Washington Law Review* 89 (2014), 1–34.
[23] B. Rubin, 'Legal Tech Startups Have a Short History and a Bright Future', *TechCrunch*, 6 December 2014; M. McKamey, 'Legal Technology: Artificial Intelligence and the Future of Law Practice', *Appeal* 22 (2017), 45–58, at 57; E. A. Rayo, 'AI in Law and Legal Practice – A Comprehensive View of 35 Current Applications', *Emerj*, 29 November 2017.
[24] M. R. Grossman and G. Cormack, 'Technology-Assisted Review in E-Discovery Can Be More Effective and More Efficient Than Exhaustive Manual Review', *Richmond Journal of Law and Technology* 17 (2011), 1–48, at 11; D. Garcia, 'Preparing for Artificial Intelligence in the Legal Profession', *Lexis Practice Advisor Journal*, 6 July 2017.

law is promoted invoking practical advances in terms of efficiency, savings, consistency in applying legal doctrines and legal harmonization.[25]

A third change relates to centralization. Under this term, reference is made to the fact that a single action – writing a bit of software code – produces legal decisions for many individuals at once.[26] These are decisions that have previously required an individualized procedure.[27] Up until recent times, enforcement was human-driven, dynamic, public and individualized. Public authorities enforcing intellectual property – judges, customs officials and police – were 'just' humans. Similarly, intellectual property could not be understood as an automated process, but as a process of weighing and balancing competing rights and interests,[28] a process taking place in an individualized fashion in public settings and administered either by judicial or administrative authorities. These features contrast with a new situation where enforcement mechanisms are automated, centralized and privatized, and big (private) players occupy the place of public authorities.

C DIGITALIZATION AND USE OF BIG DATA IN CUSTOMS CONTROL

I *Digitalization and Customs Control*

While international logistics value chains are still characterized by the abundance of manual and paper-based processes, digitalization and AI are already transforming customs control. For instance, in the area of migration control, international travellers face, more and more often, semi-automated border controls that combine biometric screening,[29] facial recognition, automated lie detection and predictive

---

[25] Perel and Elkin-Koren, note 17, at 477. For a more critical and analytic view on the phenomenon, see D. Remus and F. S. Levy Frank, 'Can Robots Be Lawyers? Computers, Lawyers, and the Practice of Law', *Georgetown Journal of Legal Ethics* 30 (2017), 501–558; A. Marwaha, 'Seven Benefits of Artificial Intelligence for Law Firms', *Law Technology Today*, 13 July 2017.

[26] Morse, note 20.

[27] As Lessig stated in his acclaimed 2000 piece, in the age of cyberspace the 'regulator is code – the software and hardware that make cyberspace as it is. This code, or architecture, sets the terms on which life in cyberspace is experienced. It determines how easy it is to protect privacy, or how easy it is to censor speech'. See L. Lessig, 'Code Is Law. On Liberty in Cyberspace', *Harvard Magazine*, 1 January 2000; also L. Lessig, *Code and Other Laws of Cyberspace* (New York: Basic Books, 1999).

[28] The same applies to other legal domains. For instance, the WTO Appellate Body has noted: 'In sum, determination of whether a measure, which is not "indispensable", may nevertheless be "necessary" within the contemplation of Article XX(d), involves in every case a process of weighing and balancing a series of factors which prominently include the contribution made by the compliance measure to the enforcement of the law or regulation at issue, the importance of the common interests or values protected by that law or regulation, and the accompanying impact of the law or regulation on imports or exports'. See Appellate Body Report, Korea – Measures Affecting Imports of Fresh, Chilled and Frozen Beef (Korea – Various Measures on Beef), WT/DS161/AB/R, adopted 11 December 2000, at para. 164.

[29] The EU has given impulse to a gigantic biometrics database, the Common Identity Repository (CIR), which interconnects border-control, migration and law enforcement systems into a

modelling.[30] Likewise, predictive analytics also transform and enhance customs risk management regarding both the control of people and the monitoring of goods.

AI functional applications, such as computer vision, natural language processing and predictive analytics, are powered by the vast amount of data available in digitalized forms. Given the importance of data, a previous step is the digitalization of customs operations, an area that is characterized by red tape[31] and the existence of a vast amount of valuable information transmitted in each transaction.[32]

In the European Union, digitalization of customs was initiated back in the late 1990s[33] and dynamically promoted in 2008 with the adoption of the decision on a paperless environment for customs and trade.[34] The 'e-Customs Decision' identified the objectives, means and framework for setting up an electronic environment for customs and trade,[35] and was followed by the electronic customs Multi-annual

---

biometrics-tracking database of EU and non-EU citizens, thus simplifying the work of customs authorities. See C. Cimpanu, 'EU Votes to Create Gigantic Biometrics Database', *ZDNet*, 22 April 2019.

[30] This is, for instance, the case of the United States system AVATAR, an automated lie detection system that makes probabilistic decisions about veracity of statements: judgements about whether someone is telling the truth thanks to sensors of eye movements, body movements and voice.

[31] According to a frequently quoted statement of the UNCTAD 2004 Trade and Development Report, 'the average customs transaction involves 20–30 different parties, 40 documents, 200 data elements (30 of which are repeated at least 30 times) and the re-keying of 60–70% of all data at least once'. See WTO, *Annual Trade Report 2019* (Geneva: WTO, 2019); also WTO, Trade Facilitation, available at www.wto.org/english/tratop_e/tradfa_e/tradfa_e.htm.

[32] Before arriving to customs, goods are declared using the 'Single Administrative Document' (SAD), which in the EU is lodged electronically on the relevant customs system. The electronic data transfer captures information about the importing shipment, such as the Commodity Code, which provides the description of the product being shipped, and the Customs Procedures Code, which describes the procedure and/or regime under which the goods are being imported. Other important data elements contained on the SAD are importing country/business unit; ship from name/DUNS; ship to name/DUNS/plant code; description; quantity; value; country of origin; country of export; HS Code; free trade agreement status; amount of duty paid; mode of transportation; category (Prod/P&A/VEH/M&E); entry/invoice detail; import-related taxes and fees.

[33] The 'New Computerised Transit System' (NCTS) set up an EU-wide electronic exchange of customs declarations in 1997. The harmonization of customs forms started well before: in 1985 the Single Administration Document defined the common data elements to be used across the then European Community. See Council Regulation No 1900/85 of 11 July 1985 Introducing Community Export and Import Declaration Forms, OJ L [1985] 197/4.

[34] Decision No 70/2008/EC of the European Parliament and of the Council of 15 January 2008 on a Paperless Environment for Customs and Trade, OJ L [2008] 23/21 [hereinafter: e-Customs Decision].

[35] Article 1 E-Customs Decision obliges the commission and member states to 'set up secure, integrated, interoperable and accessible electronic customs systems for the exchange of data contained in customs declarations, documents accompanying customs declarations and certificates and the exchange of other relevant information. The Commission and the Member States shall provide the structure and means for the operation of those electronic customs systems'.

Strategic Plan.[36] Since 2016, the Union Customs Code sets the framework on the rules and procedures for customs in the European Union.[37] Crucially, it mandates that 'all exchanges of information . . . as required under the customs legislation, shall be made using electronic data-processing techniques' and identifies 2020 as the deadline for a paperless customs union.[38]

The compromise to move towards digitalized customs management has been extended to European Union trade partners via free trade agreements. The border enforcement sections of the intellectual property chapters of those trade agreements include compromises and best efforts–type of provisions to adopt digital management systems to monitor customs procedures. For instance, in the border enforcement sections of the 2019 EU association agreements with Japan and Vietnam, the use of electronic systems for the management of customs by applications of IP holders is encouraged, and the use of risk analysis to identify goods suspected of infringing IPRs is mandated.[39]

II *Big Data, Customs Control and Risk Analysis*

In the area of customs enforcement, big data provides new knowledge, drives value creation, fosters new processes and enhances well-informed decision making.[40] Reference is commonly made to three characteristics of big data:[41] high-volume, high-speed and high-variety of information assets.[42] The fact that big data is made up

---

[36] The Multi-Annual Strategic Plan (MASP) is a joint EU commission–member states management instrument that establishes the strategic framework and objectives for implementation of the e-Customs initiative.

[37] Article 6 Regulation No 952/2013 of the European Parliament and the Council of 9 October 2013 Laying Down the Union Customs Code, OJ L [2013] 269/1 [hereinafter: Union Customs Code Decision]. See also Article 16.1 Union Customs Code Decision, establishing that 'Member States shall cooperate with the Commission to develop, maintain and employ electronic systems for the exchange of information between customs authorities and with the Commission and for the storage of such information'.

[38] Articles 16, 278 and 280 of Union Customs Code Decision mandate developing a work programme for the development of electronic systems, relying of the previously existing multi-annual strategic plan and providing a timeline for the update and creation of electronic customs systems until the end of 2020. See also Regulation No 1294/2013 of the European Parliament and the Council of 11 December 2013 Establishing an Action Programme for Customs in the European Union 2014–2020 (Customs 2020) and Repealing Decision No 624/2007/E, OJ L [2013] 347/209.

[39] See, respectively, Articles 14.51(2) of the Japan–EU EPA and Article 12.59 of the Vietnam–EU FTA and the Investment Protection Agreement.

[40] Y. Okazaki, 'Implications of Big Data for Customs – How It Can Support Risk Management Capabilities', WCO Research Paper No 39 (2017).

[41] There is no single definition of big data. See J. S. Ward and A. Barker, 'Undefined by Data: A Survey of Big Data Definitions', *arXiv*:1309.5821v1, 20 September 2013. See also Chapter 7 in this volume.

[42] TechAmerica Foundation, *Demystifying Big Data: A Practical Guide to Transforming the Business of Government* (Washington, DC: TechAmerica Foundation, 2012).

of 'extremely large data sets'[43] echoes another, implicit, characteristic: most often, big data is made of 'raw' information of both public[44] and private nature which is incomplete and imperfect.

Big data enhances the potential of descriptive, predictive and prescriptive data analytics, namely the obtention of raw data and the examination of that information with the purpose of identifying patterns, drawing conclusions, predicting the future and providing the best solution.[45] Regarding risk management in the area of customs enforcement, big data allows to predict threats, monitor trends and target high-risk transactions. Nowadays, both descriptive risk rating and prescriptive risk management have been incorporated into customs enforcement operations. This is where text analytics, data mining, statistics, natural language processing and machine learning offer valuable information and display patterns of infringing activities.

Automation and learning from past events enhance the efficiency of selecting risky cargos, in particular by identifying suspicious networks and transactions. Automation also facilitates the estimation of potential loses and damages. Additionally, image recognition is of relevance to trademark counterfeiting. In this regard, analysis and exploitation of images for automatic verification of consistency against available information is instrumental to perform customs risk management intended to fight counterfeiting.[46] Devices and software developed to spot fakes in ordinary places of commerce, such as shops,[47] can be adapted to conduct similar preliminary assessments by customs authorities.

The question that arises is how to take bigger advantage of currently existing technical capacities and amounts of data. Three aspects seem critical: First, it is necessary to ensure the quality of data regarding cargos, shipments and conveyances, and also relevant information concerning intellectual property rights. Incompleteness and heterogeneous data formats[48] make it more difficult to efficiently use information

---

[43] That may be analyzed computationally to reveal patterns, trends and associations, especially relating to human behaviour and interactions.

[44] Customs administrations compile data they already possess and data they obtain from other authorities and areas of public administration. See, for example, for internal use of customs data by the same customs authorities the case of the United States Customs and Border Protection; and, for the case of inter-agency sharing and use, the case of Hong Kong China Customs' Central Information Repository. See Okazaki, note 40, at 9, 11.

[45] L. Keyes, 'Data Analytics. How Data Analytics Can Simplify and Facilitate Trade within the European Union', Europese Fiscale Studies (2015/2016), at 4–5. On analytics, see T. H. Davenport and J. G. Harris, *Competing on Analytics: The New Science of Winning* (Cambridge, MA: Harvard Business School Press, 2007), at 7.

[46] See, more broadly, *Policy Background for Customs Risk Management: Practitioners' Guidance Document* (Brussels: European Union, 2017).

[47] Simply by scanning suspect goods, one can identify infringement. The information provided feeds and makes the system richer and more performing for future occasions. M. Arrison, 'State of the Fake: 2019 Report', Entrupy, 2019.

[48] As noted, 'developing agreed formats and standards in the exchanging of data' would increase the efficiency of trade and enhance transparency. Keyes, note 45, at 3.

for analytical purposes.[49] Second, it is also important to widen the scope of the data used for analytical purposes. In this last respect, a possibility is to go beyond data of purely customs nature and correlate such data with, for instance, tax, crime or IP-related information.[50] Third, it is also necessary to overcome country differences in terms of capacity to implement common risk criteria and standards,[51] and to efficiently address IP infringement having a border enforcement component.

III *Distributed Ledger Technologies and Localization of Traded Goods*

Distributed ledger technologies allow moving from a single administrator who controls the ledger where information is stored to a ledger shared by a network of stakeholders. None of the members of the network has autonomous control and all changes made by a member of the network are visible and transparent.[52] A well-known example of public distributed ledger technology[53] is blockchain, which enables the recording of transactions between parties in a secure and permanent way while removing intermediaries that previously verified transactions – a function that is of relevance to many economic and technological fields.[54]

Efficiency, velocity, transparency, traceability and automation are the main advantages brought by distributed ledger technologies to international logistics and commercial processes.[55] Distributed ledger technologies significantly reduce bureaucracy and paperwork,[56] and may also enable new business models[57] and

---

[49] Big data contains both structured and unstructured data formats. The use of unstructured data represents an important challenge for customs administrations, which are used to formularies and forms that are adjusted to the international standards of the WCO and the United Nations Electronic Data Interchange for Administration, Commerce and Transport. The latter is the international standard for electronic data interchange (EDI). See Okazaki, note 40, at 14.
[50] See below the example given in the case of goods in transit.
[51] For the EU, see for instance note 46.
[52] For a clear and concise explanation of distributed ledger technologies, see M. Tripoli and J. Schmidhuber, *Emerging Opportunities for the Application of Blockchain in the Agri-Food Industry* (Geneva: ICTSD, 2018), at 3–5. See also Chapter 6 in this volume.
[53] A public distributed ledger technology is an open ledger with free access.
[54] Patent families of blockchain technologies allow the observation of the technology fields where most patents are filed which, in order, are (i) payment architectures, schemes or protocols; (ii) cryptographic mechanisms or cryptographic arrangements for secret or secure communication; (iii) network architectures or network communication protocols for network security; (iv) security arrangements for protecting computers; (v) finance; insurance; tax strategies; (vi) commerce, e.g. shopping or e-commerce; (vii) digital computing or data processing equipment or methods; (viii) data processing systems or methods; (ix) network-specific arrangements or communication protocols supporting networked applications. See Y. Ménière, 'The Emerging Blockchain Patent Landscape', *Presentation at EPO Conference on Patenting Blockchain*, 4 December 2018, at 8.
[55] DHL Trend Research, *Blockchain in Logistics* (Troisdorf: DHL Customer Solutions and Innovation, 2018), at 2.
[56] Ibid., at 4.
[57] For instance, digital identities, certificates, tamper-proof documents.

enhance asset management.[58] They furthermore make it possible to obtain information in respect of manufacturing practices, quality attributes and place of origin. In the area of intellectual property, traceability is among the most visible advantages brought by distributed ledger technologies, in particular for goods protected by IPRs that identify the origin of goods (geographical indications) and for goods protected by IPRs that enable consumers to identify specific producers, characteristics and qualities (trademarks).

A particularly valuable application in the area of customs control is the possibility offered by the Internet of Things (IoT) to capture the location, condition and status of traded goods in real time.[59] This allows logistics service operators to detect irregularities affecting the cargos, improve supply chain control and detect the introduction of fake products. In order to take full advantage of distributed ledger technologies, track and trace methods should ideally allow interaction, which means that some physical devices may be embedded in the traded goods that are object of control.

Track and trace methods belong to the broader group of anti-counterfeiting technologies, which include overt and covert authentication technologies that determine whether a product is original, and allow for enhanced control within the supply chain. Regarding authentication technologies, overt technologies are accessible using human senses, such as vision and touch, thus they do not need any specific physical device,[60] while covert technologies are hidden and only accessible to technology providers, brand owners or authorized stakeholders.[61] In respect of track and trace technologies, optical methods and Radio Frequency Identification (RFID) tags stand out.[62] Both of them allow for the localization of the product along the production and distribution chain: optical technologies consist of a code that contains information on the product and is affixed on the product itself,[63] whereas RFID tags can be read by radio

---

[58] It can be used to manage the ownership of digital assets and facilitate asset transfers. See DHL Trend Research, note 55, at 6.

[59] Digitalization of trade flows and end-to-end shipment tracking are objectives of collaboration between logistics and technology companies. The goal is to allow monitoring the progress of goods through the supply chain, overview the status of customs controls, view bills of lading and other data. On the collaboration between Maersk and IBM, see 'Maersk IBM Form Joint Venture Applying Blockchain to Improve Global Trade and Digitize Supply Chain', SupplyChain247, 8 January 2018.

[60] Among the drawbacks of these technologies, mention is commonly made of easier imitation, possible reuse and false assurance. See C. Smith, *Ensuring Supply Chain Security: The Role of Anti-Counterfeiting Technologies* (Torino: UNICRI, 2016), at 16. These technologies include holograms, color-shifting inks, security threads, micro-printing, bar-code technology and watermarks.

[61] Among the drawbacks noted in respect to these technologies, mention is commonly made of easier potential imitation, possible reuse and possible false assurance. Smith, note 60, at 16.

[62] Other include EPCs, barcodes, QR codes, datamatrix codes and web portal tools.

[63] Examples in the area of medicines and tobacco control are the Council of Europe Unique Medicine Identifier 'eTACT'; see Article 15 Directive 2014/40/EU of the European Parliament

waves.[64] As it has been noted, 'smart devices can be securely tied to or embedded in the physical product to autonomously record and transmit data about item condition including temperature variation, to ensure product integrity, as well as any evidence of product tampering'.[65] In the area of pharmaceutical products, for instance, this allows to asses at the same time several types of IP infringement and the compliance with regulatory standards.

D LEGAL CHALLENGES AND OPPORTUNITIES

The control of intellectual property protected goods in transit[66] exemplifies well how existing legal challenges can be addressed resorting to AI applications and big data.

I *Opportunities*

TRIPS does not require the control of goods protected by IPRs in transit, nor the monitoring of exports. It just orders impeding the importation of counterfeit and pirated goods.[67] Building on this minimum standard, a significant number of countries has enacted legislation that goes beyond such protection,[68] thus it is nowadays usual to find countries that control exports and, to a lesser extent, the transit of IP protected goods. This is particularly the case with trademark and copyright protected goods, but some countries also monitor goods protected by other IP categories.[69]

and of the Council of 3 April 2014 on the Approximation of the Laws, Regulations and Administrative Provisions of the Member States Concerning the Manufacture, Presentation and Sale of Tobacco and Related Products and Repealing Directive 2001/37/EC, OJ L [2014] 127/1.

[64] Smith, note 60, at 17.

[65] DHL Trend Research, note 55, at 16.

[66] Terminology varies across countries. In the EU, suspensive or 'special procedures' – in the terminology used in the 2008 Modernised Customs Code – include several possibilities: transit (external and internal); storage (temporary storage, customs warehousing and free zones); specific use (temporary admission and end-use) and processing (inward and outward processing). See Article 135 Regulation No 450/2008 of the European Parliament and of the Council of 23 April 2008 Laying Down the Community Customs Code (Modernised Customs Code), OJ L [2008] 145/1.

[67] See Article 51 TRIPS, which establishes that, in respect to customs operations that must be controlled, members must allow an application to be lodged for the suspension of the release into free circulation of imported counterfeit and pirated products.

[68] For instance, pursuant to EU Regulation No 608/2013, authorities must supervise goods when declared for release for free circulation, in the cases of exportation or re-exportation, when entering or leaving the customs territory of the European Union, and when placed under a suspensive procedure or in a free zone or free warehouse.

[69] Some agreements refer not only to counterfeit and pirated goods, but to all types of trademark and copyright infringements. A smaller but increasing number of trade agreements include the obligation to control categories of intellectual property rights distinct from trademarks and

In the case of the control of goods in transit, the goal of the country of transit is to impede the arrival of products to foreign jurisdictions. This may generate tensions with two fundamental principles – the principle of territoriality of IP protection and the principle of freedom of transit of internationally traded goods. Such tension is severe in respect of the principle of territoriality, since some countries have put in place customs controls of goods in transit that disregard the status of IP protection in the country of origin and in the country of destination. In these cases, seizure and eventual destruction are decided according to the law of the country of transit, hence eroding the principle of territoriality. In the case of the principle of freedom of transit, the tension is also acute, and both legal reform and courts have qualified the cases where restriction of freedom of transit is acceptable to control goods protected by IPRs. The legal standards developed are intended to preserve the balance between adequate IP protection and the principles just referred to. As argued earlier, however, they could benefit from technological advances in the area of big data and AI.

Pursuant to EU Regulation No 608/2013, goods are suspected of infringing an intellectual property right if there are indications that where such goods are found in a member state, they are the subject of an act infringing an intellectual property right.[70] However, the mere transit of goods through a country where they are protected does not imply an infringement.[71] In response to the heated debates arising from the detention of medicines in transit,[72] EU Regulation No 608/2013 stated that 'customs authorities should, when assessing a risk of infringement of intellectual property rights, take account of any substantial likelihood of diversion of such medicines onto the market of the Union'.[73] The Court of Justice of the European Union (CJEU) linked the detention and the suspension of release of

---

copyright. This is the case of treaties that order the control of patents, designs, geographical indications, utility models and plant varieties.

[70] See Article 2.7(a) EU Regulation No 608/2013.

[71] The CJEU adopted in 2011 a seminal judicial decision on the temporary detention and eventual destruction of goods placed under a suspensive procedure. In its reply to the joined *Philips* and *Nokia* cases, the CJEU restated its previous jurisprudence, holding that the mere placement of goods under a suspensive procedure does not entitle right holders to request the detention of goods, and that no infringement of IPRs can be found if there is no evidence of the potential diversion of goods. See CJEU, Joined Cases C-446/09 and C-495/09, *Koninklijke Philips Electronics NV (C-446/09) v. Lucheng Meijing Industrial Company Ltd and Others and Nokia Corporation (C-495/09) v. Her Majesty's Commissioners of Revenue and Customs* [2011], ECR I-12435.

[72] F. M. Abbott, 'Seizure of Generic Pharmaceuticals in Transit Based on Allegations of Patent Infringement: A Threat to International Trade, Development and Public Welfare', *WIPO Journal* 1 (2009), 43–50; H. Grosse Ruse-Khan and T. Jaeger, 'Policing Patents Worldwide? EC Border Measures against Transiting Generic Drugs under EC and WTO Intellectual Property Regimes', *International Review of Intellectual Property and Competition Law* 40 (2009), 502–538; X. Seuba, *Free Trade of Pharmaceutical Products: The Limits of Intellectual Property Enforcement at the Border* (Geneva: ICTSD, 2010), at 9.

[73] See Recital 11 and Article 1.5 EU Regulation No 608/2013.

protected goods in transit to the potential diversion of those goods onto the transited market, thus only by placing the goods in the internal market can the subject matter of a specific intellectual property right be infringed.[74] Likewise, if goods are the subject of a commercial act directed to European consumers, intellectual property rights may be infringed and goods placed under a suspensive procedure may be detained. The risk of fraudulent diversion to European consumers may also arise in other circumstances, even when goods have not yet been directed towards European consumers. Customs authorities can, in effect, detain the goods or suspend their release when there are indications that commercial activities may take place in the near future or are being disguised.[75] Suspicion, based on a number of facts of the case, will suffice for that purpose. The CJEU gave a number of examples, including the destination of the goods not being declared, the lack of precise or reliable information as to the identity or address of the manufacturer or consignor of the goods, a lack of cooperation with the customs authorities, or the discovery of documents suggesting that there is a likelihood of a diversion of those goods to EU consumers.[76]

The control of the scenarios described in the paragraph above is difficult in the daily operation of customs control. Some of the examples given by the CJEU require that customs officials and/or right holders have access to information that, most often, is not publicly available. On other occasions, the volume of internationally traded goods makes it almost impossible to manage existing information. These are problems, however, that big data and AI can help to overcome. In the first case, if the use of distributed ledger technologies and track and trace technologies became general, the efficiency of control would increase exponentially. As explained by Okazaki, advanced sensor technology 'allows logistics service providers to detect any irregularities occurring in or around the cargos in transit, thus helping to enhance supply chain security. As such, a containerized cargo being once regarded as "low-risk" or "risk-free" can maintain the same condition until it is delivered at the destination unless any suspicious intervention is detected during the time of transport'.[77]

Management of data at the international level can also be instrumental in another, very practical, context. In order to protect IP, some countries have introduced legal regimes that, while allowing to take action regarding goods in transit, still differ from the EU model described earlier. An interesting, while controversial,

---

[74] Ibid., at para. 70.
[75] According to the CJEU, a customs authority can act when there are indications before it that one or more of the operators involved in the manufacture, consignment or distribution of the goods in warehousing or transit, while not having yet begun to direct the goods towards EU consumers, are about to do so or are disguising their commercial intentions. See *Philips v. Nokia*, above note 71, at para. 60.
[76] Ibid., at paras. 61 and 71.
[77] Okazaki, note 40, at 17.

alternative consists of anticipating the moment and location of the protection. This is the model followed by Switzerland, where the patent owner can impede the transit of patent-infringing goods if he can also prohibit the import into the country of destination.[78] Hence, Swiss law permits anticipating the moment of the protection that the same title holder could demand in the country of destination. Although it relates to patents, Swiss authorities justify such anticipation 'in view of the increasing international dimension of counterfeiting and piracy',[79] and in order to 'prevent Switzerland from becoming a transit country for pirated goods'.[80] In the context of trademark law, the EU has also made relevant the law of the final country of destination. In the EU, the entitlement of the trademark proprietor to detain products in transit shall lapse if, in the context of customs procedures, 'evidence is provided by the declarant or the holder of the goods that the proprietor of the registered trade mark is not entitled to prohibit the placing of the goods on the market in the country of final destination'.[81]

Naturally, should border authorities have direct and speedy access to the database of intellectual property offices from all over the world, they could also rapidly verify whether the IP owner who claims to have the right to impede importation to the country of destination is entitled to do so. It is difficult to envisage such a system to function ex officio, but it would accelerate procedures if the process were initiated at the request of an interested party. The same applies in respect to the holding made by the proprietor or consignor of the goods in the example provided regarding the EU. Advanced analytics allows to correlate internal data with other categories of data. In particular, it allows to correlate the customs situation, national intellectual property and international intellectual property protection status in the country of destination. Thus, putting existing sources of information and technologies at work for the benefit of customs authorities would make it more feasible to meet standards that, right now, are rather difficult to attain because of technical and resource-related constraints.

II *Challenges*

While big data and AI bring about new opportunities in the context of IP enforcement, including customs enforcement, new challenges also emerge. On this

---

[78] See Article 8.3 Swiss Federal Act on Patents for Inventions (PatA) of 25 June 1954 (Status as of 1 April 2019); also Swiss Federal Institute of Intellectual Property, Interpretation of the Patents Act, available at www.ige.ch/fileadmin/user_upload/recht/national/e/Auslegeordnung_Patentgesetz_e.pdf.

[79] Ibid.

[80] Ibid.

[81] See Article 10.4 and Recital 23 Directive 2015/2436 of the European Parliament and of the Council of 16 December 2015 to Approximate the Laws of the Member States Relating to Trade Marks, OJ L [2015] 336/1.

occasion, concerns arising from automation of the law and due process restrictions become also of relevance in respect of border enforcement.

In contrast to the TRIPS standard of releasing the goods that have been detained while in transit, the EU has put in place a speedy process for the destruction of goods suspected – but not confirmed – of infringing IPRs. TRIPS mandates the release of goods in case proceedings leading to a decision on the merits of the case have not been initialed or provisional measures have not been adopted within a period of ten working days after the applicant has been served notice of the suspension.[82] However, the EU has inverted the logic behind this rule and has established that the destruction of the goods will follow, without any further procedure on the merits of the case, if the alleged infringer does not respond in due time to the seizure.[83]

It is predictable that the automation of procedures will result in more cargos being detained and more notifications of such detentions being sent to the owners of the cargos. However, economic and operational difficulties to respond to this type of processes, taking place in different continents and eventually exceeding what small companies can afford, will persist. In many instances, the owner of the goods may not contest the detention because, for instance, doing so may be more expensive than the value of the parcel that has been detained, or just for lack of knowledge or lack of time to react. If other, compensatory, measures – also of a technological nature – are not introduced, due process standards, in particular the right to a fair hearing and the presumption of innocence, become clearly threatened, especially when the right holder does not even need to start procedures on the merits of the case.

Reflections made by Citron in respect of due process and algorithmic enforcement, and the need to ensure that analytical algorithms satisfy standards of review guaranteeing fairness and accuracy, are fully applicable to customs enforcement.[84] A number of actions would mitigate those concerns. First, it is necessary to improve transparency (or at least the understanding) of the algorithms that determine which cargos and goods will be detained and inspected.[85] Next, it is also necessary to allow challenging the decision and detention undertaken with the assistance of automated

---

[82] Article 55 TRIPS.

[83] EU Regulation No 1383/2003 allowed a procedure for destroying certain goods without there being any obligation to initiate proceedings to establish whether an intellectual property right has been infringed. EU Regulation No 608/2013 has made the procedure compulsory with regard to all IP infringements and orders to apply it where the declarant or the holder of the goods does not explicitly oppose destruction.

[84] D. K. Citron, 'Technological Due Process', *Washington University Law Review* 85 (2008), 1301–1333.

[85] On lack of transparency of algorithmic decision making, see Perel and Elkin-Koren, note 17, at 517–518. The central features of algorithms do not make things easy: 'Algorithms are non-transparent by nature; their decision-making criteria are concealed behind a veil of code that we cannot easily read and comprehend. Additionally, these algorithms are dynamic in their ability to evolve according to different data patterns. This further makes them unpredictable'. Perel and Elkin-Koren, note 15, at 190.

mechanisms. Finally, it must also be possible to enable public oversight of automated border enforcement.[86] In reality, these concerns are not really different from
those expressed in other areas of IP enforcement where automation has become a
common practice, as discussed earlier.

E CONCLUSIONS

Digitalization, big data and distributed ledger technologies drastically change law
enforcement. When applied to customs control, as it happens in other domains,
these technologies result in cost savings and promote more efficient and less-prone-
to-error administrative, judicial and commercial processes. Interconnectedness,
instant access to foreign databases and constant monitoring of the precise location
of goods allow to implement, for instance, standards relating to the control of goods
in transit that were difficult to meet until now. Similarly, AI functional applications,
such as image recognition, combined with the possibility to constantly and exponentially learn from past events, strengthen systems to control internationally traded
goods protected by intellectual property rights.

  Together with opportunities, challenges of both technical and legal nature also
arise. Technical challenges are still manifold and relate to aspects such as the low
quality and heterogeneous formats of digitalized data feeding AI functional applications. Legal concerns expressed in respect of algorithmic law enforcement relate to
transparency, accountability and contestability of decisions. These concerns, which
are of a general nature, are also of relevance to customs enforcement, as seen in the
case of the automation of decisions concerning goods in transit. Algorithmic law
enforcement must respond to the mentioned challenges and acknowledge in particular that intellectual property enforcement is a process of weighing and balancing
rights and interests of different nature, and not an automated process to implement a
predefined decision. Discretion and proportionality are central in the enforcement
process, but these are attributes of remedies that require human virtues and skills
that the current level of technological development does not seem capable to
replicate yet.

---

[86] For similar analysis but in the area of copyright enforcement, see Perel and Elkin-Koren, note
  17, at 476.

PART III

Safeguarding Privacy and Other Users' Rights in the Age of Big Data

9

Futuring Digital Privacy

Reimaging the Law/Tech Interplay

Urs Gasser*

A INTRODUCTION

The history of privacy is deeply intertwined with the history of technology. A wealth of scholarly literature tracks and demonstrates how privacy as a normative concept has evolved in light of new information and communication technologies since the early modern period, when face-to-face interactions were challenged by urbanization and the rise of mass communication.[1] In the beginning of the nineteenth century, a combination of societal changes, institutional developments, and technological advancements gave birth to a series of new threats to privacy. At the time, innovative technologies – such as telegraph communications and portable cameras – were among the key drivers (interacting with other factors, such as increased literacy rates) that led to growing concerns about privacy protection. These developments also set the stage for Samuel Warren and Louis Brandeis's highly influential

* Urs Gasser is Professor of Practice and Executive Director of the Berkman Klein Center for Internet and Society, Harvard Law School. Contact: ugasser@law.harvard.edu.
[1] See, e.g., C. J. Bennett, *Regulating Privacy: Data Protection and Public Policy in Europe and the United States* (Ithaca: Cornell University Press, 1992); P. M. Regan, *Legislating Privacy: Technology, Social Values, and Curiosity from Plymouth Rock to the Internet* (Chapel Hill: The University of North Carolina Press, 1995); R. E. Smith, *Ben Franklin's Web Site: Privacy and Curiosity from Plymouth Rock to the Internet* (Providence: Privacy Journal, 2000); D. J. Solove and P. M. Schwartz, *Information Privacy Law*, 5th edn (New York: Wolters Kluwer 2015); D. J. Solove, 'The Origins and Growth of Information Privacy Law', in J. B. Kennedy, P. M. Schwartz, and F. Gilbert (eds), *Fourth Annual Institute on Privacy Law: Protecting Your Client in a Security-Conscious World* (New York: Practising Law Institute, 2003), 29–83; D. Vincent, *Privacy: A Short History* (Cambridge: Polity Press, 2016); A. F. Westin, *Privacy and Freedom* (New York: Atheneum, 1967); I. R. Kramer, 'The Birth of Privacy Law: A Century Since Warren and Brandeis', *Catholic University Law Review* 39 (1990), 703–724; W. L. Prosser, 'Privacy [a Legal Analysis]', in F. D. Schoeman (ed), *Philosophical Dimensions of Privacy: An Anthology* (Cambridge: Cambridge University Press, 1984), 104–155; D. J. Solove, 'A Brief History of Information Privacy Law', in C. Wolf (ed), *Proskauer on Privacy* (New York: Practising Law Institute, 2006), 1–46.

1890 article *The Right to Privacy*,[2] which was written, in large part, in response to the combined negative effects of the rise of the 'yellow press' and the adaptation of 'instantaneous photography' as privacy-invading practices and technologies.[3] Similarly, advancements in information and communication technologies in the twentieth century, combined with other developments, such as the rise of the welfare state, challenged existing notions of information privacy and led to renegotiations of the boundaries between the private and public spheres.

Later in the twentieth century, the development, adaptation, and use of innovative technologies that enabled increased collection and use of personal information were also among the key drivers that led to the birth of modern information privacy law in the early 1970s. Starting in the United States and then extending to Europe, the increased use of computers for information processing and storage by government agencies was an important factor that led to the first generation of modern information privacy and data protection laws.[4] Anchored in a set of fair information practices,[5] many of these laws were expanded, adjusted, and supplemented over the following decades in light of evolving technologies and changing institutional practices, which – together with other factors – resulted in an ever-growing cascade of privacy concerns. In the 1990s, for instance, the widespread adoption of Internet technology as a global information and communication medium and the rise of the database industry led to a wave of legislative and regulatory interventions aimed at dealing with emerging privacy problems. More recent and more ambitious information privacy reforms, such as the revision of the influential OECD Privacy Guidelines at the international level,[6] the General Data Protection Regulation (GDPR) in the EU,[7] the proposed Consumer Privacy Bill of

[2] S. D. Warren and L. D. Brandeis, 'The Right to Privacy', *Harvard Law Review* 4 (1890), 193–220. The article had a profound impact on the development of state tort law and privacy-related causes of action. See, e.g., W. L. Prosser, 'Privacy', *California Law Review* 48 (1960), 386–423; see also D. Solove, 'Does Scholarship Really Have an Impact? The Article that Revolutionized Privacy Law', TeachPrivacy, 30 March 2015.

[3] See A. Busch, 'Privacy, Technology, and Regulation: Why One Size Is Unlikely to Fit All', in B. Roessler and D. Mokrosinska (eds), *Social Dimensions of Privacy: Interdisciplinary Perspectives* (Cambridge: Cambridge University Press, 2015), 303–323.

[4] See US Department of Health, Education, and Welfare, *Records, Computers, and the Rights of Citizens: Report of the Secretary's Advisory Committee on Automated Personal Data Systems* (Cambridge, MA: MIT Press, 1973).

[5] In essence, Fair Information Principles 'are a set of internationally recognized practices for addressing the privacy of information about individuals'. R. Gellman, 'Fair Information Practices: A Basic History', unpublished manuscript, 17 June 2016, available at http://bobgellman .com/rg-docs/rg-FIPShistory.pdf.

[6] OECD, *The OECD Privacy Framework: Supplementary Explanatory Memorandum to the Revised OECD Privacy Guidelines* (Paris: OECD, 2013).

[7] Regulation 2016/679 of the European Parliament and of the Council of 27 April 2016 on the Protection of Natural Persons with Regard to the Processing of Personal Data and on the Free Movement of Such Data, and Repealing Directive 95/46/EC (General Data Protection Regulation), OJ L [2016] 119/1.

Rights Act,[8] or the California Consumer Privacy Act[9] in the United States seek to update existing or introduce new information privacy norms for the digital age – again driven, in part, by new technologies and applications such as cloud computing, big data, and artificial intelligence, among others.

Reflecting across centuries and geographies, one common thread emerges: advancements in information and communication technologies have largely been perceived as *threats* to privacy and have often led policymakers to seek, and citizens and consumers to demand, additional privacy safeguards in the legal and regulatory arenas. This perspective on technology as a challenge to existing notions of and safeguards for information privacy is also reflective of the mindset of contemporary law and policymaking. Whether considering the implications of big data technologies, sensor networks and the Internet of Things (IoT), facial recognition technology, always-on wearable technologies with voice and video interfaces, virtual and augmented reality, or artificial intelligence (AI), information privacy and data protection challenges have surfaced among the most pressing concerns in recent policy reports and regulatory analyses.[10]

But over the decades, the development and adoption of new technologies across varying socio-economic contexts has periodically culminated in critical inflection points that offered individuals and society opportunities to re-examine and advance the notion of privacy itself.[11] Arguably, the current wave of privacy-invasive technologies marks another such inflection point. The scale and pace of society's digital transformation suggest that what is unfolding are not just gradual technological changes, but rather seismic shifts in the information ecosystem that call for a deeper rethinking of privacy.[12] The magnitude of this historical moment is reflected in an array of trends: the rise of data colonialism[13] and surveillance capitalism,[14] increased

---

[8] The White House, Administration Discussion Draft: Consumer Privacy Bill of Rights Act, 2015, available at https://obamawhitehouse.archives.gov/sites/default/files/omb/legislative/letters/cpbr-act-of-2015-discussion-draft.pdf.
[9] State of California Department of Justice, California Consumer Privacy Act (CCPA), 2020, available at https://oag.ca.gov/privacy/ccpa.
[10] See, e.g., Executive Office of the President, *Big Data: Seizing Opportunities, Preserving Values* (Washington, DC: The White House, 2014); US Federal Trade Commission, *Internet of Things: Privacy and Security in a Connected World* (Washington, DC: Federal Trade Commission, 2015); Independent High-Level Expert Group on Artificial Intelligence, *Ethics Guidelines for Trustworthy AI* (Brussels: The European Commission, 2019); OECD, Recommendation of the Council on Artificial Intelligence, OECD/LEGAL/0449, 21 May 2019.
[11] See, e.g., S. Rodotà, 'Data Protection as a Fundamental Right', in S. Gutwirth et al. (eds), *Reinventing Data Protection?* (New York: Springer, 2009).
[12] W. Hartzog and N. M. Richards, 'Privacy's Constitutional Moment and the Limits of Data Protection', *Boston College Law Review* 61 (2020), 1687–1761.
[13] N. Couldry and U. A. Mejias, *The Costs of Connection: How Data Is Colonizing Human Life and Appropriating It for Capitalism* (Stanford: Stanford University Press, 2019).
[14] S. Zuboff, *Surveillance Capitalism: The Fight for a Human Future at the New Frontier of Power* (New York: Hachette Book Group, 2019).

privacy-awareness post Facebook's Cambridge Analytica scandal,[15] AI's ability to amplify privacy risks,[16] and many more.

Some current developments already indicate or suggest shifts and innovations within privacy and data protection regimes in response to the latest changes in the socio-technological environment. For example, basic ideas of how privacy should be defined have already begun to change. At a fundamental level, for instance, some scholars propose to (re-)conceptualize privacy as trust.[17] At a more granular level, scholars have argued for a movement away from understanding privacy as attached to the individual towards a notion of group privacy.[18] In the context of genomics, for example, this idea is particularly important – the exposure of one individual's DNA data directly impacts the privacy rights of that individual's entire extended family. Similarly, privacy risks are no longer generated only by exposure of private data; rather, they can also be triggered by inferences made through analytics.[19] Thus, privacy advocates have called for regulation that protects individuals in not only the inputs but also outputs of data processing.[20]

As legal and regulatory frameworks gradually adapt to these and other facets of privacy, data-holding entities also face the challenge of figuring out the precise contours of their responsibilities to the individuals whose data they collect and process. The development of new accountability frameworks, for instance in the context of data-processing algorithms, as well as novel mechanisms to delineate the responsibilities of these entities, such as the idea of information fiduciaries,[21] also signal a potential paradigm shift in the ways information privacy and data protection are approached.

This chapter is interested in one specific cross-cutting dimension of what might be labelled as the *rethinking privacy discourse*. It asks whether and how the interplay between technology and privacy law – both systems that govern information flows – can be reimagined and organized in mutually productive ways. The chapter proceeds in four steps: (i) explaining some of the dynamics that motivate a rethinking of privacy in the modern moment; (ii) developing a historical understanding of the dominant patterns connecting the evolutions of law and technology; (iii) examining

---

[15] I. Lapowsky, 'How Cambridge Analytica Sparked the Great Privacy Awakening', *Wired*, 17 March 2019.

[16] K. Manheim and L. Kaplan, 'Artificial Intelligence: Risks to Privacy and Democracy', *Yale Journal of Law and Technology* 21 (2019), 106–188.

[17] See, e.g., A. E. Waldman, *Privacy as Trust: Information Privacy for an Information Age* (Cambridge: University Printing House, 2018).

[18] B. Mittelstadt, 'From Individual to Group Privacy in Big Data Analytics', *Philosophy and Technology* 30 (2017), 475–494.

[19] S. Wachter and B. Mittelstadt, 'A Right to Reasonable Inferences: Re-thinking Data Protection Law in the Age of Big Data and AI', *Oxford Business Law Blog*, 9 October 2018.

[20] Ibid.

[21] J. M. Balkin, 'Information Fiduciaries and the First Amendment', *UC Davis Law Review* 49 (2016), 1183–1234.

a potential way to reimagine the dynamic between these elements moving forward; and (iv) sketching elements of a pathway towards 're-coding' privacy law.

B THE MODERN MOMENT IN TECHNOLOGY

The culmination of multiple factors at the intersection among digital technologies, market paradigms, social norms, professional practices, and traditional privacy laws has prompted the urgency of the need to rethink privacy and data protection in the current moment. Among the most important drivers behind the intensified debates about the future of digital privacy as broadly defined are increasingly visible shifts in traditional power structures, more specifically towards governments with unprecedented surveillance capabilities as well as large technology companies that amass digital tracking technologies and large pools of data to develop the corresponding analytical capability to shape people's lives.[22]

From a historical perspective, it is worth remembering that it was also power shifts that triggered the emergence of the modern information privacy and data protection laws in the 1970s, when the adoption of new technologies in the form of mainframe computers created an imbalance in power between different branches of government.[23] Somewhat similarly, contemporary power struggles among governments, technology companies, and citizens/users might mark another milestone with the potential to affect the political economy of privacy in the longer term. In the United States, the significance of these changes are reflected in a backlash: a variety of developments, ranging from increased activity among lawmakers and regulators[24] to critique by leaders of tech companies themselves,[25] suggest that the 'data-industrial complex' (understood traditionally as the symbiosis between the technology companies of Silicon Valley and the US government) has eroded in the aftermath of the Snowden revelations and in light of the Facebook/Cambridge Analytica scandal, which have demonstrated how profound the effects of such power shifts can be. The ensuing flurry of proposals for privacy legislation at the local, state, and national

---

[22] Similar shifts triggered a 'rethinking' exercise about a decade ago; see H. Burkert, 'Towards Next Generation of Data Protection Legislation', in S. Gutwirth et al. (eds), *Reinventing Data Protection?* (New York: Springer, 2009).

[23] H. Burkert, 'Theories of Information in Law', *Journal of Law and Information Science* 1 (1982), 120–130.

[24] See, e.g., K. Chen, 'Yanging and Hanging onto Our Own Data', *Berkeley Technology Law Journal Blog*, 30 December 2019; M. Cantwell, 'Cantwell, Senate Democrats Unveil Strong Online Privacy Rights', *Press Release*, 26 November 2019, available at www.cantwell.senate.gov/news/press-releases/cantwell-senate-democrats-unveil-strong-online-privacy-rights; 'Senator Wicker Circulates Draft Privacy Bill', *Hunton Andrews Kurth*, 3 December 2019, available at www.huntonprivacyblog.com/2019/12/03/senator-wicker-circulates-draft-privacy-bill/; D. Shepardson, 'Trump Administration Working on Consumer Data Privacy Policy', *Reuters*, 27 July 2018.

[25] N. Lomas, 'Apple's Tim Cook Makes Blistering Attack on the "Data Industrial Complex"', *TechCrunch*, 24 October 2018.

levels can be understood as attempts to course-correct and address some of the previously less visible power shifts between public and private actors.[26]

Different manifestations and perceptions of such power shifts also fuel international and regional debates that point out the urgent need to address the privacy crisis of the digital age. This crisis has inspired the enactment of the GDPR in Europe and similar legislative efforts in other parts of the world,[27] as well as intensified global debates about 'data sovereignty', which can be understood as an immune system response triggered by the power shifts associated with the unprecedented surveillance capabilities of foreign governments and technology companies.[28]

In addition to tectonic power shifts, technology-induced changes also motivate the need to rethink privacy from within the field. A series of conceptual and definitional questions are illustrative in this respect. For example, is 'personally identifiable information' in a big data environment still a meaningful classification to trigger privacy laws?[29] What about the traditional privacy-protecting techniques, such as anonymization? In a world where volumes of ostensibly innocuous data are available on most individuals, composition effects make re-identification of individuals and reconstruction of databases possible, and even likely, in many cases.[30] How should privacy harms be defined when traditional legal standards do not easily apply to the new types of cumulative, often long-term, and immaterial effects of privacy invasions?[31] These examples are indicative of the need to revisit some of the conventional terms and concepts privacy laws have long relied upon now that they are challenged by technological advances and the socio-economic practices they enable.

Finally, in an increasingly digitally connected environment, privacy has become a complex right that requires re-evaluating the trade-offs inherent to the idea of 'privacy'. Privacy is, of course, not an absolute right; there are limits, barriers, and frequently values that are in tension with each other. Although a concept deeply

---

[26] See, e.g., 'US 50-State Statutory and Legislative Charts', IAPP, available at https://iapp.org/resources/article/us-50-state-statutory-and-legislative-charts/.

[27] See, e.g., 'Data Protection Laws of the World: Full Handbook', IAPP, 6 March 2019, available at https://iapp.org/media/pdf/resource_center/Data-Protection-Full.pdf.

[28] See, e.g., S. Couture and S. Toupin, 'What Does the Concept of "Sovereignty" Mean in Digital, Network, and Technological Sovereignty?', *GigaNet Annual Symposium*, 2017.

[29] See, e.g., P. M. Schwartz and D. J. Solove, 'The PII Problem: Privacy and a New Concept of Personally Identifiable Information', *New York University Law Review* 86 (2011), 1814–1894; E. Ramirez, 'Protecting Consumer Privacy in the Digital Age: Reaffirming the Role of Consumer Control', Keynote Address of FTC Chairwoman Edith Ramirez Technology Policy Institute Aspen Forum, Aspen, 22 August 2016.

[30] See, e.g., C. Dwork et al., 'Exposed! A Survey of Attacks on Private Data', *Annual Review of Statistics and Its Application*, 2017, 61–84; A. Fluitt et al., 'Data Protection's Composition Problem', *European Data Protection Law Review* 5 (2019), 285–292, at 285–286.

[31] See D. J. Solove and D. Citron, 'Risk and Anxiety: A Theory of Data Breach Harms', *Texas Law Review* 96 (2018), 737–786, at 745–746; 'In re U.S. Office of Personnel Management Data Security Breach Litigation', *Harvard Law Review* 133 (2020), 1095–1102.

shaped by technology, it is also directly linked to shifting social norms and normative expectations.[32] In the age of big data, the balancing act of navigating trade-offs between normative values becomes increasingly important and difficult. For example, the right to be forgotten, by prioritizing privacy interests, necessarily reduces freedom of expression and commercial interests in the data market.[33] The real challenge of privacy has now become figuring out how to balance trade-offs in a scalable manner – whether that requires developing decision trees or balancing tests – that is not merely a post hoc rationalization for a particular outcome. As the design and processes of modern technology become more sophisticated, and as big societal challenges, such as climate change or public health, increasingly rely on the collection and analysis of large amounts of data, these trade-offs will only become more pervasive and more difficult.[34]

Taken together, the modern era of digital technology has arguably pushed the need to rethink 'privacy' to become something more fundamental – a need to re-examine and potentially renegotiate the very concepts and values that society cares about in privacy. Both in terms of problem description and possible pathways forward, this may require, for example, reaching outside the frame of privacy and data protection law altogether to other areas of law and policy writ large. The interplay between technology and society and law is extraordinarily nuanced, and there are a wide variety of levellers and instruments available to help shape the societal effects of technologies in the human context.[35] More narrowly, and simplifying for the purposes of this chapter, it might be helpful to examine some archetypical response patterns from when law has responded to technology-induced information privacy concerns in the past.

C HISTORICAL PATTERNS OF INTERACTION BETWEEN LAW AND TECHNOLOGY

In considering the fundamentally defensive stance that privacy law has taken historically with regard to technology, it is important to note that law in the broader context of information and communication technology has often transcended its

---

[32] K. Nissim and A. Wood, 'Is Privacy Privacy?', *Philosophical Transactions of the Royal Society* A 376 (2018), 1–19.

[33] 'Tradeoffs in the Right to Be Forgotten', *Harvard Civil Rights–Civil Liberties Law Review*, 26 February 2012, available at https://harvardcrcl.org/tradeoffs-in-the-right-to-be-forgotten/.

[34] See, e.g., I. Graef and J. Prüfer, 'Mandated Data Sharing Is a Necessity in Specific Sectors', *Economomisch Statistische Berichten* 103 (2018), 298–301; C. L. Borgman, 'The Conundrum of Sharing Research Data', *Journal of the American Society for Information Science and Technology* 63 (2012), 1059–1078.

[35] See generally Y. Benkler, 'The Role of Technology in Political Economy: Part I', *Law and Political Economy*, 25 July 2018, available at https://lpeblog.org/2018/07/25/the-role-of-technology-in-political-economy-part-1/; Y. Benkler, 'The Role of Technology in Political Economy: Part II', *Law and Political Economy*, 26 July 2018, available at https://lpeblog.org/2018/07/26/the-role-of-technology-in-political-economy-part-2/; Y. Benkler, 'The Role of Technology in Political Economy: Part 3', *Law and Political Economy*, 27 July 2018, available at https://lpeblog.org/2018/07/27/the-role-of-technology-in-political-economy-part-3/.

familiar role as a constraint on behaviour acting through the imposition of sanctions.[36] In areas, such as intellectual property and antitrust, law has sought to engage with technology in a more nuanced way by enabling or in some cases levelling desired innovative or disruptive activity.[37] With this understanding of law as a functionally differentiated response system, and acknowledging that legal responses to technological innovation should not be understood as a simple stimulus-response mechanism, it is possible to identify a series of historical *response patterns* that characterize the evolution of privacy and data protection law vis-à-vis technological change. At a general level, three analytically distinct, but in practice often overlapping, response modes can be identified.[38]

1. When dealing with innovative technologies, the legal system – including privacy and data protection law – by default often seeks to apply the old rules to the (new) problem resulting from new technology and its uses (subsumption). One illustration of this default response mode is US courts' application of privacy torts, for instance, to address complaints about improper collection, use, or disclosure of data by digital businesses, such as Google and Facebook, because these analyses largely rely on tort conceptions of privacy advanced in the late nineteenth century.[39]
2. Where subsumption is considered insufficient due to the novelty of the issues raised by a new technology, the legal system might resort instead to innovation within its own system. One version of this response mode is to 'upgrade' existing (privacy) norms gradually, typically by setting new precedent or by adjusting and complementing current norms (gradual innovation). Proposals to introduce a tort for the misuse of personal information by data traders,[40] to provide legal recognition of data harms by extending developments from other areas of the law, such as torts and contracts,[41] to enact a Consumer Privacy Bill of Rights Act,[42] and to expand consumers' rights to access their data records within reasonable timeframes,[43] are all examples of gradual legal innovations that leave core elements of the current regulatory approach unchanged.

---

[36] J. E. Cohen, *Between Truth and Power: The Legal Constructions of Informational Capitalism* (Oxford/New York: Oxford University Press, 2019).
[37] See U. Gasser, 'Perspectives on the Future of Digital Privacy', *Zeitschrift für Schweizerisches Recht* 134 (2015), 338–448, at 368–369. On the innovation-enabling function of law, see also A. Chander, 'How Law Made Silicon Valley', *Emory Law Journal* 63 (2014), 639–694.
[38] Ibid., at 368–369.
[39] See, e.g., *Boring v. Google Inc.*, 362 Fed. App'x 273, 278–80 (3d Cir. 2010).
[40] See S. Ludington, 'Reining in the Data Traders: A Tort for the Misuse of Personal Information', *Maryland Law Review* 66 (2006), 140–193, at 173.
[41] See Solove and Citron, note 31.
[42] See The White House, note 8.
[43] M. Korolov, 'California Consumer Privacy Act (CCPA): What You Need to Know to Be Compliant', CSO, 4 October 2019, available at www.csoonline.com/article/3292578/california-consumer-privacy-act-what-you-need-to-know-to-be-compliant.html.

3. A more radical, paradigm-shifting approach is deeper-layered law reform where not only are individual norms updated, but also entire approaches or instruments are changed. In addition to the proposals already mentioned in the introduction, examples in this category include efforts to reimagine privacy regimes based on models that emerged in the field of environmental law,[44] to reformulate the current crisis as data pollution and develop social instruments that address the external harms associated with the collection and misuse of personal data,[45] to create an alternative dispute resolution scheme, such as a 'cyber court' system to deal with large-scale privacy threats in the digital age,[46] or to introduce a 'Digital Millennium Privacy Act' that would provide immunity for those companies willing to subscribe to a set of information fiduciary duties,[47] to name just a few illustrations.

Perhaps the most interesting, and arguably the most promising, approach to reprogramming information privacy and data protection law in a more fundamental sense stems from such a paradigm-shifting approach: to embrace the multi-faceted, functional role of law and reframe technology, as broadly defined, no longer (only) as a threat to privacy, but as part of the *solution space*.

Precursors of such a potential shift date back to the 1970s, when researchers under the header of 'Privacy-Enhancing Technologies' (PETs) started to develop technical mechanisms in response to privacy challenges associated with new information and communication technologies.[48] Originally focused on identity protection and technical means to minimize data collection and processing without losing a system's functionality, the scope of PETs and similar instruments have broadened over time to include encryption tools, privacy-preserving analysis techniques, data management tools, and other techniques that cover the entire lifecycle of personal data. Starting in the 1990s, PETs, one instrument in a toolbox of many more, were put into a larger context by the introduction of privacy by design, a 'systematic approach to designing any technology that embeds privacy into [both] the underlying specification or architecture'[49] and, one might add, business practices. Although still a

---

[44] See D. D. Hirsch, 'Protecting the Inner Environment: What Privacy Regulation Can Learn from Environmental Law', *Georgia Law Review* 41 (2006), 1–63.
[45] O. Ben-Shahar, 'Data Pollution', Coase-Sandor Working Paper in Law and Economics No 854 (2018).
[46] See L. M. Ponte, 'The Michigan Cyber Court: A Bold Experiment in the Development of the First Public Virtual Courthouse', *North Carolina Journal of Law and Technology* 4 (2002), 51–91.
[47] J. M. Balkin and J. Zittrain, 'A Grand Bargain to Make Tech Companies Trustworthy', *The Atlantic*, 3 October 2016.
[48] See G. W. van Blarkom, J. J. Borking, and J. G. E. Olk (eds), *Handbook of Privacy and Privacy-Enhancing Technologies: The Case of Intelligent Software Agents* (The Hague: CBP, 2003).
[49] I. S. Rubinstein, 'Regulating Privacy by Design', *Berkeley Technology Law Journal* 26 (2011), 1409–1456, at 1411–1412.

somewhat amorphous and evolving concept that seeks to integrate legal and technical perspectives, privacy by design can be understood as an important movement that promotes a holistic approach to managing the privacy challenges that result from a wide range of emerging technologies across their life cycles and within their contexts of application. The concept has been endorsed by privacy regulators from across the globe[50] and adopted on both sides of the Atlantic, with the GDPR among the most prominent recent examples.[51] In addition to research efforts and scholarly contributions that deepen, advance, and critically examine the privacy by design concept, a range of implementation guidelines and methodologies have been issued by regulatory authorities, standards organizations, and other sources to help operationalize typically abstract privacy-by-design-requirements.[52] Despite all the progress made, careful examinations of the approach have highlighted both conceptual questions[53] and implementation challenges,[54] including economic obstacles, interoperability barriers, and usability and design issues.[55] Conversely, additional work is also required to close privacy law's 'design gap', at least in practice.[56]

D REIMAGINING THE RELATIONSHIP OF LAW AND TECHNOLOGY

This relatively recent 'discovery' of technology as an approach to address the very privacy challenges it (co-)creates in the law has potential. The more technical dimensions to regulating information privacy have been the focus of intense study by computer scientists and resulted in a rich theoretical literature and numerous practical tools for protecting privacy. Yet, in the past such discussion has by and large occurred in

---

[50]   See 'Resolution on Privacy by Design', *32nd International Conference of Data Protection and Privacy Commissioners*, Jerusalem, 27–29 October, 2010; also C. Perera et al., 'Designing Privacy-Aware Internet of Things Applications', *Information Sciences* 512 (2020), 238–257; M. Veale, R. Binns, and J. Ausloos, 'When Data Protection by Design and Data Subject Rights Clash', *International Data Privacy Law* 8 (2018), 105–123; A. Romanou, 'The Necessity of the Implementation of Privacy by Design in Sectors Where Data Protection Concerns Arise', *Computer Law and Security Review* 34 (2018), 99–110.

[51]   Specifically, Article 25 GDPR requires that data controllers, in order to protect the rights of data subjects, implement appropriate technical and organizational measures designed to both embed data protection principles and integrate safeguards into data processing. See, e.g., L. A. Bygrave, 'Data Protection by Design and by Default: Deciphering the EU's Legislative Requirements', *Oslo Law Review* 4 (2017), 105–120.

[52]   See, e.g., G. Danezis et al., *Privacy and Data Protection by Design – From Policy to Engineering* (Heraklion: ENISA, 2014); European Data Protection Board, Guidelines 4/2019 on Article 25: Data Protection by Design and by Default, 13 November 2019.

[53]   See, e.g., D. K. Mulligan and K. A. Bamberger, 'Saving Governance-by-Design', *California Law Review* 106 (2018), 697–784.

[54]   S. Spiekermann-Hoff, 'The Challenges of Privacy by Design', *Communications of the ACM* 55 (2012), 38–40.

[55]   A. Tamò-Larrieux, *Designing for Privacy and Its Legal Framework: Data Protection by Design and Default for the Internet of Things* (Berlin: Springer, 2018).

[56]   See W. Hartzog, *Privacy's Blueprint: The Battle to Control the Design of New Technologies* (Cambridge, MA: Harvard University Press, 2018).

a space separate from the sphere of legal norms, regulations, policies, ethics codes, and best practices. In addition to the larger shifts mentioned earlier in this chapter, a number of *specific trends* make it now more important as well as urgent to foster knowledge sharing and integration between the two spheres and to embrace techno-logical approaches to support legal privacy across a number of different functions.

First, technological advances enable sophisticated attacks that were unforeseen at the time when many of the still-applicable legal standards for privacy protection were drafted. Computer scientists now need to develop approaches that are robust not only against new modes of attack, but also against unknown future attacks, in order to address challenges posed by next-generation privacy threats.[57] For example, database reconstruction attacks have already demonstrated that large collections of data such as the United States Census – although ostensibly confidential – are now vulnerable to discovery of a particular individual's personal, private characteristics, so new means of protection for these datasets are required.[58] Similarly, the omnipresence of predictive analytics makes it difficult for individuals to understand and control the usage of their own data, rendering traditional regulatory control paradigms increasingly ineffective against developments in technology.[59]

Furthermore, patchworks of privacy laws, the lack of interoperability among them, and different interpretations of their requirements can all result in wide variations in the treatment and protection of data across contexts and geographies, depending on the jurisdictions, industry sectors, actors, and categories of information involved. More robust frameworks for evaluating privacy threats that are based on integrated legal and scientific standards for privacy protection are required to provide more comprehensive, consistent, and robust information privacy protection, thereby furthering the end goals of the law.

Finally, traditional legal approaches for protecting privacy while transferring data, making data-release decisions, or drafting data-sharing agreements, among other activities, are time-intensive and not readily scalable to big data contexts at a time when some of the biggest global challenges urgently require more, not less, privacy-respecting data sharing. Technological approaches need to be designed with compliance with legal standards and practices in mind in order to help automate data-sharing decisions and ensure consistent privacy protection at a massive scale.[60] For example, personalization of the conventional means of ensuring privacy, such as disclosure mandates, could help incorporate more granular legal norms and requirements into an individual's privacy in a scalable fashion.[61]

---

[57] A. Wood et al., 'Differential Privacy: A Primer for a Non-technical Audience', *Vanderbilt Journal of Entertainment and Technology Law* 21 (2018), 209–276.

[58] S. Garfinkel, J. M. Abowd, and C. Martindale, 'Understanding Database Reconstruction Attacks on Public Data', *ACMQueue* 16 (2018), 1–26, at 5–7.

[59] D. D. Hirsch, 'From Individual Control to Social Protection: New Paradigms for Privacy Law in the Age of Predictive Analytics', Ohio States Public Law Working Paper No 506 (2019).

[60] M. Altman, S. Chong, and A. Wood, 'Formalizing Privacy Laws for License Generation and Data Repository Decision Automation', *Proceedings on Privacy Enhancing Technologies* 2 (2020), 1–19.

[61] C. Busch, 'Implementing Personalized Law: Personalized Disclosures in Consumer Law and Data Privacy Law', *University of Chicago Law Review* 86 (2019), 309–331, at 312.

These reasons already indicate that the need for enhanced *interoperability* between technological and legal approaches to privacy is not limited to the mechanical level of individual privacy-preserving techniques and tools and goes beyond efforts to require companies to protect privacy by embedding it into the design of technologies and business practices. Rather, the scale of the challenge of reimagining the relationship between technology and privacy – as well as the potential benefits of increased levels of interoperability between the two – becomes visible when considering the variety of interrelated functional perspectives that such an approach situated at the law/technology interface would open up when dealing with the privacy challenges of the digital age. The following questions can be raised in this context.

1. How can technological and legal perspectives be integrated more closely to enable more robust problem descriptions and analyses? Approaches like privacy by design signal a departure from binary notations of privacy and ad hoc balancing tests of competing interests toward more holistic and rigorous privacy risk assessment models that rely both on modeling approaches from information security and an understanding of privacy informed by recent theoretical advances across different disciplines. Technical research, for example, may better quantify the privacy risks associated with more traditional privacy-protection techniques like anonymization[62] and thus help establish a legal framework that articulates which privacy risks should be considered 'unacceptable'. Similarly, using both computational and sociological measures could establish a more empirical evidence base about consumers' attitudes and expectations towards privacy.[63] A growing body of interdisciplinary research demonstrates the theoretical and practical promise of such modern privacy analyses that are based in holistic analytical frameworks incorporating recent research from fields ranging from computer science and statistics to law and the social sciences.[64] Indeed, such frameworks are increasingly recognized by expert recommendations and standards.[65]

---

[62] W. H. Lee et al., 'Quantification of De-anonymization Risks in Social Networks', *ICISSIP 2017 – Proceedings of the 3rd International Conference on Information Systems Security and Privacy*, 1 January 2017.

[63] S. Barth and M. D. T. de Jong, 'The Privacy Paradox – Investigating Discrepancies between Expressed Privacy Concerns and Actual Online Behavior – A Systematic Literature Review', *Telematics and Informatics* 34 (2017), 1038–1058.

[64] For examples from research that illustrate the benefits of such a blended approach, see M. Altman et al., 'Towards a Modern Approach to Privacy-Aware Government Data Releases', *Berkeley Technology Law Journal* 30 (2015), 1967–2072; and I. S. Rubinstein and W. Hartzog, 'Anonymization and Risk', *Washington Law Review* 91 (2016), 703–760.

[65] R. M. Groves and B. A. Harris-Kojetin (eds), *Multiple Data Sources, and Privacy Protection: Next Steps* (Washington, DC: The National Academies Press, 2017); S. L. Garfinkel, 'De-identifying Government Datasets', NIST Special Publication 800-188 (2016).

2. How can legal and technological tools be combined in order to enable more effective, scalable, and accountable solutions to privacy problems, including the need for trustworthy data sharing? A wealth of research and practical examples show how emerging technical privacy solutions, including sophisticated tools for data storage, access control, analysis, and release, can act in concert with legal, organizational, and other safeguards to better manage privacy risks across the different stages of the lifecycle of data.[66] Consider, for instance, the important role encryption plays in securing access to and storage of data,[67] the technological development of a personal data store that enables individuals to exercise fine-grained control over where information about them is stored and how it is accessed,[68] the movement in AI towards transparent and explainable automated decision-making that makes technology more accountable,[69] or the development of technical ways to implement the right to be forgotten by deleting an individual's records from machine learning models efficiently.[70] Formal mathematical guarantees of privacy can also reliably lower privacy risks. Differential privacy is one such example of a mathematical framework that manages the privacy challenges associated with the statistical analysis of information maintained in databases.[71] Secure multiparty computation, to add another example, is a methodology that enables parties to carry out a joint computation over their data in such a way that no single entity needs to hand a dataset to any other explicitly.[72] While some of these technologies are still in development, others have been tested out in practice and are already recommended as best practices in selected fields of application. Real world examples include the implementation of differential privacy in the United States Census,[73] as well as the use of security multiparty

---

[66] See, e.g., 'Privacy Tools for Sharing Research Data', Harvard University Privacy Tools Project, available at https://privacytools.seas.harvard.edu/project-description.

[67] For a description of encryption standards for federal government information systems, see, for example, National Institute of Standards and Technology, Security Requirements for Cryptographic Modules: Federal Information Processing Standards, Federal Information Processing Standards Publication, FIPS PUB 140-2, 25 May 2001.

[68] See T. Kirkham et al., 'The Personal Data Store Approach to Personal Data Security', *IEEE Security and Privacy* 11 (2013), 12–19, at 12–13.

[69] S. Wachter, B. Mittelstadt, and L. Floridi, 'Transparent, Explainable, and Accountable AI for Robotics', *Science Robotics* 2 (2017).

[70] M. Hutson, 'Researchers Can Make AI Forget You', *IEEE Spectrum*, 15 January 2020.

[71] *See* C. Dwork, 'Differential Privacy', in H. C. A. van Tilborg and S. Jajodia (eds), *Encyclopedia of Cryptography and Security*, 2nd edn (New York: Springer, 2011), 338–340.

[72] See Y. Lindell and B. Pinkas, 'Secure Multiparty Computation for Privacy-Preserving Data Mining', *Journal of Privacy and Confidentiality* 1 (2009), 59–98, at 60.

[73] United States Census Bureau, 'Disclosure Avoidance and the 2020 Census', 19 December 2019, available at www.census.gov/about/policies/privacy/statistical_safeguards/disclosure-avoidance-2020-census.html.

computation to investigate pay gaps,[74] or maintain data on student outcomes in higher education.[75]

3. How can enhanced levels of interoperability between technological and legal approaches to privacy enable better matching of solutions to problems? The Harvard University Privacy Tools Project, for example, is a multidisciplinary effort to develop technical tools to address specific, identified policy needs.[76] Among other contributions, the project demonstrates, for certain categories of use cases, including data sharing in research contexts, how interdisciplinary approaches can guide actors to engage in more robust privacy risk assessments and then select the best solution from a set of integrated privacy tools, such as tiered access models, that combine both legal and technical approaches to privacy protection.[77] As another example, the LINDDUN approach, developed at Leuven University, creates a taxonomy of mitigation strategies to address privacy threats in a given high-level system and identifies effective, targeted PETs by creating data flow diagrams, mapping privacy threats, and performing risk analyses on these privacy threats.[78]

4. How can a closer integration of technical and legal concepts and applications aimed at protecting privacy make it easier to demonstrate compliance and 'measure progress' over time? Again, differential privacy is a key example of using a highly technical conception of 'privacy' to give the vague legal words used to define privacy in statutes and regulations more precision, which in turn increases the accuracy of assessment of compliance in individual cases and over time.[79] More generally, legal standards could adopt more technically robust descriptions of an intended privacy goal rather than simply endorsing traditional approaches like de-identification. This would provide a clearer basis for demonstrating whether new classes of emerging privacy technologies are sufficient to fulfil the requirements of these standards. These examples indicate how policymakers and technologists could seek to employ a hybrid of legal and technical reasoning to demonstrate a privacy solution's compliance with legal standards for privacy protection.[80]

---

[74] R. Barlow, 'Computational Thinking Breaks a Logjam', Boston University, 27 April 2015, available at www.bu.edu/articles/2015/computational-thinking-breaks-a-logjam.

[75] M. R. Warner, 'Warner, Rubio, Wyden Reintroduce "Student Right to Know before You Go Act"', *Press Release*, 7 March 2019, available at www.warner.senate.gov/public/index.cfm/2019/3/warner-rubio-wyden-reintroduce-student-right-to-know-before-you-go-act.

[76] Harvard University Privacy Tools Project, note 66.

[77] See, e.g., Altman et al., note 64.

[78] 'LINDDUN Privacy Engineering', *LINDDUN: Privacy Threat Modeling*, available at www.linddun.org/.

[79] K. Nissim et al., 'Bridging the Gap between Computer Science and Legal Approaches to Privacy', *Harvard Journal of Law and Technology* 31 (2018), 687–780.

[80] Ibid.; Nissim and Wood, note 32; A. Cohen and K. Nissim, 'Towards Formalizing the GDPR's Notion of Singling Out', *arXiv*:1904.06009, 12 April 2019, available at https://arxiv.org/abs/1904.06009.

Taken together, the integration of legal and technical approaches across different functional areas can help pave the way for a more strategic and systematic way to conceptualize and orchestrate the contemporary interplay between law and technology in the field of information privacy and data protection. The process of re-imagination through enhanced interoperability – here illustrated along four functional areas with the open-ended possibility of adding others – builds heavily upon the concept of privacy by design and is informed by related approaches such as privacy impact assessments. However, as already mentioned, this process is less focused on embedding privacy requirements into the design and architecture of individual technological systems and business practices. Rather, it is more broadly interested in finding ways to overcome the traditional interaction patterns between technology and law in order to offer new system-level opportunities to develop notions and manifestations of privacy that might only emerge after combining different substantive and methodological 'lenses'. At a moment of rethinking privacy, such an exercise might inform the evolutionary path of privacy and data protection laws at both the conceptual and implementation levels by challenging their underlying assumptions, definitions, protection requirements, compliance mechanisms, and so on.

E TOWARDS RECORDING PRIVACY LAW

Over time, enhanced interoperability between technological and legal approaches to privacy might ultimately culminate in a deeper-layered *recoding* of privacy law that transcends the traditional response patterns[81] discussed earlier in this chapter by leveraging the synergies between perspectives and instruments from both domains in order to cope with the complex privacy-relevant challenges of our future. The path towards such an outcome, however, is long and faces many obstacles given the economic, geopolitical, and other forces at play that were described earlier in this chapter.

As a precondition of any progress, such a strategy requires significant investments in interdisciplinary education, research, and collaboration.[82] Despite all the advancements made in recent years, there is much yet to be uncovered: development of novel systems of governance requires not only interdisciplinary mutual understandings but also deep inquiry into the most effective roles for law and legal governance in such a dynamic, fast-changing system. Programs designed to stimulate such collaboration and interdisciplinary learning have already started being

---

[81] See also H. Burkert, 'Changing Patterns: Supplementary Approaches to Improving Data Protection', *Presentation at CIAJ 2005 Annual Conference on Technology, Privacy and Justice*, Toronto, 2005.
[82] See, e.g., US National Science and Technology Council, 'National Privacy Research Strategy', White House, June 2016, available at https://obamawhitehouse.archives.gov/sites/default/files/nprs_nstc_review_final.pdf.

developed at universities.[83] Furthermore, technology positions in government, such as the Chief Technologist position at the Federal Trade Commission and the President's Council of Advisors on Science and Technology, to name two examples from the United States, recognize the need for experts in computer science who can inform privacy regulation and serve as models of cross-disciplinary communication and knowledge-sharing in policy circles.[84] Similarly, it is becoming increasingly important for technologists to understand legal and policy approaches to privacy protection, so that they can implement measures that advance the specific goals of such standards. Doing so will also likely require policymakers to develop mechanisms and resources for communicating their shared understanding of the interface between law and technology with privacy practitioners. Regulatory systems and institutions will also need to support additional research on policy reasoning, accountable systems, and computable policies for automating compliance with legal requirements and enforcement of privacy policies.[85]

Reimagining the relationship between technology and privacy law in the digital age can be seen as a key component of a larger effort aimed at addressing the current digital privacy crisis holistically. Under contemporary conditions of complexity and uncertainty, the 'solution space' for the multifaceted privacy challenges of our time needs to do more than treat the symptoms of discrete privacy ills. It needs to combine approaches, strategies, and instruments that span all available modes of regulation in the digital space, including technology, markets, social norms and professional practices, and the law. If pursued diligently and collaboratively, and

[83] Examples in the field of research are initiatives such as the Privacy Tools for Sharing Research Data at Harvard University mentioned earlier, which brings together computer scientists, statisticians, legal scholars, and social scientists to tackle difficult problems at the intersection of privacy technology, or the efforts by the Center on Privacy and Technology at Georgetown University Law Center, which aims to build interdisciplinary bridges between law and computer science with respect to privacy. Interdisciplinary courses in privacy at Princeton, CMU, MIT, and Harvard serve as possible sources of inspiration in the educational realm. See, e.g., Massachusetts Institute of Technology, Course: Privacy Legislation: Law and Technology, available at https://groups.csail.mit.edu/mac/classes/6.S978; Harvard Law School, Course: Comparative Online Privacy, available at http://hls.harvard.edu/academics/curriculum/cata log/default.aspx?o=69463; Carnegie Mellon University, Course: Privacy Policy, Law, and Technology, available at https://cups.cs.cmu.edu/courses/pplt-fa16; A. Narayanan, Privacy Technologies: An Annotated Syllabus, Princeton University, available at www.cs.princeton .edu/~arvindn/publications/privacyseminar.pdf.
[84] See L. Sweeney, 'Technology Science', *Federal Trade Commission Blog*, 2 May 2014, available at www.ftc.gov/news-events/blogs/techftc/2014/05/technology-science.
[85] See, e.g., D. J. Weitzner et al., *Computer Science and Artificial Intelligence Laboratory Technical Report: Information Accountability* (Cambridge, MA: MIT Press, 2007); L. Kagal and J. Pato, 'Preserving Privacy Based on Semantic Policy Tools', *IEEE Security and Privacy* 8 (2010), 25–30; H. DeYoung et al., 'Experiences in the Logical Specification of the HIPAA and GLBA Privacy Laws', in *Proceedings of the 9th Annual ACM Workshop on Privacy in the Electronic Society* (New York: ACM, 2010), 73–82; US National Academies of Sciences, Engineering, and Medicine, *Innovations in Federal Statistics: Combining Data Sources While Protecting Privacy* (Washington, DC: The National Academies Press, 2017); Groves and Harris-Kojetin, note 65.

expanding upon concepts, such as privacy by design or privacy impact assessments, as written into modern privacy frameworks like the GDPR, such a turn toward *coordinated privacy governance* could result in a future-oriented privacy framework that spans a broad set of norms, control mechanisms, and actors[86] – 'a *system* of information privacy protection that is much larger, more complex and varied, and likely more effective, than individual information privacy rights'.[87] Through such nuanced intervention, the legal system (understood as more than merely a body of constraining laws) can more proactively play the leading role in directing and coordinating the various elements and actors in the blended governance regime, and – above all – in ensuring the transparency, accountability, and legitimacy that allow democratic governance to flourish.[88]

---

[86] See C. J. Bennett and C. Raab, *The Governance of Privacy: Policy Instruments in Global Perspective* (Cambridge, MA: MIT Press, 2006).

[87] V. Mayer-Schönberger, 'Beyond Privacy, Beyond Rights – Toward a "Systems" Theory of Information Governance', *California Law Review* 98 (2010), 1853–1885, at 1883 (emphasis in the original).

[88] See M. Hildebrandt, *Smart Technologies and the End(s) of Law: Novel Entanglements of Law and Technology* (Cheltenham: Edward Elgar, 2015).

10

The Algorithmic Learning Deficit

Artificial Intelligence, Data Protection and Trade

Svetlana Yakovleva and Joris van Hoboken*

A INTRODUCTION

Commercial use of personal and other data facilitates digital trade and generates economic growth at unprecedented levels. A dramatic shift in the composition of the top twenty companies by market capitalisation speaks vividly to this point. While, in 2009, 35 per cent of those companies were from the oil and gas sector, in 2018 – just nine years later – 56 per cent of those companies were from the technology and consumer services sectors.[1] Meanwhile, the share of oil and gas companies, a pillar among traditional industries, declined to just 7 per cent. The share of digitally deliverable services in global services exports more than doubled in the last thirteen years: it increased from USD 1.2 trillion in 2005 to USD 2.9 trillion in 2018.[2]

Data also constitutes a crucial resource for the development, continuous refinement and application of artificial intelligence (AI). The availability of data and its free flow across borders are often viewed as pre-requisites for the development and flourishing of AI technology.[3] However, in the context of AI, it is not the data itself, but the knowledge and insights obtained with the help of AI algorithms from that data (in other words, the 'fruits' of the data) that constitute the main added value.

---

* Svetlana Yakovleva is a Postdoctoral Researcher at the Institute for Information Law (IViR), University of Amsterdam and Senior Legal Adviser at De Brauw Blackstone Westbroek, Amsterdam. Contact: mail@svyakovleva.com. Joris van Hoboken is Associate Professor at the Institute for Information Law (IViR), University of Amsterdam and Professor of Law at the Interdisciplinary Research Group on Law Science Technology & Society (LSTS), Vrije Universiteit Brussel. Contact: j.v.j.vanhoboken@uva.nl.
[1] UNCTAD, *Digital Economy Report 2019: Value Creation and Capture: Implications for Developing Countries* (New York/Geneva: United Nations Publications, 2019), at 17.
[2] Ibid., at 48.
[3] See, e.g., S. A. Aaronson, 'Data Minefield? How AI Is Prodding Governments to Rethink Trade in Data', in CIGI (ed), *Special Report: Data Governance in the Digital Age* (Waterloo: CIGI, 2018).

Learning, or 'digital intelligence', in the words of UNCTAD, is crucial for the market of big data. One of the upshots of this is that without the necessary infrastructure and technologies, data concerning individual persons or even aggregated data cannot by itself generate value. It is the 'learning', and not raw data itself, that constitutes a valuable economic resource and can be used in targeted online advertising, the operation of electronic commerce platforms, the digitisation of traditional goods into rentable services and the renting out of cloud services.[4] For example, personalisation, which is an important component in the production, marketing and distribution of online services, uses AI systems to transform individuals' online behaviour, preferences, likes, moods and opinions (all of which constitute personal data, at least in the European Union) into commercially valuable insights.[5] Focusing solely on data in the context of regulatory conversations on AI – both in domestic and international trade contexts – may be misguided.

AI development is at the top of the domestic and international policy agendas in many countries around the world. Just in the last couple of years, more than thirty countries and several international and regional stakeholders, including the European Union (EU), G20 and Nordic-Baltic Region adopted AI policy documents[6] revealing their ambitions to compete for dominance in AI. Digital trade provisions, including rules governing cross-border data flows, access to proprietary algorithms and technology transfers and access to open government data, have taken centre stage in bilateral, regional and international trade negotiations.[7]

Different levels of advancement in digital technologies in general, and in AI specifically, as well as the concentration of data in the hands of a few countries, make international negotiations on digital trade challenging. To illustrate the point, according to the 2019 UNCTAD Digital Economy Report, China and the United States account for 90 per cent of the market capitalisation value of the worlds' seventy largest digital platform companies and 'are set to reap the largest economic gains from AI'.[8] In contrast, the EU accounts for only 3.6 per cent of this market capitalisation.[9] The report further demonstrates that China, the United States and Japan together account for 78 per cent of all AI patent filings in the world.[10] Data – one of the key components of data analytics – is highly concentrated in Asia Pacific

4   UNCTAD, note 1, at 24 et seqq.
5   J. Crémer, Y.-A. de Montijoye, and H. Schweitzer, *Competition Policy for the Digital Era* (Luxembourg: Publications Office of the European Union, 2019), at 73.
6   For an overview, see OECD, AI Initiatives Worldwide, available at www.oecd.org/going-digital/ ai/initiatives-worldwide/.
7   S. Azmeh and C. Foster, 'The TPP and the Digital Trade Agenda: Digital Industrial Policy And Silicon Valley's Influence on New Trade Agreements', LSE Working Paper No 16-175 (2016); J.-A. Monteiro and R. Teh, 'Provisions on Electronic Commerce in Regional Trade Agreements', WTO Working Paper No ERSD-2017-11 (2017). See also Chapter 1 in this volume.
8   UNCTAD, note 1, at 8–9.
9   Ibid.
10 Ibid., at 8–9, 21.

and the United States: 70 per cent of all traffic between 2017 and 2022 is expected to be attributed to these two regions.[11] Representing 87 per cent of the B2B e-commerce, the United States is the market leader in global e-commerce, while China is the leader in B2C e-commerce followed by the United States.[12] As a result, economic value derived from data is captured by countries where companies having control over storage and processing of data reside.[13]

The high concentration of control over AI technologies, digital platforms and data in specific parts of the world raise concerns about 'digital sovereignty' related to control, access and rights of the data and appropriation of the value generated by the monetisation of the data.[14] This issue is not limited to the dynamics of negotiations between developed and developing countries. For example, the new European Commission's Digital Strategy is strongly anchored in the principles of digital sovereignty and shaping technology in a way respecting European values.[15] Public policy interests implicated by international data governance and data flows, indispensable for the global governance of AI, stretch far beyond issues of economic growth and development. They also involve a broader set of national and regional priorities, such as national security, fundamental rights protection (such as the rights to privacy and to protection of personal data) and cultural values, to name just a few. Differences in the relative weight accorded to each such priority when contrasted with the economic and political gains from cross-border data flows have resulted in a diversity of domestic rules governing cross-border flows of information, especially when it relates to personal data, and a diversity of approaches to govern the use of AI in both private and public law contexts.

Against this backdrop, this chapter's aim is twofold. First, it provides an overview of the state of the art in international trade agreements and negotiations on issues related to AI, in particular, the governance of cross-border data flows. In doing so it juxtaposes the EU and the US approaches and demonstrates that the key public policy interests behind the dynamics of digital trade negotiations on the EU's side are privacy and data protection. Second, building on the divergent EU and US approaches to governing cross-border data flows, and the EU policy priorities in this respect in international trade negotiations, this chapter argues that the set of EU public policy objectives weighted against the benefits of digital trade in international trade negotiations, especially with a view to AI, should be broader than just privacy and data protection. It also argues that an individual rights approach has limitations in governing data flows in the context of AI and should be expanded to factor in a

---

[11] Ibid., at 11.
[12] Ibid., at 15.
[13] Ibid., at 89.
[14] Ibid.
[15] European Commission, White Paper on Artificial Intelligence – A European Approach to Excellence and Trust, COM(2020) 65 final, 19 February 2020 [hereinafter: White Paper on Artificial Intelligence].

clearer understanding of who wins and who loses from unrestricted cross-border data flows in an age of data-driven services and services production.

The chapter proceeds as follows. The next section maps out the recent developments on digital trade on the international trade law landscape. The third section discusses, from an EU perspective, the limits of data protection in regulating AI domestically and as a catch-all public policy interest counterbalancing international trade commitments on cross-border data flows. The fourth section contains a brief conclusion.

B CROSS-BORDER DIGITAL TRADE AND ARTIFICIAL INTELLIGENCE

The immense potential of data to generate economic value has given rise to a so-called 'digital trade discourse', which, on the one hand, views the freedom of cross-border data flows as one of the pre-requisites of international digital trade and AI-driven innovation and, on the other hand, predicts that restrictions on data flows will hamper economic growth and undermine innovation.[16] This discourse is advanced not only by the United States, which has a strong competitive advantage in digital technologies, and the big tech companies, which invest millions of dollars in lobbying activities on digital trade, but also by the EU.[17]

Policy debates in international trade negotiations on digital trade, relevant in the AI context, revolve around the liberalisation of cross-border data flows in order to enable accumulation of large data sets to train AI systems and restrictions on those data flows in the public interest. The following subsections provide an overview of recent developments in this area.

Countries have not yet achieved a multilateral consensus on the design and scope of digital trade provisions, which have so far only appeared in bilateral and regional trade agreements and have somewhat overshadowed the multilateral efforts of the WTO in this area.[18] Although proposals on electronic commerce in the WTO increasingly focus on barriers to digital trade and 'digital protectionism',[19] the WTO has not yet made any tangible progress on this issue.[20] The discussions continue, however. In early 2019, seventy-six WTO members, including Canada, China, the EU, and the United States, started a new round of negotiations on electronic commerce at the WTO in order to create rules governing e-commerce

---

[16] UNCTAD, note 1, at 91. For overview and discussion, see S. Yakovleva, 'Privacy Protection (ism): The Latest Wave of Trade Constraints on Regulatory Autonomy', *University of Miami Law Review* 74 (2020), 416–519, at 469 et seqq. See also Chapter 3 in this volume.

[17] Yakovleva, note 16, at 473, 482; UNCTAD, note 1, at 88–89.

[18] M. Burri, 'The Regulation of Data Flows through Trade Agreements', *Georgetown Journal of International Law* 48 (2017), 407–448, at 417.

[19] A. D. Mitchell and N. Mishra, 'Data at the Docks: Modernizing International Trade Law for the Digital Economy', *Vanderbilt Journal of Entertainment and Technology Law* 20 (2018), 1073–1134, at 1111.

[20] See Chapter 1 in this volume.

and cross-border data flows.[21] It remains to be seen how these negotiations will play out. Despite a seemingly firm consensus on the use of the terms 'digital trade' and 'digital protectionism' – the axes around which the discourses governing international negotiations revolve – the value structures underlying these discourses diverge,[22] as the US and the EU examples below will illustrate. The next section on international trade law governance of cross-border data flows then explicates how trade provisions on cross-border data flows, advanced by the US and the EU, mirror this divergence.

In the spirit of its 'digital agenda', the United States has been a pioneer in including provisions on free cross-border data flows in international trade agreements.[23] The United States has managed successfully to advance broad and binding horizontal obligations enabling unrestricted data flows in the digital trade (or electronic commerce) chapters of its recent trade agreements. The Comprehensive and Progressive Agreement on Trans-Pacific Partnership (CPTPP), (where the US led digital trade discussions before its withdrawal from the TPP agreement[24]), the United States–Mexico–Canada Agreement (USMCA) and the Digital Trade Agreement with Japan examples are of trade agreements to contain a binding provision requiring each party to allow (or not to restrict) the cross-border transfer of information by electronic means, including personal information, when this activity is for the conduct of the business of a covered person.[25] The US proposal for the ongoing e-commerce talks at the WTO replicates this 'gold standard' provisions on digital trade.[26] All of the earlier mentioned free trade agreements (FTAs) also contain an exception which allows the parties to adopt or maintain measures inconsistent with this obligation to achieve a legitimate public policy objective, provided that the measure (i) is not applied in a manner which would constitute a means of arbitrary or unjustifiable discrimination or a disguised restriction on trade; and (ii) does not impose restrictions on transfers of

---

[21] European Commission, '76 WTO Partners Launch Talks on E-Commerce', *News Archive*, 26 January 2019, available at http://trade.ec.europa.eu/doclib/press/index.cfm?id=1974.

[22] Yakovleva, note 16, at 469 et seqq. See also Chapter 12 in this volume, in particular with regard to the position of China.

[23] M. Burri, 'The Governance of Data and Data Flows in Trade Agreements: The Pitfalls of Legal Adaptation', *UC Davis Law Review* 51 (2017), 65–132, at 99, S. A. Aaronson, 'Redefining Protectionism: The New Challenge in the Digital Age', IIEP Working Paper No 30 (2016), at 59; M. Geist, 'Data Rules in Modern Trade Agreements: Toward Reconciling an Open Internet with Privacy and Security Safeguards', in CIGI (ed), *Special Report: Data Governance in the Digital Age* (Waterloo: CIGI, 2018).

[24] This provision was included in CPTPP before the US withdrawal from the agreement. The version of the agreement with the United States as a party was known as the Transpacific Partnership Agreement (TPP). See Executive Office of the President, Office of the United States Trade Representative, Letter to the TPP Depository, 30 January 2017.

[25] Article 14.11(2) CPTPP and Article 19.11(1) USMCA. For other agreement containing a similar rule, see Chapter 1 in this volume.

[26] I. Manak, 'US WTO E-Commerce Proposal Reads Like USMCA', *International Economic Law and Policy Blog*, 8 May 2019, available at https://worldtradelaw.typepad.com/ielpblog/2019/05/us-wto-e-commerce-proposal-reads-like-usmca.html.

information *greater than are required* (*necessary* – in the USMCA and US–Japan Digital Trade Agreement) to achieve the objective.[27] The exception closely resembles the general exception under Article XIV(c)(ii) of the General Agreement on Trade in Services (GATS),[28] a threshold which has been particularly hard to meet in the past.[29] Similar to the general exception clause, the FTA text requires that a measure prima facie inconsistent with the data flow obligation should be subject to a two-level assessment. First, it should pass the so-called 'necessity test', where the necessity of the contested measure is assessed, based on an objective standard of 'necessity' by trade adjudicators. Second, its application should not amount to arbitrary or unjustifiable discrimination or a disguised restriction on trade (pursuant to the chapeau of the general exception provision). Under WTO case law, the 'necessity test' requires that a WTO law–inconsistent measure be the least trade restrictive of all reasonably available alternatives allowing to achieve the same level of protection of a public interest, raised by the claimant in a dispute.[30] In short, just like the GATS general exception, the FTA exception sets a high threshold for justifying a domestic measure inconsistent with relevant trade disciplines. An important difference of the earlier quoted FTA exception from the GATS general exception, however, is that it does not specify the public policy objectives that may be invoked to justify a restriction on the free cross-border data flows. In this sense, the exception is more 'future-proof', as it can rest on any public policy interest that may be implicated by the cross-border data flow obligation in the future, such as cybersecurity or even technological sovereignty (not mentioned in Article XIV GATS exception), provided of course that the measure passes the two-level assessment of the exception.

In addition, the digital trade (electronic commerce) chapters of the earlier mentioned agreements contain an article on the protection of personal information (the term used to refer to personal data in the United States), which contains a mixture of binding and aspirational provisions on the protection of privacy by the parties to the agreements.[31]

---

[27] Article 14.11(3) CPTPP, Article 19.11(2) USMCA and Article 11 US–Japan DTA contain an almost identical provision. Emphasis added.

[28] General Agreement on Trade in Services, 1869 U.N.T.S. 183; 33 I.L.M. 1167 (1994), entered into force 1 January 1995 [hereinafter: GATS].

[29] P. Delimatsis, 'Protecting Public Morals in a Digital Age: Revisiting the WTO Rulings on *US – Gambling* and *China – Publications and Audiovisual Products*', *Journal of International Economic Law* 14 (2011), 1–37; I. Venzke, 'Making General Exceptions: The Spell of Precedents in Developing Article XX GATT into Standards for Domestic Regulatory Policy', *German Law Journal* 12 (2011), 1111–1140, at 1118–1119.

[30] For more references, discussion and critique in the privacy and data protection context, see S. Yakovleva, 'Should Fundamental Rights to Privacy and Data Protection Be a Part of EU's International Trade "Deals"?' *World Trade Review* 17 (2018), 477–508; S. Yakovleva, 'Personal Data Transfers in International Trade and EU Law: A Tale of Two "Necessities"', *Journal of World Investment and Trade* 21 (2020), 881–919.

[31] Article 14.8 of CPTPP and Article 19.8 of USMCA. These articles are discussed in more detail in S. Yakovleva, 'Privacy and Data Protection in the EU- and US-led Post-WTO Free Trade

The EU largely shares the 'digital trade' discourse on the benefits of cross-border data flows for global economic growth with the United States and, in principle, supports the idea of regulating cross-border data flows in international trade agreements.[32] Largely but not completely, because there is one important point on which the EU approach diverges very significantly from that of the United States: namely, with regard to the protection of the rights to privacy and personal data. It is for this reason that the EU has until recently been cautious in including provisions on cross-border data flows in its trade agreements.[33] Understanding the EU's domestic framework on the protection of personal data and, in particular, its approach to transfers of personal data outside the European Economic Area (EEA), is essential for explaining its trade policy in the domain of cross-border data flows. Therefore, before delving into the EU's proposed provisions on the latter topic, let us first briefly discuss the EU's domestic regime for transfers of personal data outside the EEA.

The rights to privacy and the protection of personal data are protected as binding *fundamental rights* in the EU.[34] From an EU data protection law perspective, personal data is distinct from other types of information because of its inextricable link to the data source: individuals. One of the pillars of this protection, as the CJEU has ruled,[35] is the restriction on transfers of personal data outside the EEA in order to ensure that the level of protection guaranteed in the EU by the General Data Protection Regulation (GDPR)[36] is not undermined or circumvented as personal data crosses EEA borders.[37] As a consequence of the broad definition of 'personal data', EU restrictions on transfers of personal data apply to a broad range of data that can be essential for developing, fine tuning and application of AI systems. Furthermore, the restrictions also apply to mixed data sets, in which personal and non-personal data are 'inextricably linked' – which, as mentioned earlier, fall under

---

Agreements', in R. Hoffmann and M. Krajewski (eds), *European Yearbook of International Economic Law* (Berlin: Springer, 2020), 95–115.

[32] For elaborate discussion on the US and EU digital trade discourses, see Yakovleva, note 16, at 469 et seqq.

[33] For more details on the reasons for this, see Yakovleva, note 16, at 492–493. For the first time the EU included binding provisions on cross-border data flows in Article DIGIT 6 of the 2021 EU-UK Trade and Cooperation Agreement.

[34] Respectively Articles 7 and 8 of the Charter of Fundamental Rights of the European Union (2000/C 364/01), OJ L [2000] 364/1.

[35] C-362/14, *Maximilian Schrems* v. *Data Protection Commissioner and Digital Rights Ireland Ltd.* [2015], ECLI:EU:C:2015:650 [hereinafter: *Schrems*], at para. 72. This goal is now explicitly incorporated in Article 44 GDPR.

[36] Regulation 2016/679 of the European Parliament and of the Council of 27 April 2016 on the Protection of Natural Persons with Regard to the Processing of Personal Data and on the Free Movement of Such Data, and Repealing Directive 95/46/EC (General Data Protection Regulation, GDPR), OJ L [2016] 119/1.

[37] Article 44 GDPR; *Schrems*, note 35, para. 72. See also G. González Fuster, 'Un-Mapping Personal Data Transfers', *European Data Protection Law Review* 2 (2016), 160–168, at 168. Restrictions are provided for in chapter V, GDPR. For an overview of restrictions, see Yakovleva, note 31.

the scope of the GDPR.[38] The restrictions do not apply to non-personal data, including non-personal data in mixed data sets, under the condition that those can be separated from personal data. At the same time, the distinction between personal and non-personal data is not set in stone. If, due to technological developments, this anonymised data can be reidentified, it will become 'personal' and the GDPR restrictions will again apply.[39] Some scholars argue that these restrictions limit the cross-border aggregation of data and thus stifle the development of AI.[40]

The GDPR's restrictions on transfers of personal data apply when *personal data* is transferred or is accessed from outside the EEA, including when this is done for training AI systems, and in the phase of fine-tuning or cross-border application of already existing AI systems located outside the EEA to individuals located in the EEA.[41] This is because feeding an EEA individual's data to the non-EEA AI system will most likely constitute a transfer of personal data.

Turning to the intersection of the GDPR with international trade law, only one FTA to which the EU is a party includes a binding provision on cross-border data flows. The 2019 Economic Partnership Agreement with Japan (Japan–EU EPA), where such a provision was initially proposed by Japan, merely includes a review clause allowing the parties to revisit the issue in three years' time after the agreement's entry into force.[42] The EU and Japan have agreed to use a mutual adequacy decision following the route for cross-border transfers of personal data laid down in the GDPR.[43] This was due to the inability of EU institutions to reach a common position on the breadth of the data flows provision and exceptions from it for the protection of privacy and personal data, following a strong push back from academics and civil society to an attempt of including such provisions in the –

---

[38] Article 2(2) Regulation 2018/1807 of the European Parliament and of the Council on a Framework for the Free Flow of Non-personal Data in the European Union, OJ L [2018] 303/59, 28 November 2018 [hereinafter: EU Regulation 2018/1807]; European Commission, Guidance on the Regulation on a Framework for the Free Flow of Non-personal Data in the European Union, COM(2019) 250 final, 29 May 2019, at para. 2.2.

[39] EU Regulation 2018/1807, note 38, Recital 9.

[40] A. Chander and U. P. Lê, 'Breaking the Web: Data Localization vs. the Global Internet', UC Davis Legal Studies Research Paper No 378, at 40; A. Goldfarb and D. Trefler, 'AI and International Trade', NBER Working Paper No 24254 (2018), at 20–22.

[41] The notion of 'transfer' of personal data is not clearly defined in the GDPR or in the guidance of the Data Protection Authorities. It can indirectly be implied from the existing guidance on the mechanisms for transfers of personal data that a 'transfer' is understood broadly, as it also captures continuous cross-border access to EEA personal data from abroad. See European Data Protection Board, Guidelines 2/2018 on Derogations of Article 49 under Regulation 2016/679, 25 May 2018.

[42] Article 8.81 of EU–Japan EPA. The same provision is also included in Article XX chapter 16 of draft EU–Mexico FTA, negotiated roughly at the same time as the EU–Japan EPA. See also B. Fortnam, 'EU Punts on Data Flow Language in Japan Deal, Leaving Position Unresolved', *Inside US Trade*, 7 June 2017.

[43] European Commission, 'European Commission Adopts Adequacy Decision on Japan, Creating the World's Largest Area of Safe Data Flows', *Press Release*, 23 January 201.

currently stalled – plurilateral Trade in Services Agreement (TiSA) and the Transatlantic Trade and Investment Partnership (TTIP) between the EU and the US.[44]

In 2018, the European Commission reached a political agreement on the EU position on cross-border data flows. This position was expressed in the model clauses, which, in particular, include a model provision on cross-border data flows (Article A) and an exception for the protection of privacy and personal data (Article B).[45] The EU has included these model clauses in its proposals for digital trade chapters in the currently negotiated trade agreements with Australia, Indonesia, New Zealand and Tunisia,[46] as well as into the EU proposal for the WTO rules on electronic commerce,[47] which are intended to co-exist with the general exception for privacy and data protection modelled after Article XIV(c)(ii) GATS included in the same agreements.[48] The 2021 EU-UK Trade and Cooperation Agreement (TCA), however, contains provisions different and, arguably, awarding less regulatory autonomy to protect privacy and personal data, than those in the

---

[44] K. Irion, S. Yakovleva, and M. Bartl, *Trade and Privacy: Complicated Bedfellows? How to Achieve Data Protection-Proof Free Trade Agreements* (Amsterdam: Institute for Information Law, 2016), at 44–45, 59–60; M. Fernández Pérez, 'Corporarivacy Confusion in the EU on Trade and Data Protection', *EDRi*, 12 October 2016; European Parliament, Resolution of 8 July 2015 Containing the European Parliament's Recommendations to the European Commission on the Negotiations for the Transatlantic Trade and Investment Partnership (TTIP) (2014/2228 (INI)); European Parliament, Resolution of 3 February 2016 Containing the European Parliament's Recommendations to the Commission on the Negotiations for the Trade in Services Agreement (TiSA) (2015/2233(INI)).

[45] European Commission, Horizontal Provisions for Cross-Border Data Flows and for Personal Data Protection in EU Trade and Investment Agreements, February 2018, available at https://trade.ec.europa.eu/doclib/docs/2018/may/tradoc_156884.pdf.

[46] European Commission, EU's Proposal for the Digital Trade Chapter of EU–New Zealand FTA, 25 September 2018 [hereinafter: EU Proposal Digital Trade Chapter EU–New Zealand FTA], available at http://trade.ec.europa.eu/doclib/docs/2018/december/tradoc_157581.pdf; European Commission, EU's Proposal for the Digital Trade Chapter of EU–Australia FTA, 10 October 2018 [hereinafter: EU Proposal Digital Trade Chapter EU–Australia FTA], available at http://trade.ec.europa.eu/doclib/docs/2018/december/tradoc_157570.pdf; European Commission, EU's Proposal for the Digital Trade Chapter of EU–Tunisia FTA, 9 November 2018, available at https://trade.ec.europa.eu/doclib/docs/2019/january/tradoc_157660.%20ALECA%202019%20-%20texte%20commerce%20numerique.pdf; European Commission, Report of the 5th Round of Negotiations for a Free Trade Agreement between the European Union and Indonesia, 9–13 July 2018, Brussels, available at http://trade.ec.europa.eu/doclib/docs/2018/july/tradoc_157137.pdf. The EU's Proposal for Digital Trade Chapter for a Modernised EU–Chile Association Agreement only contains a placeholder for provisions on data flows (see EU–Chile FTA, 5 February 2018, available at https://trade.ec.europa.eu/doclib/docs/2018/february/tradoc_156582.pdf).

[47] WTO, Joint Statement on Electronic Commerce: EU Proposal for WTO Disciplines and Commitments Relating to Electronic Commerce, Communication from the European Union, INF/ECOM/22, 26 April 2019 [hereinafter: EU Proposal Joint Statement Initiative].

[48] See, e.g., Article X.1(2) of the EU proposal for Chapter X, 'Exceptions' of the EU–New Zealand FTA, 25 June 2019, available at https://trade.ec.europa.eu/doclib/docs/2019/july/tradoc_158278.pdf [hereinafter: Proposal for Exceptions]. This provision includes a general exception for privacy and data protection modelled after the general exception in Article XIV(c)(ii) GATS. EU proposals for 'Exceptions' chapters of other FTAs discussed in this chapter are not available as of the time of writing.

above-mentioned model clauses.[49] It is unclear whether the TCA provisions are merely outliers or represent the new model approach of the EU. Given that the above-mentioned model clauses have not been amended following the TCA and still represent the EU position in multiple ongoing trade negotiations, including those at the WTO, this chapter assumes that they still represent the EU mainstream approach and, therefore, the discussion below focuses solely on these clauses.

Model Article A provides for an exhaustive list of prohibited restrictions on cross-border data flows. Model Article B on the *protection of personal data and privacy* states that the protection of personal data and privacy *is a fundamental right* and includes an exception from the provision on cross-border data flows. The model clauses, on their face, safeguard the EU's broad regulatory autonomy, much more so than the general exception for privacy and data protection in existing trade agreements. This is made manifest in five different ways. First, as compared to the US model provision on cross-border data flows, the prohibition of restrictions on cross-border data flows in Article A is formulated more narrowly, in that it specifically names the types of restrictions that are outlawed by this provision. Second, the provisions of Article B(1) assert that the normative rationale for the protection of personal data and privacy is the protection of fundamental rights. This rationale – as opposed to economic reasons for protecting privacy and personal data – signals a higher level of protection and, therefore, arguably requires a broader autonomy to regulate vis-à-vis international trade commitments.[50] This provision is likely to be interpreted as a part of the digital trade exception for privacy and data protection in Article B(2) of the proposal. Third, the proposed exception for privacy and the protection of personal data establishes a significantly more lenient threshold – 'it deems appropriate' – than the 'necessity test' of the general exception under the GATS. Drawing the parallel with the threshold in the GATS national security exception – 'it considers necessary'[51] – one can argue that the proposed exception affords an almost unlimited autonomy to adopt measures inconsistent with Article B (2) to protection of privacy and personal data.[52] Fourth, the exception in Article B(2) explicitly recognises the adoption and application of rules for cross-border transfers of personal data – the gist of the EU's framework for transfers of personal data – as one of the measures that a party may deem appropriate to protect personal data and privacy, in spite of its international trade commitments. Fifth and finally, the

---

[49] Articles DIGIT. 6 and DIGIT. 7 of the TCA; for a critical assessment from a data protection perspective, see Opinion 3/2021 of the European Data Protection Supervisor on the conclusion of the EU and UK trade agreement and the EU and UK exchange of classified information agreement.

[50] For argumentation on this point, see Yakovleva, note 16, at 507–511.

[51] Article XIV *bis* GATS.

[52] The national security exception is the broadest of all the existing exceptions in international trade law. It is for this reason that it was labelled as 'all-embracing and seemingly omnipotent'. See J. Yeong Yoo and D. Ahn, 'Security Exceptions in the WTO System: Bridge or Bottle-Neck for Trade and Security?', *Journal of International Economic Law* 19 (2016), 417–444, at 426.

provision of Article B(2) protects the safeguards afforded by a party for personal data and privacy from being affected by any other provision of the trade agreement.

At the same time, despite these apparent strengths of the EU proposal in view of privacy and data protection, Article B suffers from at least four clear weaknesses. First, declaring that the protection of privacy and personal data are fundamental rights is EU-centric and does not leave the EU's trading partners any autonomy to choose another level of protection of these public policy interests they might see fit for their own legal and cultural tradition. Given that, as things stand now at least, the fundamental rights protection of privacy and personal data is, essentially, a European phenomenon, EU trading partners may be reluctant to commit to this level of protection in a trade agreement. Second, the exception for privacy and data protection in Article B(2) of the EU's proposal is designed for digital trade chapters and fails to clarify its relationship with the general exception for data protection, which remains intact – at least in available draft trade agreements – in which the EU has included the proposed model clauses.[53] Third, modelling an exception for privacy and data protection after the national security exception essentially creates an almost unconditional escape valve from virtually any trade commitment, as long as there is at least a remote nexus to the protection of privacy and personal data. Although this may seem justified at first glance given that privacy and data protection are fundamental rights in the EU, it creates a precedent for using this wide margin for a variety of public policy interests (other than national security), which may undermine the global rules-based trading system. Fourth, and most relevant in the context of this chapter's discussion, the public policy interests that can justify violation of Article A under Article B(2) are limited to the protection of privacy and personal data. Although this underscores the relative importance of the rights to data protection and privacy as opposed to the goal of digital trade liberalisation on the values scale, the limitation of the exception to these particular rights may have negative effects. Given that the threshold for important public policy interests, such as public morals, safety, human, animal or plant life, in the general exception clause is narrower than the threshold in model Article B(2), the regulatory autonomy to protect personal data and privacy ends up being much broader than the protection of other rights that are also recognised under the EU Charter of Fundamental Rights.[54] This elevates privacy and the protection of personal data above other rights that are equally protected[55] and may even create an incentive to – artificially – frame other public policy interests, especially those not mentioned in the GATS general exception, as protection of privacy and personal data. In the context of AI, this could steer domestic AI regulation in the EU deeper into the realm of data protection as

---

[53] Proposal for Exceptions, note 48.
[54] See, for example, Articles 2 (right to life), 6 (right to liberty and security), 37 (environmental protection) EU Charter of Fundamental Rights.
[55] K. Lenaerts, 'Exploring the Limits of the EU Charter of Fundamental Rights', *European Constitutional Law Review* 8 (2012), 375–403, at 392–393.

opposed to creating a separate regulatory framework – an issue currently discussed in the EU institutions.[56] Public policy interests, such as industrial policy,[57] cybersecurity[58] and digital sovereignty,[59] are cited as public policy interests that may require restricting digital trade in general or data flows in particular. The first is especially relevant for developing countries, for which free data flows essentially mean 'one-way flows', as these countries' data flows are constrained by the limited availability of digital technologies and of the skills necessary to produce digital intelligence from data.[60] This issue, as already mentioned, has gained prominence in the European Commission's 2020 digital strategy. In its European Strategy for Data, the European Commission stated:

> The functioning of the European data space will depend on the capacity of the EU to invest in next-generation technologies and infrastructures as well as in digital competences like data literacy. This in turn will increase *Europe's technological sovereignty* in key enabling technologies and infrastructures for the data economy. The infrastructures should support the creation of European data pools enabling Big Data analytics and machine learning, in a manner compliant with data protection legislation and competition law, allowing the emergence of data-driven ecosystems.[61]

Turning to cybersecurity interests, they may require restrictions on data flows, data localisation or restrictions on import of certain information technology products.[62] These interests are relevant for both developing and developed countries. The blurring boundary between public and private spheres in the surveillance context – where governments increasingly rely on private actors for access to data for surveillance purposes – explains why cross-border data flows may raise sovereignty concerns as well.[63]

To sum up, although the regulation of cross-border data flows, especially in the context of AI, implicates a variety of public policy interests, the EU trade policy on this topic has solely focused on one of them – namely privacy and the protection of personal data. This,

---

[56] Compare White Paper on Artificial Intelligence (note 15) with EDPB Response to the MEP Sophie in't Veld's Letter on Unfair Algorithms, 29 January 2020, available at https://edpb .europa.eu/our-work-tools/our-documents/letters/edpb-response-mep-sophie-int-velds-letter-unfair-algorithms_en.

[57] C. Foster and S. Azmeh, 'Latecomer Economies and National Digital Policy: An Industrial Policy Perspective', *The Journal of Development Studies* 56 (2020), 1–17.

[58] Mitchell and Mishra, note 19, at 1079.

[59] See European Commission, A New Industrial Strategy for Europe, COM(2020) 102 final, 10 March 2020; White Paper on Artificial Intelligence, note 15. See also K. Propp, 'Waving the Flag of Digital Sovereignty', Atlantic Council, 11 December 2019.

[60] UNCTAD, note 1, at 91.

[61] European Commission, A European Strategy For Data, COM (2020) 66 final, 19 February 2020, at 5 (emphasis added).

[62] J. P. Meltzer and C. F. Kerry, 'Cybersecurity and Digital Trade: Getting It Right', Brookings, 18 September 2019.

[63] R. D. Williams, 'Reflections on TikTok and Data Privacy as National Security', Lawfare, 15 November 2019.

arguably, has something to do with the institutional dynamics between EU institutions. However, it may not be sustainable either in the EU or in a multilateral context, such as with regard to the electronic commerce negotiations at the WTO. According to UNCTAD, the early meetings of the group on data flows at the WTO have, so far, mainly reflected the views of proponents of the free flow of data.[64] However, for these negotiations to result in concrete WTO legal norms, members will have to reach a consensus on how to balance the economic gains of free data flows with multiple competing interests, which include not only the protection of privacy and personal data – the main point of contention for the EU – but also other fundamental rights, as well as industrial policy, cybersecurity and economic development interests of other countries involved in the negotiations.[65]

In contrast to the position taken both by the United States and the EU that data flows should be free (unless their restriction can be justified by an exception), when it comes to the protection of the source code, or algorithms expressed in that source code incorporating the *learning* derived from processing of data – the position is the exact opposite. As explained in the introduction, learning, or digital intelligence, is where the real economic value of personal and other data lies. Thus, while data and data flows are viewed as 'free', the value obtained from data are up for grabs by whomever possesses the infrastructure and resources necessary to process that data. At this juncture, these entities are concentrated in the United States and China. Two recent US-led FTAs, namely the USMCA and the US–Japan Digital Trade Agreement (DTA), contain specific provisions on the protection of source code and algorithms.[66] The EU's proposal for the WTO negotiations on e-commerce also contains a prohibition on access to and forced transfer of the source code of software owned by a natural or juridical person of other members.[67] Similar provisions are included in the EU proposals for digital trade chapters of currently negotiated FTAs, such as with Mexico,[68] Australia[69] and New Zealand.[70]

C THE LIMITS OF PERSONAL DATA PROTECTION IN THE CONTEXT OF TRADE LAW POLICY ON CROSS-BORDER DATA FLOWS IN AI CONTEXT

The earlier discussion demonstrates that the only public policy interests that are fully accounted for in the exception from a proposed provision on the free cross-border flow of data in draft EU trade agreements are privacy and the protection of personal data. In

[64] UNCTAD, note 1, at 137.
[65] S. Yakovleva and K. Irion, 'Toward Compatibility of the EU Trade Policy with the General Data Protection Regulation', *AJIL Unbound* 114 (2020), 10–14, at 14.
[66] Article 19.16 USMCA; Article 17 US–Japan DTA.
[67] EU Proposal Joint Statement Initiative, note 47, at para. 2.6.
[68] Article 9 of the draft EU–Mexico FTA.
[69] Article 11 EU Proposal Digital Trade Chapter EU–Australia FTA.
[70] Article 11 EU Proposal Digital Trade Chapter EU–New Zealand FTA.

the context of AI, this mirrors the currently prevailing approach in the EU to regulate AI through the governance structure of the GDPR. This section focuses on two limitations of this approach. First, this approach is based on a distinction between personal and non-personal data, because only data that qualifies as personal falls under the EU data protection framework. The distinction is increasingly hard to make, especially in the context of AI. Second, EU privacy and personal data protection takes us to an individual rights framework that does not account for the value produced from data and the impact of applying the learning derived from AI to larger societal groups or populations.

I *Thin Borderline between Personal and Non-personal Data in AI Context*

EU law maintains a rigid distinction between personal and non-personal data,[71] in the sense that there are two different legal frameworks for personal and non-personal data. While cross-border transfers of personal data are subject to a 'border control'[72] regime, as discussed earlier, transfers of non-personal data outside the EEA are unrestricted. This distinction is increasingly unworkable in practice as it is becoming ever more difficult to draw a line between personal and non-personal (or anonymous) data, especially in the AI context.[73]

Schwartz and Solove succinctly summarise four main problems with the distinction. First, 'built-in identifiability' in cyberspace makes anonymity online a 'myth', as essentially all online data can be linked to some identifier.[74] Second, non-personal information can be transformed into personal data over time.[75] Third, the distinction between personal and non-personal data has a dynamic nature, as the line between the two depends on technological developments. Fourth and finally, the borderline between personal and non-personal data is not firm, but rather contextual, as many types of data are not non-identifiable or identifiable in the abstract.[76]

The EU regulation on a framework for the flow of non-personal data illustrates a number of those points. It specifically mentions that examples of non-personal data include 'aggregate and anonymised datasets used for big data analytics, data on precision farming that can help to monitor and optimise the use of pesticides and

---

[71] B.-J. Koops, 'The Trouble with European Data Protection Law', *International Data Privacy Law* 4 (2014), 250–261, at 257.
[72] D. J. B. Svantesson, 'The Regulation of Cross-Border Data Flows', *International Data Privacy Law* 1 (2011), 180–198, at 184.
[73] See, e.g., O. Tene and J. Polonetsky, 'Big Data for All: Privacy and User Control in the Age of Analytics', *Northwestern Journal of Technology and Intellectual Property* 11 (2013), 239–273; N. Purtova, 'The Law of Everything: Broad Concept of Personal Data and Future of EU Data Protection Law', *Law, Innovation and Technology* 10 (2018), 40–81; P. Ohm, 'Broken Promises of Privacy', *UCLA Law Review* 57 (2010), 1701–1777.
[74] P. M. Schwartz and D. J. Solove, 'The PII Problem: Privacy and a New Concept of Personally Identifiable Information', *New York University Law Review* 86 (2011), 1814–1894, at 1836–1848.
[75] Ibid.
[76] Ibid.

water, or data on maintenance needs for industrial machines'.[77] The regulation also notes, however, that '[i]f technological developments make it possible to turn anonymised data into personal data, such data are to be treated as personal data, and [the GDPR] is to apply accordingly'.[78] As can be seen, although *the very existence of this regulation is grounded on the possibility of separating the notions of personal and non-personal data*, the regulation itself suggests that such distinction is not clear-cut and requires constant reassessment.

Another limitation of a data protection approach to restrictions on cross-border data flows in the AI context is that its scope is limited to data that qualifies as personal data. However, it is not the data fed into an AI system itself, but the *knowledge* derived from the data through *learning* that integrates the value of big data into different organisational processes. Training of AI systems transforms personal data into an aggregate representation of such data, which may no longer qualify as personal data. Interestingly, some scholars have argued in this context that AI models vulnerable to inversion attacks can still be considered personal data.[79] Moreover, it is not only personal, but also non-personal – machine-generated – data that is extremely useful and valuable in AI context. As the European Commission rightly noted in its 2020 White Paper on AI:

> AI is one of the most important applications of the data economy. Today most data are related to consumers and are stored and processed on central cloud-based infrastructure. By contrast a large share of tomorrow's far more abundant data will come from industry, business and the public sector, and will be stored on a variety of systems, notably on computing devices working at the edge of the network.[80]

Although cross-border flows of non-personal data and learning produced from it may not have implications for individual rights to privacy and the protection of personal data, they may present risks for other policy objectives, such as cybersecurity or digital sovereignty. The argument in this chapter is not to suggest that cross-border flows of non-personal data should be restricted, although a possibility of such restrictions already features in the European Commission's proposal for a Data Governance Act.[81] Neither does it suggest that a strong exception for domestic privacy and data protection rules is inappropriate. Rather, it underscores the importance of assessing the implications of cross-border data flows in the context of AI against a broader set of public policy interests that matter for the EU and its trading partners in the long term. For example, Gürses and van Hoboken are doubtful that,

---

[77] EU Regulation 2018/1807, note 38, at Recital 9.
[78] Ibid.
[79] M. Veale, R. Binns, and L. Edwards, 'Algorithms That Remember: Model Inversion Attacks and Data Protection Law', *Philosophical Transactions of the Royal Society A* 376 (2018), 1–15.
[80] White Paper on Artificial Intelligence, note 15, at 1.
[81] See, e.g., Articles 5, 30 of the Proposal for a Regulation of the European Parliament and of the Council on European data governance (Data Governance Act) COM/2020/767 final.

in the context of digital services produced in an agile way where users also act as producers of such services, privacy law, traditionally centred around regulating information flows, is able to tackle the implications for individuals of such agile production.[82] They argue that such problems should not all be framed as questions of information flows and data protection, but instead addressed by other, or complementary regulatory tools, such as consumer protection, software regulation or treatment of certain services as new types of utility providers.[83]

II *Individual Rights Framework Does Not Factor in the Value of Knowledge Derived from Data*

In the digital trade discourse where unrestricted cross-border data flows are viewed as a source of tremendous – *aggregated* – value gains, not every country participating in data flows 'wins' from those data flows. Yet, the issue of who wins and who loses from unrestricted data flows is typically not raised in this discourse. As mentioned earlier, only countries that possess the necessary infrastructure and skills to refine data and extract value from large corpora of data generated in the course of the provision of online services will really benefit from the free flow of data. As a result, countries that lack these resources are merely supplying primary goods, which are worth much less than the learning that can be derived from them, just as countries that produce raw materials are rarely the largest winners when compared to countries where those materials are transformed. Just as the real value lies in the transformation of raw materials, the real value in AI lies in the value of processing the data. Against this backdrop, focusing on data instead of learning derived from data misses the point.

This brings us to the second limitation of the data protection framework being central in cross-border provision of AI, especially in the way it is designed in the EU, where personal data is primarily viewed as the subject matter of a fundamental right rather than an economic asset. This is manifested, for example, in regulatory choices that avoided recognising personal data as consideration for online services (in other words, as a form of currency) in the 2019 Digital Content Directive.[84] In its opinion on the draft of this directive, the European Data Protection Supervisor (EDPS) underscored that 'personal data cannot be *considered as a mere commodity*'.[85] Although the fact that the personal data cannot be considered as a 'mere'

---

[82] S. Gürses and J. van Hoboken, 'Privacy after the Agile Turn', in E. Selinger, J. Polonetsky, and O. Tene (eds), *The Cambridge Handbook of Consumer Privacy* (Cambridge: Cambridge University Press, 2018), 597–601.

[83] Ibid.

[84] Directive 2019/770 of the European Parliament and of the Council on Certain Aspects Concerning Contracts for the Supply of Digital Content and Digital Services, OJ L [2019] 136/1, 22 May 2019. For discussion, see European Data Protection Supervisor (EDPS), Opinion 4/2017 on the Proposal for a Directive on Certain Aspects Concerning Contracts for the Supply of Digital Content, 14 March 2017.

[85] Ibid., at 3 (emphasis added).

commodity does not mean that it cannot have economic value, viewing the protection of personal data as a fundamental right could be one of the reasons why the EU could be restrained in putting a price tag on personal data in trade negotiations on cross-border data flows.

UNCTAD stresses that platforms harnessing data generated by individuals, businesses and organisations of other countries, while based in only a few countries, raises concerns about 'digital sovereignty', in view of the control, access and rights with respect to the data and the appropriation of the value generated from monetising the data.[86] UNCTAD explains that economic value derived from data is captured by developed countries where companies having control over storage and processing of data reside.[87] It follows, that '[t]he only way for developing countries to exercise effective economic "ownership" of and control over the data generated in their territories may be *to restrict cross-border flows of important personal and community data*'.[88] Although this particular report makes an argument in the context of imbalance between developed and developing countries, given the high concentration of digital technologies in the very few developed countries, it could also be relevant in relations between those few and other developed countries. It should be emphasised that restricting the outgoing flows of personal data does not mean that those countries that impose such restrictions will have the means to process and generate value from such data within their borders. It may be about sovereignty, but it is not necessarily about endogenous economic development unless measures to ensure this development accompany the data flow restrictions.

In a similar vein, Couldry and Mejias speak about 'data colonialism', by which they mean that big data processing practices make human relations and social life overall 'an "open" resource for extraction'.[89] They compare big data to appropriation or extraction of resources[90] – another parallel between data and oil. Global data flows, they argue, 'are as expansive as historic colonialism's appropriation of land, resources, and bodies, although the epicentre has somewhat shifted'.[91] In their view, the transformation of human actors and social relations formalised as data into value leads to a fundamental power imbalance (colonial power and colonised subjects).[92] In a similar vein, Zuboff has famously labelled the business of accumulation and

---

[86] UNCTAD, note 1, at 89.
[87] Ibid.
[88] Ibid. (emphasis added).
[89] N. Couldry and U. A. Mejias, 'Data Colonialism: Rethinking Big Data's Relation to the Contemporary Subject', *Television and New Media* 20 (2019), 336–349, at 337.
[90] Ibid., at 338.
[91] Ibid., but see M. Mueller and K. Grindal, 'Data Flows and the Digital Economy: Information as a Mobile Factor of Production', *Digital Policy, Regulation and Governance* 21 (2019), 71–87, at 82, challenging this point of view.
[92] Couldry and Mejias, note 87, at 337–338.

monetising data 'surveillance capitalism', which leads not only to the accumulation of capital, but also of individual rights.[93]

There is some movement in the governance of data reflecting those concerns. A 2019 Opinion of the German Ethics Commission shows a tendency towards expanding the scope of individual rights in data beyond the non-economic rights to privacy and personal data protection. According to the commission, under certain circumstances individuals should be granted data-specific rights, which include a right to obtain an economic share in profits derived with the help of the data.[94] The potential design of a *legal framework of distribution* of economic gains from the use of data is addressed in a growing body of scholarly and policy research. This research explores frameworks or organisations acting as intermediaries between individuals and entities wishing to use (and profit from) their data, such as *data trusts* or collective data ownership (such as data funds).[95] Data trusts are viewed as an attractive tool to facilitate access to large data sets of aggregated data for the purposes of developing and applying AI, to generate trust around the use of data by various stakeholders, and as mechanisms for paying back a fair share of benefits from the use of data to individuals.[96] There is, however, little clarity regarding the structure that data trusts should take and the method for sharing value derived from the commercial use of personal data.[97] The German Ministry of Economic Affairs and the Dutch Government are investigating the possibilities of setting up data trusts in their respective countries.[98] Research on data funds views personal data as a *public resource*, drawing a parallel with natural resources that constitute the country's resource. From this perspective, data collected within a certain jurisdiction should 'belong' to that jurisdiction.[99] Data funds are viewed as a form of collective data ownership, allowing individuals to exercise control over which data is collected about them and how it is used, as well as to receive payment for commercial access to the data in the fund.[100]

[93] S. Zuboff, 'Big Other: Surveillance Capitalism and the Prospects of an Information Civilization', *Journal of Information Technology* 30 (2015), 75–89.
[94] German Data Ethics Commission, *Opinion of the Data Ethics Commission: Executive Summary* (Berlin: Data Ethics Commission of the Federal Government, 2019), at 9–10.
[95] For an overview, see UNCTAD, note 1, at 132–134.
[96] J. Hardinges, 'What Is a Data Trust? What's the Definition and How Is One Applied?', Open Data Institute, 10 July 2018; S. Delacroix and N. D. Lawrence, 'Bottom-Up Data Trusts: Disturbing the "One Size Fits All" Approach to Data Governance', *International Data Privacy Law* 9 (2019), 236–252; W. Hall and J. Pesenti, *Growing the Artificial Intelligence Industry in the UK* (London: Government of the United Kingdom, 2017).
[97] Hall and Pesenti suggesting that the trusts should take a form of a repeatable framework. Ibid.
[98] Motie Buitenweg c.s. over vormgeving van data trusts in Nederland – Initiatief nota van het lid Verhoeven over mededinging in de digitale economie, Tweede Kamer der Staten-Generaal, 35134 nr. 7, 18 December 2019, available at: www.parlementairemonitor.nl/9353000/1/j9vvi j5epmj1eyo/vl4jjboml8yr.
[99] UNCTAD, note 1, at 132.
[100] See, e.g., E. Morozov, 'To Tackle Google's Power, Regulators Have to Go after Its Ownership of Data', *The Guardian*, 2 July 2017.

These economic rights are unlikely to become a part of the EU data protection framework precisely due to their economic nature. At the same time, they could interfere with international trade disciplines which aim to facilitate the unrestricted cross-border data flows. This is why they should form part, in addition to the fundamental rights to protection of privacy and personal data, of a nuanced rebalancing of the EU's trade policy on this issue.

D CONCLUSION

The analysis in this chapter of recent developments in the governance of cross-border data flows in international trade law showed that the main public policy interests discussed in the context of EU trade policy on this issue are the protection of the fundamental rights to privacy and personal data. This chapter argued that other policy objectives, such as cybersecurity and digital sovereignty – which have recently become one of the anchors of EU's internal AI policy – should also be considered. The chapter has also shown that the individual rights–centred data protection framework has limits in governing AI both in domestic and international trade policy.

11

Panta Rhei

A *European Perspective on Ensuring a High Level of Protection of Human Rights in a World in Which Everything Flows*

Kristina Irion*

A INTRODUCTION

Pantha rhei ('everything flows') turns out to be a very fitting metaphor for how terabytes of digital data rush through the network of networks. Attributed to the philosopher Heraclitus *panta rhei* connotes that change is the fundamental essence of the universe.[1] Data flows are the undercurrent of digital globalization that transforms our societies. How data flows will likely underpin digital services in a not so distant future is vividly described in Anupam Chander's contribution (Chapter 5) in this volume. Data's liquidity tends to undermine outdated regulatory formations and erode the paradigms that used to underpin a society's conventional right to self-governance.[2] Everything is in flux.

Human rights do however remain valid currency in how we approach planetary-scale computation and accompanying data flows. As we enter 'the age of digital interdependence', a UN expert panel urges 'new forms of digital cooperation to ensure that digital technologies are built on a foundation of respect for human rights and provide meaningful opportunity for all people and nations'.[3] Today's system of human rights protection, however, is highly dependent on domestic legal

---

* Kristina Irion is Associate Professor at the Institute for Information Law (IViR), University of Amsterdam. I would like to enthusiastically thank Dr Mira Burri and her team as well as the participants of the conference 'Big Data and Global Trade Law', 16–17 November 2018, Lucerne, Switzerland. Contact: k.irion@uva.nl.

[1] Actually, it is Plato's interpretation based on an aphorism from the Heraclitean River Fragments that reads in English translation, 'On those stepping into rivers staying the same, other and other waters flow'. See D. W. Graham, 'Heraclitus: Flux, Order, and Knowledge', in P. Curd and D. W. Graham (eds), *The Oxford Handbook of Presocratic Philosophy*, Vol. 1 (Oxford: Oxford University Press, 2009), 167–188.

[2] J. E. Cohen, *Between Truth and Power* (Oxford: Oxford University Press, 2019), at 200.

[3] United Nations Secretary-General's High-Level Panel on Digital Cooperation, *Report of the UN Secretary-General's High-Level Panel on Digital Cooperation: The Age of Digital Interdependence* (New York/Geneva: United Nations Publications, 2019).

institutions, which unravel faster than the reconstruction of fitting transnational governance institutions. The transnational protection of data privacy is a case in point, which required legal reforms in order not to fall into the cracks between different domestic legal systems. Furthermore, the transnational provision of artificial intelligence (AI) is going to have a bearing on the conditions of human freedom prompting calls for a human rights–based approach to AI governance.[4]

Through the contribution in this volume it emerges that international trade law has successfully co-opted cross-border data flows as a desirable baseline for digital trade. This raises the question how the inclusion of the free flow of data in international trade law would affect the prospects for the transnational protection of human rights. As a stand-alone commitment, the free flow of data namely lacks any normative underpinning and only through the interplay with domestic legal frameworks do human rights become recognized.

In my contribution I argue that the inclusion of cross-border data flows as a new trade law discipline would be opportunistic in light of the morality to protect human rights online. International trade law, which has been criticized for the 'economization of human rights',[5] would subtly reinforce the transformative power of data flows leaving human rights enforcement to domestic institutions which in themselves have been found inferior to deal with the issues at hand. In other words, the opportunity structures offered by international trade law will not advance the construction of a global information civilization that is founded on the respect for human rights. Rather, multilevel economic governance should provide for constitutional pluralism and sufficient margin for experimentation with novel strategies to give effect to human rights in the online context.[6] I conclude with a plaidoyer for a new quid pro quo in digital trade in which the liberalization of cross-border data flows recognizes better the enhanced need for human rights accountability. This contribution intersects human rights law with international economic law, liberally borrowing from transnational legal theory and Internet governance literature. It advances its arguments through a combination of doctrinal and critical legal research with a certain predisposition to European legal thinking.

This chapter proceeds as follows: after the backdrop has been set, the following section takes a critical look at the construction of the data flow metaphor as a policy concept inside international trade law. The subsequent section explores how the respect for human rights ties in with national constitutionalism that becomes increasingly challenged by the transnational dynamic of digital era transactions.

[4] N. A. Smuha, 'Beyond a Human Rights-Based Approach to AI Governance: Promise, Pitfalls, Plea', *Philosophy and Technology* (2020).
[5] C. Breining-Kaufmann, 'The Legal Matrix of Human Rights and Trade Law: State Obligations versus Private Rights and Obligations', in T. Cottier, J. Pauwelyn, and E. Bürgi (eds), *Human Rights and International Trade* (Oxford: Oxford University Press, 2005), 95–136, at 104.
[6] E.-U. Petersmann, 'Need for a New Philosophy of International Economic Law and Adjudication', *Journal of International Economic Law* 17 (2014), 639–669, at 663.

The last section turns to international trade law and why its ambitions to govern cross-border data flows will likely not advance efforts to generate respect for human rights. In the conclusion, the different arguments are linked together to advocate for a re-balancing act that recognizes human rights inside international trade law.

B DATA FLOW AS A POLICY METAPHOR

Data is the building block of today's digital economy. As a virtual unit data can represent any type of digital infrastructure, platform, or system, that undergird an infinite range of virtual goods, services, transactions and expressions. Digital supply and value chains are ultimately representations of data which are assembled to perform varying functionalities.[7] Besides data is exponentially generated from any human and machine activity, which in turn are a key input for machine learning and algorithmic decision-making. Everything that can be expressed in data is inherently liquid because it can be de-assembled, moved across space and re-assembled again.

In social theory 'flow', 'fluidity' or 'liquidity' are used as a metaphor to connote how circulation and velocity forge a new kind of information or network society.[8] According to Castells, contemporary society is constructed around flows: 'flows of capital, flows of information, flows of technology, flows of organizational inter-action, flows of images, sounds, and symbols. Flows are not just one element of the social organization: they are the expression of processes dominating our eco-nomic, political, and symbolic life'.[9] Sociologist Deborah Lupton, by contrast, criticizes that writers on digital technologies rely on liquid concepts when discussing the circulation of digital data.[10] For Lupton, '[t]he apparent liquidity of data, its tendency to flow freely, can also constitute its threatening aspect, its potential to create chaos and loss of control'.[11] Lupton nevertheless resolves that such concep-tions can help making sense of the phenomenon. It must be conceded that the recourse to the data flow metaphor should not divert from analyzing actors, the epistemology and affordances of concrete sociotechnical systems.[12] Globalization researchers, however, consistently use the cross-border movement or flows of

---

7 Instructive on this: B. H. Bratton, *The Stack: On Software and Sovereignty* (Cambridge, MA: MIT Press, 2015).
8 T. Sutherland, 'Liquid Networks and the Metaphysics of Flux: Ontologies of Flow in an Age of Speed and Mobility', *Theory, Culture and Society* 30 (2013), 3–23.
9 M. Castells, *The Rise of the Network Society*, 2nd edn (Oxford: Blackwell, 2010), at 442.
10 D. Lupton, *Digital Sociology* (Abingdon: Routledge, 2014), at 106.
11 Ibid.
12 See, e.g., B. Bodo et al., 'Tackling the Algorithmic Control Crisis – The Technical, Legal, and Ethical Challenges of Research into Algorithmic Agents', *Yale Journal of Law and Technology* 19 (2017), 133–180; J.-C. Plantin et al., 'Infrastructure Studies Meet Platform Studies in the Age of Google and Facebook', *New Media and Society* 20 (2018), 293–310; A. Helmond, *The Web as Platform* (PhD thesis, University of Amsterdam, 2015).

persons, capital, goods and services as a conceptual lens, which is currently complemented by data flows. It is precisely the circulation of data which underpins the processes that lead to the reconfiguration of the spatial organization of social relations and transactions that characterize globalization.[13] A 2016 report by the McKinsey Global Institute proclaimed that globalization had entered 'a new era defined by data flows'.[14]

A powerful coalition of international and intergovernmental organizations, including the G7 and the G20, the Organisation for Economic Cooperation and Development (OECD) and the World Economic Forum (WEF), among others, have intensified their work on promoting cross-border data flows as an international economic policy principle. For instance, following the initiative of Japan's government on 'Data Free Flow with Trust', the 2019 G20 Osaka Leaders' Declaration states:

> Cross-border flow of data, information, ideas and knowledge generates higher productivity, greater innovation, and improved sustainable development, while raising challenges related to privacy, data protection, intellectual property rights, and security. By continuing to address these challenges, we can further facilitate data free flow and strengthen consumer and business trust. In this respect, it is necessary that legal frameworks, both domestic and international, should be respected. Such data free flow with trust will harness the opportunities of the digital economy.[15]

While the statement correctly reflects the unabated tension between cross-border data flows and domestic legal frameworks, it falls short of identifying common strategies that would mitigate this tension and thereby forging trust in legitimate cross-border data flows. The endorsement of 'Data Free Flow with Trust' perfectly encapsulates the influential narrative of innovation, growth and development associated with cross-border data flow while leaving the intricacies of protecting human rights and societal values to domestic institutions that are themselves increasingly contested in an interdependent world. From the perspective of domestic public policy, the cross-border flow of data more fittingly compares to a maelstrom that potentially erodes constitutionally guaranteed rights and societal values.

C HUMAN RIGHTS DO NOT FLOW EASILY ACROSS BORDERS

Adopted over seventy years ago, the Universal Declaration of Human Rights (UDHR) protects a canon of universal and indivisible human rights the

---

[13] D. Held et al., *Global Transformations: Politics, Economics, and Culture* (Stanford: Stanford University Press, 1999), at 16.

[14] J. Manyika et al., *Digital Globalization: The New Era of Global Flows* (Washington, DC: McKinsey Global Institute, 2016).

[15] G20, 'G20 Osaka Leaders' Declaration', 2020, available at www.consilium.europa.eu/media/40124/final_g20_osaka_leaders_declaration.pdf, at para. 11.

interpretation of which evolves with the time.[16] Already twice the UN Human Rights Council has affirmed that human rights must be protected offline and online regardless of frontiers.[17] International human rights law is addressed to states which are bound to respect and uphold the obligations in their domestic legal system. Whereas international human rights law can take different levels of commitment from non-binding to binding, its enforcement overwhelmingly takes place at the domestic level.[18] 'The multilevel human rights constitution', as Ernst-Ulrich Petersmann explains, 'remains embedded into national constitutionalism as protected by national and regional courts'.[19] Human rights thus wield universal protection from their geopolitically fragmented implementation by states. This construction has largely been workable in an offline and static world where different jurisdictions could coexist by the intuitive demarcations of territoriality. In the age of digital interdependence, however, interferences with human rights frequently take a transnational dynamic. According to Julie Cohen, domestic protections for human rights that are built on outdated regulatory formations have begun to fail comprehensively.[20] Different trends, such as the intermediation of human transactions by digital platforms, and strategies that would outsmart national legal frameworks have been held responsible for the sad state of affairs.[21] From the outset the Internet-mediated sphere has attracted much libertarianism and utopism,[22] but in hindsight too little concern about the impeding policy and regulatory challenges online.

I Who Should Be in Charge of the Internet?

In its infancy the Internet has attracted utopian ideas of a free and borderless cyberspace, a human-made global commons in the service of an international community of users. Famously, John Perry Barlow in his 'Declaration of the Independence of Cyberspace' called on governments of the world to leave the

---

[16] General Assembly of the United Nations, *Universal Declaration of Human Rights*, 3rd Session, A/RES/217(III), adopted 10 December 1948.
[17] United Nations Human Rights Council, The Promotion, Protection and Enjoyment of Human Rights on the Internet, A/HRC/RES/32/13, adopted on 18 July 2016; United Nations Human Rights Council, The Promotion, Protection and Enjoyment of Human Rights on the Internet, A/HRC/38/L.10/Rev.1, adopted 4 July 2018.
[18] One exception is the European Convention on Human Rights, which is enforceable through the European Court of Human Rights for state members of the Council of Europe.
[19] Petersmann, note 6, at 644.
[20] Cohen, note 2, at 239.
[21] Ibid.; J. van Dijck, T. Poell, and M. de Waal (eds), *The Platform Society* (Oxford: Oxford University Press, 2018).
[22] F. Turner, *From Counterculture to Cyberculture* (Chicago: The University of Chicago Press, 2006); I. de Sola Pool, *Technologies of Freedom* (Cambridge, MA: Harvard University Press, 1983).

Internet and its users alone.[23] Another proposal was to transform cyberspace into an international commons and to root Internet governance in international agreements. Analogies to Hugo Grotius' 1609 dissertation 'Mare Liberum'[24] have been offered to extend a similar regime to the Internet as is practiced today in international maritime law and space law. Despite gigantic efforts to nourish international multi-stakeholder Internet governance up to this point, this approach has never gained sufficient authority to actually deliver tangible outcomes.[25] The upshot is that the protection of individuals' human rights online has never been uploaded to a supranational level.

Simultaneously, the Westphalian nation state that derives sovereignty and jurisdiction from territory has been contested as 'an ordering device for the borderless Internet'.[26] Cedric Ryngaert and Mark Zoetekouw are looking at 'community-based systems' as jurisdictional alternatives to territory which would better respond to the peculiar nature of the Internet as a 'borderless, prima facie, non-territorial phenomenon'.[27] Correspondingly, Francesca Bignami and Giorgio Resta expect that 'the social interactions fostered by borderless digital communications should give rise to a common set of moral commitments that will gradually replace those of the nation-state'.[28] It somewhat resonates with how large user-backed digital platforms frequently invoke their community in matters that affect platform governance.[29] Lee Bygrave highlights the peculiar contribution of contract law to manage large numbers of users across countries and legal systems via terms of service, for example.[30] Whereas transnational private law could achieve private platform governance from the inside, it does not compare to an external human rights–based governance framework.

---

[23] J. P. Barlow, 'A Declaration of the Independence of Cyberspace', 8 February 1996, available at http://homes.eff.org/~barlow/Declaration-Final.html.

[24] H. Grotius and R. van Deman Golphin, in J. Brown Scott (ed), *The Freedom of the Seas* (Oxford: Oxford University Press, 1916).

[25] See L. DeNardis, 'Hidden Levers of Internet Control: An Infrastructure-Based Theory of Internet Governance', *Information Communication and Society* 15 (2012), 720–738; J. Hofmann, C. Katzenbach, and K. Gollatz, 'Between Coordination and Regulation: Finding the Governance in Internet Governance', *New Media and Society* 19 (2017), 1406–1423.

[26] F. Bignami and G. Resta, 'Human Rights Extraterritoriality: The Right to Privacy and National Security Surveillance', in E. Benvenisti and G. Nolte (eds), *Community Interests Across International Law* (Oxford: Oxford University Press, 2018), at 357.

[27] C. Ryngaert and M. Zoetekouw, 'The End of Territory? The Re-Emergence of Community as a Principle of Jurisdictional Order in the Internet Era', in U. Kohl (ed), *The Net and the Nation State: Multidisciplinary Perspectives on Internet* (Cambridge: Cambridge University Press, 2017).

[28] Bignami and Resta, note 26.

[29] R. MacKinnon, *Consent of the Networked: The Worldwide Struggle for Internet Freedom* (New York: Basic Books, 2012).

[30] L. A Bygrave, *Internet Governance by Contract* (Oxford: Oxford University Press, 2015).

II *Reactive Jurisdictional Claims*

Legal thinking moreover diverges over the question whether online activities and Internet transactions should be treated as distinct from jurisdictional claims based on geographical location.[31] To Hannah Buxbaum, conflicts about jurisdiction are a strategy where 'claims of authority, or of resistance to authority' are made by actors to advance a particular interest.[32] The beneficiaries of a global reach for that matter reflexively push back jurisdictional claims from countries where the recipients of online service are based. Frequently technology-based arguments are invoked to deny the existence of a sufficient nexus for jurisdiction and the applicability of rules interdicting certain behaviour.[33] Joel Reidenberg intriguingly warns that this in turn would disable states from effectively protecting their citizens online.[34]

Not being set in stone domestic legal institutions are reactive to the very context they are embedded in. The transnational protection of data privacy is a case in point to illustrate the crucial role of domestic legal frameworks in upholding human rights. When it became apparent that the regulation of domestic businesses no longer suffices to govern cross-border data transactions, legislators as well as courts resort to the external application of domestic laws. The European Union's General Data Protection Regulation (GDPR)[35] is a prominent example for this legal technique that refocuses the territorial scope of application to organizations that are not established in the Union as long as they collect and use personal data of individuals who are inside the Union.[36] Likewise the California Consumer Privacy Act (CCPA) applies to businesses around the whole world as long as they reach out to California residents.[37] This is how after some backlog domestic legal institutions tweak jurisdictional concepts in their quest for asserting domestic rules which would still resonate with public international law.[38]

---

[31] Well recorded is the debate between the proponents of exceptionalism and its opponents, the non-exceptionalists, arguing over the source of authority that should regulate the Internet. See, e.g., D. R. Johnson and D. G. Post, 'Law and Borders: The Rise of Law in Cyberspace', *Stanford Law Review* 48 (1996), 1367–1402; J. Goldsmith and T. Wu, *Who Controls the Internet: Illusions of a Borderless World* (Oxford: Oxford University Press, 2006), for the opposing positions.

[32] H. L. Buxbaum, 'Territory, Territoriality, and the Resolution of Jurisdictional Conflict', *American Journal of Comparative Law* 57 (2009), 631–675, at 635.

[33] Ibid.

[34] J. R. Reidenberg, 'Technology and Internet Jurisdictions', *University of Pennsylvania Law Review* 153 (2005), 1951–1974.

[35] Regulation 2016/679 of the European Parliament and of the Council of 27 April 2016 on the Protection of Natural Persons with Regard to the Processing of Personal Data and on the Free Movement of Such Data, and Repealing Directive 95/46/EC, OJ L [2016] 119/1.

[36] M. Gömann, 'The New Territorial Scope of EU Data Protection Law: Deconstructing a Revolutionary Achievement', *Common Market Law Review* 54 (2017), 567–590; C. Ryngaert and M. Taylor, 'The GDPR as Global Data Protection Regulation?' *AJIL Unbound* 45 (2019), 5–9.

[37] The California Consumer Privacy Act of 2018, AB-375, 28 June 2018.

[38] For details, see Ryngaert and Taylor, note 36.

Predictably, such reactions are bound to run into an impasse about their effect-iveness or legitimacy depending on from whose perspective one wishes to look at a particular issue. As a result, the international order now faces additional challenges, such as overlapping claims of authority and the transnational export of rules. Inquiries from the field of transnational data privacy also have shown that the extraterritorial reach of domestic rules may be overly formalistic and not matched with corresponding enforcement powers.[39] In their quest to overcome the enforce-ment fallacy domestic authorities are increasingly turning to governance by plat-forms deputizing 'multinational corporate data intermediaries to carry out and enforce their orders'.[40] Yet, asserting domestic human rights regardless of jurisdic-tion, citizenship and location of data with the help of powerful digital platforms further entrenches the power of private economic interests over the conditions of human freedom.[41]

D INTERNATIONAL TRADE LAW LAYING CLAIM TO FREE DATA FLOWS

The flow of data crucially undergirds the organization of international production, trade and investments into global value chains (GVC).[42] Activating international trade law for cross-border digital trade issues can be seen as 'forum shopping in global governance',[43] where trade venues are traditionally more conducive to eco-nomic interests than for that matter the multi-stakeholder Internet governance fora.[44] What is more, since trade rules on e-commerce could not advance under the auspices of the World Trade Organization (WTO), a number of countries have turned to preferential trade agreements instead, be they bilateral, regional or plurilateral.[45]

---

[39] D. J. B. Svantesson, 'The Regulation of Cross-Border Data Flows', *International Data Privacy Law* 1 (2011), 180–198; C. Kuner, 'Reality and Illusion in EU Data Transfer Regulation Post Schrems', *German Law Journal* 18 (2017), 881–918.

[40] P. S. Berman, 'Conflicts of Law and the Challenge of Transnational Data Flows', in P. Zumbansen (ed), *The Many Lives of Transnational Law: Critical Engagements with Jessup's Bold Proposal* (Cambridge: Cambridge University Press, 2020), 240–268.

[41] J. Barry and E. Pollman, 'Regulatory Entrepreneurship', *Southern California Law Review* 90 (2016), 383–448; Cohen, note 2, at 329.

[42] M. Burri, *Current and Emerging Trends in Disruptive Technologies: Implications for the Present and Future of EU's Trade Policy* (Brussels: European Parliament, 2017), at 11; J. P. Meltzer, 'Governing Digital Trade', *World Trade Review* 18 (2019), 23–48.

[43] See H. Murphy and A. Kellow, 'Forum Shopping in Global Governance: Understanding States, Business and NGOs in Multiple Arenas', *Global Policy* 4 (2013), 139–149.

[44] For instance, the Internet Governance Forum (IGF), see www.intgovforum.org/multilingual/; the NetMundial initiative, see https://netmundial.org/; and RightsCon, see www.rightscon.org/.

[45] M. Burri and T. Cottier, 'Introduction', in M. Burri and T. Cottier (eds), *Trade Governance in the Digital Age* (Cambridge: Cambridge University Press), 1–14, at 6. See also Chapter 1 in this volume.

The United States has been the key force behind efforts to proliferate its digital trade agenda through international trade law, albeit with a mixed record.[46] On the one hand, a new generation of mega-regional trade agreements that were negotiated between the United States and like-minded countries incorporate a new set of digital trade rules that introduce horizontal provisions on the free flow of data, such as the Comprehensive and Progressive Agreement for Trans-Pacific Partnership (CPTPP)[47] and the United States–Mexico–Canada Agreement (USMCA).[48] On the other hand, the liberalization of the cross-border flow of data has been controversial in negotiations for the EU–US Transatlantic Trade and Investment Partnership (TTIP) and for a multilateral Trade in Services Agreement (TiSA), which both stalled in 2017 over uncertainties over the stance of the incoming US administration under President Trump.

Repeated efforts to multilateralize digital trade rules through the WTO have not so far yielded tangible outcomes.[49] Initiated in 1998, the WTO Work Programme on Electronic Commerce has stalled until in early 2019 seventy-six WTO members agreed to launch negotiations on trade-related aspects of electronic commerce.[50] The resurrection of the e-commerce negotiations, however, takes place during a rather dire crisis of the multilateral forum of the WTO that has left its Appellate Body as a part of the dispute settlement system incapacitated.[51] The very capacity to adjudicate disputes, however, has oftentimes been referred to as the 'jewel in the crown' of the WTO that made it the centre of the rule-based international trading system. The timing of the negotiations seems to support Jane Kelsey's argument that e-commerce has turned into a 'proxy battleground for the future of the WTO'.[52]

Absent a broad international consensus in key areas of public interest regulation, already the General Agreement on Trade in Services (GATS)[53] curtails a member's

---

[46] See Chapter 2 in this volume.
[47] The Comprehensive and Progressive Agreement for Transpacific Partnership, available at http://international.gc.ca/trade-commerce/trade-agreements-accords-commerciaux/agr-acc/cptpp-ptpgp/text-texte/index.aspx?lang=eng. The CPTPP incorporates by reference the original Trans-Pacific Partnership Agreement (TPP) signed in 2016 and later abandoned by the incoming US administration.
[48] See Chapter 1 in this volume.
[49] For an overview of the WTO work on e-commerce, see, e.g., S. Yakovleva and K. Irion, 'Pitching Trade against Privacy: Reconciling EU Governance of Personal Data Flows with External Trade', *International Data Privacy Law* 10 (2020), 1–21; J. Kelsey, 'How a TPP-Style E-Commerce Outcome in the WTO Would Endanger the Development Dimension of the GATS Acquis (and Potentially the WTO)', *Journal of International Economic Law* 21 (2018), 273–295; S. Wunsch-Vincent, 'Trade Rules for the Digital Age', in M. Panizzon, N. Pohl, and P. Sauvé (eds), *GATS and the Regulation of International Trade in Services* (Cambridge: Cambridge University Press, 2008), 497–529.
[50] WTO, Joint Statement on Electronic Commerce, WT/L/1056, 25 January 2019.
[51] C. D. Creamer, 'From the WTO's Crown Jewel to Its Crown of Thorns', *AJIL Unbound* 113 (2019), 51–55.
[52] Kelsey, note 49, at 275.
[53] General Agreement on Trade in Services, 15 April 1994, Marrakesh Agreement Establishing the World Trade Organization, Annex 1B, 1869 U.N.T.S. 183 [hereinafter: GATS].

regulatory autonomy by subjecting public interest regulation to certain trade-conforming conditions.[54] The GATS preamble explicitly recognizes the right of a member state to regulate in order to pursue its national policy objectives.[55] This right to regulate is however confined as follows: a member may adopt a measure that is from the outset not inconsistent with its GATS commitments or, in case of a GATS inconsistent measure, to justify the measure under one of the general exceptions.[56] Even though the deregulation of services is not the objective of the GATS,[57] a member's behind-the-border regulations that aim to afford a high level of protection of human rights run the risk to be deemed protectionist under international trade rules. The EU's regulatory framework on personal data protection makes for a well-researched example. We have concluded elsewhere that 'unreservedly committing to free cross-border data flows likely collides with [the EU's] approach of affording a high level of protection of personal data as is called for by Article 8 of the Charter and as implemented by the GDPR'.[58]

With eminent cross-border trade in AI, individual and societal implications can be critically larger and more pervasive.[59] The circulation of AI raises the stakes for human rights–based governance given that the technology can be deployed fairly location-independent.[60] Not only data and machine learning code can be moved across today's digital ecosystem but the predictive outcomes of an AI system can be applied at a distance.[61] Societies have diverse set-ups of rights, freedoms and indeed also ethics. Take facial recognition systems, for example, which are the state policy in China but have prompted calls for strict regulation in Western democracies.[62] Chander rightly notes in this volume that transnational transplants of AI might prove problematic if they do not correspond to the social and legal contexts of the society it interacts with.

[54] See, e.g., M. Krajewski, *National Regulation and Trade Liberalization in Services: The Legal Impact of the General Agreement on Trade in Services (GATS) on National Regulatory Autonomy* (The Hague: Kluwer Law International, 2003).

[55] Recital 3, Preamble to the GATS.

[56] WTO Appellate Body Report, Argentina – Measures Relating to Trade in Goods and Services, WT/DS453/R, adopted 9 May 2016, at para. 6.115.

[57] P. van den Bossche and W. Zdouc, *The Law and Policy of the World Trade Organization*, 3rd edn (Cambridge: Cambridge University Press, 2014), at 515.

[58] Yakovleva and Irion, note 49, at 20; K. Irion and S. Yakovleva, 'The Best of Both Worlds? Free Trade in Services and EU Law on Privacy and Data Protection', *European Data Protection Law Review* 2 (2016), 191–208; S. Yakovleva and K. Irion, 'Toward Compatibility of the EU Trade Policy with the General Data Protection Regulation', *AJIL Unbound* 114 (2020), 10–14.

[59] See, e.g., M. Brundage et al., *The Malicious Use of Artificial Intelligence: Forecasting, Prevention, and Mitigation*, 2018, available at https://maliciousaireport.com/.

[60] See Chapter 5 in this volume.

[61] K. Irion and J. Williams, *Prospective Policy Study on Artificial Intelligence and EU Trade Policy* (Amsterdam: Institute for Information Law, 2020).

[62] L. Stark, 'Facial Recognition Is the Plutonium of AI', *XRDS: Crossroads, the ACM Magazine for Students* 25 (2019), 50–55.

The prospect that the first binding framework for the international governance of AI might be international trade law can be frightening unless WTO members retain sufficient margin for experimentation with novel strategies to give effect to human rights in the cross-border context. Susan Aaronson points at the disconnection between efforts to promote the free flow of data and efforts to promote digital human rights at national and international levels.[63] As trade agreements have gone beyond import tariffs and quotas into regulatory rules and harmonization, Kelsey has criticized that new e-commerce rules impose 'significant constraints on the regulatory authority of governments, irrespective of their levels of development, and includes matters that belong more to Internet governance, than to trade'.[64]

E CONCLUSION

Everything is in flux. Cross-border data flows are pervasive and a defining characteristic of the age of digital interdependence. So far, our global information civilization is not founded on a shared commitment to protect human rights regardless of jurisdiction, citizenship and location of data. Engendering respect for human rights remains for the foreseeable future a paramount function of domestic legal institutions which must be reactive to respond to the challenges of cross-border data flows.[65] We are also beginning to grasp that the challenges for the multi-level governance of human rights are not just about overlapping claims of authority and the transnational export of rules but go to the core of the conditions of human freedom and the democratic constitution of societies.[66]

International trade law is laying claim to the governance of cross-border digital trade and the liberalization of cross-border flow of data. From the domestic protection of data privacy and how data privacy rules may conflict with international trade law, we can draw lessons for the emerging multi-level governance of AI. With respect to AI governance, the EU's fundamental rights approach holds unique value in an international context where the other major players, like the United States and China, move ahead without paying much attention to these underlying human values. It will be important to critically assess the impact of the WTO e-commerce negotiations on the human rights–based governance of AI before the 'free trade

---

[63] S. A. Aaronson, 'Why Trade Agreements Are Not Setting Information Free: The Lost History and Reinvigorated Debate over Cross-Border Data Flows, Human Rights and National Security', *World Trade Review* 14 (2015), 671–700.

[64] Kelsey, note 49, at 256.

[65] Cohen, note 2, at 238.

[66] See, e.g., Reidenberg, note 34; H. Farrell and A. L. Newman, *Of Privacy and Power: The Transatlantic Struggle over Freedom and Security* (Princeton, NJ: Princeton University Press, 2019), at 27 et seqq.; P. P. Swire and R. E. Litan, 'None of Your Business: World Data Flows, Electronic Commerce, and the European Privacy Directive', *Harvard Journal of Law and Technology* 12 (1999), 683–702.

leviathan'[67] further restricts the policy choices not only of individual states but also of the EU itself.[68]

Where international trade rules prevail, they should provide for constitutional pluralism and a sufficient margin for domestic experimentation with novel strategies to give effect to human rights in the online context.[69] This should not be construed as an argument in favour of a uniform interpretation or even a mandate for the positive harmonization of (digital) human rights through international (trade) law.[70] Yet, trade law should not move ahead in setting the rules for cross-border trade in the era of big data and AI without recognizing the members' responsibility to take appropriate measures that would ensure that artificial intelligence and overall data governance are fully accountable to domestic human rights frameworks. Identifying strategies and approaches that effectively ground individual interests and societal values in transnational algorithmic systems ought to strike a balance between the rule of law and innovation policy that crucially undergird a robust information civilization.

---

[67] G. de Búrca and J. Scott, 'The Impact of the WTO on EU Decision-Making', in G. de Burca and J. Scott (eds), *The EU and the WTO Legal and Constitutional Issues* (Oxford: Hart Publishing, 2001).

[68] Irion and Williams, note 61.

[69] Petersmann, note 6, at 663.

[70] P. Alston, 'Resisting the Merger and Acquisition of Human Rights by Trade Law: A Reply to Petersmann', *European Journal of International Law* 13 (2002), 815–844.

PART IV

Global Perspectives on Digital Trade Governance

12

Data Regulation with Chinese Characteristics

Henry S. Gao*

Across the Great Wall we can reach every corner in the world.
The first email sent from China on 20 September 1987.

A INTRODUCTION

The regulation of data has increasingly become a common feature of trade agreements. To understand this rule framework, it is essential to first identify the main players and interests at stake. In my view, data regulation in trade agreements mainly deals with three groups of interests, each corresponding to different stakeholders. The first is the commercial interests of the companies engaged in electronic commerce. Due to the unique nature of their business, most Internet companies need unhindered data flows to conduct their business. Thus, they demand free flow of information across the globe and oppose to data localization requirements. Behind the second group of interest is the person or the consumer, who supplies the raw data to use the services provided by the Internet companies. As both the raw data and the processed data are controlled by the companies, consumers, at least to the extent they would act in their best interest, wish to ensure that their privacy and personal data are properly protected. This is where the third, and arguably the strongest, stakeholder – the state – comes into play.

The state monitors and regulates the data used by the first two groups, which involves the collection, processing, access and transfer of data. In designing the regulatory framework, the state often tries to strike a balance between the different or

* Associate Professor of Law, Singapore Management University. Contact: henrygao@smu.edu. sg. This research has been supported by the National Research Foundation, Singapore under its Emerging Areas Research Projects (EARP) Funding Initiative. Any opinions, findings and conclusions or recommendations expressed in this material are those of the author(s) and do not reflect the views of the National Research Foundation, Singapore.

even conflicting interests of the different players, by trying to ensure the protection of the privacy of personal data, while not unduly hindering the development of the economy. Faced with various threats, such as cyberwarfare and terrorism, the state also needs to ensure that public safety and national security are not compromised by rogue players roaming at large in cyberspace.

While all regulators would agree on the need to strike a balance between the clashing interests of different stakeholders, their approaches often differ in practice. Some jurisdictions prioritize the need to safeguard the privacy of their citizens. A good example in this regard is the General Data Protection Regulation (GDPR) of the European Union (EU), which recognizes '[t]he protection of natural persons in relation to the processing of personal data' as 'a fundamental right'.[1] On the other hand, some jurisdictions put the commercial interests of firms first. In the United States (US), this is reflected in the 1996 Telecommunication Act, which notes that it is 'the policy of the United States ... to preserve ... free market ... unfettered by Federal or State regulation'.[2] In contrast, national security concerns are often cited to justify restrictions on cross-border data flow, albeit in varying degrees in different countries. A recent example is China's 2017 Cybersecurity Law, which imposed several restrictions aiming to 'safeguard cyber security, protect cyberspace sovereignty and national security'.[3]

It is not easy to say which one is the best approach, as the various regulatory approaches often reflect the different legal, political, economic, social and cultural backgrounds of different countries. What is more important than passing judgement about different models, however, is to understand the inherent logic and mechanisms of the different regulatory regimes. In this chapter, I will focus on China, which is not only home to the largest e-commerce market in the world but also has one of the most tightly regulated cyberspaces. By providing a detailed analysis of the rationale and operation of 'data regulation with Chinese characteristics', the chapter seeks not only to help understand this discrete regulatory model but also to find ways to deal with such a regime at the international level.

B INTERNET REGULATION IN CHINA

The first email from China was reportedly sent on 20 September 1987 by a group of researchers at the Institute for Computer Science of China's State Commission of

---

[1] Regulation 2016/679 of the European Parliament and of the Council of 27 April 2016 on the protection of natural persons with regard to the processing of personal data and on the free movement of such data, and repealing Directive 95/46/EC (General Data Protection Regulation), OJ L [2016] 119/1, at Recital 1.
[2] Telecommunication Act of 1996, 47 U.S.C. 230(b)(2).
[3] Article 1 Cybersecurity Law of the People's Republic of China [Zhonghua Renmin Gongheguo Wangluo Anquan Fa], adopted 7 November 2016, www.chinalawinfo.com.

Machine Industry to the University of Karlsruhe in Germany.[4] On 28 November 1990, China's national domain name – '.cn' – was registered by Professor Qian Tianbai, a pioneer in the Chinese Internet industry.[5] However, it was not until 20 April 1994 that the first connection to the international network was established by China Education and Research Network, which marked the launch of the Internet in China.[6] Since then, the Chinese Internet has grown by leaps and bounds, despite occasional hiccups, such as Google's exit from China in 2009.[7] In 2013, China's e-commerce volume exceeded 10 trillion RMB and China overtook the United States as the largest e-commerce market in the world.[8] Nowadays, Chinese e-commerce giants like Alibaba are among the biggest online retailers globally and Chinese online shopping festivals, such as the Singles Day (11.11) Sale have gained loyal followers all around the world.[9] In the latest race on the research and applications of big data, machine learning and artificial intelligence (AI), China is also quickly catching up with the United States, a world leader that increasingly sees its competitive edge being narrowed.[10]

Notwithstanding the phenomenal growth in the e-commerce sector, the Internet remains under tight regulation in China. The following section provides a detailed examination of this framework, paying specific attention to the regulation of data.

I *Overview of the Regulatory Landscape*

Just like the development of the Internet in China, the evolution of the regulatory landscape in China over the past twenty years is also a remarkable journey, where the haphazard regulatory patchwork was revamped in several iterations before culminating in one of the most sophisticated regulatory frameworks the world has

---

[4] Li W., 'In the Beginning ...', *China Daily*, 17 March 2008.

[5] Ibid.

[6] State Council Information Office [Guowuyuan Xinwen Bangongshi], 'China's White Paper on the State of the Internet' [Zhongguo Hulianwang Zhuangkuang Baipishu], 8 June 2010.

[7] For a review of the background of the case and the trade law issues it raised, see H. S. Gao, 'Google's China Problem: A Case Study on Trade, Technology and Human Rights under the GATS', *Asian Journal of WTO and International Health Law and Policy* 12 (2011), 347–385; H. S. Gao, 'Googling for the Trade-Human Rights Nexus in China: Can the WTO Help?', in M. Burri and T. Cottier (eds), *Trade Governance in the Digital Age* (Cambridge: Cambridge University Press, 2012), 247–275.

[8] Ministry of Finance of the People's Republic of China, 'China's Bulk E-Commerce Transaction Value Exceeds 10 Trillion' [Woguo Dazong Dianzi Shangwu Jiaoyie Yi Chao 10 Wanyi Yuan], *China Financial and Economic News* [Zhongguo Caijing Bao], 7 August 2014.

[9] See M. Smith, 'Australian Brands Woo Shoppers at China's Singles' Day Sales', *Financial Review*, 12 November 2018; J. Lim, 'Singles' Day Sales in S'pore Doubled from a Year Before: ShopBack's Data', *Today*, 12 November 2018.

[10] T. H. Davenport, 'China Is Catching up to the US on Artificial Intelligence Research', *The Conversation*, 27 February 2019.

ever seen. With the benefit of the hindsight, we can divide the development of the regulatory framework into four stages.

The initial stage was from 1987 to 1998, when the Internet was still in its embryonic stage and the government had yet to fully fathom its potential. Thus, the world wide web largely remained as the 'wild wide web' and untangled by regulations. This does not mean that there was no regulation at all during this period. To the contrary, two important regulations were introduced in the short span of one year – the 1996 Provisional Regulations on the Management of International Networking of Computer Information Networks[11] and the 1997 Measures for Security Protection Administration of the International Networking of Computer Information Networks.[12] Yet, the regulatory framework in this period suffered from the following weaknesses: First, these regulations were very low in the legislative hierarchy, as they were provisional regulations and administrative rules issued by the executive branch, which did not have the same force as national laws issued by the National People's Congress (NPC) and its Standing Committee. Moreover, these regulations were not made with the authorization of the legislature. Thus, at least in theory, these regulations could be challenged, especially with regards to provisions that contradicted the rules in legislations of a higher rank. Second, the regulatory framework was built in a piecemeal manner. There was no central agency coordinating the powers of the different agencies and no clear delineation of jurisdictions between the different agencies. This could potentially result in gaps as well as in overlaps in the regulatory framework, making the whole system rather inefficient. Third, these regulations all focused on the Internet hardware and there was no regulation on the software, not to mention content. Paradoxically, this contributed to the exponential growth of the Chinese cyberspace at the turn of the century, where people flocked in the pursuit of freedom of speech unavailable offline.

The second stage started with the establishment of the Ministry of Information Industry (MII) on 31 March 1998, which resulted from the merger of the Ministry of Posts and Telecommunications (MPT) and the Ministry of Electronic Industry (MEI).[13] With an explicit jurisdiction over the information industry, the MII became the main regulator of the Internet in China.[14] However, other agencies

---

[11] Provisional Regulations of the State Council on the Management of International Networking of Computer Information Networks [Jisuanji Xinxi Wangluo Guoji Lianwang Guanli Zanxing Guiding], Guowuyuan Ling No 195, 1 February 1996.
[12] Measures of the Ministry of Public Security for Security Protection Administration of the International Networking of Computer Information Networks [Jisuanji Xinxi Wangluo Guoji Lianwang Anquan Baohu Guanli Banfa], Gonganbu Ling No 33, 30 December 1997, available at www.chinalawinfo.com.
[13] Li Z., 'Institutional Reforms in These Years: The Ministry of Industry and Information Technology Changed Its Name to the Ministry of Information Industry in 2008 [Jigou Gaige Zhexienian: Gongxinbu 2008 Nian you Xinxi Chanyebu Gengming Erlai]', *The Economic Observer*, 1 March 2018.
[14] Ministry of Information Industry [Xinxi Chanyebu], 'Introduction on the Ministry of Information Industry [Xinxi Chanyebu Jianjie]', 21 September 2005.

quickly stepped into the cyberspace and started to compete with MII on the regulation of various issues such as online news, audio-visual services, online media and web security.[15] While these new agencies helped to fill the void in the regulatory space, their eagerness to capture more regulatory power also heightened the risk for potential turf wars. To address this, in 2001 the State Council re-established the National Informatization Leading Group.[16] Headed by then Premier Zhu Rongji, the Leading Group tried to coordinate among the different agencies. In November 2004, the General Office of the CCP Central Committee and the General Office of the State Council issued Opinions on Further Strengthening Internet Administration, which clearly divided the jurisdiction and responsibilities of all central government ministries and agencies involved in Internet governance.[17] However, as these agencies are all of the same ministerial rank, the problem of regulatory competition remained. This did not change until 2010, when the General Office of the CCP Central Committee and the General Office of the State Council issued Opinions on Strengthening and Improving Internet Administration.[18] Pursuant to the Opinions, the Cyberspace Administration of China (CAC) was established in 2011 as a ministerial-level agency.[19] While its main jurisdiction is content regulation, the CAC also presides over the troika of Internet governance, which includes, in addition to the CAC: the Ministry of Industry and Information Technology (MIIT), which inherited the portfolio of the MII; and the Ministry of Public Security (MPS), which is responsible for Internet crimes and safety issues.[20]

The third stage in the evolution of China's cyberspace regulation was heralded in 2013 by the Third Plenum Conference of the Eighteenth Party Congress, which

---

[15] Zhu W., 'Changes, Challenges and Modernization of Internet Governance in China [Zhongguo Hulianwang Jianguan de Bianqian, Tiaozhan, yu Xiandaihua]', *Journalism and Communication* [Xinwen yu Chuanbo Yanjiu], 7 (2014), 80–127, at 81.

[16] Wang Y., 'The Origin and Implications of the Central Leading Group on Cybersecurity and Informatisation [Zhongyang Wangluo Anquan yu Xinxihua Lingdao Xiaozu de Youlai Jiqi Yingxiang]', *People.cn* [Renminwang], 3 March 2014.

[17] The General Office of the CCP Central Committee and the General Office of the State Council, Opinions on Further Strengthening Internet Administration [Zhonggong Zhongyang Bangongting, Guowuyuan Bangongting Xiafale Guanyu Jinyibu Jiaqiang Hulianwang Guanli Gongzuo de Yijian], Zhongbanfa No 32 (2004), as cited in Hu L., 'Chinese Internet Legislation before 1998 [Yijiu Jiuba Nian Zhiqian de Zhongguo Hulianwang Lifa]', 7 March 2008, available at www.ideobook.com/375/internet-legislation-1998/.

[18] The General Office of the CCP Central Committee and the General Office of the State Council, Opinions on Strengthening and Improving Internet Administration [Zhonggong Zhongyang Bangongting, Guowuyuan Bangongting Xiafale Guanyu Jiaqiang he Gaijin Hulianwang Guanli Gongzuo de Yijian], Zhongbanfa No 24 (2010), as cited in Tu C., *Generality of Broadcasting Law* [Guangbo Dianshi Falv Zhidu Gailun] (Beijing: Communication University of China Publishing House, 2011), at 62.

[19] 'The State Council Office Announced the Establishment of the National Internet Information Office, Wang Chen Is Appointed as the Director [Guoban Tongzhi Sheli Guojia Hulianwang Xinxi Bangongshi, Wangchen Ren Zhuren]', *Xinhua Press*, 4 May 2011.

[20] Wang R., 'Internet Governance in China in Two Decades [Zhongguo Hulianwang Jianguan Ershi Nian]', Tencent Research Institute [Tengxun Yanjiuyuan], 4 December 2019.

adopted the Decision of the CCP Central Committee on Several Major Issues concerning Comprehensively Deepening Reform.[21] The Decision adopted the policy of 'positive adoption, scientific development, lawful administration and ensuring security' for the development of the Internet, and called for further strengthening of Internet governance, especially the further streamlining of its leadership system. Most notably, the Decision emphasized that the objective of Internet governance shall be ensuring 'the security of national Internet and information'. This was the first time that Internet governance was elevated to the level of national security in a major Party document, and it set the tone for a new era of China's Internet regulation.

In his report to the Third Plenum Meeting, President Xi covered eleven major issues, one of them being Internet governance.[22] He emphasized that Internet and information security is 'a matter of national security and social stability, and a new composite challenge facing China'.[23] Xi also noted that the existing Internet governance system was lagging behind the rapid development of Internet technology and applications, and suffered from problems such as duplication and overlapping of agencies and their jurisdictions, mismatch between power and responsibilities, and low efficiency. According to Xi, to further strengthen Chinese Internet governance, the functions of the relevant agencies needed to be reshuffled to provide a comprehensive governance framework that covered everything from technology to content, and from ensuring everyday security to combating crimes.

Pursuant to the Third Plenum Decision, the Central Leading Group on Cyber Security and Informatization was established in February 2014.[24] The Leading Group is the third 'super agency' established after the Third Plenum Meeting, with the other two in charge of the most important topics – comprehensively deepening reform and national security, respectively. With President Xi as its head and Premier Li Keqiang as the deputy, the Leading Group has twenty-two members, which include three of the seven members of the Politburo Standing Committee and nine of the twenty-five members of the Politburo. Eleven of its members are also members of the Leading Group on Comprehensively Deepening Reform, one is

---

[21] 'Decision of the Central Committee of the Communist Party of China on Several Major Issues Concerning Comprehensively Deepening Reform [Zhonggong Zhongyang Guanyu Quanmian Shenhua Gaige Ruogan Zhongda Wenti de Jueding]', *Xinhua Press*, 15 November 2013.

[22] Xi J., 'Explanations of the Decision of the Central Committee of the Communist Party of China on Several Major Issues Concerning Comprehensively Deepening Reform [Guanyu Zhonggong Zhongyang Guanyu Quanmian Shenhua Gaige Ruogan Zhongda Wenti de Jueding de Shuoming]', *cpcnews.cn*, 9 November 2013.

[23] Ibid.

[24] 'The Member List of the Central Leading Group on Cybersecurity and Informatization – Staffed by Twelve National-Leader Level Leaders with Overlappings with Leading Group on Comprehensively Deepening Reform [Zhongyang Wangluo Anquan he Xinxihua Lingdao Xiaozu Chengyuan Mingdan 12 Zhengfu Guoji Jianzhi Shengaizu]', *guancha.cn* [Guanchazhe], 28 February 2014.

Secretary-General of the State Council at Vice Premier level, while the rest are all heads of important ministries, including the all-powerful National Development and Reform Commission. Such high-level set-up signals that cyber security and informatization have been elevated to an unprecedented level and have now become important components of the overall national security strategy.[25] While the Leading Group remains an ad hoc body, it now has an office housed at the newly restructured Cyberspace Administration of China (CAC).[26] This greatly boosted the status of the CAC among the peer ministries, as it is one of the few agencies under direct leadership of President Xi. In August 2014, the State Council even delegated its power on cyberspace content regulation to the CAC.[27] This made the CAC the most powerful agency with regard to the regulation of the Internet, and particularly with regard to Internet content.

The emphasis on cyber security was further confirmed by the 2015 National Security Law, which considers cyber security as a key component of national security and directs the state to make the 'core technology of the Internet and information, key infrastructure and the information system and data in key areas secure and controllable' in order to 'protect national cyberspace security, safety and development'.[28] Moreover, Article 77 of the law requires all citizens and organizations to make timely reports on activities that endanger national security, truthfully provide evidence relating to such activities that one knows of, and provide the necessary support and assistance to national security agencies. If enforced strictly, the provision could be used to compel netizens to report 'harmful information' or activity in cyberspace, and throw China back to the days of the Cultural Revolution, where everyone was under the constant surveillance of each other. In practice, however, this clause has not yet been employed in such an aggressive manner by the authorities.

The evolution of China's Internet regulation finally culminated in the 2016 Cyber Security law, which emphasized in the first article that cybersecurity is a matter of cyber-sovereignty and national security. The heightened role of the CAC was also further cemented by Article 8 of the law, which entrusted it with the overall responsibility for the planning and coordination of cybersecurity work and relevant

[25] Ibid.
[26] 'National Internet Information Office Restructured, State Council Delegated the Power on Internet Content Administration and Enforcement [Guojia Wangxinban Chongzu Guowuyuan Shouquan Qi Fuze Hulianwang Neirong Guanli Zhifa]', *guancha.cn* [Guanchazhe], 28 August 2014.
[27] State Council, Notice on Delegation of Power on Administration of Internet Information Content to the National Internet Information Office [Guowuyuan Guanyu Shouquan Guojia Hulianwang Xinxi Bangongshi Fuze Hulianwang Xinxi Neirong Guanli Gongzuo de Tongzhi], Guofa No 33 (2014), 26 August 2014.
[28] Article 25 National Security Law of the People's Republic of China [Zhonghua Renmin Gongheguo Guojia Anquan Fa], as adopted at the Fifteenth Session of the Standing Committee of the Twelfth National People's Congress of the People's Republic of China on 1 July 2015, available at www.chinalawinfo.com.

supervision and administration, while the other ministries, such as the MII and MPS, are only responsible for the cybersecurity administration within their own jurisdictions.

II *China's Main Internet Regulations*

From early on, the Chinese government recognized the disruptive potential of the Internet and put it under strict regulation. For example, barely two years after China was connected to the Internet, the State Council issued the very first Internet regulation – the 1996 Provisional Regulations of the People's Republic of China on the Management of International Networking of Computer Information Networks ('Provisional Regulations').[29] According to Article 3, the Provisional Regulations apply to all international networking of computer information networks within China, which is defined as 'networking of the computer information networks inside the People's Republic of China and those in foreign countries with the purpose of international exchange of information'. The key provision is Article 6, which provides that 'computer information networks shall use the international entry and exit gateways provided by the Ministry of Posts and Telecommunications in the country's public telecommunications network when they carry out direct international networking. No units or individuals shall be allowed to establish or use other channels for international networking without authorization'.

Anyone found in violation of the provision could be punished with a fine up to 15,000 RMB,[30] which was a hefty amount in 1996. With merely seventeen articles, the Provisional Regulations seem rather rudimentary, especially considering the fact that it dealt with such a complicated subject matter as the Internet. However, upon closer examination, we can say that it actually encapsulated all three aspects of Chinese Internet regulations for the decades to come.

The first is hardware regulation, which mandates that all Internet connections must go through official gateways sanctioned by the Chinese government. Such regulation enables the Chinese government to effectively control Internet connection, especially in blocking and filtering certain international websites and services.

The second is software/applications regulation, which means that even the software for Internet access must be sanctioned by the government. This is indicated in Article 10 of the Provisional Regulations, which states that all individuals, legal persons and other organizations must connect to international networks through access networks, which in turn are required by Articles 6 and 8 to connect through the Internet, i.e., those international gateways sanctioned by the MPT. This requirement is made explicit in the Implementation Rules for the Provisional Regulations ('Implementation Rules') promulgated by the Leading Group for Information

[29] Ministry of Public Security, note 12.
[30] State Council, note 11, Article 14.

Technology Advancement under the State Council on 13 February 1998.[31] After repeating the requirement to use official international gateways and the prohibition on using other gateways in Article 7, the Implementation Rules went on to state in Article 10 that all access networks to international networks shall go through the Internet and international network connections through 'any other means' are explicitly prohibited. According to Article 3.3 of the Implementation Rules, the international entry and exit gateways are 'physical information channels used for international networking'. As Article 7 already explicitly prohibits the use of other physical gateways for connection, the interpretation of the law means that the term 'any other means' shall be interpreted broadly and includes other connection methods at both the hardware and software/applications levels. In other words, the term 'any other means' includes not only other physical gateways, but also ways to connect to the Internet through software such as virtual private network (VPN). This stringent requirement is repeated in Article 12 of the Implementation Rules, which further affirms that all individuals, legal persons and other organizations must connect to international networks through the access networks and not 'any other means'.

The third category of regulation regards content. Again here, the essential rule framework on content is already found in the Provisional Regulations, which states in Article 13 that 'the organizations and individuals conducting international networking businesses shall abide by relevant State laws and administrative decrees and strictly follow safety and security rules. They shall not use international networking for law-breaking or criminal activities that may endanger national security or divulge State secrets; or producing, consulting, duplicating or propagating information that may disturb social order or pornographic information'.

This strict regulation is also duly copied into Article 20 of Implementation Rules, with two small but significant twists. First, the subject of regulation expands from those conducting international networking businesses to the access units (Internet service providers, ISPs) and users. This makes sense, as the bulk of the content online is usually created by intermediaries and end users. Second, the same article also requires the three groups to immediately report any harmful information they discover to the relevant authorities and take effective measures to prevent the dissemination of such information. This is yet another important feature of Chinese Internet regulation that differs from other countries, especially the United States, which do not impose liabilities on ISPs pursuant to the 'safe harbour' rule. As we will see later, this approach has been extended to the regulation of data in recent years.

---

[31] Information Computerization Leaders Group of the State Council, Implementation Rules for Provisional Regulations of the Administration of International Networking of Computer Information in the People's Republic of China [Zhonghua Renmin Gongheguo Jisuanji Xinxi Wangluo Guoji Lianwang Guanli Zanxing Guiding Shishi Banfa], Guoxin No 001 (1998), 13 February 1998, available at www.chinalawinfo.com.

In the sections that follow, we examine the main Chinese Internet regulations along the three themes of hardware regulation, software regulation, and content/data regulation.

1 Hardware Regulation

According to Article 8 of the Implementation Rules, the nascent Internet in China is broken down into four networks: China Public Computer Network (CHINANET), China Golden Bridge Network (CHINAGBNET), China Education and Research Network (CERNET) and China Science and Technology Network (CSTNET), which are respectively administered by the MPT, the MEI, the State Education Commission, and Chinese Academy of Sciences. Among the four, the first two are commercial networks, while the last two are non-profit networks, which provide Internet services for the universities and research institutes under their respective jurisdictions. In 2000, China Mobile, the largest mobile company in China, also received approval to build an international Internet gateway.[32] To further regulate international gateways, the MPT issued Administrative Rules on International Networking Entry and Exit Gateways for Computer Information Networks,[33] which reiterated the prohibition on international networking through self-established international networking or other means including satellite.[34] The 2000 Telecommunication Regulation[35] also stated that all international telecommunication services shall go through the approved international gateways,[36] and explicitly prohibited operating international networking business through leasing dedicated international telecommunications lines, establishing relaying facilities without permission or other means.[37] To avoid confusion as to whether Internet services were part of telecommunication services, the Telecom Regulation also explicitly stated that both Internet connection service and Internet information service are part of value-added telecom services.[38]

When China acceded to the World Trade Organization (WTO) in 2001, the hardware restriction was also copied into its Schedule of Specific Commitments for Services, which notes that '[a]ll international telecommunications services shall go through gateways established with the approval of China's telecommunications

---

[32] Ministry of Information Industry, Approval of the Agreement to Form China Mobile Internet [Xinxi Chanyebu Guanyu Tongyi Zujian Zhongguo Yidong Hulianwang de Pifu], Xinbu Dian No 48 (2000), 17 January 2000, available at www.chinalawinfo.com.

[33] Ministry of Posts and Telecommunications, Notice on Issuing the Administrative Rules on International Networking Entry and Exit Gateways for Computer Information Networks [Guanyu Fabu Jisuanji Xinxi Wangluo Guoji Lianwang Churukou Xindao Guanli Banfa de Tongzhi], Youbu No 492 (1996), 9 April 1996.

[34] Ibid., Article 2.

[35] Telecommunication Regulation of the State Council of the People's Republic of China [Zhonghua Renmin Gongheguo Dianxin Tiaoli], Guowuyuan Ling No 291, 25 September 2000, available at www.chinalawinfo.com.

[36] Ibid., Article 65.

[37] Ibid., Article 59.1.

[38] Ibid., Appendix: Catalogue of Telecommunications Business.

authorities'.[39] There was considerable confusion as to whether China's commitments include Internet services. On the one hand, its commitments on value-added telecom services seem to include all the value-added telecom sub-sectors under the Services Sectoral Classification List – that is, h. Electronic mail; i. Voice mail; j. On-line information and database retrieval; k. Electronic data interchange; l. Enhanced/Value-added facsimile services (including store and forward, store and retrieve); m. Code and protocol conversion; n. Online information and/or data processing (including transaction processing). The only restriction seems to be that the services shall be provided through a joint venture with 50 per cent cap on foreign equity. On the other hand, China's Telecom Regulations list Internet connection services and Internet information services separately from the value-added telecom services listed earlier. One may argue that one of the value-added services listed in China's schedule – online information and/or data processing (including transaction processing) – has the CPC number 843**, which corresponds to online content services in the current CPC version.[40] However, a closer examination reveals that the correspondence is only superficial, as the two Internet services under the current CPC version correspond to 75231 and 75232 in the CPC provisional list ('CPCprov'),[41] which is the basis of Services Sectoral Classification List and thus for the GATS negotiations and commitments. Class 7523 is defined in CPCprov as 'data and message transmission services', which in turn can be broken into Subclass: 75231 – data network services, and Subclass: 75232 – electronic message and information services.[42] However, according to the explanatory notes, Class 7523 only covers the necessary network services (mostly the underlying hardware) for data transmission, rather than the provision of information online. Thus, at most, China's schedule would only cover Internet connection services but not Internet information services. However, even such an interpretation cannot get around the requirement to go through officially sanctioned international gateways, which is repeated ad nauseam in the regulations mentioned above and China's GATS schedule.

2 Software Regulation

As mentioned earlier, the Implementation Rules prohibits connection to international networks through 'any other means', which could include software designed to evade

---

[39] WTO Working Party on the Accession of China, Report of the Working Party on the Accession of China, Addendum: Schedule CLII – The People's Republic of China, Part II – Schedule of Specific Commitments on Services, WT/ACC/CHN/49/Add.2, adopted 1 October 2001, at footnote 3.

[40] United Nations Department of International Economic and Social Affairs, Statistics Division, Statistical Papers, 'Central Product Classification (CPC)', Series M No 77, Version 2.1, ST/ESA/STAT/SER.M/77/Ver.2.1 (2015).

[41] United Nations Department of International Economic and Social Affairs, Statistics Division, 'CPC Versions Correspondence Tables', available at https://unstats.un.org/unsd/classifications/Econ/tables/CPC/CPCv11_CPCprov/CPCv11_CPCprov.txt.

[42] For a more detailed analysis, see Gao, note 7, at 361–362.

official international gateways in addition to hardware. This is also copied into Article 59.1 of the Telecom Regulations, which prohibits the operation of international networking businesses through any means. The 1997 Measures for Security Protection Administration of the International Networking of Computer Information Networks provides further clarification by prohibiting unauthorized access to or use of computer information networks, which could cover access to international network using unauthorized software.[43]

After Google pulled out of China in 2009, the Chinese government continued to tighten its control on cyberspace and blocked the websites of major social media (Facebook, YouTube, Twitter, etc.) and major international media (Bloomberg, Reuters, New York Times, etc.). To access these websites, many netizens resorted to VPNs. In view of this, the MIIT issued a notice in 2017, which explicitly prohibited VPNs.[44] To minimize the impact on firms, MIIT later clarified that foreign trade firms and multinational corporations could still lease dedicated lines for international networking from authorized telecom operators.[45] However, according to MIIT, such private networks can only be used for the internal office needs of the firm, and cannot be used to connect data centres or platforms abroad to conduct telecom businesses, which means that the lines cannot be leased to private consumers who are not employees of such firms. Since then, China has launched a major campaign to crack down on VPNs, and people have been jailed[46] and fined for selling and using VPN services respectively.[47]

3 Content/Data Regulation

The main content regulation is the 2000 Administrative Measures on Internet Information Services,[48] which states in Article 15 that Internet Information Service Provider shall not produce, copy, distribute or disseminate information that is contrary to the basic principles laid down in the Constitution, laws or administration

---

[43] Ministry of Public Security, Measures for Security Protection Administration of the International Networking of Computer Information Networks [Jisuanji Xinxi Wangluo Guoji Lianwang Anquan Baohu Guanli Banfa], Gonganbu Ling No 33, 30 December 1997, available at www.chinalawinfo.com.

[44] Ministry of Industry and Information Technology, Notice of the Ministry of Industry and Information Technology on Clearing up and Regulating the Internet Access Services Market [Gongye he Xinxihuabu Guanyu Qingli Guifan Hulianwang Wangluo Jieru Fuwu Shichang de Tongzhi], Gongxinbu Xinguanhan No 32 (2017).

[45] 'The Ministry of Industry and Information Technology Responded to Internet Users' Questions Such as Using VPNs [Gongxinbu Huiying Wangmin VPN deng Shiyong Wenti]', *People.cn* [Renminwang], 24 January 2017.

[46] B. Haas, 'Man in China Sentenced to Five Years' Jail for Running VPN', *The Guardian*, 22 December 2017.

[47] C. Chen, 'Chinese VPN User Fined for Accessing Overseas Websites as Part of Beijing's Ongoing "Clean Up" of Internet', *South China Morning Post*, 7 January 2019.

[48] State Council, *Administrative Measures on Internet Information Services* [Hulianwang Xinxi Fuwu Guanli Banfa], Guowuyuan Ling No 292.

regulations; is seditious to the ruling regime of the state or the system of socialism; subverts state power or sabotages the unity of the state; incites ethnic hostility or racial discrimination, or disrupts racial unity; spreads rumours or disrupts social order; propagates feudal superstitions; disseminates obscenity, pornography or gambling; incites violence, murder or terror; instigates others to commit offences; publicly insults or defames others; harms the reputation or interests of the State; or has content prohibited by laws or administrative regulations.[49]

Apparently copied from the Telecom Regulations[50] and 1996 Interim Regulations on Electronic Publications,[51] the list has remained largely constant for the past twenty years. The only addition was made in 2002, when several regulations added a new category of 'harming the social morality or the excellent cultural traditions of the nationalities'.[52] This new category, however, seems to be restricted mainly to online publications and has not been incorporated into subsequent laws and regulations. For example, neither the Administrative Measures on Internet Information Services nor the Telecom Regulations added this new category in their 2011 and 2016 amendments. It is also worth noting that such stringent regulation is not restricted to the Internet sector, as other regulations in the same period share the same restrictions on content.[53]

One apparent gap in the 2000 Administrative Measures is that the rules apply only to Internet information service providers but not the users who generate such information. This gap was filled by the 1997 Measures for Security Protection

---

[49] The translation is taken from A. S. Y. Cheung, 'The Business of Governance – China's Legislation on Content Regulation in Cyberspace', *International Law and Politics* 38 (2005), 1–38, at 13–14.

[50] State Council, note 35, Article 57.

[51] General Administration of Press and Publication, Interim Regulations on Electronic Publications [Dianzi Chubanwu Guanli Zanxing Guiding], Xinwen Chubanshu Ling No 6, 14 March 1996, available at www.chinalawinfo.com.

[52] See, e.g., Article 17, Interim Provisions of the General Administration of Press and Publication, Ministry of Information Industry on the Administration of Internet Publication [Hulianwang Chuban Guanli Zanxing Guiding], 27 June 2002; Article 14, Regulations of the State Council on the Administration of Business Sites of Internet Access Services [Hulianwang Shangwang Fuwu Yingye Changsuo Guanli Tiaoli], Guowuyuan Ling No 363, 29 September 2002; See also Article 17, Interim Provisions of the Ministry of Culture on the Administration of Internet Culture [Hulianwang Wenhua Guanli Zanxing Guiding], Wenhuabu Ling No 27, 4 March 2003; Article 19 State Administration of Radio and Television, Measures for the Administration of the Publication of Audio-Visual Programs through the Internet or other Information Network [Hulianwang deng Xinxi Wangluo Chuanbo Shiting Jiemu Guanli Banfa], Guojia Guangbo Dianying Dianshi Zongju Ling No 39, 6 July 2004, available at www.chinalawinfo.com.

[53] See Regulations of the State Council of the People's Republic of China on the Administration of Audio-Visual Products [Zhonghua Renmin Gongheguo Yinxiang Zhipin Guanli Tiaoli], Guowuyuan Ling No 165, 1 October 1994; State Council, Regulations on Administration of Films [Dianying Guanli Tiaoli], Guowuyuan Ling No 200, 1 July 1996; Regulations of the State Council on Broadcasting and Television Administration [Guangbo Dianshi Guanli Tiaoli], Guowuyuan Ling No 228, 1 September 1997, available at www.chinalawinfo.com.

Administration of the International Networking of Computer Information Networks, which expands the liability to 'any organization or individual'.[54] In judicial practice, the offense of 'Picking Quarrels and Provoking Trouble' has also been invoked on a case-by-case basis against people posting information online about various social problems. One example is the case of Zhao Lianhai, who was jailed for two-and-half years for trying to collect information about contaminated milk with a self-built website.[55] In 2013, the practice was further institutionalized when the Supreme People's Court and Supreme People's Procuratorate jointly issued a judicial interpretation, which clarifies that posting defamatory information online would be subject to the offence of criminal defamation under Article 246 of the Chinese Penal Code.[56] Moreover, in recognition of the special nature of online information dissemination, the judicial interpretation also states that the defamation would be considered to be 'serious', if the information is clicked or browsed more than 5,000 times or forwarded more than 500 times.[57] In 2015, the Penal Code was also amended to add an additional clause in Article 291, which makes it an offence to fabricate information about natural disasters or crime and spread them online, or to spread such false information knowingly online. The issue was finally sealed when the new 2017 Cyber Security Law expanded the liability for prohibited online content from organizations to individuals, which was repeated in two separate provisions (Articles 12 and 48).

One could argue that such draconian laws on netizens are rather unnecessary, especially considering the fact that, unlike the United States, the Internet information service providers are directly liable for the contents generated by users. Under the 2000 Administrative Measures, for example, the Internet information service providers are required, upon discovering prohibited information on their website, to stop the transmission, keep relevant records, and report to the relevant state authorities.[58] To give real teeth to the requirement, Article 23 of the Administrative Measures also stipulates that Internet information service providers found in violation could have their licences revoked and websites shut down.[59]

The liability for Internet information service providers was duly copied in the Cybersecurity Law.[60] Moreover, it went one step further by requiring Internet

---

[54] Ministry of Public Security, note 12, Article 5.
[55] B. Blanchard, 'China Court Sentences Melamine Milk Activist to Jail', *Reuters*, 10 November 2010.
[56] Supreme People's Court and the Supreme People's Procuratorate, Interpretation of the Supreme People's Court and the Supreme People's Procuratorate on Several Issues concerning the Application of Law in Handling Defamation and Other Criminal Cases through Information Networks [Zuigao Renmin Fayuan, Zuigao Renmin Jianchayuan Guanyu Banli Liyong Xinxi Wangluo Shishi Feibang Deng Xingshi Anjian Shiyong Falv Ruogan Wenti de Jieshi], Fa Shi No 21 (2013), 5 September 2013.
[57] Ibid., Article 2.
[58] State Council, note 48, Article 16.
[59] Ibid., Article 23.
[60] Cybersecurity Law, note 3, Article 47.

information service providers to establish mechanism to facilitate online complaints and reports.[61] A dedicated hotline and website (www.12377.cn) were also set up to handle reports on 'illegal and unhealthy information', with the first category being 'political information'.[62] In 2018 and 2019, between ten million and thirty million reports were made on average every month, with the majority being directed against major social media sites, such as Weibo, Tencent and search engines, such as Baidu.[63]

Another innovation in the Cybersecurity Law is the shift from the regulation of content to requirements on where such content, or data, shall be stored. According to Article 37, operators of critical information infrastructure are required to locally store personal information and important data collected and generated in their operations within China. If they need to send such data abroad due to business necessity, they have to first undergo security assessment by the authorities. This provision raised several concerns. First is what constitutes 'critical information infrastructure'. Article 31 defines this as infrastructure in 'important industries and fields such as public communications and information services, energy, transport, water conservancy, finance, public services and e-government affairs', as well as such 'that will result in serious damage to state security, the national economy and the people's livelihood and public interest if it is destroyed, loses functions or encounters data leakage'. Such a broad definition could potentially capture everything and is not really helpful nor does it give much guidance, which is why the same article also directs the State Council to develop the 'specific scope of critical information infrastructure'.

In 2016, the CAC issued the National Network Security Inspection Operation Manual[64] and the Guide on the Determination of Critical Information Infrastructure,[65] which clarified the scope of critical information infrastructure by grouping them into three categories: (i) websites, which includes websites of

---

[61] Ibid., Article 49.
[62] Cyberspace Administration of China (National Internet Information Office), the Center for Reporting Illegal and Bad Information [Zhongyang Wangxinban (Guojia Hulianwang Xinxi Bangongshi) Weifa he Buliang Xinxi Jvbao Zhongxin].
[63] Cyberspace Administration of China (National Internet Information Office), the Center for Reporting Illegal and Bad Information [Zhongyang Wangxinban (Guojia Hulianwang Xinxi Bangongshi) Weifa he Buliang Xinxi Jvbao Zhongxin], Acceptance of National Network Reporting in June 2019 [2019 Nian 6 Yue Quanguo Wangluo Jvbao Shouli Qingkuang], 3 July 2019.
[64] Central Leading Group on Cyber Security and Informatisation General Office, Network Security Coordination Bureau, National Network Security Inspection Operation Manual [Guojia Wangluo Anquan Jiancha Caozuo Zhinan], June 2016.
[65] Guide on the Determination of Critical Information Infrastructure (Trial) [Guanjian Xinxi Jichu Sheshi Queding Zhinan (Shixing)], in Notice on Conducting Network Security Inspections of Key Information Infrastructure [Guanyu Kaizhan Guanjian Xinxi Jichu Sheshi Wangluo Anquan Jiancha de Tongzhi], Zhongwangban Fawen No 3 (2006), Annex 1, July 2016.

government and party organizations, enterprises and public institutions, and news media; (ii) platforms, which include Internet service platforms for instant messaging, online shopping, online payment, search engines, emails, online forum, maps, and audio video; and (iii) production operations, which include office and business systems, industrial control systems, big data centres, cloud computing and TV broadcasting systems.

The CAC also laid down three steps in determining the critical information infrastructure, which starts with the identification of the critical operation, then continues with the determination of the information system or industrial control system supporting such critical operation, and concludes with the final determination based on the level of the critical operations' reliance on such systems and possible damages resulting from security breaches in these systems. More specifically, they listed eleven sectors, which include energy, finance, transportation, hydraulics, medical, environmental protection, industrial manufacturing, utilities, telecom and Internet, radio and TV, and government agencies. The detailed criteria are both quantitative and qualitative. For example, on the one hand, critical information infrastructure includes websites with daily visitor counts of more than one million people and platforms with more than ten million registered users or more than one million daily active users, or daily transaction value of ten million RMB. On the other hand, even those that do not meet the quantitative criterion could be deemed to be critical information infrastructure if there are risks of security breaches that would lead to leakage of sensitive information about firms or enterprises, or leakage of fundamental national data on geology, population and resources, or seriously harming the image of the government or social order, or national security. The potentially wide reach of the criteria was well illustrated by the case of the BGI Group, which was fined by the Ministry of Science and Technology in October 2018 for exporting certain human genome information abroad via the Internet without authorization.[66] Given the nature of their business, the BGI case could fall under the category of 'leakage of fundamental national data on . . . population', as mentioned earlier.

4 Summary

From the discussion on the remarkable evolution of Internet regulation in China over the past twenty-five years, we can distil two key trends: First, in terms of the institutional framework, we have seen the development from the period of no man's land in the 1990s to the period of proliferation of regulation and regulators with overlapping and competing jurisdictions in the first decade of the new century. Since the beginning of the current decade, however, we have seen the power of Internet regulation consolidated under the CAC, which emerged as the dominating agency presiding over the troika of Internet governance, with the MIIT and MPS

[66] An S., 'How to Conduct "Safety Check" for Exporting Data' [Shuju Chujing Ruhe 'Anjian'], *zhihu*, available at https://zhuanlan.zhihu.com/p/65413452.

playing supporting roles. Second, in terms of the substantive regulations, we have not only seen the initial gaps in the regulatory landscape being filled with more and more detailed regulation, but also the shift in the regulatory focus. At first, the regulations focused on the technology, or the hardware of the Internet. Gradually, however, the focus shifted to the software, and then to the content, and now even to the data. This moves the regulations closer and closer to the heart of the matter, as the Internet, at the end of the day, is nothing but strings of zeros and ones arranged in specific sequences. With the adoption of the Cybersecurity Law in 2016, the focus has now been shifted to security, as the Internet is increasingly regarded as the key challenge to the all-powerful control of the Party. Thus, for China, Internet or data regulation has been presently elevated to a matter of national security. To put it in the words of President Xi, 'there is no national security without cybersecurity'.[67] Moreover, he even linked the survival of the Party with the Internet, by solemnly warning in 2013 that 'unless we solve the challenge of the Internet, the Party cannot stay in power indefinitely'.[68] The key to understand data regulation in China, therefore, must be 'security'. The heightened link with security not only explains the domestic regulatory framework in China but also informs how China would deal with the issue at the international level.

C TRADE AGREEMENTS

Ever since the Declaration on Global Electronic Commerce at the Second WTO Ministerial Conference in May 1998, WTO members have been exploring ways to incorporate Internet and data regulation into trade agreements.[69] While not much success was made in the WTO collectively, individual members were able to address the issue in other fora such as free trade agreements (FTAs) and the plurilateral Trade in Services Agreement (TiSA) initiative.[70] It makes good sense to address the issue in international trade agreements, as the Internet was born with an international nature and closely linked to commerce. At the same time, however, a country's position on Internet and data regulation in trade agreements is often heavily influenced by its domestic regulatory approach, and China is no exception.

In a way, China's first encounter with data regulation in the WTO started on the wrong foot as it concerned a sensitive area: China's regulation of publications and

---

[67] 'The Central Leading Group on Cyber Security and Informatisation Held Its First Meeting [Zhongyang Wangluo Anquan he Xinxihua Lingdao Xiaozu Diyici Huiyi Zhaokai]', *Xinhua Press*, 27 February 2014.

[68] Xi J., 'Speech at the National Propaganda and Thought Work Conference [Zai Quanguo Xuanchuan Sixiang Gongzuo Huiyi shang de Jianghua]', 19 August 2013, as cited in Z. Hanhua, 'Xi Jinping Hulianwang Fazhi Sixiang Yanjiu [Study on Xi Jinping's Thoughts on Internet Legal Governance]', *China Legal Science* [Zhongguo Faxue] 3 (2017), at 7.

[69] For an overview of the issues, see H. S. Gao, 'Regulation of Digital Trade in US Free Trade Agreements: From Trade Regulation to Digital Regulation', *Legal Issues of Economic Integration* 45 (2018), 47–70.

[70] Ibid.

audio-visual products.[71] In the case, the United States complained that China has failed to grant foreign firms the right to import and distribute publication and audio-visual products. One of the key issues in the case was whether China's commitments on 'sound recording distribution services' cover 'electronic distribution of sound recordings', as alleged by the United States.[72] China disagreed with the US approach and argued instead that such electronic distribution 'in fact corresponds to network music services',[73] which only emerged in 2001 and were completely different in kind from the 'sound recording distribution services'. According to China, the most fundamental difference between the two is that, unlike 'traditional' sound recording distribution services, network music services 'do not supply the users with sound recordings in physical form, but supply them with the right to use a musical content'.[74] In response, the United States cited the panel's statement in US – Gambling[75] that 'the GATS does not limit the various technologically possible means of delivery under mode 1', as well as the principle of 'technological neutrality' mentioned in the Work Programme on Electronic Commerce – Progress Report to the General Council,[76] and argued that electronic distribution is merely a means of delivery rather than a new type of service.[77] Furthermore, the United States argued that the term 'distribution' encompasses not only the distribution of goods, but also distribution of services.[78] After a lengthy discussion covering the ordinary meaning, the context, the provisions of the GATS, the object and purpose and various supplementary means of interpretation, the panel concluded that the term 'sound recording distribution services' does extend to distribution of sound recording through electronic means.[79] China appealed the panel's findings, but they were upheld by the Appellate Body, which largely adopted the panel's reasoning.[80]

The case was also the first WTO case concerning China's censorship regime. It is interesting to note, however, that the United States did not challenge the censorship

[71] Panel Report, China – Measures Affecting Trading Rights and Distribution Services for Certain Publications and Audiovisual Entertainment Products (China – Publications and Audiovisual Products), WT/DS363/R and Corr.1, adopted 19 January 2010, as modified by Appellate Body Report WT/DS363/AB/R.
[72] Ibid., at paras. 4.49–4.71.
[73] Ibid., at para. 4.147.
[74] Ibid., at para. 4.149.
[75] Panel Report, United States – Measures Affecting the Cross-Border Supply of Gambling and Betting Services, WT/DS285/R, adopted 20 April 2005, as modified by Appellate Body Report WT/DS285/AB/R.
[76] WTO, Work Programme on Electronic Commerce, Progress Report to the General Council, S/L/74 (1999), at para. 4.
[77] China – Publications and Audiovisual Products, note 71, at para. 4.69.
[78] Ibid., at para. 7.1156.
[79] Ibid., at paras. 7.1168–7.1265.
[80] Appellate Body Report, China – Measures Affecting Trading Rights and Distribution Services for Certain Publications and Audiovisual Entertainment Products (China – Publications and Audiovisual Products), WT/DS363/AB/R, adopted 19 January 2010, at paras. 338–413.

regime per se.[81] Instead, the United States only challenged the alleged discrimination in the operation of the regime, where imported products were subject to more burdensome content review requirements.[82] Ironically, the United States even proposed, as the solution to the alleged discrimination, that the Chinese Government itself shall shoulder the sole responsibility for conducting content review, rather than outsourcing it to importing firms.[83]

With such an unpleasant experience, China took a cautious approach on the inclusion of Internet or data regulation in other trade fora. While it has signed more than a dozen FTAs so far, most of them have not included provisions on such regulations. The only exceptions are the two FTAs China signed with South Korea and Australia[84] in 2015 and the amendment of the FTA signed with Chile in 2018, which include stand-alone chapters on e-commerce. However, unlike the US FTAs, which often include provisions on free flow of data and ban on data localization requirements,[85] the earlier mentioned FTAs only address e-commerce-related issues, such as the moratorium on customs duties on electronic transmissions; electronic authentication and electronic signatures; protection of personal information in e-commerce; and paperless trading.[86] Thus, they do not really address Internet and data regulation issues as such.

A similar approach is taken by China in the WTO negotiations. Even though the United States has long been calling for rules on issues such as free cross-border data flow and ban on data localization requirements, China has ignored these issues until very recently. For example, in its communication on e-commerce jointly tabled with Pakistan before the Eleventh Ministerial Conference, China focused only on 'cross-border trade in goods enabled by Internet, together with services directly supporting such trade in goods, such as payment and logistics services'.[87] As I have mentioned in another article, this approach is a reflection of the nature of business of most Chinese Internet firms, as they tend to focus on trade in physical goods facilitated by the Internet, rather than digital products like Google and Netflix.[88] Thus, when over

---

[81] Ibid., at para. 20.

[82] *China – Publications and Audiovisual Products*, note 71, at paras. 4.72–4.85.

[83] *China – Publications and Audiovisual Products*, note 71, at para. 7.875; *China – Publications and Audiovisual Products*, note 80, at para. 72.

[84] See also H. S. Gao, 'E-Commerce in ChAFTA: New Wine in Old Wineskins?', in C. Piker, H. Wang, and W. Zhou (eds), *The China Australia Free Trade Agreement: A Twenty-first-Century Model*, (Oxford: Hart Publishing, 2018), 283–303.

[85] See Gao, note 69.

[86] See H. S. Gao, 'Digital or Trade? The Contrasting Approaches of China and US to Digital Trade', *Journal of International Economic Law* 21 (2018), 297–321.

[87] WTO General Council, Council for Trade in Goods, Council for Trade in Services, Committee on Trade and Development, Work Programme on Electronic Commerce: Aiming at the Eleventh Ministerial Conference, Communication from the People's Republic of China and Pakistan, Revision, JOB/GC/110/Rev.1, JOB/CTG/2/Rev.1, JOB/SERV/243/Rev.1, JOB/DEV/39/Rev.1 (2016).

[88] See Gao, note 86.

seventy WTO members issued a joint statement on launching the negotiations on e-commerce at the Eleventh Ministerial Conference in December 2017,[89] China declined to join. When these members decided to formally launch the e-commerce negotiations in January 2019, however, China changed its position and jumped on the negotiation.[90] In April 2019, China issued a communication on the joint statement negotiation, in which it repeated the focus on cross-border trade in goods enabled by the Internet.[91] At the same time, however, it also addressed the main concerns of the United States, including data flows, data storage and treatment of digital products, in the following manner.

First, rather than ignoring these issues as it has done in the past, China chose to face them and acknowledge them as issues of concern for some members. This itself is a positive sign, as it indicates China's willingness to engage on these issues. Second, at the same time, China also indicated that it was not ready to discuss these issues, at least not in the early stages of the negotiation. Citing the 'complexity and sensitivity' of these issues, as well as 'the vastly divergent views among the Members', China stated that 'more exploratory discussions are needed before bringing such issues to the WTO negotiation, so as to allow Members to fully understand their implications and impacts, as well as related challenges and opportunities'.[92] Such approach is all too familiar to those who follow WTO negotiations closely, as it is basically a polite way of saying 'we do not want to discuss these issues now'.

Third, in particular, China singled out the issue of cross-border data flows, by stating that '[i]t's undeniable that trade-related aspects of data flows are of great importance to trade development'.[93] Interesting to note is, however, what China did and did not say in this sentence. It did not, for example, use 'free flow of data', which is how the United States has always referred to the issue in its submissions.[94] On the other hand, it qualified 'data flow' with 'trade-related aspects'. This implies that China is not willing to address all kinds of data flows, just those related to trade. In other words, to the extent that some data flows do not have a trade nexus, they could be legitimately excluded. As I have mentioned elsewhere, this qualification could have wide implications, as it could be employed to justify restrictions on data flows in sectors that China has not made commitments, or even for those covered by

---

[89] WTO, Joint Statement on Electronic Commerce, Ministerial Conference, 11th Session, Buenos Aires, 10–13 December 2017, WT/MIN(17)/ST/60 (2017).

[90] L. Kihara, 'DAVOS – Nearly Half WTO Members Agree to Talks on New E-Commerce Rules', *Reuters*, 25 January 2019.

[91] WTO, Joint Statement on Electronic Commerce, Communication from China, INF/ECOM/19, 24 April 2019.

[92] Ibid.

[93] Ibid.

[94] See WTO, Work Programme on Electronic Commerce, Non-Paper from the United States, JOB/GC/94 (2016), which refers to 'free flow of information' in para. 2.3, and INF/ECOM/5, which refers to 'free flows of information' in section 2.

existing commitments but provided free of charge (such as Google's search engine services), as they are not 'traded'.[95]

Fourth, in an effort to turn the table, China also prefaced the discussion on these 'other issues' with the recognition that members shall have the 'legitimate right to adopt regulatory measures in order to achieve reasonable public policy objectives'. This language is reminiscent of the calls for more 'policy space', a term often employed in trade negotiations to justify special and differential treatment and resorting to exceptions clauses. As the *China – Publications and Audiovisual* case mentioned earlier has illustrated, China will, most likely, invoke the public order exception contained in the general exceptions clauses of both the GATT and GATS to justify its online censorship regime. In particular, regarding data flows, China emphasized that it 'should be subject to the precondition of security' and should 'flow orderly in compliance with Members' respective laws and regulations'. This extends China's domestic narrative of cybersecurity to the international level, which is made complete with the earlier reference for all members to 'respect the Internet sovereignty' of other members. By elevating the issue to one of 'sovereignty', China has shown the seriousness it attaches to the issue of regulating data flow.

In summary, China has made it clear that it is not yet ready to discuss these sensitive data-related issues, at least not in the early stages of the negotiations. There is a possibility that it will consider some of them further down the road, but such negotiations will not be easy given China's guarded position.

D CONCLUSION

When people discuss data regulations today, they tend to focus on two main players: the UnitedStates, which calls for free flow of data to serve the interests of firms, and the EU, which prioritizes the need for the protection of personal information and privacy of the consumers. This chapter discusses the third major player – China – which emphasizes data security and even regards it as a matter of national sovereignty. Of course, such a regulatory approach was not formed overnight. Instead, the earlier discussions have illustrated how data regulation with Chinese characteristics has evolved over the past twenty-five years. More specifically, the analyses in this chapter have shown the differing regulatory logics and approaches at two different levels – the national and the international.

First, at the domestic level, we have seen Internet regulation shifting from hardware to software, and now to content and data. The shift in regulatory focus closely follows the development of the Internet in China, where it started as a novelty that was confined to the ranks of tech-savvy geeks, then gradually expanded to the masses with the proliferation of software and apps catered to popular uses, and now permeates everyone's daily life from socializing and shopping to entertainment

---

[95] Gao, note 86.

and education. Recognizing the central role played by the Internet in modern life, Chinese regulators have shrewdly chosen to regulate data, which is the essence of cyberspace that powers everything, especially with the rise of big data and artificial intelligence. Moreover, data regulation has now been elevated to the level of national security, and the agency that is responsible for content regulation, the CAC, has also evolved into the super-agency that is almost synonymous with data regulation in China. The CAC has no responsibility in promoting the growth of the sector. Instead, its only responsibility is making sure that the cyberspace is secure and nothing unexpected pops up. It is this single-minded pursuit of security that has led to such draconian policies as Internet blockage, filtering and other restrictions on the free flow of data, forced data localization requirements and the transfer of source code. As the Internet is becoming more complicated and omnipotent, we can only expect Internet and data regulations in China to become more sophisticated and omnipresent.

Second, at the international level, due to its unpleasant experience in WTO disputes, China has for a long time been rather cautious in addressing Internet and data related issues. This approach is also reflected in its free trade agreements, which tend to avoid the Internet-related issues. Even though its most recent FTAs – especially the ones with South Korea, Australia and Chile – started to address them, they tend to focus on only e-commerce-related issues and do not really address data flows. At the same time, in contrast to its defensive position on data-related issues, China has been quite aggressive in pushing for liberalization of 'cross-border trade in goods enabled by Internet'. This reflects China's interest as the leading goods exporter and the success of its e-commerce platforms such as Alibaba. In its latest proposal on the WTO Joint Statement Initiative on e-commerce, China started to address data regulations, but they were framed as secondary issues that require 'more exploratory discussions' and are subject to each member's 'right to regulate' to achieve other policy goals, especially security.

The growth of the Internet in China over the past twenty-five years has not only led to the phenomenal growth of its e-commerce market, but also gave China the confidence and power to export its model, and to 'set the agenda and make rules for cyberspace at the international stage', as per the high-level exhortation by President Xi at the Politburo's Thirty-Sixth Collective Study Session on 'Implementation of the Internet Power Strategy' in October 2016.[96] The success of China's e-commerce sector will make the Chinese model attractive to many developing countries, as many of them are trying to emulate the accomplishments of China. However, an argument could be made that given China's huge population base and the resulting

---

[96] Xi J., 'Accelerate the Promotion of Indigenous Innovation on Internet Information Technology, Strive Unrelently towards the Objective of Building the Internet Power [Jiakuai Tuijin Wangluo Xinxi Jishu Zizhu Chuangxin, Chaozhe Jianshe Wangluo Qiangguo Mubiao Buxie Nuli]', *Xinhua News*, 9 October 2016.

enormous market, its e-commerce success story is more 'in spite of', rather than 'because of', the tight grip on cyberspace by the government. Nonetheless, given China's growing economic clout, data regulation with Chinese characteristics is something that the rest of the world must grapple with for some time to come. It is in this regard that this chapter tries to make a distinct contribution by offering a preliminary peek behind the cyber curtain, while also offering some hints on the things to come.

13

Regulatory Convergence of Data Rules in Latin America

*Rodrigo Polanco**

A INTRODUCTION

In the past two decades, the rapid development of the Internet allowed the growth of e-commerce, and together with the new digital technologies and the Internet of Things, the flow of data – both commercial and personal has increased to levels unseen before. Traditional trade rules could serve as a starting point to deal with these issues but they clearly are not enough. To provide some context, in 1994 – at the time the World Trade Organization (WTO) and its agreements were established by the Marrakesh Agreement – Mosaic was the most used web browser on the Internet. (Netscape Navigator was created the same year, and Internet Explorer was only released in 1995.)[1] Neither Google, nor Amazon or Facebook existed in 1994. The 'modern' rules of trade law were not designed having taken into account the characteristics of contemporary digital trade and data flows.

This situation has led to the regulation of electronic commerce today becoming one of the most important topics in trade law and policy. Efforts of dealing with these issues at a multilateral level started in 1998, when the WTO established a work programme on electronic commerce and at the ministerial conference that same year, members agreed on a temporary duty-free moratorium on all electronic transactions – a practice that since then has been renewed at each WTO ministerial conference.[2] Further development has been slow paced and we are still far from achieving consensus on this topic. Only in December 2017, forty-four WTO members made a joint declaration to initiate exploratory work together toward future

---

* Senior Researcher and Lecturer, World Trade Institute, University of Bern. Contact: rodrigo. polanco@wti.org.
[1] A. Schwabach, *Internet and the Law: Technology, Society, and Compromises*, 2nd edn, Legal Advisor at the Swiss Institute of Comparative Law (Santa Barbara: ABC-CLIO, 2014), at xxi.
[2] S. Wunsch-Vincent, 'Trade Rules for the Digital Age', in M. Panizzon, N. Pohl, and P. Sauvé (eds), *GATS and the Regulation of International Trade in Services* (Cambridge: Cambridge University Press, 2008), 497–529, at 498.

negotiations on trade-related aspects of electronic commerce.[3] In 2019, some countries like India and South Africa argued that the e-commerce moratorium in the WTO led to loss of revenue, as it gave such transmissions immunity from taxation, and initially opposed to the renewal of the duty-free moratorium.[4] And while there has been a new reinvigoration under the 2019 Joint Statement Initiative with currently seventy-seven WTO members on board, overall, until now, the WTO has made no substantive progress on e-commerce, and countries have not been able to agree on a multilateral regime for the treatment of e-commerce and data flows.[5]

But the lack of consensus at a multilateral level does not mean that rules for digital trade are not being created elsewhere. In fact, since the beginning of the twenty-first century, certain countries have been including provisions and even chapters on electronic commerce, as well as rules on data flows, in preferential trade agreements (PTAs). It is well known that the United States has been important in the creation and diffusion of digital trade rules, especially after the 2002 US Digital Trade Agenda and the Bipartisan Trade Promotion Authority Act of the same year.[6] Not so well known is the relevant role other actors have played in the development of these rules.[7] This contribution focuses on one group of countries of the Latin American region, which have been the most important vectors of the inclusion of e-commerce and data rules in PTAs – a group that includes Chile, Colombia, Mexico, Peru, and Panama. For the purpose of this chapter, we consider 'Latin American' PTAs those trade agreements in which at least one, or more parties, is a country from Latin America and the Caribbean region.

Besides highlighting the contribution that those countries have had in the creation and diffusion of this new rule-making, our goal is also to determine the level of regulatory convergence that Latin American countries (LACs) have on rules on digital trade and data flows. For this purpose, we understand regulatory convergence as an overarching notion that aims to reduce unnecessary regulatory incompatibilities between countries in a dynamic and incomplete process.[8] The rationale behind regulatory convergence in PTAs stems from the idea that regulatory diversity

---

[3] WTO, Work Programme on Electronic Commerce, Ministerial Decision of 13 December 2017, Ministerial Conference, 11th Session, Buenos Aires, 10–13 December 2017, WT/MIN(17)/65. WT/L/1032, 18 December 2017.

[4] K. Suneja, 'Setback for India as WTO Extends Nil Tax on E-Transmissions', *The Economic Times*, 11 December 2019.

[5] M. Burri and T. Cottier (eds), *Trade Governance in the Digital Age* (Cambridge: Cambridge University Press, 2015); S. Wunsch-Vincent, *The WTO, the Internet and Trade in Digital Products: EC-US Perspectives* (Oxford: Hart Publishing, 2006). For more recent updates, see Chapter 1 in this volume.

[6] S. Wunsch-Vincent, 'The Digital Trade Agenda of the US: Parallel Tracks of Bilateral, Regional and Multilateral Liberalization', *Aussenwirtschaft* 58 (2003), 7–46.

[7] See Chapter 2 in this volume.

[8] R. Polanco Lazo and P. Sauvé, 'The Treatment of Regulatory Convergence in Preferential Trade Agreements', *World Trade Review* 17 (2018), 575–607, at 579.

may entail significant costs that can hinder cross-border exchanges,[9] and that the maintenance of needlessly burdensome cross-border differences in regulation can result in a number of additional negative policy impacts, including higher transaction costs stemming from information asymmetries.[10] Divergent regulatory requirements can lead to duplication of procedures and costs in trade that are important for all internationally active businesses and especially so for small- or medium-sized enterprises (SMEs), for which such fixed costs can be a deciding factor in whether or not to export or invest, including across borders.[11] Lack of transparency or clarity of regulations, as well as excessive, inefficient, or ineffective regulations, create unnecessary delays or impose costs on traders and investors.[12]

Regulatory convergence mechanisms include substantive or procedural aspects that are aimed at two different types of regulatory outcomes. In some agreements, regulatory convergence aims to achieve *substantive* regulatory harmonisation (similar or equivalent regulation – 'substantive convergence'). Other agreements consider harmonisation of the *processes* by which regulations are developed, adopted, publicised, and implemented (similar or equivalent procedures – 'procedural convergence'). With different denominations,[13] both approaches are present in the PTAs examined in this chapter.

The chapter is organised as follows. After the introduction, we provide a detailed description of e-commerce and data rules found in Latin American PTAs, and their convergence or divergence. Then we briefly present the domestic frameworks of relevant LACs on digital trade–related topics, as well as their consistency with existing international commitments, with special emphasis on personal data protection. To conclude, we highlight some potential conflicts that could arise between these countries' domestic regulations and international commitments in the field.

B REGULATORY CONVERGENCE IN E-COMMERCE AND DATA FLOW PROVISIONS IN LATIN AMERICAN PTAS

The inclusion of provisions in PTAs referring explicitly to e-commerce and data flows is not a recent phenomenon, although it has evolved importantly in the past

---

[9] B. Hoekman, 'Fostering Transatlantic Regulatory Cooperation and Gradual Multilateralization', *Journal of International Economic Law* 18 (2015), 609–624, at 609.

[10] F. Chirico and P. Larouche, 'Convergence and Divergence, in Law and Economics and Comparative Law', in P. Larouche and P. Cserne (eds), *National Legal Systems and Globalization* (The Hague: T. M. C. Asser Press, 2013), 9–33, at 23–24.

[11] C. Malmström, 'Trade in the Twenty-first Century: The Challenge of Regulatory Convergence', *Speech*, 19 March 2015, at 2–3, available at https://trade.ec.europa.eu/doclib/docs/2015/march/tradoc_153260.pdf.

[12] E. Sheargold and A. D. Mitchell, 'The TPP and Good Regulatory Practices: An Opportunity for Regulatory Coherence to Promote Regulatory Autonomy?', *World Trade Review* 15 (2016), 587–612, at 592. See Chapter 3 in this volume.

[13] B. M. Hoekman and P. C. Mavroidis, *Regulatory Spillovers and the Trading System: From Coherence to Cooperation* (Geneva: ICTSD/WEF, 2015), at 2–3.

TABLE 13.1. *Latin American PTAs with e-commerce or data flow provisions*

Country	Other LACs	Developed	Developing	Total PTAs
Argentina	2	1	0	3
Bolivia	1	0	0	1
Brazil	2	1	0	3
Chile	7	5	8	16
Colombia	7	5	1	12
Cuba	1	0	0	1
Costa Rica	11	4	2	11
Dominican Republic	3	2	1	3
Ecuador	1	0	0	1
El Salvador	7	3	1	7
Guatemala	5	3	1	9
Haiti	1	1	0	1
Honduras	6	4	1	8
Mexico	6	5	2	9
Nicaragua	5	3	2	7
Panama	8	5	3	12
Paraguay	1	1	0	2
Peru	8	8	5	16
Uruguay	3	1	0	4
Venezuela	1	0	0	1

two decades. According to the TAPED dataset, 191 PTAs include provisions that are related to e-commerce and data flows, with 116 PTAs with e-commerce provisions and 86 with e-commerce chapters.[14] These provisions are highly heterogeneous and address various issues including customs duties and non-discriminatory treatment of digital products, electronic signatures, paperless trading, unsolicited electronic messages, as well as consumer protection, data protection, data flows, and data localisation.

As detailed in Table 13.1, of the total number of PTAs with e-commerce and data flow provisions the countries of Latin America have concluded 53 per cent (62 agreements, 47 chapters). Twenty-nine of these agreements have been concluded with developed countries (47 per cent of this subset) and 33 with other developing countries (53 per cent of this subset), most of them also from Latin America (26 agreements in total). The countries leading this treaty-making practice in the region

[14] All the data cited in this chapter comes from the 'Trade Agreements Provisions on Electronic-Commerce and Data' (TAPED) dataset, which includes a detailed mapping and coding of preferential trade agreement (PTAs) that include chapters, provisions, annexes, and side documents that directly or indirectly regulate e-commerce and data flows. See Mira Burri and Rodrigo Polanco, 'Digital Trade Provisions in Preferential Trade Agreements: Introducing a New Dataset', *Journal of International Economic Law* 23 (2020), 187–220 and https://unilu.ch/taped.

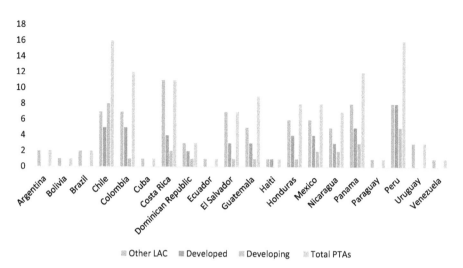

FIGURE 13.1. Latin American PTAs with e-commerce and data flow provisions

are Chile (18 PTAs) Peru (16 PTAs), Colombia (12 PTAs), Panama and Costa Rica (11 PTAs each). This is in line with the fact that the surge of PTAs having e-commerce provisions involves both developed and developing countries. 49 per cent of the PTAs with e-commerce provisions were negotiated between developed and developing countries, and 47 per cent were negotiated between developing countries.[15]

The earliest e-commerce provision in a PTA involving a Latin American country is found in the 2001 Canada–Costa Rica Free Trade Agreement (FTA), which included a Joint Statement on Global Electronic Commerce. In a non-binding fashion, it addresses several issues, like the applicability of WTO rules to e-commerce, supporting industry developments in the field, stakeholder's participation, transparency, and consumer and data protection. In 2002, the Chile–EU Association Agreement properly included e-commerce provisions in the text of the treaty on issues such as cooperation and data protection.[16] The first PTA concluded in the region having a dedicated e-commerce chapter is the 2002 Chile–US FTA. In 2006, the Nicaragua–Taiwan FTA began the inclusion of provisions on data flows as part of its cooperation commitments. The number of Latin American PTAs with such provisions has increased over the years (see Figure 13.1), simultaneously with the growing discussions on the digital economy and its move up as a topic on the policy agendas and negotiation tables.

---

[15] Country classification is according to United Nations, *World Economic Situation and Prospects* (New York: Department of Economic and Social Affairs, 2018). See also Chapter 1 in this volume.

[16] Articles 104 and 202 Chile–EU AA.

TABLE 13.2. *PTAs concluded with e-commerce provisions per region*

Type of PTA	E-Commerce provisions	E-Commerce chapters	%PTAs with e-commerce provisions
Africa	0	0	0
Americas	30	22	16
Asia	28	9	15
Europe	33	1	17
Intercontinental	98	53	52
Oceania	0	0	0

Although the number of PTAs with e-commerce and data flow provisions remains limited, the last eight years have shown a significant increase in the number of agreements with such provisions. Overall, agreements including such provisions are mainly of an intercontinental nature, but around one-third of these PTAs have at least one Latin American country as a contracting party (thirty-one treaties) and Latin America is one of the most relevant regional area with this type of treaty-making (Table 13.2).

PTAs with e-commerce provisions involving LACs have also increased their level of detail significantly over the years. Seven is the average number of PTA provisions found on e-commerce chapters in the past five years, with an average of 955 words. A treaty involving a Latin American country, the United States–Mexico–Canada Agreement (USMCA), is currently the PTA in force with the largest number of articles and words on e-commerce, as its current text has 19 articles and an average of 3,206 words. Several PTAs having a Latin American country as a party have devoted more than 11 articles and 1,900 words to these topics, like the 2017 Argentina–Chile FTA, the 2015 Pacific Alliance Additional Protocol (PAAP), the 2016 Chile–Uruguay FTA, the 2018 Australia–Peru FTA, the 2018 Brazil–Chile FTA, and both the Trans-Pacific Partnership Agreement (TPP) and the Comprehensive and Progressive Agreement for Trans-Pacific Partnership (CPTPP), whose e-commerce chapter reiterates verbatim the TPP text.

C E-COMMERCE AND DATA PROVISIONS IN LATIN AMERICAN PTAS

E-commerce and data provisions are found in the main text of several Latin American PTAs, mostly on chapters or sections dedicated to e-commerce or intellectual property (IP). When available, data flow provisions are also found in these chapters or sections, but are commonly included in chapters on specific services, mainly telecommunication and financial services. E-commerce provisions can also be found in side documents, like annexes, joint statements, and side letters. As presented in Table 13.3, Latin American PTAs represent an important number of treaties with such provisions.

TABLE 13.3. *Total PTAs and Latin American PTAs with e-commerce and data flow provisions*

Total PTAs					
Electronic commerce	Data flows	Intellectual property	Information and communication technology	Government procurement	Trade in goods
Number of provisions 116	79	153	38	68	72
% of TAPED (191 PTAs) 61	41	80	20	36	38

Latin American PTAs					
Electronic commerce	Data flows	Intellectual property	Information and communication technology	Government procurement	Trade in goods
Number of provisions 62	39	48	12	39	35
% of TAPED (191 PTAs) 33	21	25	7	20	19

In the following sections, we examine the provisions of Latin American PTAs in two main groups: (i) electronic commerce and (ii) cross-border data flows.

An assessment of the extent of legalisation of these provisions was also performed, distinguishing between 'soft', 'mixed', and 'hard' commitments. We considered as 'soft' those commitments that are not enforceable by the parties, like 'best efforts' and cooperation commitments. We classified as 'hard' those commitments that oblige a party to comply with a rule or a principle and which are enforceable by another party. Finally, we consider an agreement with 'mixed' legalisation if the treaty has both soft and hard commitments. Similarly, we included in this category references to other agreements that are only partially applicable.[17]

I *Electronic Commerce*

1 Objectives and Principles

Several Latin American PTAs with e-commerce chapters converge on explicitly stating a number of objectives like avoiding unnecessary barriers to e-commerce (37 PTAs), addressing the needs of SMEs (31 PTAs), promoting and facilitating its use

---

[17] Burri and Polanco, note 14.

(both between the parties and globally (30 PTAs), considering private participation in the development of the regulatory framework for e-commerce (15 PTAs), and the principle of technological neutrality (15 PTAs).[18] The first three objectives and principles are also commonly found in PTAs with e-commerce chapters concluded by countries outside of Latin America.

2 Applicability of WTO Rules

Although all Latin American countries that have concluded PTAs with e-commerce or data flow provisions are members of the WTO that does not necessarily mean that these countries consider that WTO law applies to digital trade. In fact, only one-third of Latin American PTAs include provisions on the applicability of WTO rules to e-commerce – twenty agreements from a total of sixty-two PTAs – with important differences of language across agreements. The first treaty including such provisions is the 2001 Canada–Costa Rica FTA, which only makes a reference to the mainten-ance of the WTO practice of not imposing customs duties on electronic transmis-sions between the parties.[19] Some treaties explicitly recognise the applicability of the WTO rules to electronic commerce, but without clearly specifying which the applicable provisions would be.[20] Certain agreements clarify the application of WTO rules to e-commerce 'to the extent they affect electronic commerce',[21] or to measures 'affecting electronic commerce'.[22] In other softer variations, countries merely reaffirm their respective commitments under WTO agreements in the respective e-commerce chapter/section.[23]

3 National Treatment (NT) and Most-Favoured Nation (MFN) Obligations

The number of Latin American agreements including provisions with explicit commitments on non-discrimination on digital trade is relatively small. In the

[18] There are different versions of the principle of technological neutrality. It is understood here as a non-discrimination principle between products delivered electronically and other modes of supply (e.g. physical delivery). See R. V. Anuradha, 'Technological Neutrality: Implications for Services Commitments and the Discussions on E-Commerce', Centre for WTO Studies and Indian Institute of Foreign Trade Working Paper CWS/WP/200/51 (2018), at 7.
[19] Canada–Costa Rica FTA, Joint Statement on Global Electronic Commerce.
[20] Article 1.2 DEPA Article 14.1(1) Central America–Korea FTA; Article 19.2(1) Colombia–Panama FTA; Article 15.03(1) Canada–Panama FTA; Article 1502(1) Canada–Colombia FTA; Article 1502(1) Canada–Peru FTA; Article 13.1 Panama–Singapore FTA.
[21] Article 16.2 Canada–Honduras FTA.
[22] Article 16.2(1) Colombia–Costa Rica FTA; Article 12.1(1) Colombia–Korea FTA; Article 15.2(1) Central America–Mexico; Article 14.1(1) Korea–Peru FTA; Article 12.1(1) Costa Rica–Singapore; Article 14.2(1) Colombia–Northern Triangle FTA; Article 14.1(1) Panama–US TPA; Article 15.1(1) Colombia–US; Article 14.01(1) Nicaragua–Taiwan FTA; Article 15.1(1) Peru–US; Article 14.1(1) CAFTA–Dominican Republic–US.
[23] Article 107.1 Colombia–EU–EU–Peru FTA.

TAPED dataset, eighteen PTAs include MFN commitments to give a treatment no less favourable on e-commerce to parties to the treaty than they accord to non-parties; and nineteen PTAs consider NT commitments to give a treatment no less favourable to other parties to the treaty than they accord domestically on e-commerce. In contrast, in the whole TAPED dataset we find thirty-five PTAs with NT and thirty-two with MFN provisions.

The large majority of these provisions are binding.[24] Following the 2015 Pacific Alliance Additional Protocol (PAAP), some agreements consider NT and MFN together, as part of a general commitment to non-discriminatory treatment of digital products. According to this provision, no party shall accord less favourable treatment to digital products created, produced, published, contracted for, commissioned or first made available on commercial terms in the territory of another party or to digital products of which the author, performer, producer, developer, or owner is a person of another party than it accords to other like digital products.[25] In certain treaties, a footnote further clarifies that to the extent that a digital product of a non-party is a 'like digital product', it will qualify as an 'other like digital product'.[26]

But the majority of Latin American PTAs consider separate paragraphs for NT and MFN. On national treatment, the most common wording goes back to the 2006 Panama–Singapore FTA, which stipulates that a party

> shall not accord less favourable treatment to some digital products than it accords to other like digital products, on the basis that the digital products receiving less favourable treatment are created, produced, published, stored, transmitted, contracted for, commissioned or first made available on commercial terms outside its territory; or the author, performer, producer, developer or distributor is a person of another Party or a non-Party; or so as otherwise to afford protection to other like digital products that are created, produced, published, stored, transmitted, contracted for, commissioned, or first made available on commercial terms in its territory.[27]

A variation of this provision uses 'may' instead of 'shall', theoretically making the commitment less binding.[28] Another variation narrows the NT as it only applies to the digitally delivered products associated with the territory of the other party or where the author, performer, producer, developer, or distributor is a person of the

[24] Only Article 10.4 Brazil–Chile FTA contains a recognition of this discussion, without a specific commitment.
[25] Article 13.4*bis* PAAP.
[26] Article 14.4 CPTPP; Article 13.4(1) Australia–Peru FTA; Article 19.4(1) USMCA.
[27] Article 13.3(2) Panama–Singapore FTA; Article 14.03(3) Nicaragua–Taiwan FTA; Article 12.4(1) Chile–Colombia FTA; Article 14.4(3) Colombia–Northern Triangle FTA; Article 12.4(3) Costa Rica–Singapore.
[28] Article 14.3(3) CAFTA–DR–US FTA; Article 15.3(3) Peru–US TPA; Article 15.3(3) Colombia–US TPA; Article 14.3(3) Panama–US; Article 14.3(2) Central America–Korea FTA.

other party.[29] A simpler recognition of NT is found in the Canada–Peru FTA, where the parties merely confirm the application of national treatment for goods to trade conducted by electronic means.[30]

Regarding MFN, some agreements stipulate that a party

shall not accord less favourable treatment to digital products created, produced, published, stored, transmitted, contracted for, commissioned or first made commercially available in the territory of another Party, than it accords to like digital products in the territory of a non-Party. Furthermore, a Party shall not accord less favourable treatment to digital products of which the author, performer, producer, developer or distributor is a person of a non-Party.[31]

A variation of this provision uses 'may' instead of 'shall', making the commitment less binding.[32]

4 Customs Duties

One of the most common provisions found in PTAs regarding digital trade (eighty-four PTAs in TAPED) is the commitment to not impose customs duties on digital products. Wu points out that this type of provision facilitates commerce in downloadable products, such as software, e-books, music, movies, and other digital media.[33] Despite being commonplace, these commitments have different wording in how the obligation is drafted. From the thirty-nine Latin American PTAs that include such provision, some agreements merely reaffirm the WTO member's practice of not imposing customs duties on electronic transmissions,[34] rather than seeking to expand it towards a WTO-plus obligation. However, the most common approach is a provision including a permanent moratorium on duty-free treatment in the PTA, meaning that no customs duties should be imposed on electronic transmissions and digital products. Yet again, this second type of provision has several variations.

Some agreements plainly stipulate that a party may not apply customs duties on digital products of the other party,[35] or in more binding terms that it 'shall not' impose customs duties on electronic transmissions,[36] or not apply customs duties, fees, or

---

[29] Article 15.4(1) Chile–US FTA; Article 15.4(3) Central America–Mexico FTA.

[30] Article 1501.1 Canada–Peru FTA.

[31] Article 15.4(2) Chile–US FTA; Article 13.3(3) Panama–Singapore FTA; Article 14.03(4) Nicaragua–Taiwan FTA; Article 12.4(2) Chile–Colombia FTA; Article 14.4(4) Colombia–Northern Triangle FTA; Article 12.4(4) Costa Rica–Singapore; Article 15.4(4) Central America–Mexico FTA.

[32] Article 14.3(4) CAFTA–DR–US FTA; Article 15.3(4) Peru–US TPA; Article 15.3(4) Colombia–US TPA; Article 14.3(4) Panama–US FTA.

[33] M. Wu, *Digital Trade-Related Provisions in Regional Trade Agreements: Existing Models and Lessons for the Multilateral Trade System* (Geneva: ICTSD/IDB, 2017), at 11, 36.

[34] Annex II, Article 2 Central America–EFTA.

[35] Article 15.3 Chile–US FTA.

[36] Article 16.4 Australia–Chile FTA.

charges on import or export by electronic means of digital products.[37] In certain agreements, the parties agree that electronic transmissions shall be considered as the provision of services, which cannot be subject to customs duties.[38] In other treaties, the parties simply agree not to impose duties on 'deliveries by electronic means'.[39]

Only a couple of agreements consider this obligation regardless whether the digital products in question are fixed on a carrier medium or transmitted electronically.[40] In several of these treaties there is an explicit distinction between digital products which are transmitted by electronic means and those whose sale occurs online but who are physically transported over the border. According to these PTAs a party shall not apply customs duties on digital products by electronic transmission, but when these are transmitted physically, the customs value is only limited to the value of the carrier medium and does not include the value of the digital product stored on the carrier medium.[41] A variation of this provision, usually found in agreements concluded with the United States, uses 'may' instead of 'shall', theoretically making the commitment less binding.[42] Certain Latin American PTAs explicitly mention that the moratorium does not extend to internal taxes or other charges. The wording of this exclusion varies across treaties. While some do not prevent a party from imposing an internal tax or charge to digital products delivered or transmitted electronically,[43] others exclude products imported/exported by electronic transmissions or means,[44] or content transmitted electronically between a person of one party and a person of the other party.[45]

5 Electronic Authentication

Thirty-seven Latin American PTAs include provisions on electronic authentication, which represent around half of the overall universe of PTAs having these provisions. Typically, they allow authentication technologies and mutual recognition of digital

[37] Article 14.4 Mexico–Panama FTA.
[38] Article 162.3 Colombia–EU–Peru FTA; Annex B, Article 1.3 Colombia–Israel FTA.
[39] Article 201.3 Central America–EU FTA.
[40] Article 1503 Canada–Peru FTA; Article 14.3(1–2) Central America–Korea FTA.
[41] Article 13.3(1–2) Panama–Singapore FTA; Article 14.03(1–2) Nicaragua–Taiwan FTA; Article 12.1(2) and 12.3 Chile–Colombia FTA; Article 14.2(2) and Article 14.4(1–2) Colombia–Northern Triangle FTA; Article 12.1(2) and Article. 12.4(1–2) Costa Rica–Singapore FTA; Article 15.2(1) and 15.4(1–2) Central America–Mexico FTA; Article 16.3 Colombia–Costa Rica FTA.
[42] Article 14.3(1–2) CAFTA–DR–US FTA; Article 15.3(1–2) Peru–US TPA; Article 15.1(2) and 15.3 (1–2) Colombia–US TPA; Article 14.1(2) and 14.3(1–2) Panama–US TPA.
[43] Article 15.04 Canada–Panama FTA; Article 19.3 Colombia–Panama FTA.
[44] Article 13.1 Peru–Singapore FTA; Article 1503 Canada–Colombia FTA; Article 14.4 Korea–Peru FTA; Article 12.2 Colombia–Korea FTA; Article 16.3 Canada–Honduras FTA; Article 13.4 PAAP.
[45] Article 14.3 CPTPP; Article 8.3 Chile–Uruguay FTA; Article 13.3 Australia–Peru FTA; Chapter on Digital Trade, Article 3 EU–Mexico Modernised Global Agreement; Article 19.3 USMCA; Article 10.3 Brazil–Chile FTA.

certificates and signatures. While earlier treaties included only best efforts commitments in this field, recent agreements include more binding and mandatory clauses. Fifty per cent of all PTAs including such provisions have been concluded by Latin American countries.

We find the earliest example of soft commitments on electronic authentication back in 2001, when Canada and Costa Rica merely acknowledged the necessity of policies to facilitate the use of technologies for authentication and for the conduct of secure e-commerce.[46] Other agreements included only cooperation commitments on electronic authentication. These comprise activities to share information and experiences on laws, regulations, and programmes on electronic signatures[47] or secure electronic authentication;[48] and to 'maintain a dialogue' on the facilitation of cross-border certification services,[49] or digital accreditation.[50]

More binding commitments on authentication and digital certificates establish restrictions on legislation, using both negative and positive obligations. According to a first group of agreements, no party may adopt or maintain legislation that (i) prevents or prohibits parties from having the opportunity to prove in court that their electronic transaction complies with any legal requirements with respect to authentication;[51] or (ii) prohibits parties to an electronic transaction from mutually determining the appropriate authentication methods.[52] Some of these treaties consider this obligation in more binding terms ('no Party shall adopt or maintain').[53] In a second group of agreements, each party has the positive obligation ('each Party shall adopt or maintain') of having domestic legislation for electronic authentication that permits parties to electronic transactions to (i) determine the appropriate authentication technologies and implementation models for their electronic transactions,

---

[46] Joint Statement on Global Electronic Commerce, Canada–Costa Rica FTA.
[47] Article 15.5(b) Central America–Mexico FTA; Article 16.10(1) Australia–Chile FTA; Article 14.8 (b) Colombia–Northern Triangle FTA; Article 14.5(b) Panama–US TPA; Article 12.5(b) Chile–Colombia FTA; Article 14.05(b) Nicaragua–Taiwan FTA; Article 13.4(b) Panama–Singapore FTA; Article 14.5(b) CAFTA–DR–US; Article 15.5(b) Chile–US FTA.
[48] Article 19.14(a)(iii) USMCA; Article 13.14(b)(v) Australia–Peru FTA; Article 11.9(b) Argentina–Chile FTA; Article 14.15(b)(v) CPTPP; Article 14.11(b) Mexico–Panama FTA; Article 13.12(b) PAAP; Article 16.5(b) Canada–Honduras FTA; Article 11.7(b)(v) Chile–Thailand FTA; Article 14.9(b) Korea–Peru FTA; Article 1507.1(b) Canada–Colombia FTA; Article 1508(b) Canada–Peru FTA.
[49] Annex B, Article 2.1(a) Colombia–Israel FTA; Article 19.7(1)(a) Colombia–Panama FTA; Article 16.7(1)(f) Colombia–Costa Rica FTA; Article 12.6(1)(a) Colombia–Korea FTA; Article 202(a) Central America–EU FTA; Article 163.1(a) Colombia–EU–Peru FTA; Article 120.1(a) CARIFORUM–EC EPA.
[50] Article 109(g) Colombia–EU–Peru FTA.
[51] Article 14.9(1) Mexico–Panama FTA; Article 13.10(1) PAAP; Article 14.7 Colombia–Northern Triangle FTA.
[52] Digital Trade Chapter, Article 6.2 EU–Mexico Modernised Global Agreement; Article 12.7 Chile–Colombia FTA; Article 15.6 Colombia–US TPA; Article 15.6 Peru–US TPA.
[53] Article 10.6(2) Brazil–Chile FTA; Article 19.6(2) USMCA; Article 13.6(2) Australia–Peru FTA; Article 11.3(2) Argentina–Chile FTA; Article 8.5(2) Chile–Uruguay FTA; Article 14.6 (2) CPTPP.

without limiting the recognition of such technologies and implementation models; and (ii) to have the opportunity to prove in court that their electronic transactions comply with any legal requirements.[54]

Further commitments on electronic signatures establish that neither party may deny the legal validity of a signature solely on the basis that it is in electronic form, either in negative ('may not maintain')[55] or positive terms ('a Party shall not deny').[56] Some agreements include exceptions to these commitments, considering that a party may require that the electronic signatures be certified by an authority or a supplier of certification services accredited under the party's law or regulations for a particular category of transactions or communications.[57] In certain cases, it is stipulated that such requirements shall be objective, transparent, and non-discriminatory and relate only to the specific characteristics of the category of transactions concerned.[58] In other agreements, it is considered that a party may deny the legal validity of an electronic signature under circumstances provided for in its law.[59]

Additional commitments on electronic authentication refer to the recognition of digital certificates, either publicly or privately issued. On public authentication, some agreements consider working towards the recognition of such certificates at a government level, based on internationally accepted standards,[60] on cooperation mechanisms between the respective national accreditation and digital certification authorities for electronic transactions,[61] or by mutual recognition agreements on digital/electronic signature.[62] On private authentication, certain treaties encourage the use of interoperable electronic trust or authentication,[63] digital certificates in the business sector,[64] and advanced or qualified certificates.[65] For that purpose, parties

---

[54] Article 11.7(e) Chile–Thailand FTA; Article 16.6(3) Australia–Chile FTA.

[55] Article 53 Chile–China FTA.

[56] Article 10.6(1) Brazil–Chile FTA; Article 19.6(1) USMCA; Digital Trade Chapter, Article 6.1 EU–Mexico Modernised Global Agreement; Article 13.6(1) Australia–Peru FTA; Article 11.3(1) Argentina–Chile FTA; Article 8.5(1) Chile–Uruguay FTA; Article 14.6(1) CPTPP.

[57] Article 10.6(3) Brazil–Chile FTA; Article 19.6(3) USMCA; Article 13.6(3) Australia–Peru FTA; Article 11.3(3) Argentina–Chile FTA; Article 8.5(3) Chile–Uruguay FTA; Article 14.6 (3) CPTPP.

[58] Digital Trade Chapter, Article 6.3 EU–Mexico Modernised Global Agreement.

[59] Article 10.6(1) Brazil–Chile FTA; Article 19.6(1) USMCA; Article 13.6(1) Australia–Peru FTA; Article 11.3(1) Argentina–Chile FTA; Article 8.5(1) Chile–Uruguay FTA; Article 14.6(1) CPTPP.

[60] Article 14.9(2) Mexico–Panama FTA; Article 13.10(2) PAAP; Article 11.7(e) Chile–Thailand FTA; Article 16.6(2) Australia–Chile FTA.

[61] Article 14.8(3) Korea–Peru FTA.

[62] Article 11.3(5) Argentina–Chile FTA.

[63] Article 10.6(4) Brazil–Chile FTA; Article 19.6(4) USMCA; Digital Trade Chapter, Article 6.4 EU–Mexico Modernised Global Agreement; Article 13.6(4) Australia–Peru FTA; Article 11.3(4) Argentina–Chile FTA; Article 8.5(4) Chile–Uruguay FTA; Article 14.6(3) CPTPP.

[64] Article 11.7(e) Chile–Thailand FTA; Article 16.6(4) Australia–Chile FTA.

[65] Article 14.9(2) Mexico–Panama FTA; Article 13.10(2) PAAP.

may endeavour to facilitate the procedure of accreditation or recognition of suppliers of certification services.[66]

6 Source Code

Overall, few PTAs include provisions referring to source code (sixteen treaties), but one third of them are concluded by Latin American countries. These clauses are largely binding prohibitions to require the transfer or access to proprietary source code of software, as a condition for the import, distribution, sale, or use of such software.[67]

In the CPTPP, the parties commit to not requiring the transfer of, or access to, source code of software owned by a person of another party, as a condition for the import, distribution, sale, or use of such software, or of products containing such software, in its territory. For these purposes, software is limited to mass market software or products containing such software, and does not include software used for critical infrastructure. However, some exceptions are considered in the same agreement, like the inclusion or implementation of terms and conditions related to the provision of source code in commercially negotiated contracts; a modification of source code necessary for a software to comply with domestic laws or regulations; and requirements that relate to patent applications or granted patents, including any orders made by a judicial authority in relation to patent disputes, subject to safeguards against unauthorised disclosure under the law or practice of a party.[68]

Later treaties have largely followed the CPTPP wording on this topic.[69] An important variation is found in the USMCA, where the protection given to source code also extends to algorithms expressed in a source code. The agreement includes a broad definition of 'algorithm', which is understood as 'a defined sequence of steps, taken to solve a problem or obtain a result'.[70] Most importantly, the USMCA considers few exceptions to the protection of source code and related algorithms, being limited to the requirements made by a regulatory body or judicial authority for a specific investigation, inspection, examination enforcement action, or judicial proceeding, subject to safeguards against unauthorised disclosure. Such disclosure shall not be construed to negatively affect software source code's status as a trade secret, if such a status is claimed by the owner. DEPA also deals with algorithms but concerning products that use cryptography and are designed for commercial applications.[71]

7 Personal Data

The protection of personal data in e-commerce or digital trade chapters of Latin American PTAs usually takes two distinctive paths: while one group of provisions

---

[66] Article 13.10(2) PAAP; Article 15.5(c) Central America–Mexico FTA.
[67] The first agreement including this type of provisions is the 2015 Japan–Mongolia FTA.
[68] Article 14.17 CPTPP.
[69] Article 13.16 Australia–Peru FTA.
[70] Article 19.1 USMCA.
[71] Article 3.4 DEPA; Article 19.16 USMCA.

Rodrigo Polanco

TABLE 13.4. *Personal data provisions in Latin American PTAs*

	Privacy issues	Consumer protection
Soft Commitments	33	33
Intermediate Commitments	34	10
Hard Commitments	22	0
Total number of provisions	44	43

deals with it from the point of view of the protection of privacy as a fundamental right (whether or how data is shared, collected, or stored, and regulatory restrictions), another group of provisions regulates the protection of such data as consumer rights. When included, agreements tend to have both privacy and consumers rights provisions, although with different levels of commitment across treaties. Both consumer protection and privacy rules are similar but different takes on the same issue. As we will see, the most binding provisions are related to privacy and not to consumer protection per se.

Few agreements, but increasing in number in recent years, explicitly exclude from the e-commerce chapter the information held or processed by or on behalf of a party or measures related to such information, including measures related to its collection.[72] These provisions put states in an asymmetrical position vis-à-vis international traders and investors, as they exclude governmental data collection and processing from the disciplines dealing with the treatment of personal data. Around half of all PTAs having these provisions have been concluded by Latin American countries (Table 13.4).

A PRIVACY ISSUES Fourty-four Latin American PTAs include provisions on privacy, usually under the concept of 'data protection'. But the way this data is protected varies considerably, a truly mixed bag of binding provisions and non-binding provisions. The 2001 Canada–Costa Rica FTA was the first of these agreements dealing with privacy issues, in a non-binding declaration which is largely programmatic.[73] Later agreements include international cooperation activities to enhance the security of personal data, like sharing information and experiences on regulations, laws, and programmes on data privacy or data protection,[74] or on the overall domestic

---

[72] Article 10.2(2)(c) Brazil–Chile FTA; Article 19.2(1)(b) USMCA; Article 13.2(3)(b) Australia–Peru FTA; Article 11.2(2)(c) Argentina–Chile FTA; Article 8.2(2)(b) Chile–Uruguay FTA; Article 14.2(3)(b) CPTPP; Article 13.2(2)(a) PAAP.

[73] Joint Statement on Global Electronic Commerce, Canada–Costa Rica FTA.

[74] Article 10.8(5) and Article 10.15(b) Brazil–Chile FTA; Article 14.5(2) Central America–Korea FTA; Article 11.5(5) and Article 11.9(b) Argentina–Chile FTA; Article 8.7(4) and Article 8.13(b) Chile–Uruguay FTA; Article 14.11(b) Mexico–Panama FTA; Article 13.8(2) and Article 13.12(b) PAAP; Article 16.5(b) Canada–Honduras FTA; Article 15.5(b) Central America–Mexico FTA; Article 14.7(2)(b) Korea–Peru FTA; Article 1507.1(b) Canada–Colombia FTA; Article 1508(b)

regime for the protection of personal information;[75] technical assistance in the form of exchange of information and experts or the establishment of joint programmes and projects;[76] maintaining a dialogue[77] or hold consultations on matters of data protection;[78] or in general other cooperation mechanisms to ensure the protection of personal data.[79]

While some Latin American PTAs merely recognise the importance or the benefits of protecting personal information online,[80] in several treaties, parties specifically commit to adopting or maintaining legislation or regulations that protect personal data or the privacy of users of e-commerce,[81] in relation to the data's processing and dissemination,[82] which may also include administrative measures.[83] Few agreements consider qualifications to this commitment, like the differences in existing systems for personal data protection,[84] or are explicit in highlighting the 'best efforts' nature of these commitments.[85]

Certain treaties add that when developing online personal data protection standards, each party shall take into account international standards[86] as well as criteria or guidelines of relevant international organisations or bodies[87] – such as the APEC Privacy Framework and the OECD Recommendation of the Council concerning Guidelines governing the Protection of Privacy and Transborder Flows of Personal

Canada–Peru FTA; Article 14.8(b) Colombia–Northern Triangle FTA; Article 14.5(b) Panama–US FTA; Article 12.5(b) Chile–Colombia FTA; Article 14.05(b) Nicaragua–Taiwan FTA; Article 13.4(b) Panama–Singapore FTA; Article 14.5(b) CAFTA–DR–US; Article 15.5(b) Chile–US FTA.

[75] Article 19.14.1(a)(i) USMCA; Article 13.14(b)(i) Australia–Peru FTA; Article 16.6(2) Colombia–Costa Rica FTA; Article 1506.2 Canada–Colombia FTA.
[76] Article 30 Chile–EC AA.
[77] Article 163.1(e) Colombia–EU-Peru FTA.
[78] Article 16.10(1) Australia–Chile FTA.
[79] Article 14.7(1)(a) Central America–Korea FTA; Annex-B, Article 2(e) Colombia–Israel FTA; Article 19.7(1)(b) Colombia–Panama FTA; Article 12.6(1)(c) Colombia–Korea FTA.
[80] Article 14.5(1) Central America–Korea FTA; Article 16.2(2)(e) Canada–Honduras FTA.
[81] Article 10.8(2) Brazil–Chile FTA; Article 19.8(1–2) USMCA; Article 13.8(1–2) Australia–Peru FTA; Article 11.5(1–2) Argentina–Chile FTA; Article 8.7(1–2) Chile–Uruguay FTA; Article 14.8 (1–2) CPTPP; Article 14.8 Mexico–Panama FTA; Article 13.8(1) PAAP; Article 19.6 Colombia–Panama FTA; Article 12.3 Colombia–Korea FTA; Article 55 Chile–China FTA (2018); Article 1506(1) Canada–Colombia FTA.
[82] Annex II, Article 1(c)(i) Central America–EFTA; Annex I, Article 1(c)(i) EFTA–Colombia FTA; Annex I, Article 1(c)(i) EFTA–Peru FTA.
[83] Article 16.6(1) Colombia–Costa Rica FTA; Article 14.7 Korea–Peru FTA; Article 16.8 Australia–Chile FTA; Article 1507 Canada–Peru FTA.
[84] Article 11.7(1)(j) Chile–Thailand FTA.
[85] Annex-B, Article 3 Colombia–Israel FTA.
[86] Article 11.5(1–2) Argentina–Chile FTA; Article 8.7(2) Chile–Uruguay FTA; Article 162.2 Colombia–EU–Peru FTA; Article 119.2 CARIFORUM–EC EPA; Article 202 Chile–EC AA.
[87] Article 14.8(2) CPTPP; Article 14.8 Mexico–Panama FTA; Article 11.7(j) Chile–Thailand FTA; Article 19.6 Colombia–Panama FTA; Article 16.6(1) Colombia–Costa Rica FTA; Article 12.1(2) and Article 12.3 Colombia–Korea FTA; Article 201.2 EU–Central America FTA; Article 16.8 Australia–Chile FTA.

Data (2013).[88] Moreover, in a couple of treaties, the parties commit to publishing information on the protections (regarding personal data) it provides to users of e-commerce,[89] including how individuals can pursue remedies and how businesses can comply with any legal requirements.[90]

Some agreements put a special emphasis on the transfer of personal data, encouraging the use of encryption or security mechanisms for users' personal information, and their anonymisation, in cases where said data is provided to third parties, in accordance with the applicable legislation.[91] Furthermore, in a couple of agreements, parties commit to encouraging the development of mechanisms to promote compatibility between different regimes, recognising that they may take different legal approaches to protect personal information. These may include the recognition of regulatory outcomes, whether accorded autonomously, by mutual arrangement, or in broader international frameworks, and the exchange of information.[92] The USMCA explicitly recognises that the APEC Cross-Border Privacy Rules system is a valid mechanism to facilitate cross-border information transfers while protecting personal information.[93]

But Latin American PTAs have also used more binding options to protect personal information online. A first option is to consider the protection of the privacy of individuals in relation to the processing and dissemination of personal data, as well as the confidentiality of individual records and accounts, as exception in specific chapters of the agreement, usually on telecommunications (to protect the privacy of non-public personal data of subscribers to public telecommunications services),[94] and financial services (adopting adequate safeguards for the protection of privacy and fundamental rights while permitting data transfer and processing).[95] Other agreements merely recognise principles for the collection, processing, and storage of personal data, without developing its content in detail.[96] The USMCA also acknowledges similar principles and the importance of ensuring compliance with measures to protect personal information and ensuring that any restrictions on

---

[88] Article 19.8(2) USMCA.
[89] Article 10.8(4) Brazil–Chile FTA.
[90] Article 19.8(5) USMCA; Article 13.8(4) Australia–Peru FTA; Article 8.7(3) Chile–Uruguay FTA; Article 14.8(4) CPTPP.
[91] Article 10.8(6) Brazil–Chile FTA; Article 11.5(6) Argentina–Chile FTA; Article 8.7(5) Chile–Uruguay FTA.
[92] Article 4.2(6)(7) DEPA Article 13.8(5) Australia–Peru FTA; Article 14.8(5) CPTPP.
[93] Article 19.8(6) USMCA.
[94] Article 18.3(4) USMCA; Article 12.4(4) Australia–Peru FTA; Article 10.3(4) Argentina–Chile FTA; Article 13.3(4) Korea–Peru FTA; Article 13.2(4) Panama–US FTA; Article 13.02(4) Nicaragua–Taiwan FTA; Article 13.2(4) Chile–US FTA.
[95] Annex 17-A USMCA; Article 10.21 Australia–Peru FTA; Annex 11-B CPTPP; Annex XVI – Financial Services, Article 8 EFTA–Colombia FTA; Article 135.1(e)(ii) Chile–EC AA.
[96] Article 11.2.5(f), footnote 1 Argentina–Chile FTA; Article 8.2.5(f), footnote 3 Chile–Uruguay FTA.

cross-border flows of personal information are necessary and proportionate to the risks presented.[97]

A second option focuses on the protection of personal data in specific sectors, like financial services. Some PTAs consider that where the financial information or financial data processing involves personal data, the treatment of such personal data shall be in accordance with the domestic law regulating the protection of such data.[98] A third option leaves the development of rules on data protection to a treaty body. For example, in the 2012 Colombia–EU–Peru FTA (which now includes Ecuador), the Trade Committee may establish a working group with the task of proposing guidelines and strategies enabling the signatory Andean Countries to become a safe harbour for the protection of personal data. To this end, the working group shall adopt a cooperation agenda that shall define priority aspects for accomplishing that purpose, especially regarding the respective homologation processes of data protection systems.[99] A fourth option allows countries to adopt 'appropriate measures' to ensure the protection of privacy while allowing the free movement of data. For that purpose a criterion of 'equivalence' is established, meaning that personal data may be exchanged only where the party that may receive it protects such data in at least an equivalent, similar, or adequate way to the one applicable to that particular case by the party that may supply them. To that end, the parties shall negotiate reciprocal, general, or specific agreements, or in a broader international framework, admitting private sector's implementation of contracts or self-regulation. Up to now, this option has only been introduced in the 2017 Argentina–Chile FTA.[100]

B CONSUMER PROTECTION Overall, forty-three Latin American PTAs include provisions on consumer protection or consumer 'confidence', explicitly applicable to e-commerce or digital trade, which are however largely non-binding. The 2001 Canada–Costa Rica FTA recognised that consumers who participate in electronic commerce should be afforded transparent and effective protection that is not less than the level of protection afforded in other forms of commerce.[101] Later agreements consider international cooperation on consumer protection, like sharing information and experiences on regulations, laws, and programmes,[102] on means

---

[97] Article 19.8(3) USMCA.
[98] Annex 10-A Australia–Peru FTA; Annex 11-A CPTPP; Annex 12-B Korea–Peru FTA; Annex 1205 Canada–Colombia FTA; Annex 12A Australia–Chile FTA; Annex 1105 Canada–Peru FTA; Annex 12.5.1 Colombia–US FTA; Annex 12.5.1 Peru–US FTA; Annex 12.5 Chile–US FTA.
[99] Article 109(b) Colombia–EU–Peru FTA.
[100] Article 11.5(7) Argentina–Chile FTA.
[101] Joint Statement on Global Electronic Commerce, Canada–Costa Rica FTA.
[102] Article 10.15(b) Brazil–Chile FTA; Article 11.9(b) Argentina–Chile FTA; Article 8.13(b) Chile–Uruguay FTA; Article 14.11(b) Mexico–Panama FTA; Article 13.12(b) PAAP; Article 12.6(1)(f) Colombia–Korea FTA; Article 14.5(b) CAFTA-DR-US; Article 15.5(b) Chile–US FTA.

for consumer redress,[103] or in confidence in e-commerce.[104] Other activities include the exchange of best practices, information or views on online protection,[105] or access to products and services offered online;[106] and maintaining dialogue/consultations[107] about the protection in the ambit of electronic commerce,[108] or especially from fraudulent and misleading commercial practices in the cross-border context.[109]

In the 2014 Pacific Alliance Additional Protocol, the parties agree to a number of additional commitments, including cooperation agreements for the cross-border protection of consumer rights; exchanging information about suppliers sanctioned for infringement of those rights; promote prevention measures and training initiatives on the protection of consumer rights in e-commerce and prevention measures; standardise the information that must be provided to consumers in this environment; and encourage e-commerce suppliers to comply with consumer protection regulations in the territory of the party in which the consumer is located.[110] Some Latin American PTAs also deal with consumer protection with reference to the adoption of domestic standards, but largely in a non-binding fashion, 'recognising the importance' of transparent and effective measures to protect consumers from fraudulent and deceptive commercial practices when they engage in e-commerce.[111] But in only a handful of agreements do the parties commit to adopting or

---

[103] Article 13.14(b)(ii) Australia–Peru FTA; Article 14.15(b)(ii) CPTPP; Article 11.7(1)(b) Chile–Thailand FTA.

[104] Article 14.3(2)(f) Mexico–Panama FTA; Article 16.5(b) Canada–Honduras FTA; Article 15.5(b) Central America–Mexico FTA; Article 1507.1(b) Canada–Colombia FTA; Article 1508(b) Canada–Peru FTA; Article 14.8(b) Colombia–Northern Triangle FTA; Article 14.5(b) Panama–US FTA; Article 12.5(b) Chile–Colombia FTA; Article 14.05(b) Nicaragua–Taiwan FTA; Article 13.4(b) Panama–Singapore FTA.

[105] Article 57.3(b) Chile–China FTA (2018).

[106] Article 10.15(c) Brazil–Chile FTA; Article 11.9(c) Argentina–Chile FTA; Article 8.13(c) Chile–Uruguay FTA; Article 14.15(c) CPTPP.

[107] Digital Trade Chapter, Article 11.1(d) EU–Mexico Modernised Global Agreement; Article 202 (c) EC–Central America FTA; Article 120.1(d) CARIFORUM–EC EPA; Article 16.10(1) Australia–Chile FTA.

[108] Article 14.7(1)(d) Central America–Korea FTA; Article 19.7(1)(f) Colombia–Panama FTA.

[109] Article 6.3(7) DEPA,; Article 16.10(1) Australia-Chile FTA; Article 14.7(1)(d) Central America-Korea FTA.

[110] Article 13.6(4–5) PAAP.

[111] Article 6.3(1) DEPA Article 10.7(1) Brazil–Chile FTA; Article 19.7(1) USMCA; Digital Trade Chapter, Article 7.1 EU–Mexico Modernised Global Agreement; Article 14.4(1) Central America–Korea FTA; Article 13.7(1) Australia–Peru FTA; Article 11.4(1) Argentina–Chile FTA; Article 8.6(1) Chile–Uruguay FTA; Article 14.7(1) CPTPP; Article 14.6(1) Mexico–Panama FTA; Article 13.6(1) PAAP; Article 16.4(1) Canada–Honduras FTA; Annex-B, Article 5.1 Colombia–Israel FTA; Article 19.4(1) Colombia–Panama FTA; Annex II, Article 1(c)(iii) Central America–EFTA; Article 16.4(1) Colombia–Costa Rica FTA; Article 12.5(1) Colombia–Korea FTA; Article 14.5(1) Korea–Peru FTA; Annex I, Article 1(c)(iii) EFTA–Peru FTA; Annex I, Article 1(c)(iii) EFTA–Colombia FTA; Article 1504.1 Canada–Colombia FTA; Article 13.2 Peru–Singapore FTA; Article 1505.1 Canada–Peru FTA; Article 14.6(1) Colombia–Northern Triangle FTA; Article 12.6 Chile–Colombia FTA; Article 15.5(1) Colombia–Peru FTA; Article 15.5 Peru–US FTA.

maintaining consumer protection laws to prescribe these practices when they cause harm or potential harm to consumers.[112] Certain treaties also recognise the importance of cooperation between the respective national consumer protection agencies on activities related to cross-border electronic commerce,[113] or exchanging information and experiences in order to enhance consumer protection.[114] Few agreements consider that the parties may evaluate the use of alternative dispute resolution mechanisms,[115] or even online dispute settlement for the protection of consumer, if feasible.[116]

But Latin American PTAs have also used more binding options to tackle consumer protection. Some establish a criterion of 'equivalence' that each party shall provide, where possible and in a manner considered appropriate, protection for consumers using e-commerce that is at least equivalent to that provided for consumers and other forms of commerce under their respective domestic laws, regulations, and policies.[117] Furthermore, the 2008 Australia–Chile FTA considers specific businesses obligations to protect consumers in e-commerce, including acting in accordance with fair business, advertising, and marketing practices, like providing accurate, clear, and easily accessible information about goods or services offered; avoiding ambiguity on intent to make a purchase; and provide easy-to-use, secure payment mechanisms and information on the level of security such mechanisms afford.[118]

II *Rules on Data*

Several Latin American PTAs include general provisions on cross-border flow of data. These are found in both electronic commerce/digital trade chapters, as well as in dedicated chapters of sectors, where data flows play a central role, like

---

[112] Article 10.7(2) Brazil–Chile FTA; Article 19.7(2) USMCA; Digital Trade Chapter, Article 7.2 EU–Mexico Modernised Global Agreement; Article 13.7(2) Australia–Peru FTA; Article 11.4(2) Argentina–Chile FTA; Article 8.6(2) Chile–Uruguay FTA; Article 14.7(2) CPTPP.

[113] Article 19.7(3) USMCA; Article 8.78(2) EU–Japan FTA; Digital Trade Chapter, Article 7.3 EU–Mexico Modernised Global Agreement; Article 14.4(2) Central America–Korea FTA; Article 13.7(3) Australia–Peru FTA; Article 11.4(4) Argentina–Chile FTA; Article 8.6(4) Chile–Uruguay FTA; Article 14.7(3) CPTPP; Annex-B, Article 5.2 Colombia–Israel FTA; Article 19.4(2) Colombia–Panama FTA; Article 16.4(2) Colombia–Costa Rica FTA; Article 12.5(2) Colombia–Korea FTA; Article 14.6(2) Colombia–Northern Triangle FTA; Article 15.5 (2) Korea–US FTA; Article 15.5(2) Colombia–Peru FTA.

[114] Article 10.7(4) Brazil–Chile FTA; Article 13.6(2) PAAP; Article 16.4(2) Canada–Honduras FTA; Article 14.4(2) Korea–Peru FTA; Article 1504.2 Canada–Colombia FTA; Article 1505.2 Canada–Peru FTA.

[115] Article 14.6(2) Mexico–Panama FTA; Article 13.6(3) PAAP; Article 16.4(3) Colombia–Costa Rica FTA.

[116] Article 10.7(4) Brazil–Chile FTA.

[117] Article 6.3(8) DEPA Article 11.7(k) Chile–Thailand FTA; Article 54 Chile–China FTA; Article 16.7(1–2)(a) Australia–Chile FTA.

[118] Article 16.7(2)(b) and Article 16.7(3) Australia–Chile FTA.

TABLE 13.5. *Data flow provisions in Latin American PTAs*

	Data flows			
	General	Financial services	Telecommunications	Data localisation
Soft Commitments	6	0	1	1
Intermediate Commitments	4	0	0	0
Hard Commitments	8	33	31	8
Total Number of Provisions	18	33	32	9

telecommunications and financial services. Around half of all FTAs including data flow provisions have been concluded by Latin American countries (Table 13.5).

Two types of data-related provisions are found on Latin American PTAs with e-commerce or digital trade chapters: (i) those referring to cross-border flow of data and (ii) those banning or limiting data localisation requirements, the former being more common, but with different levels of commitments across agreements.

1 Data Flows

There are basically two sets of provisions concerning data flows in Latin American PTAs: one binding, directly guaranteeing the free flow of data, the other non-binding, considering cross-border information flows as part of the cooperation activities between the parties. Few agreements consider some 'intermediate' type of clauses, including best endeavour provisions and commitments to future negotiations on data flows. PTAs concluded by Latin American countries are the largest group of trade agreements that include data flow provisions (thirty-nine agreements out of seventy-nine). Non-binding provisions on data flows appeared earlier. The first agreement having this type of provisions is the 2006 Taiwan–Nicaragua FTA, where as part of the cooperation activities, the parties affirmed the importance of working 'to maintain cross-border flows of information as an essential element to promote a dynamic environment for electronic commerce'.[119] A similar wording is used in later agreements concluded by Peru, Mexico, Colombia, Costa Rica, and other Central American countries.[120] An intermediate type of provision is where the parties agree to consider commitments related to cross-border flow of information in future negotiations. This type of clause is found in the 2015 Pacific Alliance

[119] Article 14.05(c) Nicaragua–Taiwan FTA.
[120] Article 1508(c) Canada–Peru FTA; Article 14.9(c) Korea–Peru FTA; Article 15.5(d) Central America–Mexico FTA; Article 16.7(c) Colombia–Costa Rica FTA; Article 16.5(c) Canada–Honduras FTA.

Additional Protocol[121] and in the Modernisation of the Trade part of the EU–Mexico Global Agreement, currently under negotiation.[122] In the latter, the parties commit to 'reassess', within three years of the entry into force of the agreement, the need for inclusion of provisions on the free flow of data.

The first agreement having a binding provision on cross-border information flows is the 2014 Mexico–Panama FTA. According to this treaty, each party 'shall allow its persons and the persons of the other Party to transmit electronic information, from and to its territory, when required by said person, in accordance with the applicable legislation on the protection of personal data and taking into consideration international practices'.[123] A much more detailed provision is found in the 2015 amended version of the PAAP,[124] which was then included in the 2016 TPP, and the TPP template has largely influenced subsequent agreements with data flow provisions.

After recognising that each party may have its own regulatory requirements concerning the transfer of information by electronic means, both the PAAP and the TPP stipulate that each party shall allow the cross-border transfer of information by electronic means, including personal information, when this activity is for the conduct of the business of a covered person. This shall not prevent a party from adopting or maintaining measures to achieve a legitimate public policy objective, provided that the measure is not applied in a manner which would constitute a means of arbitrary or unjustifiable discrimination or a disguised restriction on trade; and does not impose restrictions on transfers of information greater than are required to achieve the objective. The same provision was kept in the 2018 CPTPP, signed after the withdrawal of the United States from the TPP and in DEPA.[125]

After TPP, a similar hard rule on data flows has been incorporated into other trade agreements concluded by Chile, Argentina, Peru, Mexico, and Brazil, largely following the same wording.[126] In the 2017 Argentina–Chile FTA, there is a specific reference that the parties undertake to apply to the data received from the other party a level of protection that is at least similar to that applicable to the party from which the data originates, through mutual, general, or specific agreements.[127] In the USMCA, a footnote clarifies that a measure restricting data flows is not considered to achieve a legitimate public policy objective, if 'it accords different treatment of data transfers solely on the basis that they are cross-border in a manner that modifies the conditions of competition to the detriment of the service suppliers of the other Party'.[128]

---

[121] Article 13.11 PAAP.
[122] Digital Trade Chapter, Article XX EU–Mexico Modernised Global Agreement.
[123] Article 14.10 Mexico–Panama FTA.
[124] Article 13.11 PAAP.
[125] Article 14.11 CPTPP.
[126] Article 4.3 DEPA Article 8.10 Chile–Uruguay FTA; Article 11.6 Argentina–Chile FTA; Article 13.11 Australia–Peru FTA; Article 19.11 USMCA; Article 10.12 Brazil–Chile FTA.
[127] Article 11.6(2) and 11.5(7) Argentina–Chile FTA.
[128] Article 11.19, footnote 6 USMCA.

2 Data Localisation

In recent years, some preferential trade agreements have also started to include provisions on data localisation, either banning or limiting such requirements. An important difference with data flow provisions analysed in the previous section is that the large majority of data localisation provisions are of a binding nature. Again, PTAs concluded by Latin American countries are the largest group of trade agreements that include data flow provisions (nine agreements out of seventeen). The 2015 amended version of the Pacific Alliance Protocol includes a provision on the use and location of computer facilities, stipulating that no party may require a covered person to use or locate computer facilities in the territory of that party as a condition for the exercise of its business activity. An exception in this regard considers that nothing shall prevent a party from adopting or maintaining measures to achieve a legitimate public policy objective, provided that such measures are not applied in a manner that constitutes a means of arbitrary or unjustifiable discrimination, or a disguised restriction to trade.[129]

In 2016, the TPP considered largely the same provision on location of computing facilities, requiring in addition that such measures shall not impose restrictions on the use or location of computing facilities greater than are required to achieve the objective. The same provision was kept in the 2018 CPTPP.[130] A similar hard rule on data localisation largely following the same wording was included in the 2016 Chile–Uruguay FTA and in DEPA.[131] The 2018 Brazil–Chile FTA has a minor deviation from the TPP drafting, as it does not require that data localisation provisions are the least restrictive measure to achieve the public policy objectives. In this regard, its wording is closer to the PAAP.[132]

A more succinct version of this type of provision is found in the USMCA, which stipulates that no party shall require a covered person to use or locate computing facilities in that party's territory as a condition for conducting business in that territory, without considering any further exception.[133] One of the few provisions on data localisation that are not directly binding is found in the 2017 Argentina–Chile FTA. Under this treaty, the parties merely 'recognise the importance' of not requiring a person of the other party to use or locate the computer facilities in the territory of that party, as a condition for conducting business in that territory. To this end, the parties undertake to exchange good practices, experiences, and current regulatory frameworks regarding the location of servers.[134]

---

[129] Article 13.11*bis* PAAP.
[130] Article 14.13 CPTPP.
[131] Article 4.4 DEPA Article 8.11 Chile–Uruguay FTA.
[132] Article 9.10 Singapore–Sri Lanka FTA; Article 13.12 Australia–Peru FTA; Article 10.13 Brazil–Chile FTA.
[133] Article 19.12 USMCA.
[134] Article 11.7 Argentina–Chile FTA.

D LEGAL FRAMEWORK OF E-COMMERCE AND PERSONAL DATA PROTECTION IN LATIN AMERICAN COUNTRIES

As mentioned, a group of five Latin American countries, Chile, Colombia, Costa Rica, Panama, and Peru, have concluded an important number of trade agreements with clauses or chapters on e-commerce and data flows, representing around half of all the PTAs that include these provisions. In this section we examine whether the domestic legal framework of these countries corresponds to their international commitments, taking as a case study the regulation of data protection.

Most Latin American countries, sharing the tradition of European continental civil law, have recognised the right to the protection of personal data and the right to privacy as separate legal notions. Several Constitutions of the region recognise explicitly the right to privacy, but those of Argentina, Brazil, Colombia, Mexico, Peru, and Venezuela also include the 'habeas data', or the right to the protection of personal data. But even in countries where this mechanism is not expressly contained in the Constitution, the relevant courts have recognised the 'right to control' personal information.[135]

Chile, Colombia, Costa Rica, Panama, and Peru have also domestic regulations on the processing of personal data in both the public and private sectors. Chile was the first to introduce such framework in 1999, followed by Colombia in 2008.[136] However, in most of these countries there are concerns on the proactive application of data protection laws and regulations by their respective Data Protection Authority (DPA) – and in some cases such authority does not exist. Other challenges commonly mentioned are the harmonisation of cross-border cooperation for the protection of privacy with other DPAs and police and judicial authorities; the promotion of privacy management programmes including obligations to respond, inform, and compensate data owners in case of violation of security that affects personal information; and the enhancement of interoperability with other regional and national privacy and data protection frameworks.[137]

I *Chile*

The regulation of electronic commerce in Chile is largely contained in the general domestic legislation (e.g. Code of Commerce, Civil Code). Only in some cases,

---

[135] A. J. Cerda Silva, 'Protección de datos personales y Prestación de servicios en línea en América Latina', in E. A. Bertoni (ed), *Hacia una Internet libre de censura: Propuestas para América Latina* (Buenos Aires: Universidad de Palermo, Facultad de Derecho, Centro de Estudios en Libertad de Expresión y Acceso a la Información, 2012), 165–180, at 169–170.

[136] G. Greenleaf, 'Countries with Data Privacy Laws – By Year 1973–2019', SSRN Publication (2019), at 1, available at https://papers.ssrn.com/sol3/papers.cfm?abstract_id=3386510.

[137] C. Aguerre, 'Digital Trade in Latin America: Mapping Issues and Approaches', *Digital Policy, Regulation and Governance* 21 (2018), 2–18, at 10.

special norms have been created to respond to the challenges posed by new technologies. In 2002, Chile adopted a law on electronic documents and electronic signature (Law 19,799) which explicitly recognises the legal principles of freedom to provide services, free competition, technological neutrality, international compatibility, and equivalence of electronic support to paper support, meaning that everything contained in electronic format has the same validity as a paper document.[138] However, self-regulation of e-commerce as a complement of legal norms is still very relevant.[139]

Although rules on the protection of consumer rights were established back in 1997 (Law 19,496), these norms did not refer to e-commerce until 2004, when amendments introduced by the Law 19,955 included explicit provisions to deal with the challenges posed by digital commerce.[140] In 1999, Chile enacted the oldest personal data protection regulation in the region, the Law 19,628 'On the protection of private life', which include provisions on the treatment of personal information in public and private databases. The law has been amended a couple of times: firstly, forbidding credit risk predictions or assessments that are not based on objective data like late payments of natural or legal persons (Law 20,521 of 2011); and secondly, establishing the principle of finality in the treatment of personal data of economic, banking, financial, or commercial nature (Law 20,575). Some other sectoral laws deal with data protection, like the regulation prohibiting the inclusion of sensitive personal data in 'active transparency' public websites (Law 20,285 of 2008); or the law making all information regarding healthcare procedures and treatments sensitive data (Law 20,584 of 2015).[141]

This regulation has been criticised for its lack of enforcement, being outdated and insufficient for the expectations of both private sectors and regulators,[142] and lacking a specific and independent institution that serves to effectively protect the rights associated with data processing.[143] In response to those criticisms in June 2018, a Constitutional amendment[144] recognised the 'right to personal data protection', complementing the protection already granted to private life, as well as the honour of the person and their family.[145] A bill of law to implement this right that would

---

[138] Ley 19.799, Sobre documentos electrónicos, firma electrónica y servicios de certificación de dicha firma, published in the Official Gazette 12 April 2002.

[139] D. López Jiménez, 'La autorregulación del comercio electrónico en Chile', *Iuris Tantum Revista Boliviana de Derecho* 21 (2016), 174–208.

[140] Ley 19.496, Establece normas sobre protección de los derechos de los consumidores, published in the Official Gazette 7 March 1997.

[141] K. Lucente and J. Clark (eds), *Handbook: Global Data Protection Laws of the World* (Washington, DC: DLA Piper, 2020), at 128–129.

[142] H. J. Lehuedé, 'Corporate Governance and Data Protection in Latin America and the Caribbean', UN Production Development No 223 (LC/TS.2019/38) (2019), at 39.

[143] 'Historia de la Ley N 21.096, consagra el derecho a protección de los datos personales', *Biblioteca del Congreso Nacional de Chile*, at 3.

[144] Ley 21.096, published in the Official Gazette 16 June 2018.

[145] Constitución de la República de Chile, Article 19.4.

introduce a data protection system similar to the EU's General Data Protection Regulation (GDPR) and the creation of a DPA is still under discussion at the Chilean Congress.[146] None of the existing domestic rules mentioned earlier contain any restrictions on international transfer of data, but the bill of law currently discussed at the Congress includes certain restrictions derived from the express recognition of principles, such as consent, finality (in general terms, not only for the specific sectors mentioned earlier), proportionality, quality, security, liability, and legality of data processing.[147]

II *Peru*

Peru largely relies on general civil law to address electronic commerce issues, although it has included special provisions on e-commerce in consumer protection laws,[148] like the 'Law on Digital Signatures and Certificates' (Law 27,269 of 2000) which regulates electronic signatures and gives them the same validity and legal effect as handwritten signatures; and the 'Anti-spam Law' (Law 28,493 of 2005), which governs the use of non-solicited advertisement e-mailing.[149]

Under the 1993 Peruvian Constitution, everyone has the right that information services, computerised or not, public or private, do not provide information that affects personal and family privacy. Furthermore, the Constitution limits the right to request and receive information from any public entity, in cases where the information affects personal privacy, or those that expressly are excluded by law or for reasons of national security. The Constitution also protects bank secrecy and tax reservation, which can only be lifted at the request of the judge, the National Prosecutor, or a congressional investigative commission in accordance with the law.[150] The Peruvian Constitution establishes the guarantee of 'habeas data' (which proceeds against the acts or omissions, by any authority, official or person that violates or threatens to violate the aforementioned rights).[151] The proceedings of the habeas data were initially detailed in a separate law (Law 26,301 of 1994), but are now included in the Constitutional Procedural Code (Law 28,237).[152]

---

[146] 'Ley de datos personales fortalecerá sector de servicios digitales, pero exige ajustes a empresas', *Seguridad Digital*, 2020, available at https://seguridaddigital.emol.com/noticias/ley-de-datos-personales-fortalecera-sector-de-servicios-digitales-pero-exige-ajustes-a-empresas/.
[147] Lehuedé, note 142.
[148] UNCTAD, Intergovernmental Group of Experts on Consumer Protection Law and Policy: Consumer Protection in Electronic Commerce, 2nd Session, 3–4 July 2017, TD/B/C.I/CPLP/7, Geneva, 24 April 2017, at 14.
[149] J. A. Olaechea, 'Doing Business in Peru: Overview', *Thomson Reuter Practical Law*, 1 May 2020.
[150] Constitución Política del Perú, Article 2.5 and 6.
[151] Constitución Política del Perú, Article 200.3.
[152] J. B. B. Lartirigoyen, 'El nuevo código procesal constitucional del perú: una visión introspectiva', *Anuario de Derecho Constitucional Latinoamericano* I (2005), 353–360.

Based on the Constitutional provisions referred to earlier, the Personal Data Protection Law (PDLP – Law 29,733 of 2011) specifically protects the use of personal data of any natural person and applies to both private and state entities. In March 2013, the PDLP was complemented by a Regulation (Supreme Decree 003-2013-JUS) that develops, clarifies, and expands its requirements and set forth specific rules, terms, and provisions regarding data protection. Another statute (Law 27,489 of 2001) regulates activities related to risk centres and companies that handle sensitive personal data and information posing higher risks to individuals (like that related to financial, commercial, tax, employment or insurance obligations or background of a natural or legal person that allows evaluating its economic solvency).[153]

Peruvian PDLP was criticised for the lack of a DPA, which was finally created by Legislative Decree 1,357 of 2017. Today, the Directorate for the Protection of Personal Data is the primary agency in charge of enforcing data protection matters, which is part of the General Directorate of Transparency, Access to Public Information and Protection of Personal Data (NDPA). Yet, the fact that the DPA is not autonomous and is under the authority of the Ministry of Justice has been criticised by sectors of the civil society.[154]

The 2017 reform also strengthened the regime for the protection of personal data and the regulation of interest management. According to Article 15 of the Law 29,733 transfers of personal data beyond Peruvian territory require consent from data subjects, and they can only be transferred to jurisdictions with 'adequate' levels of data protection,[155] or to jurisdictions with lower levels, subject to a privacy guarantee from the data controller. However, some transfers of personal data are generally allowed, like those that take place as part of an international treaty on cross-border flow of personal data in which Peru is a party (which would include the PTAs mentioned in the first part of this chapter); international judicial cooperation or among intelligence agencies; those needed to execute a contractual relationship, medical treatment or a scientific or professional relation involving the owner of the personal data subject; and those conducted for bank or stock transfers trading. Notification to the DPA is required for international transfers.[156]

III *Panama*

Electronic commerce in Panama is governed by the Law 51 of 2008 (amended by Law 82 of 2012), and a couple of Executive Decrees (No. 40 of 2009 and No. 684 of

[153] Lucente and Clark, note 141, at 573.

[154] E. Artaza, 'Decreto Legislativo No 1353 La búsqueda de transparencia', *Vigilia Ciudadana Piura*, 14 December 2020, available at https://vigiliaciudadana.org/2020/12/14/decreto-legislativo-no-1353-la-busqueda-de-transparencia/.

[155] Following Article 11 Law 29,733, we should understand that 'adequate' means a sufficient level of protection guaranteed for the personal data to be processed or, at least, comparable to the provisions of that law or international standards on the subject.

[156] Lehuedé, note 142, at 46.

2013), which regulate the creation, use, and storage of electronic documents and signatures, using a registration process, as well as the supervision of providers of data storage services.[157] The regulation was based on the 1996 UNCITRAL Model Law on electronic commerce and provides for enforcement through the General Directorate of Electronic Commerce (DGCE).[158]

Until 2018, Panama did not have a law dedicated to the protection of personal data. A bill regulating this issue was introduced in the Congress in August 2018 and approved in October the same year. The Law of Protection of Personal Data (Law 81 of 2019) was promulgated only on 31 March 2019. The new law establishes that the processing of personal data may only be carried out when there is consent of the owner or when the law permits it.[159] The legislation is applicable to all databases[160] containing personal information, whether of nationals or foreigners, who are within the territory of the Republic of Panama or whose data controller is domiciled in the country. The cross-border treatment of personal data originated or stored in Panama that is confidential, sensitive, or restricted is permitted provided that the data controller and the country of destination of the data comply with protection standards that are equal or superior to those indicated in Law 81. However, the same regulation considers several exceptions to this rule – for example, when owners of the data have given their consent for the transfer and cross-border treatment; when the transfer is necessary for the execution, present or future, of a contract in the interest of the owner; when it is related to bank transfers, money, and stock market securities; when it is information required by law under international agreements or treaties signed by Panama.[161] Law 81 also establishes that those responsible or custodians of a database that transfer personal data to third parties must keep a record of them, which must be available to the newly created National Authority of Transparency and Access to Information (ANTAI), but only in case that such authority would require it. The same law also creates a Council for the Protection of Personal Data, which makes recommendations of public policies and evaluates cases entailing the protection of personal data, and also provides advice to ANTAI.[162] The actual implementation of this new law is a matter that cannot be ascertained at the moment of this writing.

[157] Lucente and Clark, note 141, at 568.
[158] K. Michalczewsky and A. Ramos, 'E-Regulación en América Latina', *Conexion Intal*, 8 March 2017.
[159] Ley 81 de Protección de datos personales en Panamá, available at https://www.gacetaoficial.gob .pa/pdfTemp/28743_A/GacetaNo_28743a_20190329.pdf.
[160] The same law defines 'databases' as an ordered group of data of any nature, whatever the form or modality of their creation, organisation or storage, which allows the data to be related to each other, as well as any type of processing or transmission of these by their custodian. Article 4.2 Ley 81 de 26 de Marzo de 2019.
[161] Ibid., Article 5.
[162] Ibid., Articles 31 and 34.

IV *Colombia*

The regulation of e-commerce in Colombia is found mainly in Law 527 of 1997 or 'Electronic Commerce Law', which establishes the 'principle of functional equivalence', between electronic signature and autograph signatures, data messages and written documents, and sets up rules for the certification of digital signatures and for the creation of certification entities. Several additional laws complement this framework on consumer protection, like the Law 1,480 of 2011, which establishes special obligations for suppliers of goods and services that are offered using electronic means like special information duties (identification of provider, characteristics of the goods, means of payment available, contract text, etc.), duties to conserve information, and procedures of filing petitions, complaints, and claims.[163]

The Colombian Constitution recognises two fundamental personal data rights: the right to privacy and the right to data rectification.[164] Personal data processing is further regulated by two statutory laws and several decrees that set out data protection obligations. The first one, the 'Habeas Data Law' (Law 1,266) was enacted in 2008, after intense discussions, and regulates the handling of information contained in some personal databases,[165] especially of financial, credit, commercial, services data collected in Colombia or abroad.

In 2012, a statutory law for the protection of personal data was enacted (Law 1,581). This statute regulates personal data processing, as well as databases including special rules for sensitive data and data collected from minors. The law further regulates data processing authorisation and procedures, and creates the National Register of Data Bases (NRDB) administered by the Superintendence of Industry and Commerce (SIC, the Colombian DPA). Law 1,581 is applicable to all data collection and processing in Colombia.[166] Under Article 26 of Law 1,581 of 2012, transfers of private or semi-private personal data must be authorised by data subjects and are not allowed to jurisdictions that the SIC regards as not providing 'adequate' levels of management of personal data. It is understood that a country offers an adequate level of data protection when it complies with the standards set by the SIC on the subject, which in no case may be less than those required by the Law 1,581. Exceptionally, beyond those cases, international transfers are allowed for exchange of financial information for transfers and banking operations; for medical, health,

---

[163] N. Barrera Silva, 'Marco regulatorio del comercio electrónico', *DocPlayer*, 18 March 2018, available at http://docplayer.es/87917391-Marco-regulatorio-del-comercio-electronico-natalia-barrera-silva-mayo-24-2018.html.

[164] Article 15 Constitución Política de Colombia.

[165] Interestingly, that law does not include a definition of 'database' and with the only exception of the title of such act, that term is not actually used in the text of the law. The notion of 'databank' is referred several times in the text, but also without any specific definition. Four years later, the Law 1,581 defined database as 'an organised set of personal data that is the subject of treatment' (Article 3.b).

[166] Lucente and Clark, note 141, at 139–140.

and public hygiene reasons; pursuant to international treaties joined by Colombia; for contracts involving the data subject and a counterpart; and when required by public interest.[167]

Despite the existing regulation, it has been criticized that Colombia still does not have successful initiatives that seek to adapt the personal data protection regime to the era of big data and the digital economy. Some scholars find fault with the fact that this law focuses on the protection of commercial and financial data and leaves normative gaps preventing the complete protection of personal data in Colombia.[168] Others have pointed out that the law is not applicable to those responsible or in charge of data processing that do not reside or are not domiciled in Colombia, even though they perform operations on personal data of persons who reside, are domiciled or located in Colombia.[169]

V *Costa Rica*

Currently in Costa Rica there is no electronic commerce law or framework that regulates all the essential aspects of online commerce. In 2013, a bill on services for the information society (or 'Electronic Commerce Law') was presented to the Legislative Assembly but has not been approved yet.[170] However, some related laws have already been enacted, such as the Law 8,454 of 2005, of certificates, digital signatures, and electronic documents.[171] Additionally, in 2017, a reform of the Regulation to the Law of Promotion of Competition and Effective Defence of the Consumer, introduced a new chapter on Consumer Protection in the Context of Electronic Commerce.[172]

Data privacy regulation in Costa Rica is contained in two laws – the Law 7,975 of 2000, 'Undisclosed Information Law', which makes it a crime to disclose confidential and/or personal information without authorisation, and the Law 8,968 of 2011 on Protection in the Handling of the Personal Data of Individuals (amended in 2016), which together with its by-laws, regulates the activities of companies that administer databases containing personal information, and recognises the 'Right to Self-Determination of Information', which includes access, rectification, cancellation,

---

[167] Lehuedé, note 142, at 42.
[168] M. Rojas Bejarano, 'Evolución del derecho de protección de datos personales en Colombia respecto a estándares Internacionales', *Novum Jus: Revista Especializada en Sociología Jurídica y Política* 8 (2014), 107–139, at 119.
[169] V. Newman Pont and M. P. Ángel Arango, *Rendición de cuentas de Google y otros negocios en Colombia* (Bogotá: Centro de Estudios de Derecho, Justicia y Sociedad, Dejusticia, 2019), at 16. However, the feasibility and the benefit of applying extraterritorial jurisdiction could also be debated.
[170] V. Sánchez del Castillo, 'Qué pasó con la ley de comercio electrónico?', *La Nacion*, 12 November 2017.
[171] Ley 8.454, published in the Official Gazette 13 October 2005.
[172] Reforma reglamento a la Ley de Promoción de la Competencia y Defensa Efectiva del Consumidor 7472, published in the Official Gazette 3 October 2017.

and opposition to the processing of personal data. The same law created the Agency for the Protection of Data of Inhabitants (PRODHAB), as the DPA and regulatory body of databases and requires the mandatory paid registration of all databases, public or private, for distribution, dissemination or commercialisation purposes.[173]

Concerning transfers of data, Law 8,968 stipulates that controllers of public or private databases can transfer personal data only if the data subject has provided express and valid consent. However, the law is not clear whether this provision relates to transfers within Costa Rica or transfers to a third country.[174] As a consequence of such unclear regulation, the transfers of personal information from a database to a service supplier, technological intermediary, or entities in the same 'economic interest group' are not considered as transfers of personal information and therefore do not need authorisation from the data subject.[175]

The local press has reported that the main weakness in the protection of information is the lack of care for the users when disclosing personal data, without reviewing the conditions of use. Additionally, the lack of registration of private-led databases (despite the fact that is a mandatory procedure) and the lack of adequate human and financial resources of PRODHAB have been criticised.[176]

E CONCLUSION

As we have seen throughout this chapter, a group of Latin American countries have pioneered the inclusion of e-commerce and data flow provisions in preferential trade agreements. These countries have done so, in a largely consistent way, with an important level of regulatory convergence on certain objectives and principles (like facilitate and promote e-commerce, avoid unnecessary barriers, and address the needs of SMEs), as well as on specific commitments, such as moratorium on custom duties, electronic authentication, source code, consumer protection, personal data, data flows and data localisation, yet, with different levels of legalisation. These principles and commitments were largely developed in the conclusion of PTAs with developed countries.

But Latin American countries have also advanced new principles on e-commerce and data flows in the conclusion of trade agreements. Around half of all PTAs including data flow provisions on telecommunications or financial services have been concluded by Latin American countries, and the 2014 Mexico–Panama FTA was the first PTA with general binding provision on cross-border information flows. Latin American PTAs are the largest group of treaties that include provisions either

---

[173] Lucente and Clark, note 141, at 146.
[174] 'Costa Rica – Data Protection', *DataGuidance*, June 2020, available at https://www.dataguidance .com/notes/costa-rica-data-protection-overview.
[175] Lucente and Clark, note 141, at 147.
[176] C. Cordero Pérez, 'Eliminación de datos personales provocó mayoría de las 133 denuncias ante agencia de protección', *El Financiero*, 3 April 2019.

banning or limiting requirements of data localisation. Additionally, the largest number of agreements including provisions on stakeholder's participation or the principle of 'technological neutrality' has also been concluded by Latin American countries. Only three PTAs explicitly recognise the principle of 'net neutrality'[177] and all have been concluded between Latin American countries.[178]

A further testimony to the creative role of Latin American countries on these topics is the announcement made on 18 May 2019 on the side lines of the Asia-Pacific Economic Cooperation (APEC) meeting of Ministers Responsible for Trade in Viña del Mar, Chile, of the start of the negotiations of a Digital Economy Partnership Agreement (DEPA) between Chile, Singapore, and New Zealand.[179] The agreement was finally concluded on 21 January 2020 covering all aspects of the digital economy to support trade in the digital era, and also going beyond existing commitments, looking at a range of emerging issues, like cross-border data flows, digital identities, artificial intelligence, electronic invoicing, and open government data.

However, the five examined Latin American countries have not all had the same consistency at domestic level, with national regulations on certain topics addressed in PTAs that lag behind what has been committed to in those agreements, particularly on the issue of data protection. The Organization of American States (OAS) has reported that a consistent and coherent regional approach to the protection of personal data has not yet emerged in Latin America. In 2015, the Inter-American Juridical Committee adopted a 'Proposal for the Declaration of Principles of Privacy and Protection of Personal Data in the Americas' with the purpose of urging the OAS member states to adopt measures to respect privacy, reputation, and dignity of people in the Americas.[180] At the same time, a group of five countries of the region that are considered to have a moderate (Chile, Colombia, Costa Rica, Peru) or limited (Panama) data protection[181] are leading the conclusion of PTAs including digital trade and data flow provisions. While these provisions are not all binding, general provisions on data flows, as well as on specific sectors (financial services and telecommunications), have become commonplace in recent years. In contrast, data protection provisions in these PTAs are largely non-binding or their scope of application is left to domestic regulations.

The different levels of commitment and approaches on these issues found in these five countries between the international and domestic regulation, as well as

[177] Net neutrality is understood here as a principle to prevent certain contents or applications on the Internet being discriminated in favour of others. C. B. Graber, 'Bottom-Up Constitutionalism: The Case of Net Neutrality', *Transnational Legal Theory* 7 (2016), 524–552.
[178] Net neutrality was also implicitly endorsed in Article 14.10 CPTPP.
[179] The text of DEPA is available at www.mfat.govt.nz/en/trade/free-trade-agreements/free-trade-agreements-concluded-but-not-in-force/digital-economy-partnership-agreement/.
[180] Inter-American Juridical Committee, Privacy and Data Protection, Eighty-Sixth Regular Session, 23–27 March, held in Rio de Janeiro, Brazil, CJI/Doc. 474/15 Rev. 2, 26 March 2015.
[181] Lucente and Clark, note 141.

their implementation (or lack thereof), potentially create the possibility of future conflicts, if some of these countries intend to change the domestic regime for data protection. If both regimes are not well-coordinated, Latin American countries could be limited in their policy space to enact rules that contradict international commitments. For example, from the group of countries mentioned earlier, only Colombia, Panama, and Peru have established a criterion of equivalence for the international transfer of personal data, meaning that those countries agree that personal data may be exchanged only where the party which may receive them undertakes to protect such data in at least an 'adequate' way to the one applicable to the party from where that data originates. In all the PTAs examined in this chapter, we find such a rule only in the 2017 Argentina–Chile FTA.

In several of these countries discussions are taking place to reform data protection laws to a model that is closer to the EU's GDPR. Up to now, the only Latin American countries the EU has determined as having and adequate levels of data protection under the GDPR are Argentina and Uruguay.[182] What would happen if other countries of the region made a policy change to be GDPR adequate and implement their own adequacy policies? Could that be a violation of PTA commitments to allow the cross-border transfer of information by electronic means that do not include such exception?[183] Is this a problem waiting to happen?

A matter for further research is to determine why these Latin American countries have pioneered the development and diffusion of electronic commerce and data flow provisions in PTAs. Is this a sort of path dependency or the influence of third countries, a reaction to particular economic interests, or rather the will to be in a position of rule-makers and not rule-takers?[184] The answers to these questions could help to shed a light on the development of new rules for digital trade.

---

[182] European Commission, 'Adequacy Decisions: How the EU Determines if a Non-EU Country Has an Adequate Level of Data Protection', available at https://ec.europa.eu/info/law/law-topic/data-protection/international-dimension-data-protection/adequacy-decisions_en.

[183] As mentioned earlier, only Peru considers that international treaties with provisions on cross-border flow of personal data in which Peru is a party may be an exception to the domestic 'adequacy' rule.

[184] See Chapter 2 Elsig and Klotz in this volume.

14

Uploading CPTPP and USMCA Provisions to the WTO's Digital Trade Negotiations Poses Challenges for National Data Regulation

Example from Canada

Patrick Leblond*

A INTRODUCTION

Policymakers face a tension between, on the one hand, generating the economic benefits associated with unfettered data flows across borders and, on the other hand, providing a trusting environment for individuals, firms and governments taking part in the data-driven economy. International trade agreements seek to regulate data flows through provisions aiming to facilitate the cross-border trade of goods and services built on data, such as data processing and other computing services.[1]

On the margins of the G20 leaders' meeting in Osaka in June 2019, twenty-three countries plus the European Union (EU) signed the Osaka Declaration on the Digital Economy.[2] The declaration states that the signatories, 'standing together with other World Trade Organization (WTO) Members that participate in the Joint Statement on Electronic Commerce issued in Davos on 25 January 2019, in which 78 WTO Members are on board, hereby declare the launch of the "Osaka Track", a process which demonstrates our commitment to promote international policy discussions'. The referred-to January 2019 Joint Statement, issued during the World Economic Forum's annual meeting in Davos, confirms the members' 'intention to commence WTO negotiations on trade-related aspects of electronic commerce'.[3] This Joint Statement is itself a restatement of a previous Joint Statement issued at the

---

* Patrick Leblond is Associate Professor and CN-Paul M. Tellier Chair on Business and Public Policy in the Graduate School of Public and International Affairs at the University of Ottawa. He is also Senior Fellow at the Centre for International Governance Innovation (CIGI), Research Associate at CIRANO and Affiliated Professor of International Business at HEC Montréal. Contact: patrick.leblond@uottawa.ca.

[1] S. A. Aaronson, 'What Are We Talking about When We Talk about Digital Protectionism?', *World Trade Review* 18 (2019), 541–577; M. Burri, 'The Governance of Data and Data Flows in Trade Agreements: The Pitfalls of Legal Adaptation', *UC Davis Law Review* 51 (2017), 65–132.

[2] See www.wto.org/english/news_e/news19_e/osaka_declaration_on_digital_economy_e.pdf.

[3] See WTO, Joint Statement on Electronic Commerce, WT/L/1056, 25 January 2019.

WTO's eleventh ministerial conference in Buenos Aires in December 2017, where some seventy-five members 'recognize[d] the important role of the WTO in promoting open, transparent, non-discriminatory and predictable regulatory environments in facilitating electronic commerce'.[4] The Buenos Aires Joint Statement indicated that the signatories would begin exploratory work toward 'future WTO negotiations on trade-related aspects of electronic commerce'.[5]

A number of discussion rounds took place in 2018 and 2019 in Geneva in order to delimit the scope of potential plurilateral negotiations on electronic commerce/digital trade. The provisions on e-commerce/digital trade found in the Comprehensive and Progressive Agreement for Trans-Pacific Partnership (CPTPP)[6] and the United States–Mexico–Canada Agreement (USMCA),[7] the North American Free Trade Agreement's (NAFTA) replacement, are currently the most detailed proposals being considered in the WTO's plurilateral negotiations on e-commerce.[8]

This is why this chapter offers a detailed analysis of these CPTPP/USMCA e-commerce/digital trade provisions that pertain to data flows in order to identify the constraints they could impose on national data regulation.[9] To do so, it uses Canada as an example, because it is a party to both trade agreements and it seeks to build a high-trust data environment for consumers and businesses.[10] The analysis leads to the conclusion that Canada's CPTPP and USMCA commitments could ultimately negate the effectiveness of future data protection policies that the Canadian federal government might want to adopt to achieve its 'trust in the digital age' objective.[11]

B CROSS-BORDER DATA FLOW AND NATIONAL DATA REGULATION

Policymakers have lots of reasons to try to link the free flow of data and data protection. According to Dan Ciuriak, 'there is a need for free flow of data,

---

[4]   WTO, Joint statement on Electronic Commerce, WT/MIN(17)/60, 13 December 2017.
[5]   Ibid.
[6]   The United States abandoned the Trans-Pacific Partnership (TPP) in January 2017 when President Donald Trump took office. The remaining eleven members, including Canada, signed the CPTPP in March 2018. The agreement entered into force on 30 December 2018, between Australia, Canada, Japan, Mexico, New Zealand and Singapore. The CPTPP entered into force in Vietnam on 14 January 2019. The agreement had yet to apply in Brunei, Chile, Malaysia and Peru at the time of writing.
[7]   The USMCA was signed by all three parties on 30 November 2018, and ratified in Canada and Mexico in the spring of 2019, and by the United States in the beginning of 2020.
[8]   The USMCA's chapter on digital trade builds on the CPTPP's electronic commerce chapter.
[9]   Besides data-related issues, Ciuriak identifies a number of other important issues related to trade in digital goods and services that the WTO negotiations should address. See D. Ciuriak, 'World Trade Organization 2.0: Reforming Multilateral Trade Rules for the Digital Age', CIGI Policy Brief No 152 (2019).
[10] On 21 May 2019, the Government of Canada published its Digital Charter, which is a set of ten principles that are 'the building blocks of a foundation of trust for this digital age'; see www.ic .gc.ca/eic/site/o62.nsf/eng/h_00109.html.
[11] Ibid.

including on a cross-border basis', because data is 'intrinsic to commercial transactions'.[12] He sees data as the 'fifth freedom' of commerce, with free movement of goods, services, capital and labour as the other four. Legal and regulatory limits on cross-border data flows can, however, act as beyond-the-border obstacles to trade.[13] For instance, Martina Ferracane and Erik van der Marel find that policies that restrict the cross-border flow of data have a negative impact on trade in digital services.[14]

In certain circumstances (for example, to protect privacy, security, competition, culture, and so on), there is a need for the regulation of data collection, access, use and transfer. For example, the use of and access to people's data should be fair, transparent, accountable and subject to individuals' explicit consent. Moreover, the use of personal data should not lead to discrimination and bias when people seek to obtain a good or a service, whether it is from the private or the public sector. Another example is the protection of proprietary business data against uncompensated commercialization by others. On the other hand, access to data should not be controlled in such a way that it limits competition and innovation.

So the big question for policy-makers is how to allow for data to flow freely across borders while maintaining a high degree of trust among individuals, firms and governments that they will not be harmed in terms of privacy, consumption (price, choice or access), competition, innovation, security and so on. Strong data protection laws and regulations are necessary to create such trust. The problem is that such laws and regulations, if developed independently from other countries, can limit the cross-border flow of data and have negative economic consequences. This is the balancing act that the countries taking part in the WTO's plurilateral negotiations on 'trade-related aspects of electronic commerce' are trying to achieve.

C THE CPTPP, THE USMCA AND NATIONAL DATA REGULATION: EXAMPLE FROM CANADA

This section analyzes the electronic commerce/digital trade chapters included in the CPTPP and the USMCA in order to determine how they may affect data regulation in Canada, in order to provide an example of the potential impact that a WTO plurilateral agreement on trade-related aspects of electronic commerce modeled on CPTPP/USMCA provisions could have on members' governments'

[12] Ciuriak, note 9, at 6.
[13] Aaronson, note 1; D. Ciuriak and M. Ptashkina, *The Digital Transformation and the Transformation of International Trade* (Geneva/New York: ICTSD/IDB, 2018); N. Cory, 'Cross Border Data Flows: Where Are the Barriers, and What Do They Cost?', Information Technology and Innovation Foundation, May 2017; M. Rentzhog and H. Jonströmer, *No Transfer, No Trade: The Importance of Cross-Border Data Transfers for Companies Based in Sweden* (Stockholm: Kommerskollegium, 2014).
[14] M. F. Ferracane and E. van der Marel, 'Do Data Policy Restrictions Inhibit Trade in Services?', DTE Working Paper No 2 (2019); see also Chapter 3 in this volume.

ability to regulate data nationally. Since the CPTPP's electronic commerce chapter provided the basis for the USMCA's digital trade chapter, the analysis focuses first on the CPTPP.[15]

I *The CPTPP*

The CPTPP contains several provisions in its chapter 14 (electronic commerce) that concern data flows.[16] Chapter 14 does not specify what types of data are covered, except to say those that are necessary for business purposes. It also preserves member states' ability to limit the free flow of data held by government entities and encourages interoperability between data privacy regimes as well as cooperation between consumer protection authorities.

Here are the CPTPP's main provisions relating to data flows:

- Consistent with the WTO's waiver on customs duties on electronic commerce, Article 14.3 prohibits the imposition of customs duties on electronic transmissions; however, it allows 'internal taxes, fees or other charges' as long as they are not discriminatory (i.e., applied equally to national as well as foreign entities).[17] As such, the CPTPP does not discriminate among various types or sources of data.
- Article 14.8 CPTPP mandates a personal data protection floor: it ensures that parties have laws and regulations that provide a minimum level of personal information protection but it is flexible as it accommodates different national approaches.[18]

---

[15] This section draws from P. Leblond, 'Digital Trade at the WTO: The CPTPP and CUSMA Pose Challenges to Canadian Data Regulation', CIGI Paper No 227 (2019).

[16] Consolidated TPP Text – chapter 14 – Electronic Commerce, Government of Canada, 30 November 2016, available at http://international.gc.ca/trade-commerce/trade-agreements-accords-commerciaux/agr-acc/tpp-ptp/text-texte/14.aspx?lang=eng.

[17] Article 14.3 CPTPP, at para. 1: 'No Party shall impose customs duties on electronic transmissions, including content transmitted electronically, between a person of one Party and a person of another Party.
2. For greater certainty, paragraph 1 shall not preclude a Party from imposing internal taxes, fees or other charges on content transmitted electronically, provided that such taxes, fees or charges are imposed in a manner consistent with this Agreement'.

[18] Article 14.8 CPTPP, at paras. 2 and 3: 'To this end, each Party shall adopt or maintain a legal framework that provides for the protection of the personal information of the users of electronic commerce. In the development of its legal framework for the protection of personal information, each Party should take into account principles and guidelines of relevant international bodies.
Each Party shall endeavour to adopt non-discriminatory practices in protecting users of electronic commerce from personal information protection violations occurring within its jurisdiction'.

- Article 14.11 protects the free flow of cross-border data for business purposes,[19] although it allows restrictions on such flows in order to achieve a 'legitimate public policy objective'.[20]
- Article 14.13 prohibits the obligation for a business to locate specific computing facilities in exchange for market access.[21] In other words, it prohibits parties from imposing data localization requirements. However, the 'legitimate public policy objective' exception also applies in this case.
- Article 14.17 prohibits requirements that source code be transferred or accessed as a condition of import.[22] The prohibition is, however, limited to mass-market software but not when it is used in critical infrastructure.[23] The prohibition also does not apply to requests for source code modification to comply with domestic laws of regulations, as long as the latter are not inconsistent with the CPTPP; that is, they are not discriminatory in nature and apply equally to domestic and foreign firm.[24]

Article 14.2(3) CPTPP stipulates that 'this Chapter shall not apply to: (a) government procurement; or (b) information held or processed by or on behalf of a Party, or measures related to such information, including measures related to its collection'. This means that prohibitions on data transfer restrictions and data localization found in Articles 14.11 and 14.13 do not apply to governments. Therefore, the requirements imposed by the federal and some provincial governments that personal information held by public bodies be kept and processed in Canada are exempted under the CPTPP. This exception is potentially important if Canadian governments wish to make more publicly collected data available for analysis (for example, for artificial

---

[19] Article 14.11(2): 'Each Party shall allow the cross-border transfer of information by electronic means, including personal information, when this activity is for the conduct of the business of a covered person'.

[20] Article 14.11(3): 'Nothing in this Article shall prevent a Party from adopting or maintaining measures inconsistent with paragraph 2 to achieve a legitimate public policy objective, provided that the measure: (a) is not applied in a manner which would constitute a means of arbitrary or unjustifiable discrimination or a disguised restriction on trade; and (b) does not impose restrictions on transfers of information greater than are required to achieve the objective'.

[21] Article 14.13(2): 'No Party shall require a covered person to use or locate computing facilities in that Party's territory as a condition for conducting business in that territory'.

[22] Article 14.17(1): 'No Party shall require the transfer of, or access to, source code of software owned by a person of another Party, as a condition for the import, distribution, sale or use of such software, or of products containing such software, in its territory'.

[23] Article 14.17(2): 'For the purposes of this Article, software subject to paragraph 1 is limited to mass-market software or products containing such software and does not include software used for critical infrastructure'.

[24] Article 14.17(3)(b): 'Nothing in this Article shall preclude: a Party from requiring the modification of source code of software necessary for that software to comply with laws or regulations which are not inconsistent with this Agreement'.

intelligence [AI] training purposes) but want to ensure that they retain control over them to protect individuals, as well as the state.

The scope of application of Article 14.2(3) CPTPP is, however, somewhat ambiguous, when it comes to subnational governments, especially part (b). This is because Article 1.3 defines 'Party' as 'any State or separate customs territory for which this Agreement is in force'. As such, it would exclude subnational governments at the provincial and municipal levels, especially since 'regional level of government' is defined separately in Article 1.3.[25] The term 'government procurement' in part (a) is less ambiguous. Article 15.2(2) CPTPP establishes the scope of application of government procurement: 'For the purposes of this Chapter, covered procurement means government procurement: (a) of a good, service or any combination thereof as specified in each Party's Schedule to Annex 15-A'. In Canada's schedule in Annex 15-A, section B deals with sub-central government entities.[26] Government procurement provisions do not apply to schools, universities, hospitals and Crown corporations for all provinces and territories except Ontario and Quebec.[27] This means that only in Ontario and Quebec (the excluded provinces) could such public entities impose localization restrictions with respect to data storage and processing in their procurement contract

Articles 14.11 and 14.13 CPTPP on the prohibition of, respectively, restrictions on cross-border data transfers for business purposes and requirements to localize the storage of data domestically, both contain an exception for a 'legitimate public policy objective'. This means that CPTPP parties, such as Canada, can restrict the in-and-out flow of data in order to pursue such an objective. The big question, however, is: what is a 'legitimate' objective? Article 14.11(3) states that a measure restricting cross-border data transfers cannot: (i) be 'applied in a manner which would constitute a means of arbitrary or unjustifiable discrimination or a disguised

---

[25] According to law professor Debra Steger, a state refers to a nation-state and does not cover subnational governments (separate customs territory refers to customs union, such as the European Union): 'No. A State is a nation state. A separate customs territory like the EU can also be a Party to a CU or an FTA under Art. XXIV GATT. University or hospital is a person or an enterprise', *Twitter*, 4 August 2018, available at https://twitter.com/DebraPS/status/1025643907097350144. This explanation was a reply to a tweet by the author: 'Calling on trade lawyers to tell me if the definition of "Party" in CPTPP Article 1.3 ("any State or separate customs territory") also covers subnational governments and their agencies or organizations (including hospitals and universities in the Canadian context). Thank you!', *Twitter*, 3 August 2018.

[26] Consolidated TPP Text – chapter 15-A – Government Procurement, Annex 15-A – Schedule of Canada, Government of Canada, 5 December 2016, available at http://international.gc.ca/trade-commerce/trade-agreements-accords-commerciaux/agr-acc/tpp-ptp/text-texte/15-a3.aspx?lang=eng.

[27] Ibid. Note 5 to section B in Canada's schedule in Annex 15-A says: 'For those provinces and territories marked by an obelisk (†), chapter 15 (Government Procurement) shall not cover the procurement of goods, services or construction services purchased for the benefit of, or which is to be transferred to the authority of, school boards or their functional equivalents, publicly-funded academic institutions, social services entities or hospitals'. Note 6 to section B applies to Crown corporations.

restriction on trade' and (ii) 'impose restrictions on transfers of information greater than are required to achieve the objective'. Article 14.13(3) offers the same limitation on the 'legitimate public policy objective' (also called general) exception:

> Nothing in this Article shall prevent a Party from adopting or maintaining measures inconsistent with paragraph 2 to achieve a legitimate public policy objective, provided that the measure: (a) is not applied in a manner which would constitute a means of arbitrary or unjustifiable discrimination or a disguised restriction on trade; and (b) does not impose restrictions on the use or location of computing facilities greater than are required to achieve the objective.

Michael Geist questions whether privacy protection would qualify under the above-mentioned exception.[28] He seems doubtful when he writes: 'the [CPTPP] restriction on the use of data localization requirements may pose an insurmountable barrier'.[29] The same conclusion would apply to Article 14.11 CPTPP on data transfers. For instance, in early April 2019, the Office of the Privacy Commissioner of Canada (OPC) released a consultation paper on transborder data flows in which it indicates that it would require a company to obtain prior consent from individuals before moving their personal data outside of Canada.[30] According to Geist, this new approach 'is a significant reversal of longstanding policy that relied upon the accountability principle to ensure that organizations transferring personal information to third parties are ultimately responsible for safeguarding that information'.[31] The OPC stated that this new approach would be consistent with Canada's international trade obligations but Geist is not so sure: 'The imposition of consent requirements for cross-border data transfers could be regarded as imposing restrictions greater than required to achieve the objective of privacy protection, given that PIPEDA [Personal Information Protection and Electronic Documents Act] has long been said to provide such protections through accountability without the need for this additional consent regime'.[32]

Andrew Mitchell and Neha Mishra, for their part, also point out that there is the potential for conflict between e-commerce or digital trade chapters in free trade

[28] M. Geist, 'Data Rules in Modern Trade Agreements: Toward Reconciling an Open Internet with Privacy and Security Safeguards', in CIGI (ed), *Special Report: Data Governance in the Digital Age* (Waterloo: CIGI, 2018).
[29] Ibid.
[30] Office of the Privacy Commissioner of Canada, 'Consultation on Transborder Dataflows', 11 June 2019, available at www.priv.gc.ca/en/about-the-opc/what-we-do/consultations/consultation-on-transborder-dataflows/.
[31] Geist, note 28. In light of the government's publication of the Digital Charter, the OPC reframed its consultation in June 2019, putting less emphasis on its interest in requiring businesses to obtain prior consent from individuals before transferring their data abroad. See Office of the Privacy Commissioner of Canada, 'Consultation on Transfers for Processing – Reframed Discussion Document', 11 June 2019, available at www.priv.gc.ca/en/about-the-opc/what-we-do/consultations/consultation-on-transfers-for-processing/.
[32] There are two federal laws that govern personal data and information in Canada. The Privacy Act sets the rules for how the federal public sector collects, uses and discloses personal information. The Personal Information Protection and Electronic Documents Act (PIPEDA)

agreements (FTAs) and WTO agreements, such as the General Agreement on Trade in Services (GATS).[33] They write that Article XIV GATS provides the basis for the general exception found in FTA provisions, such as the CPTPP's Articles 14.11 and 14.13; however, they also note that 'these exceptions may be unable to address all aspects of data flow restrictions'.[34] In addition, Mitchell and Mishra mention that 'strict scrutiny of these measures [restricting data flows] under international trade law may lead to unsatisfactory outcomes because GATS Articles XIV and XIV *bis* are limited in scope and do not facilitate consideration of Internet trust issues holistically'.[35] The above implies that general exceptions on data transfers and data localization found in the CPTPP may not offer as much policy flexibility as originally thought with respect to future laws and regulations that Canadian (federal and provincial) governments might want to put into place to govern data in order to ensure trust as well as stimulate innovation.

Given that algorithms 'drive what news content and advertising each of us sees online [and] will be used by governments to decide who receives or is denied benefits',[36] it is reassuring that Article 14.17 CPTPP does not prevent governments from regulating and supervising source codes, as long as it is not done in a protectionist way against foreign producers. Teresa Scassa notes that it is necessary to be able to access the source code of an app, software or AI in order to evaluate algorithms' performance and potential biases.[37] Such enquiries are important if governments want to protect consumers, workers and businesses from suffering the negative consequences associated with, for example, fraud or discrimination.

does the same for the private sector. See Office of the Privacy Commissioner of Canada, 'Summary of Privacy Laws in Canada', 31 January 2018, available at www.priv.gc.ca/en/privacy-topics/privacy-laws-in-canada/02_05_d_15/. PIPEDA only applies to commercial, for-profit activities. As such, it does not apply to non-profit and charity organizations, unless they conduct commercial activities that involve personal information. The OPC, which is responsible for implementing both acts, defines personal information as 'data about an identifiable individual [. . .] that on its own or combined with other pieces of data, can identify you as an individual'. See Office of the Privacy Commissioner of Canada, 'The Digital Privacy Act and PIPEDA', November 2015. As such, it indicates that the following types of information are not (generally) considered personal: information about a business or an organization; information that is not possible to link back to an identifiable person (i.e., it has been anonymized); and information that is not about an individual and whose connection with a person is too weak or far-removed.

[33] A. D. Mitchell and N. Mishra, 'Data at the Docks: Modernizing International Trade Law for the Digital Economy', *Vanderbilt Journal of Entertainment and Technology Law* 20 (2018), 1073–1134.

[34] Ibid., at 1095.

[35] Ibid.; also Creach, who writes that 'given the stringent conditions for trade restrictions to fall within the scope of GATS Article XIV (especially the necessity test), one may doubt that data-localization requirements are justifiable'. See M. Creach, 'Assessing the Legality of Data-Localization Requirements: Before the Tribunals or at the Negotiating Table?', Columbia FDI Perspectives No 254 (2019), at 2.

[36] T. Scassa, 'What Role for Trade Deals in an Era of Digital Transformation?', *CIGI*, 4 October 2018, available at www.cigionline.org/articles/what-role-trade-deals-era-digital-transformation.

[37] Ibid.

II *The USMCA*

The USMCA, unlike NAFTA, which it replaces, contains a chapter (19) on 'digital trade' (not 'e-commerce', in order to signify its broader scope) that builds on the CPTPP's chapter 14.[38] As such, the USMCA introduces a number of differences from the CPTPP. The following analysis focuses on these differences.

One significant difference with the CPTPP concerns the requirement for USMCA member states to 'adopt or maintain a legal framework that provides for the protection of the personal information of the users of digital trade'.[39] While the USMCA does not prescribe specific rules or measures that a party must take to protect privacy, it goes further than the CPTPP by providing more guidance to inform a country's privacy regime. In particular, the USMCA refers explicitly to the APEC (Asia-Pacific Economic Cooperation) Privacy Framework and OECD (Organisation for Economic Co-operation and Development) Guidelines as relevant 'principles and guidelines' when developing a legal framework for protecting personal information.[40] Unlike the CPTPP, the USMCA also mentions key principles that parties should follow as they develop their legal framework.[41]

In addition, the USMCA stipulates that the parties 'recognize the importance of . . . ensuring that any restrictions on cross-border flows of personal information are necessary and proportionate to the risks presented',[42] thereby providing some limit on the extent to which data protection legislation or regulation can constrain cross-border personal data flows. Such a standard for potentially restricting data flows in order to protect personal information is not present in the CPTPP's Article 14.8(2). As such, the USMCA provides some guidance, albeit vague, to future panel arbitrators in interpreting the 'legitimate public policy objective' exception in the case of a dispute involving limits imposed on cross-border data flows by one of the USMCA parties. The big issue in this case is what 'necessary and proportionate' mean in the context of protecting personal information? For instance, would a requirement for organizations in Canada to obtain explicit consent from individuals before the latter's data are transferred across the border to the United States be deemed necessary and proportionate?

---

[38] Government of Canada, Canada–United States–Mexico Agreement (CUSMA) – Table of Contents, 21 February 2020, available at www.international.gc.ca/trade-commerce/trade-agree ments-accords-commerciaux/agr-acc/cusma-aceum/text-texte/toc-tdm.aspx?lang=eng.

[39] Article 19.8(2) USMCA.

[40] The CPTPP's Article 14.8(3) states only that 'each Party should take into account principles and guidelines of relevant international bodies' (it does not mention any particular international body, however).

[41] The USMCA's Article 19.8(3) states: 'The Parties recognize that pursuant to paragraph 2, key principles include: limitation on collection; choice; data quality; purpose specification; use limitation; security safeguards; transparency; individual participation; and accountability'.

[42] Article 19.8(3) USMCA.

What is probably the most important difference between the USMCA and the CPTPP is the former's Article 19.17 on Interactive Computer Services, which has no equivalent in the CPTPP. According to this article, Internet service providers, social media platforms and search engines cannot be treated as information content providers for liability purposes, which means 'immunity from legal consequences for content generated by users'.[43] However, Annex 19-A(4) states: 'For greater certainty, Article 19.17 (Interactive Computer Services) is subject to Article 32.1 (General Exceptions), which, among other things, provides that, for purposes of chapter 19, the exception for measures necessary to protect public morals pursuant to paragraph (a) of Article XIV of the GATS is incorporated into and made part of this Agreement, *mutatis mutandis*'. This paragraph opens the door for potential limits on the article's scope and application but, as mentioned earlier, there is a lot of uncertainty with respect to the general exception's reach.[44] In any case, the USMCA's Article 19.17 will likely make it harder for Canadian governments to develop measures to protect individuals and consumers of social media, search engines and other user-generated content providers from the consequences of disinformation (for example, 'fake news').

Another noteworthy difference between the USMCA and the CPTPP concerns source code and algorithms. First, the USMCA's Article 19.16 gets rid of the CPTPP's Article 14.17(2).[45] This implies that all types of source code are covered by the USMCA, without exception. As Scassa notes: 'This may raise some interesting concerns given the growing government use of software and algorithms in key systems and processes'.[46] The USMCA also does not contain the CPTPP's provision on allowing requests for source code modification.[47] Instead, it offers Article 19.16(2), which does not exist in the CPTPP: 'This Article does not preclude a regulatory

---

[43] T. Israel and L. Tribe, 'Did NAFTA 2.0 Sign Away Our Digital Future?', *Ottawa Citizen*, 15 October 2018. The USMCA's Article 19.17(3) states: 'No Party shall impose liability on a supplier or user of an interactive computer service on account of: (a) any action voluntarily taken in good faith by the supplier or user to restrict access to or availability of material that is accessible or available through its supply or use of the interactive computer services and that the supplier or user considers to be harmful or objectionable; or (b) any action taken to enable or make available the technical means that enable an information content provider or other persons to restrict access to material that it considers to be harmful or objectionable'.

[44] This is why Nancy Pelosi, Speaker of the US House of Representatives, pushed, unsuccessfully, to have this provision removed at the last minute to secure the USMCA's congressional approval because she and other members of Congress were concerned that the USMCA's Article 19.17 could 'damage domestic efforts to amend the Section 230 law'. The USMCA's provision is based on Section 230 of the US Communications Decency Act.

[45] The CPTPP's Article 14.17(2) states: 'For the purposes of this Article, software subject to paragraph 1 is limited to mass-market software or products containing such software and does not include software used for critical infrastructure'.

[46] Scassa, note 36.

[47] The CPTPP's Article 14.17(3)(b) states: 'Nothing in this Article shall preclude a Party from requiring the modification of source code of software necessary for that software to comply with laws or regulations which are not inconsistent with this Agreement'.

body or judicial authority of a Party from requiring a person of another Party to preserve and make available the source code of software, or an algorithm expressed in that source code, to the regulatory body for a specific investigation, inspection, examination, enforcement action, or judicial proceeding, subject to safeguards against unauthorized disclosure'. Scassa says that the difference between the USMCA and the CPTPP provisions is 'important given that we are already facing context in which it is necessary to understand the algorithms that lead to certain decisions [for example, litigation involving autonomous vehicles]'.[48] So the USMCA improves on the CPTPP in terms of source code transparency but it is also a step back when it comes to the absence of a provision allowing requests to modify algorithms, which could be found to be biased or causing harm to people, businesses or governments. With the USMCA, unlike the CPTPP, a Canadian request for algorithmic modification could be challenged as a protectionist measure discriminating against the US or Mexican producer of the software or application.

The final difference between the USMCA and the CPTPP is with respect to the provisions on data localization ('Location of Computing Facilities'). In the CPTPP's Article 14.13, 'the Parties recognise that each Party may have its own regulatory requirements regarding the use of computing facilities, including requirements that seek to ensure the security and confidentiality of communications'[49] but 'no Party shall require a covered person to use or locate computing facilities in that Party's territory as a condition for conducting business in that territory'[50] unless it is for a 'legitimate public policy objective'.[51] For its part, the USMCA's Article 19.12 only has one provision: 'No Party shall require a covered person to use or locate computing facilities in that Party's territory as a condition for conducting business in that territory.' This means that, unlike the CPTPP, the USMCA does not allow its parties to invoke a 'legitimate public policy objective' exception to impose a data localization requirement to firms from the other two parties as a condition for providing a digital good or service in the territory. The only exception possible here is for the specific case when a digital good or service is provided to a government, because the USMCA's chapter 19 does not apply to 'government procurement; or except for Article 19.18 (Open Government Data), to information held or processed by or on behalf of a Party, or measures related to that information, including measures related to its collection'.[52] Therefore, governments can only require

---

[48] Scassa, note 36.
[49] Article 14.13(1) CPTPP.
[50] Article 14.13(2) CPTPP.
[51] Article 14.13(3) CPTPP. The CPTPP's Article 14.13(3) states: 'Nothing in this Article shall prevent a Party from adopting or maintaining measures inconsistent with paragraph 2 to achieve a legitimate public policy objective, provided that the measure: (a) is not applied in a manner which would constitute a means of arbitrary or unjustifiable discrimination or a disguised restriction on trade; and (b) does not impose restrictions on the use or location of computing facilities greater than are required to achieve the objective'.
[52] Article 19.2(3).

organizations that collect, hold or process information to locate their computing facilities in the territory when these activities are undertaken for or on behalf of a government, which is in line with current practices. However, if, for example, data deemed critical for national security reasons were held by a private organization, then the USMCA would technically require a government to allow these data to be held and processed in the other two member states' territory. As a result, these data could become accessible to the other member state governments (for example, through the USA PATRIOT Act in the United States).

III *Interim Conclusion*

With the CPTPP and the USMCA, Canada has adopted obligations that provide for the free flow across borders of data for business purposes while, in principle, protecting consumers, personal information and government-related data. However, as analyzed earlier, these two trade agreements also pose potential obstacles to Canada's ability to effectively regulate data and it is unclear how much policy flexibility they leave to the federal and provincial governments to pursue legitimate objectives and protect the vital interests of their citizens. It will ultimately be left to state-to-state dispute settlement panels in the CPTPP and the USMCA (as well as the investor–state dispute settlement mechanism in the CPTPP) to resolve this uncertainty and determine the scope of Canada's national data regulation. If dispute settlement panels were to rule in favour of cross-border data flows and impose limits on Canada's ability to ensure trust among individuals and businesses when it comes to the data-driven economy, then such decisions could undermine the CPTPP's and the USMCA's legitimacy and political support.

D KEY PROPOSALS AT THE WTO'S PLURILATERAL NEGOTIATIONS ON TRADE-RELATED ASPECTS OF ELECTRONIC COMMERCE

In April 2019, the key players in the negotiations – China, the EU and the United States – issued their proposals to the WTO's plurilateral negotiations on trade-related aspects of electronic commerce.[53] The Chinese proposal is the least ambitious. It is hortatory in nature and focuses on principles for the facilitation of cross-border electronic commerce, leaving aside data flows.[54] China's proposal is thus in

---

[53] For China's proposal, see WTO, Joint Statement on Electronic Commerce, Communication from China, INF/ECOM/19, 24 April 2019. For the European Union's proposal, see WTO, Joint Statement on Electronic Commerce: EU Proposal for WTO Disciplines and Commitments Relating to Electronic Commerce, Communication from the European Union, INF/ECOM/22, 26 April 2019 [hereinafter: EU Proposal]. For the US proposal, see WTO, Joint Statement on Electronic Commerce, Communication from the United States, INF/ECOM/23, 26 April 2019 [hereinafter: US Proposal].

[54] Specifically, Article 4.2 of China's proposal states that issues such as data flows and data storage require 'more exploratory discussions . . . before bringing [them] to the WTO negotiation'. In

line with the electronic commerce provisions contained in some of the FTAs that it has signed so far. As such, it reflects the country's desire to protect its walled-off digital realm.[55]

The EU's proposal goes much further than the Chinese one. For instance, it offers specific provisions that mandate unrestricted cross-border data flows,[56] subject to national rules deemed 'appropriate to ensure the protection of personal data and privacy'.[57] The EU's proposal also stipulates that there can be no requirement for the transfer of software source codes in exchange for market access, although it can be required for legal violations or national security reasons.[58]

The US proposal, for its part, follows closely the digital trade chapter found in the USMCA.[59] As such, it supports the EU's position on cross-border data flows, personal data protection and source codes; however, unlike the EU's proposal, which states that '[n]othing in the agreed disciplines and commitments shall affect the protection of personal data and privacy afforded by the Members' respective safeguards',[60] the US offer qualifies the limits on cross-border data flows that national data protection regimes can impose: 'ensuring that any restrictions on cross-border flows of personal information are necessary and proportionate to the risks presented' (Article 7.4), which follows USMCA's Article 19.8.3. Article 8 of the US proposal also restates, verbatim, the USMCA's provision[61] that only restrictions on cross-border data flows that 'achieve a legitimate public policy objective' are acceptable. Finally, the USMCA's Article 19.17 ('Interactive Computer Services') is transposed in its entirety into the US proposal,[62] thereby putting forward the prohibition on treating 'a supplier or user of an interactive computer services as an information content provider in determining liability for harms related to information stored, processed, transmitted, distributed, or made available by the service, except to the extent that the supplier or user has, in whole or in part, created or developed the information'.[63]

Article 4.3, the proposal adds, 'the data flow [sic] should be subject to the precondition of security, which concerns each and every Members' core interests. To this end, it is necessary that the data flow orderly [sic] in compliance with Members' respective laws and regulations'.

[55] S. A. Aaronson and P. Leblond, 'Another Digital Divide: The Rise of Data Realms and Its Implications for the WTO', *Journal of International Economic Law* 21 (2018), 245–272. See also Chapter 12 in this volume.

[56] EU Proposal, note 53, section 2.7.

[57] Ibid., section 2.8.

[58] Ibid., section 2.6.

[59] B. Baschuk, 'US WTO E-Commerce Offer Reflects USMCA Digital Trade Chapter', *Bloomberg Law*, 6 May 2019; I. Manak, 'US WTO E-Commerce Proposal Reads Like USMCA', *International Economic Law and Policy Blog*, 8 May 2019, available at https://worldtradelaw.typepad.com/ielpblog/2019/05/us-wto-e-commerce-proposal-reads-like-usmca.html.

[60] EU Proposal, note 53, section 2.8 EU.

[61] Article 19.11 USMCA.

[62] US Proposal, note 53, Article 13.

[63] US Proposal, note 53, Article 13.2.

FIGURE 14.1. Illustrating the relative positions of the main proposals to the WTO's plurilateral negotiations on e-commerce

In sum, the proposals occupy different places on a continuum that includes independent national data protection at one end and cross-border data free flow at the other, with China being close to the former pole while the United States is closer to the other pole and the EU is somewhere in between (see Figure 14.1). As analyzed earlier, the USMCA's digital trade chapter, which itself builds on the CPTPP's chapter 14, has served to inform the US position in the WTO's Plurilateral 'Trade-related Aspects of Electronic Commerce' negotiations. Should the latter ever prevail, which remains to be seen in light of the divergent key positions on offer, it will make it difficult for member states to adopt national data regulations that impose limits on the cross-border flow of data, most especially personal data.

E CONCLUSION AND OUTLOOK

As the example of Canada demonstrates herein, the CPTPP and the USMCA require their members to adopt obligations that provide for the free flow across borders of data for business purposes while, in principle, protecting consumers, personal information and government-related data. However, as analyzed above, these two trade agreements also pose potential obstacles to a member state's ability to effectively regulate data and provide a trustworthy environment for individuals, businesses and governments. The analysis shows that it is not at all clear how much policy flexibility the CPTPP and the USMCA ultimately allow governments that want to adopt new laws and regulations to, among various objectives, protect people's privacy, prevent algorithmic bias, protect critical infrastructure, ensure national security or promote domestic innovation.

For the plurilateral negotiations of an agreement on 'trade-related aspects of electronic commerce' at the WTO, this means that the US proposal, which is closely derived from the USMCA's digital trade chapter,[64] would create a lot of uncertainty as to how much limits on cross-border data flows a country could impose via its national data regulation regime, until dispute-settlement panels decide on the acceptability and legitimacy of national data rules in restricting data flows across borders.

---

[64] Chapter 19 USMCA.

To leave such crucial decisions for economy and society in the hands of unelected and unaccountable individuals seems an odd way to govern the data-driven economy's future functioning. A better approach would be to remove issues related to data regulation and standards from the WTO negotiations and push for a separate international regime to govern data and its cross-border flows.[65] Just like capital (or financial) flows are not part of the WTO's framework,[66] which limits itself to rules on trade in financial services, so should data flows be excluded from an eventual agreement on trade-related aspects of electronic commerce. The latter agreement, should it ever see the light of day, should instead focus its attention solely on the rules governing trade in digital goods and services. A separate international body (such as an International Data Standards Board) should be responsible for setting standards that regulate the creation, processing, use, distribution and transfer of data, both personal and non-personal. All countries that apply and enforce these standards would be allowed to take part in a single data area where data would be free to flow across member states' borders. The WTO's rules on digital trade would be left to deal with possible infringement of core trade principles, such as non-discrimination.

---

[65] P. Leblond and S. A. Aaronson, 'A Plurilateral "Single Data Area" Is the Solution to Canada's Data Trilemma', CIGI Papers No 226 (2019).

[66] The Financial Stability Board oversees and coordinates the various international bodies that set the standards that govern finance.

15

Data Ownership and Data Access Rights

Meaningful Tools for Promoting the European Digital Single Market?

*Florent Thouvenin and Aurelia Tamò-Larrieux**

A INTRODUCTION

The digitalization and the increase in global trade significantly impact the economy and citizens of Europe. European policymakers are well aware of these developments and wish to unlock the potential of the digital economy through the EU's Digital Single Market Strategy.[1] One core goal of this strategy, promoted by the European Commission since 2015, is the pursuit of a free flow of data within the EU. Such a free flow should encourage the creation of and access to goods and services that – in their essence – collect and process vast amounts of data.

While the free flow of data is desirable from an economic perspective, as it maximizes the use of data by businesses throughout (and beyond) the EU, an entirely free flow of personal data goes against individuals' interests to exercise some control over the collection and use of their data by third parties. Therefore, a balance between economic and individual interests must be struck by creating a regime that ensures both. We call this desired balance an 'adequate free flow of data'. The term 'adequate' implies that a European digital economy should achieve more than economic welfare and simultaneously protect the interests of European citizens and consumers, especially their fundamental rights, such as the right to personal data protection. The balancing of interests could also benefit the digital economy, as it would promote the European citizens' trust and confidence in the

---

* Florent Thouvenin is Professor of Law, Chair for Information and Communication Law and Center for Information Technology, Society, and Law (ITSL), University of Zurich. Contact: florent.thouvenin@rwi.uzh.ch. Aurelia Tamò-Larrieux is Postdoctoral Fellow at the Institute for Work and Employment Research (FAA-HSG), University of St. Gallen. Contact: aurelia.tamo@unisg.ch. This contribution was completed at the end of December 2019. Literature and EU communications published after this date could only be considered selectively.

[1] European Commission, A Digital Single Market Strategy for Europe, COM(2015) 192 final, 6 May 2015; cf. also European Commission, A European strategy for data, COM(2020) 66 final, 19 February 2020.

digital single market in order to enable the full exploitation of its potential. To achieve trust and confidence, legitimate boundaries to the free flow of data must be set.

Policymakers in the EU have debated whether the digital economy may benefit from the introduction of data ownership[2] and data access rights,[3] and legal scholars have analysed how such rights could lead to a digital economy benefitting all stakeholders. Yet policymakers and scholars have sometimes had different understandings of the term 'ownership', most often inadvertently. First, data ownership can be understood as a property right derived from civil law concepts of property in real estate and chattel, or intellectual property rights. This understanding of 'ownership' is how lawyers usually conceive the term. Second, data ownership can also be understood more broadly as a right that grants some control over data. It is this sort of ownership that non-lawyers typically have in mind when they advocate for the introduction of a 'data ownership right', most often (and again inadvertently) having only personal data in mind. With regard to personal data, this second understanding aligns with the approach taken in data protection law, namely in the EU's General Data Protection Regulation (GDPR),[4] which grants data subjects some control over their personal data. In contrast to data ownership, data access rights serve a different purpose – to empower individuals and businesses to obtain access to data that is of specific interest to them. Individuals have a legitimate interest in having access to personal data which is processed by businesses; the same is true for non-personal data that individuals have stored with a third party, such as a cloud provider. For businesses, access to data may be of key importance when offering innovative goods and services in the digital economy, as the use of specific data may be necessary to enter a new market or to remain competitive in an existing one.

In this chapter, we refrain from recapitulating the thorough academic debate on data ownership and data access rights.[5] Instead – and considering this book's broader perspective of big data and global trade – we look at the topic from a different angle and ask whether and how the concepts of data ownership and data access rights may

---

[2] See European Parliament, Resolution of 10 March 2016 on 'Towards a Thriving Data-Driven Economy' (2015/2612(RSP)), OJ C [2018] 50/50; European Commission, Towards a Common European Data Space, COM(2018) 232 final, 25 April 2018.

[3] See European Parliament, note 2; European Commission, note 2; OECD, *Data Driven Innovation – Big Data for Growth and Well-Being* (Paris: OECD Publishing, 2015), at 186–197.

[4] Regulation 2016/679 of the European Parliament and of the Council of 27 April 2016 on the Protection of Natural Persons with Regard to the Processing of Personal Data and on the Free Movement of Such Data, and Repealing Directive 95/46/EC (General Data Protection Regulation, GDPR), OJ L [2016] 119/1 [hereinafter: GDPR].

[5] For an overview, see R. H. Weber and F. Thouvenin, 'Dateneigentum und Datenzugangsrechte – Bausteine der Informationsgesellschaft?', *Zeitschrift für Schweizerisches Recht* 137 (2018), 43–74; J. Drexl et al., 'Data Ownership and Access to Data', Max Planck Institute for Innovation and Competition Research Paper No 10 (2016); F. Thouvenin, R. H. Weber, and A. Früh, 'Data Ownership: Taking Stock and Mapping the Issues', in M. Dehmer and F. Emmert-Streib (eds), *Frontiers in Data Science* (Boca Raton: CRC Press, 2018), at 111–145.

serve the goal of establishing an adequate free flow of data in the digital single market.

In the pursuit of the chapter's objective, we first map the policy goals contained within the EU's Digital Single Market Strategy. Upon this basis, we analyse how data ownership – understood as a property right – may serve the implementation of this strategy. Based on the insight that introducing property rights in data is unlikely to help implementing an adequate free flow of data, we examine in the following section of the chapter whether ownership as control over personal data is a viable alternative to the property rights approach. As a final step, we examine if, and under what circumstances, access rights to data already exist, or should be introduced, to allow individuals and businesses to use both personal and non-personal data. The last part concludes and explores paths towards strengthening data access rights, for instance, through the introduction of a compulsory licences regime.

B THE DIGITAL SINGLE MARKET STRATEGY: BASIC FEATURES AND OBJECTIVES

In a nutshell, the goal of the EU Digital Market Strategy is to ensure that individuals and businesses have access to online services and products and that the requirements of fair competition, consumer and data protection as well as copyright are being fulfilled. In addition, no geo-blocking should occur within the Union.[6] In line with the general objective of fostering the internal market, the Digital Single Market Strategy aims to 'tear down the regulatory walls and move from 28 national markets to a single one',[7] while maintaining confidence in the digital economy. In order to promote the availability of good quality and interoperable datasets, EU policymakers seek to abolish inappropriate restrictions to the free flow of data across member states. Additionally, the European Commission wants to facilitate the value generation from datasets by training their citizens in the respective fields, by cooperating with industry and universities to determine the adequate skills required for the labour market and by promoting access to and transfer of knowledge amongst the private and the public sector.[8]

These statements show that the free flow of data is a key policy goal to enable the EU to compete in the global digital economy. But limitations are necessary to create a balanced approach that takes into account the needs of businesses and individuals

---

[6] See European Commission, note 1; European Commission, Shaping the Digital Single Market, available at https://ec.europa.eu/digital-single-market/en/policies/shaping-digital-single-market.

[7] European Commission, 'Tapping the Full Potential of the Data Economy for All Europeans', *The Commission's Contribution to the Leaders' Agenda*, May 2018, available at https://ec. europa.eu/info/sites/info/files/digital-single-market-all-europeans_en.pdf.

[8] European Commission, Towards a Thriving Data-Driven Economy, COM(2014) 442 final, 2 July 2014, at 5–6; see also European Commission, note 1, COM(2020).

alike. Some of the latter fear an ever-increasing collection and unrestricted process-ing of their personal data. In light of the power and information asymmetries between data processing entities and individuals, this fear is understandable and well-founded, as individuals are left with little or no control over how their personal data is being processed.[9] Thus, an important distinction needs to be made between the free flow of personal and non-personal data.

While some individuals fear a lack of control over their personal data, they hardly care about the collection and use of non-personal data. Accordingly, Europeans seem to be quite comfortable with the free flow of non-personal data.[10] In contrast, when it comes to personal data, an arguably central foundation of the digital single market is the establishment of a 'strong, consistent and comprehensive data protection frame-work for the EU'.[11] For users to have sufficient trust and confidence in the free flow of personal data, rules governing this flow must be adopted, and the European Commission sees the GDPR as the critical building block to do so. According to the commission, the GDPR is the central piece of legislation for the development of 'innovative and sustainable data goods and services',[12] and 'the foundation for the free flow of personal data in the EU', as it 'bans prohibitions and restrictions to the free movement of personal data for reasons connected with the protection of natural persons with regard to the processing of personal data'.[13] Even if restrictions to the free flow can be justified by other reasons (e.g. under taxation and accounting laws), the GDPR is seen as an important step to abolish data localisation restrictions – i.e., rules mandating local storage or processing activities. In fact, as data localization requirements of member states are a major obstacle to the free flow of data,[14] the abolishment of such restrictions is key to promote a flourishing European data economy.[15]

---

[9] See European Commission, Special Eurobarometer 431: Data Protection, dataset available at https://data.europa.eu/euodp/en/data/dataset/S2075_83_1_431_ENG.
[10] Regulation 2018/1807 of the European Parliament and of the Council of 14 November 2018 on a Framework for the Free Flow of Non-personal Data in the European Union, OJ L [2018] 303/59, at paras. 59–68.
[11] European Commission, note 8, at 11.
[12] Ibid.
[13] European Commission, Commission Staff Working Document on the Free Flow of Data and Emerging Issues of the European Data Economy, Accompanying the Document Communication Building a European Data Economy, COM(2017) 9 final, SWD(2017) 2 final, 10 January 2017, at 10.
[14] M. Burri and R. Schär, 'The Reform of the EU Data Protection Framework: Outlining Key Changes and Assessing Their Fitness for a Data-Driven Economy', *Journal of Information Policy* 6 (2016), 479–511, at 500; M. Bauer, M. Ferracane, and E. van der Marel, 'Tracing the Economic Impact of Regulations on the Free Flow of Data and Data Localization', CIGI Paper No 30 (2016); N. Cory, 'Cross-Border Data Flows: Where Are the Barriers, and What Do They Cost', Information Technology and Innovation Foundation, 1 May 2017.
[15] European Commission, note 13, at 10; see also European Commission, Building a European Data Economy, COM(2017) 9 final, 10 January 2017, at 4–5.

Yet, while the GDPR certainly fosters a free flow of personal data within the EU by establishing a (relatively[16]) uniform regime in all EU member states, it also imposes substantial restrictions on the processing of personal data and thereby limits the free development and deployment of digital goods and services. While innovation remains possible, the GDPR has at least raised its costs, sometimes to a level making the deployment of innovative digital goods and services economically unfeasible.[17] These restrictions, however, are taken into account with the aim of protecting European citizens from the risks associated with the processing of their personal data. The tension between the free movement of personal data within the EU and the protection of the fundamental rights and freedoms of individuals is prominently highlighted in Article 1 GDPR, which addresses both goals in a separate paragraph. Interestingly, the European legislator is quite clear on the priority of the two objectives by stating that '[t]he free movement of personal data within the Union shall neither be restricted nor prohibited for reasons connected with the protection of natural persons with regard to the processing of personal data' (Article 1(3) GDPR). While it is doubtful whether this priority of objectives is actually put into action by the provisions of the GDPR, this statement supports our perspective that any (potential) regulation on personal and non-personal data should be analysed with regards to its ability to ensure an adequate free flow of data.

C DATA OWNERSHIP

I *Ownership as a Property Right*

1 State of Research

The literature on data ownership as a property right is divided: While some authors argue that the current regulatory system is inadequate to protect individuals in the digital economy, others consider it adequate (or adequate enough) and therefore do not encourage the establishment of property rights in data. A first group of authors highlights the potential threats of big data and global trade for the protection of the

---

[16] Many flexibility clauses exist within the GDPR that allow member states to 'introduce national provisions to further specify the application of the rules' of the GDPR, introduce 'sector-specific laws in areas that need more specific provisions', or 'specify rules, including for the processing of special categories of data'. See Recital 10 GDPR.

[17] Chivot and Castro criticize the negative impact of the GDPR on innovation. See E. Chivot and D. Castro, 'The EU Needs to Reform the GDPR to Remain Competitive in the Algorithmic Economy', Center for Data Innovation, 13 May 2019; N. Wallace and D. Castro, 'The Impact of the New EU's Data Protection Regulation on AI', Center for Data Innovation, 27 March 2018; see also J. Drexl, 'Legal Challenges of the Changing Role of Personal and Non-personal Data in the Data Economy', Max Planck Institute for Innovation and Competition Research Paper No 23 (2018), at 11–12; for a different opinion, see R. Bastin and G. Wantz, 'The General Data Protection Regulation: Cross-Industry Innovation', *Deloitte Inside Magazine* 2 (2015).

fundamental rights and freedoms of European citizens. Data ownership, they argue, could help cushion some of the adverse effects of the digital economy.[18] The idea behind their string of reasoning is that, by assigning data to the person to whom it refers, the individual data 'owners' are put in a better negotiating position towards companies and thus a fairer distribution of the value created by the data processing can be ensured.[19] One strong proponent of a data ownership right even argues that such a right would empower individuals to combat the 'totalitarian digital appropriation strategies' of big tech companies.[20] Yet even proponents of data ownership as a property right acknowledge that the practical implementation of such a right remains unclear.[21] In fact, so far, only abstract calls for data ownership frameworks have been proposed.[22]

A second group of authors starts from the assumption that data is a public good.[23] This means that the use of data is non-rivalrous, as data can be used by an unlimited number of individuals simultaneously, and the use of one individual does not

---

[18] M. Amstutz, 'Dateneigentum: Funktion und Form', *Archiv für die Civilistische Praxis* 218 (2018), 439–551, at 489 et seqq.; see also F. Cheneval, 'Property Rights of Personal Data and the Financing of Pensions', *Critical Review of International Social and Political Philosophy* (2018), 1–23; I. Landreau et al., 'My Data Are Mine: Why We Should Have Ownership Rights on Our Data' (Paris: GenerationLibre, 2018), at 18 et seqq.; N. Purtova, 'The Illusion of Personal Data as No One's Property', *Law, Innovation, and Technology* 7 (2015), 83–111, at 86 et seqq.; E. Tjong Tjin Tai, 'Data Ownership and Consumer Protection', *Journal of European Consumer and Market Law* 7 (2018), 136–140, at 136 et seqq.

[19] M. Amstutz, 'Dateneigentum: Eckstein der kommenden Digitalordnung', *Neue Zürcher Zeitung*, 5 September 2018; see also H.-J. Naumer, 'Dateneigentum statt Datenkapitalismus', in Stiftung Datenschutz (ed), *Dateneigentum und Datenhandel* (Leipzig: Erich Schmidt Verlag, 2019), 233–239, at 234–236; H. Zech, 'Information as Property', *Journal of Intellectual Property, Information Technology and E-Commerce Law* 6 (2015), 192–197, at 197.

[20] Amstutz, note 19 (authors' own translation from German).

[21] Ibid.; also V. Janeček, 'Ownership of Personal Data in the Internet of Things', *Computer Law and Security Review* 34 (2018), 1039–1052, at 1052.

[22] See, e.g., proposal by the Federal Minister of Transport and Digital Infrastructure of Germany, Alexander Dobrindt, who called for a 'Data Law', which includes five basic principles: (i) defining data as a material commodity; (ii) which belongs to a particular person; (iii) providing transparent information about data processing; (iv) ensuring that public data is open data, and (v) enabling individuals to have payment options instead of sharing personal data. See Bundesministerium für Verkehr und Digitale Infrastruktur, Strategiepapier Digitale Souveränität: Wir brauchen ein Datenschutzgesetz in Deutschland!, available at www.bmvi .de/SharedDocs/DE/Artikel/DG/datengesetz.html. For an overview of different ownership framework proposals, see also J. Ritter and A. Mayer, 'Regulating Data as Property: A New Construct for Moving Forward', *Duke Law and Technology Review* 16 (2018), 220–277. For other proposals, see Landreau et al., note 18, at 76 et seqq.; also Cheneval, note 18, at 16; K.-H. Fezer, *Repräsentatives Dateneigentum – Ein zivilgesellschaftliches Bürgerrecht*, (Berlin: Konrad Adenauer Stiftung, 2018).

[23] T. Heymann, 'Rechte an Daten: Warum Daten keiner eigentumrechtlichen Logik folgen', *Computer Recht* (2016), 650–657, at 652–653; W. Kerber, 'A New (Intellectual) Property Right for Non-personal Data? An Economic Analysis', *GRUR International* (2016), 989–998, at 992–993; F. Thouvenin, 'Wem gehören meine Daten? Zu Sinn und Nutzen einer Erweiterung des Eigentumsbegriffs', *Schweizerische Juristen-Zeitung* 113 (2017), 21–32, at 24; H. Zech, 'Daten als Wirtschaftsgut – Überlegungen zu einem "Recht des Datenerzeugers"',

interfere with the use of others. Against this background, introducing data ownership needs a convincing justification as such a property right would allow data owners to exclude others from using their data. According to these authors, property rights in public goods should only be granted in case of market failure, i.e. if data was not produced or used to a socially desirable degree.[24] However, in the age of big data one can hardly argue that a market failure with respect to the collection, creation, and processing of data exists. To the contrary, the exponential rise of the quantity and quality of data and its ubiquitous processing indicates that companies have enough incentives for collecting, processing, and trading data.[25] Even if incentives for the collection, processing, and trading of data exist, these activities might not lead to socially desirable outcomes. Nonetheless, it is doubtful whether these outcomes amount to an actual market failure and even more doubtful that such failure could be remedied by the introduction of propert rights in data.

A third group of authors excludes the introduction of data ownership rights from a fundamental rights perspective. They argue that the fundamental right to the protection of personal data safeguards the personality of data subjects, not their property.[26] Accordingly, a data subject cannot be 'regarded only or mainly as the owner of the data concerning him or her',[27] as such ownership would allow data subjects to trade their property rights away and thereby waive the guarantees of their fundamental rights.[28] From this perspective, granting property rights in personal data is impossible, as individuals are not free to waive or completely alienate the rights in their personal data. According to these authors, only some rights in their data could be transferred from data subjects to third parties, but not all of them.[29] For instance, a waiver of all data protection guarantees would not be permissible, but a numerus clausus of clearly defined 'leases' of personal data for specific purposes could be set in place.[30]

Computer Recht 31 (2015), 137–146, at 139; L. Determann, 'No One Owns Data', *Hastings Law Review* 70 (2018), 1–44, at 41.

[24] Drexl et al., note 5, at 2–3; W. Kerber, 'Governance of Data: Exclusive Property vs. Access', *International Review of Intellectual Property and Competition Law* 47 (2016), 759–762, at 760; Weber and Thouvenin, note 5, at 52–53.

[25] Drexl et al., note 5, at 2–3; J. Drexl, 'Designing Competitive Markets for Industrial Data – Between Propertisation and Access', Max Planck Institute for Innovation and Competition Reserach Paper No 13 (2016), at 30–31; F. Faust, 'Ausschliesslichkeitsrecht an Daten?', in Stiftung Datenschutz (ed), *Dateneigentum und Datenhandel* (Leipzig: Erich Schmidt Verlag, 2019), 85–100, at 99; Kerber, note 23, at 992–993; Weber and Thouvenin, note 5, at 52–53.

[26] S. Rodotà, 'Data Protection as a Fundamental Right', in S. Gutwirth et al. (eds), *Reinventing Data Protection?* (Berlin: Springer, 2009), 77–82, at 81; see also N. Purtova, 'Do Property Rights in Personal Data Make Sense after the Big Data Turn?', Tilburg Law School Legal Studies Research Paper No 21 (2017), at 8–9.

[27] Rodotà, note 26, at 81.

[28] Purtova, note 26, at 8; OECD, note 3, at 196.

[29] Purtova, note 26, at 8.

[30] Ibid.

With regard to the question whether the introduction of data ownership as a property right would foster an adequate free flow of data in the digital single market, other aspects are of crucial importance, namely the impact of such property rights on transaction costs and (as a result) on the use of data and the consequences for data subjects. We look in turn at these implications.

2 Analysis

A TRANSACTION COSTS The introduction of property rights in data would lead to a situation in which every transfer and use of data would have to be subject to a prior agreement with the owner of the data. First of all, the owner of the data to be used would have to be identified. Second, the potential user would have to negotiate with the owner and agree on whether and under what conditions the data can be used. Both the identification of the owner and the negotiation would lead to considerable transaction costs.[31]

Identifying the data owner might sometimes be straightforward but will more often be rather complicated. The former would be true for non-personal data which is controlled by a single entity, most often a business. The latter would apply to personal data. If one assumes that property rights in personal data would vest in data subjects, the use of large datasets containing data about a large number of individuals would quickly become very burdensome, as every data subject would have to be identified and contacted in order to negotiate the conditions for the use of their data. Although there are important differences between the transaction costs associated with the use of personal and non-personal data, the introduction of data ownership as a property right would increase transaction costs in all cases and thus hurt the free flow of data within the digital single market. With regard to personal data, one might argue that these transaction costs must be incurred to protect the interests of data subjects in having control over the use of their personal data, thus moving from a fully free flow to a somewhat restricted and more adequate free flow of personal data. Increasing transaction costs for using and trading non-personal data by introducing data ownership rights and thereby restricting the free flow of data cannot be justified.[32]

Some scholars have argued that property rights in data could (in theory) increase legal certainty and reduce transaction costs, as contract negotiations could start from a clear determination as to who owns what data.[33] However, an analysis of potential

---

[31] Weber and Thouvenin, note 5, at 53–54; Drexl, note 25, at 35.
[32] For an economic analysis of the introduction of a new property right on non-personal data, see Kerber, note 23, at 989; also Drexl et al., note 5, at 2 et seqq.
[33] See J. C. Sahl, 'Gesetz oder kein Gesetz, das ist hier die Frage – Zur Notwendigkeit gesetzlicher Regulierung in der Datenökonomie', *Privacy in Germany* 4 (2016), 146–151, at 149; Kerber, note 23, at 994–995.

criteria for allocating property rights in data shows that it is far from obvious which criteria should be applied to determine ownership, especially with regard to non-personal data.[34] While it seems intuitive that data subjects should be the owner of personal data relating to them, it is less clear if businesses collecting such data should likewise have some ownership over the data accumulated in their systems. Besides, personal data quite often relates to more than one individual; for instance, a picture of a group of people or the genetic data of one person which always of data about that person's parents, grandparents, siblings, infants, etc. Concerning the difficulties of identifying and applying a suitable criterion for allocating property rights in data, introducing data ownership rights would rather raise than reduce transaction costs and limit the free flow of data in the digital single market.

B CONSEQUENCES FOR DATA SUBJECTS The introduction of property rights in personal data would most probably have negative consequences for data subjects. Even if data controllers most often process personal data based on legitimate interests (Article 6(1)(b), (c) and (f) GDPR),[35] another important foundation for the lawfulness of processing is the data subjects' consent (Article 6(1)(a) GDPR). If the processing is based on consent, data subjects can – at least in theory – decide whether businesses may use their personal data by accepting their terms and conditions and/or their privacy policies. In doing so, they 'trade' their personal data in exchange for 'free' goods and services. However, under the current data protection regime, consent can be withdrawn by data subjects at any time (Article 7(3) GDPR), thereby enabling them to prohibit the future processing of their personal data, if they reconsider their previous decision.

Granting property rights in personal data would mean that these property rights could be transferred to third parties.[36] Given this possibility, we have to expect that businesses would request that users of their services transfer those property rights to them – just as they currently request users to allow for an all-encompassing use of their data through consent. As opposed to the situation today, however, businesses that acquire their users' property rights in their personal data would be able to exclude these users from using their personal data themselves and from exercising the limited amount of control they have today. As a result, introducing property rights in personal data would substantially weaken the position of data subjects – which is the contrary of what people advocating for such rights want to achieve. While the option to transfer ownership rights in personal data might have a positive impact on the free flow of such data, the interests of data subjects in being able to exercise some control over the processing of their personal data would be neglected.

---

[34] Thouvenin et al., note 5, at 116–117; Drexl, note 25, at 38 et seqq.
[35] F. Thouvenin, 'Datenschutz auf der Intensivstation: Befund, Diagnose und Therapie', *digma* (2019), 206–213.
[36] Thouvenin, note 23, at 26.

As a consequence, the introduction of property rights in personal data would compromise the goal of establishing an adequate free flow of data.

3 Interim Conclusion

The analysis shows that introducing data ownership as a property right does not promote the goals of the Digital Single Market Strategy. For non-personal data, granting property rights would raise transaction costs and thereby deter or at least encumber its free flow. Accordingly, legislators should not introduce any property right in such data. Moreover, there are no reasons why the free flow of non-personal data should be restricted by any other legal means. On the contrary, the full potential of non-personal data can be achieved if that data is shared amongst businesses, for instance, through the granting of access rights, as discussed later.

While property rights in personal data would also increase transaction costs, these costs could be justified with regard to the goal of protecting the interests of data subjects in having some control over the use of their personal data. However, the granting of property rights in personal data would lead to a different and quite severe problem: Since property rights in personal data could be transferred to any third party, businesses would most likely make sure that their users transfer these property rights when using their services. Consequently, data subjects would not only lose control over their personal data but businesses, as the owners of said data, could even forbid them to further use their personal data altogether. Such a scenario would undermine the policy goal of establishing an adequate free flow of personal data within the EU.

II *Ownership as Control*

1 Preliminary Remarks

The concept of 'ownership as control' is generally accepted and well-established for personal data and is usually called 'informational self-determination' or 'informational autonomy'.[37] These notions refer to the individual's right to determine which information about them is disclosed to others and for what purposes such information will be used.[38] Data protection laws are generally based on these concepts.

---

[37] See Recital 7 GDPR; also Purtova, note 26, at 6 et seqq.; H. U. Vrabec, 'Uncontrollable: Data Subject Rights and the Data-driven Economy', PhD thesis, University of Leiden (2019), at 105 et seqq. Note that the principle of 'informational self-determination' has been criticized in the literature. See H. P. Bull, *Informationelle Selbstbestimmung – Vision oder Illusion?* (Tübingen: Mohr Siebeck, 2011); Thouvenin, note 35; W. Veil, 'The GDPR: The Emperor's New Clothes – On the Structural Shortcomings of Both the Old and the New Data Protection Law', *Neue Zeitschrift für Verwaltungsrecht* 10 (2018), 686–696.

[38] German Constitutional Court (census decision) in 1983 (BVerfGE 65,1).

The GDPR is even quite explicit about this underlying rationale by stating that 'natural persons should have control of their own personal data' (Recital 7). The concept of control is most clearly expressed in the condition of consent for the lawfulness of data processing (Article 6(1)(a) GDPR) and in the individual rights of the data subjects (Articles 12 et seqq. GDPR). In the following sections, these concepts are analysed further to assess whether ownership as control is a meaningful approach to establish an adequate free flow of personal data.

2 Implementation

A CONSENT At the stage of collection, consent and the right to information are the fundamental principles within the GDPR for granting control. In order to be compliant with the GDPR, consent must represent a 'freely given, specific, informed and unambiguous indication' by the data subjects by which they state or clearly affirm their agreement with the processing of personal data relating to them (Article 4(11) GDPR). It is key that the data subjects have a real choice to agree or disagree to the data collection. Such a choice is challenged in cases of power imbalances or if consent is the condition for the performance of a contract or for the provision of a service (Article 7(4) GDPR).[39] Similarly, any form of deception, intimidation, or significant negative consequences for the data subjects if they do not consent or later withdraw consent will fail to fulfil the requirement of a freely given consent.[40]

Consent is given on an informed basis if the data subjects are able to understand who processes what data for which purpose(s), if they are made aware of their right to withdraw consent, and if they obtain information about the use of their data for automated decision-making, as well as on the risk associated with a transfer of the data to an unsafe third country.[41] More often than not, the necessary information is provided in the controllers' privacy policy or as a specific part of the general terms of service. In either case, the information must be provided in an intelligible and accessible form, using clear and plain language (Article 7(2) GDPR).

Due to the complexity of digital goods and services, being adequately informed about the data processing is very challenging and it can be argued that due to an overload of consent notices, data subjects no longer make active, informed choices

---

[39] See Article 29 of Article 29 Working Party, Guidelines on Consent under Regulation 2016/679, 28 November 2017 [hereinafter, Working Party 29 Consent Guidelines], at 5–6; E. M. Frenzel, 'Art. 7 DSGVO: Bedingungen für die Einwilligung', in B. P. Paal and D. Pauly (eds), *Datenschutz-Grundverordnung*, 2nd edn (Munich: C. H. Beck, 2018), 107–115.

[40] Ibid.

[41] Working Party 29 Consent Guidelines, note 39, at 13.

but merely agree to such notices when they are asked to do so.[42] Because users often 'blindly' agree to notices that pop up on their screens, the ability to withdraw consent (Article 7(3) GDPR) at any given time becomes (at least in theory[43]) an important redress mechanism for such situations and extends the control of data subjects beyond the stage of data collection to the entire data lifecycle.

B DATA SUBJECTS' RIGHTS Next to consent, data subjects' rights provide individuals with control over the use of their data, which is why they are also referred to as 'control rights'.[44] These rights apply notwithstanding whether the processing is based on consent or if another legal basis applies (see Article 6(1)(b-f) GDPR).

Data subjects' rights include

- the right to information (Articles 13 and 14 GDPR), which lists the (comprehensive) information that data controllers must provide to data subjects when collecting their data;
- the right access (Article 15 GDPR), which grants data subjects the right to get a copy of the personal data (in a commonly used electronic format) from the data controller and the right to obtain similar information on the processing of their data as provided for under the right to information;
- the right to rectification (Article 16 GDPR), which empowers data subjects to rectify inaccurate or complete incomplete personal data;
- the right to erasure (Article 17 GDPR), which allows data subjects to have their data erased by the data controller in specific circumstances, namely if the data subject withdrew consent or if the data is no longer necessary for the purposes it was collected for;
- the right to restriction of processing (Article 18 GDPR) in specific circumstances, namely if the accuracy of the data is contested or if the data subject has objected to the processing;
- the right to data portability (Article 20 GDPR), which enables data subjects to receive their data in a machine-readable format or to transmit it to any third party;
- the right to object (Article 21 GDPR) to data processing which is based on public or legitimate (private) interests on grounds relating to their particular situation;

---

[42] B. Schermer, B. Custers, and S. van der Hof, 'The Crisis of Consent: How Stronger Legal Protection May Lead to Weaker Consent in Data Protection', *Ethics and Information Technology* 16 (2014), 171–182, at 171–172.

[43] See B. Custers, 'Click Here to Consent Forever: Expiry Dates for Informed Consent', *Big Data and Society* 3 (2016), 1–6. Custers describes the practical challenges that the withdrawal of consent faces in the data economy. He notes that users typically do not withdraw consent to free accounts but merely stop using the service.

[44] Vrabec, note 37, at 111.

- and the right not to be subject to automated decision-making (including profiling) when such an automated decision produces legal effects or similarly significantly affects a data subject (Article 22 GDPR).

Boundaries to these data subjects' rights are set within the GDPR, either within the data subjects' rights themselves or through Article 11 GDPR. The latter limits the rights of the data subject when the data controller is unable to reidentify a data subject within its datasets. While the rights to access, rectification, erasure, restriction, and portability do not apply in such cases, the data subjects' right to information, to objection, and to not being subject of automated decision-making still prevail (Article 11(2) GDPR).

3 Analysis

When personal data is being processed, the GDPR provides a some control to data subjects: Consent is one of the two most important lawful bases of processing, thereby handing the decision whether personal data is processed to the data subject. In addition, data subjects have a well-developed set of rights that allow them to be informed about, to exert some control and quite often also to inhibit the processing of their data by the data controller.

However, the GDPR only provides an amount of control. Most importantly, the lawfulness of the processing can be (and often is) based on the legitimate interests of the controller or public interests; in these instances, the processing of personal data is warranted without the consent and even against the will of the data subject.[45] Besides, control is also limited, as many of the data subjects' rights come with essential restrictions. For instance, the right to erasure is only granted if one out of a limited set of situations is given, namely if personal data is no longer necessary in relation to the purpose for which it was collected (Article 17(1)(a) GDPR), if the data subject withdraws consent and there is no other legal grounds for the processing (Article 17(1)(b) GDPR), or if the data has been unlawfully processed (Article 17(1) (d) GDPR). Another example is the right to data portability, which is limited if the personal data is necessary for the performance of a task carried out in the public interest or in the exercise of official authority vested in the controller (Article 20(3) GDPR).

By providing a limited amount of control to data subjects, the GDPR aims to strike a balance between facilitating the free flow of personal data and ensuring that

---

[45] F. Ferretti, 'Data Protection and the Legitimate Interests of Data Controllers: Much Ado about Nothing or Winter of Right?', *Common Market Law Review* 51 (2014), 843–868, at 856. In cases where processing is based on legitimate interests pursuant to Article 6(1)(b-f) GDPR and the conditions for the right to erasure (Article 17 GDPR) to restriction (Article 18 GDPR) or to object (Article 21 GDPR) toare not met, personal data may be processed even if data subject opposes such processing.

data subjects can exercise control with respect to the processing of their data (Recital 7 GDPR). Thereby, the law balances conflicting interests of data subjects and data controllers and aligns them with the ideal of an adequate free flow of personal data. The ideal of a 'free flow' is achieved by establishing a (mostly) harmonized data protection law framework within the EU, while the adequacy of the free flow is guaranteed by enshrining the notion of ownership as (adequately limited) control over personal data.

Compared with the property rights model, ownership as control takes a more balanced approach. In particular, data access rights are seen as a way forward to enable a more (adequate) free flow of personal data within the EU.[46]

D DATA ACCESS RIGHTS

I *Access by Individuals*

1 Access to Personal Data

Data subjects have a legitimate interest in having access to personal data others process about them. Therefore, the GDPR provides data subjects with a right to receive information about the purposes of the processing, the categories of personal data being processed, as well as – if determinable – the period for which the data will be stored (Article 15(1) GDPR). Amongst others, such access empowers individuals to verify the lawfulness of the processing of their personal data (Recital 63 GDPR). More important – from the perspective of the free flow of data – is the right of data subjects to receive a copy of their data from the data controller; if such request is made by electronic means, the controller shall provide the data in a commonly used electronic form (Article 15(3) GDPR). Where possible, the controller should even grant data subjects remote access to a secure system, which provides them with direct access to their personal data (Recital 63 GDPR). The right to obtain a copy is only restricted if such right adversely affects the rights and freedoms of others (Article 15(4) GDPR), namely if providing a copy of the data would harm trade secrets or intellectual property rights (Recital 63 GDPR). At least theoretically, data subjects are thus able to collect and later use all the data that others have about them.

The explicit and fully fledged right to obtain a copy of the personal data is closely linked to the right to data portability,[47] which the GDPR grants on top of the right of access if the processing is carried out by automated means (Article 20 GDPR). The latter allows data subjects to (re)claim the personal data they provided to the

---

[46] See also H. Richter and R. M. Hilty, 'Die Hydra des Dateneigentums – eine methodische Betrachtung', in Stiftung Datenschutz (ed), *Dateneigentum und Datenhandel* (Leipzig: Erich Schmidt Verlag, 2019), 241–259, at 256; European Commission, note 2; OECD, note 3.

[47] Vrabec, note 37, at 216.

controller in a structured, commonly used and machine-readable format (Article 20 (1) GDPR). Data subjects may themselves receive their personal data, transfer it, or have it, directly transmitted to another controller, if technically feasible. However, the scope of the right to data portability is restricted to data 'provided' by the data subject and to the instances of processing based on consent or a contract.[48] As a consequence, all data inferred from the personal data or information predicted by data controllers, will not be subject to this right.[49] However, the right of access, which is not restricted to data provided by the data subject, may empower data subjects with a right to get a copy of this data all the same.

2 Access to Non-personal Data

Individuals might also have legitimate interests in having access to non-personal data (e.g. text documents, spreadsheets, presentations, or other files that do not contain personal information) that they stored with a service provider, such as a cloud storage or a webmail provider. Such data will most often be processed on a contractual basis. These contracts grant users access to the service providers' servers to upload and access their files. The applicable terms of service of cloud service providers usually state that the users own the files and that they have a right to access their files, while cloud providers most often reserve the right to access, store, and scan these files (see for instance the terms of service of Dropbox or Google Drive). If the terms of service do not explicitly provide for a user's right of access, courts might derive such right from the underlying contract given that granting access to one's data is the very nature of such contracts. Accordingly, users should have a right to access non-personal data they provided to a service provider in most cases.

If non-personal data has been stolen, e.g., by hacking a user's device, criminal sanctions apply. In addition to these sanctions, tort law may give users a right to reclaim their non-personal data from the ones that stole it from them.[50] Even if such claims may be difficult to enforce in practice, the legal basis for access is given.

---

[48] The term 'provided' can be interpreted restrictively, meaning that it concerns only personal data that the data subject explicitly provided in an explicit form, or extensively, including data that the controller collects upon consent or according to a contract (e.g. GPS, cookies, preferences). See P. De Hert et al., 'The Right to Data Portability in the GDPR: Towards User-Centric Interoperability of Digital Services', *Computer Law and Security Review* 34 (2018), 193–203, at 199; P. De Hert, 'The Future of Privacy: Addressing Singularities to Identify Bright-Line Rules That Speak to Us', *European Data Protection Law Review* 4 (2016), 461–466. De Hert argues that when dealing with fundamental rights, we should favor the interpretation that is most beneficial for individuals. Likewise, the Working Party 29 in its Guidelines on the Right to Data Portability argues for a broad interpretation of the term 'provided'. See Article 29 Data Protection Working Party, Guidelines on the Right to Data Portability, 13 December 2016 [hereinafter, Working Party 29 Data Portability Guidelines].
[49] De Hert et al., note 48, at 199.
[50] For a legal analysis under Swiss law, see Weber and Thouvenin, note 5, at 58–59; with reference to M. Eckert, 'Digitale Daten als Wirtschaftsgut: digitale Daten als Sache',

3 Analysis

Although the law does not provide for a general right of access to all sorts of data, individuals seem to be able to get access to 'their' data in most instances where access can reasonably be required. At the same time, data controllers and processors may only process their personal data in accordance with the requirements of the GDPR. Accordingly, from the perspective of the individuals, an adequate free flow of their data seems to be granted (at least in theory).

This is especially true when personal data is being processed as data subjects can draw upon the various control rights established in the GDPR, as discussed earlier. Next to the right of access, the right to data portability is seen as a powerful means to strengthen individual control.[51] In theory, this right should ensure that data subjects 'play an active role in the data ecosystem'[52] and enable them to break up service lock-ins in the digital economy (especially in social media). In this sense, data portability is seen as a means to foster competition,[53] while simultaneously ensuring an adequate free flow of personal data. However, it is more than doubtful that these goals can be achieved, since the vast majority of data subjects have so far only reluctantly made use of their individual rights.[54] Also, the mere right to data portability will hardly suffice to overcome the strong network effects which exist in some sectors, especially in social media platforms.[55] Nevertheless, the right of access and the right to data portability may prove useful for switching providers in other sectors, such as email or cloud storage providers.

Schweizerische Juristen-Zeitung 112 (2016), 245–249 and U. Hess-Odoni, 'Die Herrschaftsrechte an Daten', *Jusletter*, 17 May 2004. Weber and Thouvenin (note 5, at 59) provide also references to German literature elaborating on the right to reclaim stolen data; amongst others, see T. Hoeren, 'Dateneigentum – Versuch einer Anwendung von § 303a StGB im Zivilrecht', *Multimedia und Recht* 8 (2013), 486–491.

[51] Recital 68 GDPR.

[52] Working Party 29 Data Portability Guidelines, note 48, at 4, footnote 1.

[53] Ibid., at 3–4; De Hert et al., note 48, at 195.

[54] See J. Ausloos and P. Dewitte, 'Shattering One-Way Mirrors: Data Subjects Access Rights in Practice', *International Data Privacy Law* 8 (2018), 4–28, at 5; Vrabec, note 37, at 257 et seqq. Note that there is not much data available on the number of requests (e.g. access, restriction, portability) made by data subjects to individual data controllers. Search engine providers only publish the number of erasure requests received, e.g., Google publishes erasure requests made in every country. See Google, 'Requests to Delist Content under European Privacy Law', Google Transparency Report, available at https://transparencyreport.google.com/eu-privacy/overview?hl=en. Data protection authorities in the EU have noticed an increase of complaints brought forward by individuals, see, e.g., Commission nationale de l'informatique et des libertés (French Data Protection Authority), Presentation of the 2018 Activity Report and 2019 Issues of the French Data Protection Authority, 15 April 2019, available at www.cnil.fr/en/presentation-2018-activity-report-and-2019-issues-french-data-protection-authority. Note that websites such as www.datarequests.org/ have been created to facilitate obtaining access to personal data from companies. It remains unclear whether such sites have led to an increase of data subjects' requests.

[55] European policymakers have recently proposed legislative initiatives to tackle some of these issues, e.g., by means of the Digital Services Act (DSA) and Digital Markets Act (DMA). See

When non-personal data that belongs to a particular individual is being processed, data can most often be accessed based on contractual norms and sometimes based on tort law. While these access rights are much less comprehensive than the access rights for personal data, the latter may promote access to non-personal data for two reasons. First, because service providers have to build their systems in a way that allows them to extract the personal data of their users to comply with the right of access granted in data protection law, they need to build their systems in a way that enables them to identify and distinguish personal from non-personal data. Within this process non-personal data that belongs to an individual, such as text documents, can be identified and extracted as well. Second, it is often hard (or even impossible) to distinguish personal and non-personal data, and both types of data are often present in a single file, e.g. in a document that contains information about its author or in an email that always contains information about recipient and sender (at least in the metadata). Accordingly, it might be easier for service providers to provide all the data that belongs to an individual (whether personal or non-personal) if the said individual requests access to their personal data. It, therefore, seems that the current legal situation should also ensure an adequate free flow of non-personal data that belongs to an individual.

II *Access by Businesses*

1 Preliminary Remarks

Until today there are no general data access rights for businesses, neither with regard to data held by other businesses nor for data held by government agencies. But, of course, businesses can grant each other access to data on the basis of a contract. The default for businesses, however, seems to be that data is regarded as an asset that should not be shared with others. The general approach of collecting and analysing data in-house and via sub-contractors, and ensuring that this data stays within organizations and is not traded with other businesses,[56] is an essential impediment to the free flow of data and harms the overall digital economy.

As a public good, data could be used by an unlimited number of businesses simultaneously and the use by one business would not interfere with the use of others. Accordingly, granting access rights to businesses would be a meaningful way to enable broader use of data, unravel its potential, and foster competition. While this applies to all sorts of businesses, it is especially true for start-ups and small- and medium-sized enterprises (SMEs), which could benefit from the access to data for developing innovative digital

European Commission, Proposal for a Single Market for Digital Services (Digital Services Act) Amending Directive 2003/31/EC, COM(2020) 825 final, 15 December 2020; European Commission, Proposal on Contestable and Fair Markets in the Digital Sector (Digital Markets Act), COM(2020) 842 final, 15 December 2020.
[56] European Commission, note 13, at 15.

goods and services.[57] It is therefore not surprising that both the European Commission[58] and the OECD[59] are promoting the digital economy via access rights.

Even if no harmonized legal framework granting access rights for businesses exists, some sector-specific regulations can remedy specific problems. Besides, competition law contains generally applicable rules that may allow businesses to request access to data in some situations. More recently, the introduction of compulsory licences has been promoted in the literature as a new and promising way to establish access rights for businesses.

2 Implementation

A SECTOR-SPECIFIC REGULATIONS There are three types of sector-specific regulations granting access rights to data: (i) regulations granting government agencies access to data held by businesses; (ii) regulations that provide businesses access to data held by government agencies; and (iii) regulations providing businesses access to data held by other businesses. The first type of access rights ensures that government agencies have access to the data they need to perform their tasks and to take well-informed decisions.[60] Such access rights are common in many EU member states[61] but they are not the subject of this chapter, the enquiry of which is limited to access rights of businesses. The second type of access rights is a means to make better use of the data collected by government agencies by enhancing the reuse of such data. The third type mainly aims at fostering competition.

The most prominent example of the second type of access rights is the EU's Public Sector Information Directive.[62] According to this directive, this data must be

---

[57] Drexl et al., note 5, at 8.
[58] European Commission, note 2; see also Richter and Hilty, note 46, at 256.
[59] OECD, note 3.
[60] A. Früh, 'Datenzugangsrechte: Rechtsrahmen für einen neuen Interessensausgleich in der Datenwirtschaft', *sic!* 10 (2018), 521–539, at 528 et seqq. with reference to European Statistical System, 'Access to Privately Held Data', Position Paper, November 2017.
[61] In France, for instance, the government has a right to access privately held data that are relevant for establishing public statistics (Article 19 Loi 2016-1321 du 7 octobre 2016 pour une Répulique numérique, NOR: ECFI1524250L, JORF 0235 du 8 octobre 2016, texte 1). Overall, France has been pushing for access rights to privately held data in various sectors, such as for scanner data of retailers, in order to improve the quality of the standard Consumer Price Index, for mobile phone data to measure the mobility of people within local areas, or for data on tourist accommodations offered by individuals on the Internet. Other EU member states – such as Italy, the Netherlands, and Poland – are likewise establishing regulations allowing statistical authorities to access scanner data of large retailers and supermarkets. In Estonia, government agencies have access to data from smart electricity meters in order to produce electricity consumption statistics of households and businesses and accordingly plan for future electricity needs. See European Statistical System, note 59, at 8 et seqq.
[62] Directive (EU) 2019/1024 of the European Parliament and of the Council of 20 June 2019 on open data and the re-use of public sector information PE/28/2019/REV/1, OJ L 172, 26.6.2019, p. 56–83.

freely available for reuse and public sector bodies are not allowed to charge more than marginal cost for such reuse.[63] However, one could argue that if private businesses profit from data provided by the government, the general public should in return obtain some benefits from the data that businesses generate through the use of government data, or that at least government agencies obtain access to such data at marginal costs.[64]

The third type of access rights is not very widespread, at least until today. A case in point is the maintenance work on cars which often depends on access to data about the car. This case is governed by Regulation 715/2007 of the EU.[65] In order to foster competition in the market for car maintenance, manufacturers of cars must provide unrestricted and standardized access to specified information to repair workshops through websites using a standardized format in a readily accessible and prompt manner (Article 6 Regulation 715/2007). For doing so, the manufacturers can charge a 'reasonable and proportionate fee' (Article 7 Regulation 715/2007). Another example is the EU Directive 2015/2366 on payment services in the internal market,[66] which enables payment service providers to get access to data held by banks in order to facilitate their market access.[67]

B COMPETITION LAW In addition to sector-specific regulations, competition law contains generally applicable rules that may arguably serve as access right. In practice, however, competition law is not a workable solution, for several reasons:[68]

---

[63] European Commission, 'Digital Single Market: EU Negotiators Agree on New Rules for Sharing of Public Sector Data', *Press Release*, 22 January 2019.

[64] Früh, note 59, at 525–526. In order to prevent public sector information being locked in by private companies that work for the government, the EU will establish safeguards that will reinforce transparency and limit the conclusion of agreements which could lead to exclusive reuse of public sector data by private partners. See European Commission, note 62.

[65] Regulation No 715/2007 of the European Parliament and of the Council of 20 June 2007 on Type Approval of Motor Vehicles with Respect to Emissions from Light Passenger and Commercial Vehicles (Euro 5 and Euro 6) and on Access to Vehicle Repair and Maintenance Information, OJ L [2007] 171/1; C. König, 'Der Zugang zu Daten als Schlüsselgegenständen der digitalen Wirtschaft', in M. Hennenmann and A. Sattler (eds), *Immaterialgüter und Digitalisierung: Junge Wissenschaft zum Gewerblichen Rechtsschutz, Urheber- und Medienrecht* (Baden-Baden: Nomos, 2017), 89–104, at 94.

[66] Directive 2015/2366 of the European Parliament and of the Council of 25 November 2015 on Payment Services in the Internal Market, Amending Directives 2002/65/EC, 2009/110/EC and 2013/36/EU and Regulation (EU) No 1093/2010, and Repealing Directive 2007/64/EC, OJ L [2015] 337/35 [hereinafter: Directive 2015/2366].

[67] Article 35 Directive 2015/2366.

[68] For an overview of the failures of competition law to grant access to privately held data, see J. Drexl, *Data Access and Control in the Era of Connected Devices*, Study for the European Consumer Organisation (Brussels: BEUC, 2018), at 4 and 36 et seqq.; Drexl et al., note 5, at 9–10; Früh, note 59, at 532 et seqq.; A. Früh, 'Zum Bedarf nach Datenzugangsrechten', *Jusletter IT Flash*, 11 December 2017; B. Lundqvist, 'Big Data, Open Data, Privacy Regulation, Intellectual Property and Competition Law in an Internet of Things-World: The Issue of Access', in M. Bakhoum et al. (eds), *Personal Data in Competition, Consumer*

First, with regard to access rights, competition law only comes into play in respect of businesses with a dominant position; even if this condition is met, access can only be requested in case of an abuse of such dominance (Article 102 TFEU). Second, the traditional criteria for defining the relevant market are not very helpful for defining markets in the data economy.[69] Third, and most importantly, competition law cases take a very long time to be decided, sometimes up to ten years.[70] It is obvious that businesses requesting access to data need much faster procedures to enforce their rights. Therefore, competition law is not a meaningful way for granting access to data.

C COMPULSORY LICENCES A promising way forward for ensuring access to data is the granting of compulsory licences as known in intellectual property law. As opposed to competition law, where courts define the conditions of granting a licence ex post, the conditions of such compulsory licences are defined ex ante. The difficulty here rests in establishing a system that considers the interests of all businesses involved, the one requesting and the one granting access, especially the latter's interest in securing its trade secrets.[71]

A general right of access to data would have to be regulated in a generally applicable body of law. A suitable and convincing approach is introducing such a right in trade secrets law. This previously quite heterogeneous body of law has recently been harmonised by the EU's Trade Secrets Directive.[72] The directive contains an expansive notion of trade secrets embracing all secret information (i.e. information not generally known or readily accessible) that has commercial value because it is secret and is subject to reasonable steps to keep it secret.[73] This definition encompasses most data held by businesses. Accordingly, amending trade secrets law would be a promising way to introduce general compulsory licences for granting access to data. While such an approach would be rather broad, compulsory licences could also be granted in sector-specific regulations, such as in telecommunications or energy acts, or in a potential regulation of platforms, covering search

---

Protection and Intellectual Property Law: Towards a Holistic Approach? (Berlin: Springer, 2018), 191–214, at 202–203.

[69] Drexl, note 67, at 36; Lundqvist, note 67, at 202–203.

[70] Früh, note 59, at 535; for an illustrative example, see R. Podszun, 'Lizenzverweigerung – Ernstfall im Verhältnis von Kartell und Immaterialgüterrecht', in P. Matousek, E. Müller, and T. Thanner (eds), *Jahrbuch Kartell- und Wettbewerbsrecht* (Wien: Neuer Wissenschaftlicher Verlag, 2010), 57–76.

[71] Früh, note 59, at 528, 530; A. Wiebe, 'Von Datenrechten zu Datenzugang – Ein rechtlicher Rahmen für die europäische Datenwirtschaft', *Computer und Recht* 33 (2017), 87–93, at 92.

[72] Directive 2016/943 of the European Parliament and of the Council of 8 June 2016 on the Protection of Undisclosed Know-How and Business Information (Trade Secrets) against Their Unlawful Acquisition, Use and Disclosure, OJ L [2016] 157/1 [hereinafter, Directive 2016/943].

[73] Article 2(1) Directive 2016/943.

engines or social media providers. In any case, access rights should not be granted for free. Rather, any business making use of its right of access should pay a fair, reasonable, and non-discriminatory (FRAND) compensation to the business that has collected, stored, and curated the data.[74]

Even if compulsory licences are considered a meaningful way of granting access to data, many things are still unclear. For example, one would have to define the conditions for granting such a licence and its scope (i.e., the data which is covered), as well as the purpose for which the data may be used if access is granted.[75] Today's case law contains some hints to address these important questions – the need for having access to data for entering a secondary market.[76] Other conditions could relate to single source data situations or some degree of market power of the business that should grant access. Also, one would have to decide whether a compulsory licence includes the right to get a copy of the data or whether such right should be limited to using and analysing the data on the machines of the trade secret owner. Lastly, and most importantly, even if compulsory licences are considered a suitable mechanism for granting access rights, it remains unclear if granting such licences is justified.

The most important argument in favour of introducing compulsory licences is undoubtedly the fact that data is a public good, as discussed earlier. Also, the business of most companies is not selling data to their customers but providing services that are based on data. As a consequence, granting access to data does not necessarily have a negative impact on the market share of the business that has to provide access. If this should be the case, one could consider restricting access to businesses that are not direct competitors but active in a secondary or even in an entirely different market.

The most important argument against granting access rights is the risk of undermining incentives for collecting, storing, and curating data. However, for the time being, it is hard to imagine that well-defined access rights would actually undermine such incentives to a relevant degree.

3 Analysis

Access rights for businesses are a meaningful way to enhance the free flow of data in the digital single market in order to foster innovation and strengthen the competing power of European companies. While competition law is not a workable solution,

---

[74] European Commission, note 13, at 39; Früh, note 59, at 537; Früh, note 67.

[75] Früh, note 67.

[76] Lundqvist, note 67, at 202–203 with reference to Joined Cases C-241/91 and C-242/91, *Radio Telefís Eireann (RTE) and Independent Television Publications Ltd (ITP)* v. *Commission of the European Communities* [1995], ECLI:EU:C:1995:98; C-418/01, *IMS Health GmbH & Co. OHG* v. *NDC Health GmbH & Co. KG* [2004], ECLI:EU:C:2004:257; T-201/04, *Microsoft Corp.* v. *Commission of the European Communities* [2007], ECLI:EU:T:2007:289.

two complementary approaches seem quite promising: First, trade secrets law could be amended to include compulsory licences, which allow businesses to claim access to data held by other businesses. Given the very broad scope of application of trade secrets law, this approach would allow to establish a general right of access to data. In order to protect the interests of businesses that have to grant access, relatively strict conditions would have to be designed and businesses requesting access would have to pay an appropriate licence fee. Second, sector-specific regulations could grant specific access rights. In such regulations, the conditions for claiming access could be modified and be either stricter or more lenient than in trade secrets law and certainly more specific, also with regard to the calculation of the licence fee. In addition, there might be situations in which access should be granted for free or only if the businesses involved grant each other access on a mutual basis (cross-licence). The combination of these two approaches would allow for a comprehensive regime of access rights, ensure an appropriate balancing of interests, and help establish an adequate free flow of data amongst businesses in the digital single market.

For the free flow to be fully adequate the interests of the individuals represented in the data must be taken into account as well. This is ensured by the application of the GDPR, which regulates virtually all processing of personal data by businesses (Article 2(1) GDPR), including the granting of access to such data. Access to personal data can thus only be granted in accordance with the requirements of the GDPR, namely the principles of transparency and purpose limitation (Article 5 (1)(a) and (b) GDPR), the conditions for the lawfulness of processing, namely consent of the data subjects or legitimate interest of the data controller (Article 6 (1)(a) and (f) GDPR), the information duties (Articles 13(1)(e) and 14 GDPR), and (if applicable) the conditions for the transfer of personal data to third countries (Articles 44 et seqq. GDPR).

If these requirements are met, one can certainly say that granting access to data through compulsory licences is a promising way to establish an adequate free flow of data in the digital single market. Given that many questions still need to be answered, it is also an avenue that deserves further research.

E CONCLUSION

In order to unlock the potential of the digital economy, the EU promotes its Digital Single Market Strategy. A core aspect of this strategy is establishing an adequate free flow of data within the Union. This adequate free flow balances economic interests of businesses of an entirely free flow of all types of data and individual interests to have some control of the collection and processing of personal data. To achieve this balance, different regulations have been set in place, such as the Trade Secrets Directive, the Open Data, some sector-specific regulations granting access rights, and, above all, the GDPR.

These regulatory attempts have been accompanied by a policy discussion on data ownership and data access rights. As shown in this contribution, data ownership can be understood both as a form of property and as a form of control. Both concepts are not equally fit to achieve the goal of establishing an adequate free flow of data within the digital single market. The introduction of data ownership as a property right for personal and non-personal data would increase transaction costs and impede the trading and the use of data. Such a right would thus hinder the EU's goal of achieving a free flow of data. Additionally, in terms of processing personal data, ownership as a property right does not aid individuals to remain in control of their personal data. To the contrary, such ownership rights would substantially weaken their position, as businesses could acquire these rights and exclude the data subjects from using their own personal data. Therefore, the concept of ownership as a property right can be dismissed as a model to help achieve the goals of the Digital Single Market Strategy. The concept of ownership as control has been implemented in the GDPR for the processing of personal data and has the potential to balance economic and individual interests. From an economic perspective, the harmoniza-tion of rules and the prohibition of data localization restrictions enhance the free flow of personal data. In contrast, the necessity to comply with the data protection principles (Article 5 GDPR), the need to establish a basis for the lawfulness of all processing of personal data (Article 6 GDPR) and the increased compliance duties of data controllers limit the processing activities and require the establishment of costly organizational and technical solutions to enable data subjects to make use of their individual rights (e.g., right of access and erasure). From an individual perspective, however, these limitations and in particular the (limited) control over how data about them is collected, as well as the options to interfere with the processing of said data at a later stage, are welcomed by many. It remains to be seen, however, whether individuals will actually exercise their (limited) control and whether the current approach of data protection law is able to strike an appropriate balance between economic and individual interests. While some doubts remain, the GDPR can be seen as a first step towards establishing an adequate free flow of personal data within the digital single market.

To achieve the goal of an adequate free flow of data within the EU, individuals and businesses should have access to the data necessary to pursue their interests. For individuals, access to their personal data is key to ensure informational self-determination. Such access is granted by the GDPR, in particular through the right of access and the right to data portability. In most cases, individuals also tend to have sufficient means to access non-personal data that belongs to them. Businesses should have access and be able to use personal and non-personal data as seamlessly as possible in order to develop innovative goods and services and strengthen their competing power, both within the EU and on a global level. The goal of a fully free flow of data, however, must be balanced against the interest of individuals in the protection of their personal data and the interest of businesses in the protection of their trade secrets. Accordingly, a business' access to personal data held by another business must only be granted in accordance with the GDPR. If these requirements are met or do not apply (as in the case of non-personal data), access to and use of data should be fostered. One way forward is the introduction of additional sector-specific access rights. Another, more all-encompassing and possibly more promising way, is to establish a general right of access to data which is protected as a trade secret by introducing compulsory licences in trade secrets law. Obviously, such licences would only be granted if certain conditions are met, and if an appropriate licence fee is paid. But the mere existence of such licences and the enforcement on a case-by-case basis could help to open up datasets which have been sealed behind corporate walls despite the fact that the data could be useful for others. Overall, the introduction of compulsory licences to grant access to data would allow for the balancing of interests of the businesses holding data with the interests of other businesses that need access to such data to enter a market, develop innovative goods or services, or remain competitive.

16

Data Is Different, So Policymakers Should Pay Close Attention to Its Governance

Susan Ariel Aaronson[*]

A INTRODUCTION

The founders of Stitch Fix and Strava understood something basic about people. Humans like to use data to connect with other people and to compare with their peers. Based on those insights, these entrepreneurs were able to build two new digital service companies. Both Stitch Fix (a clothing service) and Strava (a social network) rely on personal data to provide services to their customers. Stitch Fix clients first answer a detailed questionnaire about their clothing likes and dislikes. In return, these customers receive clothes and style recommendations designed by stylists and artificial intelligence (AI) to help them look and feel better about themselves.[1] Meanwhile, runners, cyclists and triathletes turn to Strava to measure their performance and instantly compare it to others around the world.[2] The two companies could not succeed without the relatively free flow of data across borders. Data flows move across borders when individuals, companies or governments authorize data to be transferred from one country (the source of data) to another country where the data may be processed or used.[3]

[*] Susan Ariel Aaronson is Research Professor, George Washington University, Director of the Digital Trade and Data Governance Hub, and GWU Cross-Disciplinary Fellow. She is also Senior Fellow at the Centre for International Governance Innovation (CIGI). Contact: saaronso@gwu.edu. The chapter is based on a paper originally published in 2018 by the Centre for International Governance Innovation entitled 'Data Is Different: Why the World Needs a New Approach to Governing Cross-Border Data Flows'. The permission to publish by CIGI is kindly acknowledged.

[1] https://support.stitchfix.com/hc/en-us/articles/204222994-What-is-Stitch-Fix-How-Does-it-Work-FAQ.

[2] www.strava.com/about.

[3] United States International Trade Commission, Digital Trade in the US and Global Economies, Part 1, Investigation No 332-532, Publication 4415, July 2014; United States International Trade Commission, Digital Trade in the US and Global Economies, Part 2, Investigation No 332-540, Publication 4485, September 2014; J. Nicholson and R. Noonan,

Firms have long relied on data to improve the efficiency and quality of goods and services. However, today market actors also utilize data to create entirely new services, such as personalized healthcare, and sectors such as apps, Internet-connected devices (Internet of Things, IoT), cloud service providers and AI. These sectors are the foundation of the data-driven economy: an economy built around the collection, preservation, protection, implementation and understanding of many different types of data. Although no one has exact figures, a significant portion of the data-driven economy is built on personal data – that is, data by and about people or a person.[4]

The data-driven economy portends major changes for the ability of individuals to shape their destiny and autonomy. Firms active in the data-driven economy are dependent upon data, much of which is personal data. According to the US National Institute of Standards (NIST), in the past, personal data was something that researchers had to ask for, store, analyze. Because it was not easy to collect personal data, scholars struggled to get sufficient information to do a full analysis. But today almost all our daily activities are data-collection opportunities, thanks to the mobile Internet, the IoT, and other data-driven technologies. Moreover, in the past, people could control their data to some extent because researchers, whether firms or individuals, had to obtain, or at least go through the motions of obtaining, consent. However, with the data-driven economy, people whose data is collected and used have provided their personal data without fully informed consent. To put it differently, despite mechanisms to opt in or out of data collection, people do not understand that in return for providing data that firms then monetize, they receive the many free services presented by digital technologies.[5] In this sense, while the mission of data-driven firms, such as Stitch Fix and Strava may be to help customers, their strategy for so doing may also conflict with long-accepted ideas about autonomy.[6]

Compared to Alibaba or Google, Stitch Fix and Strava are small players in the data-driven economy, but they are not atypical. Many of these firms see providing data services as akin to providing a public good. For example, Google's corporate mission is 'to organize the world's information and make it universally accessible and useful'.[7] Not surprisingly, researchers and policymakers now believe that data is

---

Digital Economy and Cross-Border Trade: The Value of Digitally-Deliverable Services (Washington, DC: US Department of Commerce, 2014), at 1.

4   World Economic Forum, *Personal Data: The Emergence of a New Asset Class* (Geneva: WEF, 2011); D. Ciuriak, 'The Economics of Data: Implications for the Data-Driven Economy', Centre for International Governance Innovation, 5 March 2018.

5   Australian Government Productivity Commission, 'Data Availability and Use', Productivity Commission Inquiry Report: Overview and Recommendations No 82 (2017).

6   P. D. König, 'The Place of Conditionality and Individual Responsibility in a "Data-Driven Economy"', *Big Data and Society* (2017); J. F. Childress, 'The Place of Autonomy in Bioethics', Hasting Center Report No 20 (1990), 12–17.

7   www.google.com/search/howsearchworks/mission/.

the most traded good or service. In 2016, the McKinsey Global Institute asserted that the value of data flows has overtaken the value of global trade in physical goods.[8] According to the World Economic Forum, 'the world produces 2.5 quintillion bytes a day, and 90 per cent of all data has been produced in just the last two years'.[9]

To succeed in the data-driven economy, companies and researchers need access to significant amounts of data – what economists term 'economies of scale'. Policymakers in many countries want to encourage these scale economies with shared norms and rules, but they also want these norms and rules to explicitly limit trade in some types of data to ensure the safety and privacy of their citizens. In elaborating this rule framework decision-makers must develop a process that reassures their citizens that the rules-based system is transparent, accountable and open to citizens' input.[10] With shared norms and rules, the Internet would be less likely to fragment; more people would have greater access to information; and individuals could create and share more information.[11] Individuals might also be better able to obtain rents from their personal data and have some modicum of control over its use. However, policymakers around the world disagree on how and where to develop such shared rules.[12]

Many executives and policymakers argue that trade agreements are the appropriate venue in which to govern cross-border data flows, because they believe that when information flows across borders, these flows are essentially traded.[13] They have negotiated e-commerce and digital trade chapters for this purpose. Herein, we distinguish between e-commerce (goods and services delivered via the Internet and associated with a transaction) and 'digital trade', which includes 'e-commerce' as well as new data-based services, such as Stitch Fix, or social platforms, such as Twitter.[14]

---

[8] J. Bughin, 'The Ascendancy of Digital Trade: A New World Order?', *OECD Business Brief*, 2016.

[9] V. Thirani and A. Gupta, 'The Value of Data', *World Economic Forum: Industry Agenda*, 22 September 2017.

[10] S. A. Aaronson, 'The Digital Trade Imbalance and Its Implications for Internet Governance', CIGI Global Commission on Internet Governance Paper No 25 (2016).

[11] Ibid.

[12] D. Castro and R. Atkinson, 'Beyond Internet Universalism: A Framework for Addressing Cross-Border Internet Policy', Information Technology and Innovation Foundation, September 2014, at 2; The World Bank, *World Development Report 2016: Digital Dividends* (Washington, DC: The World Bank, 2016).

[13] Aaronson, note 10; J. Meltzer, 'The Internet, Cross-Border Data Flows and International Trade', Brookings Institution Issues in Technology Innovation No 22 (2013).

[14] National and international organizations have not agreed on a common definition of digital trade. According to the OECD, digital trade can be defined as all cross-border trade transactions that are either digitally ordered, facilitated or delivered (see OECD and IMF, 'Measuring Digital Trade: Results of OECD/IMF Stocktaking Survey', BOPCOM 17/07 (2017), at 4). The United States defines digital trade as goods and services delivered via the Internet and/or associated technologies (see R. F. Fefer, S. I. Akhtar, and W. M. Morrison, 'Digital Trade and US Trade Policy', Congressional Research Service Report R44565 (2019)). The

While countries have begun to build a regulatory environment for e-commerce, it is unclear how to build an effective enabling environment for data. Many developing countries are not yet ready for such rule-making. After all, the bulk of firms like Strava and Stitch Fix are being created in middle-income and wealthy countries.[15] In many developing countries, business people are hobbled by obstacles such as unstable Internet connections, limited funding, inadequate numbers of researchers, and complementary policies, and infrastructure.[16] Moreover, while many countries have open data strategies for government-funded or public data, others have not yet figured out how to ensure that when firms mine the personal data of their users, they protect it from misuse, theft, or human rights violations. Firms that do not adequately protect the data that they collect, monetize, and share could lead users to experience problems such as identity theft, manipulative marketing or discrimination.[17] Users deserve a chance to shape new rules and to influence how firms use data.[18]

This chapter examines the new role of data in trade and explores how trade in data differs from trade in goods and services. Clearly, data is different and may need a distinct set of rules. Although there are six different types of data, we focus on two types: public data and personal data (information that relates to an identified or identifiable individual). We then examine several analogies used by analysts to describe data as an input, which can help us understand how data could be regulated. Next, we discuss how trade policymakers are regulating trade in data and how these efforts have created a regulatory patchwork. Finally, we suggest an alternative approach noting that any agreement must be built by and for the people whose data serve as its foundation. Before trade negotiators try to develop rules regarding cross-border data flows, they must acknowledge the special character of data and focus first on creating an effective enabling environment, then built trust in that new economy by empowering people around the world to control their data.

government of Australia notes 'electronic commerce (e-commerce) and digital trade refer to the trade of goods and services using the Internet including the transmission of information and data across borders' (see https://dfat.gov.au/trade/services-and-digital-trade/pages/e-commerce-and-digital-trade.aspx). I could not find an official Canadian definition, but Canada used the term digital trade in its most recent WTO reform proposals.

[15] WTO, *World Trade Report 2018: The Future of World Trade: How Digital Technologies Are Transforming Global Commerce* (Geneva: WTO, 2018).

[16] C. Golobski, 'Capitalizing on Industry 4.0 in Africa', Brookings Institution: Africa in Focus, 3 July 2018, available at www.brookings.edu/blog/africa-in-focus/2018/07/03/capitalizing-on-industry-4-0-in-africa/.

[17] UNCTAD, 'Data Protection and Privacy Legislation Worldwide', available at https://unctad.org/en/Pages/DTL/STI_and_ICTs/ICT4D-Legislation/eCom-Data-Protection-Laws.aspx.

[18] S. A. Aaronson and P. Leblond, 'Another Digital Divide: The Rise of Data Realms and Its Implications for the WTO', *Journal of International Economic Law* 21 (2018), 245–272.

B THE PECULIARITIES OF DATA AND THE ROLE OF DATA IN TRADE

Data and information have long been a key component of trade, but as noted earlier, data has also created new forms of trade. However, cross-border data flows are quite different from trade in goods or other types of services for many reasons: First, many services from payroll to data analytics rely on access to cross-border data flows. These data flows may yield a good or a service, or both.[19] Second, trade in digital services differs from trade in other services because suppliers and consumers do not need to be in the same physical location for a transaction to occur. Third, trade in data is fluid and frequent, and location is hard to determine on the borderless network. Trade in the same set of data can occur repeatedly in nanoseconds – for instance, when millions of people download Drake's latest song. As a result, researchers and policy-makers may find it hard to determine what is an import or export. They may also struggle to ascertain when data or data sets are subject to domestic law (such as intellectual property law) and what type of trans-border enforcement is appropriate.[20] Fourth, when data flows across borders, it may or may not be affiliated with a transaction. Hence, it is hard to describe some of these flows as 'traded'.[21] Fifth, economists generally agree that many types of data are public goods, which governments should provide and regulate effectively. Furthermore, when states restrict the free flow of data, they reduce access to information, which in turn can diminish economic growth, productivity and innovation domestically and globally.[22] Such restrictions can also affect the functioning of the Internet.[23] Sixth, trade in data occurs on a shared platform (the Internet) that is held in common. Seventh, and as earlier mentioned, much of the data flowing across borders and powering new sectors is personal data – digital data created by and about people. While they may benefit from services built on that data, the people who are the source of it do not control it. Data is their asset, yet they cannot manage, exchange and account for it.[24]

---

[19] A. Ariu, 'Services vs. Goods Trade: Are They the Same?', National Bank of Belgium Working Paper Research No 237 (2018).

[20] E. Goldman, 'The Open Act: Significantly Flawed but More Salvageable Than SOPA/ PROTECT IP', *Ars Technica*, 12 December 2011; B. de la Chapelle and P. Fehlinger, 'Jurisdiction on the Internet: From Legal Arms Race to Transnational Cooperation', CIGI Global Commission on Internet Governance Paper No 28 (2016).

[21] Nicholson and Noonan, note 3; US Department of Commerce, *Measuring the Value of Cross-Border Data Flows* (Washington, DC: US Department of Commerce, 2016), at 3.

[22] K. E. Maskus and J. H. Reichman, 'The Globalization of Private Knowledge Goods and the Privatization of Global Public Goods', *Journal of International Economic Law* 7 (2004), 279–320, at 284–285; OECD, 'Economic and Social Benefits of Internet Openness', OECD Digital Economy Papers No 257 (2016).

[23] J. Force-Hill, 'The Growth of Data Localization Post Snowden: Analysis and Recommendations for US Policymakers and Industry Leaders', *Lawfare Research Paper* 2 (2014), 1–40, at 32; L. Daigle, 'On the Nature of the Internet', CIGI Global Commission on Internet Governance Paper No 7 (2015).

[24] WEF, note 4, at 11.

Recent surveys show that people around the world are increasingly concerned about how firms use, protect, control and trade personal data. A 2018 poll of 25,262 Internet users in twenty-five countries found that half of Internet users surveyed are more concerned about their online privacy than they were a year ago, reflecting growing concern around the world about online privacy and the power of social media platforms.[25] Citizens want their governments to strengthen data protection laws and to beef up enforcement. In 2017, the Australian government stated that 'governments that ignore potential gains through consumer data rights will make the task of garnering social license needed for other data reforms more difficult'.[26]

In sum, cross-border data flows may not fit the traditional definition of trade. Policymakers should thus at least question whether the traditional model of trade rules needs reforms to reflect the specificities of data.

C NEW USES FOR DATA REQUIRE NEW WAYS OF THINKING ABOUT DATA

When individuals try to describe how firms are using data to reorder markets, they often compare data to other longstanding inputs to the provision of goods and services. In so doing, they hope to create greater understanding of the import and value of data. As an example, the World Economic Forum describes data as the oxygen of digital life.[27] In contrast, *The Economist* describes data as a new type of raw material, such as oil, on par with capital and labour.[28] However, law professor Lauren Scholz notes that this analogy is not helpful because the supply of oil is limited and only one actor can use a given portion of oil at one time. However, if you have access to data, then you can use it to create information and value.[29] Other analysts describe data as a form of capital, which can be shared and leveraged within and between organizations.[30] They note that the big data firms, such as Google, Facebook, Amazon, Uber, Stitch Fix and Strava, commodify and monetize data, creating new revenues and/or functions for the company.[31]

---

[25] Centre for International Governance Innovation, *2018 CIGI-Ipsos Global Survey on Internet Security and Trust* (Waterloo: CIGI, 2018).
[26] Australian Government Productivity Commission, note 5, at 2.
[27] M. Sönmez, 'Could Japan Become a Role Model for the Fourth Industrial Revolution?', *World Economic Forum*, 2 July 2018, available at www.weforum.org/agenda/2018/07/could-japan-become-a-role-model-for-the-fourth-industrial-revolution/; 'Data Is Oxygen of Digital Life: Mukesh Ambani', *Governance Now*, 16 February 2017, available at www.governancenow.com/news/regular-story/data-oxygen-digital-life-mukesh-ambani.
[28] 'Special Report: Data, Data Everywhere', *The Economist*, 27 February 2010.
[29] L. H. Scholz, 'Big Data Is Not Big Oil: The Role of Analogy in the Law of New Technologies', *Tennessee Law Review* 86 (2019), 863–893.
[30] 'The Rise of Data Capital', *MIT Technology Review*, 21 March 2016; J. Sadowski, 'Companies Are Making Money from Our Personal Data but at What Cost?', *The Guardian*, 31 August 2016.
[31] Sadowski, note 30; World Economic Forum, note 4.

Meanwhile, some other scholars posit that we should think about data as labour, as in the early phases of the industrial revolution. We provide our data for free to firms that turn around and monetize this information. But you and I, like the workers of yore, lack bargaining power and are unable to meaningfully negotiate over payments for our data. Most of us are not sufficiently protected from misuse of our personal data or violations of our privacy. In this way, we are denied a share of the economic value of our data, just as workers in the early industrial age. We are facilitating a massive transfer of wealth from ordinary people to the tech titans.[32] In search of evidence, two scholars traced the AI supply chain and found invisible labour, outsourced or crowdsourced, hidden behind interfaces and camouflaged within algorithmic processes. They note '[s]ometimes this labor is entirely unpaid, as in the case of the Google's reCAPTCHA. In a paradox that many of us have experienced, to prove that you are not an artificial agent, you are forced to train Google's image recognition AI system for free, by selecting multiple boxes that contain street numbers, or cars, or houses'.[33] Moreover, these scholars note that treating data like capital exacerbates inequality and limits the productivity gains from big data and AI. They suggest that we should organize collectively to form a 'data labor union' that would bargain for fees for assessing our data. The union could certify data quality and guide 'users to develop their earning potential'. Meanwhile, data collectors 'must allow users to understand, withdraw, and transfer their data across competitors'.[34] Only by organizing collectively can we control how our data are used.

Still other scholars argue that personal data is a form of property that individuals can assert rights to control and to access.[35] This concept underpins the European Union's General Data Protection Regulation (GDPR). The notion that data is a form of personal property that people should be able to control also undergirds other countries' approaches, such as those of Brazil and China.[36]

---

[32] E. Posner, 'On Cultural Monopsonies and Data-as-Labor', 31 January 2018, available at http://ericposner.com/on-cultural-monopsonies-and-data-as-labor/.

[33] K. Crawford and V. Joler, *Anatomy of an AI System: The Amazon Echo as an Anatomical Map of Human Labor, Data and Planetary Resources* (New York: AI Now Institute and Share Lab, 2018), available at https://anatomyof.ai/, at section XVIII.

[34] I. A. Ibarra et al., 'Should We Treat Data as Labor? Moving beyond "Free"', *Proceedings of the American Economic Association*, 1 (2018), 1–5, at 3–4.

[35] T. Scassa, 'Considerations for Canada's National Data Strategy', Centre for International Governance Innovation, 5 March 2018, available at www.cigionline.org/articles/consider ations-canadas-national-data-strategy; B. Wylie, 'Governance Vacuums and How Code Is Becoming Law in Data Governance in the Digital Age', in CIGI (ed), *Special Report 2018: Data Governance In the Digital Age* (Waterloo: CIGI, 2018), 86–91, D. Breznitz, 'Data and the Future of Growth: The Need for Strategic Data Policy', Centre for International Governance Innovation, 19 April 2018, available at www.cigionline.org/articles/data-and-future-growth-need-strategic-data-policy.

[36] M. Ramey, 'Brazil's New General Data Privacy Law Follows GDPR Provisions', Covington and Burling, 20 August 2018, available at www.insideprivacy.com/international/brazils-new-general-data-privacy-law-follows-gdpr-provisions/.

If we view data as property, then corporations would have to pay the data generators (you and I) for permission, collection and use of data. The big firms would probably not offer services for free if we had to pay. Moreover, firms would then have an incentive to keep data accurate and carefully stored.[37] But law professor Lisa Austin warns that if you think about data as property, you have to balance the ownership claims of the owners of personal data with those of the firms processing and monitoring that data.[38] Nor can we ensure that our private information is not misused. As law professor Teresa Scassa has noted, privacy laws are ill fitted to a context in which data is a key economic asset.[39]

Finally, the UK government has introduced the notion that data is similar to infrastructure. In a paper prepared for the National Infrastructure Commission, the authors noted 'the managed and built environments increasingly depend upon data in real time. New mechanisms for the assembly, management and processing of data provide a new impetus for thinking how the data is best managed so that society can best utilize its resources, solve the most problems and provide the most social good for most people'.[40] In this view, government plays an important role providing and regulating data and promoting its sharing and consumption.[41]

Except for data as property, these analogies have not significantly influenced national and international regulations. Moreover, these analogies miss an important aspect of the nature of personal data. It is a by-product of our thinking, actions and simply living. It is not one thing, and thus, we should not simply view it as a resource, or as our property, capital, labour, or infrastructure.

There are no reliable statistics about the types, value and amounts of data exchanged across borders and what percentage of cross-border data flow consists of personal data. Both Canada[42] and in the United States,[43] are trying to estimate the value of these flows. Despite the lack of exact numbers, we can hypothesize that a significant portion of the data exchanged across borders is personal data. People's ability to control their data, like other issues of autonomy, is becoming a civil rights issue.[44] According to Ravi Naik, individuals' rights to data protection 'have too often been ignored, and it is taking a groundswell of citizen activism to flip the script and hold power to account by individuals asking for their data and determining its use. We

---

[37] Breznitz, note 35.
[38] L. Austin, 'We Must Not Treat Data Like a Natural Resource', *Globe and Mail*, 9 July 2018.
[39] Scassa, note 35, at 9.
[40] P. Kawalek and A. Baya, 'Data as Infrastructure', A Report for UK National Infrastructure Commission UK, 14 December 2017, at 1.
[41] Ibid.
[42] Statistics Canada, 'The Value of Data in Canada: Experimental Estimates', 10 July 2019, available at www150.statcan.gc.ca/n1/pub/13-605-x/2019001/article/00009-eng.htm.
[43] US Department of Commerce, note 26.
[44] König, note 6; S. A. Aaronson, 'Data Minefield: How AI Is Prodding Governments to Rethink Trade in Data', in CIGI (ed), *Special Report: Data Governance In the Digital Age* (Waterloo: CIGI, 2018).

are at a watershed moment of a citizen-led demand for data rights, with the hallmarks of a new civil rights movement enmeshed within it'.[45] Some countries, such as Chile, Colombia, Mexico, Turkey and Ecuador, are making personal data protection a constitutional right, although they differ as to the efficacy of enforcement.[46]

Truth is, these analogies can only go so far in guiding public policy because the new economy is behaving in ways that few of us understand. For example, the market for data is opaque: we really do not know how firms use our data. In these conditions, data holders/gatherers can deny or grant access to data; they do not have to let people know what data they have collected, whether it is accurate, how they use it and if they sell it.[47] In opaque markets, policymakers should develop policies that facilitate transparency and accountability, as counterweights to opacity. Breznitz argues in this sense that governments must establish the market for data and set the rules for how data are gathered and used.[48] Meanwhile, the Australian Productivity Commission says that governments must move markets from a system based on risk aversion and avoidance (which is not working) to one based on transparency and confidence in data processes.[49]

Despite their flaws, two of these analogies may be useful to trade policymakers, as they seek to develop rules governing cross-border exchange of data. First, at the national level, developing country policymakers who see data as a form of basic infrastructure could be more willing to establish data plans. Smart management of all types of data will enable more people to benefit from such data and to create new data-driven services attuned to specific economies and cultures. In contrast, the data as labour analogy might help trade policymakers as they attempt to bridge national strategies and create international rules governing data. In the late nineteenth century, many industrializing states developed national regulations to improve work conditions and protect workers from the vagaries of globalization. These regulations helped raise wages, which in turn led to improvements in labour productivity and greater trade. But not all states adopted such worker protections and trade policymakers feared a race to the bottom among states competing for lower wages and working conditions. The members of the League of Nations established an International Labour Organization (ILO) with rules that would help them find common ground to improve workplace conditions, facilitate peace and encourage trade.[50] We may need a similar organization to help mitigate the differences among national data approaches, if not the WTO.

---

[45] R. Naik, 'Let's Take Back Control of Our Data – It's Too Precious to Leave to the Tech Giants', *The Guardian*, 3 October 2017.
[46] O. Molina, 'Personal Data Protection Is a Constitutional Right in Chile', *IAPP*, 22 June 2018, available at https://iapp.org/news/a/personal-data-protection-is-a-constitutional-right-in-chile/.
[47] Breznitz, note 35.
[48] Ibid.
[49] Australian Government Productivity Commission, note 5, at 2.
[50] M. Huberman, *International Trade and Labor Standards in History* (New Haven, CT: Yale University Press, 2002); International Labour Organization, *Rules of the Game: A Brief Introduction to International Labor Standards* (Geneva: ILO, 2014).

D THE CURRENT STATE OF RULES GOVERNING CROSS-BORDER DATA AND THE RISE OF DATA REALMS

Policymakers have been trying for years to create global rules to govern cross-border data flows both at the World Trade Organization (WTO) and in bilateral and regional trade agreements. The multilateral trade forum of the WTO includes several agreements that address issues affecting data and digital trade. They include the Information Technology Agreement; the Agreement on Trade-Related Aspects of Intellectual Property Rights (TRIPS); and the General Agreement on Trade in Services (GATS). The GATS is the most relevant to the new data-driven services; it has chapters on financial services, telecommunications, computer and media services. But the GATS predates the invention of the Internet and World Wide Web and says nothing explicitly about cross-border data flows. Nonetheless, the WTO panels and the Appellate Body have interpreted the agreement as applying to various online services. While they acknowledge that the agreement is technically neutral – that it was written to apply to changing technologies – academics, business leaders and various governments, including the United States, have argued that the WTO's rules need both amplification and clarification to apply to new data-driven services, such as those provided by Stitch Fix and Strava.[51] Meanwhile, WTO members established a work programme on e-commerce in 1998 and have agreed to waive customs duties on electronic transmissions. They also appear to have made progress on negotiations on data, as a leaked text reveals.[52]

At the Eleventh WTO Ministerial Conference in Buenos Aires in December 2017, Australia, Japan and Singapore, with the support of sixty-seven other WTO members, launched the E-Commerce Joint Statement Initiative. They hoped to encourage a consensus on what members should negotiate and how.[53] To further that effort, countries issued proposals and background papers. A group of African countries, also supported by India, advocated keeping the discussions within the WTO's current exploratory work programme, which has conducted work on e-

[51] M. Burri, 'Should There Be New Multilateral Rules for Digital Trade?' Think Piece for the E15 Expert Group on Trade and Innovation of the ICTSD and WEF, 2013; H. Lee-Makiyama, 'Future-Proofing World Trade in Technology: Turning the WTO IT Agreement (ITA) Into the International Digital Economy Agreement (IDEA)', ECIPE Working Paper No 4 (2011); WTO, Work Programme on Electronic Commerce: Ensuring That Trade Rules Support Innovative Advances in Computer Applications and Platforms Such as Mobile Applications and the Provision of Cloud Computing Services, Communication from the United States, S/C/W/339, 20 September 2011; S. A. Aaronson, 'What Are We Talking about When We Talk about Digital Protectionism?', *World Trade Review* 18 (2018), 1–37.

[52] WTO, Work Programme on Electronic Commerce, Ministerial Decision of 13 December 2017, WT/MIN(17)65, WT/L/1032, 18 December 2017. Bilaterals.org released this draft text in February 2021, which I confirmed was correct with WTO secretariat staff. https://www.bilaterals.org/IMG/pdf/wto_plurilateral_ecommerce_draft_consolidated_text.pdf.

[53] All WTO documents relevant to e-commerce discussions are available at www.wto.org/english/tratop_e/ecom_e/ecom_e.htm.

commerce-related topics within various WTO bodies, such as its Council for Trade in Services and Council for Trade in Goods.[54] Overall, not only is there a lack of consensus on e-commerce issues among the members but also it is often apparent that many of the members do not understand the differences, nor do they clearly distinguish between e-commerce and the provision of data-driven services.[55]

Despite this, on 25 January 2019, some seventy-six WTO members agreed to commence dedicated e-commerce talks. The announcement of this initiative was not greeted with universal acclaim. While business groups lauded it, civil society organizations and international labour groups came out against the talks and argued that a new agreement could threaten jobs, privacy and data security.[56] The members of the WTO did not only disagree about whether or not these talks should proceed, they also disagreed about the scope of the talks.[57] Many states – including the United States, Canada, China, Japan, the EU, Australia, Brunei, Hong Kong, Kazakhstan, Korea, Mongolia, New Zealand, Singapore, Chinese Taipei, Thailand, Georgia, Iceland, Liechtenstein, Moldova, Montenegro, Norway, Russia, Switzerland, Macedonia and the Ukraine – are keen to move the talks forward. With regard to data flows in particular, while the United States, Canada, the EU and Brazil generally want to create interoperable and universal rules and limit barriers to cross-border data flows, Russia and China are more concerned with maintaining internal social and political stability and are more open to using domestic regulation to limit such flows.[58] Developing countries are also divided. Policymakers and business leaders in most countries acknowledge that traditional e-commerce could help their farmers and firms trade directly with consumers around the world.[59] So, they are willing to negotiate 'e-commerce', but many are leery of negotiating data-driven services, given that they may lack domestic data-driven firms.

Meanwhile, the United States, the EU, Australia, Canada and other nations have placed language governing cross-border data flows in e-commerce chapters of their free trade agreements. As the data-driven economy has expanded in importance, the US, Mexico, Canada, the EU and Japan have recently renamed the newer versions of these chapters 'digital trade' chapters. Nations are also negotiating and agreed to digital economy specific agreements such as the Digital Economy Agreement of

---

[54] WTO, Work Programme on Electronic Commerce, Communication from the African Group, WT/MIN(17)/22, 6 December 2017.

[55] L. Kihara, 'China and US among 76 WTO Members Pushing for New E-Commerce Rules', *Reuters*, 25 January 2019; 'E-Commerce: A New Initiative Aims to Modernise Global Trading Rules', *The Economist*, 31 January 2019.

[56] H. Monicken, 'US China over 70 Others Announce Intent to Launch E-Commerce Talks', *Inside US Trade*, 31 January 2019.

[57] *The Economist*, note 55.

[58] Aaronson and Leblond, note 18.

[59] UNCTAD, *Information Economy Report 2017: Digitalization, Trade and Development* (Geneva: UNCTAD, 2017); UNCTAD, 'UNCTAD B2C E-Commerce Index 2018: Focus on Africa', *UNCTAD Technical Notes on ICT for Development* No 12 (2018).

Australia and Singapore, US Japan Digital Economy Agreement, and the Digital Economy Partnership of Chile, New Zealand, and Singapore.[60]

The first agreement, the Comprehensive and Progressive Trans-Pacific Partnership (CPTPP) went into effect in 2019 among eleven nations bordering the Pacific including Australia, Japan, Mexico, Chile and Canada. These nations agreed to the free flow of data across borders as a default, with limited exceptions. All signatories also must adopt a minimum level of privacy regulation. In contrast, the EU–Japan Free Trade Agreement (FTA), which also went into effect in 2019, puts personal data protection at its core. The EU–Japan Free Trade Agreement is the first FTA of the EU that includes rules on data but it also ensures that personal data is adequately protected not only under the agreement but additionally through an adequacy decision of the European Commission – the first such decision under the GDPR heightened standards of data protection.[61]

The US government next used CPTPP, whose e-commerce chapter is identical to that negotiated under the Transpacific Partnership Agreement (TPP) as a building block for the renegotiation of the North American Free Trade Agreement (NAFTA). NAFTA 2.0, now called the United States–Mexico–Canada Agreement (USMCA), has several interesting elements designed to promote data-driven economic growth. It seems designed to promote AI and other data-driven services. First, the USMCA contains a proper chapter on 'digital trade' (chapter 19), rather than one on e-commerce. Secondly, like CPTPP, it bans mandated disclosure of source code. But differently from the CPTPP, it also promotes AI by encouraging the parties to provide public information (information developed or provided to public entities) in a machine-readable and open format that can be 'searched retrieved, used, reused, and redistributed'.[62]

While the United States and Canada have made regulating barriers to cross-border data flows a priority, the EU has made personal data protection a priority. The EU will only sign FTAs that contain language regarding the free flow of data if its FTA partner(s) adequately protect personal data. These nations must go through a process of becoming 'adequate'. Specifically, these states must create independent government data protection agencies, register databases with those agencies and, in some instances, obtain prior approval from the European Commission before personal data processing may begin.[63] This process is both time-consuming and

---

[60] For details, see Chapter 1 and 2 in this volume.

[61] S. A. Aaronson, 'The Digital Trade Imbalance and Its Implications for Internet Governance', CIGI Global Commission on Internet Governance Paper No 25 (2016); European Commission, 'International Data Flows: Commission Launches the Adoption of Its Adequacy Decision on Japan', *Press Release*, 5 September 2018.

[62] Article 19 USMCA.

[63] European Commission, 'European Commission Endorses Provisions for Data Flows and Data Protection in EU Trade Agreements', *European Commission: Daily News*, 31 January 2018; European Commission, 'Questions and Answers on the Japan Adequacy Decision', *Memo*, 17 July 2018; European Commission, 'Horizontal Provisions for Cross-Border Data Flows and

expensive, as the EU's digital trade partners must devote resources to data protection, a difficult choice for nations with limited governance expertise or funds.

Meanwhile, policymakers in China restrict the free flow of data and information not only across borders but also within China. In so doing, Chinese officials maintain social stability and the power of the Communist Party.[64] However, China participated in the negotiation of Regional Comprehensive Economic Partnership (RCEP), a mega-regional trade agreement. RCEP includes Australia, Indian, Japan, South Korea and New Zealand as well as the nations of the Association of Southeast Asian Nations (ASEAN).[65] The RCEP' allows member states to impose whatever national regulatory restrictions they wish, as long as they are applied in a non-discriminatory way (are applied equally to domestic and foreign businesses).The provisions are not disputable.[66]

Thus, the three big digital markets – the United States, EU and China – have taken different approaches to cross-border data flows. This patchwork approach is causing another problem for many nations. Nations, such as Canada, Mexico and Australia, that have or seek to build strong trade relationships with the big three must choose which approach they would follow.[67] Countries that choose more than one such market will face high regulatory costs, as their costs of compliance would rise, given different standards.[68]

In a recent scholarly study, the WTO secretariat confirmed this patchwork of rules. It examined regional trade agreements that have incorporated specific provisions related to e-commerce. They found significant heterogeneity among the seventy-five chapters that explicitly address e-commerce. For example, these FTAs have different objectives, scope and definitions. The FTAs also define and

for Personal Data Protection in EU Trade and Investment Agreements', February 2018, available at https://trade.ec.europa.eu/doclib/docs/2018/may/tradoc_156884.pdf.

[64] Aaronson and Leblond, note 18. See also Chapter 12 in this volume.

[65] J. Panday, "RCEP's Digital Trade Negotiations Remain Shrouded in Secrecy', Electronic Frontier Foundation, 16 May 2017, available at www.eff.org/deeplinks/2017/05/rcep-negoti ations-remain-shrouded-secrecy; Australian Government Department for Foreign Affairs and Trade, 'Barriers to Australian Trade and Investment in Regional Comprehensive Economic Partnership (RCEP Countries)', 2018, available at www.dfat.gov.au/trade/agreements/negoti ations/rcep/Pages/barriers-to-australian-trade-and-investment-in-regional-comprehensive-eco nomic-partnership-rcep-participating-countries.aspx.

[66] Asia Trade Center, 'E-Commerce and Digital Trade Proposals for RCEP', Working Paper (2016); Asia Trade Center, 'TPP11 and RCEP Compared', Policy Brief No 17-12 (2017) and P. Leblond 'Digital Trade: Is RCEP the WTO's Future?' Centre for International Governance Innovation, 23 November, available at https://www.cigionline.org/articles/digital-trade-rcep-wtos-future..

[67] Aaronson and Leblond, note 18.

[68] A Carson, 'European Regulators, FTC Unveil Cross-Border Data Transfer Tool', IAPP News, 7 March 2014, available at https://iapp.org/news/a/european-regulators-ftc-unveil-cross-border-data-transfer-tool/; A. Carson, 'EU and APEC Officials Agree to Streamline BCR/CBPR Application Process', IAPP News, 26 May 2015, available at https://iapp.org/news/a/eu-and-apec-officials-agree-to-streamline-bcrcbpr-application-process/.

limit different barriers to trade, and most importantly, some thirty-eight of the seventy-five have different provisions related to the domestic legal framework in which e-commerce takes place. Finally, some forty-four of the seventy-five include language on personal data protection but again with very different definitions and obligations.[69]

Developing countries are likely to have the most problems adapting to the data-driven economy. These countries will be customers of AI and other data-driven sectors, rather than producers. According to Kai-Fu Lee, a venture capitalist and former computer scientist, the bulk of profit from the data-driven economy and particularly AI will go to the United States and China: 'AI is an industry in which strength begets strength: The more data you have, the better your product; the better your product, the more data you can collect; the more data you can collect, the more talent you can attract; the more talent you can attract, the better your product. It's a virtuous circle, and the USA and China have already amassed the talent, market share and data to set it in motion'.[70]

Finally, many developing countries have not yet adopted effective rules protecting personal data online or established rules for the use of public data. Based on data from 2017 the UNCTAD reports that 57 per cent of all countries (some 107 countries of which 66 were developing or transition economies) have put in place legislation to secure the protection of data and privacy. In this area, Asia and Africa show a similar level of adoption, with less than 40 per cent of countries having a law in place. Some 21 per cent of countries have no law at all; and 10 per cent are in the process of drafting legislation.[71] Moreover, most of adopted legislation contains rules that are not consistent with either the OECD Guidelines for the Protection of Personal Information and Transborder Data Flows[72] or EU's GDPR.[73]

Moreover, some countries hoard and refuse to share publicly held data with their citizenry.[74] In general, data gains value as it is shared, but it has little value if governments hoard it. While there is little empirical proof, open data appears to have important spillover effects including increasing civil discourse, improved public welfare and a more efficient use of public resources. But many states lack right to information laws or do not allow their citizens to view or comment on the

[69] J.-A. Monteiro and R. Teh, 'Provisions on Electronic Commerce in Regional Trade Agreements', WTO Working Paper No 11 (2017). For a more recent enquiry, see Chapter 1 in this volume.
[70] K.-F. Lee, 'The Real Threat of Artificial Intelligence', *The New York Times*, 24 June 2017.
[71] UNCTAD, note 17. UNCTAD had no data for 12 per cent of the countries reviewed.
[72] OECD, *Guidelines for the Protection of Personal Information and Transborder Data Flows* (Paris: OECD, 1980; updated in 2013).
[73] Consumers International, *The State of Data Protection Rules around the World: A Briefing for Consumer Organizations* (London: Consumers International, 2018), available at www .consumersinternational.org/media/155133/gdpr-briefing.pdf.
[74] The World Bank, note 12, at 241–247; B. Dennis, 'Scientists Are Frantically Copying US Climate Data Fearing It Might Vanish under Trump', *The Washington Post*, 13 December 2016.

data they hold.[75] So not only is there a patchwork for FTAs but there is also a patchwork of approaches to governing various types of data as well.

Without sufficient understanding and interaction with data-driven firms and their customers, developing country policymakers may struggle to effectively advocate for their short- and long-term interests in the data-driven economy. Zimbabwe provides an example: the government signed a strategic cooperation framework agreement with a Chinese start-up, CloudWalk Technology, for a large-scale facial recognition programme. Zimbabwe will export a database of their citizens' faces to China, allowing CloudWalk to improve their underlying algorithms with more data. The government allegedly agreed to the system to improve public safety, while the company wanted to improve the accuracy of its facial recognition system which was based on Chinese faces and needed a wider range of facial types. However, the government of Zimbabwe could use this system to more closely monitor its citizens, which could undermine social stability and trust.[76] While such a situation may be rare, it provides a strong rationale for Zimbabwe and other countries to develop and debate a strategy for protecting personal data.

E A PATH FORWARD

Humans have long exchanged data between borders, but never have they traded so much data or benefited from so many new services built on data. These new services may make us smarter, richer, more flexible and more efficient. But not all countries or people are ready to participate in this brave new world. The OECD recently noted that 'governments and stakeholders have a responsibility to shape a common digital future that improves peoples' lives and boost economic growth for countries at all levels of development, while ensuring that nobody is left behind'.[77] However, for governance to succeed and be trusted, it needs to be built on shared norms and rules.

Policymakers should first work at the national level to develop a national strategy for data and then move towards interoperability of approaches rather than harmonization. They must find a way to conduct discussions on data governance that build public trust, consistent with the multi-stakeholder processes embedded in other forms of Internet governance. Against this backdrop, this chapter suggests five steps for moving forward, summarized below.

---

[75] World Wide Web Foundation, *Open Data Barometer – Leaders Edition* (Washington, DC: World Wide Web Foundation, 2018); Centre for Law and Democracy, 'Global right to information by indicator', available at www.rti-rating.org/country-data/by-indicator/Indicators.

[76] I. Hogarth, 'AI Nationalism', 13 June 2018, available at www.ianhogarth.com/blog/2018/6/13/ai-nationalism; S. Jie, 'China Exports Facial ID Technology to Zimbabwe', *Global Times*, 12 April 2018.

[77] OECD, 'Going Digital in a Multilateral World: An Interim Report to Ministers', Executive Summary Meeting of the Council at Ministerial Level, 30–31 May 2018, available at www.oecd .org/going-digital/project/going-digital-interim-overview.pdf.

Step 1: Encourage States to Develop Plans for the Regulation and Exchange of Different Types of Data

Given the complexity of data, its role in new services and the importance of data to economic health and political stability, every nation should develop a strategy for how public and personal data are to be used and exchanged across borders (a national data plan). The plan should focus on ensuring that most public data sets are open, and personal data, especially personally identifiable information,[78] is adequately protected. Such a plan should address issues of ownership, control, equity (i.e. that the data is developed and analyzed in an even-handed manner) and monetization of data (who can earn money for data and how). Policymakers will also have to address issues related to the cloud and data transfer – how a country can control the transfer of data that might include personally identifiable information or data that is important for national security.[79]

It will not be easy for most states to develop such a plan. Policymakers will need guidelines, incentives and technical assistance. Most advanced economies are in the early stages of developing such plans, as they wrestle with disinformation, ethics of AI and digital disruption of various sectors. But some nations/trade blocs are way ahead. The EU, for instance, has developed an EU-wide data strategy focusing on types of data, giving citizens in the EU some control over use of their data. The EU has also established a road map which enables EU policymakers to monitor member states' progress.[80] Meanwhile, the UK, Canada and Australia are in the process of developing their own data plans to match their digital trade strategies. Mexico, Australia and Brazil have too put forward public data or data innovation strategies and Canada is in the process of developing one.[81] In addition, some countries are putting in place plans to facilitate the development of data-driven sectors. As an example, the seventy-five members of the Open Government Partnership pledge to develop plans to make public data open to all. The D7 is a group of countries

---

[78] Personally identifiable information (PII) is information that, when used alone or with other relevant data, can identify an individual. PII may contain direct identifiers (e.g. passport data) that can identify a person uniquely, or quasi-identifiers (such as race) that can be combined with other quasi-identifiers to recognize an individual.

[79] Scassa, note 35.

[80] European Commission, Commission Staff Working Document on the Free Flow of Data and Emerging Issues of the European Data Economy Accompanying the Document Communication Building a European Data Economy, SWD(2017) 2 final, COM(2017) 9 final.

[81] For Brazil, see 'Estratégia Brasileira para a transformação digital: e-digital', available at www .mctic.gov.br/mctic/export/sites/institucional/estrategiadigital.pdf; for Canada, see Government of Canada, 'Innovation, Science and Economic Development Canada: Government of Canada Launches National Consultations on Digital and Data Transformation', 19 June 2018, available at www.canada.ca/en/innovation-science-economic-development/news/2018/06/government-of-canada-launches-national-consultations-on-digital-and-data-transformation.html; for Australia, see Australian Chamber of Commerce and Industry, 'The Digital Economy: Opening up the Conversation', 30 November 2017, available at www.australianchamber.com.au/wp-content/uploads/2018/01/digital_economy_strategy_submission.pdf.

(Estonia, Israel, New Zealand, South Korea, the UK, Canada and Uruguay) committed to encouraging the data-driven economy and e-government.[82]

International trade and development organizations, such as the World Bank and UNCTAD, could work with civil society groups skilled in data issues (such as Privacy International or the Open Government Partnership) to bring these issues to the fore and provide technical assistance.

Step 2: Give People Greater Voice and Greater Control over Their Data

For the data-driven economy to succeed it must be built on a foundation of trust, and users must have legal protections and greater control over their data. A growing number of data protection plans include some element of consumer control over personal data. Policymakers should call for an international meeting to establish an interoperable approach to data protection and control, which allows nations to evolve their own complementary approaches. The meeting should be attended by a diverse set of individuals, firms and agencies involved in privacy and data protection issues, and it should be tasked to build on existing principles, such as the APEC and OECD Privacy Principles.[83] The organizers of such a meeting could establish a website that will be 'marketed' by participating governments. The architects of the site could then ask netizens to crowdsource ideas about how to build on these existing principles while simultaneously empowering people to control their personal data.[84] Companies and data protection officials have already found some common ground on helping companies that move data globally to transcend different regulatory strategies.[85] But there seems to be a growing sense that the US approach is too focused on ensuring that personal data can be utilized as a commercial asset, while the EU has put its citizens first and protect their personal data as a matter of a fundamental right.

Step 3: Clarify the Rules and Exceptions to the Rules, So Nations Do Not Restrict Cross-Border Data Flows More Frequently or Broadly than Necessary

Like other treaties, a data-driven economy agreement should include exceptions to the rules. Nations can use the exceptions to 'excuse' violations to the agreement when they pursue other important policy objectives. (Figure 16.1 shows that governments have a wide range of reasons to restrict cross-border data flows.) Countries can only use these exceptions, however, if they do so in the least trade distorting manner. Yet, so far, there is no clear model that policymakers can follow to distinguish between legitimate and trade-distorting data flow regulation. The current language in trade

---

[82] See www.digital.govt.nz/digital-government/international-partnerships/d7-group-of-digital-nations/.
[83] For an overview of data protection laws and regulations, see Consumers International, 'Digital Index: Data Protection and Privacy', available at https://digitalindex.consumersinternational .org/search/category/data-protection-and-privacy/subcategory/personal-data-protection/page/1.
[84] WEF, note 4.
[85] Carson, note 68.

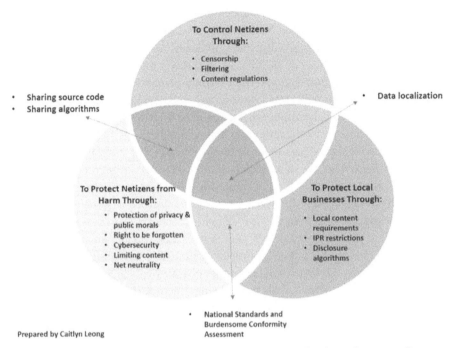

FIGURE 16.1. Why and how do governments restrict cross-border information flows?
Prepared by Caitlyn Leong

agreements is vague and states must rely on trade disputes to develop clarity and some degree of legal certainty. However, there have been few disputes to provide guidance and policymakers have not yet agreed on updating the WTO law language with regard to the general exception clauses or other specific exceptions.

Policymakers should begin by delineating how and when nations can use the exceptions to limit cross-border flows in the name of protecting domestic security or cybersecurity. For example, some governments, such as India, Brazil, the United States and the UK, have called on companies to provide backdoors to encrypted communications to help law enforcement. However, such an encryption backdoor would undermine trust and the effectiveness of encryption as a tool for keeping individuals, firms and governments safe online.

Step 4: Provide Clarity on What Types of Practices Should Be Banned
Because They Are Trade Distorting

Beyond data localization and taxation of e-commerce, there is little agreement as to what measures distort cross-border data flows.[86] For example, many Western

---

[86] WTO, note 52; Aaronson, note 51.

countries believe that censorship is a trade barrier, which can undermine the many benefits of the Internet. Yet, no trade agreement discussing cross-border data flows mentions censorship, filtering or Internet shut-downs as a barrier to trade that should be regulated. Many states censor, filter or shut down the Internet for a variety of reasons, including safeguarding government authority, fighting terrorism, maintaining national security or protecting local businesses. When they censor, filter or shut down the Internet, they determine what data will be available within their borders.[87] Authoritarian states are not the only states that censor data. The Indian government, the world's largest democracy and a technology leader, has had fifty-four Internet shut-downs, more than any other nation in 2017. Human rights groups view these shut-downs as an intentional form of censorship which distorts the free flow of data. These shut-downs have also huge economic costs, estimated at some $3 billion for the period 2012–2017 for India alone.[88] Brookings scholar Darrell West estimated that globally, Internet shut-downs cost some $2.4 billion in 2015 alone.[89] Policymakers must find common ground on defining and regulating these practices or they cannot reap the benefits of economies of scale on data. Such practices may also create costly spillovers, such as reducing Internet stability and hampering scientific progress.[90]

Step 5: Delineate How Nations Should or Should Not Respond to State Actions That Distort Cross-Border Data Flows

Trade agreements allow signatories to respond to the trade distorting practices of their partners with compensatory practices. The agreement should clearly state that party responses should be limited and proportional in such instance and define accordingly the legal test. Moreover, any agreement should also clearly state that adopting protectionist strategies, such as tariffs and quotas, or turning to strategies, such as malware, are inappropriate responses, which could reduce cross-border data flows, are prohibited. According to trade scholar Patrick Leblond, 'Ideally, the response should increase the costs of doing business and penalize proscribed practice, but not penalize the sources of data'.[91] Data protectionism will beget

---

[87] A. Chander and U. P. Lê, 'Breaking the Web: Data Localization vs. the Global Internet', UC Davies Legal Studies Research Paper No 378 (2014).

[88] R. Kathuria et al., *The Anatomy of an Internet Blackout: Measuring the Economic Impact of Internet Shutdowns in India* (New Delhi: Indian Council for Research on International Economic Relations, 2018).

[89] D. West, 'Internet Shutdowns Costs Countries $2.4 Billion Last Year', Brookings Report, 6 October 2016, available at www.brookings.edu/research/internet-shutdowns-cost-countries-2-4-billion-last-year/.

[90] S. Box, 'Internet Openness and Fragmentation: Toward Measuring the Economic Effects', CIGI Global Commission on Internet Governance Paper No 36 (2016).

[91] P. Leblond, email to author, 10 July 2018.

further data protectionism and undermine the utility of the Internet.[92] We may be seeing evidence of this digital trade wars already between the United States and the EU: After the US Secretary of Commerce Wilbur Ross called the EU approach to data protection trade distorting in May 2018,[93] the EU proposed tax and regulatory policies to challenge what some see as the monopolistic control of US Internet giants.[94]

F CONCLUSION

The world is awash with data and there is no consensus on how to regulate it. The five outlined steps can help nations prepare for future negotiations and build value from data. These ideas will not address all the issues that arise in regulating cross-border data flows, and any new approach is likely to face many challenges, especially from those vested in the existing organizations and approaches to governing data. But clearly, we are stuck in a rut on trade and must creatively address the trade and non-trade dimensions of cross-border data flows. Policymakers from a wide range of countries may be more willing to compromise if they see that their citizens will benefit from clear, interoperable rules and from receiving funds for their data. Moreover, this approach could help firms accommodate national differences regarding ethics of data usage, disinformation and other upcoming regulatory issues. It could also give developing countries greater leverage in the discussions on data flows, where they would ordinarily be 'rule takers'.[95] Finally, these ideas could help more countries better integrate data-driven firms and their traditional firms. By collaborating and rethinking the process of global rule-making on data, we will be better able to achieve the change we wish to see in the world – where people have greater autonomy and control over their data and data drives equitable growth.

---

[92] Box, note 90; OECD, note 21.

[93] W. Ross, 'EU Privacy Laws Are Likely to Create Barriers to Trade', *Financial Times*, 30 May 2018.

[94] European Commission, 'Digital Taxation: Commission Proposes New Measures to Ensure That All Companies Pay Fair Tax in the EU', *Press Release*, 21 March 2018.

[95] Aaronson and Leblond, note 18.

Index

small- and medium-sized enterprises (SMEs), 70,
     135, 269–270, 274–275, 298, 332–333
small services–oriented economies, 66
smart city, 117
smart contracts, 133–134, 138–139
SMEs. *See* small- and medium-sized enterprises
Snapchat, 147
Snowden, Edward, 199–200
social media, 345
socialism, 256–257
software regulation, 255–256
Solove, Daniel J., 225
source code, 108–109, 224, 281, 305, 308
     transparency of, 99
South Africa, 268–269
South Korea, 33, 138
South Korea–United States FTA, 24–27
Sovrin, 147
spam control, 36–37
Spotify, 140–141
SPS. *See* Sanitary and Phytosanitary Measures
stakeholders, 5–6, 8, 63–64, 77, 106, 138–139, 145,
     152, 157–158, 180, 186–187, 212–213, 229,
     245–246, 317, 354
Standard Contractual Clauses, 86–87
Stitch Fix, 340–343, 345–346, 349
Stone, S., 79
Strava, 340–343, 345–346, 349
supercomputers, 1–2
Superintendence of Industry and Commerce
     (SIC), 296–297
Supreme People's Court (China), 257–258
Supreme People's Procuratorate (China), 257–258
surveillance capitalism, 197–198, 228–229
Swedish National Board of Trade, 64–65
Switzerland, 189–190
Szabo, Nick, 133–134

Taiwan–Nicaragua FTA, 288–289
takedown requests, 180–181
TAPED *See* Trade Agreements Provisions on
     Electronic Commerce and Data
     (dataset)
tariff losses, 109
tariffs, 176
TBT. *See* Agreement on Technical Barriers to
     Trade
TDM. *See* Text and Data Mining
technological advances, 187–188, 195–196, 205
technological protection measure (TPM), 162, 173
Telecommunication Act (US), 246
Telecommunication Regulation (China), 254–256
Telecommunications Reference Paper, 110
Tencent, 258–259

terrorism, 245–246
Tesla, 119
Text and Data Mining (TDM), 161,
     169–176
text-as-data analysis, 53–55
TFA. *See* Trade Facilitation Agreement
TFP. *See* total factor productivity
TikTok, 115–116
TiSA. *See* Trade in Services Agreement
Total factor productivity (TFP), 71
TPM. *See* technological protection measure
TPP. *See* Transpacific Partnership Agreement
trade agreements, 214–215, 245. *See also* Free Trade
     Agreements; preferential trade
     agreements
Trade Agreements Provisions on Electronic
     Commerce and Data (dataset)
     (TAPED), 20–21, 58–61, 270–271,
     275–276
trade conflicts, 17
trade distortions, 69
Trade Facilitation Agreement (TFA), 15–16,
     137–138
trade finance, 134, 152–154, 156
     coordination costs, 135–136
Trade in Services Agreement (TiSA), 219–220,
     238–239, 261, 349
trade rules, 3, 15, 24, 85, 111–112, 116–117, 176,
     238–241, 345
     digital, 20, 36, 40, 238–240, 268–269
     international, 122, 239–240, 242
     traditional, 268
Trade Secrets Directive (EU), 335–336
trade wars, 358–359
trade-inhibiting effects, 64–65
Tradelens, 135
transaction costs, 269–270, 323–325
Transpacific Partnership Agreement (TPP), 27–28,
     55–56, 273, 289, 351
transparency, 31–32, 38, 99–100, 107–108, 119,
     129–130, 156, 191–192
     active, 291–293
     of blockchain, 139
     cooperation on, 47–48
     ensuring, 210–211
     facilitation of, 348
     GATS and, 92–93
     importance of, 140–141
     industry developments in, 272
     lack of, 269–270
     principles of, 337
     requirements of, 14
     of source code, 266
     treaty design, 58–60

Milton Keynes UK
Ingram Content Group UK Ltd.
UKHW020828120424
440787UK00022B/181